Legal Stuff, Small Print, and Copyright

This is a cookbook. I make no health claims or medical claims, at all… ever. Even if I do happen to make something that *looks* like a claim of some kind, I didn't. It was an accident. I *do* claim, however, that the recipes are yumtastic! While the whole book is mired in a fairly specific philosophy I've picked up and massaged over the years, I only claim that they've benefitted me. Because this is a litigious world, I cannot claim these recipes will benefit you in any way, short of bringing a satisfying smile to your face 'cause they're just so gosh darned yummy!

Point being: I'm not a doctor, nutritionist, naturopath, or any kind of chemist or biological specialist. My degree is from the Culinary Institute of America. It essentially qualifies me to peel carrots, really quickly.

Listen to your doctors!

About the Nutrition

I take great pride in offering the most thorough nutritional analysis I've ever seen… anywhere. I do my best to give accurate nutritional information for each ingredient, in addition to adding the values and offering totals, plus total macronutrient count per serving. I want people to feel that they can tweak the recipes and know how the removal of a single ingredient will impact the overall nutritional value. I also feel it encourages the understanding of individual ingredients and where the macronutrients are coming from.

This is a good-faith promise that the information is as accurate as I know how to make it. The majority of the information comes from the United States Department of Agriculture's Nutrient Database for Standard Reference release 21 (also known as USDA SR-21). When the information is unavailable from the USDA, I do my best to find current information. However, I make no promises of the accuracy of the information, just that it's as good as I'm able to make it (and that it's very honorably presented).

Copyright

Assembled in the United States of America and Mexico

ISBN 978-0-9863444-0-4

First Printing, 2015

www.DJFoodie.com

Thanks!

Without the assistance and support of my parents, I could not have started this project. They noted how serious I was taking this way of life and supported my decision to walk this direction. Thank you, Mom and Dad! I love you!

I want to thank Dixie Vogel, from Low-Carb Zen. On a lark, about a week into this whole blogging thing, I submitted a recipe to a website (LowCarbZen.com) that looked interesting. I was curious. Dixie wrote me back, and we began an exchange of emails. Since then, she's consistently shared my recipes with her hundreds of thousands of fans on Facebook, which has been nothing short of another miracle. Beyond that, Dixie's initial words of wisdom and support have also given me the confidence to really push this project as far as I have so far. Dixie, you'll never really know how much you carried me through those early weeks and months. Aside from Dr. Gundry, you're probably the second most influential person in my life... whom I have never met. At a time when it was scary venturing down this path, you made me feel valid. Thank you!

I want to thank the Low-Carbing Among Friends team, past, present and future members. I see great things coming from this group. I'd specifically like to thank Jennifer and Ian Eloff for having the confidence to bring a new little blogger aboard your successful cookbook authoring team. I'd also like to extend a hearty thank you to George Stella for writing this wonderful foreword. Yes, Chef. Thank you, Chef!

I also want to thank Maria Luisa Dorbecker, Ken Priest, and Horacio Sobarzo Romo, friends who stepped in to help with photography when my fingers were dripping with bacon grease. Extra special thanks to Horacio, who went above and beyond, coming up with the graphic designs for this book! *Gracias, amigo mío. Ustedes son los mejores!*

Thanks to Dr. Gundry, the man with the words that convinced me to change. Thank you, sir! My parents may have given me life, but... you've extended it! Thank you!

Finally... last, but certainly not least... Thank you, T! I don't think this book would've existed without you!

SLOW
and
STEADY

o o o

WINS
the
RACE

Table of Contents

RECIPES

Foreword

My name is George Stella, and my family and I have been living a low-carb lifestyle for over fifteen years. I've written six cookbooks and have hosted a few dozen low-carb cooking shows on Food Network.

However, things weren't always like this. A little over fifteen years ago, I weighed 467 pounds, and I was sick—very sick. I had congestive heart failure and more due to obesity, and worse yet, my family of four had followed suit, weighing a half a ton collectively!

What came next changed our entire lives. My family lost over 550 pounds eating low-carb, and within a year of losing the weight, we were featured in magazines and countless television shows. I even had my own show on Food Network called *Low-Carb and Lovin' It!*

What started as something we had given one month turned into a way of life that we follow to this very day!

Why do I tell you all this? Because after all these years, this lifestyle still has me so energized that I feel the need to shout from the rooftops that another true low-carb guru has emerged with the most exciting new low-carb cookbook ever: DJ Foodie!

To say DJ is my friend is an understatement; he's more like my long-lost son. It is my greatest pleasure and honor to tell the world that my good friend DJ Foodie has broken the mold and written here—let the adjectives rip!—the most modern, comprehensive, fun, funny, interesting, and pertinent low-carb cookbook ever written by someone who is passionate, relatable, and approachable, someone who has been there and done that. DJ is truly on a mission to help others, and this is rare to find today!

DJ, like me, is a real chef, but we have so many more similarities from our growing-up years that it's no wonder I love this guy:

I was inspired to cook by my mother and DJ by his grandmother. I started cooking in a restaurant at age thirteen; he started at fourteen. DJ attended the Culinary Institute of America (CIA) and a decade earlier (or more perhaps) I was teaching students from the CIA on their externships. Unfortunately, DJ and I also both became obese but, fortunately, were able to learn about low-carb and use our cooking knowledge to save our lives! However, most of all, like me, DJ found a calling in his weight-loss success and has made it a life mission to share, teach, and help anyone who will listen that fresh, healthy, low-carb foods can change their lives too!

It is for all these reasons and more that I am proud to consider DJ Foodie not only a friend but also a member of my family. In this his newest cookbook, not only does DJ share his tested and tasty low-carb recipes, but he also demonstrates his knowledge and firsthand experience in a fun and inviting way everyone will relate to.

What are you waiting for? Go ahead! Start eating and feeling better than you ever have before—this book is your ticket to the show!

George Stella

George Stella, a professional chef for over thirty years, is an official spokesman for the Junior League's Kids in the Kitchen initiative to empower youth to make healthy lifestyle choices. He has appeared on numerous television and news shows, including two seasons of his own show, *Low-Carb and Lovin' It* on the Food Network, and has written six bestselling cookbooks. Connecticut born, he has spent more than half his life in Florida, where he lives today with his wife of over thirty years, Rachel.

You can catch up with George, his family, and other families eating fresh, healthy foods at...

www.StellaStyle.com

Before !!

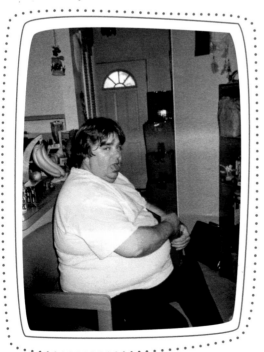

After !!

Preface

Before I get into my story, I just want to point out that these pages contain guidelines that forever and dramatically changed my life. I wholeheartedly believe that the words contained within this book can help anyone, short of the most dedicated athlete. If you're just in need of losing a few pounds, this book will help you. If you're in need of losing more than a hundred pounds, this book will help you *a lot*… and the ride should be sweet.

I also want to point out that these changes have taken me from a severely overweight man, who feared diabetes and was very likely depressed, and they have not only returned me to health, but there were all kinds of unexpected side effects!

I look younger; there are no more seatbelt extensions; I feel younger; I no longer have sleep apnea; I have more opportunities and more friends; stress is less stressful; I go further/faster; I do more, and I eat better and enjoy it more; I have increased libido and stamina, clearer eyes, better vision, smoother skin, and I can reach my feet to tie my shoes. I LIKE exercising, I smile more, clothes actually fit, I have sharper wits, I'm not hot all the time (no more sweat stains!), I'm social, I no longer crave sweets, and I don't always look disheveled.

Put simply: it's been my experience that life improves in unexpected ways. It's *far* more fulfilling and… life has treated me… in kind.

My Story

I have always had an intense relationship with food. I love the stuff! I love to eat it, obviously, but I also love to talk about it, look at it, smell it, read about it, play with it, cook it, shape it, and… whatever else you can do with the tasty stuff. I mean, my last name is "Foodie" for crying out loud. It's no wonder!

screech

Before !!

Ok, let's try this again.

Hi. My name is Kenneth Eric Williams, but my family has called me DJ since I was born. It's a name in honor of my two grandfathers, David and John. The *Foodie* name came around 1998, when I hosted an online radio show, well over five years prior to the invention of the word *podcast*.

Ultimately, this book isn't about me. I'm the inspiration and the proof that it worked for me, but the details of my life aren't that significant, really. The important parts are: I'm real. This really happened. This really worked.

In short… I was fat. Then, I wasn't!

When I was younger, I was never fat, but I think it was

obvious that I was capable of being fat. As a kid, I always saw myself as chubby, but I've never seen a childhood photo of me being chubby. I think that was just in my mind.

When I was a kid, I was asked what I wanted to be when I grow up. I said, "A chef!" I think it's because my grandmother is an amazing cook, and I loved that about her. For as long as I can remember, I've wanted to be a chef. Gifts from a very early age involved items like cookbooks and egg slicers. At fourteen, I got a job working in the best restaurant in town. It was just a weekend job, but it was a start, and it was real food too! Excellent mixed baby greens were washed and dried by these very hands. Raspberry sauce was swirled onto dessert plates. My young fingers plunged into boiling water to grab out the occasional stray green bean. I started very young.

Two days after my eighteenth birthday, I moved to New York, where I attended the Culinary Institute of America. I was young, but it was college, and I did learn quite a lot. I took an extended externship at Wolfgang Puck's second restaurant, Postrio, in San Francisco, in 1992. I worked under Anne and David Gingrass, an amazing culinary duo. They likely formed the core of my knowledge base and organizational structure. Any success I have or have ever had in this industry, I owe to them.

ahem

But again, this isn't about me.

Moving forward about seven years…

I had my talk show starting in late 1998. *The MasterCook Show* ran until early 2000. This was the first time I was outside of a fast-paced kitchen but was also still around food. My partner and I would cook and take hundreds of photos (one of each step), to run as slides during the show, then discuss them on the air, while sharing the images online. My rear end began its slow and consistent widening around this time.

After *The MasterCook Show* came the Manager of Special Projects at Allrecipes.com—another food-based desk job involving cooking. This and the talk show were both *enormously* rewarding jobs, and I was very fortunate to have had them, but… I wasn't exercising, and I wasn't eating properly. My posterior continued to increase its mass.

The dot-bomb bubble exploded around this time, and I floundered… hard. As a well-paid dot-bomber, unemployment paid much more than going back to restaurants, and I had house payments to make. I couldn't find anything interesting in the culinary computer world. My bottom gained more inches, and my stress levels increased.

Cut to three years later…

I'd always wanted to live abroad. My folks own a house down in Mexico. Mexico just seemed like a logical next step, as there was a safe landing pad, people I knew, and I spoke some Spanish.

So I moved to Mexico, where I bought some land, built a house, and started a catering business, all while working a full-time job as a website builder. Oh man, life was *stressful!* I was barely able to cope with my days. My job was demanding, my house was an endless battle, my catering company was a lot tougher to handle than I'd thought (language barriers, different laws, schedule conflicts with my day job, etc.). I had no real social life to speak of. It was all work and stress and… pizza and bags of Butterfingers. I was quickly heading toward a major disaster.

I was struggling to breathe. I'm 5' 8 ½" and was over 350 pounds. I volunteered with the local organic farmer's market (where I'd started as a food vendor, as a local caterer). I would attend the meetings with these wonderfully healthy and vibrant people, and work to spread the message of healthy and organic farming practices. I, by contrast, was this overweight, sweaty oaf of a man, straining and heaving just so I could sit upright. I would get distracted in the meetings by the sounds and depth of my own breathing. About every thirty or forty breaths, my body would require a big, gulping inhalation. I'm sure people noticed I wasn't getting enough air and was always struggling to breathe. I was constantly hearing the ubiquitous question, "Dude, are you all right?"

Food—my love, my pride, my joy, my training and schooling, my profession… my reason for living—was killing me.

I was going to the gym occasionally. I would try and eat less. I did silly things like the Subway Diet. Nothing seemed to work, and I'd just wallow, sad and alone, with a comforting pan of lasagna and a medium-sized pile of Reese's Peanut Butter Cups.

Hey, at least the TV was good. *Monk* was on and… I like *Monk*.

I knew I was broken. I knew I was overextended. I knew I was diabetic, and I knew I was losing my vision. I knew my feet had weird, prickly sensations all the time. I knew my back hurt. I knew I had all kinds of crazy abdominal pains all the time. I knew I was dying, but… I also knew that I couldn't stop working. I couldn't stop trying to make my catering company a success. I knew I couldn't stop paying my bills. I knew I couldn't budge, fold, or show weakness. I had to stay the course.

I couldn't go to a doctor because a doctor would force my hand. I couldn't really commit to a diet because I couldn't deal with my own life as it was, much less the addition of new rules, restrictions, and a complete and total removal of the one thing that brought me peace: food. Sweet, delicious food.

I'm a good cook, but I'm a lousy businessman. I made a substantial series of lousy business decisions and essentially ran out of money. I was making *just* enough money from my website job to pay the bills, but… I had to drop the catering business. I couldn't carry it any longer. My knees hurt too much anyway.

Losing my catering company really hurt. I was already broken, but now…

It was the first time in my life when I had no direct connection to food. I was in another country, without my lifelong career in food, I owned a house in a crumbling market, and I was almost as tall lying down as I was standing up. I was sad… and had lost my way. I didn't know what to do.

I knew it was time to make some difficult decisions. I reevaluated my priorities. I had a tendency to do too many things and put too many *huevos* in too many baskets. Trying to be a financially successful rock-star chef in Mexico had eluded me. I needed to fix *me.* I also knew I had to make it a priority. In fact, it had to be *the* priority.

I had to mend what I had broken—no matter what.

I'd just lost my business, so I suddenly had spare time. I used that time to read about blood sugar. I knew I was diabetic. So I read about controlling blood sugar through diet. My theory was I could get my health under control through my diet. I hadn't really thought a whole lot about weight loss at this point. My goal was to not be sick or, at the very least, not die anytime soon. This was me fighting for my life.

I was slowly arming myself with what was turning out to be a low-carb way of eating. I didn't really know it at the time, but I was glued to the idea of controlling blood sugar through low-glycemic and low-carb foods. Even though I was studying and preparing for a big change, I was still making my world-famous sweet corn, potato, and bacon chowder and downing it by the gallon, polishing it off with a box of doughnuts that I'd secretly bought.

Even at this point, I was still knowingly, *blatantly* sticking the dagger deeper into my chest.

Finally, I read a book that my mother gave me: *Dr. Grundy's Diet Evolution* (Three Rivers Press, 2008). It was recommended to her by our family doctor. Reading this book was one of the defining moments in my life. Every word, every sentence, every concept and idea were being burned into my psyche, like… well, like my life depended on it. I inhaled it like I had last night's greasy sack of Tacos al Pastor and a big bowl of sugar-coated fruity pops.

(Notice how my love of food, *good* food, had devolved into all-out carbage? I was deep in the throes of addiction, at that point.)

A New Direction...

I read the book in one afternoon. My way of eating has permanently changed since that day, March 18, 2010.

On that day, I sat and wrote out my life goals. It incorporated documenting my pain, with a plan for the future, for health, but also with a professional tie-in. I am, at my core, what I do. I love food. What can I say?! Basically, it was, "Eat well and write about it!" That's what I find myself doing—four years and nearly 150 pounds later.

There is a lot of personal drama, desperation, frustration, and anxiety all wrapped up in the passage above. It's my story and it's a bad one, but there are worse. I've spoken with people who can no longer even walk because of their weight. Their solution? Keep eating more carbage. They, like me, believed it was the only way to kill the pain—of being them… being overweight.

As it turns out, I did not have diabetes (Thank God!), but there are millions of people who aren't so lucky. There are people dying every day due to cancer, heart conditions, and diabetes… all largely due to lousy diets.

My story is intended to connect, inspire, and motivate. It's my belief that people don't make a change unless they need to. Usually that means that the situation they are in must be worse than the effort required to change it. Isn't that just the darnedest thing?

People will intentionally keep doing the horrible thing that they know is horribly bad… until it becomes *so* awfully, terribly bad that they have no choice but to fix it (or die or lose a limb). Sometimes people befuddle me.

However, having been there, I get it.

Whatever your situation, wherever you think you're at, I believe I can offer some insight… and yummy recipes!

Please, though, I implore you: Don't let things get so bad that you're forced to change them. Please. Be proactive and stop the downward slide… before you hit bottom.

Please.

A Look at the Old Direction

If you've been on my website, you have likely seen this passage there, but it bears repeating here. Feeling as if I was literally dying, in pain, having lost my career and health, on March 18, 2010, I wrote:

I feel terrible, I look terrible, and I'm terribly unhealthy.

I have peaked at 352 pounds about a week ago. I look like someone who has just eaten the Stay Puft Marshmallow man, except that I feel even heavier.

My lower back hurts when I walk, to the point where I need to sit down after walking about five hundred feet. My ankles always hurt, and I think I'm diabetic. I'm not positive, and I'm too chicken to go to the doctor, but I have problems that indicate this. Mostly, I just pee at night—a lot. Beyond that, I'm just very unhealthy feeling. There is a "suck," a sense of a medical "squeezing" of my soul. It can get powerful sometimes.

I have what I call my "ring of pain." It starts with the organs under my final right rib and crosses my rib cage into the organs under my final left rib. Apparently these organs don't have any sensation of their own. It's got to be the areas surrounding the organs being constantly pressured by my gut and my ribcage as I sit at my desk and work all day.

Either that or it's something far more nefarious, like cancer.

Ahhhhhhhhhhhhhhh...

...ignorance is bliss!

I could go on and on with gripes, complaints, pains, ticks, tocks, and issues. I have little doubt that I will as this story progresses, but I suppose I should talk a little about what I'm doing.

I'm writing.... I'm documenting.... I'm journaling.

I'm not sure why, exactly. I have grand visions of this turning into a cookbook, filled with inspiration, recipes, and a true-to-life story about how a man came back from the depths of hell—how he was able to conquer his vices, organize his thoughts, and create a fulfilling life for himself. That man, I hope, will be me.

As I said, I'm very unhealthy and overweight. I should go to the doctor but am afraid of what I'll learn. I tell myself that if I can just get my eating and exercise under control that I'll visit a physician when I "feel better." I'm not sure what this means precisely, but it's fair to say that I haven't felt better in a very long time.

I'm without a career, friends, health, happiness, a girl, and a healthy outlook. I don't have anything much left to lose... except my life. It's really about the only thing I have left to lose!

I need to take stock of my life. I need to work toward friends, happiness, health, family relationships, career, and improving my healthy outlook.

My hope is that this journal will document this process, that it will take some of my random blatherings and slowly but surely gel into a cohesive and uplifting story of a man who got it right, after seemingly intentionally doing everything wrong from the moment he turned eighteen.

To begin...

I have been trying like mad to lose weight. I've been doing a horrible job and have been teetering between 338 pounds and 352 pounds. I'm about 5' 9". So this isn't good. I have no muscle. I'm a disgusting, blubbery whale. Yuck.

Before !!

 I was saving this for later...

I've been trying to walk. I try and walk about a mile, every other day. I walk with my puppies to the beach and back. It's a grueling hour, and I hate it. It's hard; my back hurts; I have to sit all the time, but I can never find anywhere to sit, just the occasional rock. I'm starting to learn the good spots.

It's embarrassing to be out in public, walking my dogs, all fat and sweaty, in clothes that don't fit, while I rock out to outdated music on my iPhone. I'm the guy I want to laugh at on the street but don't because I'm mature enough to recognize that the guy is trying to make it better. He's trying to make improvements!

Then... I laugh at him anyway. Fat bastard. I'm that guy!

The days I don't walk, I tell myself that it's good to let my muscles relax. Then I eat way way too much cereal, pasta, or some other kind of sugary, fatty sweet concoction.

Without the walks, I'd be 400 pounds by now. So I suppose I'm at least teasing and taunting the right thing to do. I'm testing the waters. They are cold but inviting.

This past weekend, I forced myself to read a book by a heart surgeon. It was a book on a diet evolution. It spoke to me and made me want to try something radically different. However, it was also something I felt was manageable, appropriate, and understandable. The end result would be a healthy person, at least physically, and with the capacity to live another sixty years. It's good health and longevity... and that, to me, tastes better than all the meat lover's pizza and chocolate-coated fruity nibblets in the world.

Today, I have started on my path.

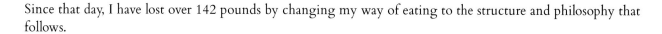

Since that day, I have lost over 142 pounds by changing my way of eating to the structure and philosophy that follows.

I really need to emphasize that I do not see this as a diet, in the modern sense. That word really irks me in what it has come to mean today. A "diet" has become something you do to get into "bikini shape" after adding a warming layer of adipose tissues over the winter. A "diet" will blast the pounds and you'll lose weight... while you're on the diet. If you go back to eating whatever it was you were eating in the first place, you'll go back to having that toasty layer of insulation!

Diet was originally defined as "food and drink regularly provided or consumed." I prefer this original definition, as opposed to the modern twist. Given the origins, a diet consisting of whole, largely unprocessed, and low-glycemic foods is a complete and total life change for the better. Within that context, I accept the word *diet.*

Now that we've all seen where I've been and what drove me to arrive *here*, let us jump into the book!

After!!

Introduction

I had the idea for a cookbook and blog, several years before I actually started it. This book was released near the beginning of 2015. I started my blog on August 10, 2012. However, on March 21, 2010, while weighing about 340 pounds, I wrote:

I think I have decided to try and write a formal cookbook.

Here's what I've been focusing on regarding food and what to eat. Basically, it has to be delicious in order for me to survive this diet. *Has to be.* According to Dr. Gundry (of *Dr. Gundry's Diet Evolution Fame*), I was born in a time and have a genetic structure that requires me to seek out the delicious flavor and ease of the almighty carbohydrate. I need to change that and convince my body that vegetables are where it's at. With strong flavors from ingredients like vinegar, spices, mustard, etc., I'll be able to build a strong, varied, and flavorful set of recipes without needing breads, pastas, or more simple and direct forms of sugar, like sugar, honey, etc.

Delicious is number 1.

It must taste good. If it doesn't taste good, it won't be here.

Number 2: Ease of preparation.

I'm busy. Chances are you're busy. I'm also not a rich man, so I can't afford to hire someone to do the legwork for me, nor can I afford a long laundry list of expensive ingredients. Yes, they will be in here, peppered in, but for the most part, I will create very functional, useful, simple, quick, and easy recipes. So far, this seems like a lot of soups, salads, stir-frys, etc. That's fine. If a big bowl of warm chicken salad and greens, if tasty and easy to prepare, fits the bill, helps me drop weight and extend my life, so be it! I want that! In time, I have no doubt that I will layer in more composed dishes, but I suspect the overwhelming majority of the people who want to lose weight are already upset about the work involved. I'm not going to pile onto that by making things needlessly complex.

I also live in Mexico, so it's going to be very difficult for me to find certain ingredients. I wouldn't even know where to begin looking for "grass-fed flank steak" in Mexico. I'm sure it exists, but I don't know how to find it. I'm going to have trouble finding organic unsweetened almond milk and finely ground almond meal. It's going to be tough finding carb-free pastas and non-Dutch cocoa powder.

Point being, whatever I come up with will be easier for you than for me, unless you're in a more rural part of Mexico than I am. If I can do it, you can do it.

There will be times you'll want to entertain, show off, play with the food, learn, experiment, etc. That will all be in here. I want people to explore and expand their skills and tastes. I want to offer beautiful ideas, as well as a variety of tastes from different cultures, but for the most part, simple, easy, cost effective, and *delicious*.

Number 3: Efficient.

I will try to organize this material into a slice of information that is easy to absorb and follow. So, rather than just a flat list of recipes, I would like to believe I'll have full shopping lists of ingredients and especially a pantry, full calendars, and sections of recipes designed for specific phases of the diet. I want to incorporate schedules. For example, Sunday's might require four hours of cooking, but the rest of the week will be easy, easy, easy. The alternative to this would be a daily scramble, resulting in twenty hours of time, the majority being wasted effort. It has to fit into your schedule in order to work. So far, each of my starter dishes requires about ten minutes to prepare and has virtually no advanced preparation. That's a good trend!

However, in order to have the variety I think people like, we'll need to change that up and create some effortless routines.

Number 4: Never leave the diet.

This is designed as a lifestyle change intended to make you feel better, look better, have more confidence, and live a longer life.

Supermodel Kate Moss is quoted as saying, "Nothing tastes as good as skinny feels."

This has been bouncing around my head for the past few days. At a glance, it's kind of clever, but it's also a bit sad. In order for this to work, it needs to be rooted in the positive. This feed needs to be desired. People should *want* to eat... not *have* to eat. Food needs to be delicious and healthy, without the sense that you've given something up.

This book will explore that very idea.

Four directives:

1. Delicious
2. Easy and cost effective
3. Efficient and time saving
4. Never strays from the diet, while still allowing for some "legal cheats"

I have to admit that this is a daunting task.

Why I Believe this Works

Back in the time before time, humans grew on the earth with the birds and the trees and the chickens and the bees. This was a period of time before agriculture and baking and low-carb diets. This was a time when everything was symbiotic with everything else.

This ecosystem provided nourishing and nutritious foods filled with vitamins and minerals, and good quality fats and proteins. Part of the symbiosis was everything ate everything else in a generally consistent pecking order, with the humans generally at the top. One of the little clues that something was filled with nutrients was just a little sugar… to make it sweet and to give a small burst of energy when consumed. Humans developed a taste for sweets in accordance with the flora being provided, or rather, the flora was providing a touch of sweet because the flora knew it was a good way to spread their seeds.

Eventually, the humans got wise and figured out how to plant the seeds and tend to them, creating an agricultural system allowing for endless renewable foodstuffs!

The meddling humans knocked symbiosis all out of whack.

They developed agriculture faster than their human bodies were able to adapt to the change. They discovered they could manipulate the plants to increase the sweet sensation. They discovered they could dry and refine the plants for longer-term storage. More of that sweet sensation occurred and more refining occurred, resulting in a whole bevy of new products, such as beer and bread!

All the while, the human body… stayed more or less, approximately, the same.

Humans, evolved within and amongst its finite world, unwittingly detached and placed themselves above their natural connection, allowing for excess… above and beyond what the human body was accustomed to. Silly humans!

See, when the human body is given carbohydrates, it quickly converts them to glucose. Glucose is burned for energy (thinking, running, breathing, etc.). Whatever isn't needed right away is absorbed by the pancreas, which kicks out an appropriate amount of insulin, which in turn runs around taking the excess glucose and shoving it into your jiggly rear, hips, and gut… where it's stored for future energy.

This system worked really well and allowed for all kinds of variables within the ecosystem at the time. Today, the human body is *surrounded* with carbs. And more carbs and… then more carbs! The pancreas throws out insulin, where the energy is saved for later, but while this sugar dance is playing out, more carbs are ingested! The pancreas throws out more insulin! Then, this all stops, but the blood is now filled with insulin, frantically doing its best to handle the situation. With no new carbs coming in, all the sugar is taken from the blood and stored. Now, there's no more sugar in the blood. Poor human! You're tired. You're listless and… probably feeling a little depressed. Something sweet will cure that!

"Ahhhhhh. Life is good again!" thinks the human body, still unchanged from a time before time.

See, in the time before time, the fruits in the trees didn't have as much sugar. They weren't stripped of their skins and their shells and their fibers. These things all work in concert to keep the show going! Without these things, the pancreas freaks out and dies or the body resists the efforts of the insulin, causing diseases like diabetes, as well as metabolic syndrome, and liver and heart diseases. Also, obesity (yeppers—you get fat).

Oh… poor humans. What have you done to yourselves?!

Stop it. Eat like you're from the ecosystem in which you live. Return to symbiosis and you'll live longer, feel better, look younger, feel younger, run further, run faster, and, in all likelihood, lose that infernal jiggle.

Paleo versus Low-Carb

I've been interacting with a larger growing collection of people online for about a year and a half, at this point. I'm constantly asked, "Which is better, Paleo or low-carb?"

Let me just say, there are no clear, easy answers where my opinion is concerned. I can't just say, "Paleo is better," and leave it at that because it's not. I *love* Paleo but feel it has flaws. I *love* low-carb, but I also feel it has flaws. Beyond my own opinion, different diets are going to affect different people differently. Bodies are different due to medical conditions, damage done by previous diets, gender, age, etc. Even the desire to adhere to one over the other is different and will influence how well it works for any given individual.

What works for me may not work for you.

First, I think we should discuss what it means to "diet." If you're looking to lose weight or remedy some kind of medical condition, there is a good chance that you've been doing something wrong. You've been eating the wrong things or lounging around, watching the boob tube far too often. If you were to go on a super restrictive, hardcore, barebones diet for thirty days… Yep! Weight loss would ensue! If you were to go back to the same old habits from before, the weight would return, usually and unfortunately with a few bonus pounds, which will be increasingly more difficult to remove. If you diet and then go back to old habits and then diet again and then return to old habits… not only will things get worse, but permanent damage may occur as well.

Albert Einstein once defined *insanity* as, "doing the same thing over and over again and expecting different results." I love this definition, as it so succinctly states the obvious while shining a big light on most peoples' insanities.

Point being, if you want to remedy your situation, you have to make a lifelong change. This means you must restrict something. You just have to! You *will* need to eliminate something. This is why and how *all* restrictive diet plans work. Every plan out there works, because it eliminates something from the equation. If you were to sustain yourself on any given plan, forever, you'd drop to the new weight that that particular set of rules allows for… and you'd stay there forever, provided you continue adhering to it.

Return to old habits? You get the old muffin top dangling over your pants again!

The goal for any person, really, is to find what works best for them while still finding gratification in their meals. (That said, food is fuel, and while it should be gratifying, seeing it as a form of entertainment is something of a dodgy business.)

Once you've decided that you're going to restrict, good luck with the selection process! There are a near-infinite number of options to choose from. You can opt to count calories or count carbs, or pay close attention to your fat-to-protein-to-carb ratio and keep your fats super high. You can eat only vegetables. You can eat just cabbage and Twinkies (although, this will kill you eventually).

Pick the most rewarding one and stick with it forever. Or continue to learn and refine as time goes on. This is what I do.

It's important to say that not all calories are equal. It has to do a lot with insulin. I'm not a science geek and don't claim to be, but having lost near 150 pounds by decreasing the insulin in my blood, I would stake my life on that belief. If pushed, I can also point out tons of literature to support this stand (like *Wheat Belly*, for example). What I'm providing you with here is ultimately a cookbook and less of a nutrition book. While this book covers some important basics, it is far from exhaustive. Read books like *Good Calories/Bad Calories* or the easier read *Why We Get Fat and What to do About It*, both by Gary Taubes.

See, here's the thing. We all know calories, right? A calorie is a measurement of heat energy. One calorie will raise the temperature of 1 gram of water by 1 degree Celsius. Think of calories like gas for cars. Interestingly, like cars, you can put 1 gallon into some cars and they'll go 10 miles (like my 20-year-old beater), or you can put a gallon into other cars, and they'll go 60 miles. Same gas, very different results. A lot has to do with the efficiency of the car... or the biology/physiology of the car. A gallon of gas is not always equal. A calorie is not always a calorie.

The most overly simplistic illustration I can offer is this:

- 1700 calories a day of doughnuts, pizza, pasta, and most cereal will likely keep a 135 pounds woman at about the same weight for life. She won't gain or lose, but she will likely spend most of her life feeling hungry, as her blood sugar rises and falls, cresting and collapsing.
- 1700 calories a day of salmon, broccoli, blueberries, and almonds will likely cause a 135 pounds woman to lose weight—and she'll never feel hungry or unsatisfied! Realistically, this woman should probably eat well over 2000 calories in order to sustain her body weight; she's eating a wider range of nutrient-dense foods and doesn't have the hunger pangs and cravings that go along with low blood sugar.

See, starches and sugars convert to glucose in the blood. Excess glucose is stashed as fat, to be used another day. The pancreas recognizes the excess glucose and sends out the fat storing hormone insulin to go save that stuff for future bursts of energy. Remove the starches and sugars to remove the insulin. Remove the insulin, and the body stops stashing food on your rear end. In fact, instead, your body starts to *use* that butt energy, rather than stash it! YAY!

Carb calories trigger the body's response to save energy in your love handles. Without those carb calories, the body doesn't save as much in your love handles and, instead, burns fat, followed by burning the energy stored in your love handles. Make sense?

At the very least, I'm a very strong believer in reducing carbohydrates, regardless of your dietary leanings. This does play heavily into my vote for the low-carb camp.

However, again, not all carbs are equal either.

There are three macronutrients: fat, protein, and carbohydrates. Fat is pretty much fat, protein is pretty much protein, and carbs are a bit different. It's as if the nutrition people of yore had plenty of coffee the day they defined *fat* and *protein*. Someone must have switched it to decaf on the day they worked to define *carbohydrates*. They kind of threw in the towel too quickly, in my opinion. It's as though they rationalized, "Fat was easy to define; protein was easy to define. It's late; we're tired; let's just call everything that's left over carbs! Let's just say this: 'Carbohydrates are defined as anything that isn't a fat or a protein.'"

Some interesting things about carbohydrates…

Carbohydrates are the only macronutrient not required to live. If you were to cut out fat… you'd die. No protein? Death. Remove the carbs? You live! It'd be challenging, and you'd have to really work to get all your essential nutrients (by eating raw organ meats, for example), but you could live a full, long, and healthy life.

Carbs are things like starches, sugars, fibers, sugar alcohols, plus a whole range of other goofy, multisyllabic terms that no one understands, except those that speak Latin… and that one super-pumped guy, babbling in the corner.

It's because of this that *some* carbs are considered good carbs, whereas others are labeled as bad. Sugar, corn syrup, sucrose, fructose, honey, maple syrup, fruit juice concentrate, etc., are all the bad carbs, in my opinion. Starch is another one, which is why potatoes, rice, and grains are often shunned. Fiber, on the other hand, has no impact on blood sugar, so it produces no insulin, and there's the added benefit of bulk (literally extra volume or size), gut health, and it helps move things along! Then, we get into the sugar alcohols, which are compounds like maltitol, xylitol, sorbitol, and erythritol (the -itols). These impact blood sugar to varying degrees and turn into glucose more quickly than others. This is based on the glycemic index, a measurement of how foods affect blood sugar levels.

The overarching point is this: carbs aren't necessarily evil. They are often paired with nutrient-dense foods. Many of the carbs, such as fiber, are actually even beneficial. Even the plain, simple sugars have their place. It's important to understand how each of these different carbohydrates works within the body, because there are pros and cons of each. This book focuses largely on reducing those carbs that raise blood sugars (sugars and starches) and increase insulin levels.

Lower the sugar in the blood (to stable levels) and you'll reduce the fat-storing hormone insulin, and your body will burn the stored fat instead.

Paleo

Paleo is essentially "eating like our ancestors." Eat like a hunter/gatherer. Eat like a caveman. Eat things that were only available ten thousand years ago. Minimally process the ingredients before eating. Rustic cooking techniques are strong within the Paleo community. The idea here is these foods are the foods that existed when we were developing as humans. Thus, these are the foods we're genetically designed to eat. Prior to agriculture and the domestication of animals, the human diet was meat, fish, eggs, low-starch veggies, fruits, nuts, and seeds. Grains weren't grown in massive fields. They weren't milled and stripped of their fiber. Humans didn't develop with grains or orange groves, or grocery stores filled with coconut flour and honey.

If you held a hand-whittled bow and arrow to my head and asked me to choose an ideology between Paleo and low-carb, I'd say Paleo. *True* Paleo. This is an abrupt answer to a life-or-death situation, mind you, and needs some explaining.

The beating heart of Paleo is that it incorporates fresh, whole foods, minimally processed. Paleo also ties in exercise, but like our ancestors might have, not a ten-mile run or sixty minutes of high-impact jazzercise. It's a lot of steady, continuous movement, followed by short blasts of extreme output, like jumping really high and hard (to escape a lion) or lifting a really massive boulder (which has just rolled into your living room). It's about your body fighting the wild, or at least acting as if it is.

Here is where I get so bent out of shape over Paleo: honey. I hate you, honey! You've very much and very sincerely ruined what feels like an otherwise beautiful, harmonious, and symbiotic philosophy.

Paleo has been tampered with. Its seemingly crystal-clear edges have been sanded down, hacked. Because bees were around and making honey ten thousand years ago, it's been decreed by the Paleo community: "HONEY GOOD!"

Now, don't get me wrong. Honey *is* good. It clearly serves a valuable role in the world. It's the result of bee pollination… from which we get the sweet, tasty bee liquid, which brave and enterprising cave folk probably *did* indulge in—from time to time… rarely.

I also believe honey is better than refined sugar. It's got a few extra nutrients, volumetrically, it's quite a bit sweeter, so a little goes further than regular sugar, and it pretty much never goes bad. *However*, it's sugar. I don't care which way you slice and dice it. Spin it as hard as you want to—the simple fact remains that my body *loves* to stash excess honey on my butt. It gives me a quick boost of energy and then stashes the rest… right square on my rear.

My frustration with honey is the result of reading hundreds of sickeningly sweet Paleo cookbooks that time and time again spin the idea that honey is an acceptable excess—it is plain wrong. This, my friends, grows old, resulting in a resentment that's potentially even a bit stronger than it really has any right to be.

See, ten thousand years ago, Grok and Groll couldn't just walk into a grocery store and pluck jars of raw honey off the shelf. When I ask myself *What's Paleo?* I ask myself, *Would I be willing to fend off thousands of bees to get my honey?* Remember, this is at a time when there were no hospitals.

So, the answer is nope, not bloody likely!

The same is true with maple syrup. Sure, those trees existed, but I somehow doubt that Grok got up and turned the tap on his maple tree for that morning's almond-meal pancakes. Grok just wasn't that sophisticated. I simply don't believe our bodies were designed for blasts of sugar in this manner. At least, not consistently, year after year after year…

The same is true with dried dates. I mean, they are just concentrated sugar. Sure, it's a fruit, but it's a *super* sweet fruit, which has been dried and concentrated! They have been accepted by the Paleo community because they are fruit and can be dried by the sun. But come on. We're talking about a time before agriculture. I don't see Cro-Magnon folks resting their Medjool dates on rocks until they concentrated their sweet flavor for tomorrow's coconut-date-maple muffins.

Full Discloser: I would eat a dozen Coconut-Date-Maple Muffins. They would be *delicious!* I'd eat them with my whole face! Our bodies *want* these kinds of things and are hardwired for sugar, which is *why* we want it! But, remember, in order to get that sugar (to stash on our butts for potential times of famine), we had to fend off large animals, bees, climb trees, lift rocks, and generally do everything we could not to starve, get injured, or die. The sweet taste is for survival, but we've refined and bottled that stuff. We are now continuing to create reasons for pouring it on our tapioca-and-arrowroot waffles, with extra-sweet and super-tasty caramelized organic apples.

This is the Paleo slippery slope. Because certain things existed back in time, they're considered acceptable foods… even though they didn't really exist in the *same way* that they do today. This frustrates me to no end.

Honey… I hate you.

Low-Carb

Low-carb is a method I personally followed, and it allowed me to lose almost 150 pounds within a fairly short span of time. It *clearly* works, but if you're following the overall theme, it's that too many of the wrong carbohydrates will cause weight gain, regardless of your philosophy.

Probably my biggest beef with low-carb is that it has a tendency to portray itself as gluttonous. Whereas a quick glance at Paleo suggests whole foods, foraged by rock-scaling, tree-climbing cave people, low-carbers present low-carb eating as stacks of steak, eggs, and bacon-y cream and cheese sauces… with a whisper of spice and a broccoli floret. To be perfectly honest, I do it all the time too! I definitely play into this view quite often. It's the low-carb sales pitch: "Come on, Sally! Think about it… you can eat as much bacon as you want! BACON!!!!"

This is potentially where I'm even sharing some insight into my own personal issues. It's often hard to see outside yourself, so what I'm sharing could be very centered around me and my views, and I'm casting a negative light on something simply because of my own weaknesses, when the reality is low-carb, just like any other dietary plan, works when you work it.

A traditional low-carb plan actually has some amazing features built into it. Aside from induction (20 "net" carbs per day, or less), there is a slow increasing of carbs during the Ongoing Weight Loss (OWL) period, which allows for the ability to fine-tune and increase the intensity, should you have that inclination. No such concept exists within Paleo. There is the carb ladder, which suggests starting with meats, eggs, simple leafy greens, and low-carb veggies. Then, over a span of time, add in heavy dairy. Then, a while later, add in nuts and seeds, then berries, stone fruits, and melons, then lighter forms of dairy. Later, layer in the legumes (not allowed on the Paleo diet because raw legumes are toxic; thus it's inferred that our ancestors didn't eat them), finally start adding in sweeter fruits, and last… grains. This is an interesting progression that never rules out any particular food group. They are all allowed—provided you've earned the right to step up a rung!

I actually really love this approach and breakdown because it offers a path of intensity and restriction options. If things are stalling, climb lower on the ladder. If things are going well, step up a rung! This also does a fantastic job at helping people identify specific groups that they may disagree with for some reason. One that isn't clearly identified is the nightshade family, which probably should be a rung, but it isn't…

By and large, low-carb seems more willing to accept frankenfoods (synthetic and/or highly refined foods that never existed until we created them). I *do* feel these have held me back, personally. Lately, in fact, many healthy-based corporations seem to be embracing these more and more (something I'm personally a bit disappointed with). I've mostly phased them out. Looking through some of the more die-hard low-carb websites, you'll see things like polydextrose, wheat protein isolate, high gluten flours, acesulfame potassium, sucralose, glucomannan, xanthan gum, glycerin, xylitol, oat fiber, etc. Many die-hard low-carbers have an arsenal of chemicals, so that they can make foods… just like the processed foods they used to eat before starting low-carb! (I know! I have such a laboratory, myself!)

Low-Primal

Through my own personal experiences teetering between low-carb and Paleo, I've arrived at my current eating style, which I've lovingly dubbed "Low-Primal" = Low-Carb + Primal (Paleo + Dairy) + Erythritol. It's a blend. It could be said it's even served with a tiny side dish of raw. To be clear, Low-Primal is pure rationalization. It's a very modern spin; it embraces the ideas of both Paleo and Low-Carb, while allowing for some minimal processing. It's my way. It's what I feel is the best combination—for me—that I've found, that I can live with, is entrenched in rules I understand, and comes complete with chutes and ladders, allowing me the option to vary the intensity, should I ever choose to.

I don't often bake coconut flour muffins, and the erythritol is mostly for my coffee. Low-Primal, to me, combines the best aspects of each of the various ideologies while staying within natural ingredients that existed in nature tens of thousands of years ago and that currently exist in modern configurations. It also allows me to eat foods that look and taste a lot like the foods my fellow humans are eating today. This gives me a sense of comfort… in numbers.

I know how to be more restrictive and gain intensity, but I haven't fully marched that way, just yet… even though I know I'm going to have to someday. For now, Low-Primal is where I sit, and I may sit here for life. It's a pretty tasty, varied way to be! Someday, I may remove dairy or nuke anything sweet. I may opt to include more raw ingredients or boost my fermented foods. Someday. Maybe.

Going Low-Primal is a trek and an adventure. It's somewhere you'll never arrive at, but you'll always work to get to. It's a search and one that requires Low-Primal Participation.

Low-Primal Participation

When I was younger, I attended a speech at a somewhat odd university I was visiting… on a boat. Yep, it was a university on a boat. A big boat… on the Baltic Sea, no less! The speech was philosophical in nature. The topic was happiness. The guy prattled on about drugs and direct wiring to the pleasure sensors of the mind, chocolate, alcohol, cocaine, etc. He talked about rats running through heated mazes and across electrified fields in search of cheese. He really went through just about every pleasure-giving act that can be foisted upon a person (or rat). It was interesting how he'd start with a topic, describe how deeply pleasurable it would be, and then… beat it to death. He would deconstruct the sensation and point out convincing reasons why it's not true happiness.

In the end, after knocking pleasure silly, he left us all with one last thought, a perfect coda to an otherwise frustrating speech.

He said that he's looked far, wide, up, down, and at everything under the sun. If there's any single description for *happiness* that he's able to live with, it is this: "Happiness is participation in anything which brings fulfillment."

Then… he bowed.

Really, if you want to deconstruct that saying, you can kill the word *happiness* because we already know that it's happiness that we're talking about. You can pretty much nuke *fulfillment* also. That's really just reiterating that we're talking about happiness, and we already know this. That leaves, "Participation in anything." "Anything" isn't narrowly defined enough for me, so… let's throw that out too.

This leaves us with: "participation"—preferably *voluntary* participation.

ahem

You need to participate in your own story. Sitting with a bag of popcorn and a pint of ice cream in the fridge while watching *Roseanne* reruns is not participating. It's… sitting and widening. Trust me, I know.

Walking for twenty minutes every day. *That* is participating.

Driving through a take-out joint and picking up a greasy sack of burgers and fries is not participating. It's living outside the experience.

I'm not demonizing burgers. I *am*, however, saying that a greasy sack of soulless burgers wolfed down on the drive home is not participating. There's a world of difference between that and the conscious experience of finding an organic, local, whole-food burger and being present while you eat it.

To be clear, having a conscious ritual of purchasing the best burger and fries, from an elite location, with a bun made from stone-ground grains, house-aged beef, and local, organic tomatoes; taking the time to stop and notice the nooks and crannies on the bun and paying close, careful attention to the doneness of the meat, and the coarseness of the grind; enjoying the spicy notes permeating your olfactory system while you take slow bites, enjoy the moments, and share them with friends and family—this, to me, is participation. The act isn't blind. It's conscious, deliberate, and enjoyed for very clear and specific reasons.

Going to the store and selecting ripe vegetables and talking to the butcher about how to cut and freeze pork chops from the pork loin that is on sale is participating.

Watching *Cupcake Wars* on the Food Network is… well, ok. I like that show too. I like to see how they decorate and work in the theme. I usually watch it while jogging on the treadmill (horse and carrot).

Reading this book? That's participating.

Cooking, especially if it's something new, is participating. It's not tuning out and throwing stuff in the microwave. It's paying attention to the way a peeler is peeling a carrot and trying to do it a little faster with each pass. It's trying to peel the carrot while the sauce simmers away, rather than peeling the carrot *and then* putting the sauce on to simmer.

Being present and aware of the things you're doing will help you understand the changes. This, in my opinion, will make them lasting and permanent. Drifting through them or pushing through them to kill a quick ten pounds is murky, out of focus, and not participating. And you'll likely gain back fifteen.

Lifting weights is participating. Yoga is participating.

Going to a farmer's market and asking what goat cheese tastes like from the farmer that very likely coagulated it him/herself is participating.

I'm not saying you need to do all of these things at once. I sure didn't! I started by changing my diet and walking. Nothing too dramatic, but once I started… I never stopped. I looked for new ways to participate and challenge myself. *Slowly*. Very slowly… too slowly for some, in fact!

I'd walk a mile and sit ten times during that mile. The next day, I'd walk a mile and challenge myself to sit… only nine times! Then… eight times. Then… seven times! Before I knew it, I could walk a mile without sitting! Then, I started to time myself. Then, I started to focus on my stride, then, my posture.

For the most part, for the real lessons and true ongoing change, participation is a key component to moving toward a healthier, low-primal way of life.

Right about now, you're probably thinking, *Ugh! I have to not only change what I eat, but I have to participate too? Whatever that means.*

The idea here is that you should *want* to and that it should be fun—and fulfilling. It's a system designed to bring about happiness!

I've peeled a million potatoes. I'm sure of it. Probably twice as many carrots. Needless to say, I've peeled *a lot* of *many* things in my life. Peeling a fifty-pound sack of potatoes is mindless drudgery; it's not fun. How do you make that fun? Invite some buddies and race! I can't tell you how many potato-peeling challenges I've taken. (I've even won some of them.) Point being, there are ways to make anything engaging or fun. Find your way.

Low-Primal Rules

Some say you should eat five or six small meals a day. Others insist intermittent fasting, extended periods of time without a meal, is the way to go. Many, including my doctor, insist that a big breakfast is better than a big dinner.

I'm not sure what the answer is, in terms of what's right. Everyone seems to think their general consensus is the right one. I'm going to throw caution to the wind and say…

Rule 1. Eat when you're hungry.

I should clarify: eat when you're *hungry*, not when you're *craving*. This isn't a free ticket to the all-you-can-eat buffet. Learn to tell the difference. One is your body saying, "Hey. You, up there! We're out of food. Feed us!" The other feels similar but tends to be slightly irrational, stronger, strangely persistent, and with a tantrum-y vibe. It's vital to understand the difference.

Eat when you're *hungry*… not just craving like a lunatic. Craving and hunger are very different creatures.

I personally eat twice a day most of the time. A big cup of coffee in the morning, usually blended with some grass-fed butter and MCT Oil, and then sweetened with an erythritol sweetener blend.

Then, I usually have a small lunch. This is usually Poorly Cooked Eggs with sautéed veggies swirled in. Other times it's sausage, cheese, and sliced tomatoes or unsweetened Greek yogurt with fresh berries and powdered erythritol swirled in, or a small salad, crust-less quiche, quickie veggie cream soups, etc.

Dinner is where my big meal usually comes in. This is generally more composed and has two or three parts—chicken with a salad, for example, or steak with a red wine cream sauce and broccoli.

I rarely drink anything other than water or coffee, and only coffee in the morning. I drink *a lot* of water.

If I'm hungry, I do snack, but snacks are limited, as I'm rarely hungry!

My big go-to snacks are sliced salami or yogurt. I know many like nuts. Nuts are fine, but not too many. Lately, I've been noshing on a lot of sunflower seeds. They're hard for me to put them down. I love them so! The big issue with nuts and seeds: people want to keep going. Try not to eat more than a quarter of a cup at a time.

Again, eat when you're hungry. *Only* when hungry.

Rule 2. Eat less than thirty <u>net</u> carbs per day.

This is straight from a traditional low-carb induction period, but with a little extra allowance. The traditional number is twenty, but I'm allowing thirty, simply because I am presenting clean foods, and I don't want people to feel strapped to steak and eggs. Thirty carbs a day allows for *huge* variety! That said, if you want to increase the intensity, cut back to twenty… or ten. Any lower than ten and variety, as well as a rich assortment of nutrients, becomes harder to attain.

If you're losing weight quickly, feel free to up it 5 or 10 net carbs for a week or two. Continue adjusting up or down to maintain a comfortable pace, while maintaining a nice healthy variety or meals.

I experimented with zero carbs for a thirty-day period. However, without the fiber in the foods, there were some unexpected and uncomfortable consequences. Additionally, carbs are often intertwined with nutrient density. A pure meat, bacon fat, and egg diet may be effective for short-term losses, but it's not terribly interesting or varied and doesn't have all the nutrients required to live (unless you opt to start eating raw offal meats to supplement the nutrients lost from vegetables). I feel thirty is a very solid and reliable number and is a bit of a sweet spot.

"Net" carbs are traditionally defined as the total number of carbohydrates minus fiber.

Some people just count all carbs, whereas others deduct fiber and all sugar alcohols (I'll get into these, later).

I like to think of carbs in terms of how much sugar it gets converted into. Perhaps it's silly, but the visualization of the actual little piles of white granulated sugar surging through my veins really helps me put this into perspective.

First, realize that sugar isn't just sugar. Starch is also sugar. Many carbs are converted into sugar (glucose, if you want to get technical) in your blood. There's a scale called the glycemic index, which assigns a value to an ingredient or food based on how quickly a food converts to glucose in the blood.

Thirty grams of net carbs for the day is roughly the equivalent of three tablespoons (just under 45 mL) of pure granulated sugar, spread throughout the day. So, while thirty grams may feel low, it's still near three tablespoon-sized piles of refined, crystalline evil.

My personal rule for a "net" carb…

Net Carbs = Total Carbs, minus fiber, minus 50 percent the value of a sugar alcohol (except for erythritol)

So, let's say that we are looking at a sugar-free strawberry jelly.

One serving size is 1 tablespoon (17 grams or 15 mL).

1 Tbsp has 5 total carbs
2 g of fiber
2 g of sugar alcohols
1 g of sugar

It is sweetened with the sugar alcohol xylitol.

In this case, I would count one serving as two net carbs. The assumption, in this case, is that the fiber and sugar come naturally from the berries. The extra 2 grams of xylitol boost the sweetness, while still impacting blood sugar (just nowhere near the level of sugar). In reality, xylitol has a small impact on blood sugar and is also natural. On the other side of the sugar alcohol spectrum is something like maltitol, which is found in a huge array of "sugar-free" candies and impacts blood at levels near sugar. As a result, I tend to merge and blend *all* sugar alcohols into one fuzzy and inaccurate lump-sum of *half*. If you want precision in your net-carb counts, the information is available. Do a little research on sugar alcohols, sugar-free sweeteners, and the glycemic index.

Stevia, erythritol, and oligosaccharides are all sweeteners with a glycemic index of zero. They don't impact blood sugar, so they don't count at all. This is where exceptions come in. These are the sweeteners I use; these are the sweeteners my recipes and their nutrition are based on.

Rule 3. Never eat more than ten net carbs per hour.

This is more a cautionary guideline than a hard-and-fast rule, although feel free to treat it like a hard and fast rule. It is a good one. The goal with this whole way of eating is to stabilize the blood sugar and insulin and repair metabolism. If you know you can eat upward of thirty net carbs a day, and eat steak with steak and a side of steak, then polish it off with 7 1/2 teaspoons (30 grams or 38 mL) of granulated sugar, you're going to cause a spike in blood sugars. Keep it level, even. As I said, it's just a guideline.

Rule 4. Eat clean, whole foods. No grains. Nothing refined or overly processed.

This is another guideline, but certainly something to strive for.

Our food production and refining methods have far outpaced our own evolution. Our bodies aren't designed for a life watching TV while eating a milky bowl of chocolate-frosted sugar bombs (even though it may feel like it!). Our bodies are designed to eat wild berries and leaves, fish and fast, stringy birds—our bodies are also designed to chase the stringy birds and run from the giant cats.

What our modern lifestyle has done is stopped us in our tracks. It has given us countless ways to ingest the pure, refined stuff. Nowadays, we strip out the beet and… eat beet sugar!

What Can You Eat?
What Should You Avoid?

You can eat pretty much anything when you're eating Low-Primal, as long as it isn't full of carbs, comes from a box, can, or bag… or comes from the middle part of your grocery store. Fresh, whole foods are on the outside of grocery stores—veggies, nuts, meats, seeds, seafood, fruits, eggs, dairy, and mushrooms.

To generalize and simplify it: zero to very low starch and zero to very low sugar. This means no grains, a small amount of fruits, virtually no legumes (green beans and snap peas make the cut. Peanuts also fall into an ambiguous gray area [I tend to avoid them]), and in an easy-to-remember and roundabout way: nothing "white." This means no bread, no pasta, no rice, and no potatoes (white or otherwise, although some sweet potatoes are often acceptable in moderation). Also, to paint a clearer picture: no bananas, no tortillas, no beans, and so on. Except, you know, when it's under thirty net carbs and the alternative is a full-blown binge.

You can eat any meats (bacon!) and eggs, in virtually any amount, as well as most all veggies, especially the leafy, green ones; cheeses; other dairy products, such as cream and butter; and healthy oils, like lard, olive, and coconut.

To be more specific…

Meats

Most any and all muscle meats, in any amounts.

However, be aware that eggs, some organ meats (offal), and some seafood have small amounts of carbohydrates. You can still eat substantial portions of these ingredients, but you will need to count those carbs toward your daily limit.

Some examples:

- Eggs = approximately half a carb each
- Shrimp = about 4 carbs per pound (so about 1 carb per 4 large shrimp)
- Oysters = about 2.5 carbs each
- Beef Liver = about 1 carb per ounce (28g) (16 carbs per pound (454g))

Also, some other meaty things to watch out for…

Bacon, ham, sausages, salami, deli meats, etc.—you'll need to read the packages for these products. Again, you may eat substantial portions of these items, but you'll need to shop around and find a product that suits your way of eating. This category of meat product often has sugar in their brines, marinades, and cures, as well as carb-y and wonky fillers and preservatives in some of the sausages and highly processed lunch meats. Talk to your butcher.

Fruits, Vegetables, and Legumes

Eat your vegetables! Vegetables have a lot of nutrients that aren't found in muscle meats. In order to get all necessary nutrients *just* from meats, you'd have to eat a really wide variety of meats, including organ meats, often raw and/or undercooked.

Eat your vegetables. They're delicious, and they're good for you! One of the biggest myths of a low-carb diet is that you can't eat vegetables. That simply isn't true.

Eat them. They're not only allowed, they're encouraged!

Greens If it's a leaf, eat up! I personally believe that it's impossible to eat enough green, leafy vegetables to really cause a problem. So, salad greens are essentially a totally free pass, though, to begin, you should always stay under thirty grams a day, but a giant bowl of spinach tossed with a bit of oil, salt, pepper, and a squirt of lemon is unlikely to ruin anyone's day.

Fruits On the other end of the spectrum are fruits. Fruits are highly nutritious, but they tend to be combined with lots of fructose. Pay close attention to the amounts of fruit you eat, because too much of the wrong ones can definitely add up!

(**Note:** carb amounts are based on 100 grams [roughly 4 ounces] of "average" raw fruit or vegetable, except where otherwise noted. USDA-21 Database)

Alfalfa sprouts	0	Avocado	2.17	Brussels sprouts	5	Honeydew melon	8.28
Broccoli rabe/rapini	0	Zucchini/Summer Squash	2.17	Raspberries	5.45	Peaches	9
Mushrooms	1	Eggplant	2.37	Strawberries	5.6	Peas	9
Asparagus	1.49	Tomatoes	2.74	Casaba melon	5.67	Oranges	10
Radish	1.72	Cauliflower	2.86	Rutabagas	5.7	Plums	10
Celery	1.82	Cucumber	2.99	Celeriac/Celery root	5.77	Apple	12
Greens/Lettuces		Peppers	3.05	Pumpkin	6.03	Blueberries	12
Endive	.19	Cabbage	3.29	Carrots	6.25	Leeks	12
Watercress	1	Green Beans	3.64	Beets	6.62	Pears	12
Boston/Butter	1.23	Jicama	3.92	Spaghetti Squash	6.93	Pineapple	12
Romaine	1.28	Broccoli	3.95	Watermelon	7.15	Parsnips	13
Mesclun/Mixed	1.29	Okra	4	Cranberries	7.27	Cherries	14
Spinach	1.47	Tomatillos	4	Onions	7.5	Beans, fava (cooked)	14
Iceberg	1.99	Fennel	4.27	Papaya	7.89	Potatoes, red	14
Arugula	2	Blackberries	4.86	Cantaloupe	7.99	Beans, kidney (cooked)	16
Chard	2	Artichokes	4.94	Kale	8	Beans, navy (cooked)	16
Collard	2	Turnips	4.92			Corn, sweet yellow	16
Mache	2					Grapes	16
Mustard	2					Potatoes, russet	17
						Sweet Potatoes	17
						Beans, pinto (cooked)	18
						Bananas	20
						Beans, garbanzo (cooked)	20

Dairy

All dairy is acceptable, but the lower-carb ingredients are at the top of the list. I'm going to stick with 100 grams/4 ounces (by weight) portions, for consistency. For visualization purposes, 4 ounces of cream is about a half a cup (120 mL).

Butter	0	Blue cheese	2.22	Cream cheese, full fat	3.88
Brie	.42	Provolone cheese	2.35	Feta cheese	4
Goat cheese	1	Ricotta cheese, full fat	2.84	Half and half	4.13
Cheddar cheese	1.23	Heavy cream	2.94	Plain yogurt, full fat	4.49
American cheese	2	Sour cream, full fat	3.48	Skim milk	4.87
Mozzarella cheese, whole milk, low moisture	2	Parmesan cheese	3.52	Milk	5.33
		Cottage cheese, full fat	3.56	Swiss cheese	5.33

Dairy is one of those topics that is a bit tricky to present within a low-primal way of eating. Traditional low-carb has limits set on dairy. The logic, as I understand it, is to limit a combination of both calories and carbs.

The core issue with dairy is it's filled with calories and also goes down easily. It's very easy to get carried away with dairy and simply drink buckets of cream and inhale blocks of cheese.

With a low-primal lifestyle, you will be able to eat more calories than on the Standard American Diet (SAD) and lose or maintain a healthy weight. *However*, calories still count. Additionally, dairy does contain carbs, mostly in the form of lactose (milk sugars). I should also point out that you should always purchase the full-fat versions of these products. Food is essentially made of fat, protein, and carbohydrates. If you remove the fat, you need to replace that fat with something. Manufacturers add sugar to enhance the flavor and mouthfeel lost by the elimination of fat.

I don't want to govern people. I eat dairy when I want to and completely skip it at other times. I suggest eating dairy whenever you want and as much as you want, but not like it's going out of style. As you get closer to your goal, you may need to cut calories… which may mean the elimination of some dairy. Don't worry about that though. That's another book (probably titled "Low-Paleo").

Personal note: I use almond milk in place of regular milk. It has about .5 net carbs per 100 gram/4 ounce portion. That's roughly ten times fewer carbs than standard milk.

Spices and Herbs

Because spices and herbs are used in such small quantities (while also packing a punch), rather than list them all at four ounces, I'm going to list them at around one teaspoon (5 mL).

Basil, fresh, chopped	.01	Fennel seed	.24	Cumin seed	.66
Chives, fresh	.01	Coriander seed, ground	.26	Black pepper	.76
Cilantro, fresh, chopped	.01	Thyme, ground	.27	Cardamom, ground	.8
Oregano, fresh, chopped	.01	Basil, dried, ground	.28	Tarragon, ground	.86
Green onions	.04	Ginger, fresh	.32	White pepper	.86
Parsley	.04	Paprika	.38	Garlic, fresh, chopped (about 1 carb per clove)	.93
Dill weed, fresh	.05	Oregano, ground	.42	Allspice, ground	1
Rosemary, fresh	.05	Curry powder	.5	Pumpkin pie spice	1.08
Sage, fresh	.1	Vanilla extract	.5	Poultry seasoning	1.1
Tarragon, fresh	.1	Cloves, ground	.54	Ginger, ground	1.16
Thyme, fresh	.1	Cinnamon, ground	.56	Onion powder	1.5
Sage, ground	.14	Nutmeg, ground	.56	Garlic powder	1.89
Parsley, dried	.15	Cayenne pepper	.6		
Caraway seed	.24	Mace, ground	.6		

Nuts and Seeds

Nuts are one of the ingredients that are generally discouraged during the early parts of a low-carb diet. Some are higher in carbs than others. Again, the primary issue, is that nuts are difficult in terms of portion control. Most people, when they sit down to eat a bowl of nuts, rarely stop at just a quarter cup. They'll just keep eating, while totally losing track of themselves. Nuts are also fairly calorie dense.

However, nuts are also rich with amino acids, which are the building blocks of protein and the nutrients your body uses to build muscle. Nuts are also high in magnesium (magnesium helps keep blood pressure normal, bones strong, and the heart rhythm steady), while also being high in healthy fats.

Nuts can be a good thing if used sparingly. I personally very rarely eat nuts, but I *love* to add them to salads for texture (instead of those filthy croutons). In a pinch, I will also dig macadamias.

Seeds tend to be a great thing. I love sunflower seeds (which happen to make a great flour, as an alternative to almond flour, for those with nut allergies). Also, I'll use ground flax or chia seeds in various pastries and breads.

For these, I'm going to focus on a single ounce (28 grams), the idea being one ounce is a nice little snack.

To put things into perspective, one ounce is about a quarter cup (60 mL) of whole almonds.

Flax seeds	.44	Coconut, dried, unsweetened	2.24	Cashews	8.4
Pecans	1.12	Peanuts	2.24	Chestnuts	12.32
Brazil nuts	1.38	Pine nuts	2.24		
Macadamia nuts	1.4	Poppy seeds	2.24		
Chia seeds	1.68	Pumpkin seeds	2.52		
Coconut, raw meat	1.68	Almonds	2.8		
Hazelnuts	1.96	Sesame seeds	3.08		
Walnuts	1.96	Sunflower seeds	3.08		
		Pistachios	5.04		

Fats and Oils

Fats and oils are all zero carb, but I want to take this opportunity to point out some fats that are better than others, and also suggest some that should be avoided entirely.

Also, because my core training and information base is in cooking, it seems only natural to present the following fats and oils in terms of their smoke point. A *smoke point* is the temperature at which an oil burns and smokes, producing toxic fumes, nasty free radicals, and icky, bitter tastes. Higher smoke points mean the oils can be used for high-heat cooking, such as frying. Lower smoke points mean mellow cooking methods or no heating at all (which means they can be used for salad dressings, some sauces, etc.).

Good Fats				Bad Fats
Flaxseed oil	225°F (107°C)	Cocoa butter	400°F (204°C)	Margarine
Butter, whole	250 to 300°F (121 to 149°C)	Almond oil	420°F (216°C)	Shortening
		Hazelnut oil	431°F (221°C)	Canola oil
Sesame oil, unrefined	350°F (177°C)	Palm oil	455°F (235°C)	Corn oil
Coconut oil, unrefined	352°F (177°C)	Coconut oil, refined	450°F (232°C)	Soybean oil
Lard	370°F (188°C)	Sesame oil, semirefined	450°F (232°C)	Cottonseed oil
Olive oil, extra virgin	375°F (191°C)	Olive oil, extra light	468°F (242°C)	Vegetable oil
Olive oil, virgin	391°F (199°C)	Butter, clarified (ghee)	485°F (252°C)	

Snacks

I think it's important to have a bag of tricks in your arsenal, just in case the lunatic Crave Gremlins are banging down your door. While you should never ever go off plan, it's unrealistic to assume it will never happen. It's better to have a backup plan for just such an occasion, because a pint of ice cream will just cause problems, feed the fire of cravings, and will likely knock you out of *ketosis* (the state your body enters to burn your stored fat for energy, rather than glucose... "Fat Burning" vs. "Sugar Burning"), requiring you to start all over again.

No cheating–it can take two to four days to get back into ketosis!

The following are quick one- to ten-minute snack ideas that can get you through a strong craving.

First and foremost, have a big glass of water. This will help create a feeling of fullness, along with the satisfaction of having a little snack.

This collection is by no means exhaustive. There are countless ideas on the Internet, including on my own website. These are just some of the most simplistic and basic. However, they will all work in a pinch. They range from salty to sweet to crunchy. Most cravings should be fed with this list. Also, several are portable, meaning you can have a bag of protein shake powder in a purse, backpack, glove compartment, desk drawer, etc., in addition to a bag of nuts or some jerky. Ideally, you will have a meal plan so you have an idea about what happens if you choose to go off plan. A smart plan B is always wise. Keep these around and close. You never know when the Crave Gremlins are gonna get you!

- A big glass of water
- Deli meats and cheese (Roll these up in a lettuce leaf with a squirt of mustard. Yum!)
- Hard-boiled egg
- A handful of nuts
- Small bowl of plain Greek yogurt with berries or sugar-free jam or jelly swirled in (Not too big—this can be a dangerous snack. Portion control is tough, but this snack is acceptable if you're careful.)
- Protein shakes (Look for very low- or zero-carb whey protein.)
- Pepperoni sticks
- Pork rinds
- Sunflower seeds in the shell
- Scrambled eggs
- Celery sticks or other raw vegetables, with or without cheese or creamy dips
- Sliced mozzarella and slices of tomato with a sprinkle of salt and pepper (I'm a big fan of this.)
- Cooked sausages (There are a million flavors to choose from.)
- Beef or turkey jerky
- String cheese (I always have string cheese close by.)
- Sugar-free Jell-O
- Low-carb snack bars (**Note:** Most low-carb/sugar-free snacks and meal replacement bars use really fuzzy logic. They often have malitol, sorbitol, and/or vegetable glycerin, each of which computes wildly differently in the blood than other sugar alcohols. These can knock you out of ketosis and cause a major stall. *However*, they are *much* better than a pint of ice cream. I do not recommend these for the first two weeks, nor do I particularly believe in them while actively losing weight. However, I believe they are acceptable in an emergency, compared with the alternative, and are completely fine for maintenance.)

Sweeteners

I'm asked some variation of the question "What is the best sweetener?" several times a day. "What is the best sweetener?" is almost like asking someone their religion or political leanings these days.

People tend to have strong and often fierce beliefs in this realm. Someone who has educated themselves into a locavore, raw honey–dipped corner is *very* unlikely to ever change their stance on the subject… and will defend that stance to the end. I've seen serious fights break out in chat rooms and on social media networks over things like honey versus Splenda.

Some of the time, I see these feuds and chuckle. These sweeteners don't really benefit us in any meaningful way. They don't really have vast quantities of nutrients. Distilled down, it's just sugar versus nothing, really. Empty and void of any meaningful nutrients, they either raise blood sugar or just casually pass through the body. I sometimes like to think it's like people fighting over which is the most healthy cigarette brand or the best beer for attaining a lovely "beer figure." I'm sure there's an answer to the question... but I think the real answer is "None."

I'm honestly not completely sure I understand the passion with which people defend their sweeteners, but as someone whose been attacked by the honey lovers, or the stevia freaks or the maple fanatics, I know how devoted some people are. For them, it's a simple universal topic that encapsulates larger dietary philosophies... and can even be used to help frame larger ideologies—someone that rubs manuka honey all over a recent burn is coming at the world from a very specific place. They'll defend that place.

Let me just say that we don't *need* sweeteners at all. Yep. I'm a big party pooper! I know. I'm no fun, but I want this to be seen as an honest and sincere presentation. It's hard to act as if these ingredients or the sweet taste is necessary. It absolutely has its place in history and evolution, and there are some benefits, as mentioned earlier in the book (helps spread seeds, pollination, gives energy to store as fat for our ancestors, etc.), but really, if we *really* back up to a place of pure health and survival... sweeteners are totally unnecessary for our physiology. In fact, there are some schools of thought stating that even just the simple taste of "sweet" will cause an insulin response. The body knows some sugar has just entered the body, so it proactively secretes insulin to manage it. When it doesn't find the sugar, it takes the existing glucose in the blood and stashes it in the fat deposits anyway, dropping blood sugar and causing cravings. This logic is one of the reasons behind the claims that diet sodas don't "work."

There are loads of studies based on various sweeteners and the release of insulin. Technically, there have been studies done showing that sucralose, the primary sweetener in Splenda, does not cause insulin to respond. At bare minimum, this suggests that the proactive release of insulin based purely on the taste of sweet is a bit of a myth or only applies to some sweeteners. Yet it persists, and there are always exceptions.

When I began my big change, I began with a zero-sweets experiment, lasting about six weeks. I *highly* recommend everyone try and eliminate sweets from their diet for a period of thirty days. This means nothing sweet in the coffee. No chocolate. No fat bombs or one-minute muffins. No pies, panna cotta, or ice cream.

It's *amazing* how the sweet taste in broccoli stems begins to reveal itself. Who's ever tasted a sweet bell pepper and thought it tasted sweet? Try eliminating all sweets for thirty days... *and then* bite into a pepper. Sweet, right? Almost like an apple.

A grand experiment, it's like rebooting the sense of taste.

For the most part, sweet things are interpreted as high-energy foods and bitter things are considered poisonous. It's these traits that have helped us taste our way through history. This is another way in which we've evolved with the world around us; it guided us toward the energy and nutrient-dense foods, while warning us against the poisonous ones.

Now that we've got an established food system, we know that the bitter leaves of endive are better and more nutrient dense than, say, a tablespoon of sugar, which may supply a shorter burst of energy but that's about it; however, I think it would be a challenge to find a person who would agree that the sugar is healthier than the endive.

Common Natural Sweeteners

Sugar

Now that we've talked a bit about the sensation of "sweet," let's talk a bit about sugar.

Sugar is that white granular stuff that we all know and love. Because we all know it and love it, our culture—and many others—has grown up around it. This means that cookie, cake, and ice cream recipes have been formulated and refined over hundreds of years, based on the characteristics of sugar. The characteristics of sugar reach much further into our tasty sweets than one might initially discern. Sure, the stuff is sweet, but it's got a point at which it dissolves in water. It's got a point at which it melts. It's got a point at which it caramelizes. It's got a point at which it will become gooey and stretchy, based on the temperature it's at or was at. It's got a point at which it will crack and shatter if dropped on the floor. An oversimplification, but it's the sugar in cookies that gives them their nice golden-brown color. It's even got specific and unique hygroscopic properties. Anyone that's ever poured sugar on cut strawberries and let it sit for thirty minutes knows about its ability to pull yummy red juice from the sliced berries.

Sugar is a friendly word, especially compared to the less friendly sounding *sucrose*, which is friendlier than the even less friendly sounding *saccharose*. Each of these names is just common table sugar, a disaccharide composed of the monosaccharides glucose and fructose (about fifty/fifty).

Sugar is *delicious!* It sends a quick and immediate message to the brain, "SWEET, LOVING DELICIOUS-NESS! ENERGY! WHEE!!!!" See, this reaction is evolutionarily advantageous. It's what kept us going in the time before time. Our present-day body doesn't know that we've extracted the sweet white stuff from beets and a really, really tall, thick grass. We've distilled the flavor down to a pure crystal, without any nutrition. *Yum!*

The actual roots of sugar go back many thousand years, starting simply as sugar cane juice. Over time, refinement techniques improved. Sugar, as we know it, has more or less been a part of most cultures for about five hundred years, with its popularity increasing dramatically ever since. In the mid 1800s, the process became completely mechanized, allowing for substantial amounts to be inexpensively produced. Present-day Americans consume about 152 pounds (69 kg) of sugar per person, per year. This is between a third and a half a pound (.19 kg) a day… every day. This is roughly a cup (240 mL) of sugar. This is about 190 carbs… *purely* from sugar. Interestingly, the USDA suggests we eat about 300 carbs per day, every day. So, aside from our sugar intake, the USDA suggests we eat a *further* 110 carbs. That's just astounding to me. Mind-boggling, even!

But this system is broken. The evidence is all around us.

This is *a lot* of sugar, and there are increasing claims that sugar is bad for us. I know, right?! Go figure!

Sugar is a prime suspect in the increasing cases of obesity, diabetes, cardiovascular disease, dementia, macular degeneration, cancer, and tooth decay. I think we all know that sugar is pretty closely linked to just about all medical conditions, in one way or another.

Yet we are all hardwired to enjoy the taste of sweet. It's in our physiology. We desire it because, from an evolutionary standpoint, it means nutrients.

I've made my peace with all of this by using sweeteners that don't impact my blood sugar but still taste great, giving my instinctual yearning for sweet something to snack on. I see nothing wrong with pleasure!

Because sugar is the norm, the familiar ingredient, the devil we know, it's what every single other sweetener is compared to. As endlessly frustrating as it is to say, there simply is no equal that I've found. Every other sweetener I've run across tastes different. They've *all* got different characteristics and properties, but some come closer than others.

Here is where I'm going to derail this book, a bit... and plug my blog. Outside this book, I have an ongoing blog consisting of hundreds of blog posts and recipes.

www.DJFoodie.com

Within those posts is a large series based entirely around the concept of sweeteners. I cover all the heavy hitters in great detail. I encourage you to pop onto my website and seek it out. It's well worth the read!

What follows is the most-concentrated, highly important stuff.

Erythritol

Erythritol, a sugar alcohol, is easily my favorite base sweetener. It's a natural, (mostly) noncaloric sugar alcohol, while actually having no sugar and no ethanol, a.k.a., booze. It's a by-product of fermenting the sugars in some fruits. It's got a chemical structure similar to sugar and similar to alcohol, while having a rating of zero on the glycemic index, which suggests it has no impact on blood sugar whatsoever. There's also no effect on cholesterol or triglycerides. In the body, most erythritol is absorbed into the bloodstream in the small intestine and then, for the most part, excreted unchanged in the urine. About 10 percent enters the colon. Because 90 percent of erythritol is absorbed before it enters the large intestine, it does not normally cause laxative effects, as are often experienced after consumption of other sugar alcohols (such as xylitol and maltitol). Roughly one fourth of a cup of the stuff can be eaten at once without much issue. Also, unlike sugar, it doesn't contribute to tooth decay!

However, it's *far* from perfect all on its own. First of all, it's name, phonetically air-rith-ritt-all. Bleh. It *sounds* like a chemical, even though it's actually a naturally occurring compound. If I'm in polite company, dinner with friends and family, and the word *erythritol* comes out of my mouth, people look at me like I've just poured saccharose (sugar) in my coffee or poured some of that horrifying dihydrogen monoxide (water) into my pancake batter. The point being, names that sound like chemicals tend to worry people, even though they are completely harmless. If erythritol had a common usage/happy shiny name, it would be *far* better received.

For years, I've tried to come up with a better name for it. The sound my mind always arrives at is: smappy. I don't know why, but that's what my brain calls it, and I think it would blend into a conversation if I said that I added smappy to my ice cream. Erythritol would get accusing glares—*smappy*, on the other hand, just sounds tasty!

Anywho, smappy is 70 percent as sweet as sugar. If I'm reading a recipe that asks for one cup of sugar, I'll actually need about one and a half cups of smappy. This is one clear and immediate way in which it's different than sugar. It has the same appearance but isn't as sweet.

If you taste it, you'll also notice a cooling sensation in your mouth, not entirely unlike the sensation felt when enjoying a breath mint or brushing one's teeth. This only occurs in the crystalline state, so don't worry about it cooling your coffee. The cooling sensation is gone when it's been dissolved, which is much harder to do with smappy than with sugar. Because of smappy's stubbornness dissolving, many people powder or pulverize the granulated smappy in a strong blender or coffee grinder; making the granules smaller helps them dissolve more quickly. I typically grind my own smappy.

Smappy does not caramelize. In order to use it in anything caramel tasting, it needs to be blended with something that *does* caramelize. (Personally, I like to brown butter to get a caramel flavor.)

Finally, smappy has a nasty habit of crystallizing when it cools if used at too high a concentration (which is easy to do, since it takes *extra* to sweeten something as much as sugar does). What this means is, if smappy is used in a super-sweet confection, like a fudge, it will melt just fine and look like a spectacular syrup, but when it cools, it will form back into small grainy crystals, resulting in a fudge that feels like it's spent the day at the beach. Along with the gritty texture will be that nice, cooling sensation in the mouth.

However, in small amounts, where the erythritol is more evenly distributed and suspended in and amongst other ingredients, it will stay dissolved and not have the cooling sensation.

It's for all these seemingly bizarre quirks and behavioral traits that erythritol isn't that great of a sweetener all on its own. *However*, it does make for a fantastic base for a blend. All my favorite low- to zero-net-carb sweeteners are based on erythritol, with other things peppered in to help it caramelize, boost sweetness, decrease crystallization, etc.

Smappy is a naturally occurring molecule found in fruits/ such as pears, watermelons, and grapes; it is also present in some drinks, like sake and wine, and sauce such as soy sauce.

It is usually made, at an industrial level, through a fermentation not unlike that of beer or wine. The liquid is then purified, reduced, turned to solid crystals, and separated from any remaining liquids.

Smappy is my favorite single base sweetener. PERFECT in a blend!

Stevia

Speaking of intimidating names, let's dig into *stevia rebaudiana*, which is the species of stevia known for its sweet leaves. It's relatively easy to grow. The leaves can be dried and added to things like teas and other beverages, fruits, salads, and various desserts. It's essentially got zero carbs and zero calories, but is also not really a direct replacement for sugar, as many of the characteristics and bulk are missing from the equation.

Most mainstream stevia is highly refined, removing all the fiber and nutrients. Some extracts and tinctures from high-quality, whole-leaf stevia contains an array of these sweet compounds, as well as many antioxidants. There are also many products that go even further to isolate a single steviol glycoside called *Rebaudioside A*, which is about three hundred times sweeter than sugar. It is this highly refined compound that is most commonly sold and promoted under the *stevia* name.

Some people love stevia, and there's a lot to love. At its heart, it's a plant. It's sweet tasting, noncaloric, and has no impact on blood sugar. It's about as perfect a natural sweetener as there is. Used as a leaf, it's hard to fault. That said, it needs to be grown, harvested, maintained, used fresh and/or dried, and still requires some level of processing to boost taste. This can be done by steeping the leaves like tea, straining away the actual leaves, and sweetening with the remaining liquid. Others make a tincture by steeping the leaves in a strong alcohol, such as vodka, for a few days. This is then heated for thirty minutes, allowing much of the alcohol to evaporate. It's then strained and the remaining liquid is used as a sweetener. Both methods create a nice sweetening option, but as with all things stevia, less is often considered more. Too much stevia can translate acrid.

See, stevia has a tendency toward bitterness or a strong licorice flavor. A little bit tends to give a faint and long-lasting sweet taste, whereas anything approaching an actual, clear, and immediately obvious sweet taste tends to be accompanied by a slightly less obvious bitter taste, which many struggle with (including myself). This makes stevia great in blends. For my tastes, standard stevia extracts need something else to balance them out.

One quick note: Many stevia products are blends and mixes. Because of the wide variety of the blends, it's hard to describe the various behavioral quirks in various recipes. Some forms are liquid, others are highly concentrated powder, and others are blends. Some bake well and others will caramelize (most won't). Some have bulk; others don't. Some are better than others. Read the labels to understand their potency. Most of the time they state how much to use to replace specific amounts of sugar.

In general, if you're buying a granular or powdered version of it and it comes in anything much larger than a saltshaker, it's likely a blend designed to function like sugar. These require a bit of reading to understand what they really contain. I'm a fan of stevia blends bulked out and balanced with smappy. However, beware of any mixed with dextrose or maltodextrin. Those are both essentially glucose (sugar) and have an impact on blood sugar. Even if the product claims to have zero carbs, it's because the serving size is usually miniscule (I've seen serving sizes listed as low as 1/4 tsp [for something like stevia, this is likely less than 1 gram]). Labeling laws allow carbs on a nutrition facts label to be set to zero if under .5 grams within the set serving size. This can mean that the total number of carbs can approach upwards of one hundred carbs per cup while still legally being able to state that it's zero carbs. Fun, huh?

Just because it's a stevia product doesn't mean it's not pumped full of "sugar" and isn't highly, *highly* processed. Read the labels and understand the blends and the logic behind labeling laws. You may very well be ingesting a stevia product, but it's highly refined and tastes great because of all the sugar.

Millions love this sweet leaf and pick up tinctures or make their own blends. Stevia is a great thing, but it can be heavily tampered with. Know what's in the box.

Honey

Honey is nature's sugar. Honey has been used and hunted by humans for at least eight thousand years. It has been in use for about as long as writing has been. In addition to being a food, it's also used as a medicine and has rich religious and philosophical significance. In terms of broad human evolution, it's relatively new, but it's been a part of our experience for thousands of years.

In terms of pure function, it's a bit sweeter than regular sugar (by volume), with approximately the same impact on our blood sugar. Honey will cause just as much of an insulin secretion as good ol' fashioned table sugar (raw honey has a much lower GI though). While certainly a natural food and quite delicious, it's really got no immediate benefit for the human body, short of helping to store fat on our rears for the potential times of famine and starvation. Beyond this, there are some benefits of honey over refined table sugar. Aside from water and various forms of sugar, the remaining .17 percent is various vitamins and minerals. These are not massively meaningful amounts. If I had to choose between sugar and honey, I'd pick honey (and raw honey, at that), but it's not a landslide victory. It's really just sugar as far as the body is concerned.

Honey does have some medicinal properties, but being that this book is about tasty goodness and blood sugar, I'm going to acknowledge that they exist and promptly move on.

crosses arms, makes a wish, and briskly nods head

Probably the most important aspect in regards to honey is how it compares to sugar from a functional standpoint. Honey is sweeter and denser than sugar (meaning less needs to be used), higher in calories, more acidic, and contains about 20 percent water. It's also got a sugar profile closer to high fructose corn syrup (about 40 percent fructose and 30 percent glucose, plus some water and a few other things). Processed honey has a glycemic index of about 75 to 85 (higher than table sugar). Interestingly, raw honey clocks in closer to 30. In any event, these differences all suggest it's going to behave somewhat differently in a recipe than sugar. It's going to have an impact on leaveners (both yeast and sodium bicarbonate). It's going to add moisture and boost sweetness above that of standard table sugar. It's also going to brown foods more quickly. Most of these things aren't a huge issue for small baking tasks, but as the amounts grow, suddenly things can get wonky pretty quick.

Substitution tip: In general, use about 3/4 of a cup (180mL) for every cup of sugar being replaced. Also, reduce other liquids by about 1/4 cup (60mL) for every cup of honey being used. Finally, lower the oven temperature by about 25°F (4°C) to prevent over browning.

Ultimately, this is probably the best overall sweetener to replace sugar in a recipe, in terms of function. It *is* sugar for the most part. With the tweaks listed above, just about any recipe can be converted (err on the side of less additional liquid, and add a bit more as it needs it). As long as you're not concerned about blood sugar, honey is behaviorally and ethically probably your best bet, unless you're bothered by irritating and offending honeybees, which some people are! This is why honey isn't classified as vegan.

However, if you're paying attention to blood sugar and carbs, stay away. I only use honey when I need a tiny blast of actual sugar for yeast-leavened recipes or, as mentioned before, if I need a bit of something sticky to glue things, like nuts, together. Mostly it takes up space in my pantry, but I am glad it's there when I need it. Honey does a great job of staying stable for years on the shelf.

Yacon Syrup

Yacon syrup is one that I don't see mentioned very often. It's expensive and hard to find, but it's a sweetener with a very low glycemic index. I've seen GI ratings of 0 and 1 for this sweetener. It's similar to coconut sugar, in that it's got inulin. Yacon syrup is made from a Peruvian yam. It's made in a manner similar to maple syrup, through evaporation. It looks and tastes a lot like molasses. It's dark, thick, and… well, syrupy. It's not something I'd put in my coffee, but if I were looking to make a brown-sugar blend, this would be my pick. I'd mix this into a mixture of erythritol, inulin, and a bit of stevia for, essentially, a noncaloric, zero carb, zero GI brown sugar. Sweet, huh?

Because of its strong flavor, I wouldn't really consider this a direct replacement for sugar. It's more a complement to other sweeteners. but isn't a great sweetener on its own. I'd bet it would be a *wonderful* addition to something like a BBQ sauce or in a glaze for a piece of grilled, gingery salmon! I've tried it, and it is definitely quite tasty! I'd take this over coconut sugar or molasses. It should be perfect for diabetics as well as low-carbers. Even Paleo people should agree this is an acceptable sweetener.

It baffles me why this isn't discussed more often. There isn't a lot of info on it, and again, it's hard to find and is expensive—maybe that's why it isn't discussed more.

For those of you with an extra buck or two in your pockets, I suggest picking some up and playing with it.

Common Synthetic Sweeteners

Synthetic sweeteners tend to be frowned upon in the general landscape. People use them, but rarely do they do so proudly. You'd have to look pretty hard to find someone who really stands behind saccharine or develops recipes with aspartame and actively works to promote them. It's much hipper to cook with raw honey than it is to use an isomalt/Ace-K blend. Synthetic sweeteners take a lot of abuse (largely from the sugar industry), yet they're relatively inexpensive, easy to find, and *millions* of people are buying them. While it may not be en vogue to load up a protein shake with sucralose (most easily recognized as the brand Splenda), millions are. Maybe you?

I know I've done it!

I'm an open-minded guy. I'm not here to preach. I'm just here to share my thoughts and experiences and tell you what I know. If you love to bake with Splenda, go for it! If you love to bake with honey, do it! All I ask is that you inform yourself and become aware of the issues. Do it *thoughtfully*. Just because we feel like we know something doesn't mean we can't learn something new—and change our minds. Our bodies may also need something different at different points in time. Sometimes, it isn't even up to us at all.

So, it's with this that I say… meh. Some synthetic sweeteners don't bother me. I think they're fine.

OH NO! All the cave people just closed the book on me. That makes me sad, but I tend to think the "natural" in the natural versus synthetic has some unfair advantages. The general assumption is, if it's here, it's supposed to be here, and it must be good for us. It's from the earth, right?

That simple line of logic can be tough to argue against.

But let's consider: Do you ever think about pouring some snake venom on a stack of pancakes? Would you consider adding some poison oak leaves to a sauce to enhance the flavor? I know I haven't.

Just because something is natural doesn't mean it's good for us. There are *plenty* of things that are natural that I wouldn't bake into a sheet of Garlic-Herb Fauxcaccia. (p. 470)

Even the idea of processed versus raw/natural is endlessly challenged. If something is processed, it's pure evil. Or terms like *minimally processed* are thrown around to suggest, somewhat sheepishly, that… well, yeah. It was processed… kinda… but only a little bit.

So, here's my take on the whole thing. It's about balance. I live in a city and have a car I use to find good stores that carry great food but buy some of my food from the dinky little bodega on the corner when I run out of the good food I pick up elsewhere. I'm a modern dude, deeply entrenched in this world. I am firmly on the grid. However, I fantasize about building my own home from dirt (earth bags), running electricity via solar power and my stove on coconut shell briquettes, growing my own foods via organic standards, and raising chickens for meat and eggs. I romanticize these ideas quite often. Yet, I own no land, I have no green thumb, and I'm afraid of chickens. (They will peck out my eyeballs while I sleep. I just know it!)

In my own life and in terms of my own diet, I have learned that I do better when I eat closer to the food chain. I have discovered that I do better when I eat fresh broccoli and grass-fed beef, instead of a diet of boxed pasta and canned tomato sauce with a fruity-sugar-cereal chaser.

I do feel that, the more I balance my existence with my planet and fellow humans, the more my health increases, along with confidence, thought patterns, relationship health, etc. Slowly but surely, I am testing the waters and continually finding that I'm marching in that direction. So when faced with a choice between a popular sucralose blend and honey, you'd *think* I'd choose honey.

But no. The popular sucralose blend wins.

By pursuing synthetic foods, we may find something wonderful for our bodies. We may find ways to feed nations of hungry folks. We may find foods that both nourish and repair. We may discover a food with a flavor better than bacon! We may not, I confess, but I support the efforts, and I'll keep testing and tasting.

My point is this: boxed, processed, and synthetic foods are cheaper, last longer, and save time for people. They also pave the way for some areas of potential progress. They aren't going anywhere anytime soon either.

Remember sugar, that seemingly harmless, processed natural crystal? I do not understand why it's so innocently pumped into our foods and glossed over by the masses when *millions and millions* of people are having heart issues, diabetes, dementia, extreme obesity, feeding their cancers, etc. It's even acknowledged regularly, by individuals, groups, and the media, yet it just goes on and on. Sucralose (the concentrated sweetener in Splenda), on the other hand, is blasted by people for being synthetic and artificial when it's *far* less destructive than pure cane sugar. (Bearing in mind, the sugar industry would disagree.)

Again, my overall point with this entire Sweeteners section is: sweets aren't necessary. Honey, sugar, sucralose, erythritol, etc.—our bodies aren't really designed for the level of sweets and carby things that our culture dictates. This is very much a case of picking your poison. I know I'm no fun, but really, the culture is a bit out of whack on this one. Our balancing act is currently tipping.

I realize I'm writing a lot about the topic of sweeteners while also repeatedly stating that they're not necessary. As a public blogger, one of the first questions anyone asks is, "What's the best sweetener?" Sweeteners aren't going anywhere, so it behooves me to at least cast a well-meaning light on the topic.

Sucralose

Sucralose is probably the most common sweetening alternative out there right now. Artificial, natural, processed, etc., sucralose is the "sugar-free" sweetener in most homes in 2015. You probably know it by its bright yellow bags and its small yellow packets. The common sucralose blend is actually a product blending sucralose, dextrose, and maltodextrin.

Sucralose is a synthetic and artificial sweetener. It doesn't exist in nature. It is manufactured by the selective chlorination of sucrose (table sugar), which substitutes three of the hydroxyl groups with chlorine.

I don't typically use sucralose blends because of the fillers, but I do occasionally use liquid sucralose and I'm also no stranger to sucralose-based products. I've got sucralose-based jams in the fridge as I type this. I've also got some of those sugar-free coffee syrups, which are sweetened with sucralose. I think they're delicious. I find sucralose to have a very nice taste. It's very slightly "hollow" in my opinion, but it's quite a clean, nice sweet. Being that it's about six hundred times as sweet as sugar, a tiny bit goes a very long way. This means it's super cheap and can boost the sweetness in just about anything. Aside from the controversy and the fact that it philosophically rubs some people the wrong way, it's actually a great sweetener. It's also heat stable, so it's good for baking.

However, in baking it's got no substance to it. A cup of sugar takes up the space of my fist, in terms of pure volume. This can be replaced by a few drops of liquid sucralose, maybe taking up the same space as the tip of my pinky. What do you think this does to a cake? A lot of volume and texture is going to go missing. Now, technically, sugar is a liquefier, in baking terms, so a lot of that bulk can be made up by adding more liquid, but because it tends to start life as a dry crystal, people don't often make that connection.

As time moves on and I engage in more earthly symbiosis, I'm finding that I'm slowly phasing these things out. I'm replacing sucralose-based syrups with xylitol-based syrups. I have no major logic for doing so, other than the "it exists on earth" argument, which, snake venom aside, still carries weight with me.

It is delicious, it's everywhere, it's cheap, and it's in loads of tasty products.

Meh. It's fine… just not too much!

Sweetener Odd and Ends

These are the sweeteners that don't quite fit into the other categories. The riff-raff. The ragamuffins. The disorganized leftovers, such as inulin, polydextrose, and fructo-oligosaccharides.

Inulin

Inulins are a group of naturally occurring polysaccharides, most often extracted from chicory. It is used as energy storage in many roots and rhizomes, much in the same way we store fat for energy. It also helps some 36,000 species of plant withstand cold and drought, just how we convert carbs to stash as fat on our own bodies! It's found in high concentrations in the roots of chicory, but also in agave, artichokes, asparagus, bananas, various onions, yacon, jicama, and even wheat.

In terms of function, it's essentially a fiber. It's sweet tasting but only about 10 percent as sweet as sugar. It's a bit chalky and with a slightly tart but pleasant aftertaste. I personally love this stuff.

Inulin is not digested by enzymes in humans. As a result, it's used in some foods to reduce calories, increase fiber, as well as increasing the probiotic effects. It promotes the growth of beneficial intestinal bacteria. It also increases calcium absorption. I like to think of it as a big sweeping broom for my digestive tract. This stuff really is just all good!

It's got a lot of a boons: it's able to replicate some of the mouthfeel of fat; it adds bulk and sweet taste; it can improve the stability of foams and emulsions; and it can take the place of fats, sugars, and flours!

Again, it should be said that this fructan does act like a fiber in the body. Too much can cause various gastric issues. I've personally never experienced any, but people with sensitive tracts may want to tread lightly.

I use it to add bulk to homemade erythritol blends. See, erythritol tends to crystallize in concentrations that are too high, so something else needs to be added to somewhat dilute the erythritol. Then, toss in some concentrated stevia for a sweet boost, and you've got yourself a *wonderful*, homemade natural sweetener that looks, tastes, and works a *whole* lot like sugar!

The downside is it's hard to find and expensive. The qualities and sweetness levels also tend to vary.

Oligosaccharides

Oligosaccharides are very much like inulin. They are both fructans coming from roughly the same places and doing roughly the same things. Their chemical formation is a bit smaller and simpler than inulin's, which is a polysaccharide. I'm going to focus mostly on something called fructo-oligosaccharides (FOS).

Fructo-Oligosaccharides (FOS)

FOS is about 30 to 50 percent as sweet as sugar. FOS is actually made by degrading inulin and is more soluble than inulin; it is often added as a probiotic to dairy products like yogurt. The yacon and sunchoke both have the highest concentration of FOS.

Both FOS and inulin are used as supplements to help promote gut health. Again, I just see it as a big broom for my digestive tract. Keeps things clean and running!

Like inulin, this is something I would use to add bulk and to extend something, like erythritol, to make my own homemade blends. This can create something that is not only sweet tasting, but is also actually healthy. So maybe the taste of sweet *can* have some perks.

Polydextrose

Polydextrose, or Poly D for those who like street slang, is like the synthetic form of inulin. Also a polysaccharide, it's also classified as a soluble fiber. It's commonly used in foods to add bulk, fiber, and/or to replace sugar, fat, and/or starch. Yep, it's another fun one that finds its way into all sorts of things!

Polydextrose is made from dextrose (glucose, the stuff the body uses for energy), probably from corn and sorbitol (a low glycemic sugar alcohol). It's a white powder and really tastes like nothing. Maybe slightly sour but… mostly just nothing. It's got little to no effect on blood sugar and really reacts much more like a fiber in the system, like a big synthetic broom for the gut. I've read studies suggesting this is solid at promoting gut health (not as good as inulin) and to keep bowels moving along but without the gastric distress accompanying other higher fiber treats. That said, I've read anecdotal evidence that too much of this stuff can cause some gut-wrenching issues. I've never had an issue with it, but not too much!

Back in my very earliest days of low-carb, long before I discovered some of my favorite store-bought blends, I made my own homemade sugar blend. It was a pulverized blend of erythritol, polydextrose, and a refined stevia powder. This created something that measured like sugar, tasted sweet, had bulk, and never crystallized. It was a great sweetener. It even did a good job of mimicking the mouth-feel of sugar.

This stuff is relatively cheap. It's got about 24 net carbs per packed cup (240 mL) and about 200 calories. Because of its humectant nature, it really needs to be kept sealed. I was already living in Mexico when I started making this, and it would suck the water out of the air and result in an almost natural candy making. The mixture would get hard and slowly kind of ooze and melt together into blobules. As long as it's stored in an airtight container and used within a reasonable time frame (weeks or months, as opposed to years), you'll be fine.

My personal opinion is that this stuff is fine, although it is highly processed.

Sweetener Blends

Ok, here's the grand finale: how to make your own sweetening blends. HUZZAH!

Our goal is to create a cup (240 mL) of sugar replacement. We're going to create something with the sweetness and bulk of sugar, with a clean, sweet taste and very few of the drawbacks that are associated with many existing blends. Keep in mind that none of these are as good as sugar, in terms of taste and behavior. If you're comparing it to sugar, you'll be disappointed. However, these are *excellent* alternatives, without the hard hits that your blood sugar takes from sugar. It should also be said that the blends work together to form a synergy. They tend to help emphasize the benefits of the sweetener/bulking agent, while decreasing the negative qualities.

All sweeteners I've seen have printed on the box, bottle, or jar how much of it equals a similar amount of sugar in terms of sweetness. It doesn't always say "a cup" (240 mL) but will do say something like "1 1/2 tsp (7.5 mL) smappy equals 1 tsp (5 mL) sugar." This suggests that 1 1/2 cups (360 mL) of smappy equals 1 cup (240 mL) of sugar, but in reality, as the amounts increase, things can get a bit dicey, and the ratio starts to crumble. As a simple comparison, though, it works.

The first thing is to understand how much of the sweetener you're working with is required to make a cup (240 mL) of sugar's sweetness. Some of the time, with potent sweeteners, it's only a tiny bit, measured in grams or drops. Other times, it's quite a bit more. Before proceeding with any mixing and matching of your own, know how much of it equals the sweetness of a cup (240 mL) of sugar.

Now, what we need to do is mix and match a variety of sweeteners in order to equal both the sweet potency of the blend as well as the volume. If you have a sugar cookie recipe asking for 1 cup (240 mL) of sugar replacement and substitute a few drops of liquid sucralose, it's likely to have poor results. Now, in a liquid, like coffee, or even a liquid base, like ice cream, it doesn't matter as much, but the bulk is very important to some recipes.

We need to maintain that bulk.

What follows will be a bunch of ideas. This is a stab at creating a variety of blends for a variety of purposes. None will be perfect, but they're a great place to start.

Tasty versus Goodness

I really see the sugar-free sweetener world as having two mainstream dominant super-potent sweeteners: sucralose and stevia. If I had to do a double-blind taste test, sucralose wins. I don't love it alone, but I prefer the taste to stevia. Stevia just has a bitter taste to me, which is less pleasant than the somewhat hollow or empty sweetness that I get from sucralose. However, stevia is going to win every argument put forth about health and nature simply because it comes from a leaf (somewhere in there).

So, I'm going to create a split in my naming convention. Sucralose blends will be known as "Tasty," and Stevia blends will be known as "Goodness," henceforth.

Tasty blends will often be less expensive than their Goodness counterparts. They're likely to be more synthetic in nature and are likely to be the better tasting of the blends. Goodness blends will be as close to nature as I can make them, without concern for costs.

Even though I personally believe that the Tasty ones are less expensive and taste better, I'm still likely to mix up a batch of Goodness for myself. I often call myself a "gateway cave hippy." It's the best way I can describe my desire to be open to things while trying to stay closer-ish to nature and eat like Grok.

Finally, all of my blends contain erythritol, so they will all be *Smappy* based.

Basic Tasty Smappy

Basic Tasty Smappy is designed for simple applications. It's cheap, easy to make, and tastes great! It's good in most applications. This runs the risk of crystallizing in super-sweet recipes but is fine as a standard sweetener. This would be great for coffee or iced tea. This would be good to give a sweet kick to a pancake batter. It's great for adding a touch of sweetness to *any* savory dish. Really, what we're trying to do is limit the high concentrations of erythritol. So this sweetener should work for most things, where sugar is needed, provided the end result isn't super sweet. We have another blend for that.

Here's the recipe:

1 cup (240 mL) erythritol
14 drops liquid sucralose

That's it! Put it in a bowl and stir it up. You can now use this mixture like you would for sugar, one cup (240 mL) to one cup (240 mL).

Here's how to arrive at this conclusion…

Erythritol is about 70 percent as sweet as sugar. This means that one full cup (240 mL) of erythritol is going to be equal to the sweetening power of 7/10 of a cup (168 mL) of sugar, even though it takes up the full volume of one cup (240 mL) of sugar. So we need to add 3/10 of a cup's (72 mL) worth of sugary sweetness, without adding any extra volume. This is where the zero-carb liquid sweetener sucralose comes in. The brand I'm using suggests each drop is one teaspoon's (5 mL) worth of sugar. (Remember, if you use a different brand, this number is important.) There are about 14 teaspoons (72 mL) in 3/10 a cup (72 mL). So we add the 14 drops to the erythritol, and we now have something with both the volume and sweetness of one cup (240 mL) of sugar. BOOM!

Make sense?

Actually, what I like to do is put it into a coffee grinder and powder it. Because erythritol is so stubborn to dissolve, I tend to pulverize it. This, somewhat confusingly, changes its volume. When you powder the smappy, it increases in volume, because of all the air that's just been added to it. What I usually do is just weigh it. The weight is consistent, whether it's full of air or not. Imagine a cup of sugar, or a cup of Basic Tasty Smappy, as being 200 grams, or just over 7 ounces. If you powder it, but you need a cup of granulated sugar for something, just to be safe, weigh it. However, if you never powder it, then it's fine to keep the granular Basic Tasty Smappy and measure it, one for one, to sugar.

Basic Smappy Goodness

1 cup (240 mL) erythritol
1/8 tsp (.63 mL) powdered stevia

Mix it up. Powder it if you want to. That's it!

Again, we're just trying to replace that 3/10 of a cup (72 mL) of sugar, but this time doing so with the stevia. The stevia powder I'm using is highly concentrated and suggests 1/2 teaspoon (2.5 mL) is enough to replace a full cup (240 mL) of sugar. If you do a bit of math, the real numbers are actually .15 teaspoon (.75 mL), but 1/8 is close enough and I've seen 1/8 of a teaspoon measuring spoons. I suppose you'd want i*t* *he*aping. If you've got a very accurate scale, you'd want about 192 mg worth of powdered stevia to make up that 3/10 of a cup (72 mL).

This stuff may sound a bit intimidating at first, but it's really not. It's all basic math based on stuff printed on the labels. It takes a bit of extra knowledge to know things like how many teaspoons are in a cup and so on, but that information is just a quick online search away. My goal with this is less to lock people into a specific recipe and more to give them the keys to make their own blends, combining their favorite products. These blends I'm describing are merely examples. Good examples optimized by math, though, not your personal tastes.

Tasty Smappy: Baking Blend

Now, here's a sugar blend that's better for baking. Really, it's just as good as the Basic Tasty blend, but it's a bit more complex, a bit more costly, and certainly a bit stranger. *However*, it's also very tasty and will work fabulously in your muffins, cakes, and cookies. Again, the idea is a cup of sugar replacement.

1/2 cup (120 mL) erythritol
1/2 cup (120 mL) polydextrose
31 drops liquid sucralose

Mix in a bowl, and/or powder in a Vitamix or coffee grinder.

This one uses polydextrose to bulk out the erythritol. Erythritol, in too high a concentration, tends to crystallize when it cools, resulting in a gritty texture and a "cooling" sensation. This is why recipes that are super sweet tend to exhibit this behavior. By using a bit less and adding the bulk of the polydextrose and the sweetness of the liquid sucralose, we get a blend that's more suited to sweet things like super-sweet cakes, cookies, frostings, some ice creams, etc.

This particular blend is probably the tastiest of them all. It's got the best behaviors. It's also the cheaper blend. However, it's not without its faults.

The polydextrose adds about 12 carbs to the mix per full cup (240 mL). That's a clear downside. It's also got a bunch of super-strange-sounding synthetic oddities in it.

Another downside is the Poly D tends to fight with fat. It won't cream with butter, for example. It'll clump up and misbehave. My little workaround has always been to cream the butter without the sweetener and distribute the Tasty Smappy Baking blend in with the other dried ingredients. This dilutes the behavioral quirks of all the sweeteners and turns out a nice baked treat.

This one will caramelize and can be used for some hard candies, although I wouldn't really recommend it. The fiber is likely to cause some gastric distress and the Poly D's water-sucking properties will make it sticky and hard to store. In general, I feel okay saying that hard candies should pretty much be avoided while following a low-primal way of eating. The best are going to have some carbs and create gastric issues, and the worst, well… they won't be any good.

Smappy Goodness: Baking Blend

1/2 cup (120 mL) erythritol
1/2 cup (120 mL) inulin
1/4 tsp (1.25 mL) stevia (scant)

Mix it up. Powder it if you want to. That's it!

This time the erythritol makes up 35 percent of the sweetness of the cup (240 mL) of sweetener blend. Look for a nice organic inulin FOS blend, which is roughly 40 percent as sweet as sugar (being quite natural, apparently batches vary and it's an inconsistent product). This suggests the 1/2 cup (120 mL) supplies a further 20 percent of sweetness, leaving us to replace the remaining 45 percent with the stevia. This would be just under 1/4 teaspoon (1.25 mL) of stevia. If you were to make your own stevia products, you could combine the inulin and erythritol and adjust the sweetness with your own blend. If it contains water, then you'd omit some water-based liquid in whatever recipe you're working on.

This one is zero net carbs and measures cup (240 mL) for cup (240 mL), like sugar. It's good for baking and higher levels of sweet. It will also caramelize. I've had fewer issues with this blend creaming with butter, but again, I've grown into the habit of mixing my dried sweeteners and thickeners in with other dried ingredients. For whatever reason, wheat, corn, and sugar products all seem easy to use, whereas similarly ground and refined nuts, sweeteners, and other odds and tubers tend to be *far* more fickle and misbehave more readily. Mixing all the dried ingredients together saves me often.

All of this is a relatively imperfect science, as products come and go, change configurations, etc. My aim is just to set you on the path of discovery.

If you like xylitol, for example, using the logic in this passage, you should be able to do a bit of research to figure out how strong it is in relation to sugar and then make up the difference with another sweetener. You could do the same with isomalt and make your own isomalt blends, should you have that desire.

Some blends work better for some applications than others. To date, I have not found, made, or even heard of a single sugar replacement that is an exact match for sugar (but I will give a nice plug for Swerve® Sweetener, an erythritol/oligosaccharide blend, I personally feel is the best sugar replacement on the market, today [www.SwerveSweetener.com]).

In any event, once you start venturing down the road of homemade blends, you, like me, are pioneering.

Light Brown Smappy: Baking Mix

1 cup (240 mL) of either of the two Smappy Blend, Baking Mixes
1 tsp (5 mL) yacon syrup

In an electric mixer, mix the ingredients until well combined.

This will have a slightly muddy and wet texture. That's fine. I wouldn't make too much of it and would really just drizzle a bit of yacon into whatever it was that I might be making. You could also use one teaspoon (5 mL) of blackstrap molasses instead of yacon, but it adds about 5 net carbs to the whole recipe.

Dark Brown Smappy: Baking Mix

1 cup (240 mL) of either of the two Smappy Blend, Baking Mixes
1 Tbsp (15 mL) yacon syrup

In an electric mixer, mix the ingredients until well combined.

Again, this will have a slightly muddy and wet texture, and as with the above, I wouldn't make too much of it and would really just drizzle a bit more of yacon syrup into whatever it was that I might be making. You could also use 1 tablespoon (15 mL) of blackstrap molasses, but it adds about 15 net carbs to the whole recipe.

What Else Can I Eat?

There are a million ingredients available outside these lists. There are obscure fruits and vegetables that are likely delicious and appropriate. There are also some condiments, sauces, and spice blends that are completely appropriate. The issue with these is, they vary from company to company. This is where label-reading skills play a role. This is where seeking out products with ingredients you can pronounce plays a roll.

There are also products, like sweeteners, which I tend to think are mostly harmless. And there are more refined products, like coconut flour, almond meal, hazelnut flour, ground chia, arrowroot, baking soda, and all the other loosely Paleo-friendly ingredients that are *mostly* okay. These also vary from brand to brand. Read the labels. If you ever want to know my specific opinion about a brand or product, I'm easily found by email, my blog, or, better yet, my Facebook page, where I'm often found hamming it up with folks.

I am here to help… even beyond the scope of this book.

Just ask!

Bag of Tricks

Reading Labels

Knowing how to read Nutrition Facts labels and understanding what they mean is vital to success, both short and long term. This can be complicated and can involve knowledge of weights and ingredients, including some that sound like science experiments. In time, on my blog or in future books, I'm sure I'll cover all of that, but for now, I want to very simply present the most important information.

I'm going to present a low-carb distillation of the Nutrition Facts panel (within the scope of how I see a low-primal way of eating). Yes, I'm leaving all kinds of information out of the equation. However, what I'm about to discuss gets most new folk a good 80 percent of the way there. We'll explore details, nuance, and exceptions in another venue at another time. For now, I want to be clear without muddying the waters.

Here's a Nutrition Facts Label for a fictitious brand of delicious low-carb (not low-primal) flour tortillas. It's kind of complex and involved. I *wanted* something kind of complex and involved for this example, so let's dive in.

Looking at this monster, it's no wonder so many are confused by what these labels contain!

Before looking at any Nutrition Facts panel, you must know your daily net carb allowance. In this case, for anyone reading this book, the answer starts at 30.

The second question you need to ask yourself is, "How much do I plan to eat?" Without knowing how much you plan to eat, you're entering a calculation that has no logical conclusion. It's like the problem: "A train is going to Las Vegas. How many minutes until it arrives?" Impossible to answer without knowing its speed!

Many of you may be rolling your eyes at this point, thinking "That's too much! Can't I just skip flour and sugar?" Sure. Yes. Sure you can, and you'll achieve some level of success too. However, it's my belief that this knowledge is imperative in arriving at permanent and life-changing goals. You need to participate in the experience. You need to understand the metrics. In the grand scheme of things, this miniscule little bit of effort will pay significant unforeseen dividends down the line. I don't often promise or guarantee things, but if you learn this information and pay attention to it, you'll carry with you the keys to success. I promise.

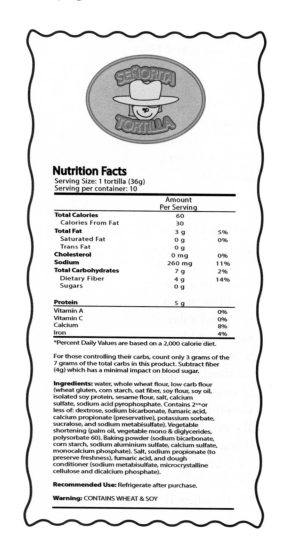

Nutrition Facts
Serving Size: 1 tortilla (36g)
Serving per container: 10

	Amount Per Serving	
Total Calories	60	
Calories From Fat	30	
Total Fat	3 g	5%
Saturated Fat	0 g	0%
Trans Fat	0 g	
Cholesterol	0 mg	0%
Sodium	260 mg	11%
Total Carbohydrates	7 g	2%
Dietary Fiber	4 g	14%
Sugars	0 g	
Protein	5 g	
Vitamin A		0%
Vitamin C		0%
Calcium		8%
Iron		4%

*Percent Daily Values are based on a 2,000 calorie diet.

For those controlling their carbs, count only 3 grams of the 7 grams of the total carbs in this product. Subtract fiber (4g) which has a minimal impact on blood sugar.

Ingredients: water, whole wheat flour, low carb flour (wheat gluten, corn starch, oat fiber, soy flour, soy oil, isolated soy protein, sesame flour, salt, calcium sulfate, sodium acid pyrophosphate. Contains 2% or less of: dextrose, sodium bicarbonate, fumaric acid, calcium propionate (preservative), potassium sorbate, sucralose, and sodium metabisulfate). Vegetable shortening (palm oil, vegetable mono & diglycerides, polysorbate 60). Baking powder (sodium bicarbonate, corn starch, sodium aluminium sulfate, calcium sulfate, monocalcium phosphate). Salt, sodium propionate (to preserve freshness), fumaric acid, and dough conditioner (sodium metabisulfate, microcrystalline cellulose and dicalcium phosphate).

Recommended Use: Refrigerate after purchase.

Warning: CONTAINS WHEAT & SOY

Again, the key questions to ask:

- **What's your daily net carb allowance?**
- **How much do you plan to eat?**

Here's a simplified label for the same fake product. This one has a lot of the intimidation removed or faded out, but it's still got the information *we* need. My goal is to reduce and remove the anxieties of these labels and point out the most immediately meaningful parts; Serving Size, Total Carbohydrates, and Fiber. I'll get into variations later. For now, focus on Serving Size, Carbohydrates, and Fiber.

In this case, a single tortilla contains 7 total carbs. However, because net carbs don't include the fiber, we can deduct 4. Carbs (7) minus Fiber (4) equals Net Carbs (3).

One tortilla counts as 3 net carbs. If I still ate these tortillas, this implies I can personally eat about 10 (3x10=30, which allows for a cup of coffee and lots of steak and chicken cooked in butter) a day. Yay! While this may seem like common sense, many go cross-eyed when they see these labels. People are also often deceived by the labels, sometimes because of intentionally deceptive labeling and other times, frankly, because people see what they want to see.

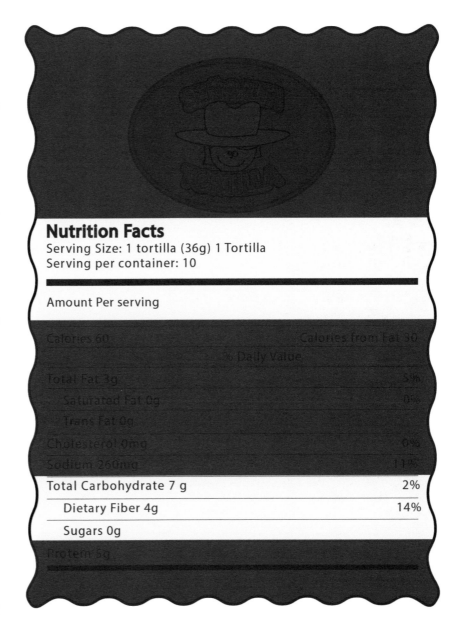

Nutrition Facts
Serving Size: 1 tortilla (36g) 1 Tortilla
Serving per container: 10

Amount Per serving

Calories 60   Calories from Fat 30
                    % Daily Value

Total Fat 3g   5%
    Saturated Fat 0g   0%
    Trans Fat 0g
Cholesterol 0mg   0%
Sodium 260mg   11%

Total Carbohydrate 7 g	2%
Dietary Fiber 4g	14%
Sugars 0g	

Protein 5g

This is where the second question becomes important: "How much of this thing are you going to eat?"

These particular tortillas aren't that big. They're not like those giant burrito blankets that were so yummy back in the day. These are lil' guys. It's highly unlikely that I'm going to sit and eat just one. It's more likely that I'll eat two or three.

Fuzzy Logic: Somehow, some kind of strange, mutant mathematics start to occur at about this point in the game. Logic breaks down. People that have taken the time to sit and read the label know there are 3 carbs per tortilla. So they'll eat one, 3 carbs. No problem. So, they'll eat another one. 3 carbs. No problem! Ok, just one more… it's just 3 carbs!

Here's the mutant math: if I were to walk up to any of these folks and ask them how many carbs were collectively within their three tortillas, almost every time, I suspect they'd all innocently retort, "Three!"

You know it's true.

I hate to be the bearer of bad news, but 3+3+3 almost never equals 3. More often than not, three tortillas, each at 3 net carbs, is going to be *nine* carbs. Plus, there's the filling too! Meat's ok. You get a pass, but… how many net carbs are in that cheese? Did you read the label? What about in the sour cream? Did you pay attention? What about the salsa? That's another couple carbs!

It's very easy to pile on the goodies, and with each new addition comes a few more numbers to pile onto our calculation.

With 9 net carbs already being used by the tortillas, we're left with 21 of our original 30. But don't forget breakfast! Or lunch! You probably had a few carbs there too.

Product note: I used a tortilla for the Label Reading passage because it's easy for people to picture individual tortillas, whereas two tablespoons (30 mL) of coconut milk is more of a liquid idea and tougher to visualize. Additionally, I wanted something with a complex label. However, I want to stress that processed foods, such as these faux tortillas, are not recommended for the first two weeks of weight loss and probably not even until you've reached your goals. They're known to cause stalls in some, as delicious and convenient as they may be.

At this point, you may be feeling squeezed, like I'm suggesting that you count every little carb and eat only 30 per day. While this may be true, and certainly reads as true, I'm far from insisting it. My aim is long-term success, and my hope is that I'm giving you the tools to climb up and down this ladder at your own pace, to suit your own goals and sensibilities. Thirty is simply a great place to start, but it's not the only place to start.

Start at 200 per day if you like! That's fine. But learn how to utilize these skills. Learn how to read the label, ignore the other complicated stuff, and simply laser focus on the serving size, carbs, fiber, and sometimes, the sugar-alcohols. Block out, zone out, tune out, or otherwise totally ignore that other stuff for now.

At 200 carbs a day, there stands a good chance you'll stop losing weight at some point. You'll probably stall. Then, you'll need to go to 190. Thankfully, you'll have developed the skills to make that transition painlessly and seamlessly. Then, perhaps to 180. Some people do really well at 180. Some do well at 100. Others do well at 500 (although probably not many). It seems to be that the sweet spot for many is around 40 to 60, but that's just an anecdotal estimate from reading lots of message boards and participating in bazillions of Facebook chats.

I'm currently at about 30 to 35 per day, after having lost near 150 pounds, and… the food is absolutely delicious at this level.

Won't you join me?

Hidden Carbs

What is a hidden carb? Well, based on the term, it seems reasonable to assume it's a carbohydrate that you can't see! I tend to give it a slightly broader scope than that. I define it more along the lines of "foods that have a greater impact on my blood sugar than I was anticipating." This can occur for any number of reasons, from too-loose labeling laws, to intentionally deceptive labeling techniques and, of course, to complete and total ignorance on my part.

As of the writing of this book, I've personally lost 142 pounds by maintaining a low-carb way of eating. I've got some skin in the game. Along the way, I've learned quite a bit and have successfully been tripped up by hidden carbs. I know the downside of these evil, shady, invisible gremlins.

True Story: I had been eating well and losing consistently and happily. Then, almost like walking into a solid concrete wall, I stopped losing. I stalled. I hit a weight that I simply could not move through. I was stuck. Immobile. Going nowhere. Over time, this started to shake my confidence. It made me want to give up. Why continue to limit what I'm eating if it's not going to work?!

(**Flawed Thinking Alert**: Don't fall into this trap of thinking! It's important to remember: If you're not losing, you're *maintaining*. It's a whole lot better than gaining.)

For the life of me, I couldn't figure it out. I was eating clean, unprocessed foods, all under 30 grams of net carbs per day. In fact, I was even focused on spreading the carbs out throughout the day. What could it be?! Rather than give up, I stuck to my guns and started to dissect my diet. This pursuit took on a soul-searching vibe. Whatever it was, it was preventing me from losing, and I was using it a lot because I was consistently stuck. There was no sense of being stuck some of the time. I felt endlessly glued to a giant immovable wall of jiggly adipose tissue. I started to eliminate things from my diet. I eliminated sweet things. I eliminated tomatoes. I eliminated cheeses. Still stuck. Nothing.

AHHHHHHHHHHHHHHHHHHHHHHHH!!

Then, it hit me like a ton of bricks. I *knew* what it was… or at least, what it had to be! I'd eliminated pretty much everything else.

Chicken powder.

Maybe I'm a total whackadoo, but early on, I'd formed a bad habit of adding a tasty, yummy powdered chicken bouillon base to almost everything. I added it to soups, salad dressings, seasonings for meats, etc. It had slowly manipulated its way into becoming my salt. Reading the label indicated that it had zero net carbs, so it must be ok… right? Plus, it's just chicken, so it's *got* to be good… *right*?!

Nope. Not at all. I'm a dumb-dumb.

My little green-lidded jars listed a teaspoon (5 mL) as the serving size. This was said to have zero carbs. However, I went to Costco, where they had a big tub of the stuff. This had a tablespoon (15 mL) listed as the serving size… and listed 2 grams of carbs per tablespoon (15 mL). Aha! BUSTED!

A little more light reading indicated the second ingredient listed on the label was… SUGAR! Followed quickly by cornstarch, as well as maltodextrin—all rich with carbs! There's also the infamous "natural flavorings," which could mean almost anything.

Needless to say, I stopped using it entirely. About three days later, I experienced a massive WHOOSH! I lost about ten pounds that week. YAY!!!

I also got back my sweet things, tomatoes, and cheese. Over time, I've rolled back the chicken base, but sparingly.

This is a story that highlights my own ignorance, and also what I feel is misleading labeling. Two grams per tablespoon may not seem like a lot, but if you're staying within a 30-gram range, 2 grams is not an insignificant percentage of the daily allotment! It could also be 2.49 grams per tablespoon, but there's no requirement to list this extra fraction.

Another *big* area to expose is sugar free.

Yes, there are carbs that just flat-out don't get included on labels. However, combined with this lack of information is a second information vortex: the polyols or sugar alcohols.

I'm a fairly new low-primal author, but it doesn't take long to figure out that a significant percentage of people who adopt this way of eating are looking for ways to keep their chocolate. They want to lose weight, eat well, have their cake, and eat it too—literally. This tells me that there is a lot of sugar-free candy being purchased and eaten (usually made with sorbitol or malitol). There are a lot of cakes and cookies being made with a common powdered sucralose blend (sucralose, dextrose, and maltodextrin). There are a lot of sugar-free, diabetic friendly, low-carb protein bars giddily being noshed upon with vegetable glycerin.

HOLY GADZOOKS, BATMAN!

There's a myth that sugar alcohols are ok. Another common definition for a net carb is: **Total Carbs – Fiber – Sugar Alcohols = Net Carbs.**

It's simple, easy to wrap your head around, and makes for quick math at the grocery store. Unfortunately, and *especially* for those people who are still eating sugar-free candies, cakes, bars, cookies, ice cream, pudding mixes, etc., it's going to cause a stall eventually. It's not really accurate. It's an oversimplification, and… it's simply not true.

My personal general definition of a net carb is: Total Carbs – Fiber – (Sugar Alcohols/2) = Net Carbs

I know I covered this before, but it's a core piece of information and I wanted to show it from a slightly different angle. This second mention is… *reinforcement*.

Anywho, I count sugar alcohols as 50 percent off, not 100 percent off. So if something says it has 10 grams of sugar alcohols, I *do* take half off, to 5 grams, but I definitely count the full 5.

For me, there is only one exception to this rule, which is when the sweeteners are erythritol, pure stevia (the concentrated stuff, not a blend), and/or oligosaccharides (sweet-tasting fibers). Anything else I count 50 percent. These three sweeteners get a full, 100-percent discount in my personal calculation. I suppose liquid sucralose, aspartame, saccharin, and acesulfame potassium (Ace K) also each get a pass, but for whatever reason,

I rarely pay attention to these, nor do I eat them very often (the way I tend to eat pushes these fairly low in my world). Each sugar alcohol is different. Some are technically *more* than 50 percent and some are less, but they mostly all hover between 70 percent and 30 percent. For simplicity's sake, I stick with a nice round 50 percent with the three exceptions listed above.

Finally, I tend to avoid things made with malitol and/or sorbitol, for two reasons.

1. There are lower-carb alternatives. Why have a chocolate bar made with malitol, when I can find one sweetened with erythritol?

2. These sugar alcohols cause gastric distress. They will upset your tummy, especially if you eat too much. Stevia will not, and it takes large amounts of erythritol to cause any gastric distress (I've personally never noticed it but have read rumors).

Some people are stricter than this and just count all carbs, including fiber and all sugar alcohols. Truth be told, this is probably the easiest to understand, the most basic, and probably the safest approach, but it also tends to be more restrictive. My suggestion is to pick a method and apply it consistently and then climb up and down that particular ladder as your weight adjusts.

Consistency combined with continued education and refinement of the method is key.

Finally, a warning, red-flag alert: honey, agave, yacon syrup, powdered sucralose blends, vegetable glycerin, most all sugar alcohols and starchy fillers, booze, refined grains, and molasses will all potentially likely cause a stall. There are little hidden carb land mines spread all over the place… even (and often *especially*) in foods that are labeled sugar free.

Cravings

Cravings are horrible, evil realities of a changing way of eating. I believe it's a combination of simply missing foods that you're comfortable with, in addition to your body screaming out for more sugar and starch. Your body is so accustomed to certain consistent blasts of sweet energy that to almost completely cut it off sends the body into some kind of retaliatory state. It yearns for starches. It begs for sugar. It twists thoughts, suggesting a quick little dip into the cookie jar won't hurt anyone… it's just one… then you can go back to starving me, you spiteful human, you!

In my experience, my own mind is powerful, tricky, deceptive, and downright manipulative. It's almost as if I'm in some strange form of invisible pain. It feels like I'm going to just die if I don't have a soda. It just does! IT JUST DOES!

It's totally irrational. I'm not going to die. I'm not going to be sick. Precisely zero will happen if I skip that soda. Very few worlds have collided because a large order of French fries was declined. In the moment, it will feel like everything is going wrong and the stress and the pressure of this way of eating, and everything else going on in life, is just too, too much… *I need a slice of pizza. The pizza will return me to a feeling of comfort.*

And it will too! If you eat that pizza, you'll be happy! You'll be glad you did, and you'll feel normal and comfortable… for a while… probably thirty minutes or so. Then, some devious little gremlin will pop up on your shoulder and whisper, "Psst. Hey. Want a cookie?"

Many people experience *serious* cravings near the beginning of their weight-loss journey, usually within the first week. The craving gremlins are fierce and will stop at nothing to get fed. DON'T FEED THEM! DON'T DO IT. NO MATTER WHAT!

In my case, the cravings never really appeared until later. For me, at about six weeks in, I would have carb-mares. I'd have sleepless nights when I would literally fantasize about pizza crusts and hamburger buns. Yep! Crusts and buns—not the toppings and not the thick, juicy burger patty, but the crusts and buns. I couldn't stop! I'd shut my eyes and a kaleidoscope of luxurious breadstuffs would spin through my mind, beckoning, calling my name.

I don't think I slept during week six. I was a little angry and grumpy and tired and listless, but I trusted I was on the right path and stayed the course.

You *must* stay the course. If you do, if you rid your body of the sweet memories of these sweet, satisfying food-stuffs, you will stop having cravings. You'll stop fantasizing about foods. You will begin to develop a natural hunger, which will ask you for food when you need it, not when the shady little goblins demand it.

This way of eating, when done right and done well, eliminates cravings. You'll never ever feel as if you're starving. You just have to push through those walls of cravings to get to the meadow of peace. It's there. I promise you!

Warning: The Crave Gremlins only hibernate, unfortunately. They're still there; they're merely asleep. If you eat a full sugar candy bar, you will awaken them and they will beg for more. They'll cry and scream until they're fed! It's been my experience that with long periods of good behavior, the Crave Gremlins will go back to sleep after a day or two of good behavior on your part, but in the beginning, it can take a week or more. Be warned and try not to wake them!

Stalls

You will stall. I hate to say it, but... you will. There will be periods of time with no movement on the scale whatsoever. In fact, even if you are on your absolute best behavior, you may gain a pound or two—overnight! The body is a fickle creature. Perhaps you had a bit too much salt the night before, and you've retained a lot of water. It happens!

One time when it's very likely that you'll stall is at about one to two weeks into this way of eating. You'll very probably lose a lot of weight quickly. This is almost all water. A low-primal way of eating tends to be a bit of a diuretic, so you carry around less water. Once it's gone, then the actual fat burning and true weight loss begins, but there seems to be a wall that many hit after the initial loss.

Stay the course. The weight *will* continue to come off, but you need to stay the course. Do not give in. Do not give up... no matter what.

Do not worry about the day-to-day fluctuations. If you gain three pounds in a week but lose four, you've lost a full pound that week! The idea is to eat properly and to pay attention to the trends. As long as you are losing weight month over month, you have nothing to worry about.

No matter what, even if you've seen no changes on the scale, stay the course. Keep doing what you're doing.

Your body is just adjusting. Your losses will begin again.

There are also other factors to consider. If you've been exercising, it's possible you're adding muscle. Muscle is denser and weighs more than fat. So, if you gain a pound of muscle and lose a pound of fat, there's no movement on the scale, but you're happier, healthier, and have certainly lost an inch!

Myth: I once read a theory about stalls. I don't quite know where it came from, but I've seen it echoed from time to time. I like this little story, as it helps me stay focused.

I've read that the body doesn't like a lot of dramatic change. It prefers stasis. It's quite content with the size it's grown accustomed to. Any big changes, whether they are gaining weight or losing it, are something that the body wants to resist. It wants to stay the same—where it's at right now, here. If you begin to lose a lot of weight, your body just assumes that it's only temporary and does what it can to help maintain your size and shape. So while you're trying to shrink your fat cells, your body starts to replace that lost volume… with water! It tries to keep the fat cells nice and plump for you, so that when you start eating your "normal" diet, it won't need to change much of anything. Your fat cells have been kept nice and plump for you, ready and waiting. Nice, isn't it?

You need to fight through this. Stay the course. Carry that jiggly-puff water weight around with you. Eventually, your body will get it. It will concede that you've made some kind of change and that it now needs to give in and release the excess water.

WHOOSH!!!

It's been my experience that a long stall is often followed with a big WHOOSH of weight loss, sometimes upwards of five pounds within a single twenty-four-hour period.

In my case, it's common after I've taken a break from exercise. It's always a bit maddening when I return to a good fitness regime. This always coincides with a slightly tighter eating routine. Yet there I go—working out, eating properly, sleeping well—life is good, yet… the scale is stuck, pegged, at the same weight it has been for *two weeks*!

Usually, when I'm about to freak out and run through a wall, I'll drop three to five pounds within about forty-eight hours. Somehow… it just happens!

I choose to believe in the myth.

Fun fact: Muscles swell with water when stressed or sore, while they're healing. This can look like a stall or weight gain, but it's actually a good thing! This effect decreases as the muscles get used to the routine and the weight will drop as the soreness dwindles.

If you *do* stall for more than a month, and you see no changes in inches either, then there stands a very good chance that you're getting some carbs from somewhere, and you'll need to look harder at your diet. This is where tracking and label-reading skills can really come in handy. Eliminate certain foods, to find the hidden carbs, or simply remove 5 net carbs from your daily allocation.

Finally, there also stands the chance that you're just really close to your own personal goal and that you need to start exercising to blast off that last little bit. You could also look into the glycemic index and perhaps remove some of the ingredients with a higher glycemic index. Alternately, and unfortunately, you may need to dissect your diet and lower your carbs again, possibly even your calories at this point. At the end of the day, calories do still count!

Exercise

Obviously, exercise is good for you. You should exercise. However, don't kill yourself. Don't exercise to excess, and don't do anything outside of a proper form or routine. It's best to consult a trainer or a doctor for personal routines and instruction.

My stake in the ground on this topic, for now, is to start: simply walk. Just walk. Walk for thirty minutes a day. If you're already doing more than that, then I'll stay out of it. Keep doing what you're doing! Just do it a little better every day!

In reality, the biggest component is diet. You can do more than 80 percent of the hard work simply by changing your diet. Exercise does have an influence on weight loss, but not as big of an influence as many seem to believe. It's a small factor, from a biological standpoint.

Conventional wisdom would have us believe that if we can burn an extra 3,500 calories per week, that we'll lose 1 pound (.45 kg) of fat. This equates to an extra loss of 500 calories per day, over the span of seven days, and assumes the loss is purely from fat deposits. While this is mostly true, it's not the entire story.

A *very* general way to determine how many calories you burn in a day is to multiply your weight by 11. (I tend to think it's closer to 15, for Low-Primalists, but... I can't prove it. Let's call it an *edumahunch*.)

Let's assume we're discussing a 150-pound woman named Fiona. Fiona burns about 1,650 calories a day by doing nothing. This suggests she can eat 1,650 calories and watch TV all day, and never gain weight. It's perfectly balanced. This equates to about 70 calories an hour, while holding a remote control.

Now, let's assume Fiona does one hour of high-impact jazzercise. According to standard fitness calculators, Fiona has just burned about 476 calories. If you deduct the 70 calories she would've lost anyway, we're still at 407 calories. Even if Fiona does this for one full hour, seven days a week, without a rest day, at 2.849 calories, she's *still* not up to the 3,500 excess calories, and this assumes 100 percent of any weight loss that did occur comes entirely from fat deposits (this tends to be mostly true, while low-carbing) and it assumes Fiona didn't eat anything extra to compensate. Typically people that exercise a lot tend to eat more.

To create a deficit equal to those 407 calories from her hour of jazzercise, Fiona could've just skipped a slice of mud pie.

On January 21, 2009, the Cochrane Collaboration pooled forty-three different studies, including almost 3,500 people. The goal was to determine whether exercise would help overweight people lose weight. Granted, this is a pool of information and just a generalization, but it's very compelling information. Those that restricted their food intake via a dietary plan lost a range of between 6.2 lbs. (2.8kg) and 29.9 lbs. (13.6kg), without exercise. Those that merely exercised, without restricting foods also lost weight, but only between 1.1 lb. (.5kg) and 8.8 lbs. (4kg), on average. Those that both focused on a dietary plan *and* exercise lost an average of between 7.5 lbs. (3.4kg) and 38.9 lbs. (17.7kg). As you can see, the exercise *does* help, but diet has the far greater impact.

Why do I share this? I don't want to undermine the benefits of exercise. This information is here to help frame the importance of a proper diet. Diet is key. However, I do believe exercise is very important for a variety of reasons not completely related to weight loss.

Exercise reinforces your change in routine. If you have just gone for a nice long walk, it's a lot less likely that you'll come home and have a hamburger with sweet, sugary condiments, a thick toasted bun, and greasy fries. It's more likely that you'll have a salad with a nice piece of chicken and some cheese and maybe a nice creamy salad dressing.

To me, exercise is participating in this way of life. It's being involved in the improvement of your own health and well-being. It creates a stronger, more well-developed, happier person with a longer life span.

Other reasons why consistent, even basic, movement and exercise is good for you:

- Benefits the cardiovascular system—heart health!
- Benefits the brain—cardiovascular activity can even help grow new brain mass.
- Builds muscle and more muscle means more calories are being burnt… even while just sitting around.
- Increased quality of sleep.
- Lowers insulin levels.
- Increases feelings of happiness—physically active people have greater general feelings of excitement and enthusiasm, especially on days when they are physically active.
- Improved self-image.

There's no denying that exercise is good. I'm a strong believer in exercise.

I personally started by walking. I walked about a mile a day for about three months. That's all I did, but I got better at it. Finally, after three months, I had lost a significant amount of weight and was feeling good enough about myself to actually… join a gym! Start small if you have to, but start!

If you start walking for twenty minutes every day (or thirty minutes every other day), within two to three weeks, you'll notice a significant boost in your mood. This is a result of increased endorphins, a decrease in cortisol, and changes to dopamine and serotonin. Aside from giving the mind time to stop focusing on day-to-day stresses, these changing compounds will help decrease depression and boost motivation.

As of this writing, my personal typical routine has evolved from walking. Presently, it involves quite a bit of heavy lifting combined with a lot of movement and balance—yoga, plyometrics, rock climbing, jogging, kick-boxing, etc. I'm constantly up to new things.

Start small, with the best you've got, even if it's just 5 feet a day or requires a swimming pool. Move your body.

In addition to those benefits, there's a saying that I really like about exercise because it's so true:

Change your diet and reduce your carbs to look good in your clothes.
Exercise to look good naked!

How to Cook

I think it's vitally important to cook the majority of your meals. It's a great way to participate in this way of life. It's also less expensive than eating out. It has the potential to take more time, but with a little practice and organization, great meals can be planned for and created in very little time overall.

Planning

First, a lot of it comes down to planning. You should have a sense of what you plan to cook and eat, including amounts and times. The actual act of planning may seem like a time crunch, but it will save you countless hours in the long run.

Have a strong sense of what you plan to make for the week or even for the month. Have lists organized and ingredients purchased. Know what dishes will go with the other dishes and on what days.

Next comes the single greatest educational tool I know of…

Practice!

Cooking is something that takes time to learn. I've been cooking since I was a child and still learn every day. Practice and routine will help you learn to cook. Some people burn water and others are old pros, but all can and will learn more by getting into the kitchen and burning stuff. Our best lessons are learned from our mistakes, so don't be afraid to make some. If you can, eat your mistakes too!

In order to take stock of your way of eating, you'll need to spend more time in the kitchen. In my experience, cooking 95 percent of my meals has saved me time and money. Sure, it requires more effort, but so did countless trips to the doughnut shop. Those pizza-delivery tips added up too!

Practice, practice, practice. It's a good thing any which way you look at it. Do not be afraid to study, read, learn, and take risks!

Then start honing your skills with a nasty word I like to call…

Discipline

This is a terrible word. Yuck. Who wants discipline? It sounds like work and like something I'd totally like to avoid. However, here's a little secret—discipline is a real time-saver and a reducer of stress!

When cooking, there's a loose protocol that I always follow:

- **If cooking from a recipe, read the recipe.** Read it from top to bottom and visualize the steps you'll need to take. This is important. Imagine starting a recipe, getting it halfway completed, and then noticing that the eighth step suggests, "Marinate overnight," but you've got your mother-in-law coming for dinner in thirty minutes. Whoops! Should've read that recipe!

- **In order of priority, always start the long projects first.** If you're going to make a complex soup and a simple salad, sure, making the salad might seem easy and where you want to start—just throw together and set aside, right?—but you're doing yourself a disservice. Start the soup. Get it simmering away and developing flavors. It's always better to have the complicated and time-consuming things done first and in process. Worst-case scenario, your visiting Spanish cousins can help throw together the salad at the last minute, when they arrive, but if that soup isn't done… *No soup for you!* I can't stress enough how important it is to start the big projects first. Save the little, quick, simple, easy projects for last. That salad would've wilted anyway…

- **When cooking, save yourself steps.** It may sound silly, but walking around your kitchen, opening the refrigerator repeatedly, getting one ingredient at a time, as you need it, reaching into low cabinets for pots and pans over and over… It wastes a lot of time. All these little steps add up. Stop it! Think ahead a little bit. If you've read your recipes and thought through the steps you need to take, you should have a fairly strong sense of what you'll need to use throughout the cook. When reaching into the cabinets, grab all the pots and pans you'll need for the day. When looking for spices and other pantry items, grab everything you'll need, all at once. Make a nice tight little pile near where you plan to work. Do the same thing with your refrigerated items. Open the door once, save a little on the electric bill, and grab everything you'll need. Unless it's going to rot, wilt, or melt, get it out; a head of broccoli sitting on the countertop for thirty minutes isn't going to hurt anyone. You'll save some time, and the broccoli is just happy to feel some warm air on its florets anyway. Point being, do as much as you can, in consolidated steps. Do more in less time. If you always strive for this, in a very short while, you'll clearly see the benefits. Plus, it'll become second nature!

- **Be organized and consistent.** This is may be too much information, but it's a bit of a mantra for me. There's a French term in professional kitchens that is relentlessly pursued and followed. That term, or concept, is *mise en place.* It means "things in place." I'm not sure how relevant this is to the home cook, but it's a concept that runs deeply through my veins, so I imagine it's worth sharing. Ultimately, it's a term that suggests everything has its place in your kitchen during the preparation of food—the way you prioritize yourself and travel through your kitchen, etc. They say *mise en place* is physical just as much as it is mental. There are serious, die-hard cooks, sweating in fast-paced kitchens in Manhattan right now, who will swear, as they dance through their routines, that *mise en place* has taken on an almost spiritual nature for them. It is the keystone for any good cook. Be organized and consistent. If you have a salt-shaker and want to season your food, put the saltshaker back where it belongs. It has a place. Always… *always* return the saltshaker to its rightful home in your kitchen. Imagine you're about to burn something on the stove, and you need to season it right before you remove it. You reach for the salt, and… IT'S NOT THERE! Now, you've very probably burned your food, *and* you're now wasting time trying to find the salt. If the salt had been where it belonged, you'd have a quick and almost effortless meal. This extends to how you organize your kitchen, from the canned goods in the cabinets to the way you stack your bowls under the counter. It's important that these things stay in the same spots as much as possible. Keep things clean, organized, and within reach as you cook. It will save you time and make for better food.

- **Clean as you go—or, put another way, "Work clean!"** This has a double meaning. First, there are always going to be moments, between cooking and preparing, when you can wash a dish or two. If you put a pot on the stove to start boiling and there's no immediacy in any of your next steps, take a moment to scrub a dirty pot. Always use little breaks to wash and dry dishes. If you plan to use it again, leave it out and put it in your pile of things to use. If you're done with it, put it away (hopefully with a lot of other stuff, at the same time—putting things away, one at a time, can also take extra time). It's also intended to imply you should keep things sanitary. Wash your lettuces and melons. Wash your hands. Don't cut raw chicken on a cutting board then cut salad tomatoes on the same board, with the same knife, without washing it. This is a quick way to make people sick. And, even though I've already said it, wash your hands! Dirty hands are the number one reason for food-borne illnesses. Work clean!

Part of discipline extends to managing time.

Restaurants function because they are efficient machines. A well-run restaurant has everything prepped and ready to go for service. When an order comes in, the chef can grab everything that he/she has prepared and quickly whip up a fantastic meal for the guests. Most of the time and effort goes into the preparation, making stocks and sauces, and precooking some of the vegetables and peeling the potatoes. The final assembly is always the easy part. *À la minute!*

Some of this preparation takes place days or weeks in advance and is stored accordingly, until it is needed.

Once a Month Cooking

There's a concept called "Once a Month Cooking." If you search on the Internet, you'll find all sorts of great information about it (it's often abbreviated as OAMC). I've personally been doing this for years without realizing it had a name. I just called it "efficiency" or "my training."

The core idea being you set aside a day, once a month, and cook for a small army. Portion and package that food, then store it in the cupboard, refrigerator, and, most importantly, the freezer.

If you've got food, all ready to go, just a defrost away, it's unlikely you'll ever let yourself down! Thanks to planning ahead and preparing some good meals and surrounding yourself with healthy options, you're setting yourself up for a lifetime full of success.

What I always do is cook the stew or soup or casserole, then refrigerate it to cool it, chilling it thoroughly. It's vital that you cool it all the way prior to packaging. If it's still warm, the heat may expand and create problems. There are also issues with bacteria. I make sure to cool it thoroughly. Then, I portion it and vacuum pack the individual portions or put them into restaurant to-go containers. (You can go to a restaurant supply store and buy sleeves full of small containers in virtually every possible size.) Fill them up, stack them up, and freeze! If you are cooking for two or six, package away the amount that will feed the people you're feeding. You may need to purchase a separate deep freezer, but the cost will be made up in time.

Things I often make and freeze are:

- meat and fish (I'm a big fan of buying large cuts of meat, then butchering it myself. This is far more economical, while also allowing me to decide how big of a steak or piece of fish I want.)
- soup bases, stocks, and broths
- sauces
- meatballs and meatloaves

- sausages
- shredded cheese (Many pre-shredded cheeses are filled with starches to prevent clumping. Grating your own is more cost effective *and* lower carb! I store these in plastic containers in the fridge. I never freeze cheese.)
- ice cream/sorbets/yogurts
- casseroles (My freezer is full of vacuum-packed "bricks" of foodstuff.)
- crepes/wraps
- low-primal breads
- shredded/pulled meats
- bacon bits
- stuffed/rolled meats

Odds and Ends

The only other two things that seem appropriate to list here might be:

- **Make a checklist.** When I have a lot to do, I make a list. This may sound like overkill, but it's actually a great exercise. First, it forces you to think through every little thing you need to do, including the details, but it also minimizes stress. You can plainly see everything that needs to be done. Finally, it's a ton of fun to strike the pen though the items as you cross them off, one by one. I love that!

- **Seasoning. Cook things properly, in the right order, and season as you go**. In general, food should be cooked properly. I could make the case that it's better to *under*cook your foods than it is to *over*cook your foods. Undercooked foods tend to have more nutrients; your body needs to work harder to process them (meaning you'll probably absorb less sugar into your bloodstream), you'll have more texture and color, and more vibrancy of flavors. There are many people who eat purely raw foods and swear by it. Work toward a fresher style in your kitchen. Also, salt, sugar (or more specifically a sugar equivalent, like erythritol), and acid (lemon juice, vinegar, wine, etc.) are all flavor enhancers. If you are making a recipe involving multiple steps, throw a little smattering of salt or a light squeeze of lemon juice into each step. Allow these flavor enhancers to permeate the food and get deeper into whatever it is that you might be cooking. This goes *a great* distance toward making food worth talking about. Season as you go, even if the recipe doesn't fully call for it—always season, taste, and cook things properly.

- **Always Taste Everything.**

How does it all work?

Throughout this book, I've made a fairly extensive list of ingredients that you can use, and I have also tried to organize them in such a way that plucking out the best ones for your diet should be easy.

The next section outlines a meal-plan calendar for two weeks, a shopping list, and is followed with over two hundred recipes. My goal is to leave you with a clear plan that can be followed to the letter. However, I also want to plant the seeds for future successes, so I think it's important to know how to plan your own meals and mix and match ingredients.

Menu Planning

Let's be honest, picking, planning, budgeting, shopping, cooking, and cleaning all takes time. I see menu plans all the time. I see menu-planning services that can be signed up for. I even see my own sample menu plans and… my only question is: who's going to cook all that for me?!

What I *love* about menu plans is the immediate promise and possibility they provide. I can look at a menu plan, with recipe ideas and nutrient breakdowns, and immediately get it, but the very real reality of it is, three different meals a day, plus snacks, desserts, beverages, and any sides and sauces that may go along with it is time consuming. Who really has time for all of that? I'm about as fast a cook as there is, and even I don't have the time or wherewithal to cook up all that is presented in all these menu plans.

However, within them is the clear and obvious promise of success and variety, and for that, they are *invaluable*.

Let's take a look at the fourteen-day menu plan on the next two pages.

The goal: 30 net carbs or less per day

Sample Menu Plan: Week 1

	Monday	Tuesday	Wednesday	Thursday	Friday	Saturday	Sunday
Breakfast	Pancakes (96)	Granola (106)	Baked Eggs (98)	French Toast (108)	Chia Fauxtmeal (118)	Crab Frittatas (110)	Apple Pancakes (112)
Net Carbs	3.16	9.73	3.4	4.38	6.28	1.88	8.25
Lunch	Turkey Meatball Soup (178)	Cobb Salad (194)	Curried Chicken Salad (186)	Shrimp, Mango, Tomato (190)	Chilled Flank Salad (198)	Taco Soup (157)	Pizza Pucks (212)
Net Carbs	7.41	3.94	10.02	8.36	5.34	6.84	7.87
Snack Options	1/2 cup sliced strawberries (42g or 120 mL)	Pork Rinds	Eggnog (89)	1/4 cup sunflower seeds (35 g or 60 mL)	Hardboiled Egg	Pepperoni Sticks	1/4 cup pecans (27 g or 60 mL)
Net Carbs	5	0	3.12	4	.5	1	1.25
Dinner	Meat Lover's Lasagna (228) The Great Wedge (193)	Jambalaya (172) Miracle Cauli-Rice (320)	Chicken Puttanesca (246) ZOODLES! (226)	Singapore-Style Noodles (230)	Thai Hot and Sour Shrimp (150) Miracle Cauli-Rice (320)	Pork Carnitas (238) Cheddar Taco Shells (478) Salsa Guacamole	Spatchcock Chicken (264) Green Beans, Almonds, Peppers (343) Orange-Rosemary Compound Butter (372)
Net Carbs	9.17	8.67	9.47	9.97	8.67	11.46	9.37
Dessert	Coco-Cocoa-Walnut Bark (404)	Triple Chocolate Everything Wads (412)	The Famous Mock Danish (400)	Sweet 'n' Spicy Fat Bomb (416)	Lemongrass-Scented Coconut-Lime Sorbet (406)	Mexican Wedding Cookies (442)	Raspberry Mocha Sorbet (432)
Net Carbs	1.13	3.04	2.95	1.7	3.87	5	1.5
Total Net Carbs	25.87	25.38	28.96	28.41	24.66	26.32	28.24

Sample Menu Plan: Week 2

	Monday	Tuesday	Wednesday	Thursday	Friday	Saturday	Sunday
Breakfast	Poorly Cooked Eggs (116)	Bacon Wedgie (103)	Eggy McFoo (114)	Blueberry Bread Pudding (456)	Chia Fauxtmeal (118)	Blueberry-Cream Cheese Eggy McFoo (454)	Ham & Swiss Frittata (102)
Net Carbs	6.31	3.16	4.69	7.34	6.28	6.83	7.18
Lunch	Italian Turkey Club (202)	Sausage, Tomato, Mozzarella (188)	Sandwich Wraps (216)	Spicy Stuffed Burger (204)	Greasy Pork Sandwich (210)	Greatest Salad Ever! (180)	Salad Niçoise (196)
Net Carbs	8.56	5.65	5.23	6.58	6.28	7.42	7.57
Snack Options	Celery Sticks / Savory Fat Bomb (384)	Sliced Mozzarella / Sliced Tomato	Strawberry-Kiwi Popsicles (402)	String Cheese Sticks	Sausages	Hardboiled Egg	Packaged Snack Bar
Net Carbs	3.2	5	4.83	4	2	.5	3
Dinner	Baked Salmon with Fennel, Leeks, and Cauliflower (242)	Sweet Thai Chili Wings (124) / Über Crack Slaw (286)	Spicy Burger Casserole (240) / Sweet 'n' Creamy Coleslaw (200)	Stuffed Pork Chops (278) / Green Beans Tapenade (310)	Ropa un Poco Vieja (268) / Miracle Cauli-Rice (320)	Herb Pork Tenderloin Roast (234) / Garlicky Baby Broccoli with Bacon (328)	Brisket with Shrooms and Fennel (244)
Net Carbs	8.49	9.19	9.17	5.57	6	8.9	9.14
Dessert	Salted Brown Butter Fat Bomb (414)	Raspberry-Cream Cheese Swirl Frozen Custard (418)	Frosted Carrot Cake OMM with Pecans (396)	Chocolate OMM (392) / Crème Anglaise (458)	Almond Joy Thumbprint Cookies (438)	Sparkling Gelled Layered Strawberries and Cream (450)	Blackberry-Basil Sorbet (408)
Net Carbs	3.22	6.57	5.25	4.96	4.88	3.33	2.74
Total Net Carbs	29.78	29.57	28.91	28.45	25.44	26.98	27.14

Planning Your Own Menu

Here's where the *real* menu planning exists. The previous two plans are a myth. They look and sound plausible, but, they may or may not be real… like bigfoot, the yeti, and mermaids (unicorns are real).

The reality is, I'm personally a big time repeat eater. It's efficient, and as long as I'm getting diverse foodstuffs every seventy-two hours or so, I'm happy.

Rather than making pancakes on Monday and granola on Tuesday, I'm more likely to bake a double batch of granola and enjoy it for three or four straight days. On the fourth day, I'll bake twelve Individual Swiss Cheese and Ham Frittatas. This will be enough for four days. I've cooked twice but have enough breakfast food for twelve days (eight days' worth of granola, plus four days' worth of fritatta). This kind of system allows for a lot of granola ready to be eaten on a rainy day! On top of that, when I *do* get around to making the pancakes, rather than just making a batch, I'll actually toss together a *big* batch of the powdered ingredients, so that when the time comes, I just scoop some out, add an egg or two, a little butter, and some liquid, and I've got a quick batch of pancakes. None of this looks terribly interesting on a menu plan grid, but it's the reality of my life… and very possibly yours.

The funny part here is that even this is a lie. I don't *eat* breakfast—for shame!

Now, I may be unique in that I only eat twice a day. Lunch is either breakfast or lunch foods. Truthfully, on a daily basis, I have Bulletproof® Coffee for breakfast, along with a good multivitamin and some fish oil. Then, I typically have "brunch," then, dinner, and very often… ice cream. That's really the snapshot of my personal day. Some of the time, brunch is granola and frittatas, but other times, lunch can be something like sausages from the store, with some fresh tomatoes on the side. The next day, maybe some tomatoes, mozzarella, and bacon bits tossed with some lemon juice, olive oil, salt, and pepper. I'm also a big fan of tossing something like cauliflower in a pot with some chicken broth, some bacon bits, and a few cloves of garlic. I put a lid on it and let it simmer for 30 minutes. Then, I puree it in a blender with some cream and a small handful of Parmesan cheese. I can pretty much do the exact same thing with broccoli (10 minutes), tomatoes (30 minutes), zucchini (10 minutes), etc. The process is the same but different colors, flavors, and nutrient blends. It's also all pretty quick, has water for bulk as well as hydration, and a good mix of fat, proteins, and good carbs. I'm also inclined to make a big batch of Herby Sandwich Bread and make sandwiches for four days—different kinds but basically all just sandwiches, some hot and some cold.

Dinner is usually something like a big soup or stew, like Sopa sin Tortilla. I'll make a big batch, freeze three-quarters of it in frozen containers, and eat the rest over two nights. The third night will be something like a quick, warm salad, such as the Greatest Salad Ever. Then on the fourth night, I'll make something like a big batch of Bacon-Wrapped Pizza-Stuffed Chicken. I'll eat one portion, chill the rest, and vacuum pack it for the freezer. As I cook, my freezer slowly fills with meals, portioned ready to be heated on a night where I've got big plans, I'm too busy, I've got a hot date, I want to watch a movie, or I'm just feeling particularly lazy and that troublemaker Alf is about to eat another cat.

I almost never snack. I just honestly never feel the need. Thankfully, this way of eating suppresses appetite. It becomes somewhat "self-policing," in time. When I first started, I did eat a lot of fat bombs though. They're easy to make and store well in the fridge.

Early on and for reasons that are beyond me, I got into the habit of making ice cream. Years on, I still make a batch or two a week.

Sugar-free ice cream is perfect for low-primalists in that it's easy to portion, it typically has a nice portion of satiating fat, it freezes, so it's in greater danger of being eaten than it is of going bad, and the ice cream category allows for near-infinite variety. When I make a batch of ice cream, it typically makes about eight portions (I have a slightly larger ice cream maker than most). As a result, I'll make something like a Dark Chocolate and Almond Butter Swirl on Sunday and stash it in the freezer. I'll eat one at the end of each day. As I'm making dinner, I'll pull one from the freezer and put it in the fridge to soften. I'll make dinner, eat dinner, watch a few *Three's Company* reruns, and then enjoy a nice, smooth, and softened ice cream. The following Sunday, I'll make a big batch of Strawberry Cream Cheese… which now gives me a selection of eight Strawberry and one Chocolate Almond. By doing it this way, I eventually wind up with a huge selection of flavors as I toss different ingredients into a basic frozen custard base.

Given my personal lifestyle and approach to eating, my own weekly menu plan might look repetitive and boring to a casual observer, but as the system churns along, the freezer gets loaded up with sauces, soup bases, ice cream flavors, casseroles, different meats and sausages, and a month in… I've got a massive variety built up, all ready to go. The overall system is simply in need of an occasional artichoke, when things begin to feel a bit stale. If I'm having guests or I'm going to cook for family, then I'll use one of the more elaborate recipes. If I'm just feeling spunky, in the mood to cook, or in need of a change of pace, I'll rock out a big Thai Feast. Like most of you, I've got my thirty things I make over and over, and I love them, but I'm also a massive fan of options and variety.

Yum.

Here's a typical week for me:

	Monday	Tuesday	Wednesday	Thursday	Friday	Saturday	Sunday
Breakfast	Bulletproof® Coffee	Bulletproof® Coffee	Bulletproof® Coffee	Bulletproof® Coffee	Bulletproof® Coffee	Bulletproof® Coffee	Bulletproof® Coffee
Net Carbs	.1	.1	.1	.1	.1	.1	.1
Brunch	Granola (106)	Granola (106)	Italian Club Sandwich (202)	Italian Club Sandwich (202)	Italian Club Sandwich (202)	Italian Club Sandwich (202)	Cream of Cauliflower Soup (160)
Net Carbs	9.73	6.69	8.56	8.56	8.56	8.56	8.42
Dinner	Bacon-Wrapped Pizza-Stuffed Chicken (294)	Bacon-Wrapped Pizza-Stuffed Chicken (294)	Greatest Salad Ever! (180)	Sopa sin Tortilla (168)	Sopa sin Tortilla (168)	Über Crack Slaw (286)	Über Crack Slaw (286)
Net Carbs	3.35	3.35	7.42	7.58	7.58	7.69	7.69
Dessert	Raspberry Cream Cheese Frozen Custard (418)	Raspberry Cream Cheese Frozen Custard (418)	Raspberry Cream Cheese Frozen Custard (418)	Raspberry Cream Cheese Frozen Custard (418)	Raspberry Cream Cheese Frozen Custard (418)	Raspberry Cream Cheese Frozen Custard (418)	Raspberry Cream Cheese Frozen Custard (418)
Net Carbs	6.57	6.57	6.57	6.57	6.57	6.57	6.57
Total Net Carbs	19.75	16.71	22.65	22.81	22.81	22.92	22.78

A suggestion that I make all the time on my blog and in comments and email responses to people goes something like this:

1. Identify your meal needs. If you're like me, you'll need roughly eight recipes to satisfy an entire week's worth of eating. Aside from the coffee, my own needs are three brunch recipes, four dinner recipes, and one dessert recipe. These are made in larger portions and enjoyed over several days. Some may have more time or a stronger desire for immediately varied variety. In that case, feel free to seek out seven breakfast, lunch, snack, dinner, sides, and dessert recipes. Forty-two different recipes a week is *sure* to prevent boredom!

2. Make a grid that looks like mine but with empty boxes. Just draw it out on a piece of paper. It doesn't need to be perfect, just somewhat grid-like. Put the days at the top and the meal types on the left.

3. Find recipes to fill your needs. You're looking for recipes that are 10 net carbs or less. Thumb through this book, look through my blog, ask Google, seek out other authors and bloggers, and compile a list of eight (or forty-two) recipes you'll try the following week. Think about your schedule and budget. Find recipes that are quick, simple, budget friendly, adventurous, spicy, sophisticated, bacon friendly, OAMC (once a month cooking), etc. Make sure to find recipes with clear nutritional analysis. Also, be sure to plan ahead and anticipate curveballs. It's *always* good to have a freezer full of backup meals. Once you've found the recipes that fill your needs, plop them in their slots on your grid. Make sure you know where to find the recipes as well. Make notes on your grid.

4. Make a shopping list. Go shopping!

5. Cook!

In anticipation of the following week, use the same system and even some of the same recipes. Make a grid. Chances are good that you've got some extra meals from the previous week, so you can put those in some of new slots. Layer in five of the same recipes from the prior week and look for two new recipes. Add those. Make a shopping list, go shopping, and get cooking!

Something like this is fairly simple discipline but builds in awareness of the foods being eaten; it anticipates future needs. It considers time constraints, budgets, number of people being fed, dietary needs, etc. It also builds in ways to keep the system evolving by introducing new recipes. I'll be the first to admit it takes a little bit to get started, but once it begins rolling along, it becomes second nature.

Shopping List

This is my stab at providing a unified list, but… this is no easy task! There are so many thoughts and opinions on all of this, ranging from cost issues (That's *way* too expensive!), to location issues (I can't find that in my area!), to dietary issues (OMG! That's not gluten-free!!), to philosophical issues (How could you!? That's artificial!!). Within all of your varying opinions are my own opinions, backed by my own thoughts and experiences. I've been at this for over four years now, and I've evolved! My thoughts and experiences are wildly different now than they were four years ago. I've learned loads in that time, and my opinions have changed. However, I also remember my mindset when I started. Some of the things I now avoid really helped to get me started!

In order to produce a clean list, my plan is to create a solid list of product categories that I've either used or believe to be quality products. Each of you will disagree with some items on this list. I actually no longer work with some of the items on this list, but, again, I also know my mindset when I first started. I'm including many of the things I enjoyed in the beginning, things I've long since phased out.

Each of these products can be found online. With some foresight and bargain hunting, many of these can be found in bulk, inexpensively, and often with free shipping.

* Products with an asterisk are products I currently use. Those without an asterisk are products I likely used early on in my own personal weight loss but have cut them from my own habits for a variety of reasons, from stalls to philosophical changes to simply changing my habits to a point where it's no longer a useful ingredient or product to me. Everything on this list has value to someone.

I should point out that this list is an abbreviated guide. If you visit my website and/or directly ask me, I'll send you an updated printable list that contains specific products, including brand names and items not listed here. Because products can come and go, I didn't want to include specific brands, except where there's a very clear recommendation with staying power.

Check out my website for a richer, up-to-date, print-friendly list, including produce, dairy, nuts, meats, etc.

www.DJFoodie.com/ShoppingList

Low-Primal Powdery Stuff

* Coconut Flour
* Almond Flour
* Hazelnut Meal/Flour
* Glucomannan Powder (a thickener)
* Arrowroot Starch/Flour (a thickener)
* Tapioca Flour (a thickener good for baking)
* Stevia-Sweetened or Unsweetened Whey Protein Powder (typically vanilla)
* Gelatin Powder (I prefer grass fed.)
* Cocoa Powder
* Ground Chia Seeds (I typically grind my own in a coffee grinder.)
* Ground Flaxseed Meal (I typically grind my own in a coffee grinder.)

These are all things I currently eat and use. They more or less form the backbone of anything that I use to bake and/or make sweets—muffins, pancakes, breading, thickeners, etc. This is my concentrated list of goodness. Low-Primal suggests it's Paleo friendly while also being fairly low on the glycemic index. The arrowroot and tapioca flours are both higher carb starches, but used in small amounts, they provide some wonderful texture to baked goods and various sauces.

Nonlow-Primal Powdery Stuff

Soy Flour
Oat Fiber
Resistant Wheat Starch
Gluten Free Oat Flour
* Xanthan Gum
Guar Gum
Wheat Protein Isolate 5000
Wheat Protein Isolate 8000
Vital Wheat Gluten
Lupin Flour
Peanut Flour

These are all things that I used pretty heavily in my early low-carb'ing days. They're largely grain- or legume-based flours or thickeners. I still own most of these, but I haven't used them in several years. However, I should point out that these are all *wonderful* products. There are loads of recipes containing these ingredients. These are the kinds of ingredients you can buy to make a loaf of bread… that actually looks like a loaf of bread, not a shady Paleo knockoff. These are all completely valid in their own right and well worth looking into.

Baking Mixes/Prepared Powdery Stuff

Low-Carb Flours and Bake Mixes
Sugar-Free Gelatin Desserts
Sugar-Free Pudding Desserts

These are premade blends—muffins, breads, pizza crusts, pancakes, etc. There are hundreds if not thousands of products on the market. Many are delicious, but I confess to preferring individual ingredients and making my own blends. These are well engineered, convenient, and great to have around for a lazy day.

Also, there are the two gelatin and pudding products. These are artificially flavored and sweetened. The pudding blends, in particular, also have starches in them to help them thicken. I *loved* these in my early days, but found the starch would slow me down. I eventually fazed them out.

In general, I've personally moved on from the various mixes and just have the raw ingredients. If I want to make pancakes, I mix together four or five different ingredients, rather than reaching for a box of bake mix. It takes longer, but it's far more flexible and ultimately a less expensive approach. If I wanted Jell-O or pudding, I'd also make them from scratch, using plain gelatin and/or eggs or other low-primal thickeners. However and again, these *are* great products and *perfect* for someone starting out. Just work to faze them out, over time. Someone with crutches always hopes to put them down someday.

Low-Primal Sweeteners
* Swerve Sweetener (a premade blend and my personal favorite: www.SwerveSweetener.com)
* Erythritol
* Inulin
* Tagatose
* Yacon Syrup (For making brown sugar)
* Xylitol Honey
Stevia Products

Nonlow-Primal Sweeteners
* Liquid Sucralose
* Sugar-Free Syrups (like you'd see at a coffee shop)
Polydextrose Fiber

Fats/Oils
* Lard (I typically use bacon fat, though.)
* Olive Oil (look for the real deal; a lot of what is available isn't actually pure olive oil.)
* Coconut Oil
* Butter
Red Palm Oil
Ghee

In all honesty, I use bacon fat for most all cooking… even a lot of baking. I also use a lot of butter. I typically use extra virgin olive oil for salads and salad dressings. Coconut oil gets used for stronger-flavored dishes, like curries and other exotic and spicy things. I've never used red palm oil, but it's known to be a good one—just be aware it's got some sustainability issues attached to it. Ghee is also a wonderful high-smoke point fat, but it's just so expensive, I never actually purchase it. If I needed some, I'd just make it from butter. (Ghee is little more than toasty-flavored clarified butter.) Finally, I'm not sure if this belongs here, but, on a personal note, I'm a fan of fish oil and MCT oil (the latter of which finds its way into my coffee, most mornings!).

Condiments
* Reduced Sugar Ketchup
* No-Sugar-Added Jams and Jellies
* Xylitol Pancake Syrup
* Sugar-Free BBQ Sauce
* Tomato Sauce
* Salsa
* Almond Butter
* Peanut Butter
* Mustard
Hot Sauce
Coconut Aminos

Condiments are great. They're quick and simple. Reach into the fridge, pull out some low-sugar ketchup, and an accidently overcooked steak suddenly becomes delicious again! I love to use these things in a pinch and use many of them frequently. Some of the time, I make my own, but when I'm feeling lazy, I like knowing I've got some pasta sauce floating around or hot sauce or… pancake syrup. Perfect *and* is a great excuse to use that little shelf in the fridge!

Prepared Products
* Erythritol-Sweetened Chocolate Bars
* Erythritol-Sweetened Snack and Protein Bars
* Xylitol Breath Mints
Low-Carb Tortillas
Low-Carb Pita Breads

These are some of the bready-er things and sweets. There are full-blown loaves of bread and bagels and cookies and crackers on the market. Feel free to explore each of these products. For whatever reason, I never delved too deeply into them, usually making something if I really wanted it. However, I *did* buy a lot of pitas and tortillas in my early days.

Today, I still enjoy chocolate bars and tend to enjoy these as snacks, the same with the snack bars. Both are treats I enjoy from time to time—I sneak them into movie theaters. I also love Xylitol Breath Mints. They're tasty, and they make my breath smell like wintertime in the forest.

Canned Stuff
* Coconut Milk
* Pumpkin Puree
* Black Organic Soybeans
* Erythritol-Sweetened Soda

Stuff in cans is good to have around. Both coconut milk and pumpkin puree get used fairly often around the

Foodie household. Combine the two with some sweetener for a delicious smoothie!

The black soybeans are actually super great. I probably go through a can every month, on average. I don't eat a lot of soy or soy products, but organic non-GMO black soybeans are one I use for bulk in chili, soups, or refried beans. Paleo enthusiasts probably hate me right now, but I don't eat them often and they're *shockingly* black bean–like!

I almost never drink soda, but I tend to have some on hand for random urges or visitors. I prefer a naturally sweetened soda over most other diet sodas.

Other Stuff

* Almond Milk, unsweetened
* Cacao Nibs
* Shirataki Noodles and Rice
* Chia Seeds
* Apple Cider Vinegar
* Flavor Extracts and Oils
Cacao Butter
Erythritol-Sweetened Chocolate Chips
Kelp Noodles

This is just a list of odds and ends. I use unsweetened almond milk almost daily. I use a lot of flavorings to stretch flavors in fat bombs, ice creams, and things like muffins. For example, if I want a strawberry muffin, I'll use a little strawberry flavoring plus some actual strawberries. I get all the strawberry flavor, some real fresh fruit, but a nice big drop in the fructose levels. YAY! I use them to stretch certain flavors.

I'm also a big chia seed nut. I make flour with the seeds, as well as a wide variety of puddings and porridges. One of my absolute favorite new ingredients!

The rest are noodles and rice replacements. I love the *shirataki* rice, blended with cauli-rice. The Kelp and *shirataki* noodles take some getting used to though. I think they're *wonderful* in Asian preparations with lots of ginger and spice, plus other contrasting colors and textures. A bowl of *shirataki* noodles with some Alfredo sauce, in my mind, is just… ick. However, stir-fried with some sesame oil, ginger, black pepper, coconut aminos, sesame seeds, cabbage, broccoli, beef, and green onions. Bring it on!

LET'S GET COOKING!!!!

ALWAYS

o o o

TASTE

o o o

EVERYTHING

BEVERAGES

○ ○ ○

Don't underestimate the power of water. I have a gallon pitcher that lives in my fridge. I drink from it all day, and I fill it again before bed.

Water is hydrating, which is vital for energy, concentration, and mood. It's filling! The best response to a craving is a big glass of cold water. It helps flush out waste and bacteria. It's excellent for skin. Let's face it: you need the stuff! We are all mostly made of water. As it leaves our bodies, we need to be constantly replacing it to survive. I even have a water bottle I carry with me most places. It's almost like my binky... I feel a bit lost without it now. (Don't tell anyone!)

I drink coffee in the morning, water all day long, and decaf tea at night. On rare occasions, I throw a little variety in the mix, so here are some ideas to mix it up.

HORCHATA

SERVES: 12 · · · PREP: 30 MIN · · · COOK: 5 MIN · · · TOTAL: 12 HRS

aprx 12 cups (3 L) **water**, divided

1 3/4 cups (420 mL) **blanched almonds**

3/4 cup (180 mL) **cashews**

1/2 cup (120 mL) **white sesame seeds**

2 tsp (10 mL) finely chopped **fresh lime zest**

2 sticks **cinnamon**

1 tsp (5 mL) **freshly grated nutmeg**

1 1/2 cups (360 mL) **sugar replacement** (to taste)

1 Tbsp (15 mL) **vanilla extract**

1/2 tsp (2 mL) **salt**

Pronounced OR-CHA-TA, this is one of my absolute favorite beverages, going as far back as I can remember. I knew it to be a sugar-and-spice rice-based beverage from Mexico, but it actually has its roots in Spain. This particular configuration is more Central American in nature, resembling the horchatas of Nicaragua, Honduras, and Venezuela, but it still just tastes like "liquid rice pudding" to me!

1. In a medium pot, bring approximately 5 cups (1.2 L) of water to a boil.

2. In a large bowl, place the zest, almonds, cashews, sesame seeds, cinnamon, and nutmeg.

3. Once the water comes to a boil, pour it over the nuts, seeds, and spices (reserving the last three ingredients in the list above for later). Cover the bowl and let stand overnight, in the refrigerator.

4. The next day, get a second large bowl. Place a large sieve in it, and then line the sieve with 3 layers of cheesecloth, with the four corners hanging over the edge of the sieve. Additionally, get about 3 to 4 cups (720 mL to 960 mL) of water and place next to a blender.

5. Scoop the chilled nut mixture into a blender. You will likely need to do this in batches. Add enough to fill the blender about halfway, and add enough water to keep the mixture moving. Blend each batch for 2 to 3 minutes or until it's very fine and no longer gritty. Pour the liquid into the second bowl, through the cheesecloth. Repeat this process until all of the nut mixture has been blended.

PER SERVING
CALORIES: 214.88
FAT: 17.73
PROTEIN: 7.39
CARBS: 40
FIBER: 3.84
SUGAR ALCOHOLS: 30
NET CARBS: 6.16

MORE FACTS: P. 495

6. Stir the liquid gently around the cheesecloth until the majority has been strained through. Grab the four corners of the cheesecloth, folding them together above the liquid and then twisting them to force the remaining liquid from the solids inside the cheesecloth. Discard this bundle of solids.

7. Add the remaining 3 to 4 cups (720 mL to 960 mL) of water to the strained liquid. Whisk in the sweetener, vanilla, and salt until dissolved. Adjust sweetness to personal preference. If it's too thick, add more water. The mixture will settle, with some of the solids sinking to the bottom. This is fine. Simply stir it before serving! Chill.

8. Serve with ice, if preferred.

Watermelon Agua Fresca

SERVES: 10 · · · PREP: 15 MIN · · · COOK: 0 MIN · · · TOTAL: 15 MINS

8 cups (1.9 L) **seedless watermelon cubes or balls**, divided

6 cups (1.4 L) **water**

1/2 cup (120 mL) **sugar replacement**

1/4 cup (60 mL) freshly squeezed **lime juice**

1/2 tsp (2 mL) **salt**

An *agua fresca* is a beverage that combines various ingredients with healthy portions of water and sweetener to stretch and extend the tastes of the goodies (horchata is actually an *agua fresca* as well). This technique can be done with many other ingredients, such as pineapple, lime, Jamaica flowers (hibiscus), tamarind, oat, rice, orange, almond, mango, strawberry, watermelon, passion fruit, prickly pear, cucumber, etc. These are combined and blended with other herbs and spices, sweetened, and then diluted, often strained, and then served. It is a great, inexpensive, and absolutely flavorful beverage.

1. Place 6 cups (1.4 L) of the watermelon into a blender. Add the lime juice, sweetener, salt, and just enough water to cover the watermelon in a blender. Puree the mixture until smooth.

2. Optional: Place a fine strainer over a large bowl or nonreactive pot and strain the liquid, removing any thick pulp that may be left behind. This will make for a thinner and more consistent beverage.

3. Place the liquid in a large pitcher, jug, or punch bowl. Add the remaining water and whisk. Taste and adjust seasoning. Add the remaining melon, chill, and drink!

PER SERVING
CALORIES: 38.33
FAT: 0
PROTEIN: .83
CARBS: 21.33
FIBER: .83
SUGAR ALCOHOLS: 12
NET CARBS: 8.5

MORE FACTS: P. 496

Coconut, Orange, and Chia

SERVES: 2 · · · PREP: 5 MIN · · · COOK: 0 MIN · · · TOTAL: 30 MINS

1 1/3 cups (320 mL) **unsweetened almond milk**

2/3 cup (160 mL) **unsweetened coconut milk**

2 Tbsp (30 mL) **sugar replacement**

1 Tbsp (15 mL) **chia seeds**

1 Tbsp (15 mL) **fresh orange juice**

2 tsp (10 mL) **yacon syrup** (or blackstrap molasses)

1/2 tsp (2 mL) finely chopped **fresh orange zest**

a dash of **salt**

I was strangely resistant to chia seeds for years. I had a large bag, procured from the local organic market, which stared at me that whole time. It just seemed far too close to what my mind considered "health food" for me to give it a shot. My mind is very often wrong and should be more open to new ideas. A move to another country and a fresh bag prompted my first foray into the world of chia via a breakfast pudding. I immediately fell in love and began adding it to everything, including *this* wonderful beverage!

1. In a medium bowl, whisk together the ingredients until the sweetener dissolves and it's well combined.

2. Wait about one minute and whisk again. Wait about two minutes, and whisk one more time. The chia has a tendency to sink and clump together unless it is mixed a few times and has absorbed some water.

3. After about 5 to 7 minutes of periodic stirring, refrigerate.

4. The beverage is ready after about 30 minutes. Serve with ice, if preferred.

PER SERVING
CALORIES: 203.98
FAT: 19.01
PROTEIN: 3.68
CARBS: 26.25
FIBER: 2.68
SUGAR ALCOHOLS: 15
NET CARBS: 8.58

MORE FACTS: P. 495

Spiced Masala Chai Tea

SERVES: 4 ··· PREP: 5 MIN ··· COOK: 25 MIN ··· TOTAL: 30 MIN

Calling this Spiced Masala Chai Tea is approximately thrice redundant. It's really just *Masala* Chai. Masala means "spice mix" in most of Southeast Asia. In Indian Hindi, *chai* means "tea." "Spiced Masala Chai Tea" is like saying Spiced Tea... in a few different ways, all at the same time. Fun, right? I love Spiced Masala Chai Tea. It's an extremely charismatic tea, with wild, exotic scents and powerfully delicious flavors. It's most commonly known as a sweet, warm black tea. It's made by steeping spices and tea in milk, sweeteners, and water. It's yum!

2 cups (480 mL) **water**

1/4 cup (60 mL) **sugar replacement**

1/2 tsp (2 mL) **vanilla extract**

1/2 tsp (2 mL) ground **cinnamon**

1/4 tsp (1 mL) ground **cloves**

1/4 tsp (1 mL) ground **cardamom**

1/4 tsp (1 mL) ground **black pepper**

1/4 tsp (1 mL) ground **fennel seeds**

1/4 tsp (1 mL) ground **nutmeg**

1/4 tsp (1 mL) **salt**

1/2 tsp (2 mL) grated **fresh ginger**

2 cups (480 mL) **unsweetened almond milk**

4 **black tea bags**

1. In a medium saucepan, bring all the ingredients except the tea and almond milk up to a slow simmer.

2. Once it simmers, remove from the stove and allow it to steep for 15 minutes.

3. Return to the stove, add the almond milk, and bring the liquid back to a low simmer and add the tea.

4. Remove the tea from the stove, and allow it to steep for a further 5 minutes.

5. Strain the tea through a fine sieve and serve.

PER SERVING
CALORIES: 22.5
FAT: 1.75
PROTEIN: 1
CARBS: 16.5
FIBER: .5
SUGAR ALCOHOLS: 15
NET CARBS: 1

MORE FACTS: P. 495

Spicy Hot Chocolate

SERVES: 2 · · · PREP: 5 MIN · · · COOK: 5 MIN · · · TOTAL: 10 MIN

1 cup (240 mL) **unsweetened almond milk**

3/4 cup (180 mL) **heavy whipping cream**

1 tsp (5 mL) **vanilla extract**

1/4 cup (60 mL) **sugar replacement**

3 Tbsp (45 mL) **unsweetened cocoa powder**

1/2 tsp (2 mL) **cinnamon**, ground

1/2 tsp (2 mL) **ancho pepper, New Mexico chili, or cayenne**, powdered

a dash of **salt**

1 shot (30 mL) **espresso** (optional)

The word *chocolate* comes from the Aztec word *xocolatl*. Xocolatl (meaning "bitter water") was an ancient beverage of cocoa beans, maize, various spices, honey, and chili. This was a special drink, reserved for warriors and nobles. It's generally believed that this wasn't a sweet concoction and that sugar and cream was added by the Europeans many years later. This hot beverage pays homage to its Latin origin while being simple enough to make and modernized for it to be reminiscent of a comforting cup of cocoa, but with a faint, titillating tickle near the back your throat.

1. Place your almond milk, cream, and vanilla on the stove, and slowly bring it up to a very low simmer.

2. While the milk is heating, combine all your dry ingredients and blend them together.

3. Once the milk is hot, quickly whisk in the dry ingredients until they are well blended, the sugar replacement has dissolved, and a nice foam has formed.

4. Pour the liquid into two mugs and, optionally, top with whipped cream and some cocoa powder.

5. To make it a hot chili mocha, you can add a shot of espresso.

Perfect for a hot little kick on a cold winter's day!

PER SERVING
CALORIES: 361.07
FAT: 36.53
PROTEIN: 14.61
CARBS: 34.98
FIBER: 3.71
SUGAR ALCOHOLS: 30
NET CARBS: 6.27

MORE FACTS: P. 495

Luxurious Eggnog

SERVES: 8 · · · PREP: 15 MIN · · · COOK: 15 MIN · · · TOTAL: 2 HRS 20 MIN

I somewhat famously ate *zero* carbs for thirty days after reading about one of the Grateful Dead's early soundmen, Owsley "Bear" Stanley. Believing vegetables to be toxic, he claimed to have eaten nothing but meat, eggs, butter, and cheese for over fifty years. He believed insulin did enormous damage to the body, so he avoided all carbohydrates for the majority of his life. He believed he aged slower than most who ate a "normal" diet. During my thirty-day stint, I needed a variety of foods to keep it interesting. There was a bottomless jug of eggnog on hand at all times. Who says this stuff is seasonal? It's perfect for neutralizing a craving, and it's tasty, filling, and satisfies the sweet tooth!

2 1/2 cups (600 mL) **heavy whipping cream**

1 1/2 cup (360 mL) **unsweetened almond milk**

1 **vanilla bean**, split lengthwise (or 2 tsp [10 mL] vanilla extract)

1/2 tsp (2 mL) ground **cinnamon**

1/4 tsp (1 mL) freshly ground **nutmeg**

1/3 cup (80 mL) **sugar replacement**

a dash of **salt**

6 large **whole eggs**

1. In a medium saucepan, combine cream and almond milk.

2. Scrape the seeds from the vanilla bean. Add the bean and seeds to the milk and cream. Add the cinnamon and nutmeg, and then bring the milk to a slow simmer. Remove the milk from the heat, and whisk the sweetener and salt into the milk. Make sure it dissolves.

3. In a separate bowl, whisk the eggs well. Very, very slowly, pour the hot milk mixture into the eggs. While slowly pouring, whisk quickly, so as to incorporate the hot liquid evenly, without cooking or scrambling the eggs. Once the liquid has been incorporated into the eggs, pour the milk–egg mixture back into the saucepan and return to a low heat.

4. Stir consistently until the eggnog thickens. The temperature should be between 165 and 175°F (74 and 79°C). Whatever you do, do not boil this mixture.

5. Strain the eggnog and chill.

PER SERVING
CALORIES: 322.14
FAT: 31.93
PROTEIN: 3.57
CARBS: 13.38
FIBER: .27
SUGAR ALCOHOLS: 10
NET CARBS: 3.12

MORE FACTS: P. 496

Cucumber-Ginger Water

SERVES: 16 · · · PREP: 5 MIN · · · COOK: 0 MIN · · · TOTAL: 5 MIN

1 one-inch piece (2.5 cm) **fresh ginger**

1 (301 g) **English cucumber**

1 gallon (3.8 L) **cold water**

a dash of **salt**

While I'm clearly a fan of plain old water, I often hear people insist, "But… I don't like the taste of water!" Ultimately, anything you eat or drink has some water in it. It doesn't need to be pure water. A bowl of soup is mostly water. Coffee is mostly water (though its diuretic nature isn't strong enough to counteract the water it contains). However, don't underestimate what a little boost of a few ingredients can do to change the taste of that boring old cup of water. Try smooshing a few berries into it, or a squeeze of orange or a sprig of rosemary. This is just one fun idea of millions, and it's perfect for a hot summer's day!

Serve with some lime wheels!

1. Peel and juice the ginger. A great way to do this is to place a small and fine sieve over a large bowl. Then, grate the ginger using the weird, bumply side of your cheese grater. If you have a ginger grater, so much the better! Alternately, puree it in a food processor or blend it with one cup of water (these last two options will result in a cloudier beverage, but it's no less tasty). Strain through the sieve.

2. Wash the cucumber, and then slice it very thin. This is best done with a mandolin or some kind of vegetable slicer (such as an attachment for a food processor). Add the cucumber to the bowl.

3. Add the water along with a dash of salt. Mix. Serve chilled.

PER SERVING
CALORIES: 3.46
FAT: 0
PROTEIN: 0
CARBS: .85
FIBER: .11
SUGAR ALCOHOLS: 0
NET CARBS: .74

MORE FACTS: P. 496

Chocolate Shake with Chocolate Sauce

SERVES: 4 · · · PREP: 15 MIN · · · COOK: 15 MIN · · · TOTAL: 30 MIN

Chocolate sauce

1/4 cup (60 mL) **unsweetened cocoa powder**

1/3 cup (80 mL) **heavy whipping cream**, divided

3 Tbsp (45 mL) **sugar replacement**

a dash of **salt**

Chocolate Shake

4 cups (960 mL) **ice cubes**

3 cups (720 mL) **heavy whipping cream**

1 recipe **chocolate sauce** (about 1/2 cup [120 mL])

1/4 cup (60 mL) **sugar replacement**

a dash of **salt**

In a perfect world, a great chocolate shake is made with a wonderful ice cream, but there are virtually no quality sugar-free ice creams on the market. The closest national brand that I'm aware of is SO Delicious. While dairy free, it doesn't lack in flavor and uses an excellent blend of ingredients. There are also some local shops and small-scale companies putting out excellent products. I might also suggest pouring my Crème Anglaise into an ice cream machine. It'll make for a really tasty vanilla! Though I can't rely on a good ice cream, I still wanted to include a good ol' fashioned chocolate shake with things you'll find pretty much anywhere. Make some extra sauce, just to have it around the house for a periodic chocolate milk or a Bulletproof® Mocha in the morning!

1. For the Chocolate Sauce, heat all the ingredients (omitting half the cream) over medium heat, whisking until just below simmering, thick, and well combined. You can thin it out with the cream. You may not use it all. Adjust to your personal preference. Remember, it will thicken as it cools!

2. Drizzle a small amount of chocolate sauce onto the edges of four glasses.

3. Add all the ice cubes, the remaining cooled chocolate sauce, cream, sweetener, and a dash of salt to a blender. Blend until desired consistency. Pour into the 4 glasses. Top with whipped cream and a sprinkle of cocoa powder if so desired.

4. Note: To give a fuller flavor, you can freeze almond milk or coconut milk into ice cube trays and use these. Can also use almond milk/coconut milk instead of cream for a nondairy chocolate shake.

PER SERVING
CALORIES: 696.42
FAT: 74.46
PROTEIN: 5.23
CARBS: 35.21
FIBER: 1.81
SUGAR ALCOHOLS: 26.25
NET CARBS: 7.13

MORE FACTS: P. 496

Sweet Lassi

SERVES: 1 · · · PREP: 5 MIN · · · COOK: 0 MIN · · · TOTAL: 5 MIN

1 cup (240 mL) unsweetened **plain Greek yogurt**

1/2 cup (120 mL) **ice cubes**

2 Tbsp (30 mL) **sugar replacement**

1/2 tsp (2 mL) **rose water**

scant 1/4 tsp (1 mL) ground **cardamom**

a dash of **salt**

Sweet lassi (pronounced LAHH-SEE) is a sweetened Indian drink made from yogurt. This is a beverage from my childhood, like horchata. It's sweet and tart, with a taste that I simply couldn't place for most of my life, even after decades in professional kitchens. Finally, one day, Google came along with all the answers. ROSE WATER! I'd always been able to place the cardamom but never the rose water. Oh, that was such a load off!

1. Place the yogurt, ice, sweetener, rose water, cardamom and salt in a blender.

2. Puree until smooth. Serve topped with a tiny dash of ground cardamom, toasted almond slivers, and/or a few saffron threads. Enjoy on a warm summer day!

PER SERVING
CALORIES: 260.78
FAT: 22.02
PROTEIN: 8.03
CARBS: 40.17
FIBER: .07
SUGAR ALCOHOLS: 30
NET CARBS: 10.1

MORE FACTS: P. 495

BREAKFAST & BRUNCH

○ ○ ○

As I understand it, breakfast is the most important meal of the day. Breakfast, for me, is usually quite simple. I often make granola over the weekend and have a big bag of it lying around. I'll throw some in a bowl with some almond milk and a few blueberries. With a double-large mug of Bulletproof® Coffee? Double YUM! I'm also a huge fan of eggs. It's a tie between frittatas and my Poorly Cooked Eggs silliness; both are made frequently. While I don't often make pancakes, I *do* bake little cakes, like the Bacon Pancake contained herein. I simply use the same batter, and add cranberries and orange zest, or chunks of ham, or strawberries and toasted almonds. I bake them up and coat with butter, syrup, jam, and/or berry goo! Did I mention chia? I LOVE a nice bowl of Chia Fauxtmeal in the morning.

GRAIN-FREE PANCAKES

SERVES: 4 · · · PREP: 5 MIN · · · COOK: 15 MIN · · · TOTAL: 20 MIN

1/4 cup (60 mL) **coconut flour**

1/4 cup (60 mL) **almond flour**

1/4 cup (60 mL) **vanilla whey protein** powder (sweetened with stevia)

1/4 cup (60 mL) **sugar replacement**

2 tsp (10 mL) **baking powder**

Dash salt

4 large **eggs**

1/4 cup (60 mL) melted **butter**

2 Tbsp (30 mL) **butter**, **ghee** or **lard** (for pan/griddle)

It's at this point in the book that I unleash the "mega-batter": the simple and easy to remember ratio for the gooey substance I use for making a variety of simple quick-breads, from pancakes, to muffins, to layers within desserts. One part of me feels its cheating to use the same recipe over and over again, in different configurations, whereas another part of me feels the need to showcase its seemingly endless uses! Here it is, in one of its most basic forms ... the humble pancake.

1. In a medium mixing bowl, sift together coconut flour, almond flour, protein powder, sweetener (if powdered), baking powder and salt.

2. Add eggs and melted butter. If using a liquid sweetener, add it now. Mix until combined. If the batter is still too thick, add a little cream, coconut milk, almond milk, or even water to thin.

3. Heat a heavy griddle or fry pan that is greased with a little butter or bacon fat on a paper towel. Pour a small amount of batter (approx 1/4 cup [60 mL]) into pan and tip to spread out or spread with spoon. When bubbles appear on surface and begin to break, turn over and cook the other side. Repeat this process until all the batter is gone.

4. Garnish the pancakes with butter, your favorite syrup, jelly, fresh berries and/or whipped cream.

PER SERVING
CALORIES: 319.5
FAT: 25.75
PROTEIN: 15.75
CARBS: 21.91
FIBER: 3.75
SUGAR ALCOHOLS: 15
NET CARBS: 3.16

MORE FACTS: P. 495

Baked Eggs with Spinach, Sun-Dried Tomatoes, and Goat Cheese

SERVES: 4 · · · PREP: 10 MIN · · · COOK: 15 MIN · · · TOTAL: 25 MIN

1/4 lb. (114 g) **spinach**, washed and stems removed

1 Tbsp (15 mL) **butter**

8 large **eggs**

1/4 cup (60 mL) **sun-dried tomatoes in oil**, oil drained off, sliced into strips

1/4 cup (60 mL) crumbled **goats cheese**

1/4 cup (60 mL) heavy **whipping cream**

2 sprigs fresh **thyme**, stems removed

salt and freshly cracked **pepper, to taste**

Baked eggs are a remarkably simple yet elegant way to enjoy breakfast or brunch. While I'm presenting a version with spinach, tomatoes, and goats cheese, it should be said that this is simply an idea. The same concept could be applied to a mixture involving cooked mushrooms, chorizo, and *queso fresco*, just as it would with asparagus, bacon, and parmesan cheese. The point is, place some eggs in a small ramekin, top with your favorite toppings, dust with a touch of salt and pepper, and then bake to desired doneness!

1. Preheat oven to 400 F (204 C).

2. Place a large pot of water on the stove to boil over high heat. Gather a bowl with ice cubes and water, as well as a colander or strainer. Once the water boils, add a liberal amount of salt. Place spinach into the boiling water and stir for about 30 seconds. Remove the spinach with the strainer and immediately plunge it into the ice water. When it is thoroughly cooled, remove the spinach and squeeze it, by clinching it in your fists (or with a cloth), until all the water has been squeezed out. You should have a lump of dried cooked spinach. Coarsely chop this spinach and set aside. (**Note:** frozen spinach will work for this. Just make sure it's defrosted and very well squeezed, to have any extra water removed.)

3. Butter the inside of four porcelain ramekins (or any

PER SERVING
CALORIES: 327.38
FAT: 22.7
PROTEIN: 19.7
CARBS: 4.87
FIBER: 1.06
SUGAR ALCOHOLS: 0
NET CARBS: 3.81

MORE FACTS: P. 497

oven-safe dish, appropriate for single servings). Break 2 eggs into each of the 4 ramekins. Evenly divide the sun-dried tomato strips, goat cheese, and coarsely chopped spinach between the 4 dishes. Drizzle 1 tablespoon (15 mL) of heavy cream over the top of each dish, followed by garnishing with fresh thyme leaves and a light dusting of salt and pepper. Push the sun-dried tomatoes down, so they are somewhat preserved. Being dried, they can burn if overly exposed to the hot oven; a cream/egg coating will help this.

4. Bake for 8 to 12 minutes or until eggs have achieved desired doneness. Serve straight from the oven!

TORTA DI ROTELLO

SERVES: 12 · · · PREP: 50 MIN · · · COOK: 50 MIN · · · TOTAL: 2 HR 10 MIN

3 cups (720 mL) **almond flour**

1 tsp (5 mL) **arrowroot** (optional)

1/2 tsp (2 mL) **salt**

4 large **eggs**, divided

2 Tbsp (30 mL) **butter**

1 lb. (454 g) **spinach**, washed and stems removed

1/2 lb. (227 g) **cream cheese**

1/2 lb. (227 g) whole milk, low-moisture **mozzarella**

1/4 lb. (114 g) grated **parmesan cheese**

3/4 lb. (341 g) sliced genoa **salami**

4 each **roasted peppers**, dried with paper towels

3/4 lb. (341 g) sliced **turkey breast**

salt and **pepper**, to taste

PER SERVING
CALORIES: 529.61
FAT: 42.01
PROTEIN: 29.45
CARBS: 12.15
FIBER: 4.32
SUGAR ALCOHOLS: 0
NET CARBS: 7.83

MORE FACTS: P. 498

I'm honestly not sure what *Rotello* is, short of it being a blend of salami, turkey, spinach, peppers, and cheese rolled in puff pastry and baked. When I was younger, I worked in a grocery store deli, where this was made daily, and it sold like hot cakes! I've never forgotten this strange, potentially Northern Italian rolled pastry. One day, on a lark, I tried to research it... and came up dry! Maybe its origin is in West Seattle? Whatever it is, or wherever it came from, it's simply *amazing* reconfigured as a pie—perfect for a special brunch with family and friends! It's a big pie, with dense and rich slices. Can easily serve 12!

1. Preheat oven to 325°F (163°C).

2. In a food processor, place the almond flour, arrowroot, salt, 1 egg (saving the other 3 for filling), and butter. Pulse the ingredients until they come together and form a dough. Do not puree. (If you don't have a food processor, cut the butter into the dry ingredients and then mix the egg in until a dough is formed.) Cover the dough with a moist towel and let relax in the refrigerator for 30 minutes.

3. While the dough relaxes, place a large pot of water on the stove to boil over high heat. Gather a bowl with ice cubes and water, as well as a colander or strainer. Once the water boils, add a liberal amount of salt. Place spinach into the boiling water stir for about 30 seconds. Remove the spinach with the strainer, and immediately plunge it into the ice water. When it is thoroughly cooled, remove the spinach and squeeze it by clinching it in your fists (or with a cloth), until all the water has been squeezed out. You should have a lump of dried, cooked spinach. Coarsely chop this spinach and set in a medium-sized mixing bowl. (**Note:** Frozen spinach will work for this. Just make sure it's defrosted and very well squeezed, to have any extra water removed.)

4. In the medium-sized mixing bowl, combine the spinach, 3 remaining eggs, and cream cheese, with a bit of salt and pepper. Set aside.

5. Grease a 9-inch (23 x 5 cm) pie pan. With a rolling pin, roll the dough into a large circle (I like to do this between two greased sheets of parchment paper). Place the sheet of dough into the pie pan, forming it to the base of the pan. Crimp the edges of the crust. Work with one hand on the inside of the edge, and one hand on the outside, and use the index finger of your inside hand to push the dough between the thumb and index finger of your outside hand to form a U or V shape. Then, continue the same motion all around the pie plate, spacing your flutes about an inch apart. The height of the fluted crust should increase the depth of the pie by at least an extra half inch.

6. Spread one-third of the spinach mixture on the bottom of the pie pan. Spread one-third of the mozzarella and the Parmesan on the spinach mixture. Evenly spread 1/2 pound (227g) of the Genoa salami on the cheese layer. Evenly lay 2 of the dry roasted peppers over the Genoa salami. Spread another one-third of the spinach mixture over the top of the peppers. Distribute a second one-third of the cheeses over the spinach. Layer the turkey evenly over the cheese. Spread the remaining spinach mixture on the turkey. Set aside a small handful of the remaining cheeses. Cover the spinach with the rest of the cheese (minus the small handful). Layer the remaining salami over the cheese, followed by the remaining peppers. Finally, garnish with the small handful of cheese.

7. Bake the torta for roughly 50 minutes or until the crust is golden brown and the center of the pie is bulging. Remove from the oven and allow to rest for 30 minutes before slicing. Serve hot or chill for later.

ROSEMARY, HAM, AND SWISS FRITTATAS

SERVES: 4 · · · PREP: 10 MIN · · · COOK: 30 MIN · · · TOTAL: 40 MIN

1/2 cup (120 mL) real **bacon** bits

1/2 lb. (227 g) **ham**, cubed

1/2 lb. (227 g) **swiss cheese**, cubed

1 Tbsp (15 mL) chopped fresh **rosemary**

4 large **eggs**

1 1/4 cups (300 mL) heavy **whipping cream**

2 Tbsp (30 mL) **dijon mustard**, whole grain

salt and freshly cracked **pepper** to taste

Like Poorly Cooked Eggs (p. 116), this is another breakfast vehicle for a wide variety of taste sensations and nutrients. In essence, a mixture of ingredients is assembled, potentially partially cooked, and then placed into muffin cups. These are then filled with an egg mixture and baked. What follows is just one simple example, but there is an endless variety of options. Don't limit yourself to just this one.

I personally use two 6-cup Teflon pans. I bake twelve, eat four, and package the other eight for the next two mornings. An easy way to make breakfast for three days!

1. Preheat oven to 400°F (205°C).

2. In a mixing bowl, mix together your bacon, ham, Swiss cheese, and chopped rosemary.

3. If you have seasoned Teflon or nonstick muffin pans, fill each of the twelve cups with a portion of the ham and cheese mixture. If you don't have nonstick or Teflon, spray the trays or butter them heavily, then fill with the ham and cheese mixture.

4. In the original mixing bowl, whisk together your eggs, cream, mustard, and a small amount of salt and pepper.

5. Evenly pour the egg mixture into each cup.

6. Bake for about 23 to 28 minutes or until puffy and golden brown. Remove from oven and let rest for 5 minutes. They will fall, but they will also be easier to move around. Serve!

PER SERVING
CALORIES: 689.64
FAT: 55.65
PROTEIN: 41.48
CARBS: 7.55
FIBER: .37
SUGAR ALCOHOLS: 0
NET CARBS: 7.18

MORE FACTS: P. 497

BACON PANCAKE WEDGIE

SERVES: 4 · · · PREP: 2 MIN · · · COOK: 2 MIN · · · TOTAL: 20 MIN

Here we have the mega-batter again. This is a different configuration of this batter. In this case, I've got the same batter, but I've added bacon bits to it and have used bacon fat, rather than the original butter. I've also poured the batter in to an 8-inch cake pan, rather than making pancakes with them. The idea here is that anything can be used in this batter. Berries? Nuts? Citrus zest? Ham and cheese? Chili flakes? All are tasty options! I like to make the batter, fold in a few ingredients, set a timer, and bake while I perform my various morning tasks. About the time I'm ready for the day, I've got a fresh cake all ready for me!

1/4 cup (60 mL) **coconut flour**

1/4 cup (60 mL) **almond flour**

1/4 cup (60 mL) **vanilla whey protein powder** (sweetened with stevia)

1/4 cup (60 mL) **sugar replacement**

2 tsp (10 mL) **baking powder**

a dash of **salt**

4 large **eggs**

1/4 cup (60 mL) **melted bacon fat**, divided

1/2 cup (120 mL) real **bacon bits**

1. Preheat oven to 350°F (177°C).

2. In a medium mixing bowl, sift together coconut flour, almond flour, protein powder, sweetener (if powdered), baking powder, and salt.

3. Add eggs, 3 tablespoon (45 mL) of melted bacon fat, and the bacon bits. If using a liquid sweetener, add it now. Mix until combined. If the batter is still too thick, add a little cream, coconut milk, almond milk, or even water to thin.

4. Grease an 8-inch (20x5 cm) cake pan with the remaining tablespoon (15 mL) of bacon fat.

5. Pour the batter into the cake pan and bake for 23 to 28 minutes or until golden brown. Remove, slice, and serve hot!

6. Garnish the pancakes with butter, your favorite syrup, jelly, fresh berries, and/or whipped cream! With this particular configuration, I love a good sugar-free orange marmalade!

PER SERVING
CALORIES: 319.5
FAT: 23.25
PROTEIN: 21.75
CARBS: 21.91
FIBER: 3.75
SUGAR ALCOHOLS: 15
NET CARBS: 3.16

MORE FACTS: P. 498

Orange - Walnut Strata

SERVES: 10 · · · PREP: 15 MIN · · · COOK: 1 HR 15 MIN · · · TOTAL: 2 HR 45 MIN

1/4 cup plus 2 Tbsp (90 mL) **coconut flour**

1/4 cup plus 2 Tbsp (90 mL) **almond** flour

1/4 cup plus 2 Tbsp (90 mL) **vanilla whey protein powder** (sweetened with stevia)

3/4 cup (180 mL) **sugar replacement**, divided

1 Tbsp (15 mL) **baking powder**

a dash of **salt**

1 fresh **orange**

14 large **eggs**, divided

1/4 cup plus 2 Tbsp (90 mL) melted **butter**

1 lb. (454 g) **cream cheese**

1 cup (240 mL) coarsely chopped **walnut** bits

1 tsp (5 mL) **vanilla extract**

1 1/2 cup (360 mL) heavy **whipping cream**

It is so often the case that a gluten-free, or even more extreme a grain-free, diet intimidates people because they fear they will lose bread. "Loss of bread" likely tops the list of anxieties people feel when they consider going grain free. I am here to tell you, my friends, that all is not lost. Bread is an option. Good bread too! Here we having something called a *strata*, which is a form of layered bread pudding. Normally, a strata is a savory dish, alternating slices of bread with eggs, veggies, meats, and cheeses. It's similar to a quiche or frittata, but occasionally slightly more composed. I wanted to present a strata but opted to go sweet. This is up there with the best of bread puddings but with the addition of an orange scent, a bit of tang from the cream cheese, and a nice texture from the walnuts.

1. Preheat oven to 350 F (177 C).

2. In a medium mixing bowl, sift together coconut flour, almond flour, protein powder, 1/4 cup plus 2 tablespoons (90 mL) sweetener (if powdered), baking powder, and salt.

3. Zest the orange peel with a zester or vegetable peeler. Make sure just to get the orange part, not the bitter pith. Chop the zest and add to the powder in the mixing bowl. Juice the orange, and set the orange juice aside.

4. Add 6 of the eggs and the melted butter to the mixing bowl. If using a liquid sweetener, add it now. Mix until combined. Use the orange juice to adjust and thin out the batter. It should look like a thick pancake batter.

5. Grease the inside of a large loaf pan (a 1 1/2-pound loaf pan, 5" x 9" x 3" [23 x 13 x 8 cm]). Pour the batter into the pan and bake for 24 to 28 minutes or until golden brown.

PER SERVING
CALORIES: 570.5
FAT: 51.31
PROTEIN: 19.29
CARBS: 28.54
FIBER: 3.25
SUGAR ALCOHOLS: 18
NET CARBS: 7.29

MORE FACTS: P. 498

6. While the loaf bakes, in a small mixing bowl, combine 2 of the eggs, 3 tablespoons (45 mL) of the sweetener, walnuts, cream cheese, vanilla extract, and a dash of salt. Set aside.

7. In a separate medium-sized mixing bowl, whisk together the remaining 6 eggs, the remaining 3 tablespoons (45 mL) sweetener, and the heavy cream with a dash of salt.

8. Once the loaf is done, remove it from the oven and allow to rest for 10 minutes. It should pop right out of the pan. With a knife parallel to the cutting board, cut the loaf into 3 even and thin strips, so the surface area stays the same but you now essentially have three thinner "loaves" stacked on each other. Separate them and let them cool. This takes about 2 minutes.

9. Spread half of the cream cheese mixture on top of the smallest slice (the bottom-most slice from the narrow end of the pan). Spread it evenly and then place the middle slice on top of it. Then, spread the second half of the cream cheese mixture evenly onto the middle slice. Place the top slice onto the cream cheese. You should have a giant double-decker sandwich at this point.

10. Clean out the loaf pan and grease it again. Pour about one-quarter of the egg mixture into the bottom of the pan. Gently lower the double-decker sandwich into the loaf pan. Now, gently weigh down the strata with a small brick wrapped in foil, or a butter dish with a plate on top of it. Pour in as much of the egg mixture as will fit. The bread needs a little time to absorb it, and the weight helps to keep it from floating. Place it in the refrigerator with the weight still on the top. Every 15 minutes, check it and add a bit more egg mixture, as the strata slowly drinks it up. Continue this process until all the egg mixture is in the loaf pan or the strata stops absorbing it. The pan will be very full when complete.

11. Bake the strata at 325°F (163°C) for about 50 minutes or until golden brown and the center bulges. Remove and allow to rest for 30 minutes before removing from pan and slicing.

12. Serve garnished with your favorite syrup, sugar-free marmalade, berries, sweetened sour cream, and/or confectioner's sweetener!

Spiced Nut-N-Honey Granola

SERVES: 4 · · · PREP: 5 MIN · · · COOK: 1 HR 15 MIN · · · TOTAL: 1 HR 20 MIN

1 cup (240 mL) chopped **pecans**

1/2 cup (120 mL) chopped **walnuts**

1/2 cup (120 mL) slivered **almonds**

1/2 cup (120 mL) flaked unsweetened **coconut**

1/2 cup (120 mL) **almond flour**

1/4 cup (60 mL) **flax meal** (or ground chia seed)

1/4 cup (60 mL) **pepitas** (pumpkin seeds)

1/4 cup (60 mL) **sunflower seeds**

1/4 cup (60 mL) melted **butter**

1/2 cup (120 mL) **sugar replacement**

1 tsp (5 mL) **honey**

1 tsp (5 mL) **cinnamon**

1 tsp (5 mL) **vanilla exract**

1/2 tsp (2 mL) **nutmeg**

1/2 tsp (2 mL) **salt**

1/4 cup (60 mL) **water**

I *love* granola and have loved it for as long as I can remember. Typically, granola is made from various sweetened grains and the occasional nut. I've opted to nut it up and remove the grains. The end result is precisely as tasty as its grainy counterpart, but with nowhere near the blood sugar impact. I have added a small amount of regular old honey, because the tiny amount of sugar will melt and dry on the nuts. When it cools, it will act as an adhesive, helping to hold the whole thing together. Break it apart, stash in a bag or container, break up the clusters, and enjoy on its own or with some almond milk... A wonderful way to start the day!

1. Preheat oven to 250°F (121°C).

2. In a large bowl, combine all the ingredients. Mix very well.

3. Place a piece of parchment paper on a baking tray and grease it. Spread the granola on the tray. Place a second piece of parchment on the granola. With a rolling pin, roll the granola to compress it into a firm and even sheet. Remove the top piece of parchment and discard.

4. Bake for about 60 to 90 minutes or until evenly golden. Remove from the oven and allow to fully cool. Break into pieces and save; I personally make large batches, doubling and tripling these numbers. I store the clusters in large gallon-sized sealable plastic bags. Delicious with almond milk and a berry or two!

PER SERVING
CALORIES: 765.77
FAT: 71.97
PROTEIN: 20.29
CARBS: 52.23
FIBER: 12.24
SUGAR ALCOHOLS: 30.27
NET CARBS: 9.73

MORE FACTS: P. 499

Coconut Flour OMM French Toast

SERVES: 4 · · · PREP: 10 MIN · · · COOK: 30 MIN · · · TOTAL: 40 MIN

1/4 cup (60 mL) **coconut flour**

1 Tbsp (15 mL) **sugar** replacement

2 tsp (10 mL) **baking powder**

dash **salt**

8 large **eggs**, divided

3/4 cup (180 mL) unsweetened **almond milk**, divided

1 tsp (5 mL) **vanilla** extract

1/4 cup (60 mL) melted **butter**

1/2 cup (120 mL) heavy **whipping cream**

1/4 cup (60 mL) **butter**

This recipe will introduce the concept of the One-Minute Muffin (OMM), which is a form of muffin designed for the microwave. In this case, the batter is nuked, forming soft little pucks of delight. They are then coated in egg batter, fried in butter, and drenched in butter and syrup! For those wanting to skip the microwave, simply bake them at 350°F (177°C) for about 13 to 15 minutes. I personally prefer them this way, but it takes longer. I leave it to you to decide!

1. Mix together your coconut flour, sweetener (if it's powdered; if it's a liquid, add with the liquids), baking powder, and a dash of salt.

2. In a separate bowl, whisk together 4 of the eight eggs. Add only 1/4 cup (60 mL) of the almond milk and the vanilla. Whisk. Add your dry ingredients to your wet ingredients and whisk, while pouring in your melted butter.

3. Grease 12 microwaveable safe containers, which are fairly wide. I used 8 oz (240 mL) ramekins, but you could also use flat bottomed soup bowls, wide coffee mugs, etc. You could even use tall coffee cups and simply cut your muffins in half. Divide the batter between the 12 containers. Microwave your muffins. For each muffin, add a minute to the microwave. I did 2 batches of 6, with 6 minutes on the timer for each batch. Total: 12 minutes. (baking will likely take a similar amount of time)

4. While your muffins are nuking, in a large and wide

PER SERVING
CALORIES: 490.45
FAT: 44.41
PROTEIN: 15.75
CARBS: 11.31
FIBER: 3.19
SUGAR ALCOHOLS: 7.75
NET CARBS: 4.38

MORE FACTS: P. 498

mixing bowl, whisk together your remaining 4 eggs, 1/2 cup (120 mL) of almond milk and 1/2 cup (120 mL) of heavy cream.

5. As your muffins come out of the nuker, pop them out of their containers and let them cool for about 1 minute, just long enough to keep them from cooking the egg mixture. When they are cool enough, add them to the egg mixture and allow to sit for a few minutes; flipping them occasionally. They are somewhat fragile. You can fairly easily grab and flip them around, but do so gently. They will absorb the egg mixture.

6. When they have absorbed some of the egg mixture, heat a large skillet, sauté pan or flat-top griddle over medium-low heat. Add some of your fresh butter and melt it. Everyone has their own method for doing this. So, I'm just going to say... Fry your muffins like French toast. Keep warm in the oven until they are all ready Serve!

Mini Crab, Asparagus, and Pepper Frittatas

SERVES: 8 · · · PREP: 15 MIN · · · COOK: 20 MIN · · · TOTAL: 50 MIN

1 small (74 g) **red bell pepper**

1 bunch (227 g) **asparagus spears**, tough stem ends removed

1 Tbsp (15 mL) **butter**

2 tsp (10 mL) roughly chopped **fresh tarragon**

3 large **eggs**

1 cup (240 mL) **heavy whipping cream**

1/2 lb. (227 g) **lump crab meat**, drained and shells removed

salt and freshly cracked **pepper**, to taste

These fun little snacks are intended for a morning or early afternoon event. They're incredibly easy to make, attractive, and delicious! They taste somewhat like a full and creamy crab cake—yum!

1. Preheat oven to 425°F (220°C).

2. Remove the seeds from the bell pepper. Dice the bell pepper into very small pieces, roughly the size of small peas. Set aside.

3. Cut the top inch off 24 stalks of asparagus (optional). With the remaining asparagus, slice small coins, each about 1/4-inch (1/2 cm) slice. Each little coin will be roughly the same size as the bell peppers.

4. Heat a sauté pan over high heat. Add the butter to the pan, and swirl it around. Quickly add the peppers and asparagus. Season with salt and pepper. Toss in the fresh tarragon. Toss it all together and make sure it tastes good by sampling the mixture. Adjust seasoning. After about 1 minute, place the ingredients on a room-temperature plate or pan. Set aside.

5. In a bowl, whisk together the eggs and cream. Add a small amount of salt and pepper.

6. In a separate bowl, mix together the fresh lump crab and vegetable mixture.

7. Grease two 12-cup mini muffin pans. Evenly divide the crab-veggie mixture between each of the 24 cups. Pour the egg mixture into each cup, filling it just over 3/4 of the way. Place a raw asparagus spear in the top of each muffin cup.

PER SERVING
CALORIES: 179.78
FAT: 16.68
PROTEIN: 9.48
CARBS: 2.74
FIBER: .86
SUGAR ALCOHOLS: 0
NET CARBS: 1.88

MORE FACTS: P. 499

8. Bake for 15 to 18 minutes or until the eggs puff evenly and slightly brown on the top. Remove from the oven. They will fall a little. Do not be alarmed. Let set for a further 5 minutes before serving.

9. **Note:** This recipe is for a total of 24 mini frittatas. However, for a full muffin-sized frittata, reduce the temperature to 375°F (190°C) and bake about 10 minutes longer.

Caramelized-Apple Topped Grain-Free Pancakes

SERVES: 4 · · · PREP: 10 MIN · · · COOK: 10 MIN · · · TOTAL: 20 MIN

1 medium (161 g) **apple**

1/4 cup (60 mL) **butter, ghee, or lard** (for sautéing and pan/griddle), divided

a dash of **cinnamon**

a dash of **nutmeg**

a dash of **salt**

1/4 cup (60 mL) **coconut flour**

1/4 cup (60 mL) **almond flour**

1/4 cup (60 mL) **vanilla whey protein** powder (sweetened with stevia)

1/4 cup (60 mL) **sugar** replacement

2 tsp (10 mL) **baking powder**

4 large **eggs**

1/4 cup (60 mL) melted **butter**

1/4 cup (60 mL) chopped toasted **walnuts**

Here's the mega-batter again! There is virtually nothing different about these compared to the plain pancakes recipe, short of the addition of a few ingredients, along with a special message. That message is this: apples and other fruits aren't going to kill you. In fact, they're delicious and filled with nutrients! So many low-carbers fear fruits, and I feel that's a bit much. Depending on your personal situation, the occasional apple is not only healthy, but it also removes some of the stress and anxiety around restrictions. Throwing some tasty caramelized apples on a pancake is going to taste great and boost your variety too!

1. Preheat a medium sauté pan over medium-high heat

2. While the pan is heating, cut the apples into 1/4-inch (1/2 cm) cubes. Peeling is optional.

3. Once the pan is hot, add some fresh butter and quickly swirl it around the pan. It should lightly brown around the edges but not burn. Quickly add the apple cubes and coat with butter. Turn the heat to medium, and evenly distribute the apples along the bottom of the pan, so that a single layer of apple cubes is formed. Sprinkle a dash of cinnamon, nutmeg, and salt onto the apples.

4. After about 1 minute, one side of the cubes will take on a nice caramel color. Toss the apples, so that most have a new side facing down. Allow them to sit for about 1 minute. Continue cooking and tossing until they are nicely browned on the outside but not overcooked, soft, and mushy. The process should be fairly quick, taking about 3 to 4 minutes. Place the browned apple cubes on a plate to cool. Set aside.

PER SERVING
CALORIES: 469.63
FAT: 35.31
PROTEIN: 16.69
CARBS: 28.04
FIBER: 4.69
SUGAR ALCOHOLS: 15
NET CARBS: 8.35

MORE FACTS: P. 499

5. In a medium-sized mixing bowl, sift together coconut flour, almond flour, protein powder, sweetener (if powdered), baking powder, and salt.

6. Add eggs, melted butter, and half the caramelized apples. If using a liquid sweetener, add it now. Mix until combined. If the batter is still too thick, add a little milk, cream, coconut milk, almond milk, or even water to thin.

7. Heat a heavy griddle or fry pan greased with a little butter or bacon fat. Pour a small amount of batter (approximately 1/4 cup [60 mL]) into pan and tip to spread out or spread with spoon. When bubbles appear on surface and begin to break, turn over and cook the other side. Repeat this process until all the batter is gone.

8. Garnish the pancakes with more butter, your favorite syrup, toasted walnuts, and the remaining caramelized apples.

Eggy McFoo

SERVES: 1 · · · PREP: 5 MIN · · · COOK: 20 MIN · · · TOTAL: 25 MIN

2 Tbsp (30 mL) **flaxseed** meal (or ground chia)

2 Tbsp (30 mL) **almond flour**

1/2 tsp (2 mL) **baking powder**

a dash of **salt**

2 large **eggs**

1 tsp (5 mL) melted **butter, ghee,** or **lard**

3 oz. (85 g) **ham**

2 oz. (57 g) **cheddar cheese**

I was daydreaming about breakfast sandwiches one morning and wondered what would happen if I poured batter into a ramekin, then placed a bit of ham and cheese in the middle of the batter, and topped it with a bit more batter. My theory was it would bake together something like one of those famous fast food breakfast sandwiches. *I was right!* The end result is a *delicious* self-contained little breakfast sandwich of sorts. The batter is extra eggy to compensate for the lack of eggs in the filling. A perfect way to start the day!

1. Preheat oven to 350°F (177°C).

2. In a small mixing bowl, combine flax or chia with the almond flour, baking powder, and salt. Mix together. Add the eggs and fat, and mix. Set aside. You want the batter to sit for about 4 minutes. It will slightly thicken.

3. While the batter thickens, grease a ramekin or other ovenproof small baking pan, such as a large muffin pan, potpie pan, etc.

4. Cut your ham, cheese, and/or other fillings into shapes that will fit your ramekin or baking pan. This can be cubes, circles, squares, dice, etc. A blob of cream cheese with ham and broccoli will taste quite nice, for example. Just be sure that the filling isn't too wet, so nothing with more moisture than cream cheese.

5. Pour half the thickened batter into the baking pan or ramekin. Place your filling in the center of the batter, without any of it touching the rim. It needs to be completely detached from the edge. Cover the filling with the remaining batter.

6. Bake for 23 to 28 minutes or until golden. Remove from the oven and allow to set for about 5 minutes before removing from the pan. Enjoy breakfast!

PER SERVING
CALORIES: 676.89
FAT: 49.77
PROTEIN: 44.03
CARBS: 10.19
FIBER: 5.5
SUGAR ALCOHOLS: 0
NET CARBS: 4.69

MORE FACTS: P. 499

McFoo

POORLY COOKED EGGS

SERVES: 6 · · · PREP: 15 MIN · · · COOK: 10 MIN · · · TOTAL: 25 MIN

12 large **eggs**

3 cups (720 mL) heavy **whipping cream**

1 Tbsp (15 mL) **butter**

1 bunch (227 g) **asparagus**, tough stem ends removed then sliced into little 1/4–inch (.6 cm) coins

1/2 lb. (227 g) **ham**, cubed

1/2 lb. (227 g) **cheddar cheese**, cubed

salt and **pepper** to taste

This is easily one of my favorite and most-cooked recipes. I cook some version of Poorly Cooked Eggs at least once a week. The name is my little joke, in that I know overcooked eggs would get me screamed at in professional kitchens, but... my mom burned 'em growing up. So I like them like that!

This recipe is for a specific variety, but the fact is there are a million combinations, and they're each quite tasty in their own right. It's a fantastic way to add a variety of tastes and nutrients to a quick morning breakfast. Poorly cooked eggs are designed to be nourishing, quick, tasty, and... generally unattractive!

1. Place a large nonstick pan on the stove, over medium-high heat.

2. Whisk together your eggs and heavy cream. Add a touch of salt and pepper. Set aside.

3. Add butter to the preheated nonstick pan. Quickly add your asparagus and sauté for 2 minutes. Season with a little salt and pepper. Add your ham and sauté for a further 2 minutes. Add your egg mixture and let sit for one minute. Then, with a wooden spoon or heat-resistant plastic spatula, stir the eggs. Let sit for another minute. Repeat this process until the eggs are cooked to just under the desired doneness.

4. Add your cheese, and stir the eggs. Let sit for one minute. Serve!

PER SERVING
CALORIES: 789.69
FAT: 73.79
PROTEIN: 25.1
CARBS: 7.15
FIBER: .85
SUGAR ALCOHOLS: 0
NET CARBS: 6.31

MORE FACTS: P. 500

Here are a few variation ideas:

Pizza: Use pizza toppings, and then top with pizza sauce and cheese!
Chester Copperpot: chopped Anaheim, banana, and chipotle chilies with some queso fresco
Puttanesca: garlic, onions, olives, anchovies, capers, tomatoes, and chili flakes
Old Classic: broccoli, ham, and cheddar
Primavera: peppers, mushrooms, zucchini, spinach, onions, and garlic
New Classic: Romanesco, pancetta, caper berries, artichokes, and manchego
Seafood: crab and shrimp with leeks, bacon, and peppers
Seefood: ham, bacon, chicken sausage, peppers, olives, capers, broccoli, sun-dried tomatoes, and Parmesan
Italian Turkey Club: sliced turkey breast, roasted peppers, and pesto
Greek: peppers, onions, olives, garlic, tomatoes, and feta
Smoked Fish: smoked salmon, cream cheese, red onions, dill, and capers
Taco: ground meat, salsa, sour cream, olives, cheddar cheese, and avocado
Funky Chicken: chicken, spinach, walnuts, chives, and Roquefort cheese

This list could continue, almost forever.

Terrible, overcooked, brown, terrifyingly delicious, tasty, outstanding, comforting and poorly cooked eggs!

Nutty Chia Fauxtmeal

SERVES: 1 · · · PREP: 2 MIN · · · COOK: 2 MIN · · · TOTAL: 20 MIN

1/2 cup (120 mL) unsweetened **almond milk**

2 Tbsp (30 mL) heavy whipping **cream**

2 Tbsp (30 mL) sugar-free **pancake syrup**

1/4 tsp (1 mL) **vanilla** extract

1/4 cup (60 mL) **hazelnut meal/flour** (substitute almond flour)

2 Tbsp (30 mL) **chia seeds**

1 Tbsp (15 mL) **slivered almonds**, toasted

1 Tbsp (15 mL) chopped **pecans**, toasted

1/4 tsp (1 mL) ground **cinnamon**

dash **nutmeg**

dash **salt**

Frankly speaking, I really thought chia seeds were little more than squirrel food and resisted them for years. One day, on a lark, I picked some up and whipped up a similar recipe. It blew... my... mind! Be willing to bring chia seeds into your world. I think you'll be glad you did!

Chia seeds are essentially flavorless and create a pleasant pudding-like texture as they absorb liquids. The actual seeds have a texture not entirely unlike the little achenes on the outsides of strawberries. This recipe is intended to give not only the taste and texture of a morning's bowl of oatmeal, but the comfort as well!

1. Combine then heat almond milk, cream, pancake syrup, and vanilla (you can do this on the stove; I do it in the microwave, by pressing the "Beverage" button). You want it hot but not necessarily scalding.

2. While the liquid heats, combine the chia, nut meal, nuts, spices, and salt. Mix them up a bit.

3. When the liquid is hot, pour it over the top of the chia seed–nut mixture and stir. It's good to stir the chia about every minute or two for the first 4 or 5 minutes. Then, just let it sit there and gel. Maybe stir it once more. After about 20 total minutes of the chia absorbing the liquid, it will be perfect. Feel free to garnish with some more nuts and a sprinkle of cinnamon. Eat!

PER SERVING
CALORIES: 474.64
FAT: 43.26
PROTEIN: 11.21
CARBS: 17.62
FIBER: 11.34
SUGAR ALCOHOLS: 0
NET CARBS: 6.28

MORE FACTS: P. 497

Appetizers & Snacks

○ ○ ○

As mentioned earlier in the book, snacks and appetizers can play a large role in curbing cravings and managing hunger. Ideally, we're never hungry... but it's going to happen from time to time. While most snacks tend to be easy, handheld nibbles, there are also more complex vittles, which can be prepared in advance, served prior to a meal, as a mini-meal between meals, and also to serve while entertaining. Social gatherings are always a bit of trouble for someone following a healthier set of guidelines than most. Being able to host and present tasty foods that everyone will enjoy is a wonderful way to bring everything into a luscious harmonious focus.

○ ○ ○

Whole Artichoke

SERVES: 4 · · · PREP: 5 MIN · · · COOK: 35 MIN · · · TOTAL: 40 MIN

12 cups (2.9 L) **water**

3 cups (720 mL) **white wine**

1 cup (240 mL) **lemon Juice**

1/4 cup (60 mL) **salt**

5 **garlic cloves**, sliced

5 to 10 (15 g) **thyme sprigs**

1 **bay leaf**

1 Tbsp (15 mL) **peppercorns**

4 medium **artichokes**

I LOVE ARTICHOKES!! I vividly recall my first artichoke. I was about twelve years old, eating at the Wawona Inn, inside Yosemite National Park. It was love at first bite!

Artichokes are very easy to deal with, but a little extra care will take a good artichoke and transport it into a dynamite thistle! Artichokes contain a taste-inhibiting acid called *cynarin*. Because of this sensation-repressing behavioral quirk, it's been my experience that poaching artichokes in an acidulated water is the way to go! Counterbalance the sweet with a bit of tart to bring the whole thing back together. In short, add some flavor to that water! Don't just steam or boil it, but give the liquid some personality. What we're actually going to do is create a light, quick, and dirty "court bouillon," which is an acidic and flavorful poaching liquid. It absolutely translates into a more flavorful and enriching artichoke experience!

1. In a large pot, add the water, wine, lemon juice, salt, garlic, thyme, bay leaf, and peppercorns.

2. With kitchen scissors, cut the small, sharp thorns off the tips of each leaf. With a knife, cut the top off the artichoke, removing the sharp thorns and creating a flat, clean top. With a knife, trim the cut end of the stem. As each is prepared, place it in the pot and spin it in the acidulated water—the artichokes want to turn brown; the water will slow down the oxidation.

PER SERVING
CALORIES: 60
FAT: 0
PROTEIN: 4
CARBS: 13
FIBER: 7
SUGAR ALCOHOLS: 0
NET CARBS: 6

MORE FACTS: P. 502

3. Once all the artichokes are prepared, place a lid on the pot and put it on high heat until it begins to simmer. Turn the temperature to low, and allow the artichokes to poach for about 35 minutes. Be sure to turn the artichokes every 10 minutes, so they cook evenly (they have a tendency to float on the top). Poach until a small, sharp paring knife is easily inserted into the base and the leaves peel off easily.

4. Remove the artichokes from the poaching liquid and set upside down in a colander for about 1 minute to allow any excess liquid to drain off.

5. Serve with any number of dipping sauces. Melted butter is a common one, as is mayonnaise, or mayonnaise with a bit of fresh garlic. This would also be delicious with a Rouille (p. 376) or a Béarnaise sauce (p. 382).

Baked Coconut Shrimp

SERVES: 4 · · · PREP: 15 MIN · · · COOK: 15 MIN · · · TOTAL: 30 MIN

1/2 cup (120 mL) **unsweetened** shredded **coconut**

3 Tbsp (45 mL) **almond flour**

1 Tbsp (15 mL) **tapioca flour**

1 large **egg**

1 Tbsp (15 mL) **coconut milk**

1 Tbsp (15 mL) **lime juice**

1 tsp (5 mL) **fresh lime zest**, minced

1 lb. (454 g) **shrimp (16/20)**, peeled, with the tails left on, and deveined

salt and **pepper** to taste

This is one of those dishes that is incredibly simple but somehow feels incredibly complex. It's literally just peeled shrimp tossed with some eggs, then tossed in coconut and baked! It's only very slightly more complex than that, but that's the general idea. I had several friends over the day I made this one, and not only was it gone before I had a bite, but it was unanimously declared the day's favorite as well!

1. Preheat oven to 400°F (204°C).

2. Grease a baking tray (I like to use parchment paper instead of greasing), and set aside.

3. In a large mixing bowl, combine coconut, almond flour, tapioca flour, and a bit of salt and pepper. Mix and set aside.

4. In a medium mixing bowl, whisk together the egg, coconut milk, lime juice, and lime zest with a bit of salt and pepper. Quickly add the shrimp to this mixture before the lime juice "cooks" the egg. Toss the shrimp in the egg mixture and evenly coat.

5. Remove a shrimp and place it in the larger bowl, tossing in the dry ingredients until it is well coated. Carefully grab the shrimp by its tail and lay it on the baking tray. This will give it a loosely dusted look when it's baked. If you'd like more coconut to adhere to the shrimp, you can press it into the shrimp in the palm of your hand. This will give it more of a coconut-shell appearance, with more crust and texture. The first is a lighter option; the latter is heavier. There are no wrong answers. Repeat this step until all the shrimp are coated.

PER SERVING
CALORIES: 242
FAT: 12.83
PROTEIN: 26.41
CARBS: 7.57
FIBER: 2.71
SUGAR ALCOHOLS: 0
NET CARBS: 4.86

MORE FACTS: P. 501

6. Bake until the shrimp begin slightly turning golden and are cooked through (should still be very slightly translucent in the center), about 10 to 12 minutes. Remove and serve with dipping sauce.

7. **Note:** I served this with Pineapple Salsa (p. 355). Sweet Thai Chili Sauce (p. 349) would also be an excellent option!

Sweet Thai Chili Wings

SERVES: 4 · · · PREP: 15 MIN · · · COOK: 40 MIN · · · TOTAL: 2 HRS

2 lb. (908 g) **wings and drumettes**

1/4 cup (60 mL) **Sweet Thai Chili Sauce (p. 349)**

salt and **pepper** to taste

Wings are just about tailor-made for low primal. They're crunchy, fatty, handheld, messy little bones. It's hard not to feel a bit primal while gnawing on some osseous matter. While the obvious use for wings is Buffalo style, that's been done to death (combine equal volumetric parts fresh butter, cayenne, and Tabasco in a bowl, and toss the hot wings until the butter melts; serve with blue cheese dressing and celery sticks). The reality is, wings are awesome with just about anything.

Baked or fried, while they're freshly hot, toss them in a large bowl with:

- Fresh herbs, chopped garlic, and Parmesan
- BBQ sauce
- Favorite hot sauce, such as Sriracha
- Curry powder, lime juice, minced garlic, and cilantro
- Fish sauce, minced ginger, chilies, minced garlic, lime, cilantro, and basil
- Mustard, capers, and chives
- Teriyaki sauce and hot sesame oil
- *Your favorite invention here*

1. Set up a large steamer (I have an 8-quart [8.5 L]), with about an inch (2.5 cm) of water at the bottom. Some people add aromatics (fresh garlic, lemongrass, lime leaves, and ginger) to the water to infuse a bit of aroma. This is optional. Bring the water to a boil.

2. If your wings have tips, clip them at the joint with a chef's knife or kitchen scissors. Save for stock or discard.

3. Evenly distribute the wings and drumettes within the steamer basket. Cover and allow the wings to steam for 10 minutes. Remove the chicken and place on a clean towel or bed of paper towels to dry. Put in the refrigerator until completely chilled through, 60 to 90 minutes.

PER SERVING
CALORIES: 533.93
FAT: 36.45
PROTEIN: 40.97
CARBS: 16.88
FIBER: .34
SUGAR ALCOHOLS: 15
NET CARBS: 1.5

MORE FACTS: P. 500

4. Preheat the oven to 450°F (232°C).

5. Cover a baking tray with foil and place in the oven.

6. Season the wings with a bit of salt and pepper. Take the hot tray out of the oven and quickly spread the wings in an even layer around the pan. Place it back in the oven and allow to bake for about 15 to 20 minutes. When the wings begin to turn golden, turn them over to bake the opposite side. When the wings are nice, golden, and crispy, remove them from the oven.

7. Immediately place the wings and chili sauce in a large mixing bowl with a bit of salt and pepper. Toss the wings to coat with sauce. Serve!

Bacon-Cheddar BBQ Pork Sliders

SERVES: 4 · · · PREP: 30 MIN · · · COOK: 15 MIN · · · TOTAL: 45 MIN

1 1/2 lb. (681 g) **ground pork**

2 Tbsp (30 mL) **Dijon mustard**

3 **garlic cloves**, minced

1 Tbsp (15 mL) **paprika** (preferably smoked)

1 tsp (5 mL) ground **cayenne pepper**

1 tsp (5 mL) chopped **fresh thyme**

12 slices (300 g) **raw bacon**

1 small (110 g) **onion**, sliced into strips

12 **mini One-Minute Cheddar Buns (p. 472)**

3/4 cup (180 mL) **Sweet 'n' Tangy BBQ Sauce (p. 356)**

1 cup (240 mL) Sweet 'n' **Creamy Coleslaw (p. 200)**

salt and **pepper** to taste

This idea just came to me out of the blue. I wanted something scrummy and simple. I wanted the kind of thing that anyone would look at and think, "That's something I can get behind!" I wanted something that would appeal to anyone, regardless of their dietary preferences (minus vegetarianism, mind you). The idea was actually inspired by a "game day" mentality, something *perfect* for Monday Night Football, any man cave, or really anyone who likes an excellent little burger... or three!

Note: each slider is about 4.7 net carbs.

1. In a mixing bowl, blend together pork, mustard, garlic, paprika, cayenne, thyme, and a little salt and pepper. Mix well and then divide into twelve 2-ounce (56 g) balls. Press each ball into a small patty. Set aside.

2. Fry up the bacon (I usually do this on a rack over a rimmed cookie tray, in the oven). Baking bacon at about 400°F (205°C), for about 15 to 18 minutes, is a great way to get lots of bacon for very little effort. Keep in mind that different thicknesses can really vary the times. Pay attention to it as it bakes. (Don't burn it!) When the bacon comes out, cut each one in half, at the middle point. Save the bacon grease for the next step.

3. Place a sauté pan over medium-high heat. Add about 2 tablespoons (30 mL) of the bacon grease to the pan. Quickly add your onions to the pan with a little salt and pepper. Cook the onions until they have caramelized and turned a nice shade of brown. Lower and slower is better (and yields a softer and more charismatic onion), but high heat is fine as well. Keep the onions warm but set aside.

PER SERVING
CALORIES: 1,165.52
FAT: 95.86
PROTEIN: 64.31
CARBS: 26.22
FIBER: 12.18
SUGAR ALCOHOLS: 0
NET CARBS: 14.04

MORE FACTS: P. 501

4. Season your pork patties with a little salt and pepper. Cook them like you'd cook a hamburger (everyone has their way of doing this… in a pan, over a grill, in a George Forman grill, etc. I recommend high heat and don't overcook them). Baste them with a little BBQ sauce as they cook.

5. Split your buns in half and then toast them. Spread a small amount of BBQ sauce on the tops and bottoms.

6. Assemble 12 small sliders with the bun bottoms, a pork patty, 2 half slices of bacon, caramelized onions, coleslaw, and a lid!

7. Call your friends!

THAI GRILLED BEEF SKEWERS

SERVES: 6 · · · PREP: 15 MIN · · · COOK: 15 MIN · · · TOTAL: 1 HR 30 MIN

1 1/2 lb. (681 g) **beef tenderloin, sirloin, or rib eye**, cut into strips

1/4 cup (60 mL) **fish sauce**

1 Tbsp (15 mL) minced **fresh ginger**

4 **garlic cloves**, minced

1 Tbsp (15 mL) minced **lemongrass**

2 Tbsp (30 mL) freshly squeezed **lime juice**

1 Tbsp (15 mL) **yacon syrup** (optional)

1 Tbsp (15 mL) **sugar replacement**

18 **bamboo skewers**, soaked in water for 30 minutes

salt, pepper, and **chili flakes** to taste

2 Tbsp (30 mL) **coconut oil**, for grilling

I *love* these things. I'm a fish sauce fanatic but confess that it's amongst one of the most bizarre and stinky ingredients in existence. It's bizarre to me that such a pungent ingredient has stood the test of time!

Fish sauce is like salt or soy sauce in Thailand. It's used everywhere and in everything, but to me, fish sauce is weird. For one, it's called "fish sauce" (*Nam Pla*), which is bad enough to make me want to leave the room. I like fish, and I like sauce, but sauce made out of fish? Too unusual! It's also *fermented* fish (usually anchovies), which is extra icky. It's a lot of fresh, little boney fishes mixed with salt. It's covered, then left to sit in the sun for about a year. Sometimes, they uncover it to let it air out and get a tan. After several more months, it's squished, and the liquid is removed. Fish sauce! It's a pungent brown liquid. It's salty, and it stinks like that weird cheese you're afraid to try... mixed with old fish! If you have a really hot pot and add some fish sauce to the bottom of the pot, the odors stemming from the hot fish sauce vapor might make you exit the kitchen. You're almost certain to tear up and complain. I know I do!

The weirdest thing about fish sauce, though, isn't what it is or how it's made... or how it smells. The strangest thing is that... IT'S DELICIOUS!!!

PER SERVING
CALORIES: 333.1
FAT: 24.5
PROTEIN: 22.91
CARBS: 6.31
FIBER: .03
SUGAR ALCOHOLS: 2.5
NET CARBS: 3.78

MORE FACTS: P. 501

1. Mix the ingredients together in a bowl, except the salt, pepper, chili flakes, coconut oil, and skewers. Let marinate in the refrigerator for an hour.

2. When ready to cook, thread the beef on the bamboo skewers.

3. Preheat a grill.

4. Season the beef with salt, black pepper, and chili flakes (or, instead, add a bit of Thai chili paste to the marinade).

5. Once the grill is hot, brush it with coconut oil and quickly place your beef on the grill. Grill each skewer until it's nicely seared and cooked to your desired doneness. Serve!

Fish sauce is weird

Stuffed Bacon-Wrapped Shrimp

SERVES: 4 · · · PREP: 15 MIN · · · COOK: 25 MIN · · · TOTAL: 40 MIN

1 lb. (454 g) **shrimp** (16/20), peeled, with the tails left on, and deveined

1 lb. (454 g) **raw Italian sausage** (spicy or sweet)

8 slices (200 g) **bacon**

salt and **pepper** to taste

On my website, I have a bit of a famous—dare I say infamous?—recipe. In many serious BBQ competitions, various forms of a smoked bacon–wrapped jalapeño are served and judged, known as the mighty "Atomic Buffalo Turd". Not a terribly glamorous name, but the name is likely a large part of its infamy. They are chorizo-stuffed jalapeños, wrapped in bacon, and then slowly smoked… OUTSTANDING! I wanted to do something similar but a little less aggressive and a bit more family friendly. Welcome to these Italian sausage-stuffed shrimp… wrapped in bacon! I've redubbed these: UBTs: Underwater Buffalo *Things*, or, well… use your imagination.

1. Preheat oven to 350°F (177°C).

2. Hold the shrimp on a cutting board with the removed-vein side down. Do your best to somewhat flatten it; it will want to curl. The exposed portion of the shrimp is roughly 3 inches (7.5 cm). Make two very shallow incisions about an inch (2.5 cm) in and an inch (2.5 cm) apart. You do not want to cut through the shrimp, or even make a hole to the deveined side. You are simply trying to cut through the connective tissue that encourages the curve to take place. These two tiny incisions should help the shrimp lay flat. Flip the shrimps over, so that the deveined side is now facing up and the shrimp are now lying flat. Season the shrimp with a very light sprinkle of salt and pepper.

PER SERVING
CALORIES: 576.31
FAT: 40.79
PROTEIN: 47.4
CARBS: 4.31
FIBER: .07
SUGAR ALCOHOLS: 0
NET CARBS: 4.24

MORE FACTS: P. 500

3. Count your shrimp. You should have about 18 of them, but you may have as few as 16 or up to 20. Divide your sausage into portions that match the number of shrimp. (I'm going to assume you have 16 shrimp just to simplify the instructions.) Your sausage may be in its casings. If so, simply cut one end of each link and squeeze out the contents, like a tube of toothpaste. Make 16 one-ounce (28 g) balls with the sausage. Then, roll each ball into the shape of a two-inch (5 cm) cigar. Press the sausage cigars into the deveined portion of each shrimp.

4. Normally a strip of bacon is about 6 inches (15 cm) long. Cut your 8 strips into 3-inch (7.5 cm) halves. Place each one on a cutting board. Place the flat edge of a chef's knife on the slice, and push your palm onto the blade while sliding the blade away from you. This has the effect of squishing the bacon, making it thinner, wider, and longer. Repeat this process until all the bacon has been thinned and enlarged.

5. Wrap each piece of bacon around each shrimp, preferably with the end of each bacon strip ending underneath the shrimp, so that the weight of the shrimp will hold the strip in place. Place each shrimp, bacon-seam side down, on a parchment or foil-covered baking tray.

6. Bake for approximately 20 to 25 minutes or until the bacon has started to turn golden and the sausage is cooked all the way through. Serve! These would be delicious with a Rouille (p. 376) or a Béarnaise sauce (p. 382).

MINIATURE CRAB CAKES

SERVES: 6 · · · PREP: 20 MIN · · · COOK: 20 MIN · · · TOTAL: 40 MIN

1/2 lb. (227 g) firm, fresh, **raw white fish** (cod, halibut, sole, shrimp, scallop, lobster, etc.)

1 large **egg**, chilled

1/2 cup (120 mL) **heavy whipping cream**

1 lb. (454 g) **lump crab meat**, drained and shells removed

1 small (74 g) **red bell pepper**, seeded and finely diced

4 whole (60 g) **green onions** (scallions), cut lengthwise into thin strips and divided

1 tsp (5 mL) **smoked paprika**

1/2 tsp (2 mL) **cayenne pepper**, ground

1 cup (240 mL) **pine nuts**

1/4 cup (60 mL) **fresh whole butter**, divided

salt and fresh-cracked **pepper** to taste

I'm really super proud of these crab cakes. I kinda feel like this is a full-blown reinvention of the low-primal crab cake! A standard crab cake is usually crab, which is held together with lots of breadcrumbs and eggs and/or mayonnaise. I thought to use mousseline.

Mousseline is basically a catchall term meaning whipped cream is involved. In this case, it's a fish mousseline, or even more specific to the pictures, a *shrimp* mousseline! (The stuff you'll find on shrimp toast or within the shrimp-stuffed dishes at dim sum.) Mayonnaise, a common binder for crab cakes, is an egg and fat emulsion. Shrimp Mousseline is an egg, shrimp, and fat emulsion—kinda similar, but it'll hold its shape better and… tastes like shrimp! A perfect complement for a crab cake!

1. Before you do anything, chill your food processor bowl and blade. The mousseline needs to be made in a cold environment.

2. Add your fish/shrimp/whatever (I use shrimp for this recipe) to your food processor with a small amount of salt (about 1/2 teaspoon [2 mL]), pepper, and an egg. Turn the food processor on. Through the hole in the top, slowly drizzle in your cream until it is well blended. You'll have something that looks like paste. You may need to scrape down the edges and puree for another moment or two. Scrape your mousseline into a chilled bowl, and add your crab, bell pepper, green onions, cayenne, paprika, and a small amount of salt (about 1 teaspoon [5 mL]) and pepper. Mix well. Set your crab

PER SERVING
CALORIES: 498.89
FAT: 40.26
PROTEIN: 29.11
CARBS: 6.91
FIBER: 1.97
SUGAR ALCOHOLS: 0
NET CARBS: 4.94

MORE FACTS: P. 502

mixture in the fridge.

3. Place your pine nuts in a plastic bag—a one-gallon Ziploc would work nicely. Roll over the bag with a rolling pin or crush the nuts with a mallet or the bottom of a pan. You want them crushed but still somewhat whole. You're going to use them as a crust. Once the pine nuts are crushed, pour them into something like a pie pan; you want a wide-bottomed bowl or pan. A fairly small casserole dish would work as well.

4. Portion 1- to 1 1/2-ounce (42 g) balls of the crab mixture and place them in the pine nuts. Roll them around, so they are evenly coated with the pine nuts. Pick up each pine nut–crusted crab ball and shape it into a little puck in the palm of your hand. It should be about 1-inch (2.5 cm) thick. Set them aside.

5. Preheat oven to 350°F (177°C).

6. In two large ovenproof sauté pans, melt 2 tablespoons (30 mL) of butter in each pan. Over medium heat, place some crab cakes into each pan. There should be about a 1/2-inch (1.2 cm) gap between each cake. If you don't have room for all of them, don't worry. Lightly brown one side of each cake, then turn over. Lightly brown the other side. Once both sides have been browned, remove them and place them on a cookie tray. Continue with remaining crab cakes and place them on the baking tray.

7. Bake the whole tray for 10 minutes in the oven. Remove. Serve!

CHINESE SPARE RIBS

SERVES: 6 · · · PREP: 10 MIN · · · COOK: 3 HRS · · · TOTAL: 3 HRS

Plus optional overnight

2 slabs (4.5 kg) **pork spare ribs** (about 5 lb. per slab)

1/4 cup (60 mL) **rice wine vinegar**

1/4 cup (60 mL) **soy sauce** (or coconut aminos)

1/4 cup (60 mL) loosely packed **raisins**

2 Tbsp (30 mL) **sesame seeds**, divided

2 Tbsp (30 mL) **sugar replacement**

1 Tbsp (15 mL) **sesame oil**

1 Tbsp (15 mL) **crushed chilies** or **chili paste**

1 Tbsp (15 mL) **Chinese Five-spice**

1 Tbsp (15 mL) chopped fresh **ginger**

4 **garlic cloves**

salt and **pepper** to taste

Note: I struggled to find the correct macronutrient amounts for the ribs. My guess is that the calories and fat are less than half the amount shown here. My belief is that these numbers include the fat, before it is rendered out, as well as the inclusion of the bone, which is not eaten.

PER SERVING
CALORIES: 1,530.39
FAT: 96.265
PROTEIN: 145.3
CARBS: 13.66
FIBER: 1.14
SUGAR ALCOHOLS: 5
NET CARBS: 7.47

MORE FACTS: P. 502

This could just as easily be in the main dishes section, but I confess to loving the idea of beginning my meal with a few ribs! Ribs, by design, are easy to make into small portions of just 3 or 4 ribs, or whole racks can be served. Note that this recipe contains raisins, a naturally high-sugar ingredient. It's a relatively small portion, considering the size of the overall recipe, only contributing about 5 carbs per portion. The ingredient is completely optional but will add some of the character that would usually be found in a hoisin-type sauce. If you choose to omit the raisins, add an extra tablespoon or two of your preferred sweetener. I also want to point out that these keep quite well and are the kind of thing I'm likely to vacuum pack and freeze for a rainy day. Just be sure they are fully chilled before vacuum packing and reheat in foil, at about 250°F (121°C) for 20 to 30 minutes. DELISH!

1. To begin, wash the ribs and pat them dry.

2. You'll want to peel the membrane off the inside (boney side) of the slabs. This can be tricky to start, but once a corner has been loosened, the rest usually rips right off. The membrane is a slightly shiny, thick, paper-like layer covering the ribs. Slide a small knife into one corner of the rib, just between the meat and membrane. I usually use a butter knife for this (a sharp knife may cut through the membrane, when I see this as more of a "prying" effect). Jiggle, push, and shove the knife between the meat and membrane, sliding it from side to side, until roughly 1 inch (2.5 cm) of membrane has been loosened enough to hold on to. With a towel, grab the flap and, with consistent force, peel the membrane off the inside of the slab. It should come off in one nice tear. If it doesn't, continue the prying and pulling process until the entire membrane has been removed. Discard the membrane, cut the slab in half (creating two half-racks), set the slabs aside, and repeat for the second slab.

3. In a blender or food processor, puree vinegar, soy sauce, raisins, 1 tablespoon (15 mL) of the sesame seeds, the sweetener, sesame oil, chilies, five-spice, ginger, and garlic.

4. Season both slabs with salt and pepper. Then, rub the marinade all over the ribs. Wrap them in plastic, with the marinade, and allow them to marinate for about an hour, but overnight if possible.

5. Turn oven to 300°F (149°C).

6. Wrap ribs in foil packets with the marinade. Place them meaty side down on a baking tray in the oven. Allow them to bake for about 2 hours.

7. After two hours, remove them from the oven. Carefully unwrap them and pour off the liquid that has accumulated. Save this liquid and skim the fat off the surface, leaving just the juices.

8. Place the ribs back on the baking tray, meaty side up, and place them back in the oven. Allow them to cook for another 30 minutes. The ribs are done when the meat pulls back from the bones. The racks will be very flimsy, and the meat easily separates from the bones. It will be soft and tender. If the meat is still tough, let it go for 15 more minutes, basting with the liquid.

9. When they are done, cut the ribs with a knife, between every one or two ribs. Serve 3 or 4 ribs per plate. Drizzle with the remaining juices and garnish with the remaining sesame seeds.

Sweet Thai Chili Shrimp

SERVES: 4 · · · PREP: 5 MIN · · · COOK: 5 MINS · · · TOTAL: 10 MINS

oil for frying (coconut or lard)

1/2 cup (120 mL) **coconut flour**

1 Tbsp (15 mL) **tapioca flour**

1 large **egg**

2 Tbsp (30 mL) **club soda** (or water)

1 lb. (454 g) **shrimp (31/35)**, peeled and deveined

1/4 cup (60 mL) **Sweet Thai Chili Sauce** (p. 349)

2 Tbsp (30 mL) fresh, chopped **cilantro**

8 large (45 g) **lettuce leaves** (butter, romaine, cabbage, ice burg, etc.)

salt and **pepper** to taste

This is easily one of my favorite dishes on the planet. I actually snatched this concept from a restaurant called Sweet Basil in Vail, CO, back in the mid-nineties. It was a tempura-fried rock shrimp, tossed with sweet Thai chili sauce. Let's just say that I played a little game called "one for me, one for them" every night I made that mind-blowing dish! Because of the sugar and flour, I'd long considered this a distant memory... until now!

1. Set up a fryer for the shrimp. Ideally the temperature is set at 350°F (177°C). This can be done via deep-frying or panfrying. In all cases, I usually use a candy thermometer to test the temperature. If deep-frying, fill the fryer with enough oil for frying (several cups worth at least; some recommend filling the vessel by two-thirds). If panfrying, you want a layer of oil about 1/2 inch (1.2 cm) thick in the bottom of the pan. Be careful not to burn the oil, as you can use it again when it cools.

2. Combine coconut flour, tapioca flour, and a bit of salt and pepper. Add the egg and stir, while adding the club soda. Add enough to make a thick pancake batter.

3. Grab a large mixing bowl and line it with paper towels. Also grab a handheld strainer of some kind—a slotted spoon, a metal spider (a kind of mesh sieve/strainer, with a handle), etc. Make sure these are both close and ready.

4. Add the shrimp to the batter and toss around so that they're evenly coated. With your hands, reach in and grab the shrimps. With your fingers close to the surface of the oil, gently drop the shrimps into the oil one at a time. You don't want them to clump together. If your hand is too high, you'll splash, and if it's too low, you'll burn your fingers. Just carefully release each shrimp into the surface of the oil. Fry until crisp and golden, about 2 to 3 minutes.

PER SERVING
CALORIES: 238.92
FAT: 5.21
PROTEIN: 28.01
CARBS: 29.24
FIBER: 6.74
SUGAR ALCOHOLS: 15
NET CARBS: 7.47

MORE FACTS: P. 502

5. Remove the shrimp with the handheld strainer and place in the bowl with the towels. Sprinkle with a bit of salt and pepper. Let the shrimp drain for about 30 seconds. Remove the towels from the bowl, leaving the shrimp. Add the Thai chili sauce and the cilantro. Toss to coat evenly, and then distribute evenly between the lettuce leaves, like tacos. Serve!

Tod Man Pla (Thai Fish Cakes)

SERVES: 6 · · · PREP: 20 MIN · · · COOK: 15 MINS · · · TOTAL: 35 MINS

1 1/2 lb. (681 g) firm, fresh, **raw white fish** (cod, halibut, sole, shrimp, scallop, lobster, etc.)

3 **large egg whites**

1 Tbsp (15 mL) minced **fresh ginger**

4 **garlic cloves**, minced

1 Tbsp (15 mL) **Red Curry Paste** (p. 484)

1/4 cup (60 mL) **fish sauce**

10 **kaffir lime leaves**, cut into very thin strips (lime zest is an acceptable substitute)

1/2 lb. (227 g) **green string beans**, ends and string removed, cut into thin little disks

1 small (74 g) **red bell pepper**, seeded and cut into small dice

2 Tbsp (30 mL) **oil** (for sautéing, such as coconut, or ghee)

salt and freshly cracked **pepper** to taste

Some names, for me, just seem unfortunate. That these are called *fish cakes* is unfortunate. Something about the name doesn't really elicit visions of fresh fish blended with a spicy curry paste, vegetables, and a bit of egg, then panfried. Instead, it elicits visions more in the spirit of something Bugs Bunny might give to Elmer Fudd. The idea of a *fish cake* feels a bit cartoonish and filled with ulterior motives. These fish cakes are Thai, which somehow renders the whole thing exotic... and cartoonish.

Because I detest the name *fish cake*, I'm going to call these Tod Man Pla, which is what they're really called by the street vendors that hock these tasty cakes on the streets of Thailand.

1. In a food processor, place your fresh fish, egg whites, ginger, garlic, curry paste, and fish sauce. Puree the mixture until it is a smooth, frothy paste. Transfer the mixture to a bowl. Fold in your lime leaf strips, green bean disks, and red bell pepper dice. Season with a bit of salt and pepper.

2. Heat a skillet or large sauté pan over medium heat. These are often deep-fried, but I opt to cook them like pancakes (less mess, less need to use a lot of fat/oil, for the purposes of frying). You can do it in any manner you see fit.

3. Add your oil to the pan. When the oil ripples, place little plops of paste into the oil (I like to use a small ice cream scooper for this). Press down a bit, to flatten them out. They'll cook more quickly and evenly.

4. When one side is nice and golden brown, flip them to cook the other side.

5. When they are cooked through, serve!

PER SERVING
CALORIES: 189.66
FAT: 5.73
PROTEIN: 26.15
CARBS: 4.77
FIBER: 1.55
SUGAR ALCOHOLS: 0
NET CARBS: 3.21

MORE FACTS: P. 503

Bacon-Wrapped Rose-mary-Skewered Scallops

SERVES: 6 · · · PREP: 10 MIN · · · COOK: 10 MINS · · · TOTAL: 20 MINS

18 sprigs **fresh rosemary**

9 slices (225 g) **raw bacon**

18 jumbo (504 g) **sea scallops**

salt and **pepper** to taste

These delightfully and deceptively quick and simple little scallop skewers come bacon wrapped and skewered with fresh rosemary twigs! The saltiness of the bacon really complements the sweet scallop flavor. The rosemary skewer simply imparts a mild herby twist to the whole thing, while also helping to keep the bacon in place. I personally seared these in a hot pan, but in retrospect probably would've done them on a grill. I don't remember my logic for using a pan. The good news is, both methods would work!

Note: I topped these off with some Orange-Rosemary Compound Butter (p. 372) that I had in my freezer. Fantastic combo!

1. Remove the leaves from the bottom portion of the fresh rosemary sprigs. Save the leaves for another recipe.

2. Cut the slices of bacon in half, so that each slice of bacon is half as long. You should now have 18 short slices of bacon. Wrap each slice of bacon around a scallop. Skewer the scallops with the bare end of the rosemary twig, so that it holds the two bacon flaps in place.

3. Preheat a large nonstick sauté pan over medium-high heat.

4. Season the scallops with a small amount of salt and pepper. Place the scallops in the pan, with a flat side down. Try to keep them from touching one another. You may need to do this in two batches. You won't need any extra oil, because the fat from the bacon quickly renders into the pan.

5. You do want a fairly high heat for this, so that the surface of the scallop sears and you get a nice color, without overcooking the scallop. After about 2 minutes, flip the scallops and brown the other side.

6. Remove from the pan and serve. These are nice sitting on top of a nice basic salad, or served by themselves.

Shrimp Scampi

SERVES: 4 · · · PREP: 5 MIN · · · COOK: 5 MIN · · · TOTAL: 10 MIN

Shrimp scampi is one of the best, tastiest little appetizers in existence. It's extra wonderful because of how quick and easy it comes together. This elegant little dish can literally be thrown together in minutes. It's little more than shrimp, garlic, wine, herbs (usually parsley), and butter. It's wonderful nicely plated all by itself, as it is when the tails are removed and it's served as a mound of shrimp served over a bed of Spaghetti Squash (p. 223) for dinner.

1 lb. (454 g) **shrimp (16/20)**, peeled, with the tails left on, and deveined

1/4 cup (60 mL) **cold butter**, divided

8 **garlic cloves**

2 Tbsp (30 mL) **dry vermouth**

1 Tbsp (15 mL) fresh **lemon juice**

1 Tbsp (15 mL) sliced **chives**

salt and **pepper** to taste

1. Heat a large nonstick pan or skillet over medium-high heat.

2. Wash and drain shrimp in strainer, and dry thoroughly by letting air dry or blotting with a towel. Season the shrimp with a little bit of salt and pepper (I also like a touch of chili flakes).

3. Add 1 tablespoon of butter to the pan and swirl around. Immediately add the shrimp, and swirl the pan around, to coat with butter. Now, lay each shrimp in an even layer in the pan and allow them to cook for about 1 minute. Turn the shrimp over, and cook on the other side for about 1 minute. Add the garlic, vermouth, and lemon juice, and again, swirl the pan around. Let simmer for about 1 minute.

4. Cut your remaining butter into about 12 small cubes. Keeping the pan over the burner, endlessly swirl the shrimp around, constantly moving them, and add 1 small cube of butter every 10 seconds, for 2 minutes. The slow addition of cold butter will make a slightly thickened sauce. Taste the sauce and adjust with salt and pepper. It should be tart and quite garlicky. Finally, add the chives, give it one last swirl, and serve!

PER SERVING
CALORIES: 240.77
FAT: 13.27
PROTEIN: 22.72
CARBS: 4.34
FIBER: .09
SUGAR ALCOHOLS: 0
NET CARBS: 4.26

MORE FACTS: P. 501

Blackened Chicken Tenders

SERVES: 6 · · · PREP: 10 MIN · · · COOK: 15 MINS · · · TOTAL: 25 MINS

2 Tbsp (30 mL) **paprika**

1 Tbsp (15 mL) **freshly cracked black pepper**

1 Tbsp (15 mL) **cayenne pepper**

4 **garlic cloves**, minced

2 tsp (10 mL) chopped **fresh thyme**

1 tsp (5 mL) chopped **fresh oregano**

1 Tbsp (15 mL) **salt**

2 tsp (10 mL) **sugar replacement**

1 1/2 lb. (681 g) **boneless and skinless chicken breasts**, cut into strips

1/2 cup (120 mL) **fresh whole butter** (one stick), melted

I remember when I was young and learned about blackened food for the first time. Something about intentionally burning the surface of the food, in a really, really searing hot pan to enhance the flavor, really stuck with me. I think this is one of those foundational concepts that made me think about flavor as something bigger than the goodness that teases my nose and tongue. You can manipulate it. You can use techniques, interesting blends of spices and herbs, and fats and temperatures to change the way the final dish looks, tastes, and feels in the mouth. A lot to think about for an eight-year-old boy! But... I did!

These are spicy and cozy, hot but familiar—really, just flat-out delicious and the kind of thing I could eat a basket of. In this case, I served them with a cool ranch dressing, but you could really eat them plain, on a salad with some blue cheese, or even stacked up in a po' boy!

1. Preheat a large iron skillet (or a big sauté pan if you don't have a large iron skillet) over medium-high heat.

2. In a large bowl, mix the paprika, pepper, cayenne, garlic, thyme, oregano, salt, sweetener, chicken, and melted butter. Coat the chicken with an even layer of spice and melted butter. Be quick, before the butter solidifies because of the cold chicken.

3. Add your chicken strips to the hot pan, leaving space between each piece. Do not add too many to the pan at once, or else they will not blacken; they will just simmer and steam. In a hot pan, the butter will melt off the cold chicken and fry/blacken the surface of the chicken. If you need to do this in a few batches, that's fine. Wipe out the pan between each batch, but also always make sure the pan is very hot before you add the chicken. This will help it blacken and also help prevent the chicken from sticking to the pan.

PER SERVING
CALORIES: 283.64
FAT: 18.5
PROTEIN: 24.86
CARBS: 4.59
FIBER: 1.43
SUGAR ALCOHOLS: 1.33
NET CARBS: 1.83

MORE FACTS: P. 503

4. When one side is nice and black, turn it over and blacken the other side. Adding a small amount of flavorless oil (lard, for example) to the pan may help cook the chicken more evenly, even if it's slightly less authentic.

5. Once the chicken tenders are cooked through, serve!

Wrapping **stuff in** bacon is my **favorite!**

BBQ'D BACON-WRAPPED BASIL SHRIMP

SERVES: 6 · · · PREP: 20 MIN · · · COOK: 15 MINS · · · TOTAL: 35 MINS

This combines several of my favorite things: grillin' stuff, wrappin' stuff in bacon, and shrimp! It's also got some fun little twists, like the addition of some BBQ sauce and a fresh basil leaf. Familiar and comfortable, yet different and with a slight basil kick!

1. Marinate the shrimp in the BBQ sauce for about 20 minutes.

2. Preheat the grill.

3. While the shrimp is marinating, cut eat slice of bacon into thirds. This will result in 18 approximately two to three-inch (6 cm) slices of bacon. Squish each slice of bacon with the side of a knife or the bottom of a pan. Don't tear it up. You want 18 nice thin "sheets" of bacon.

4. Set each sheet of bacon on a cutting board, and place a basil leaf on top of each sheet.

5. Place a marinated shrimp above each basil leaf. Season with a small amount of salt and pepper (chili flakes are a nice addition too).

6. Wrap each slice of bacon around the shrimp, and use a thin premoistened skewer to hold the bacon in place. You can also put up to 3 per skewer, for a different look.

7. Brush the oil on the grill to help prevent sticking. Grill the shrimps over medium-high heat until the bacon is crisp and the shrimps are cooked through.

8. Serve!

1 lb. (454 g) **shrimp** (16/20), peeled and deveined

1/4 cup (60 mL) **Sweet 'n' Tangy BBQ Sauce** (p. 356)

6 slices (150 g) **raw bacon**

18 **fresh basil** leaves

18 **bamboo skewers**, soaked in water for 30 minutes

salt, **pepper**, and **chili flakes** to taste

2 Tbsp (30 mL) **coconut oil** for grilling

PER SERVING
CALORIES: 244.45
FAT: 17.1
PROTEIN: 18.44
CARBS: 3.02
FIBER: .52
SUGAR ALCOHOLS: 0
NET CARBS: 2.21

MORE FACTS: P. 503

GRILLED CHICKEN SATAY

SERVES: 6 · · · PREP: 15 MIN · · · COOK: 15 MIN · · · TOTAL: 30 MIN

Plus optional overnight

1 1/2 lb. (681 g) **boneless skinless chicken breasts**, cut into strips

4 **garlic cloves**, minced

1 Tbsp (15 mL) minced **fresh ginger**

2 tsp (10 mL) **Red Curry Paste** (p, 484)

1/4 cup (60 mL) unsweetened **coconut milk**

2 tsp (10 mL) ground **turmeric**

1 Tbsp (15 mL) freshly squeezed **lime juice**

18 **bamboo skewers**, soaked in water for 30 minutes

salt, **pepper**, and **chili flakes** to taste

2 Tbsp (30 mL) **coconut oil**, for grilling

I remember being a kid and eating this stuff. To this day, chicken satay is probably one of my favorite things to eat. Maybe it's the chicken, but *maybe* it's the peanut sauce! As a kid, our local restaurant always served it with peanut sauce and a sweet-spicy cucumber salad. The chicken skewers were always resting on a slice of white toast, which had been cut into nine squares, each square absorbing the bright yellow grease dripping from the satays. This was my favorite part. And the chicken.

Oh, and the Peanut Sauce (p. 379) was my favorite!

1. Marinate the chicken with the garlic, ginger, curry paste, coconut milk, turmeric, and lime juice. Cover and refrigerate the chicken for a few hours, up to overnight.

2. Thread the chicken on the bamboo skewers, weaving the skewer in and out, down the center of each strip of chicken.

3. Preheat a grill.

4. Season the chicken with salt, black pepper, and chili flakes.

5. Once the grill is hot, brush it with coconut oil and quickly place your skewers on the grill. Grill each until it's nicely seared and cooked through. Serve with peanut sauce (p. 379)!

PER SERVING
CALORIES: 200.52
FAT: 9.28
PROTEIN: 24.61
CARBS: 2.17
FIBER: .17
SUGAR ALCOHOLS: 0
NET CARBS: 2

MORE FACTS: P. 500

Soups &
Stews

○ ○ ○

I LOVE SOUPS! I cannot say it any more simply or plainly than that. Soups are an amazing way to get a wide variety of tastes, textures, and nutrients, all at the same time. Soups tend to be simple to make. Soups, being mostly water, are incredibly filling. Soup is a very common lunch in my world—just a big bowl of soup, whether it be chowder, a vegetable soup, or a creamy broccoli. It's a well-balanced meal, all in one big comforting bowl of yum!

ALBONDIGAS

SERVES: 6 · · · PREP: 15 MIN · · · COOK: 30 MIN · · · TOTAL: 45 MIN

1/2 lb. (227 g) **ground beef, pork, or turkey**

1/2 lb. (227g) **raw Mexican chorizo**

1 large **egg**

1 Tbsp (15 mL) **ground chia seed** (optional)

6 **garlic cloves**, chopped and divided

2 tsp (10 mL) ground **cumin**

1 tsp (5 mL) ground **coriander seed**

1/2 tsp (2 mL) ground **cinnamon**

6 cups (1.4 L) **chicken broth**

1 medium (110 g) **onion**, diced

1 medium (91 g) **tomato**, diced

2 ribs (101 g) **celery**, diced

1 small (72 g) **carrot**, peeled and diced

1 Tbsp (15 mL) **lard** or other cooking oil

1/4 bunch (25 g) **fresh cilantro**, very coarsely chopped

salt and **pepper** to taste

I started working in restaurants at the age of fourteen. I've spent most of my life since then in professional kitchens in both the United States and Mexico. One mainstay of the professional kitchen is the "family meal." This is where a staff member cooks something basic and in large quantities to feed the entire restaurant staff (or hotel staff, as the case may be). Albondigas is one of those meals that makes regular appearances, as it's easy to make, filling, comforting, and filled with loads of good veggies. This Mexican meatball soup is always a winner!

1. In a medium-sized mixing bowl, combine ground meat with chorizo, egg, ground chia seeds (the chia helps retain moisture and texture, but it's still delicious without!), half of the chopped garlic, cumin, coriander, cinnamon, and a bit of salt and pepper. Mix well.

2. In a large soup pot, bring the chicken broth, onion, tomato, celery, and carrot up to a slow simmer. The soup should take about 30 minutes from this point.

3. While the soup simmers, form 24 small meatballs. Each should weigh just under an ounce.

4. Heat a large sauté pan or skillet over medium-high heat. Add lard to the pan, and quickly coat the bottom of the pan. Evenly distribute the meatballs around the pan and get a nice browning on their surface. Sear all sides. Once the meatballs have been seared, place them in the pot with the chicken broth. Allow the broth to simmer for roughly 20 more minutes.

5. In the moment before serving, stir in the fresh cilantro. Taste the soup and adjust seasoning with salt and pepper. Serve!

PER SERVING
CALORIES: 341.69
FAT: 25.4
PROTEIN: 19.25
CARBS: 8.1
FIBER: 1.88
SUGAR ALCOHOLS: 0
NET CARBS: 6.3

MORE FACTS: P. 509

Thai Hot and Sour Shrimp

SERVES: 4 · · · PREP: 15 MIN · · · COOK: 40 MIN · · · TOTAL: 55 MIN

1 lb. (454 g) **shrimp (16/20)**, peeled, with the tails left on, and deveined

2 Tbsp (30 mL) **coconut oil**, divided

1 medium (110 g) **onion**, diced

4 **garlic cloves**

1 one-inch (22 g or 2.5 cm) piece of **galangal** (Thai ginger—ginger is an acceptable substitute), peeled and sliced into 8 chunks

1 **lemongrass stalk**, rough chop from the white portion

3 **kaffir lime leaves**, roughly chopped (or 1/2 tsp [2 mL] fresh lime zest)

1 **red Thai chili**, roughly chopped

5 cups (1.2 L) **chicken broth**

1/2 lb. (227 g) **crimini, shiitake, oyster, or button mushrooms**, washed and sliced into wedges

1 small (118 g) **green zucchini**

2 Tbsp (30 mL) **fresh lime juice**

2 Tbsp (30 mL) **fish sauce**

1/4 bunch (25 g) **fresh cilantro**, very coarsely chopped

1/4 bunch (25 g) **fresh basil**, very coarsely chopped

salt and **pepper** to taste

PER SERVING
CALORIES: 224.07
FAT: 8.72
PROTEIN: 27.77
CARBS: 7.59
FIBER: 1.4
SUGAR ALCOHOLS: 0
NET CARBS: 6.27

MORE FACTS: P. 504

One of my absolute favorite soups meals is the famous *Tom Kha Gai*, which means "Chicken with Galangal." I only mention this because this particular soup tends to have a similar taste sensation, except… with shrimp! If you've enjoyed the famous Thai soup and you enjoy shrimp, then move this to the top of your list! This one has a base of *fantastic* and incredibly flavorful shrimp broth, which is made from fresh shrimp shells and other aromatics. I like to make this and freeze it when I've got excess shrimp shells. Then, making a quick batch of this soup becomes easy!

Note: Because about half of the ingredients are strained out of this recipe, I omitted them from the nutrition, which likely makes the nutrition on this recipe slightly suspect but mostly accurate.

1. Peel and devein the shrimp, setting the shrimp shells aside.

2. In a large pot, heat 1 tablespoon (15 mL) coconut oil over medium heat. Add the shrimp shells and quickly stir to cook them. They burn easily, so keep them moving. Cook until they are red in color and lose any ammonia aroma. Add onion, garlic, galangal (or ginger), lemongrass, lime leaf (or a small amount of fresh lime zest), chili, and a bit of salt and pepper. Cook for about 3 minutes or until onions are slightly translucent. Add chicken broth to the pot. Simmer.

3. Once the shrimp stock has simmered for about 30 minutes, strain it. Discard shells. This is when I will often chill the broth and then freeze it. If continuing, place the stock back on the stove to slowly simmer.

4. Heat a large sauté pan over high heat. Once hot, add the remaining coconut oil, zucchini, and mushrooms with a bit of salt and pepper. Sauté until cooked through but still slightly firm. Add to the shrimp broth.

5. Add the raw shrimp to the shrimp broth. Allow the vegetables and shrimp to simmer for about 1 to 2 minutes. Add the lime juice, fish sauce, and a bit of salt and pepper. Taste the broth and adjust seasoning. When the shrimp is cooked through, about 1 more minute, add the fresh cilantro and basil. Serve.

Curried Chicken and Apple "Mulligatawny"

SERVES: 8 · · · PREP: 15 MIN · · · COOK: 40 MIN · · · TOTAL: 55 MIN

2 Tbsp (30 mL) **ghee** or **coconut oil**

1 lb. (454 g) **boneless chicken**, light or dark meat, cubed

1 small (110 g) **onion**, diced

2 ribs (101 g) **celery**, diced

1 small (72 g) **carrot**, diced

4 **garlic cloves**, minced

2 tsp (10 mL) grated **fresh ginger**

1 Tbsp (15 mL) **yellow curry powder**

6 cups (1.4 L) **chicken broth**

2 medium (322 g) **apples** (such as golden delicious)

1 Tbsp (30 mL) **fresh lemon juice**

1 tsp (15 mL) minced **fresh lemon zest**

1/4 bunch (25 g) **fresh cilantro**, very coarsely chopped

salt and **pepper** to taste

PER SERVING
CALORIES: 195.32
FAT: 6.9
PROTEIN: 18.84
CARBS: 14.13
FIBER: 2.56
SUGAR ALCOHOLS: 0
NET CARBS: 11.66

MORE FACTS: P. 505

I'm always a big fan of diverse flavors. I also love sneaking fruit into my diet, even though it's got loads of fruit sugars. A loose rule of recipe writing, for me, involves creating recipes that fall under 10 net carbs per serving, but a step over the line for a bit of apple seems reasonable. If the carb count is too high for you, simply use one apple, rather than two. It'll still be excellent, while dropping the net from near 12 to about 8.5 grams. I tend to feel that a little bit of apple isn't going to dramatically impact my blood sugars, while also allowing me to feel like I'm eating fruit! It's a freeing feeling. It's with these ideas that I assembled this quick Mulligatawny-influenced soup.

1. Heat a large soup pot over medium-high heat.

2. Add the ghee or coconut oil, and coat the bottom of the pan. Add the chicken, along with a bit of salt and pepper. Allow the chicken to sear and caramelize a bit. After about 2 or 3 minutes, when the chicken is nicely browned, add the onion, celery, carrot, garlic, ginger, and curry powder, with a bit more salt and pepper. Turn the heat down to low. Stir to combine the ingredients and allow to cook for about 5 more minutes or until the onions are translucent. Add the chicken broth and bring up to a simmer. Simmer for about 30 more minutes or until the chicken is tender.

3. Dice the apples (peeling them is optional). Place the diced apple into a bowl and add the lemon juice and a small amount of salt and pepper. Mix to coat the apples with the juice.

4. Once the soup is ready and the chicken is tender, add the apples and any juice that may have collected, along with the lemon zest and cilantro. Stir to combine. Taste and adjust seasoning.

5. Serve while the apple and cilantro is still fresh and vibrant!

Smoked Salmon Chowder

SERVES: 6 · · · PREP: 15 MIN · · · COOK: 40 MIN · · · TOTAL: 55 MIN

2 cups (480 mL) **chicken stock or broth**

1 small (110 g) **onion**, diced

2 (101 g) **celery ribs**, diced

4 **garlic cloves**, minced

1 bay leaf

4 slices (100 g) **raw bacon**, chopped

1 cup (240 mL) cubed **Hubbard squash**, cut into 1/4- to 1/2-inch (1 cm) cubes

1 small (74 g) **red bell pepper**, seeded and diced

1 tsp (5 mL) **smoked paprika** (nonsmoked is fine)

2 1/2 cups (600 mL) **heavy whipping cream**

1/2 lb. (227 g) **smoked salmon**, cut into cubes

salt and **pepper** to taste

The definition of chowder is pretty elusive. The only clear trend among all chowder is that they are always hot and always cooked for a good long time. They're usually pretty thick and chunky. I'd originally thought that they needed fish or seafood, but there are clearly vegetarian chowders. I'd also thought perhaps they needed to be creamy, but... the Manhattan chowder has no dairy. So... what makes a chowder, a chowder? This, I think, is the mystery of the universe.

Squash note: I curiously happened to see a big pile of Hubbard squash, wrapped in nice precut packages in the local grocery store. I cut some really nice cubes out of it for this chowder, but you could really use any of the following: Kabocha squash, pumpkin, delicata, butternut, acorn, buttercup, etc. You could even use sweet potatoes. The method remains the same, but the flavor will vary somewhat, as will the carb amount. My suggestion would be to stick with Hubbard or Kabocha, if you can.

1. Place a soup pot over medium-low heat. Add chicken stock, onions, celery, garlic, and bay leaf. Bring to a simmer.

2. In a sauté pan, over medium heat, cook the bacon until the bacon is crispy. Strain out the bacon and set aside. Also, remove about half of the bacon fat and save for another day.

3. In the still-hot sauté pan, add your squash and a little salt and pepper. Sauté over high heat to get a little caramelization on the squash cubes.

PER SERVING
CALORIES: 195.32
FAT: 6.9
PROTEIN: 18.84
CARBS: 14.13
FIBER: 2.56
SUGAR ALCOHOLS: 0
NET CARBS: 11.66

MORE FACTS: P. 505

4. Once the squash cubes begin to develop a nice brown color on the exterior, add your bell peppers, paprika, and a little salt and pepper. Sauté for about 3 more minutes. Dump the ingredients into the soup pot and continue simmering. Reduce temperature to low.

5. Add cream to the chowder. If your salmon is hot smoked (looks like cooked salmon), add it to the chowder at this point. Also, add your bacon bits. Allow the chowder to simmer on low for about 45 minutes.

6. If you're using cold-smoked salmon (soft, bright orange, and moist), add it after the chowder has simmered for about 45 minutes. Allow it to simmer in the soup for about 5 minutes.

7. Taste, adjust seasoning, and serve!

TACO SOUP

SERVES: 8 · · · PREP: 15 MIN · · · COOK: 30 MIN · · · TOTAL: 45 MIN

This particular soup has two interesting points. One is a bit of a personal secret. Though listed as a soup made essentially from ground beef and a fresh, home-made salsa, the reality is... when I make this at home, I purchase little tubs of fresh salsa from the produce department and toss it in. Easy, quick, and fresh!

The second point is slightly controversial in a book focused largely on primal ideologies. Corn is a grain and grains are a no-no, and I know this. Anything I say from here on in is a rationalization. However, I rationalize, "Baby corn has a very low carbohydrate content compared to the adult variety. It's also a tip of the hat to a corn tortilla shell... without which... this isn't much of a taco!" For purists, feel free to leave out the baby corn. It'll still be quite tasty without it!

1. In a large soup pot, brown ground beef. If you're using a very lean ground beef, you may want to start with your favorite cooking fat, but with most standard ground beefs, you won't need any additional fat. Season with a bit of salt and pepper. Continue cooking and breaking up until completely broken apart, cooked, and slightly browned.

2. Add the chopped tomatoes, baby corn, onion, garlic, jalapeños, lime juice, cilantro, chicken broth, and a bit more salt and pepper. Bring to a simmer, and then turn the heat to low and allow it to simmer for about 20 minutes.

3. Divide between 8 bowls, garnish with a dollop of sour cream, slices of fresh avocado, and some grated cheddar cheese. Serve!

1 lb. (454 g) **ground beef** (80 lean/20 fat)

2 **large** (364 g) **ripe tomatoes**, diced

1 14-oz. can (392 g) **baby corn**, drained and cut into 1/2-inch (1.2 cm) portions

1 small (110 g) **onion**, diced

4 **garlic cloves**, minced

1 (7 g) **jalapeño pepper**, diced and seeds removed

2 Tbsp (30 mL) **freshly squeezed lime juice**

1/2 bunch (50 g) **cilantro**, washed, large stems removed, and chopped

6 cups (1.4 L) **chicken broth**

1 cup (240 mL) **sour cream**

2 whole (272 g) **avocados**, peeled and sliced

1 cup (240 mL) **shredded cheddar/Colby cheese blend**

salt and **pepper** to taste

PER SERVING
CALORIES: 360.28
FAT: 26.95
PROTEIN: 17.21
CARBS: 10.68
FIBER: 3.84
SUGAR ALCOHOLS: 0
NET CARBS: 6.84

MORE FACTS: P. 506

Manhattan Chowder

SERVES: 6 · · · PREP: 30 MIN · · · COOK: 30 MIN · · · TOTAL: 60 MIN

4 lbs. (1.8 kg) small to medium **clams** (Quahog, Littleneck, or Cherrystone)

4 slices (100 g) **raw bacon**, chopped

4 **garlic cloves**, minced

1/2 tsp (2 mL) **chili flakes**

1 cup (240 mL) good quality **white wine**

1 small (110 g) **onion**, diced

1 small (74 g) **red bell pepper**, diced

2 (101 g) **celery ribs**, diced

1 small (72 g) **carrot**, peeled and diced

2 (364 g) **large ripe tomatoes**, diced

2 cups (480 mL) **chicken stock or broth** (maybe a bit more)

1 **bay leaf**

10 springs **fresh thyme**

salt and **pepper** to taste

This is another recipe breaking the 10-net-carbs guideline, which is odd in that more than half the carbohydrates in this recipe come from animal protein: the clams! Most animal protein is zero carb, with the exception of some organ meats. However, some seafood can register higher, with the bivalve mollusks, like clams, oysters, and mussels, being some of the highest. This is here because it's delicious, it's a good introduction to seafood, it's a full meal and can be adjusted to contain less clams, and finally... because I cooked it and took a picture!

1. Discard any clams that are open or that don't immediately shut when tapped. Place the clams in a large bowl in the sink, with cold water slowly pouring into them from the tap. Leave the tap water at a very slow trickle for about 20 minutes. This will give the mollusks time to spit out any trapped sand.

2. While the water trickles, place a large pot on medium-high heat. Add the bacon and cook until brown and crispy. Once crispy, strain the bits and save the fat. Leave any residual fat in the pot.

3. Return to the clams. Lift them up and out of the water, one at a time. Scrub them under the cold, running tap water and set aside. Continue this process until they are all free of sand, cleaned, and scrubbed.

4. Place a colander or strainer in a large bowl and have it close by.

PER SERVING
CALORIES: 371.09
FAT: 10.7
PROTEIN: 43.36
CARBS: 18.2
FIBER: 2.12
SUGAR ALCOHOLS: 0
NET CARBS: 15.59

MORE FACTS: P. 506

5. Return the original large pot (with bacon fat residue) to the stove, over medium heat. Add about 1 table-spoon (15 mL) of the strained bacon fat, garlic, and chili flakes. Cook for about 30 seconds or until the chili and garlic is aromatic. Add the clams and quickly stir to coat with spicy bacon fat. Pour the wine over the clams and cover with a lid. After about 2 minutes, turn the heat to low. Let the clams steam for about 3 more minutes or until they are all opened. Pour the clams into the strainer, making sure you save and reserve the clam juice. Spread the clams evenly on a tray and place them in the fridge to cool.

6. Wash the original pot and place it back on the stove, over medium heat. Add roughly 2 tablespoons (30 mL) of the reserved bacon fat. Then add the onion, bell pepper, celery, and carrots with a bit of salt and pepper. Stir and cook until the onions are translucent. Add the tomatoes, chicken broth, bay leaf, thyme, and the reserved clam juice. Bring to a simmer. Once a very low simmer is achieved, turn the pot to low and place a lid on it. Allow it to cook for 20 more minutes.

7. While the chowder cooks, get the clams from the fridge and remove them from their shells. If they are large, chop them into smaller pieces. Discard the shells.

8. After 20 minutes on the stove, add the clams. If the soup is very thick and not broth-y enough, add a bit more chicken broth to adjust the consistency. Adjust the seasoning, place the lid on the pot, and allow it to return to a very low simmer. Once the first bubble percolates to the surface of the chowder, turn it off and allow it to sit for 5 minutes.

9. Serve!

CREAM OF ROASTED GARLIC, CAULIFLOWER, AND BACON

SERVES: 6 · · · PREP: 20 MIN · · · COOK: 50 MIN · · · TOTAL: 1 HR 10 MIN

4 slices (100 g) **raw bacon**, chopped

12 **garlic cloves**, sliced into 1/16-inch (1 mm) to 1/8-inch thick "chips"

1 head (840 g) **large cauliflower**, stem and leaves removed, and cut into small florets

2 cups (480 mL) **chicken stock or broth**

1 1/2 cups (360 mL) **heavy whipping cream**

salt and **pepper** to taste

This soup is *amazing*. This is the kind of taste experience that makes me want to go out at night, pick a random table in a nice restaurant, and... dance on it. It's that good! The big trick is not burning the garlic. You want it sweet and roasted, with a nice flavor throughout the soup, but it goes from caramelized to *burned* at the snap of a finger. Go slow. Go low.

Make it. It's worth it. You'll be glad you did!

1. In a sauté pan, over medium heat, cook the bacon until crispy. Remove the bacon from the bacon grease and set aside, leaving the grease in the hot pan.

2. Over very low heat, in the pan with the bacon grease, add the garlic chips and let them slowly fry and turn a light golden brown—the slower, the better. This can take upwards of 30 minutes and require some careful attention (though you should do other things while it cooks). Do not let this burn or turn too dark. It becomes bitter very quickly. Remove the garlic from the bacon fat and set aside on a paper towel to dry.

3. Add 1/2 of the remaining bacon fat to a medium-sized soup pot and add about 3/4 of the cauliflower florets. Add some salt and pepper to the pan, and fry the cauliflower in the bacon fat for about 3 minutes, until just a little color is added to the cauliflower. Add the chicken stock to the soup pot. Let simmer for 30 minutes or until very soft.

4. While the soup is simmering, place the original sauté pan, with the remaining bacon fat, on the stove over medium heat. Add the final 1/4 of cauliflower florets and season with a little salt and pepper.

PER SERVING
CALORIES: 329.81
FAT: 29.82
PROTEIN: 6.83
CARBS: 11.92
FIBER: 3.5
SUGAR ALCOHOLS: 0
NET CARBS: 8.42

MORE FACTS: P. 505

5. When the cauliflower in the sauté pan is cooked and slightly browned, add the bacon and roasted garlic.

6. Add the cream to the soup pot, and season with a little salt and pepper.

7. Do not let the soup boil. When it is very hot, puree in a blender until smooth. Adjust seasoning with salt and pepper, and consistency with more warm chicken stock if it needs it.

8. Divide the soup between several bowls, then garnish with the cauliflower florets, bacon, and garlic chips.

Fantasy Island of Delight!

BOUILLABAISSE

SERVES: 8 · · · PREP: 20 MIN · · · COOK: 30 MIN · · · TOTAL: 50 MIN

1/2 cup (120 mL) **extra virgin olive oil**, divided

1 cup (240 mL) good quality **white wine**

1 small (110 g) **onion**, peeled and diced

4 each **garlic cloves**, minced

2 medium (182 g) **tomatoes**, diced

1 bulb (234 g) **fennel**, diced

1 **bay leaf**

1/2 tsp (1 mL) **saffron** threads

1 tsp (2 mL) chopped **fresh thyme**

1/2 tsp (1 mL) **fresh orange** zest (peel)

1/2 tsp (1 mL) ground **cayenne pepper**

1 1/2 lb (681 g) **halibut fillets**

32 medium-sized (454 g) **clams**, fresh and alive

32 medium-sized (454 g) **mussels**, fresh and alive

1 lb. (454 g) **shrimp**

4 fillets (681 g) **dover sole**

1 cup (240 mL) **Rouille** (p. 376)

salt and fresh cracked **pepper**, to taste

PER SERVING
CALORIES: 573.62
FAT: 29.1
PROTEIN: 59.67
CARBS: 11.09
FIBER: 1.5
SUGAR ALCOHOLS: .03
NET CARBS: 9.55

MORE FACTS: P. 507

Bouillabaisse is a French seafood stew, originating over 2,500 years ago, in the southeastern part of France. It's usually a blend of both fish and shellfish. The core focus is on using very fresh seafood. The fish should almost *wiggle*, as it's cooked. Additionally, it should use very local seafood, which can be tough for the people of cities like Denver, CO. As a result, *TRUE* Bouillabaisse can really only come from France and use French seafood, French herbs, and French vegetables.

Alas, my version ... is a cheap knockoff!

Bouillabaisse has another eccentricity: It's a stew, but it's very often served with the goodies strained out and served separately from the broth. The broth is often served as a first course, with bread and Rouille (p. 376), which is a mayonnaise made from saffron and cayenne. The seafood is often served separately!

Now, because the overwhelming majority of us are not in France, and we don't eat bread, I've had to modify my recipe to be somewhat neutral in geography and lower in carbs. If you have both the access and the desire to add sea creatures such as eel, sea urchin, octopus, scorpion fish, and spider crabs, definitely, completely, totally throw it in there (in due time, of course). I have opted out of these regional specifics, knowing the local grocery store is unlikely to carry these things. However, by no means does that diminish the time, care, and attention that went into creating this really quick-to-make and amazing bowl of fresh brothy seafood!

Next time you've got company over, give this a shot. Oh's and ah's will abound!

1. In a large pot, add your 1/4 cup (60 mL) of olive oil, wine, onion, garlic, tomato, fennel, saffron, cayenne, orange zest, thyme and bay leaf, with a little salt and pepper. Put it on the stove over medium-low heat with a lid and allow it to simmer. Allow it to simmer for about 20 minutes. This will soften everything and allow all the flavors to meld together.

2. While the broth simmers, soak your fresh clams and mussels in a bowl of cold water, with a slow, steady stream of cold water dropping from the faucet into the bowl. This helps remove a touch of extra saltiness and sand. Let this sit with the water dripping on it. Pick your clams and mussels out of the bowl, by scooping them up with your hands, and transferring them to another bowl. Any sand or debris should be left at the bottom of the original bowl. Wash the original bowl. Place the new bowl of clams and mussels under the slow stream of cold water. Transfer your clams and mussels one more time. With a wet towel, pull the beards from the mussels. This is done by grabbing the beard with the towel and pinching hard between your fingers, then deliberately pulling OUT and towards the hinge. You may also want to scrub the outside of your mussel shells, if there are a lot of funky little barnacles, debris, and other riddles and games attached to them. Once your clams and mussels are clean and happy, pull them up and out of the bowl and place them on a dry towel or in a colander to drip dry.

3. Peel your shrimp and remove the big vein running through the back.

4. Cut your fish into appropriate sizes. Large bite sized chunks is fine, but I opted for larger fillets. I thought it looked nicer when it was in the bowl and tends to retain more moisture, with these cooking methods

5. Place a large sauté pan on the stove over high heat.

6. Season your thick halibut fillets with salt and pepper. Also coat them with olive oil (2 tbsp (30 mL)). Place them in your hot sauté pan and get a nice brown color on one side. When the first side has color, turn the fish over and sear the other side. When the second side of halibut has a nice sear, add your clams and mussels to the pan and shake everything around. Let sit for 30 seconds and then dump the halibut, clams and mussels into the pot with the broth. Place the lid on the pot and allow it to continue simmering.

7. While that simmers, quickly clean out your hot sauté pan and keep it hot on high heat.

8. Season your shrimp and sole with salt and pepper. Coat them with olive oil (2 Tbsp [30 mL]) and place into the hot sauté pan to get a little color. You may need to do this in batches. Once one side sears, flip them over and sear the other side. Once both sides are seared, add them to the pot with the broth and replace the lid.

9. Allow the whole pot to simmer for about 3 to 4 more minutes. From the moment you started cooking your halibut, to the moment the Bouillabaisse is added to the bowls, should be about 12 minutes. It goes quickly! Evenly divide your Bouillabaisse into bowls. Serve with Rouille!

LAZY CIOPPINO

A true Cioppino *(pronounced CHUH-PEE-NO)* is made from super fresh seafood, but ... unwanted and leftover seafood on the San Francisco wharf. This means crabs missing legs, lobster sans claws, small unwanted shrimps and clams that may or may not ever open, etc. It's all fresh and "catch of the day," but... is akin to the meager late night selection offered (often discounted) at the local grocery store.

Traditionally, these super fresh, imperfect scraps were tossed, bones, shells and all, into a bubbling hot cauldron of olive oil, tomatoes, wine, garlic, and other aromatics like herbs and lemon. These would gurgle all day and would be scooped and served, as people donned bibs, demanded and devoured bowls of the stuff.

This recipe, as presented, is actually a quick or "Haste Cioppino" ... potentially even referred to as a "Lazy Cioppino," because it's been shelled, beheaded, and made easy to eat. Bib not required!

While I jokingly refer to myself as being in my hundreds, I do genuinely have a good 25 years of professional experience. I can appreciate what slow heat and mellow time can do to a bowl of acidic seafood. However, I've also acquired a taste for raw scallops and medium rare shrimp. I love the vibrancy of super fresh herbs, with their aromas *just being* released by the heat. Truth be told, my palate has changed and I tend to prefer fresh vibrancy over aged and broken down stew.

In the end, both ways are excellent and tasty, but I'm opting to keep this recipe fresh!

1/2 cup (120 mL) **extra virgin olive oil,** divided

1 cup (240 mL) **white wine,** good quality

1 small (110 g) **onion,** peeled and diced

4 each **garlic cloves,** minced

2 medium (182 g) **tomatoes,** diced

1 bulb (234 g) **fennel,** diced

2 ribs (101 g) **celery,** diced

1/2 tsp (2 mL) **chili flakes**

1 **bay leaf**

32 medium-sized (454 g) **clams,** fresh and alive

32 medium-sized (454 g) **mussels,** fresh and alive

1 lb (454 g) **shrimp**

1 1/2 lb (681 g) **halibut fillets**

3 tbsp (45 mL) **fresh lemon juice**

1 tsp (5 mL) chopped **fresh thyme**

1/2 tsp (2 mL) **fresh lemon** zest (peel)

salt and fresh cracked **pepper,** to taste

PER SERVING
CALORIES: 404.62
FAT: 17.6
PROTEIN: 43.3
CARBS: 11.23
FIBER: 1.76
SUGAR ALCOHOLS: 0
NET CARBS: 9.47

MORE FACTS: P. 508

1. In a large pot, add 1/4 cup (60 mL) of the olive oil, wine, onion, garlic, tomato, fennel, celery, chili flakes, and bay leaf, with a little salt and pepper. Put it on the stove over medium-low heat with a lid and allow it to simmer. Allow it to simmer for about 20 minutes. This will soften everything and allow all the flavors to meld together. (**Note:** should you decide to use crab or lobster, now would be the time to add to the pot. Just make sure it's split, cleaned and/or cracked.)

2. While the broth simmers, soak your fresh clams and mussels in a bowl of cold water, with a slow, steady stream of cold water dropping from the faucet into the bowl. This helps remove a touch of extra saltiness and sand. Let this sit with the water dripping on it. Pick your clams and mussels out of the bowl, by scooping them up with your hands, and transferring them to another bowl. Any sand or debris should be left at the bottom of the original bowl. Wash the original bowl. Place the new bowl of clams and mussels under the slow stream of cold water. Transfer your clams and mussels one more time. With a wet towel, pull the beards from the mussels. This is done by grabbing the beard with the towel and pinching hard between your fingers, then deliberately pulling OUT and towards the hinge. You may also want to scrub the outside of your mussel shells, if there are a lot of funky little barnacles, debris and other riddles and games attached to them. Once your clams and mussels are clean and happy, pull them up and out of the bowl and place them on a dry towel or in a colander to drip dry.

3. Peel shrimp and remove the big vein running through the back.

4. Cut your halibut into appropriate sizes. Large bite sized chunks is fine, but I opted for larger fillets. I thought it looked nicer when it was in the bowl. (**Note:** *Other fish is good, as well. Get whatever is fresh!*)

5. Place a large sauté pan on the stove over high heat.

6. Season your thick halibut fillets with salt and pepper. Also coat them with olive oil (2 tbsp [30 mL]). Place them in your hot sauté pan and get a nice brown color on one side. When the first side has color, turn the fish over and sear the other side.

7. When the second side of halibut has a nice sear, add your clams and mussels to the pan and shake everything around. Let sit for 30 seconds and then dump the halibut, clams, and mussels into the pot with the broth. Place the lid on the pot and allow it to continue simmering.

8. While that simmers, quickly clean out your hot sauté pan and keep it hot on high heat.

9. Season shrimp with salt and pepper. Coat them with olive oil (2 tbsp [30 mL]) and place into the hot sauté pan to get a little color. Once one side sears, flip them over and sear the other side. Once both sides are seared, add them to the pot with the broth. (**Note:** *I'd add large sea scallops at this point, and cook them in the same way.*)

10. Sprinkle the lemon juice, lemon zest, and fresh thyme over the top of the ingredients in the pot and give it a quick stir. Replace the lid and allow the whole pot to simmer for about 3 to 4 more minutes. From the moment you started searing your halibut, to the moment the Cioppino is added to the bowls, should be about 12 minutes. It goes quickly! Evenly divide your Cioppino into bowls and serve!

CHUH-PEE-NO, NOT BOOYAH-BASE

Sopa Sin Tortillas

SERVES: 8 · · · PREP: 30 MIN · · · COOK: 2 HR · · · TOTAL: 2 HR 30 MIN

8 cups (1.9 L) **chicken stock or broth**

2 **pork tenderloins**, cut into halves and cleaned (or 2 1/2 lbs. (1.1 kg) equivalent pork shoulder, cut into 4 large chunks)

1/2 Tbsp (8 mL) ground **cumin**

1 tsp (5 mL) ground **coriander**

1 Tbsp (15 mL) **lard** or favorite cooking oil

2 large (364 g) **ripe tomatoes**, coarsely chopped

1/2 seven-oz. can (98 g) **chipotle peppers in adobo sauce**

1 medium (110 g) **onion**, diced

4 **garlic cloves**, peeled

1/4 cup (60 mL) **freshly squeezed lime juice**

1 bunch (100 g) **cilantro**, washed and chopped

2 whole (272 g) **avocados**, peeled and sliced

1 1/2 cup (360 mL) **pork rind pieces**

1 cup (240 mL) **sour cream**

1 cup (240 mL) cubed **Monterey jack cheese**

salt and **pepper** to taste

PER SERVING
CALORIES: 429.58
FAT: 22.65
PROTEIN: 41.34
CARBS: 12.49
FIBER: 4.92
SUGAR ALCOHOLS: 0
NET CARBS: 7.58

MORE FACTS: P. 507

I live at the tip of Baja California Sur, in Mexico. There are hundreds of restaurants here. They pretty much all have some variation on the following dishes: Caesar salad, tortilla soup, and fish tacos. Tortilla soup is one of my favorite things to eat, on this here earth. Unfortunately, in a land of tortillas, alas, I cannot eat them. Thus, this soup has been renamed "Soup without Tortillas," or in Spanish, *Sopa sin Tortillas*!

1. Place the chicken stock into a medium-large soup pot. Place the pot on the stove, over medium heat.

2. Season the pork with a mixture of cumin, coriander, salt, and pepper.

3. Preheat a large sauté pan on the stove. Add lard or your favorite cooking oil, and quickly spread it around the bottom of the pan. Add the pork to the sauté pan and sear the outside of the pork. When one side is nice and browned, sear a new side. When the pork has been nicely browned on all sides, add to the chicken stock.

4. In a blender, puree the tomatoes, chipotles in adobo, onion, garlic, lime juice, and cilantro.

5. Add the tomato mixture to the chicken stock. Watch the soup mixture. When it begins to simmer, turn the heat down to a low simmer. Allow to simmer for roughly 2 hours, stirring and turning the pork occasionally.

6. When the pork is soft and tears easily with a fork, remove the pork and cut into large bite-sized chunks.

7. Season the soup base to taste. Add a little more salt and perhaps a touch more lime juice (I tend to like a lot in mine).

8. Divide the soup base and pork into 8 bowls. Garnish with optional garnishes of: cheese, sour cream, avocado, fresh cilantro, crumbled pork rinds, fresh diced onions, and/or fresh limes!

Curried Cauliflower

SERVES: 6 · · · PREP: 15 MIN · · · COOK: 20 MIN · · · TOTAL: 35 MIN

1 one-inch (22 g or 2.5 cm) **piece of ginger**, divided

2 Tbsp (30 mL) **ghee** or **coconut oil**, divided

3 **garlic cloves**, diced

1 tsp (5 mL) **garam masala**

2 tsp (10 mL) **ground turmeric**

1 tsp (5 mL) **ground cumin seed**

1 tsp (5 mL) **ground coriander seed**

1 tsp (5 mL) **chili flakes**

1 head (840 g) **large cauliflower**, chopped and divided

2 cups (480 mL) **vegetable stock**

1 13.5-ounce can (381 g) **coconut milk**

1 tsp (5 mL) **lemon juice**

6 sprigs fresh whole **cilantro leaves**, stems removed

salt and **pepper** to taste

PER SERVING
CALORIES: 210.20
FAT: 17.65
PROTEIN: 4.61
CARBS: 12.66
FIBER: 4.26
SUGAR ALCOHOLS: 0
NET CARBS: 8.4

MORE FACTS: P. 508

This is one of those "throw it in the pot and blend it" kind of soups I tend to make for lunch. It's quick to make, hard to mess up, and totally tasty! It's got a little spice and is very warming on a cold winter's day.

The garnish is obviously not required, and I rarely make such a thing for myself, but for those looking to impress, you can top it off with a little roasty-toasty cauliflower!

Tip: For a silky smooth soup, you can also run it through a very fine mesh strainer. However, this is far from required. Only recommended for the brave individual that likes super smooth soups and lots of extra dishes to do!

1. Preheat oven to 350°F (177°C).

2. Peel ginger and slice into two pieces, one twice as big as the other. Chop the big piece into a few large chunks and set aside. Slice the smaller piece into very thin, noodle-like strands. Set aside for the garnish.

3. Place a medium-sized soup pot, over medium heat. Add half of the ghee or oil to soup pot. Add garlic, larger ginger pieces, garam masala, turmeric, cumin, coriander, chili flakes, and a bit of salt and pepper. Stir until garlic is translucent and spices are aromatic (2 or 3 minutes). Add cauliflower to the pot and add some salt and pepper. Add vegetable stock to the pot. Cover the pot, turn to low heat, and simmer for 15 minutes.

4. While the soup simmers, melt the remaining ghee (or oil) over medium heat in a medium sauté pan. Add the thin noodle-like ginger to the pan and toss, coating it with fat. Add the cauliflower garnish to the pan, and season with salt and pepper. Toss the cauliflower in the pan to evenly coat with the fat. Place the pan in the oven to roast. Roast until cauliflower is soft and browned.

5. After the soup has simmered for 15 minutes, add the can of coconut milk and lemon juice. Season soup with salt and pepper while stirring. Once the soup begins to simmer, remove from heat. Puree the soup in a blender until smooth. If the soup is too thick, thin with more veggie stock.

6. Remove the garnish from the oven (if you haven't already), and toss with fresh cilantro leaves.

7. Place the soup in bowls, evenly dividing the roasted cauliflower garnish. Spoon any remaining flavorful browned fat onto the top of the soup. Serve!

Jambalaya

SERVES: 8 · · · PREP: 30 MIN · · · COOK: 60 MIN · · · TOTAL: 1 HR 15 MIN

2 Tbsp (30 mL) **unsalted butter**

1 medium (110 g) **onion**, diced

4 **garlic cloves**, peeled

1 (50 g) **celery rib**, diced

1 small (74 g) **green bell pepper**, diced

1/2 tsp (1 mL) **guar gum** (optional)

1/2 tsp (1 mL) **xanthan gum** (optional)

2 cups (480 mL) **chicken stock or broth**

2 (364 g) **large ripe tomatoes**, coarsely chopped

1 lb. (454 g) **ham**, diced

3 **bay leaves**

1 Tbsp (15 mL) **chili powder**

2 tsp (10 mL) chopped **fresh thyme**

1 1/2 lb. (681 g) **whole boneless chicken breasts** (or equivalent thigh meat, skin optional)

4 **Andouille links** (340 g) (or other Creole/Cajun smoked sausage; I often use Spanish chorizo), sliced into thick rings

1 lb (454 g) **shrimp (16/20)**, peel and deveined

salt and **pepper** to taste

PER SERVING
CALORIES: 417.46
FAT: 18.79
PROTEIN: 48.8
CARBS: 8.36
FIBER: 2.1
SUGAR ALCOHOLS: 0
NET CARBS: 6.27

MORE FACTS: P. 504

A jambalaya recipe is whole big thing. It's this and that, with a touch of the other. It's a big, gurgling hot cauldron of anything from alligator and rabbit to ham, shrimp, and tomatoes. It got its roots in the Caribbean, Africa, Spain, France, and the southern United States, depending who you ask... There is literally no end to the way this can be made. No set combination of ingredients is defined as jambalaya. It's more a concept... and a *delicious* one at that!

Funky Gums Note: Because Jambalaya normally has the rice mixed into it, the starch thickens it and it's a thicker meal. This version is more like a stew, which can be served with rice or a rice substitute (p 316). (I know people that love it on pasta too!) Because of this, you can add a little guar and xanthan gums, which will thicken it slightly. This is totally optional, but a nice way to throw a little more viscosity at it. I'm ok with a thinner stew base, but some good folks really seem to require a thicker consistency.

Paleo Alternative: In place of the two gums, you could make an arrowroot slurry by adding 2 tablespoons (30 mL) arrowroot powder to 1/4 cup (60 mL) water or cold chicken stock and whisk it in, and then whisk the slurry into the stew base once it first comes up to a simmer. This will add about 14 net carbs to the recipe, or about 2 extra net carbs, per serving.

1. In a large soup pot, over medium heat, add the butter to melt. Add the onions and garlic. Stir until onions and garlic are translucent, about 3 minutes. Add celery and bell pepper, and stir for another 3 minutes. If you choose to add the guar and xanthan gums, sprinkle them over the top of the vegetables while stirring. You want to spread it evenly and stir quickly to prevent clumping. Add chicken stock, tomatoes, ham, and bay leaves.

2. Place a large sauté pan on high heat on the stove. While the pan heats, in a mixing bowl, mix together the chili powder, thyme, and some salt and pepper. Dredge your chicken breasts in this mixture and coat evenly. Set aside. Add your slices of sausage to the pan, so their cut surfaces are facedown and evenly cover the bottom. This will add a nice color and flavor to the face of the sausage and will also pull some of the fat out of it, for the pan. When the edges of the sausage start to look nice and browned, flip each slice and brown the other side. When the sausages are cooked, remove, and add them to the soup pot. Immediately (don't let the empty sauté pan with the sausage fat burn!), add the chicken breasts to the hot sauté pan and cook them in the fat left behind by the sausages. Brown both sides of the chicken, and then add the seared but mostly raw chicken to the soup pot. Adjust the temperature of the soup pot to maintain a low and slow simmer. Cover the soup pot and allow to simmer for about 45 minutes. Check the chicken breasts with a fork. You will know the chicken is done when it tears easily with a fork.

3. When the chicken is ready, add the shrimp to the mixture and stir. With a fork, break the chicken into large chunks in the soup pot. Cover, and let simmer for 5 more minutes.

4. Adjust seasoning, check that the shrimp has been cooked through, and serve.

Sinful Crimini of Mushroom Soup

SERVES: 6 · · · PREP: 10 MIN · · · COOK: 30 MIN · · · TOTAL: 40 MIN

8 slices (200 g) **raw bacon**, chopped

1 medium (110 g) **onion**, diced

2 **garlic cloves**, minced

1 lb. (454 g) **crimini (portobello with the gills removed or button) mushrooms**, washed and sliced into little wedges

1 1/2 cups (360 mL) **chicken stock or broth**

2 Tbsp (30 mL) **Worcestershire sauce**

1 tsp (5 mL) chopped **fresh rosemary**

3/4 cup (180 mL) **heavy whipping cream**

1/4 cup (60 mL) **parsley leaves**, washed

3 Tbsp (45 mL) **extra virgin olive oil**

salt and **pepper** to taste

This soup is fantastic! It's so rich and creamy. With these baby portobello mushrooms, it almost becomes *meaty*. It's a wonderful soup that can be served for any meal, whether it be a simple dinner for one, the full family, or a special occasion!

Note: This could easily be vegetarian, by using vegetable stock rather than the chicken stock. Remove the bacon and just use a little olive oil for cooking the veggies. You could even make it completely vegan by using a blend of almond and coconut milk.

It also couldn't hurt to throw some nice Italian parsley leaves on top, or puree a small handful of spinach into the soup. You could even add some pine nuts for a little more textural contrast.

1. Cook the bacon in a medium-sized pot deep enough to cook the soup. When crispy, strain the bacon bits and set aside. Save fat for another day, but do not clean the pot.

2. Sweat and lightly caramelize the onions and garlic in the pot with the film of bacon fat. Add a touch of salt to help pull the water out. Add the mushrooms and a little more salt. Sauté for 15 minutes or until mushrooms are cooked. Remove and set aside enough mushrooms to use as a garnish later. Add the stock, Worcestershire sauce, and half the bacon bits. If you have any herbs, tossing some rosemary or thyme in would be delicious. Simmer for about 10 to 15 minutes. The mixture should be like wet mushrooms and not very soupy. Add the cream and bring to a simmer. Remove from heat and puree in a blender.

PER SERVING
CALORIES: 353.04
FAT: 32.83
PROTEIN: 7.66
CARBS: 7.84
FIBER: 1.15
SUGAR ALCOHOLS: 0
NET CARBS: 6.69

MORE FACTS: P. 510

3. While blending, adjust seasoning with salt and pepper. If soup is too thick, adjust consistency with more cream or warm chicken stock. A touch of sour cream sounds delightful as well, but it's not what I usually use. This is an "eyeball it" step. Use your discretion. The end result should be a pleasant-colored tan, creamy soup.

4. Dish into bowls and garnish with bacon bits, mushrooms, fresh herbs, and swirls of extra virgin olive oil and/or bacon fat.

Mexican Gazpacho

SERVES: 8 · · · PREP: 20 MIN · · · COOK: 5 MIN · · · TOTAL: 25 MIN

2 lb. (908 g) **fresh assorted tomatoes**, cut into chunks

1 (301 g) **English cucumber**, peeled, seeded, and cut into chunks

1 small (70 g) **sweet red onion**, cut into chunks

1 small (74 g) **red bell pepper**, seeded and cut into chunks

4 **garlic cloves**

2 Tbsp (30 mL) freshly squeezed **lemon juice**

2 Tbsp (30 mL) **red wine vinegar**

1/4 cup (60 mL) good quality **extra virgin olive oil**

1/4 lb. (114 g) **cherry tomatoes**, washed, dried, and halved or quartered

8 sprigs (20 g) fresh **cilantro**, stems removed

1/4 cup (60 mL) **sour cream**

1/2 tsp (2 mL) ground **cumin**

1 whole (136 g) **avocado**, peeled and sliced

salt and **pepper** to taste

Gazpacho is an ancient chilled vegetable soup hailing, *probably*, from Spain. It's essentially a variety of peak-of-season vegetables that is then pureed raw and poured into a bowl. I'll confess to not loving the concept of a gazpacho. It really sounds like a thick V-8 to me. However... when it's done right, and the vegetables are truly at their peak, probably home grown, bought from a local farm or farmer's market, there's a living vibrancy to it that's just unmistakable. It's a fantastic soup for any summer day!

Because I'm in Mexico, I'm going to give this one a subtle Latin flair! My recipe is garnished with a light salsa, some cilantro leaves, and a cumin crema!

1. In a blender, combine the tomatoes, onions, cucumbers, bell peppers, garlic, vinegar, and lemon. Season with a small amount of salt and pepper. Puree. While the blender is pureeing the soup, slowly pour in the olive oil. Taste and adjust seasoning.

2. **Optional Step:** Strain the soup through a fine mesh sieve. This will give it a smoother texture.

3. Divide the soup into 8 soup bowls.

4. In a separate bowl, toss together the cherry tomatoes, salt, pepper, and cilantro leaves. Split this mixture eight ways, and place a small amount in the center of each bowl.

5. In another bowl, mix the cumin with the sour cream. Some sour creams are thicker than others. If it's too thick, you can add a small amount of water to thin it out. Spoon the cumin crema in a circle, around the tomato garnish.

6. Top the soup with thin slices of ripe avocado. Serve!

PER SERVING
CALORIES: 151.49
FAT: 10.81
PROTEIN: 3.87
CARBS: 11.39
FIBER: 3.52
SUGAR ALCOHOLS: 0
NET CARBS: 7.87

MORE FACTS: P. 509

TURKEY MEATBALL SOUP KALE AND ROASTED PEPPERS

SERVES: 6 · · · PREP: 15 MIN · · · COOK: 30 MIN · · · TOTAL: 45 MIN

2 Tbsp (30 mL) **butter**, divided

1 small (110 g) **onion**, diced and divided

4 **garlic cloves**, minced and divided

1 lb. (454 g) **ground turkey**

1 large **egg**

1 Tbsp (15 mL) **ground chia seed** (optional)

1 Tbsp (15 mL) **fresh chopped sage**

1/2 lb. (227 g) **kale**, washed and very roughly chopped

2 small (148 g) **roasted bell peppers**, peeled, seeded, and sliced

6 cups (1.1 L) **chicken broth**

salt and **pepper** to taste

Interestingly, this was conceived of as a holiday-themed soup. From the green and red colors and the hearty use of winter kale, to the fact that turkey is a common holiday fowl, this soup was inspired by all things chilly, wintry, and celebratory. Aside from the actual forming of the meatballs (which, frankly, could just as easily be treated like the ground beef in the Taco Soup [p. 157]), this goes quick, has fantastic nutrients, and is quite tasty on a cold, snowy day!

1. In a sauté pan, over medium-high heat, sauté half of the onions and garlic, in 1 tablespoon (15 mL) of butter. Add a little salt and pepper. Sauté for about 5 minutes. A little brown color is fine. Once this is done, set aside.

2. Mix together the turkey, egg, optional ground chia, fresh sage, salt, pepper, and onion mixture. Combine well with your hands.

3. Roll small meatballs with your hands, about 1/2 to 3/4 ounces per ball (about 15 to 20 g).

4. In a large soup pot, over medium-high heat, sauté the meatballs in the remaining 1 tablespoon (15 mL) of butter. Once the surface of the meatballs are nice and browned, turn the heat to low, and add the remaining half of the onions and garlic. After about 3 to 5 minutes, the onions will be translucent. Add the kale and peppers, and sauté for about 3 more minutes. Season with a bit of salt and pepper.

5. Add the chicken broth and allow to simmer for roughly 20 minutes or until the meatballs are completely cooked through.

6. Taste, adjust seasoning, and serve!

PER SERVING
CALORIES: 210.82
FAT: 11.52
PROTEIN: 17.72
CARBS: 9.29
FIBER: 1.12
SUGAR ALCOHOLS: 0
NET CARBS: 7.41

MORE FACTS: P. 505

Salads

○ ○ ○

I never in my life thought I'd love salad or eat as many salads as I do. It could be said that two things happened:

1. My definition of a salad has changed.
2. My palate has also changed.

A salad to me was always iceberg lettuce, tomatoes, and some kind of nonfat dressing. Basically, a big ol' plate of "why bother." Now, a salad is a common and quite regular meal for me, but... my salads today are nothing like the salads I was given as a kid. Now they're full of a wide variety of different lettuces and vegetables, raw or cooked, untouched or highly manipulated, loads of cheeses, fats, meats, nuts, herbs, and other sweet and tart flavors. A salad is no longer that little weird bowl at the beginning of the meal, but it is now, more often than not, the *entire* meal.

GREATEST SALAD EVER!

SERVES: 4 · · · PREP: 10 MIN · · · COOK: 10 MIN · · · TOTAL: 20 MIN

4 cups (960 mL) **mixed baby greens,** washed

1 lb. (454 g) **fresh mozzarella,** cubed

1 lb. (454 g) **fresh tomatoes,** cubed

16 **fresh basil** leaves, hand torn

1/4 cup (60 mL) **balsamic vinegar**

1/4 cup (60 mL) **extra virgin olive oil**

4 5 to 6 oz. (605 g) **boneless chicken breasts,** cubed (or equivalent thigh meat, skin optional)

2 **garlic cloves,** minced

8 slices (200 g) **raw bacon,** chopped

salt and **pepper** to taste

I probably eat this salad at least once a week, and have for a few years. It's probably the backbone of my entire outlook on this way of eating. It's fresh, warm, comforting, delicious, a little sweet, and a little dangerous; it has no Frankenfoods; it's a combination of cooked and raw ingredients; plus... it has BACON!

This salad also illustrates the power of the warm salad. It's a quick and easy full-fledged meal. Throw a variety of cooked ingredients into a bowl along with some raw ingredients, and you've got a super nutrient-dense and instantly delicious dinner!

Try pancetta with cut-up hard-boiled eggs, tomatoes, spinach, lemon juice, and a bit of fresh rosemary or a mix of endive, radicchio, and watercress with some pesto, roasted peppers, thinly sliced raw onions, and spicy Italian sausage! This concept can be twisted to form numerous different meals, all while maintaining an interesting variety. Try beef with fish sauce, fresh mint, basil, ginger, and thinly sliced romaine, peppers, and onions! Go a bit Thai! YUM!

1. In a large salad bowl, add greens, mozzarella, tomatoes, and large pieces of hand-torn basil leaves, keeping the tomatoes on the side of the bowl, in a nice pile. Season the tomatoes with a little salt and pepper (the salt will pull the tomato juice from the tomatoes, which will mix with the salad later).

2. In a cup, place the olive oil and balsamic vinegar. Set the vinaigrette aside.

3. In a medium bowl, mix the cut chicken with the chopped garlic. Season the chicken with a little salt and pepper.

PER SERVING
CALORIES: 933.43
FAT: 69.78
PROTEIN: 59.72
CARBS: 9.68
FIBER: 2.26
SUGAR ALCOHOLS: 0
NET CARBS: 7.42

MORE FACTS: P. 512

4. In a sauté pan, over medium heat, cook the bacon until it is crispy. Remove the bacon from the bacon grease and set aside, while leaving the grease in the hot pan. Add the seasoned chicken to the hot bacon fat and cook until the chicken is cooked through. At the last minute, add the bacon back into the chicken, simply to warm it up.

5. Pour the vinaigrette over the top of the salad in the salad bowl.

6. Pour the hot chicken, bacon, and bacon fat over the tomatoes in the salad bowl.

7. Quickly toss the salad, serve, and eat! It should slightly wilt and have a great sweet bacon taste!

Seriously, just the best salad, ever!

Cucumber Mint Salad

SERVES: 8 · · · PREP: 10 MIN · · · COOK: 0 MIN · · · TOTAL: 20 MIN

2 (602 g) **English cucumbers**, sliced into very thin rings

1 small (110 g) **red onion**, very thinly sliced

1/4 cup (60 mL) plain, full fat **Greek yogurt**

2 Tbsp (30 mL) **freshly squeezed lime juice**

1/4 cup (60 mL) **fresh mint**, leaves sliced thin

salt and **pepper** to taste

I'm not going to mislead you, dear friends. I find cucumbers as exciting as I find garden gnomes. They hold virtually nothing over me. I understand that they exist and that some people *love* them for a variety of reasons. I recognize the passion that *can* exist. Alas, I have no passion for cucumbers. However, I run a recipe-based website, and I need to fill certain holes and use certain ingredients and appeal to the people that *do* have a cucumber passion. This recipe is for those folks.

(I secretly loved this salad when I made it... and continually dipped my fingers in the bowl for another mouthful. Don't tell anyone!)

1. In a large salad bowl, combine and mix all the ingredients.

2. Allow it to rest and macerate for about 10 minutes.

3. Mix it one more time.

4. Serve!

PER SERVING
CALORIES: 27.37
FAT: 0.72
PROTEIN: 0.48
CARBS: 5.01
FIBER: 0.45
SUGAR ALCOHOLS: 5
NET CARBS: 4.56

MORE FACTS: P. 510

COLORFUL ASIAN SLAW

SERVES: 6 · · · PREP: 15 MIN · · · COOK: 0 MIN · · · TOTAL: 25 MIN

This stuff is absolutely addictive! With a helpful slicing tool, like a plastic Japanese mandolin (watch your fingers!), something like this can be whipped up in just a few minutes. This is cold and perfect for a box lunch paired with something like a chilled chicken breast. It would also be excellent as a potluck salad. Not only is it bright and colorful, but the sweet crunch combined with the stronger ginger and sesame flavors will also have everyone asking for the recipe.

1. In a large salad bowl, combine and mix all the ingredients, except the sesame seeds.

2. Allow it to rest and macerate for about 10 minutes.

3. Mix it one more time.

4. Serve, garnished with the sesame seeds.

1 small head (304 g) **Napa cabbage**, shredded

2 small (148 g) **red bell peppers**, seeded and sliced thin

1 small (72 g) **carrot**, peeled and sliced into very thin strips

1 cup (240 mL) **snow peas**, sliced into very thin strips

1 small (110 g) **red onion**, sliced thin

4 whole (60 g) **green onions (scallions)**, sliced thin

1/4 cup (60 mL) **soy sauce (or coconut aminos)**

1/4 cup (60 mL) **rice wine vinegar**

1 Tbsp (15 mL) chopped **fresh ginger**

4 **garlic cloves**, minced

2 Tbsp (30 mL) **sesame oil**

2 Tbsp (30 mL) **sugar replacement**

2 Tbsp (30 mL) toasted **black sesame seeds** (or regular toasted sesame seeds)

salt and **pepper** to taste

PER SERVING
CALORIES: 132.41
FAT: 6.59
PROTEIN: 2.95
CARBS: 16.07
FIBER: 3.17
SUGAR ALCOHOLS: 5
NET CARBS: 7.9

MORE FACTS: P. 511

Green Beans, Asparagus, and Heartichoke Salad

SERVES: 4 · · · PREP: 15 MIN · · · COOK: 5 MIN · · · TOTAL: 20 MIN

1 bunch (227 g) **asparagus**, fibrous ends removed

1/2 lb. (227 g) **green beans**, ends removed

8 whole (222 g) **artichoke hearts in oil**, drained and cut into 8 wedges, each

1/4 cup (30 mL) **toasted pine nuts**

1 Tbsp (15 mL) coarsely chopped **capers**

2 **garlic cloves**, crushed

2 tsp (10 mL) chopped **fresh oregano** (and/or thyme, rosemary, sage, or marjoram)

1/4 cup (60 mL) **good quality extra virgin olive oil**, divided

2 Tbsp (30 mL) **freshly squeezed lemon juice**

salt and **pepper** to taste

This is a fun little salad or side dish. It's very basic in its ingredients but has *amazing* flavors! When I first thought of the idea, I called it Green Things Salad. I'm not quite sure why, as a "green thing" to me is usually parsley or some other kind of herb; this does have some oregano, but it's not an overly herby salad. Because of the blanch-and-shock method being used, the veggies hold their incredibly bright green color, even though they are cooked. It's really just a well-cooked blend of asparagus, green beans, and artichoke hearts. Brilliant! (In reference to the color, of course.)

1. Place a medium-sized pot with about a gallon (3.8 L) of water on the stove to boil. Once it boils, add about a scant 1/4 cup (50 mL) of salt.

2. The idea is to cut the beans and asparagus on the bias. Imagine an asparagus stalk. Rather than cutting it straight down, turn the stalk 45 degrees and cut every 1/4 inch (6 mm) or so. You'll wind up with little diamond-shaped pieces of asparagus. Kinda fun! Now, imagine doing an even more exaggerated version of that! Turn it about 80 degrees, and cut about every 2 millimeters. This should result in long thin strips of asparagus! If you do the same thing with the green beans, you've got something thin, attractive, a bit different, and something eager to be coated with a simple lemon-herb dressing! Cut the asparagus and green beans on a very strong bias, resulting in thin strips about 1 to 1 1/2 inches (3 cm) long.

3. Place a colander or food strainer in an empty sink. Also, gather a medium-sized bowl filled about halfway with ice water. Have both of these ready and waiting.

4. Drop your beans and asparagus into the boiling water and stir to submerge. Allow to cook for about 30 to 45

PER SERVING
CALORIES: 276.09
FAT: 28.06
PROTEIN: 4.96
CARBS: 14.41
FIBER: 6.48
SUGAR ALCOHOLS: 0
NET CARBS: 7.94

MORE FACTS: P. 513

seconds (1 to 1 1/2 minutes if left whole or largely whole). Immediately pour the contents through the strainer and then transfer the veggies into the ice water to chill completely through.

5. While the veggies chill, in a medium-sized salad bowl, add the artichoke hearts, capers, pine nuts, chopped oregano, garlic, lemon juice, and olive oil. Strain the veggies from the ice, and maybe even blot with a paper towel to get the extra water off of them. Add the dried and chilled green beans and asparagus to the salad bowl. Toss all the ingredients with a bit of salt and pepper. Taste, adjust seasoning, and serve!

CURRIED CHICKEN SALAD

SERVES: 4 · · · PREP: 15 MIN · · · COOK: 0 MIN · · · TOTAL: 15 MIN

1 1/2 lb. (681 g) **cooked chicken meat**, diced

1/2 small (35 g) **red onion**, diced

1/2 cup (120 mL) diced **celery**

1/4 cup (60 mL) chopped **raisins**

2 tsp (10 mL) **curry powder**

1 cup (240 mL) **mayonnaise**

1/4 cup (60 mL) **toasted slivered almonds**

2 tsp (10 mL) **fresh lemon juice**

1/2 bunch (50 g) **cilantro**, washed, large stems removed, and chopped

salt and **pepper** to taste

I have a habit of buying those roasted chickens at the grocery store. I usually eat half and then pick the other half and toss it into stir-frys, eggs, soups, and... this recipe right here! Skin, dark meat, oysters, and all—point being: leftover chicken around my house is *always* a good thing! It's yum! One could also just take four chicken breasts and/or thighs, coat them with a little olive oil, salt and pepper, roast them at about 400°F (204°C) until done (about 15 minutes, with an internal temperature of 165°F [74°C]), let them cool, and then cut them up. That's another way to get the chicken. You could also use canned! I usually eat this in a lettuce leaf, like a wrap or taco, but you could also use some form of low-primal bread if you'd like.

Note: For those with a higher tolerance to carbs, you can double the raisins and even toss some diced apple into this. FANTASTIC!

> Just a whisper of raisins!

1. Combine.

2. Eat.

3. Smile!

PER SERVING
CALORIES: 685.4
FAT: 48.91
PROTEIN: 50.01
CARBS: 11.93
FIBER: 1.85
SUGAR ALCOHOLS: 0.06
NET CARBS: 10.02

MORE FACTS: P. 513

Thai Cucumber Salad

SERVES: 8 · · · PREP: 10 MIN · · · COOK: 0 MIN · · · TOTAL: 40 MIN

When I posted to my blog a recipe for the surprisingly popular Thai Fish Cakes (p. 138), I included a small little note suggesting that people serve this with a Thai cucumber salad, followed by brief instructions for assembly. Interestingly, I received a few comments on those brief instructions, with people actually trying it and suggesting it was, indeed, a perfect pairing! Here it is, in full recipe form!

Variations: I've seen many variations on this. Fun additions are toasted peanuts, red Thai chilies, shredded carrots, slivered red bell peppers, green mango, lime juice, cilantro leaves, mint leaves, etc.

1. In a large salad bowl, combine and mix all the ingredients.

2. Allow to sit and macerate for at least 30 minutes, mixing occasionally. This is *really* excellent if left to sit overnight.

3. Mix it one more time.

4. Serve!

2 (602 g) **English cucumber**, sliced into very thin rings

1 small (110 g) **red onion**, very thinly sliced

2 **jalapeño peppers**, seeds removed and thinly sliced

1/4 cup (60 mL) **rice wine vinegar**

1/4 cup (60 mL) **sugar replacement**

2 Tbsp (30 mL) **fish sauce**

1 tsp (5 mL) **salt**

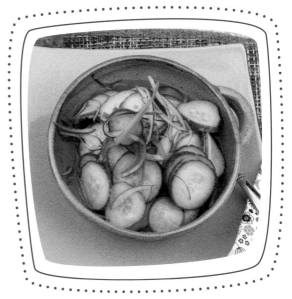

PER SERVING
CALORIES: 21.63
FAT: 0.01
PROTEIN: 0.37
CARBS: 12.45
FIBER: 0.73
SUGAR ALCOHOLS: 7.5
NET CARBS: 4.22

MORE FACTS: P. 511

Sausage, Tomato, and Fresh Mozzarella Tower

SERVES: 4 · · · PREP: 15 MIN · · · COOK: 10 MIN · · · TOTAL: 25 MIN

1 lb. (454 g) **raw Italian Chicken Sausage** (p. 480)

1 lb. (454 g) **assorted fresh tomatoes**

1 lb. (454 g) **fresh mozzarella cheese**

2 Tbsp (30 mL) **chopped capers**

2 Tbsp (30 mL) **fresh lemon juice**

1 tsp (5 mL) minced **fresh lemon zest**

2 tsp (10 mL) chopped **fresh oregano**

2 **garlic cloves**, minced

1/4 cup (60 mL) **extra virgin olive oil**

salt and **pepper** to taste

Note: Obviously, you don't need to stack this like the Leaning Tower of Pisa. Perhaps just arrange them in three small stacks instead.

PER SERVING
CALORIES: 696.65
FAT: 53.11
PROTEIN: 42.35
CARBS: 7.89
FIBER: 2.24
SUGAR ALCOHOLS: 0
NET CARBS: 5.65

MORE FACTS: P. 512

I must have just come fresh off of a Jenga tournament, as I opted to make a chicken and cheese tower and call it salad. The funny part is, it reminded me of my younger days working in restaurants, at a place and time where the name of the game was "tall food." So many things seemed based around culinary architecture. I remember a specific salad which combined nothing more than local, seasonal tomatoes sliced and stacked as high as possible, alternating planks of fresh grilled olive and herb bread. It was a sight to behold! Poor waiters...

1. Form the Italian sausage into 12 small patties, each weighing just over an ounce (38 g).

2. Slice the tomatoes into 12 or more slices and set aside. Slice the mozzarella into 12 slices and set aside.

3. In a small mixing bowl, combine capers, lemon zest, lemon juice, oregano, garlic, and olive oil, with a bit of salt and pepper.

4. Heat a large sauté pan or skillet over medium-high heat. When the pan is hot, place the sausage patties in the pan (you shouldn't need to add any oil; the sausage will have plenty of fat), making sure they are spread evenly and barely touching one another (you may need to do this in two pans). Once they are seared a nice golden, flip them and sear the other side. Turn the heat down to medium low and allow them to continue cooking until cooked through (about 4 to 5 minutes).

5. While the sausages cook, distribute the tomatoes on 4 plates. Season the tomatoes with a bit of salt and pepper. Layer the fresh mozzarella slices over the tomatoes, and season them with salt and pepper.

6. When the sausages are cooked through, place 3 of them on each stack of mozzarella and tomatoes. With a spoon, mix the caper dressing and drizzle equal portions over the top of each sausage patty. Serve warm!

Shrimp and Mango Stuffed Tomato

SERVES: 8 · · · PREP: 15 MIN · · · COOK: 5 MIN · · · TOTAL: 20 MIN

2 lb. (908 g) **shrimp** (31/35), peeled and deveined

2 Tbsp (30 mL) **coconut oil**

4 small (454 g) **tomatoes** (about 1/4 lb. each)

1 (70 g) **sweet red onion**, very thinly sliced

1 small (74 g) **roasted red bell pepper**, seeded and very thinly sliced

1 small (392 g) **mango**, peeled, cored, and sliced thin

2 Tbsp (30 mL) **fresh lime juice**

1/2 bunch (50 g) **cilantro**, washed, large stems removed, and chopped

salt and **pepper** to taste

PER SERVING
CALORIES: 186.23
FAT: 5.43
PROTEIN: 23.82
CARBS: 9.69
FIBER: 1.70
SUGAR ALCOHOLS: 0
NET CARBS: 8.36

MORE FACTS: P. 512

This is another walk on the wild side with tropical fruits. Again, I love to use these fruits in recipes, but within reasonable amounts—enough to give satisfaction and eliminate the sense that certain foods are "off limits." Frankly, I find it hard to believe that anyone's day had ever been ruined by excess of mangos. Sure, as a general rule, it's probably not wise to eat loads of fruit sugar, but mango is delicious, sweet, and wonderful in salads with seafood! As an interesting side note, it's also fairly low glycemic, so even though it's higher in carbs, it'll absorb more slowly than, say, a banana.

1. Preheat a large sauté pan or skillet over high heat.

2. Season the shrimp with salt and pepper. Add the coconut oil to the hot pan and swirl to coat the pan. Add the shrimp to the pan and sauté. These shrimp will cook quickly, so don't overcook them. Cook until translucent but still slightly opaque, or desired doneness. Place the shrimp on a large plate, spread them evenly, and place in the fridge to cool.

3. Wash the tomatoes and carefully remove the stem end. Cut them in half and scoop out the seeds (you can save this for sauce, juice, or soup, or discard). Season the insides with a bit of salt and pepper. Place each in the center of eight different plates.

4. In a large mixing bowl, combine the onion, roasted peppers, mango slices, lime, and cilantro with a bit of salt and pepper. Mix well. Allow to sit for about 10 minutes, marinating and macerating.

5. Remove the chilled shrimp and add to the bowl with the salad. Taste, adjust seasoning, mix, and evenly divide the salad between each of the 8 tomato halves. Serve!

Mixed Greens with Blackberries, Bacon, and Goat Cheese

SERVES: 4 · · · PREP: 10 MIN · · · COOK: 0 MIN · · · TOTAL: 10 MIN

I like a good salad. I like bacon. I like free time. I like berries. When I have a salad that has bacon and berries, and is quick and easy to make, it zooms right to the top of my favorite salads list. There's no deep mystery to this salad. There's no salad dressing that needs to be made. There's only the basic natural alchemy emanating from the right ingredients, pulled together at the right time, and tossed in a bowl. This sweet, salty, and crunchy salad is fantastic and can go on just about any table in the land.

1 cup (240 mL) **fresh blackberries**, washed

4 cups (960 mL) **mixed greens**, washed and dried

1/4 cup (60 mL) **fresh mint leaves**, washed and dried

1/4 cup (60 mL) real **bacon bits**

1/4 cup (60 mL) **broken walnut halves**

2 Tbsp (30 mL) **balsamic vinegar**

1/4 cup (60 mL) **extra virgin olive oil**

1/4 cup (60 mL) **goat cheese**

salt and **pepper** to taste

1. In a large salad bowl, add your blackberries. With a sturdy fork, squish the berries, so that they are somewhat smooshed. You want them to be broken up enough to release some blackberry juice, but not so broken up that they no longer look like blackberries. Do a partial smoosh. (Yes, I use only the most technical of terms. *wink*)

2. Add the rest of the ingredients to the bowl, except the goat cheese. Toss lightly.

3. With your fingers, break up little pieces of the goat cheese all over the top of the salad. Toss it lightly.

4. Serve.

PER SERVING
CALORIES: 327.78
FAT: 28.61
PROTEIN: 11.48
CARBS: 9.63
FIBER: 3.39
SUGAR ALCOHOLS: 0
NET CARBS: 6.24

MORE FACTS: P. 513

GREEK SALAD

SERVES: 8 · · · PREP: 15 MIN · · · COOK: 0 MIN · · · TOTAL: 15 MIN

1 lb. (454 g) **fresh assorted tomatoes**, cut into thin slices or wedges

1 (301 g) **English cucumber**, seeded and cut into small cubes

1 small (70 g) **sweet red onion**, very thinly sliced

1 small (74 g) **red bell pepper**, seeded and cut into small cubes

1/4 cup (60 mL) chopped **Kalamata olives**

2 tsp (10 mL) chopped **fresh oregano**

2 **garlic cloves**, minced

2 Tbsp (30 mL) **fresh lemon juice**

2 Tbsp (30 mL) **red wine vinegar**

1/2 cup (120 mL) **extra virgin olive oil**

1 lb. (454 g) **feta cheese**, cut into cubes

salt and **pepper** to taste

This is a salad made of myriad colors, flavors, and textures. I think it's very pretty, very healthy, and full of nutrients. I have some friends that grow sprouts and supply local restaurants. The first day I made this salad, they brought over some lovely sunflower sprouts for me. (**Side note:** sprouts are awesome foodstuffs and one of the only things people eat while it's still alive!) I confess to distrusting pickled cheese, but... I had a request for Greek salad and whipped this up. I tasted it and thought it was fantastic. Someday, should I ever get over my fear of feta, I'm sure I'd love a bowl for lunch!

1. Assemble all your ingredients, except the feta, in a salad bowl. Allow to sit for 5 to 10 minutes, so it can absorb the flavors and soften a bit.

2. Add the feta cheese, and carefully toss the salad. Try not to break apart the cubes of feta.

3. Divide the salad between 8 plates or bowls. Garnish with fresh parsley or sprouts.

PER SERVING
CALORIES: 307.53
FAT: 25.66
PROTEIN: 10.9
CARBS: 9.34
FIBER: 1.8
SUGAR ALCOHOLS: 0
NET CARBS: 7.54

MORE FACTS: P. 513

THE GREAT WEDGE

SERVES: 6 · · · PREP: 15 MIN · · · COOK: 0 MIN · · · TOTAL: 15 MIN

Iceberg lettuce is little more than crunchy water. It doesn't have much to it, but I've come to one logical conclusion. This is the salad that gets fed to men that don't like salads. *This* salad is like the steak of salads! I have to assume that a vegetarian would look at this like a steak, right? It's a man salad, for a man. Sure, a woman can order and eat the steak of salads, but a man can order the Great Wedge and still feel like a man. So, for those of you out there facing feeding picky eaters, people who won't eat their salads, here's one to put in front of them. The Great Wedge... the steak of salads!

1 small head (324 g) **iceberg lettuce**, washed

2 oz. (56 g) **quality Roquefort cheese**, crumbled

1/2 lb. (227 g) **cherry tomatoes**, washed, dried, and halved or quartered

1/4 cup (60 mL) **real bacon bits**

1/4 cup (60 mL) **parsley leaves**, washed

1 Tbsp (15 mL) **extra virgin olive oil**

1/2 cup (120 mL) **Blue Cheese Dressing (p. 365)**

salt and **pepper** to taste

1. Cut the iceberg lettuce into quarters. Often, the core will be "rusty." Cut off the rust, but leave each core quarter intact, as it's what holds all the leaves together.

2. In a small mixing bowl, combine Roquefort cheese crumbles, tomatoes, parsley, bacon, olive oil, and a bit of salt and pepper. Toss them together and set aside.

3. Place a wedge of lettuce, with the round side of the wedge on the bottom, on each of four plates. Divide the tomato mixture over the top of the 4 wedges and then drizzle a healthy portion of blue cheese dressing over each plate. Finally, season the whole plate with a bit more salt and pepper. Serve!

PER SERVING
CALORIES: 237.06
FAT: 20.04
PROTEIN: 10.02
CARBS: 5.81
FIBER: 1.7
SUGAR ALCOHOLS: 0.02
NET CARBS: 4.09

MORE FACTS: P. 512

The Famous Cobb Salad

SERVES: 6 · · · PREP: 15 MIN · · · COOK: 0 MIN · · · TOTAL: 15 MIN

1 cup (240 mL) chopped **Belgian endive**

1 cup (240 mL) coarsely chopped **watercress**

1 cup (240 mL) shredded **iceberg lettuce**

1 cup (240 mL) shredded **romaine lettuce**

4 cooked and chilled **chicken breast halves** (344 g) (skin on if possible)

12 slices (336 g) **bacon**, precooked and crispy

2 **hard-boiled eggs**, peeled and chopped or cut in half

1/4 lb. (114 g) quality **Roquefort cheese**, crumbled

1/2 lb. (227 g) **cherry tomatoes**, washed, dried, and halved or quartered

2 whole (272 g) **avocados**, peeled and sliced or diced

4 whole (60 g) **green onions** (scallions), sliced

2 **garlic cloves**, minced

1 Tbsp (15 mL) **Dijon mustard**

1 Tbsp (15 mL) **freshly squeezed lemon juice**

2 Tbsp (30 mL) **red wine vinegar**

1/4 cup (60 mL) **good quality extra virgin olive oil**

salt and **pepper** to taste

PER SERVING
CALORIES: 395.33
FAT: 31.74
PROTEIN: 28.86
CARBS: 8.45
FIBER: 4.49
SUGAR ALCOHOLS: 0
NET CARBS: 3.95

MORE FACTS: P. 514

Here we have the famous Cobb salad. It's not really known where this particular salad originated, but it generally seems to be attributed to the Brown Derby restaurant in the late 1920s or 1930s. It's a ninety-year-old salad, and... it's great for a low-primal way of life! It's got a wide mixture of salad greens, vegetables, and healthy fats from a variety of ingredients. In fact, the odd assortment of ingredients, while building a truly healthy and wonderful combination of fats and nutrients, is a bit puzzling to me. After having made it and combing through information about the salad, I really have begun to subscribe to the idea that Robert Howard Cobb (the owner of the Brown Derby) was hungry late one night and raided his kitchen. He grabbed a little of this and a little of that, combining a random assortment of freshly prepared ingredients, tossed them into a bowl, and topped it all with salad dressing.

Note: This recipe implies you have a few precooked, chilled, ready-to-go ingredients. Pay close attention to the list of ingredients, as the salad can be a bit time consuming just gathering the stuff!

1. In a large salad bowl, or nicely presented in four smaller salad bowls, start by mixing the endive, watercress, iceberg, and romaine lettuces. Layer the chicken, bacon, eggs, cheese, tomatoes, avocadoes, and green onions on the top. Be sure to season the tomatoes with a little salt and pepper.

2. In a separate bowl, whisk together the garlic, mustard, lemon juice, vinegar, and oil with a bit of salt and pepper. Whisk it well to form a slightly creamy consistency. The mustard should help form an emulsified red wine vinaigrette. Taste and adjust seasoning.

3. Pour the dressing over the salad and serve!

The Famous Salad Niçoise

SERVES: 4 · · · PREP: 15 MIN · · · COOK: 10 MIN · · · TOTAL: 25 MIN

2 Tbsp (30 mL) **Dijon mustard**

2 Tbsp (30 mL) **freshly squeezed lemon juice**

4 sprigs chopped, **fresh tarragon leaves**

1 **garlic clove**, minced

2 Tbsp (30 mL) finely diced **shallots**

2 tsp (10 mL) chopped **capers**

1/2 cup (120 mL) **extra virgin olive oil**

1/2 lb. (227 g) **green beans**, ends removed

4 cups (960 mL) **butterhead (a.k.a., Boston or Bibb) lettuce**

1/4 cup (60 mL) coarsely chopped assorted **French olives**

1/2 lb. (227 g) **cherry tomatoes**, halved or quartered

16 **boneless anchovy filets**

4 (672 g) super fresh **tuna steaks** (yellowfin [ahi] or albacore)

1 Tbsp (15 mL) **lard, olive oil,** or **ghee**

4 **hard-boiled eggs**, peeled and chopped or cut in half

salt and **pepper** to taste

PER SERVING
CALORIES: 365.86
FAT: 12.15
PROTEIN: 49.51
CARBS: 11.58
FIBER: 4.01
SUGAR ALCOHOLS: 0
NET CARBS: 7.57

MORE FACTS: P. 514

Much like the Cobb salad, salad Niçoise is also up for interpretation. The term *Niçoise* simply means it's a dish made with the type of foods a chef in Nice, France, might use. This very likely implies it's going to be fresh, in-season produce; fresh and locally caught fish; and some kind of tasty salad dressing. Some clearly common ingredients are tuna and anchovies. Other usual suspects are green beans, tomatoes, and potatoes. There tends to be a wide assortment of pickled goodies, like olives, capers, and artichoke hearts, as well as hard-boiled eggs, carrots, red beets, golden beets, radishes, cucumbers, green onions, red onions, white onions, celery, shallots, garlic, etc.

I think the point is, if it's fresh, in-season, and yummy, throw it in there!

1. Place a medium-sized pot of water on the stove to boil.

2. In a mixing bowl, whisk together garlic, Dijon, lemon juice, shallots, capers, and fresh tarragon, with a little salt and pepper. While whisking your mustard mixture, slowly pour in your oil. This should emulsify (blend the oil in) the dressing, creating something thicker and creamier than a "broken" vinaigrette (one that is separated). Set aside.

3. Get a bowl of ice water and set it near your sink.

4. Heavily season your boiling water with salt (about 2 tablespoons [30 mL]). Add green beans to the water and allow to boil until cooked about 95 percent of the way done. They should still be a bit crunchy; this should take somewhere between 2 and 5 minutes, depending on the thickness of the beans and personal preference. When the beans are cooked, strain them out of the boiling water and immediately place them into the bowl of ice water. Set aside to chill.

5. In a large salad bowl, add your torn or sliced lettuce, olives, tomatoes, and anchovies (as well as anything else you might choose to add to this concoction). At this point, your green beans should be thoroughly chilled. Pull the green beans from the ice water and shake off any extra moisture. Add them to the bowl. Add about 3/4 of your dressing to the bowl with a little salt and pepper. Mix well and then distribute between four different plates.

6. Preheat a sauté pan or skillet on the stove over high heat. Season tuna with salt and pepper.

7. Add oil to the pan and swirl it around, being careful not to burn it. Place the tuna steaks into the hot pan. They should not touch one another. Sear each side of each piece of tuna for about 30 seconds. Merely sear the outside, leaving the center completely raw. Once all sides are seared, remove them from the pan.

8. Slice each tuna steak and fan it over the top of each salad. Drizzle the remaining vinaigrette over the tuna. Garnish with hard-boiled eggs and serve!

Famously Fishy!

Chilled Soy-Lime Flank Steak Salad

SERVES: 4 · · · PREP: 15 MIN · · · COOK: 10 MIN · · · TOTAL: 25 MIN

1 1/2 lb. (681 g) **beef flank, tenderloin, sirloin, or rib eye**, cut into 4 portions

2 Tbsp (30 mL) **coconut oil** or **ghee**

4 cups (960 mL) **shredded romaine lettuce**

1 small (74 g) **red bell pepper**, seeded and cut into thin slices

1 small (70 g) **sweet red onion**, cut into thin slices

1/4 bunch (25 g) **cilantro**, washed and large stems removed

1 Tbsp (15 mL) **toasted sesame oil**

1 Tbsp (15 mL) **spicy chili oil**

3 Tbsp (45 mL) **avocado, macadamia,** or a **light olive oil**

1 Tbsp (15 mL) **sugar replacement**

2 Tbsp (30 mL) **fresh lime juice**

3 Tbsp (45 mL) **Japanese soy sauce** (shoyu) or **coconut aminos**

2 tsp (10 mL) grated **fresh ginger**

2 Tbsp (30 mL) **sesame seeds**, toasted

salt and **pepper** to taste

PER SERVING
CALORIES: 699.6
FAT: 56.94
PROTEIN: 39.57
CARBS: 11.86
FIBER: 2.77
SUGAR ALCOHOLS: 3.75
NET CARBS: 5.34

MORE FACTS: P. 511

This is a really simple salad that came about as a request for a nice sack-lunch idea. The idea is to cook a portion of meat and chill it (chicken, pork, shrimp, etc., in place of the flank would work with the flavors as well). Alternately, use a leftover piece of meat. The salad can be assembled, with the meat placed on the top, in a portable container with a lid. I tend to like slicing it in advance, as it makes eating it on the run a little easier. Flank steak also tends to have a reputation of being a little on the tough side. As a result, I tend to cook it closer to a rare and slice it thin. These tricks help keep it tender and pleasantly beefy. The sweet and salty dressing is really intended to be packed up in a separate container. When it's time to eat, drizzle the dressing on the salad and enjoy!

1. It's always better to cook a warm and relaxed piece of meat. Set your flank on the countertop about an hour (and up to 4 hours) before cooking if possible.

2. Preheat a large sauté pan over medium-high heat. Season the flank steak with salt and pepper.

3. Add coconut oil or ghee to the hot pan, and swirl it around to coat the bottom of the pan. When the oil's surface begins to ripple, place flank pieces into the pan to sear one side. Do not crowd the pan. Try and keep each piece of flank steak from touching any other piece. This helps them sear. Turn the heat down to a medium low, and allow to continue searing on the stove top, about 6 minutes. Once one side of flank is seared, flip the flank steaks over and sear the other side for a further 5 or 6 minutes. At this point, I would generally consider the meat cooked, but you may want to go longer, depending on personal preference and thickness of the meat.

4. Place the steaks on a plate (do not stack them). Put the meat in the refrigerator until chilled completely through.

5. While the meat is chilling, assemble the lettuce, bell peppers, onions, and cilantro. You may either mix these ingredients together, or nicely layer and evenly divide onto plates or into containers.

6. In a small mixing bowl, mix the oils, sweetener, lime juice, soy (or coconut aminos), ginger, sesame seeds, and a bit of salt and pepper with a whisk. Make sure it is mixed well and your sweetener is dissolved. Distribute into four smaller containers or cups.

7. Remove the flank from the refrigerator when it is chilled. Slice it very thin, against the grain, and place it on top of the salad. Cover and save for later… or serve and eat!

Note: Make sure you whisk the dressing right before pouring into each alternate container; if you don't, the oil will almost all be poured into the first container, because the oil will float to the top. For an even pour, make sure the dressing is recently whisked.

Sweet 'n' Creamy Coleslaw

SERVES: 8 · · · PREP: 10 MIN · · · COOK: 0 MIN · · · TOTAL: 30 MIN

8 cups (1.9 L) **cabbage**, shredded (about 1/2 head)

1/4 cup (60 mL) peeled and grated **carrot**

1/2 cup (120 mL) **mayonnaise**

2 Tbsp (30 mL) **fresh lemon juice**

2 Tbsp (30 mL) **sugar replacement**

salt and **pepper** to taste

This is a basic salad. It's literally mayonnaise with a little sweetener, tossed with shredded cabbage and carrots. That's it! I've seen all kinds of variations over the years though. Shredded raw broccoli (and stems) with cabbage, carrots, raisins, and almonds, for example. Raw sliced onions are another common addition. Just about anything is improved with the addition of bacon! Poppy seeds, celery seeds, sesame seeds, and pecans; dried cranberries; apples, orange juice, and orange zest—whatever you can dream up, really. My suggestion is start with a good base and toss in the stuff you love!

1. In a large salad bowl, combine cabbage, carrot, mayonnaise, lemon juice, and sweetener with a bit of salt and pepper. Allow the slaw to macerate for 20 minutes.

2. Serve.

PER SERVING
CALORIES: 113.17
FAT: 10.43
PROTEIN: 1.34
CARBS: 9.51
FIBER: 2.38
SUGAR ALCOHOLS: 4.22
NET CARBS: 2.91

MORE FACTS: P. 510

Lunch

Lunch is always a quick and easy meal for me. It's usually fairly small and almost never "composed." Nine times out of ten, it's a few sausages, a soup, or a salad... and that's it. The tenth time, it's usually something a bit more elaborate because I've got guests, or I'm just in the mood to change it up. Here are a few ideas that broaden the idea of a soup or salad for lunch!

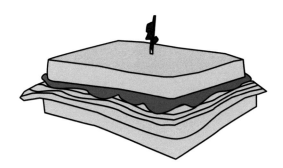

Italian Turkey Club

SERVES: 6 · · · PREP: 2 MIN · · · COOK: 1 MIN · · · TOTAL: 3 MIN

1 sheet **Garlic–Herb Fauxcaccia** (p. 470)

1/2 cup (120 mL) **Pesto alla Genovese** (p. 386)

1 1/2 lb. (681 g) **sliced turkey**

12 slices **cooked bacon**

1 medium (91 g) **tomato**, sliced thin

salt and **pepper** to taste

I've always thought the idea of making a *super* sandwich and then cutting it into portions was a great and clever idea. This technique can be used to make different-sized sandwiches for different members of the family, or it can be used to make a series of premade sandwiches for the same person. Since I've started doing this, I've done it often. And this is where the idea becomes less a specific recipe (even though it is one) and more a general concept for a larger sandwich idea.

Note: Deli meats can have a lot of fillers, sugars, and preservatives. Look for fresh, preferably in-house meats from the local deli or butcher. There are some quality brands, with excellent options, but this often means reading the labels and looking for simple, short, and easy to pronounce ingredients lists.

1. This is best done with a long, sharp, serrated knife. Butterfly the sheet of bread, splitting it into a top half and a bottom half. As you cut, the key is keeping the knife at precisely the midpoint between the top and bottom, and making sure that it's *always* perfectly parallel to your cutting surface. If the blade tilts up or down, then it will begin to slice up or down. Ultimately, you want two equal thicknesses to the top and bottom halves.

2. Once both halves have been split, spread an equal amount of pesto on the inside of both the top and the bottom.

3. On the bottom, evenly lay out the turkey, followed by the bacon, and finally the tomatoes. Sprinkle a little salt and pepper on the tomatoes and then place the top on the whole thing, with the pesto side facing the tomatoes.

4. Cut out sandwiches! This is designed for 6 substantial sandwiches, but a variety of numbers are possible. Cut out 48 little mini sandwiches for a party. Enjoy!

PER SERVING
CALORIES: 627.54
FAT: 47.53
PROTEIN: 41.01
CARBS: 12.58
FIBER: 4.01
SUGAR ALCOHOLS: 0
NET CARBS: 8.56

MORE FACTS: P. 516

Spicy Cheese-Stuffed Burger

SERVES: 6 · · · PREP: 20 MIN · · · COOK: 20 MIN · · · TOTAL: 40 MIN

1/4 cup (60 mL) **ghee**, **bacon fat**, or **lard**, divided

1 (65 g) **Poblano pepper**, seeds removed and diced

1 **jalapeño pepper**, seeds removed and diced

3 **garlic cloves**, diced

1 small (110 g) **onion**, diced

1 1/2 lb. (681 g) **ground beef**

1 large **egg**

2 tsp (10 mL) ground **cumin**

1 tsp (5 mL) ground **coriander seed**

8 oz. (227 g) **Oaxaca cheese**, grated

1 cup (240 mL) **sour cream**

1/4 bunch (25 g) **fresh cilantro**, large stems removed, divided

2 medium (182 g) **tomatoes**, sliced

1 whole (136 g) **avocado**, peeled and sliced

salt and **pepper** to taste

Burgers seem custom tailored to the lunchtime experience, but the issue of the bun always rears its ugly head. I say... ditch the bun! There's no need for it. We've all been eating with forks and knifes since we were old enough to hold them. If you absolutely must have buns, try using the One-Minute Cheddar Buns (p. 472). *Many* people, including the famous In-n-Out Burger, make it "Protein Style" and simply use a thick stack of iceberg lettuce leaves in place of the bun. I mean, who's to say a simple patty can't be delicious served solely with complementary ingredients? Why not place a patty on a salad? Why not get fancy and stuff it? So many ways we can go with a burger for lunch...

1. Place a sauté pan over medium heat on the stove. When it is warm, add 1 tablespoon (15 mL) of your cooking fat. When the oil begins to ripple in the pan, add the Poblanos and jalapeños. Season with a bit of salt and pepper. Sauté until soft, about 3 or 4 minutes. Set aside to cool.

2. Add another 1 tablespoon (15 mL) of your cooking fat to the original pan. Add onions and garlic. Season with a little salt and pepper. Cook for about 7 to 10 minutes or until soft and caramelized. Turn off the heat and set aside.

3. In a mixing bowl, add beef, egg, cumin, coriander, and warm onion mixture. Combine mixture well.

4. Form ground beef mixture into 12 roughly 2 1/2-ounces (71 g) balls. Press the balls with your palms to make them into thin and round patties. Carefully lay 6 of the patties on a plate, cutting board, or countertop.

5. In a separate mixing bowl, combine cooked peppers with the Oaxaca cheese.

PER SERVING
CALORIES: 496.33
FAT: 41.77
PROTEIN: 20.6
CARBS: 9.21
FIBER: 2.72
SUGAR ALCOHOLS: 0
NET CARBS: 6.58

MORE FACTS: P. 515

6. With the cheese, compress and form 6 disks or pucks that are a bit smaller than the beef patties. Place each cheese puck in the center of each beef patty. Place the second set of 6 beef patties on top of the cheese and carefully seal the beef around the cheese. Do not allow any holes to appear during this process, or the cheese will melt and make a mess in the pan. A cheese leak is best avoided.

7. Preheat a large sauté pan over high heat on the stove. While the pan is heating, season the outside of the patties with a little bit of salt and pepper.

8. Add your remaining 2 tablespoons (30 mL) of cooking fat to the pan. When the oil ripples, add your patties to the pan, so that they are not touching. If they are too crowded, the pan will cool down and you won't get a nice sear. You may need two pans for this.

9. Sear the outside of your patties, moving them around the pan to try and get a nice brown sear on the outside. Lower the heat to medium low and allow the patties to cook for about 5 minutes. Flip them and allow them to sit, sear, and cook on the other side for about 5 minutes.

10. While the patties cook, coarsely chop half the cilantro and add to a mixing bowl with the sour cream. Add a little salt and pepper, as well as enough water to thin the sour cream to the consistency of pancake batter. Set aside.

11. Slice tomatoes and place on 6 individual plates. Season with a bit of salt and pepper. Add sliced avocados to the top of the tomatoes. Drizzle the sour cream mixture around the plate. When the patties are nicely seared on both sides, place them in the center of each plate. Garnish with the remaining cilantro. Serve!

PULLED PORK

SERVES: 8 · · · PREP: 20 MIN · · · COOK: 9 HR · · · TOTAL: 24-ISH HR

1/4 cup (60 mL) **yellow mustard**

2 Tbsp (30 mL) **yacon syrup**

1 small (110 g) **onion**, cut into chunks

12 **garlic cloves**, tips removed

1 (2.7 kg) **pork butt**, bone in (also known as shoulder or Boston butt) (about 5 to 6 lb.)

2 Tbsp (30 mL) **paprika**

2 Tbsp (30 mL) **salt**

1 Tbsp (15 mL) **cayenne pepper**

1 Tbsp (15 mL) chopped **fresh thyme**

1 Tbsp (15 mL) **fresh cracked black pepper**

I almost always have some pulled pork lying around. I tend to pick it, chill it, vacuum pack, and freeze it. A very common lunch for me is the Pulled Pork Bowl, which is pulled pork warmed in a bit of BBQ sauce and then topped with spicy hot link, some coleslaw, and a bit of melted cheese. One of my favorite lunches!

1. In a blender or food processor, puree the mustard, yacon, garlic, and onion to make a paste.

2. Wash the pork shoulder and pat it dry. Rub the mustard paste all over the outside of the pork, pushing it into any crevices that may exist. Create as thick a layer as is possible.

3. Mix the spices (the remaining ingredients) in a bowl. Liberally coat the pork with this dry rub. If you have any that doesn't stick, save it and add the rest of it the following morning.

4. Wrap the pork in plastic wrap (or even better, vacuum pack it). Refrigerate it overnight.

5. The next morning, prepare your smoker. Preheat to between 215 and 235°F (102 and 113°C) (this can be done in an oven without smoke, and still tastes great, but it loses that smoky quality). Depending on your approach to the smoking process, you can soak some hickory or other aromatic wood chips in some water at this point. Finally, put a drip pan filled with water on the rack beneath where the pork will go. Some of this water will evaporate, helping maintain moisture and forming the outer layer of crust (known as *bark*) on the surface of the meat. It will also catch any fat, rather than causing flare-ups in the fire… or just making a big mess. Even if this is done on a pan in an oven, include a pan of water under the rack containing the pork.

PER SERVING
CALORIES: 834.7
FAT: 62.16
PROTEIN: 59.52
CARBS: 8.14
FIBER: 1.61
SUGAR ALCOHOLS: 0
NET CARBS: 6.53

MORE FACTS: P. 516

6. Take the pork out the refrigerator and unwrap it. Coat it with any remaining dry rub.

7. Oil a rack inside the smoker. Place the pork in the smoker (not too close to the main heat source; either set it to the side of the flame, or use a heat deflector between the meat and flame) and close it up, maintaining the indirect heat somewhere between 215 and 235°F (102 and 113°C), by feeding the fire and controlling air flow with your damper (or just set the oven to this temperature and relax).

8. Smoke the meat, occasionally adding aromatic chips to the fire, for roughly 1 1/2 hours per pound of meat. So, a 6 pound (2.7 kg) pork butt will smoke for approximately 9 hours.

9. Once the pork has reached a temperature around 200°F (93°C), remove it, place it somewhere warm, and cover it with foil and a heavy towel. Let it relax for 1 hour, to let the juices within it reabsorb into the meat.

10. Pull and serve!

ChupaChorueso: Cheese-Stuffed Cheese with Mexican Sausage

SERVES: 1 · · · PREP: 10 MIN · · · COOK: 10 MIN · · · TOTAL: 20 MIN

4 oz. (114 g) **cheddar cheese**, grated

2 oz. (56 g) **hot pepper Monterey jack cheese**, grated

2 oz. (56 g) **queso fresco**, crumbled

4 oz. (114 g) **raw Mexican chorizo**, crumbled and cooked

This is not a real recipe. It's not indigenous to Mexico, and it's not rooted in some lost culinary lore. It was actually invented by a guy named Howard Tayler with a web comic known as *Shlock Mercenary*. *ChupaQueso* started as a bit of a gag term, designed to embody all things greasy and cheesy, but with a decidedly south-of-the-border slant to it. It slowly evolved into this cheese-crisp thing, as Mr. Tayler began to veer into the land of the low-carb himself. The ChupaQueso became a real thing. Fried cheese... stuffed with cheese! I've stepped it up a notch and thrown chorizo into the mix, dubbing the new invention the *ChupaChorueso* (pronounced Choopa ChorAYso). Yes, I know that's not the correct phonetic pronunciation, but... let's be fair, it's not a real recipe. It's a caricature of one!

I couldn't stop giggling like a buffoon, as I made this silly thing. Cheese-and-chorizo-stuffed cheese—it's about as indulgent a thing as I can imagine.

1. Heat a large nonstick sauté pan over medium heat. Evenly sprinkle your grated cheese around the base of the pan. Depending on the size of your pan, you may need to occasionally adjust the pan over the burner, to ensure that it cooks evenly (this means moving the pan around the burner). Continue to cook over low–medium heat. The cheese will melt together. It will eventually begin to fry and darken.

2. Once the cheese has a firm, crispy look to it but before it burns, sprinkle your queso fresco, pepper jack, and cooked chorizo down the center, as if it were a racing stripe.

PER SERVING
CALORIES: 1,384.76
FAT: 113.82
PROTEIN: 79.85
CARBS: 7.34
FIBER: 0
SUGAR ALCOHOLS: 0
NET CARBS: 7.34

MORE FACTS: P. 515

3. With a heat-resistant plastic spatula or wooden spatula, pry the edge of the cheese disk up, and then loosen the entire thing from underneath. Fold the two flaps over the filling in the center and turn the heat down to very low. Cook for about 2 minutes.

4. Flip the ChupaChorueso and cook for a further 2 or 3 minutes on the other side or until the cheese filling has melted. Serve!

 Fried Cheese, Stuffed with Cheese, Stuffed with Sausage. Quintessential Keto!

Greasy Pork Sandwich

SERVES: 1 · · · PREP: 10 MIN · · · COOK: 12 MIN · · · TOTAL: 22 MIN

2 Tbsp (30 mL) **flaxseed meal** (or 1 1/2 Tbsp [23 mL] ground chia seed)

2 Tbsp (30 mL) **almond flour**

2 large **eggs**

1 tsp (5 mL) **melted butter**

1/2 tsp (2 mL) **baking powder**

3 slices (84 g) **deli ham**

3 slices (84 g) **bacon**, precooked and crispy

2 Tbsp (30 mL) **heavy whipping cream**

1 Tbsp (15 mL) **bacon fat** or **butter**

salt and **pepper** to taste

One random day, I had a desire for a deeply heavy and greasy fried pork sandwich. I don't know why. I just wanted something wonderful and amazing, but that somehow felt bad... dirty... wrong. What I came up with is nothing short of spectacular! It's little more than a blend of a basic square one-minute muffin, which is then split in half, loaded with a bit of ham and crispy bacon, and then dipped into an egg bath. From there, it's fried like French toast!

1. In a flat-bottomed glass or china bowl (preferably square and about the surface area of sandwich bread), mix the flax (or chia), almond flour, 1 of the eggs, butter, baking powder, and a bit of salt and pepper. Microwave this for 60 to 90 seconds on high. Let the bread sit for a further 60 seconds. Remove from the microwave and slice into two halves (a top and a bottom).

2. Line the bottom with ham and bacon. Place the top on the sandwich.

3. In a separate bowl (I used a pie tin), whisk your second egg and cream, with a little salt and pepper.

4. Add sandwich to the egg mixture and coat it evenly, flipping it over and pushing it into the egg mixture so that the bread absorbs the egg, like a sponge. It may take a few minutes, but just keep flipping it. Eventually, most of it gets absorbed, and you have a nice egg-coated sandwich.

5. Heat a skillet or sauté pan over medium-low heat. Add bacon fat or butter and swirl it around. Add sandwich to the pan, and allow it to turn golden brown on one side. Flip it and cook the other side. Turn the heat down to low and allow it to cook for about 4 to 6 minutes on either side, until it's cooked through.

6. Cut into tasty quarters and eat!

PER SERVING
CALORIES: 474.64
FAT: 43.26
PROTEIN: 11.21
CARBS: 17.62
FIBER: 11.34
SUGAR ALCOHOLS: 0
NET CARBS: 6.28

MORE FACTS: P. 516

Pizza Pucks

SERVES: 4 · · · PREP: 20 MIN · · · COOK: 25 MIN · · · TOTAL: 45 MIN

1/4 lb. (114 g) **regular cream cheese** (not low-fat), softened

2 large **whole eggs**

1/2 cup (120 mL) grated **Parmesan cheese**, divided

3/4 lb. (341 g) **mozzarella** (whole milk, low moisture), grated and divided

1 tsp (5 mL) chopped **fresh oregano**

4 **garlic cloves**, minced

1/4 lb. (114 g) **raw Italian Chicken Sausage** (p. 480)

1 cup (240 mL) **Marinara Sauce (p. 358)**

1/4 cup (60 mL) **real bacon bits**

24 thin slices (48 g) **pepperoni**

salt, **pepper**, and **chili flakes** to taste

In my pickle of a pursuit for the perfect pizza, I've decided to play with a fairly common approach toward low-carb deep-dish pizza making. The idea is, in short, to make a thick crust-like creature consisting of cream cheese, cheese, and eggs. This is par-baked; then it is topped with pizza toppings, then baked again. My conclusion? It was *very* good and certainly hit the spot. It tasted like pizza. That is to say, it tasted like pizza *toppings*. Imagine ordering a fantastic pizza, with all the stuff you love, then asking for triple exxxtra cheese. When it arrives, pick off only the cheese and toppings, and devour with glee. That is what this tasted like. SHAZAM!

1. Preheat oven to 375°F.

2. In a mixing bowl, combine the cream cheese, eggs, 1/4 cup (60 mL) of Parmesan cheese, and 1/2 lb. (227 g) of the grated mozzarella with the fresh oregano and minced garlic.

3. If you're not using a nonstick muffin pan, grease 12 muffin cups. If your trays are nonstick, don't worry about it. Spoon equal amounts of "crust batter" into the base of 12 muffin cups.

4. Bake in the preheated oven for 12 to 15 minutes or until the edges of the "crusts" begin to lightly turn brown. Remove from the oven. While hot, with the back of a teaspoon, push the centers of the newly puffed crusts downward, making a bit of a well in the center, with higher "crust walls" around the rim.

5. In a sauté pan, cook the sausage and break it up with a spoon, until it resembles cooked ground beef.

PER SERVING
CALORIES: 638.32
FAT: 49.41
PROTEIN: 39.64
CARBS: 9.26
FIBER: 1.38
SUGAR ALCOHOLS: 0
NET CARBS: 7.87

MORE FACTS: P. 515

6. Fill the center of crusts with a spoonful of marinara sauce and an even distribution of your toppings: the cooked sausage, bacon bits, and pepperoni. Finally, dust the toppings with the rest of your two cheeses.

7. Bake for 12 more minutes.

8. Remove from the oven and let rest for about 10 minutes prior to popping the pizza pucks from their trays and serving.

Famed hockey player Wayne Gretzky is famous for having said, "I skate to where the puck is going to be, not where it has been."

CHICKEN NUGGETS

SERVES: 8 · · · PREP: 15 MIN · · · COOK: 15 MIN · · · TOTAL: 30 MIN

1 cup (240 mL) **high smoke point oil** (see recipe notes)

1 1/2 cup (180 mL) **almond flour**

1 cup (240 mL) finely grated **Parmesan cheese**

2 tsp (10 mL) chopped **fresh oregano** (thyme, rosemary, sage and/or marjoram)

4 **garlic cloves**, minced

1 large **egg**

1 1/2 lb. (681 g) **boneless chicken** (I used breast, but thigh will work, as well; skin is optional), cut into cubes

salt, pepper, and **chili flakes** to taste

Here's a fun one, and one that's likely to delight the whole family! I had some friends over when I made this and asked them to honestly let me know if they could tell that they'd been low-primal'd. They all agreed that there was no lack of flavor and that they were as good, if not better than, the real thing. These are a bit messy to make, but I agree with my *amigos*. They were outstanding. In fact, I was frankly caught a little off guard by how wonderful these little chicken nibblets turned out to be. They were golden brown, flavorful, had a spectacular texture, and were full of moist and juicy goodness.

Fat note: Good high smoke point oils for frying are: coconut oil, lard, palm oil, and ghee. Avoid hydrogenated or partially hydrogenated oils and man-made trans fats. Processed oils like canola, corn, vegetable, and soybean should be avoided.

1. Preheat your oil to a temperature between 325 and 350°F (163 and 177°C), in a wide skillet over medium-low heat.

2. While the oil heats, in a large and wide-mouthed bowl, mix your almond meal, Parmesan cheese, oregano, garlic, salt, pepper, and optional chili flakes. (I actually used a large, wide Tupperware with a lid.) Remove half the mixture and set aside in a small bowl.

3. In third bowl, whisk together your egg with 2 tablespoons (30 mL) cold water. Add a little salt and pepper.

4. Add your cubed chicken to the eggs and mix well.

5. To the best of your ability, spread the almond flour mixture evenly along the bottom of your large bowl or container.

PER SERVING
CALORIES: 570.29
FAT: 49.42
PROTEIN: 27.95
CARBS: 5.62
FIBER: 2.29
SUGAR ALCOHOLS: 0
NET CARBS: 3.34

MORE FACTS: P. 516

6. Evenly drop the chicken cubes around the almond flour mixture, so that they don't touch one another.

7. Dust the tops of the cubed chicken with the remaining almond flour mixture.

8. Shake the chicken. If you've got a lid, add the lid and shake, shake, shake, señora. Otherwise, just get in there and make sure the nuggets are evenly coated. If all the dredge doesn't fully stick, just let it sit for a few minutes, then give it another mix. Some of the moisture will continue to collect on the surface of the chicken and little more will stick. Alternately, you can literally just "squeeze" it on, by applying pressure with your palms.

9. Once the nuggets are evenly coated, carefully drop them evenly into their own spots within the heated oil. At this point, you probably want to increase the temperature of the burner, as the chicken will lower the temperature of the oil. (However, be careful not to let the oil go much higher than 350°F [177°C]).

10. As one side turns golden brown, flip them to the other side. Continue frying and turning until they are cooked through and golden brown.

11. Remove them from the oil with a slotted spoon and place on a towel to absorb any extra fat.

12. **Note:** If you chose to do a deep fry, rather than a pan fry, as long as your oil never goes above 350°F (177°C), you can strain it through a coffee filter and reuse one more time. BE CAREFUL not to burn yourself.

13. Serve!

SANDWICH WRAPS

SERVES: 2 · · · PREP: 10 MIN · · · COOK: 0 MIN · · · TOTAL: 10 MIN

8 **All-Purpose Crepes (p. 476)**

2 Tbsp (30 mL) **Dijon mustard**

6 (31 g) **lettuce leaves**, washed and dried

4 slices (112 g) **deli ham**

4 slices (112 g) **cheddar cheese**

4 slices (32 g) **cooked bacon**

1 small (91 g) **tomato**, cut into 10 wedges

salt and **pepper** to taste

Sandwich wraps can mean a lot of things to a lot of people. In this recipe, I'm using my all-purpose crepes, but anything can be wrapped or used as the wrapper. For example, slices of deli meat can be used as the wrapper. Lay one out and spread condiments on it. Follow this with lettuce, tomatoes, sliced onions, olives, or whatever other accouterments you may have in mind. Many also use large lettuce leaves as the wrapper.

1. Lay down the two crepes, side by side, on a flat surface. Imagine an envelope with its flap open. Spread the mustard evenly over each crepe, with the exception of a 1-inch (2.5 cm) "flap" at the top. Leave this dry. Next, lay 3 lettuce leaves within each crepe. Then, layer 2 slices of ham, 2 slices of cheese, 2 slices of bacon, and, in a straight line near the center of each crepe, place 5 small tomato wedges. Season each tomato wedge with a small amount of salt and pepper.

2. Run fingers through some water, just enough to get them wet. With your wet fingers, make the dry portion of the crepe flap slightly moist.

3. Tightly roll the crepe and fillings, away from yourself, toward the flap. Stop when the damp flap is completely held down by the rest of the wrap.

PER SERVING
CALORIES: 477.11
FAT: 33.3
PROTEIN: 36.01
CARBS: 7.215
FIBER: 1.985
SUGAR ALCOHOLS: 0
NET CARBS: 5.23

MORE FACTS: P. 515

4. Let the wrap sit on top of the flap for about 1 minute, while it slightly seals.

5. Cut each wrap into pieces, and lay them attractively on a plate (or just eat the things!).

6. Eat the things!

Pasta

o o o

Pasta is a tricky one. I know I personally love it. It's a very common meal type in that it tends to be quick to throw together, inexpensive, and filling. The drawback, of course, is that it's going to create havoc on your blood sugar and really has no nutrients to speak of. Delicious, cheap, and comforting to be sure, but for the most part, there's nothing else good about it, from a *healthy* standpoint.

I've done my best to present a fun and varied assortment of pasta ideas in an effort to showcase about eight different directions that pasta can go under the low-primal umbrella. Each of these ideas are fun, tasty, relatively easy to throw together, quite filling, *and* nutritious!

Note: There are a wide variety of pastas on the market catering to a variety of dietary philosophies. Some are better than others. Some function as stated, whereas others do not. When experimenting with the various pastas or pasta flours on the market, please do some reading about them to determine if they *truly* fit your needs. Not all products are exactly what they claim to be. Do your research.

Chicken Noodles with Asparagus, Artichokes, and Pine Nuts

SERVES: 4 · · · PREP: 20 MIN · · · COOK: 15 MIN · · · TOTAL: 35 MIN

2 cups (480 mL) **chicken stock or broth**

3/4 cup (180 mL) **ice cubes**

3 Tbsp (45 mL) **egg white powder**

6 oz. (168 g) chilled **skinless chicken breast**, cubed

1/2 cup (120 mL) **fresh whole butter**, cut into about 12 cubes and divided

4 **garlic cloves**, chopped

1 bunch (227 g) **asparagus**, cut into thin slices

3 whole (83 g) **artichoke hearts in oil**, drained and cut into 8 wedges each

1/4 cup (60 mL) **pine nuts**, toasted

1 Tbsp (15 mL) coarsely chopped **capers**

1/4 tsp (1 mL) **crushed red chili flakes**

1/4 cup (60 mL) grated **Parmesan-Reggiano**

16 leaves **fresh basil**, hand torn

salt and **pepper** to taste

This is my twist on a recipe from Rocco DiSpirito, as presented on *Rachel Ray*. What we have here is a chicken emulsion, not entirely unlike a very long and thin chicken sausage. Imagine a hot dog but much, much thinner, much, much longer, and without a casing to hold it all together. That is essentially what this "pasta" is! A really, really, really, really long chicken wiener!

Note: This was based on a video which can be seen on Rachel Ray's website, along with a poorer version of a different video on my own website.

1. Bring a large pot of water to a boil and season well with salt.

2. In a small saucepan, bring some chicken stock to a boil. Turn the heat to medium-low and place on a burner out of the way. Our goal is to reduce this stock by about 75 percent (resulting in about 1/2 cup [120 mL] of super-reduced chicken stock).

3. In a blender, puree the egg white powder and ice until the powder has dissolved. Add the raw chicken and puree until the mixture is smooth and consistent. Place the chicken batter into a squeeze bottle (or emptied plastic squeezable ketchup/mustard bottle) and place in the refrigerator. Keep this mixture chilled until time to cook it.

PER SERVING
CALORIES: 390.52
FAT: 35.89
PROTEIN: 19.65
CARBS: 7.62
FIBER: 2.76
SUGAR ALCOHOLS: 0
NET CARBS: 4.86

MORE FACTS: P. 517

 Literally, Chicken Noodles!

4. Fetch a bowl of ice water and set nearby.

5. Holding your finger over the hole of the squirt bottle, swing the bottle in the air to push as much of the batter toward the tip of the bottle as is possible. Holding the tip over the water, with even pressure, squeeze a thin and consistent stream of chicken into the boiling water, while moving in a circular fashion. This will create a long thin ribbon or "noodle." Once you're happy with the length of the noodle or it snaps naturally, allow it to simmer for about 1 minute. It cooks quickly! Remove and place into the ice water. Repeat this process until all the chicken is cooked.

6. Once all the noodles have been cooked and chilled, drain and place on a towel to dry completely.

7. Place a large sauté pan on the stove over high heat. Place 2 of the butter cubes into the hot pan with the garlic and sauté until the garlic is aromatic and *just* begins to turn golden.

8. Add the asparagus to the pan with a little salt and pepper. Toss to coat with butter and garlic.

9. After about 1 minute, add the artichoke, pine nuts, capers, and chili flakes. Sauté for about 1 minute.

10. Add the reduced chicken stock to the pan and toss to coat the ingredients. Add a cube of butter and keep mixing the ingredients. Once you add the butter, the pan needs to keep moving to help the butter melt and thicken the sauce, rather than melting and creating an oil slick on top. Moving the butter around will emulsify it into the chicken stock, thickening it, enriching it, and giving it a bit of a sheen. When the previous cube is about half melted, add another cube. Continue this process until all the butter is absorbed into the sauce.

11. Add the pasta and toss to coat.

12. Season with a bit of salt and pepper and then give one final toss with leaves of fresh basil and grated Parmesan cheese.

13. Divide between 4 plates or pasta bowls and serve!

Stir-Fried Peanut Chicken with Kelp Noodles

SERVES: 4 · · · PREP: 15 MIN · · · COOK: 15 MIN · · · TOTAL: 30 MIN

24 oz. (680 g) **kelp noodles**

1 Tbsp (15 mL) freshly squeezed **lime juice**

1/4 large (210 g) **bunch broccoli**, including stalks, cut into florets

1 1/2 lb. (681 g) **boneless chicken**, cut into strips

4 **garlic cloves**, minced

1 Tbsp (15 mL) minced **fresh ginger**

2 Tbsp (30 mL) **coconut oil**

1 small (74 g) **red bell pepper**, seeded and sliced very thin

1 large (72 g) **carrot**, peeled and cut into thin strips (or grated with grater)

1/2 medium (55 g) **red onion**, very thinly sliced

1/2 cup (120 mL) **Peanut Sauce** (p. 379)

1/4 bunch (25 g) **cilantro**, washed and large stems removed

2 whole (30 g) **green onions** (scallions), cut lengthwise into thin strips

1/4 cup (37 g) chopped **peanuts**, toasted

salt and **pepper** to taste

PER SERVING
CALORIES: 454.08
FAT: 22.76
PROTEIN: 43.63
CARBS: 18.16
FIBER: 5.8
SUGAR ALCOHOLS: 2.25
NET CARBS: 10.12

MORE FACTS: P. 517

This surprisingly tasty entry uses a noodle made of kelp. Yep! That weird stuff that floats around beaches, washes up on shore, and generally makes the thought of swimming in it make my skin crawl.

However, these read like a low-primalist's dream food. A four-ounce portion has just one carb, and it's all fiber. It's also got only 6 calories, is high in iodine (YAY, thyroid function!) and other minerals, and is also considered good eating by the raw and Paleo communities. In a sense, it's just water held in place with seaweed fiber, and flavored with just a touch of seaweed salt. No cooking is done or required. Open a bag and eat up!

Yes, you can eat these right out of the package. There are many that love these things and swear by them. People pop the bag, cut up the noodles, slather them with cucumbers and avocados, and chow down. Not only is this possible and acceptable, but it's also quite common! I think from my personal vantage point, I'll need to rise to that particular occasion. I'm more a regular ol' noodle type dude, and these hard, elastic strands just kind of weirded me out. I read and read and discovered that prolonged exposure to acid will start to soften them, somewhat. I rinsed them in warm water, cut them into manageable strands, and then tossed them with fresh lime juice, where they sat on the counter for about an hour. Interestingly, liquid pooled at the bottom, which I poured off. The noodles did, indeed, soften somewhat. Cooking them with other ingredients really whipped them into a nice noodley shape! In the end, I think these are kind of a fun product to play with. The flavor is very mild and easily canceled out by other ingredients and can be tamed into something wonderful like... Stir-Fried Peanut Chicken with Kelp Noodles!

Purchase note: I personally purchased my noodles online, but I also noticed they sell them at the local Asian grocery store. I assume they can be found in some stores but suspect they can be a bit of a challenge to find. I do recommend them, though, if you're up for something kind of different!

1. Rinse your kelp noodles under warm water to wash off any extra salt or liquid from the packaging. Cut your noodles into manageable lengths with a knife or food scissors. Toss your noodles in the lime juice, cover, and set aside. The longer they sit, the softer the noodle will be. I recommend about an hour, but the entire step is completely optional. When ready to use, pour off any liquid that may have accumulated at the bottom of the bowl.

2. Another optional step: I personally like my broccoli a bit on the undercooked and crunchy side. I stir-fry raw florets into this and find the end result to be quite tasty and crunchy, but if you like your broccoli cooked through, boil some salted water and add your broccoli. Let it cook for about 2 minutes, then strain out and set aside. Your broccoli will be about halfway cooked, and it will finish in the stir-fry later.

3. Mix together your chicken, garlic, and ginger in a bowl with a little salt and pepper.

4. Note: I might suggest splitting all your ingredients into two halves and either doing this in two hot pans at the same time, or in 2 quick batches. It goes quickly and will help to keep things hot and moving around the bottom of the pan. If the pan sits still for more than a moment, you run the risk that things will stick and burn.

5. Heat a large sauté pan or wok (if you have one) over high heat. The hotter the better. The next few steps are going to be hot, fast, and smoky. Be ready with your chicken and vegetables, all cut and ready to throw in the pan.

6. First, start by adding coconut oil to the pan and swirl it around. Immediately add your chicken pieces. Sprinkle them around the bottom of the pan to create a flat, single layer of chicken. Let the pan sit for about 2 minutes, letting the chicken turn nice and brown. Add your broccoli to the pan. Toss it into the chicken, and allow the chicken and broccoli to cook for about 2 minutes. Add your thinly sliced bell peppers, carrots, and red onions. Toss these into the pan. Season with a bit of salt and pepper, and then allow to cook for about 1 minute. Add your noodles and peanut sauce. This will be a bit of a challenge to mix, but just smoosh it all together over the heat until it is evenly mixed. Taste and adjust seasoning with a bit more salt and pepper.

7. Divide the mixture between four plates or bowls, and garnish with fresh cilantro, thinly sliced green onions, and chopped, toasted peanuts.

8. Enjoy!

ROASTED SPAGHETTI SQUASH

SERVES: 6 · · · PREP: 10 MIN · · · COOK: 45 MIN · · · TOTAL: 55 MIN

Spaghetti Squash is not, contrary to popular opinion, a racquet sport played in a four-walled court with a small rubber ball and a bowl of pasta. It is, however, a delicious winter vegetable, also known as Squaghetti. This oblong squash tends to be fairly large and is usually yellow. Within, it is a firm flesh and seeds, similar to that of a pumpkin. Where a spaghetti squash suddenly becomes a little extra interesting is in what happens to the flesh when it is cooked. It becomes... pasketti!

1 roughly 5-lb. (2.3 kg) **spaghetti squash**
1/4 cup (60 mL) **fresh whole butter**, softened
salt and **black pepper** to taste

1. Preheat oven to 375°F (190°C).

2. Cut your spaghetti squash into two even halves with a large, sharp knife. Be very careful when doing this, as it's got thick, firm flesh, and it likes to roll around.

3. Once it's been cut in half, scrape the seeds out with a spoon. You can save the seeds and dry them out if you like. They're like pepitas (pumpkin seeds). I usually just throw them out though (I'm lazy).

4. Rub two tablespoons (30 mL) of the softened butter on the exposed fleshy bits of each squash half. Get a nice, even layer on both halves.

5. Season the flesh with a good bit of salt and pepper.

6. Place the two halves, flesh-side down, into a casserole pan or a cookie tray with a rim.

7. Roast in the oven for about 45 minutes or until soft (larger ones can take over an hour). Stick a knife into the rind and see if it enters easily. When it does, it's done. Remove from the oven!

8. Here, you can scrape the strands out with a fork and serve them as is or with some kind of sauce. Alternately, you can also cut the halves into individual crescents and let people scrape their own threads from their portion. In all cases, be careful—they're hot, heavy, and a little bit awkward. Enjoy!

PER SERVING
CALORIES: 108.67
FAT: 7.33
PROTEIN: 1
CARBS: 10
FIBER: 2
SUGAR ALCOHOLS: 0
NET CARBS: 8

MORE FACTS: P. 517

CREPE FETTUCCINE WITH TOMATOES, FRESH MOZZARELLA, AND PESTO

SERVES: 4 · · · PREP: 15 MIN · · · COOK: 5 MIN · · · TOTAL: 20 MIN

15 **All–Purpose Crepes** (p. 476)

2 Tbsp (30 mL) **olive oil**

1 lb. (454 g) **assorted fresh cherry tomatoes,** cut into halves and quarters

1/2 tsp (1 mL) **crushed red chili flakes**

1/4 cup (60 mL) **Pesto alla Genovese** (p. 386)

1 lb. (454 g) **fresh mozzarella**, removed from water and cubed (or use bocconcini)

1/4 cup (60 mL) **Parmesan–Reggiano cheese,** grated

16 leaves **fresh basil**

salt and **fresh cracked pepper** to taste

These little crepe noodles come about as close as I've come to a noodle that pulls from the flavors you give it. They have a wonderful texture (not as slide-y as a good noodle but still quite nice!). They hold up well on the end of a fork, they can be cut into a variety of shapes and sizes, they're super low carb, and they are just flat-out delicious! Do they hit the same spot as a store-bought box of delicious grain-based horror? Nope! Not quite, but... SOOOOO close.

Worth the effort. I promise you!

Note: The crepe recipe is a fantastic recipe. For a good year, I'd make a batch or two at the beginning of the week and just use the sheets for wraps, pasta, casseroles, and desserts. I can't stress enough how versatile and awesome these crepes really are.

PER SERVING
CALORIES: 846.33
FAT: 60.1
PROTEIN: 46.61
CARBS: 9.51
FIBER: 1.41
SUGAR ALCOHOLS: 0
NET CARBS: 8.1

MORE FACTS: P. 518

1. Stack the crepes into little stacks of 4 or 5; then roll them into fairly tight little logs. Slice each crepe every 1/2 inch (1 cm) for something approximating a fettuccine noodle. You could double that for something like a pappardelle, or go much thinner for a linguini or even an angel hair. Once cut, pick the noodles up and "fluff" them, so that they are a nice little pile of noodles. Set aside.

2. Place a large sauté pan on the stove, over medium-high heat and add the oil. Once the oil ripples, add the cherry tomatoes and chili flakes with a little bit of salt and pepper. Cook in the oil for about 1 minute.

3. Add the pesto and noodles, and toss to coat. Cook for about 1 minute.

4. Add the fresh mozzarella and toss. Cook just long enough for the cheese to begin melting.

5. Divide between four plates. Garnish with Parmesan cheese and fresh basil. Serve!

Zucchini Fettuccini, A.K.A., Zoodles!!!

SERVES: 4 · · · PREP: 5 MIN · · · COOK: 2 MIN · · · TOTAL: 30 MIN

4 small (472 g) **green zucchini and/or summer squash**, cut into zoodles

1/4 cup (60 mL) **real bacon bits**

1 Tbsp (15 mL) **oil/fat** (like olive oil, ghee, or bacon fat)

salt and **pepper** to taste

PER SERVING
CALORIES: 69
FAT: 4.62
PROTEIN: 4.46
CARBS: 4.02
FIBER: 1.46
SUGAR ALCOHOLS: 0
NET CARBS: 2.56

MORE FACTS: P. 517

Zoodles! I just love saying that. It's impossible to say the word *zoodles* and not crack a smile. Try it. I dare you! Did you smile? Told you!

There are all kinds of tools for cutting zoodles. The most basic is a standard vegetable peeler. Just peel the zucchini, deeper and deeper. You'll create a series of imperfect but flat, wide "zoodles," which will resemble green pappardelle. Alternately, you can use something like a spiral-cut machine or tool. I personally don't like these much and prefer to go with a more standard flat mandolin, creating thick strips of zucchini, stacking the strips on one another, then cutting them into 1/3-inch strips with a knife. This approach gives me a heartier zoodle, with a bit more texture and bite. However, you can make them thinner, thicker, etc. It's all personal preference.

1. If you haven't already, cut your zoodles, using any method you would like. Once your zoodles have been cut, season them with salt and pepper. Toss them around, so that they are evenly coated with the seasoning. Set them aside for about 20 minutes while you focus on other things. The salt will pull some of the moisture out of the zoodles and will also macerate them. They will become soft and pliable all on their own, without any cooking at all. Pour off any excess water that may develop.

2. Heat up a large nonstick sauté pan over medium-high heat.

3. I personally don't use oil for this. I have a big favorite nonstick pan I use, but you can add something like olive oil, bacon fat, or ghee. I almost always have bacon bits lying around. Instead of using oil, I'll throw those into the pan, where some of the bacon fat will render out. Once I see the bits starting to fry, I will evenly spread my zoodles around the bottom of the pan. Toss them in the pan to mix the bacon and bacon fat into them, then spread them flat on the bottom of the pan. Let them sear for about 30 seconds to a minute.

4. Toss them one more time, spread them out, let them sear for about 30 seconds longer, and then serve!

Zoooooooooooooooodles!

Meat Lovers' Lasagna

SERVES: 12 · · · PREP: 30 MIN · · · COOK: 1 HR · · · TOTAL: 1 HR 30 MIN

1 1/2 lb. (681 g) **chicken breasts, scaloppini style**

1 Tbsp (15 mL) **olive oil**

1 lb. (454 g) **ground beef**

1 lb. (454 g) **raw Italian sausage**

3 cups (720 mL) grated **Parmesan cheese,** divided into two parts

1 cup (240 mL) **whole-milk ricotta cheese**

2 large **whole eggs**

2 lbs. (908 g) **whole milk, low-moisture mozzarella,** grated

15 **All-Purpose Crepes** (p. 476)

1 26-oz. jar (737 g) **no-sugar-added pasta sauce**

salt and pepper to taste

This recipe still has a lot of dairy, but it is also completely wheat free. Sheets of lasagna would definitely work in this recipe, but... so do my crepes! In fact, as I was eating this and sharing it with friends, I asked them if they felt like they were eating something *other* than lasagna. *None* of them batted an eyelash. It was lasagna in every way they know. I agreed. It was soooo good too!

Chicken note: It's my understanding that you can buy scaloppini style chicken breasts in many supermarkets. I'm in the habit of slicing and pounding my own. If you can't find it at the store, you can ask the butcher or pound your own. To do this, cut a chicken breast in half, as if you're butterflying it. Cut it all the way through. Then place each half between two pieces of plastic wrap and whack at it with a meat mallet, the back of your knife, or the bottom of a pan. You want to pound it thinner and wider, until it's about 1/4-inch (3/4 cm) thick.

1. Preheat oven to 350°F (177°C).

2. Season your thinly sliced chicken with salt and pepper; then coat with olive oil.

3. Preheat a large sauté pan over high heat. Once it is hot, add your chicken pieces, in one layer (may need to do in two or three batches). Cook for about 90 seconds on one side; then flip and cook the other side until the chicken is cooked. Remove it and set aside. When all the chicken is cooked, add your ground beef to the pan and brown it with a little salt and pepper. Set aside. Next, sauté the Italian sausage. If it's in a casing, cut one end of each sausage, then squeeze the sausage out of its casing. Break the meat up in the pan. The fat from the meat should be enough to keep it from sticking. When it is cooked, set it aside.

PER SERVING
CALORIES: 798.14
FAT: 53
PROTEIN: 57.76
CARBS: 6.08
FIBER: 1
SUGAR ALCOHOLS: 0
NET CARBS: 5.08

MORE FACTS: P. 518

4. In a bowl, combine ricotta cheese, eggs, and half of the grated Parmesan. Mix and then divide into four rough sections in the bowl.

5. Spray the bottom of a 13" x 9" (33 x 23 x 5 cm) pan. Add a small amount of sauce to the bottom of the pan. Place three crepes on the bottom of the pan. Evenly spread one-quarter of the sauce mixture over the crepes.

6. Evenly spread your ground beef over the sauce. Evenly spread one-quarter of the ricotta mixture over the beef. Evenly spread one-quarter of the shredded mozzarella over the ricotta mixture. Place three more lasagna noodles on top of the mozzarella. Repeat these steps, layering the lasagna, next with the chicken and then the Italian sausage, until all the crepes have been used. On top of the final three crepes, spread the remainder of the sauce, ricotta mixture, the rest of the mozzarella, and finally, the remainder of the grated Parmesan cheese.

7. Bake for about an hour or until cooked through and nice and browned on the top.

8. Remove from the oven and let rest for about 20 minutes prior to slicing and serving.

Singapore-Style Noodles

SERVES: 4 · · · PREP: 15 MIN · · · COOK: 15 MIN · · · TOTAL: 30 MIN

16 oz. (454 g) **tofu shirataki noodles, angel hair** (nontofu is fine too!)

1/4 large (210 g) **bunch broccoli**, including stalks, cut into florets

1 lb. (454 g) **boneless chicken**, cut into strips

1 lb. (454 g) **shrimp (16/20)**, peeled and deveined

2 Tbsp (30 mL) **yellow curry powder**, divided

4 **garlic cloves**, minced

1 Tbsp (15 mL) minced **fresh ginger**

4 large **whole eggs**

2 Tbsp (30 mL) **coconut oil**

1 small (74 g) **red bell pepper**, seeded and sliced very thin

1 cup (240 mL) **mung bean sprouts**

1/2 medium (55 g) **onion**, very thinly sliced

1/4 bunch (25 g) **cilantro**, washed and large stems removed

2 whole (30 g) **green onions** (scallions), cut lengthwise into thin strips

salt and **pepper** to taste

PER SERVING
CALORIES: 462.6
FAT: 17.93
PROTEIN: 57.69
CARBS: 15.98
FIBER: 6.01
SUGAR ALCOHOLS: 0
NET CARBS: 9.97

MORE FACTS: P. 518

When I was younger, I worked in a sort of strange restaurant. It seemed to want to be all things to all people, serving a wide range of high-end foods, including ingredients like sea urchin and goose liver, while also offering ornate bar foods in the expensive, cold, and fancy social gathering area, where beautiful people would ignore the sporting events on the walls. Our menu had both pizza and sushi.

Good food… weird place! While it was a hopping joint at the time, I believe it's the only restaurant I've ever worked in that doesn't still stand today.

In any event, we had a few sushi chefs on hand. They had a boss, the lead sushi chef, whose complicated name was a challenge to pronounce. He was lovingly dubbed "Tamale Cauliflower" by the crew. Tamale was a dutifully honorable and stoic Japanese man. His sushi and his creations were well above any I've ever seen. I learned *a lot* from Tamale. He could do things I've never seen duplicated by any other chef, and he knew it. Between orders, he would sit and read the paper, which would get you fired in most places. Tamale was the only man I've ever known, in any kitchen, anywhere, who could not only get away with sitting and reading a paper while working but could make it look like it was part of his job description. He could sit and quietly read while emanating a paradoxically strong, busy demeanor.

Somewhere, somehow, I'd managed to convince Tamale that he shouldn't isolate himself so much and that he should contribute to the team. It's not that Tamale was standoffish. Tamale was an incredible guy, but he just radiated something tough to penetrate. He lived by his own rules. I somehow managed to reach in there and convince him to cook dinner for the staff, if even only occasionally.

Once a month, Tamale made Singapore Noodles for a group of about forty people. He'd show up early, and quickly, quietly, calmly, and effortlessly float around, gathering the ingredients. Then he would methodically slice everything into perfect little strips, ribbons, and cubes. He'd sort the ingredients into perfectly lined rows, set up on a large bamboo tray. He'd carry the tray to the wok station, crank the massive industrial wok to high, and then Tamale would... *dance*! That's the only way I know to describe it. Between working the water flow with his knees, shucking and jiving while tossing the ingredients into a thousand-degree wok hovering above a rocket engine, Tamale's whole being just grooved into this amusing, amazing 12-minute burst of curry powder, shrimp, and vegetables. It was really quite a sight to see from a man who never smiled, never frowned, never showed any kind of display... of any kind.

Yet, once a month, Tamale would dance and give us Singapore Noodles. They were good too!

1. Rinse your *shirataki* noodles under warm water, for about 2 to 3 minutes, to wash off liquid from the packaging. Set in a strainer to allow them to drip dry. Many people, including myself, like to sauté these in coconut oil for about 5 minutes prior to doing anything with them. It tends to tighten them up and dry them out. The end result is, in my opinion, a more appealing noodle from both a taste and texture perspective. This step is optional, but one I recommend. Sauté over high heat until dry and "squeaky." Set aside.

2. Another optional step: I personally like my broccoli a bit on the undercooked and crunchy side. I stir-fry raw florets into this and find the end result to be quite tasty and crunchy, but if you like your broccoli cooked through, boil some salted water and add your broccoli. Let it cook for about 2 minutes, then strain out and set into ice water. Your broccoli will be about halfway cooked, and it will finish in the stir-fry later.

3. Mix together your chicken, shrimp, garlic, ginger, and one-third of your curry powder in a bowl with a little salt and pepper. Set aside.

4. In a separate bowl, whisk your eggs with about one-third of your curry powder and a little salt and pepper. Set aside.

5. **Note:** I might suggest splitting all your ingredients into two halves and either doing this in two hot pans at the same time or in two quick batches. It goes quick and will help to keep things hot and moving around the bottom of the pan. If the pan sits still for more than a moment, you run the risk that things will stick and burn.

6. Heat a large sauté pan or wok (if you have one) over high heat. The hotter the better. The next few steps are going to be hot, fast, and smoky. Be ready with your chicken/shrimp and vegetables, all cut and ready to throw in the pan.

7. First, start by adding coconut oil to the pan and swirl it around. Immediately add your chicken/shrimp pieces. Sprinkle them around the bottom of the pan to create a flat, single layer of meat. Let the pan sit for about 2 minutes, letting the ingredients turn nice and brown on one side.

8. Add your broccoli to the pan. Toss it into the chicken/shrimp and allow to cook for about 2 minutes.

9. Add your thinly sliced bell peppers, bean sprouts, and onions. Toss these into the pan. Season with a bit of salt and pepper, and then allow to cook for about 1 minute.

10. Add your eggs and mix to scramble the eggs around the ingredients. Allow it to sit and cook, then toss, sit, and cook, then toss. You want little pieces of egg visibly cooked onto the ingredients. If you over mix, it'll just stir in and get lost.

11. Add your noodles and toss. Add your remaining curry powder. Taste and adjust seasoning with a bit more salt and pepper.

12. Divide the mixture between four plates or bowls, and garnish with fresh cilantro and thinly sliced green onions.

13. Enjoy!

Main Dishes

o o o

Welcome to the heart of the book! While I will often make a soup or salad as my meal, there are times when something bigger, bolder, more complex, more impressive, or more composed is desired. This is where the following collection comes from, with a focus on variety. Some recipes are challenging, some are diverse, and many are quite simple, with a few slower-cooker and one-pan meals thrown in for good measure. I really tried to cover all bases, leaving no one with the sense that low-primal is boring or *ever* without variety!

Herb Pork Tenderloin Roast

SERVES: 6 · · · PREP: 5 MIN · · · COOK: 30 MIN · · · TOTAL: 45 MIN

2 Tbsp (30 mL) **olive oil, lard or bacon fat**

1/2 Tbsp (23 mL) chopped **fresh rosemary**

1 tsp (5 mL) chopped **fresh thyme**

1 tsp (5 mL) chopped **fresh oregano**

1 tsp (5 mL) chopped **fresh lemon zest**

1 Tbsp (15 mL) freshly squeezed **lemon juice**

4 **garlic cloves**, minced

2 **pork tenderloins** (1.1 kg), cleaned of sinew and extra fat (about 1–1/4 lb., each)

salt and **pepper** to taste

This is a very simple and basic pork roast, but a few ideas make it kind of a fun roast. A good butcher will happily trim and tie this for you, but you can also tie it yourself. As a general rule, I'm a minimalist when it comes to meats like this. Like the Prime Rib (p. 236), I tend to find a high-quality piece of meat and simply season it with salt and pepper. I like my meat to taste like meat, rather than being hidden by the other seasonings. That said, I know people love the different tastes, so I'm upping the ante on this one by doing a very basic herb blend. The same blend would be lovely on a nice piece of beef or chicken as well. A light coating would be quite tasty on some fish too!

The big trick with this roast is that it's actually two tenderloins, reversed and tied together. Most tenderloins are quite thin, cook quickly, and are often a bit dry. By tying them together, it creates a thicker and more even roast, which gives a larger margin for error. Additionally, by tying your own, you can put a thin layer of herbs between the two roasts.

1. Preheat oven to 400°F (204°C).

2. In a large mixing bowl, whisk together the oil, rosemary, thyme, oregano, lemon zest, lemon juice, and minced garlic.

3. Add trimmed tenderloins to the bowl and evenly coat with the herb mixture. If the tenderloins have been tied together, use your finger to push some of the herbs between the two pieces.

PER SERVING
CALORIES: 249.88
FAT: 8.14
PROTEIN: 39.78
CARBS: 1.17
FIBER: .16
SUGAR ALCOHOLS: 0
NET CARBS: 1.01

MORE FACTS: P. 526

4. If the tenderloins have not been tied, tie them together with the thin end touching the thicker end of the other, and vice versa. This will result in a very even thickness across the roast. With butcher's twine, tie and tighten the twine around the roast every 1 1/2-inches (4 cm).

5. Preheat a large ovenproof skillet or sauté pan. While this heats, season the outside of the pork roast with salt and pepper. Once the pan is hot, place the roast in the pan and sear one side. Once one section is seared, roll the roast and sear another section. Continue rolling and searing until the outside has a very nice golden sear.

6. Place the entire pan in the oven. After about 20 minutes, insert a meat thermometer into the thickest part of the roast, to test the temperature. When the temperature is about 135°F (57°C), remove the pan from the oven and set in a warm place. If it's not ready, let it continue to roast, checking the temperature every few minutes, until it is ready. Cover the pan with foil and allow the pork to rest for about 10 minutes.

7. With a knife or kitchen shears, remove the twine. Slice and serve!

PRIME RIB

SERVES: 8 · · · PREP: 15 MIN · · · COOK: 5 HR · · · TOTAL: 9 HR 45 MIN

1 10-lb. (4.5 kg) **prime rib**, bone in (about 4 ribs)

1/4 cup (60 mL) **fat** (tallow, ghee, bacon fat, etc.)

salt and **pepper** to taste

A prime rib is the big granddaddy of feasts. It's the juicy mountain of meat around which a feast of sides bows in its honor. In my world, this is reserved for special occasions, such as large family gatherings and/or the holidays. My family tends to like it well done, and as a result, I always overcook mine. I eat the least-cooked center cut, and Grandma gets the toastiest well-done end! A good prime rib needs nothing more than salt and pepper, time to relax before roasting, and time to relax after roasting. Beyond that, the lower and slower the temperature, the more moist it will be! The best roasts come down to the quality of the meat. For a magnificent meal such as this, I suggest going for the best!

PER SERVING
CALORIES: 1,164
FAT: 98
PROTEIN: 64
CARBS: 0
FIBER: 0
SUGAR ALCOHOLS: 0
NET CARBS: 0

MORE FACTS: P. 525

1. Most prime ribs are trimmed and tied by the butcher. However, if it is not, trim off any excess fat, leaving a good 1/4 (3/4 cm) inch of fat on the exterior. Tie the roast tightly with butcher's twine between each rib.

2. Leave the roast at room temperature for 4 hours. The warmer the roast, the more relaxed the muscle and the better the roast will be.

3. Preheat the oven to 450°F (232°C).

4. Rub the outside of the roast with melted fat or oil. The best options would be a warm liquid beef tallow, ghee, or bacon fat. However, most any fat will do. Olive oil would be fine, for example.

5. Season the outside of the roast with a liberal amount of salt. It's a large piece of meat and can withstand a good deal of salt. Roughly 3 tablespoons (45 mL) of standard salt or upwards of a 1/3 cup (80 mL) of coarser grinds, such as kosher or some sea salts. Layer it evenly on the outside, along with as much freshly ground black pepper as you'd like.

6. Place the roast, fat side up, on a roasting pan and place in the oven. Roast for 20 minutes to sear the outside.

7. After 20 minutes, turn the oven down to 200°F (93°C). After about 3 hours, check the internal temperature by inserting a meat thermometer into the thickest part of the roast. For a medium rare, you want the internal temperature to be about 125°F (52°C). A 10-lb. (4.5 kg) roast will take between 4 and 5 1/2 hours. Check every 30 minutes until it reaches the desired doneness.

Internal Temperature:

The prime rib will continue to cook and add about 5°F (2.5°C) after it's been pulled from the oven as it rests. This is called "carry over" cooking. To reach the desired doneness, remove the rib when it has reached the following internal temperature.

- **Rare:** 120°F (49°C)
- **Medium Rare:** 125°F (52°C)
- **Medium:** 130°F (54°C)
- **Medium Well:** 135°F (57°C)
- **Well:** 150°F (65°C)

8. I usually remove the prime rib at about 130°F (54°C), although my grandmother would prefer I go further. This results in a nice even medium. Her end is cut and seared in a pan and throw in the oven for an additional 5 minutes, but everyone else is quite happy with their cut!

9. Once the rib is removed from the oven, cover it with a foil tent and place it somewhere warm, to allow it to rest for 30 minutes, while the rest of the sides and sauces are assembled.

10. With a knife or kitchen shears, remove the twine. Slice and serve!

PORK CARNITAS

SERVES: 8 · · · PREP: 5 MIN · · · COOK: 8 HR · · · TOTAL: 8 HR 20 MIN

1 approximately 5 to 6 lb. (2.5 kg) **pork butt**, bone-in (also known as shoulder or Boston butt)

12 **garlic cloves**, sliced into thin slivers

1/2 cup (120 mL) **fresh lime juice**

salt and **pepper** to taste

A more traditional Mexican carnitas recipe will be fried in lard. Large pieces of pork are lightly seasoned and then fried until the meat is crunchy on the outside and soft, moist, and tender on the inside. This is then set aside to relax while the rest of the accouterments are assembled. It is then pulled, picked, and/or chopped into bite-sized pieces, when it is then loaded into a warm, handmade corn tortilla, topped with salsas and pickles, and enjoyed.

This version is somewhat simplified to allow for a delicious pork carnitas flavor, without the dangers involved with frying large pieces of pork in scalding hot lard.

1.   With a sharp, thin knife, like a boning knife, repeatedly stab the pork shoulder so 30 or so holes are made, running through most of the pork shoulder. This will help the flavors get a bit deeper into the meat.

2.   In a large bowl, combine the garlic and lime juice. Place the pork in the large bowl and season with upwards of 2 tablespoons (30 mL) salt and pepper to taste. Make sure the pork is evenly coated with lime juice and seasonings. Allow to sit for an hour.

3.   Turn on your slow cooker and set it to low.

4. Place the pork and all liquids into the slow cooker. Place the lid on the cooker and cook for 8 hours. Once cooked, carefully remove the pork from the slow cooker and remove the shoulder blade. Strain off the liquid and set aside.

PER SERVING
CALORIES: 812.32
FAT: 61.5
PROTEIN: 58.57
CARBS: 2.82
FIBER: 0.07
SUGAR ALCOHOLS: 0
NET CARBS: 2.75

MORE FACTS: P. 520

5. **Optional crispy tip:** If you want the little crispy bits, preheat the oven to 450°F (232°C). Pull the meat apart with two forks, or chop it with large knife. Spread it evenly on a baking tray. With a spoon, evenly drizzle some of the fat floating on the top of the strained liquid over the top of the pork. About 1/4 cup (60 mL) of fat should do it. Place the tray of pork into the oven and bake for about 8 to 12 minutes or until the top layer is crispy. Stir and continue crisping, until the desired crispiness is achieved. Remove from the oven and place in serving container.

6. Drizzle some of the remaining juice and fat over the meat for extra moisture if needed.

7. I suggest serving with Cheddar Taco Shells (p. 478) or lettuce leaves. The photo on the previous page is taken with purple cabbage leaves, salsa, sour cream, avocado, and cilantro.

Spicy Burger Casserole

SERVES: 8 · · · PREP: 20 MIN · · · COOK: 45 MIN · · · TOTAL: 1 HR 15 MIN

2 small (148 g) **red bell peppers**, stems removed and seeded

2 (130 g) **Poblano peppers**, stems removed and seeded

1 cup (240 mL) **water**

1/2 cup (120 mL) unsweetened **almond milk**

1/4 cup (60 mL) **fresh whole butter**

2 Tbsp (30 mL) **fat** (olive oil, butter, or even bacon fat!)

1 medium (110 g) **onion**, diced

2 **jalapeño peppers**, seeds and ribs removed, finely diced

4 **garlic cloves**, minced

2 lbs. (908 g) **ground beef** (80 lean/20 fat)

1 tsp (5 mL) ground **cumin seed**

1 tsp (5 mL) ground **coriander seed**

1 1/2 cups (360 mL) **almond flour**

1 lb. (454 g) **cheddar cheese**, grated and divided

salt and **pepper** to taste

Here's a really nice casserole. It has a few different moving parts, but it actually comes together quite quickly. Ultimately, it's a one-pan meal, which can be easily assembled the night before, chilled, and tossed into the oven just before dinner. This is also the kind of meal that would be nice frozen, before it's cooked. The dish would be assembled warm and then thoroughly chilled in the refrigerator. Then it would be tightly wrapped in plastic wrap and frozen. Defrost before baking.

1. Preheat oven to 350°F (177°C).

2. On a baking tray, place your bell peppers and Poblanos in the oven to roast. Roast them for about 10 minutes, just enough to soften.

3. Place a medium-sized saucepan on the stove with the water, almond milk, and butter. Bring to a slow simmer.

4. While waiting for the almond water to simmer, in a large sauté pan, over medium heat, add your fat, onions, garlic, and diced jalapeños, along with a little bit of salt and pepper. Sauté until the ingredients are soft and lightly colored (about 5 minutes). Once soft, add the ground beef. Season with the cumin, coriander, and a bit of salt and pepper. Cook and break apart with a wooden spoon until the meat is cooked, browned, and flavorful. Line the bottom of a 13" x 9" casserole pan (32.5 x 23 cm) with the ground beef.

5. Whisk the almond flour into the simmering almond-water mixture. Then, whisk in half of the grated cheddar cheese. Taste and adjust seasoning with a bit of salt and pepper.

6. Remove the peppers from the oven, if you haven't already. Flatten and layer the Poblano peppers on top of the beef.

PER SERVING
CALORIES: 735.88
FAT: 60.66
PROTEIN: 38.44
CARBS: 9.43
FIBER: 3.43
SUGAR ALCOHOLS: 0
NET CARBS: 6

MORE FACTS: P. 520

7. The almond flour mixture should be roughly the consistency of mashed potatoes. If it's too thick, add a bit of water or almond milk to thin it out. Spread the mixture evenly over the top of the peppers.

8. Top the almond meal mixture with the roasted red peppers.

9. Coat the top of the pan with an even layer of the remaining cheddar cheese. At this point, place, uncovered in the oven to bake (or in the refrigerator to chill). It is ready when the top is nicely golden brown, about 25 to 30 minutes. Serve!

Baked Salmon with Fennel, Leeks, and Cauliflower

SERVES: 6 · · · PREP: 5 MIN · · · COOK: 25 MIN · · · TOTAL: 30 MIN

1 (108 g) **lemon**

1/4 cup (60 mL) **extra virgin olive oil**, good quality

1 large head (840 g) **cauliflower**, cut into large florets

1 bulb (234 g) **fennel**, cut into 6 wedges

1 **white part** (89 g) **of a leek**, cut into 6 disks

1 **side** (1.4 kg) **of salmon** (or two smaller ones, about 3-lbs.)

1/4 cup (60 mL) whole grain **Dijon mustard**

salt and **pepper** to taste

This is quick and easy one-pan dish. On some level, it's probably got several fancy ingredients, but the simplicity and ease in which it comes together really counterbalances some of the cost. Additionally, it tends to translate as a somewhat special meal when it actually hits the dinner table. Light and tasty!

1. Preheat oven to 450°F (232°C).

2. Peel the very outer layer of the lemon. You want just the very outer yellow layer, the zest, not the white pith. Peel off strips of lemon zest with a vegetable peeler. Slice the strips into very thin noodles.

3. Boil a small amount of water. Add your lemon zest to the boiling water and boil for 30 seconds. Strain out the zest and set aside. This act kills a lot of the bitterness that can come from fresh lemon zest. It mellows it.

4. Cut your lemon in half and juice it into a large mixing bowl. Add your lemon zest strips and olive oil. Whisk together.

5. Add to the bowl the cauliflower, fennel, and leek disks. Carefully coat them with the lemon vinaigrette, being careful not to damage the leek disks or fennel wedges. Season with salt and pepper.

6. Line a large baking pan with parchment paper. Evenly distribute the vegetables on the parchment, so that it's one layer. Leave the rest of the lemon vinaigrette in the bowl. Place the vegetables in the oven for about 10 to 12 minutes to roast.

PER SERVING
CALORIES: 569.76
FAT: 36.85
PROTEIN: 49.42
CARBS: 13.91
FIBER: 5.42
SUGAR ALCOHOLS: 0
NET CARBS: 8.49

MORE FACTS: P. 522

7. While the vegetables roast, place the salmon in the bowl with the lemon vinaigrette. Season with salt and pepper.

8. When the vegetables are almost roasted through, remove them. Lay the raw salmon over the top of the cooked vegetables and place the tray back into the oven. Quickly spread the Dijon mustard over the salmon. Place the salmon back in the oven and bake for a further 7 to 10 minutes for thinner sides of salmon, or upwards of 15 for a larger, thicker side. The vegetables should be soft and lightly roasted and the salmon cooked until just opaque in the center, about a medium rare to medium.

9. Serve!

Serving note: I didn't think it needed at the time, but a nice vinaigrette with lemon juice, olive oil, and a mixture of fresh tarragon, dill, and/or chives with a touch of salt and pepper would be nice drizzled over this dish.

Brisket with Shrooms and Fennel

SERVES: 8 · · · PREP: 10 MIN · · · COOK: 10 HR 20 MIN · · · TOTAL: 10 HR 30 MIN

16 sprigs **fresh rosemary**

12 **garlic cloves**

5 lb. (2.3 kg) **beef brisket**, fat trimmed off

1/2 cup (120 mL) **red wine**, good quality

1/4 cup (60 mL) **balsamic vinegar**

2 lbs. (908 g) (about 24 large) **whole crimini (or button) mushrooms**, dirt removed with brush

2 bulbs (468 g) **fennel**, cut into 8 wedges each

2 Tbsp (30 mL) **olive oil**

salt and **pepper** to taste

Like the preceding salmon recipe, this is a one-pan dish, but it also involves tinkering with the pan somewhere in the middle. The end result is a delicious, soft, and tender beef brisket, with a slightly sweet rosemary jus, roasted mushrooms and fennel. Simple but somehow elegant!

Easier-ish note: The method described will result in something incredibly delicious. However, if you simply throw everything except the fennel into a casserole dish with a lid and bake it at 300°F (149°C) for about 4 hours, it'll taste almost as good. Just add the fennel when there's only about 20 minutes to go; otherwise, it will turn to mush.

1. Preheat oven to 225°F (121°C).

2. In a casserole dish, form a small bed of rosemary sprigs about the same size as the brisket. Place the garlic cloves onto the rosemary.

3. Season the brisket with salt and pepper. Place the brisket on the bed of rosemary and garlic. Pour the wine and balsamic vinegar over the top of the brisket. Place in the oven and roast, basting the brisket with the liquid about every 30 minutes. Total, the brisket will slowly cook for about 10 hours.

4. When the meat is close to done, in a medium-sized mixing bowl, combine the mushrooms and fennel with the oil. Season with salt and pepper, and mix to coat the vegetables with the seasoning and oil.

PER SERVING
CALORIES: 890.03
FAT: 66.15
PROTEIN: 55.04
CARBS: 12.03
FIBER: 2.89
SUGAR ALCOHOLS: 0
NET CARBS: 9.14

MORE FACTS: P. 520

5. Check the internal temperature of the meat by inserting a meat thermometer into the thickest part of the brisket. Once the thermometer reads 190°F (88°C), remove the meat.

6. Turn the oven to 450°F (232°C).

7. Leaving the meat in the dish, carefully pour the juices into a cup and set aside.

8. Evenly distribute the seasoned fennel and mushrooms around the meat, with some of it on top of the meat. The vegetables should be one layer in the pan. Brush some of the juice onto the vegetables. Place the pan in the oven and roast for about 20 minutes or until the fennel is soft and the mushrooms are cooked through. Remove the pan, set it in a warm place, and cover it. Allow it to rest for about 20 minutes.

9. While the vegetables roasted, the juice may have formed a layer of fat on top of it. You can very gently pour this off or whisk it into the sauce. I personally like some, but not more than a 1/4 to 1/2-inch layer (1 cm).

10. Slice the meat very thin, against the grain. Serve with the veggies and the juice from the pan.

CHICKEN PUTTANESCA

SERVES: 4 · · · PREP: 10 MIN · · · COOK: 20 MIN · · · TOTAL: 30 MIN

1/4 cup (60 mL) **extra virgin olive oil**, divided

4 (681 g) **boneless chicken breasts** (skin optional)

4 **garlic cloves**, minced

1 small (110 g) **red onion**, diced

1/2 cup (120 mL) pitted and very coarsely chopped **assorted Italian olives**

1 Tbsp (15 mL) coarsely chopped **capers**

4 **boneless anchovy filets**, coarsely chopped

1/2 tsp (1 mL) **crushed red chili flakes**

1 lb. (454 g) **assorted fresh tomatoes**, diced

salt and **pepper** to taste

Pollo alla Puttanesca literally means "Whore's Style Chicken." It's essentially just chicken with Sugo alla Puttanesca (whore-ish sauce) draped over the top of it. The sauce is a mixture of tomatoes, olives, capers, anchovies, garlic, and chili flakes. If you're a bit squeamish of the anchovies, bacon bits will do in a pinch!

Whatever the case, whatever the origin of the strange name, it is, no doubt, a tasty dish!

Preparation note: This recipe goes quickly, so have everything chopped and ready to go before you even start heating the pan.

Photo note: Served over a bed of Zoodles (p. 226).

1. Preheat oven to 450°F (232°C).

2. Preheat a large ovenproof sauté or skillet over high heat.

3. Coat the chicken breasts with 2 tablespoons (30 mL) of oil and season both sides with salt and pepper.

4. Place the chicken breast in the hot pan and sear them. When one side is nice and golden brown (about 2 minutes), turn them over and place the entire pan in the oven. Let roast in the oven for about 6 to 8 minutes.

5. When the breasts are firm to the touch, remove the pan and place it on a hot burner on the stove. Quickly remove the chicken breasts from the pan and place them on plates.

6. Add your remaining oil, garlic, onions, anchovies, olives, capers, and chili flakes to the pan. This will likely cook *quickly*. You want to lightly fry these ingredients in the oil for about 1 minute.

PER SERVING
CALORIES: 386.23
FAT: 20.51
PROTEIN: 38.6
CARBS: 9.46
FIBER: 2.55
SUGAR ALCOHOLS: 0
NET CARBS: 6.91

MORE FACTS: P. 519

7. Add the tomatoes to the pan with a bit of salt and pepper. Still over high heat, cook the sauce until the tomatoes are just cooked and the sauce is thick, about 2 more minutes.

8. Divide the sauce between the chicken breasts and serve!

 That's a randy sauce!

Seared Scallops with Almond-Parsnip Mash & Blackberry Beurre Rouge

SERVES: 4 · · · PREP: 30 MIN · · · COOK: 5 MIN · · · TOTAL: 35 MIN

20 jumbo (560 g) **sea scallops**

1 Tbsp (15 mL) **cooking fat** (such as ghee, olive oil, bacon fat, lard, etc.)

2 Tbsp (30 mL) **butter**

20 fresh **blackberries**, washed

2 **fresh sage leaves**, very thinly sliced and divided

1/4 cup (60 mL) **toasted slivered almonds**

1/2 full recipe **Almond-Parsnip Mash** (p. 342)

1 full recipe **Blackberry Beurre Rouge (p. 346)**

salt and **pepper** to taste

PER SERVING
CALORIES: 537.84
FAT: 35.9
PROTEIN: 28.68
CARBS: 21.78
FIBER: 6.24
SUGAR ALCOHOLS: 0
NET CARBS: 15.54

MORE FACTS: P. 519

This one is a bit of a departure. It's higher carb than most, but it's a real-foods based recipe with lots of good stuff in it. For the primal enthusiasts or those allowing for a bit more carbs than a super-low daily carb count will allow, this kind of dish is perfect. If I had to be brutally honest, it's here because it tastes great, I loved the idea, and I think the picture is pretty. That said, it's excellent for a special occasion or served as a smaller appetizer. In all cases, a fun, sweet, and buttery little dish!

Note: This recipe assumes you've got the Beurre Rouge and Mashed Parsnips being held warm on the side. This is incredibly quick and easy and really only requires scallops, sage, blackberries, butter, and toasted almonds. This part goes really quickly. When you're done, the scallops should be a beautifully seared medium rare. From there, simply assemble the plate and serve!

1. Preheat a large sauté pan or skillet over medium-high heat. You really need to make sure there is space between each scallop in the pan. Don't crowd the pans! As a result, you may need two pans over medium-high heat. If you crowd the pan, they won't sear. Instead, they'll just simmer, the juices will come out, and you'll have pasty-white erasers. It's crucial that the pans be hot and that there is plenty of space for the scallops to sear without bumping into one another and/or cooling down the pan.

2. Rub the scallops with fat, salt, and pepper.

3. Place the scallops evenly around the pan(s), with the flat sides down. Allow them to sit and sear for about 2 minutes, picking up a nice caramelization. At this point, add the butter and let it melt around the pan (trying not to disturb the scallops).

4. After they are nicely colored, flip them over and start searing the other side. Also, add the blackberries, the toasted almonds, and half of the sage leaves. Allow the pan to sit and continue searing for about 2 more minutes.

5. Place a nice dollop of the mash in the center of each of four plates. Drizzle a healthy amount of the Beurre Rouge around the dollops. Then, remove the scallops from the pan and quickly place 5 of them around each dollop of mash. Garnish each plate with the warm blackberry and almond mixture. Finally, sprinkle a bit of the fresh sage around the plates. Serve!

Coq au Vin

SERVES: 4 · · · PREP: 30 MIN · · · COOK: 2 HR 30 MIN · · · TOTAL: 3 HR

1 large (about 6 lb.) (2.7 kg) **chicken**, cut into 8 pieces

1/4 lb. (114 g) **salt pork** (or bacon), cut into cubes

1 lb. (454 g) **mushrooms**, dirt removed with brush

16 (128 g) **pearl onions**, peeled

2 large (144 g) **carrots**, peeled and cut into chunks

2 cups (480 mL) **burgundy wine**

4 **garlic cloves**, crushed

1 (50 g) **celery rib**, cut into chunks

10 sprigs **fresh thyme**

1 **bay leaf**

1/4 cup (60 mL) **whole butter**, cut into about 12 cubes

salt and **freshly cracked black pepper** to taste

Coq au Vin simply means "Cock with Wine" in French. It's a dish employing a cooking technique known as *braising*, which essentially means "cover and simmer in liquid," the idea being to break down the tough tendons and stringy nature of an old rooster. This ancient recipe is just a hair over the normal 10-carb goal (at about 12 carbs per massive serving), but it's also all good whole and real foods.

1. Season your chicken with salt and pepper. Set aside.

2. Over medium heat, in a large sauté pan or skillet, brown your salt pork cubes (or bacon is a fine substitute). Cook until crispy and golden. Remove the pork from the skillet and place into a large pot with a lid or Dutch oven.

3. Quickly add your chicken to the hot pan, skin side down. Only add enough chicken to cover the bottom of the pan in a single, uncrowded layer. You may increase the heat to high. Sear the skin side of the chicken pieces until golden and then place on top of the pork, in the larger pot. Continue searing the chicken until it is all seared.

4. In the same sauté pan/skillet, with the hot pork and chicken fat, add your mushrooms with a bit of salt and pepper. Cook until the edges brown a bit, and then add to the pot with the chicken.

5. In the same sauté pan/skillet, add your pearl onions and carrots. Cook long enough to brown the outside of these two ingredients, about 5 minutes. Add to the pot with the chicken.

6. Deglaze the hot sauté pan/skillet by adding your red wine to the pan. This will quickly boil, picking up flavor from the bottom of the pan. After about 1 minute, pour this warm mixture over the top of your chicken.

PER SERVING
CALORIES: 1,154.31
FAT: 75.13
PROTEIN: 79.69
CARBS: 14.84
FIBER: 2.83
SUGAR ALCOHOLS: 0
NET CARBS: 12.01

MORE FACTS: P. 521

7. To the chicken pot, add your garlic, celery, thyme, and bay leaf. At this point, you can refrigerate the whole pot as is and let it marinate overnight. This is optional but does develop more flavor.

8. About 2 1/2 hours prior to dinnertime, place the pot of chicken on the stove over medium heat. Bring to a very low simmer, then adjust the heat to low, maintaining the super slow simmer. Allow to simmer for about 2 hours or until the chicken is quite tender and tears easily.

9. Strain the liquid out of the chicken by either carefully pouring it out (using the lid or a large spoon to hold back the chicken) or placing a colander in a large bowl and dumping the entire pot into the colander. Either way, put the chicken back into the pot and keep it warm.

10. Place the braising liquid into a saucepot and place over high heat to boil. Once the liquid has reduced by about half and has noticeably thickened, turn the heat down to very low and whisk a single cube of butter into the sauce. Keep whisking, so that the butter will emulsify into the sauce, thickening and enriching it, rather than simply melting and floating on the top, like an oil slick. Once the first cube of butter is about 75 percent melted, add a second cube of butter. Keep whisking. When the second cube of butter is about 75 percent melted, add your third cube of butter. Keep adding the butter in this manner, continually whisking, until your sauce is thick, shiny, and luscious.

11. Divide your chicken and vegetables between four plates or bowls and drizzle the sauce over each.

12. Serve!

Smoked Paprika Chicken

SERVES: 4 · · · PREP: 5 MIN · · · COOK: 6 TO 8 HR · · · TOTAL: 8 HR

1 lb. (454 g) **assorted fresh tomatoes**, cut into rustic chunks

2 small (148 g) **piquillo peppers,** peeled, seeded, and cut into rustic chunks

1 medium (110 g) **onion,** cut into rustic chunks

2 Tbsp (30 mL) **red wine vinegar**

1 Tbsp (15 mL) **smoked paprika** (regular is fine)

1 Tbsp (15 mL) chopped **fresh thyme**

4 **garlic cloves,** minced

1 approximately 3 lb. (1.3 kg) **whole chicken**

1/4 cup (60 mL) **blanched and slivered almonds,** toasted

salt and **pepper** to taste

Slow cookers are new to me. I call the technique braising, which is essentially cooking something slowly in a pool of liquid. The method is not new, but this piece of equipment is. I wanted to see how well a whole chicken would hold up and threw in some fun flavors, inspired by the Spanish Romesco sauce (p. 378). In the end, I was completely flabbergasted by not only how flavorful it and the juices were, but also by how fall-off-the-bone tender the chicken was without being totally dry. An excellent recipe, and quick and simple to boot!

Note: I typically use peppers from a jar or can. The Spanish piquillo peppers would be excellent and are fairly easy to find. I also strongly suggest the smoked paprika. While this would be delicious with standard roasted red bell peppers and an unsmoked paprika, it really becomes a new dish with the piquillo peppers and smoked paprika. Don't worry about buying the smoked paprika just for this dish. If you're anything like me, you'll find you start adding to almost everything!

1. Turn on your slow cooker and set it to low.

2. In a medium mixing bowl, combine the tomatoes, peppers, onion, and red wine vinegar. Season with a bit of salt and pepper. Taste, adjust seasoning, and pour half of the mixture in the bottom of your slow cooker. Set the rest aside.

3. In a small mixing bowl, combine smoked paprika, fresh thyme, and garlic with salt and pepper. Mix.

4. Making sure the chicken has its giblets removed, coat the chicken with the paprika and thyme mixture. Add the chicken to the slow cooker, with the breast side facing up. Pour the remaining tomato mixture over the chicken.

PER SERVING
CALORIES: 828.3
FAT: 57.82
PROTEIN: 61.15
CARBS: 13.02
FIBER: 4.14
SUGAR ALCOHOLS: 0
NET CARBS: 8.87

MORE FACTS: P. 521

5. Cover and allow to cook on low for 6 to 8 hours.

6. Serve, along with the veggies and broth. Garnish with the toasted almond slivers.

Slow Cooker Cochinita Pibil

SERVES: 8 · · · PREP: 15 MIN · · · COOK: 9 HR · · · TOTAL: 1 DAY

1 (140 g) **orange**

1 3.5 oz. box (about 1/3 cup) (80 mL) **achiote paste**

2 **jalapeño peppers**, seeds removed

2 tsp (10 mL) ground **cumin seed**

1 tsp (5 mL) ground **coriander seed**

1 tsp (5 mL) ground **cinnamon**

1/2 tsp (2 mL) ground **cloves**

1/2 bunch (50 g) **cilantro**, washed and stems removed

12 **garlic cloves**, sliced into 1/8th inch (1 mm) thick "chips"

1/2 cup (120 mL) freshly squeezed **lime juice**

1 (2.7 kg) **pork butt**, bone-in (also known as shoulder or Boston butt, about 5 to 6 lbs.)

3 **banana leaves** (optional but recommended)

salt and **pepper** to taste

I have a weird fascination with *Cochinita Pibil* (Pit Buried Baby Pig). This is a near ancient dish, harking from the Mayan people in the Yucatan peninsula of Mexico. If you've never had it, stop what you're doing, start making some calls, and track down the ingredients. There are only two truly odd ones (achiote paste and banana leaves), with only one being an absolute must (the achiote).

If I had to compare it to something, it most closely resembles pulled barbecue pork from the Eastern part of North Carolina. It's a somewhat spicy and tart flavor. Recipes vary, but it's usually a shredded pork with sour orange and achiote paste (a paste made from the *annatto* seed). It's easily one of my favorite things on this planet. Easily!

1. With a vegetable peeler, peel 6 nice strips of just the outer orange rind, trying not to get any of the white pith. The strips should be about 3/4" x 3" (1.5 x 7 cm). Set aside. Juice the orange and set aside. Discard the rest of the orange.

2. In a blender, combine orange juice, rind, achiote paste, lime juice, jalapeños, cumin, coriander, cinnamon, cloves, cilantro, garlic, salt, and pepper. Puree until smooth.

3. With a paring knife or a sharpening steel, deeply puncture the pork, making twenty to thirty deep holes around the entire surface of the meat.

PER SERVING
CALORIES: 850.14
FAT: 62.05
PROTEIN: 59.42
CARBS: 10.51
FIBER: 2.69
SUGAR ALCOHOLS: 0
NET CARBS: 7.82

MORE FACTS: P. 524

4. In a large bowl or storage container with a lid, liberally rub the achiote mixture from the blender all over the outside of the pork, pushing some into the holes of the pork as well. Pour any remaining marinade over the top of the pork. Cover and refrigerate overnight.

5. **Highly suggested but optional step:** You will want three nice, clean, and uncracked sections of banana leaves about 1 1/2 x 3 feet (1/2 x 1 m). Line the inside of your slow cooker with banana leaves, making sure that large flaps hang over the outside of it.

6. Place the pork in the slow cooker, and pour the marinade over the top of the pork. If you used banana leaves, wrap the flaps over the top of the pork, to completely cover it, making a nice tidy little package.

7. Turn the cooker to low and cook for 8 to 9 hours.

8. When the meat can be easily shredded with a fork, remove it from the slow cooker and shred. Add enough of the remaining juice to keep it nice and moist.

9. **Optional step:** I *love* the juice at the bottom. Many simply discard it at this point, but I will put it in a pan and slowly reduce it until it's like a thin barbecue sauce. Then, I drizzle it over the top of my meat. With the pickled onions and some salsa… it's *fantastic!*

10. Serve with lime pickled onions (thin slices of red onion, soaked in lime juice and salt for at least 20 minutes) and Cheddar Taco Shells (p. 478).

Slow Cooker Brisket 'n' Cabbage

SERVES: 8 · · · PREP: 5 MIN · · · COOK: 8 HR · · · TOTAL: 1 DAY 8 HR

1/4 cup (60 mL) **coarse kosher** or **sea salt**

1 Tbsp (15 mL) **black peppercorns**

1/4 **cinnamon stick**

2 **bay leaves**

2 whole **cloves**

2 whole **allspice berries**

2 whole **juniper berries**

1 small (110 g) **white onion**, diced

2 ribs (101 g) **celery**, diced

1 small (72 g) **carrot**, peeled and diced

2 Tbsp (30 mL) **Dijon mustard**, whole grain

5 lb. (2.3 kg) **beef brisket**

1 large head (908 g) **green cabbage**

salt to taste

This idea came to me as a request for more slow-cooker recipes, right around the same time I was asked a question about why corned beef is "corned" (it's related to what are often referred to as "corns" of coarse salt crystals). I thought it would be fun to take some of the flavors of that dish and do a quicker marinated brisket (rather than the week or two brining period it can often take). Once marinated, cook it low and slow with some cabbage. It is divine!

1. In a spice or coffee grinder, grind salt with pepper, cinnamon, bay leaves, cloves, allspice, and juniper berries.

2. In a blender, combine onion, carrot, and celery with the whole grain mustard. Puree together. If there isn't enough liquid from the vegetables, add just enough water to get them started.

3. Rub the trimmed brisket with the spice blend. Then, in a large bowl, coat the brisket with the pureed onion paste, making sure it's well coated. Cover or wrap tightly in plastic wrap and place in the refrigerator overnight, up to 24 hours.

4. The next day, cut the green cabbage into 8 wedges, cutting through the stem end at the bottom, so that each wedge is still held together by the core. Line the bottom of a slow cooker with the cabbage. Season each wedge with just a bit of salt and pepper as you add it.

5. Place the brisket, fat side up, on top of the bed of cabbage. Pour any juices from the bowl over the top of the beef and cabbage.

6. Cover and allow to cook on low for 8 to 10 hours.

7. Slice and serve with the jus and a wedge of cabbage!

PER SERVING
CALORIES: 831.92
FAT: 63.24
PROTEIN: 52.91
CARBS: 10.11
FIBER: 4.1
SUGAR ALCOHOLS: 0
NET CARBS: 6

MORE FACTS: P. 522

Chicken with Pancetta and Mushrooms

SERVES: 4 · · · PREP: 10 MIN · · · COOK: 15 MIN · · · TOTAL: 30 MIN

1 cup (240 mL) **chicken stock or broth**

8 leaves **fresh sage**, divided

1 lb. (454 g) **crimini or button mushrooms**, halved or quartered

2 cups (480 mL) **cubed eggplant**

1/4 cup (60 mL) **olive oil**, divided

4 **garlic cloves**, minced

1 Tbsp (15 mL) coarsely chopped **capers**

4 (681 g) **boneless chicken breasts** (skin optional)

8 slices (100 g) **pancetta**, sliced into strips

1/2 cup (120 mL) **chilled whole butter** (one stick), cut into about 12 cubes

salt and **pepper** to taste

This one started life as *Saltimbocca di Pollo*, which is an Italian dish loosely translated as "chicken that jumps into your mouth." It's usually chicken rolled up with prosciutto and sage, and then cooked. I'm not a big fan of cooked prosciutto and tend to prefer cooked pancetta (similar to bacon but not smoked). So I came up with this *Saltimbocca*-inspired dish intended to be cooked fairly fast and furious. It may look complicated and exotic, but it all comes together quite quickly and *tastes* amazing!

1. Place the chicken stock in a small saucepan on the stove and bring it to a slow boil. The goal is to reduce it by half.

2. Preheat oven to 400°F (204°C). Have a small baking tray or pan for 4 chicken breasts close and ready to go.

3. Chop 4 leaves of the sage and add it to a medium-sized mixing bowl. To the bowl add the mushrooms, eggplant, 3 tablespoons (45 mL) of the olive oil, garlic, and capers. Season the mixture with salt and pepper, and set aside.

4. Heat a large sauté pan or skillet over high heat. Season the chicken breasts with salt and pepper. Add the remaining 1 tablespoon (15 mL) of oil and swirl around the pan. Sear both sides of the chicken breasts so that they are nice and golden.

5. While the chicken is searing, check the mushroom mixture. Some water may have formed from the eggplant. Pour any extra liquid into the sink.

PER SERVING
CALORIES: 615.24
FAT: 44.24
PROTEIN: 41.93
CARBS: 6.44
FIBER: 2.2
SUGAR ALCOHOLS: 0
NET CARBS: 4.24

MORE FACTS: P. 520

6. As soon as the chicken is nicely seared, place the 4 breasts on your small baking tray. Immediately add your mushroom mixture to the hot sauté pan and scatter it evenly along the bottom. While the mushrooms cook, quickly place 1 sage leaf on each chicken breast, followed by 2 slices of pancetta. Place the tray in the oven and allow to bake.

7. Once the mushroom and eggplant are mostly cooked, add your reducing chicken stock to the hot pan. This should immediately boil and let off a lot of steam. Stir the mushrooms. Turn the heat off the pan and add a small piece of cold, fresh butter to the pan and swirl it around. When one piece of butter is about halfway melted, add a second piece of cold, fresh butter. When that second piece is halfway melted, add a third piece. Keep swirling in the cold, fresh pieces of butter until it has created a lovely and luxurious mushroom chicken jus. This is done in this manner so that the butter is incorporated into the jus, without simply melting and forming an oil slick on the top of the stock. This slow, cold swirling method emulsifies it into the stock in a method known as *monté* (pronounced mont-tay).

8. Remove the chicken from the oven when it has cooked through (about 6 to 8 minutes, depending on size of breasts and time in the pan during the searing process).

9. Divide the sauce between 4 plates or bowls and add a chicken breast to the top of each. Serve!

Ham 'n' Cheddar Chicken

SERVES: 2 · · · PREP: 10 MIN · · · COOK: 20 MIN · · · TOTAL: 35 MIN

1 large (118 g) **chicken breast**, boneless and skinless

2 slices (56 g) **ham**

1/2 cup (120 mL) grated **cheddar cheese**

4 slices (100 g) **raw bacon**

salt and **pepper** to taste

I'm a big fan of wrapping things in bacon (as evidenced by several of the recipes in this book). A bacon wrapper accomplishes several things. 1. It adds moisturizing fat to the dish, which somewhat "self-bastes" as it cooks. 2. It adds some salt to the dish, enhancing the flavors. 3. It adds a touch of smokiness, which adds some character. 4. It also holds things together, forming an actual wrapper of food! 5. It can also be quite pretty! In this case, I took some classic favorite flavors and married them all into one tasty dish.

Note: Recommended to be served with the Dijon-Caper Cream Sauce (p. 362) and maybe garnished with some chives. Outstanding!

1. Preheat oven to 425°F (218°C).

2. Butterfly the chicken breast (or buy it that way). Lay the chicken breast on a flat cutting board. Place a knife parallel to the cutting board, about 1/2 inch (1.3 cm) above the surface. Slice into the breast, maintaining a slice that is parallel to the cutting board and essentially cuts the breast in half. However, do not cut through the entire breast. Also, be careful not to tear the meat or slice either side too thin. Both top and bottom halves should be equal in thickness. You want to stop slicing just prior to slicing through the opposing side of the breast. Once you've sliced almost through the breast, you can open it, like a book. You essentially want to create a thin sheet of chicken.

3. Once you've got a thin sheet of chicken breast, place it between two sheets of plastic wrap and pound it even thinner. You can use a mallet, rolling pin, or even the bottom of a saucepan. Just be careful to hit it flatly and evenly, or else you will make deep divots or holes in the chicken. Ideally, the chicken will be a thin and even sheet of chicken breast when you are done.

PER SERVING
CALORIES: 444.92
FAT: 33.86
PROTEIN: 30.51
CARBS: 2
FIBER: 0.28
SUGAR ALCOHOLS: 0
NET CARBS: 1.72

MORE FACTS: P. 525

4. Very lightly season the chicken with salt and pepper.

5. Place your slices of ham on the chicken.

6. Evenly distribute the cheese over the slices of ham.

7. Roll your chicken into a log. Try and roll it as tightly as possible. Set it aside.

8. Set your 4 bacon slices on a cutting board, and cut them all in half. This will result in 8 short slices of bacon. Stretch them out a bit.

9. Lay one slice of bacon on the cutting board; then offset a second slice of bacon. The top and bottom should match, but the slice should be next to the original. Continue this shingling process until you have a sheet of bacon slices.

10. Preheat a large ovenproof sauté pan, over medium-high heat.

11. Lay the chicken log at the top of the sheet of bacon, making sure it's perpendicular to the strips of bacon. Tightly roll the log into the bacon sheet, making sure there is a clean seam at the bottom of the finished log.

12. Once the log is complete and the pan is hot, carefully place the seam side down in the sauté pan. Let it sear for about 30 seconds, then place the entire pan in the oven. Allow it to bake for roughly 20 to 30 minutes, depending on the size and thickness of the log.

13. Once the chicken has an internal temperature of 160°F (71°C), remove from the oven and allow to rest in the pan for 10 minutes before slicing.

14. Slice and serve!

Paella Mixta

SERVES: 8 · · · PREP: 20 MIN · · · COOK: 30 MIN · · · TOTAL: 1 HR

16 medium-sized (224 g) **clams**, fresh and alive

1 head (840 g) **large cauliflower**

4 (202 g) **celery ribs**, cut into large dice

2 small (148 g) **red bell peppers**, seeded and cut into large dice

1 small (110 g) **onion**, cut into large dice

1/2 cup (120 mL) **frozen peas and carrots**

4 **garlic cloves**, minced

1/2 tsp (1 mL) **crushed red chili flakes**

1/2 tsp (1 mL) **saffron threads**

4 (340 g) **Spanish chorizo links** (or a hot Italian sausage)

1 (1.3 kg) **whole chicken**, cut into 8 pieces

2 cups (480 mL) **hot chicken stock or broth**

16 (454 g) **shrimp (16/20)**

salt and **pepper** to taste

PER SERVING
CALORIES: 564.18
FAT: 31.18
PROTEIN: 54
CARBS: 13.59
FIBER: 4.56
SUGAR ALCOHOLS: 0
NET CARBS: 9.03

MORE FACTS: P. 523

Paella is a traditional rice dish from the eastern coast of Spain. Roughly two hundred years of history are behind the flavors and concepts in this dish, from the ingredients and method, right on down to the traditional paella pan that is often used. As with many of my recipes, the idea is to remove the carbs, while maintaining a mind-bendingly delicious recipe! This particular recipe would be called a *mixed* paella because of the combination of land and sea. In this case, I'm substituting the rice with grated cauliflower and the beans with green peas (I'm always looking for an excuse to slip a few of these into things ... look away, Paleo people! *wink*). The end result is a quick one-pan meal fit for the whole family!

Note: This recipe is traditionally made with saffron, a spice that comes from a flower called the saffron crocus. It's the most expensive spice, by weight, on the planet, which suggests I should offer an alternative for those unwilling or unable to spring for a pinch of saffron. Ground turmeric, annatto seed, and/or paprika will make for a sincere replacement, but will do little more than impart the color. The flavor will be lost. However, skipping it altogether would still result in an absolutely delicious meal.

1. Before doing anything, soak your fresh clams in a bowl of cold water with a slow, steady stream of cold water dripping from the faucet into the bowl. This helps remove a touch of extra saltiness and sand. Let this sit with the water dripping in it.

2. Remove the leaves and core from the cauliflower.

3. With a cheese grater, grate the cauliflower over the largest grate section. An alternative is to put it into a food processor and pulse the cauliflower until it's the size of small grains; you don't want to puree it, which is why I like the cheese-grater method.

4. In a large mixing bowl, combine the grated cauliflower, celery, bell pepper, onion, peas, carrots, garlic, chili flakes, and saffron. Season with a bit of salt and pepper. Mix and set aside.

 262 MAIN DISHES

5. Cut each sausage link in half. Set aside.

6. Heat your largest, widest pot or pan over high heat.

7. Season the chicken with salt and pepper. Line the bottom of the hot pot with the chicken, skin sides down. If you'd like to add some oil, you may, but the chicken skin has its own fat that cooks right out. No extra oil is required. Sear both sides of the chicken.

8. Once the chicken is seared on both sides, remove it from the pot and quickly add the cauliflower mixture to the pan. Stir the cauliflower mixture in the pan. Push the sausage links into the cauliflower rice mixture. Place the chicken on top of the faux rice. Add the hot chicken broth to the pan and cover it. Once it boils, turn the heat to medium-low and allow the pan to simmer for about 4 to 6 minutes.

9. While the chicken simmers, pick your clams out of the bowl by scooping them up with your hands and transferring them to another bowl. Any sand or debris should be left at the bottom of the original bowl. Wash the original bowl and set aside; we'll use it one more time. Place the new bowl of clams under the slow stream of cold water.

10. Peel your shrimp and remove the big vein running through the back. Set aside.

11. Transfer your clams one more time. Once your clams are clean and happy, pull them up and out of the bowl, and place them on a dry towel or in a colander to drip dry.

12. Open the lid of the pot and evenly place the shrimp along the top of the pot, pushing them down into the liquid. Follow this by doing the same thing with the cleaned clams. Replace the lid and allow it to simmer for about 6 more minutes or until the shrimp are cooked through and the clams open. Discard any clams that do not open. Serve!

OVEN-ROASTED SPATCHCOCK CHICKEN

SERVES: 2 · · · PREP: 10 MIN · · · COOK: 50 MIN · · · TOTAL: 1 HR

2 tsp (10 mL) **fresh thyme**, chopped

2 tsp (10 mL) **fresh rosemary**, chopped

2 tsp (10 mL) **fresh oregano**, chopped

1/2 tsp (2mL) **crushed red chili flakes**

4 **garlic cloves**, minced

1/4 cup (60 mL) **light oil** (such as coconut, olive, or ghee)

1 (1.4 kg) **whole chicken**

salt and **pepper** to taste

This chicken recipe involves a process called *spatch-cocking* or *spattlecocking*, a process where the backbone of a whole chicken is removed and the bird is flattened and cooked.

Spatchcocking a bird is a great way to go for a few reasons:

- The bird cooks faster. Because it's flat and thin, it gets direct heat from both sides, while also cooking more evenly.
- It usually tastes better. With a whole bird, not a lot of seasoning usually makes it into the cavity. It's just tough to get in there and season it. However, with a spatchcocked bird, you can season one side, flip it over, and season the other!
- It's often a bit easier to get a crispy skin. Because this lies flat, even in a big pan or on a grill, the skin gets an even and direct blast of heat, crisping it up!
- It's a little easier, in my opinion, to handle a spatchcocked chicken. It's been flattened and just cuts up more easily. A whole bird is round and likes to wobble and roll around.

Serving size: The recipe is for an about 3-lb. (1.4 kg) bird, which would feed 2 to 3 people. Add a few herbs and get a 4 or 5-lb. (2 kg) bird for 4 people. Adjust cooking time accordingly.

PER SERVING
CALORIES: 1,695.49
FAT: 130.17
PROTEIN: 114.2
CARBS: 2.91
FIBER: 0.51
SUGAR ALCOHOLS: 0
NET CARBS: 2.4

MORE FACTS: P. 521

1. Preheat oven to 450°F (232°C).

2. Combine your herbs, chili flakes, garlic, and oil. Mix and then pour half into a large mixing bowl while reserving the other half for later.

3. Place bird on the cutting board with the backbone down. Stick a large chef's knife into the cavity, just to one side of the backbone, pushing the entire length of the knife through, so that the tip is sticking out near the neck. Then, with force, push the knife straight through the ribcage. I move the knife to the other side of the backbone and repeat. Two swift moves and the backbone pops right out! Alternately, with tough kitchen shears, you can cut through the ribs on both sides of the spine. While the inside cavity is facing up, position the chicken so the drumsticks are pointing away from you. Use a paring knife to make a small cut in the white cartilage that conceals the top of the breastbone. Bend both halves of the carcass backward at the cut to expose the breastbone. It should pop right up through the cut. Run your thumbs or index fingers down both sides of the breastbone to separate it from the meat; then, pull the bone out. The breastbone may break into two pieces when you pull it out, especially if you haven't separated it well enough from the breast meat using your fingers. No big deal, just pull out the two pieces. Now that the breastbone and spine have both been removed, your bird should easily lie flat.

4. Place the chicken in the bowl with the herb oil. Coat the chicken, evenly and well, with the herb oil. At this point, it's not uncommon to let the bird marinate in the herbs for a few hours, up to overnight. This step is optional.

5. Season both sides of the bird with salt and pepper.

6. Preheat a large skillet or ovenproof sauté pan (large enough for the whole bird to easily fit in the bottom of the pan). The pan needs to be very hot. Once the pan is very hot, place your chicken in the pan with the skin side down.

7. Place the whole pan in the oven and allow it to roast until a thermometer in the deepest part of the leg reads 160°F (71°C). Start checking at about 30 minutes. Depending on the size of the bird, it will be ready between 35 and 50 minutes. When it is the correct temperature, remove the pan and turn the bird over, so that the skin is now facing up. Cover with foil and leave somewhere warm for about 10 minutes. This will let the bird relax, the juices will settle, and the chicken will continue cooking on its own, from the internal heat still in the chicken.

8. Drizzle some of the fresh herb oil over the top. Cut and serve!

Cuban Stuffed Pork Loin

SERVES: 6 · · · PREP: 10 MIN · · · COOK: 1 HR · · · TOTAL: 1 HR 10 MIN

1 (140 g) **fresh orange**, washed

1 (67 g) **fresh lime**, washed

1/2 cup (120 mL) **kosher salt** (or 5 Tbsp [75 mL] standard table salt)

3 lbs. (1.4 kg) center cut **pork loin**, boneless

1/2 cup (120 mL) coarsely chopped **assorted olives with pimento**

1/4 cup (60 mL) coarsely chopped **raisins**

1 Tbsp (15 mL) coarsely chopped **capers**

4 **garlic cloves**, minced

2 tsp (10 nL) coarsely chopped **fresh oregano**

1 Tbsp (15 nL) ground **cumin seed**

2 Tbsp (30 mL) **fat** (lard, ghee, bacon fat, etc.)

salt and **pepper** to taste

PER SERVING
CALORIES: 506.56
FAT: 30.34
PROTEIN: 46.45
CARBS: 7.9
FIBER: 1.03
SUGAR ALCOHOLS: 0
NET CARBS: 6.87

MORE FACTS: P. 523

I'm a big fan of mixing things up and dipping into a variety of different tastes and cultures. So many times I hear about steak and eggs being all we can eat. People often use boredom as a reason to cheat. So, by introducing and playing with a lot of different flavors, it decreases the sense that there are limits. The only limits are your creativity! Combined with this book, most all real-food based ingredients, and all the inspiration and ideas the Internet can offer, you should never ever feel bored. Problem solved!

In this case, I went for a Cuban flavor profile, which has some really interesting tastes to it.

Note: The brining step isn't required, but it really helps to create a deeply moist and flavorful roast. I highly recommend it. It only takes a few extra moments and a bit of timing. It's worth it. This is perfect served with the Coconut Cauli-Rice (p. 322) and Orange Mojo (p. 354)!

1. In a medium-sized saucepan, bring 1 1/2 cups (360 mL) of water to a boil.

2. While waiting for the water to boil, with a zester or a vegetable peeler, remove the very outer layer of about half of both the orange and lime. Do your best not to get any of the bitter white pith underneath the fragrant orange and green outer layers of rind. Coarsely chop this for a total of about 1 total tablespoon of the two mixed zests. Place the zest into a small container with a lid and save for later. Juice the lime and orange, and place the juice in a large bowl or plastic container (large enough for the pork and about 5 cups of liquid).

3. Add 2 1/2 cups (600 mL) of very cold ice water (with a lot of ice) to the mixed citrus juice.

4. Once the water is boiling, whisk the salt into the boiling water until it completely dissolves. Pour this mixture into the ice water and citrus juices. Whisk this in. This should result in a cold liquid with a few small, remaining half-melted ice cubelets.

5. Butterfly the pork loin, so that you have a large rectangular sheet of pork loin. Place the pork in the brine. Cover and refrigerate overnight, and up to 24 hours.

6. About 90 minutes prior to serving, preheat an oven to 325°F (162°C).

7. In a small mixing bowl, add the citrus zest you saved along with the olives, raisins, capers, garlic, and fresh oregano.

8. Remove the pork from the brine and wash it off in the sink. Discard the brine. Dry the pork with a towel and lay flat.

9. Evenly spread the olive mixture on the sheet of pork. Roll the pork into a log, like a cinnamon roll. With butcher's twine, tie the roast into a tight cylinder. Season the outside of the log with the ground cumin and a light dusting of salt and pepper.

10. Place a large, ovenproof sauté pan (large enough to hold the roast with room to spare) on the stove, over a medium-hot temperature, to begin preheating.

11. When the pan is hot, add the fat to the pan and swirl it around to coat the pan. Immediately place the seam side of the pork in the pan and sear it. Once a nice golden color has developed, roll the log about 45 degrees and sear a nice section of the roast. Continue this process until the whole roast has a nice golden color and is seared. Place the whole pan with the roast in the oven.

12. Allow the pork to roast for about 35 minutes or until the internal temperature is 140°F (60°C).

13. Once the pork has reached the desired temperature, remove it from the oven. Cover with foil and place in a warm place to relax for about 15 minutes.

14. Remove the twine with a knife or kitchen shears, slice, and serve!

ROPA UN POCO VIEJA

SERVES: 8 · · · PREP: 20 MIN · · · COOK: 8 HR · · · TOTAL: 8 HR 20 MIN

2 medium (182 g) **tomatoes**, diced

2 small (148 g) **red bell peppers**, peeled, seeded, and sliced into strips

1/2 cup (120 mL) coarsely chopped **assorted olives with pimento**

1 small (110 g) **onion**, sliced

4 **garlic cloves**, minced

2 tsp (10 mL) coarsely chopped **fresh oregano**

2 **bay leaves**

1 5- to 6-lb. (2.5 kg) **pork butt**, bone in (also known as shoulder or Boston butt)

1 Tbsp (15 mL) ground **cumin seed**

2 Tbsp (30 mL) **fat** (tallow, ghee, bacon fat, etc.)

salt and **pepper** to taste

Ropa Vieja was actually made for me the first time in Mexico, by a Venezuelan woman. I'd never heard of *Ropa Vieja* prior to that. While it looked delicious and smelled amazing, it's one of many recipes with a strange name that makes me wonder which way is up. *Ropa Vieja* really means "old clothes" in Spanish. What an odd name for a recipe, right? Typically, this Spanish dish is made from super heavily cooked beef, until it completely breaks down into tasty yumminess, but I'd had this lovely pork shoulder that I'd bought from a local farmer kicking around my freezer, and I wanted to try something different. So, I took this Spanish–North African–Caribbean–Cuban dish as inspiration and made it with that lovely shoulder (which is actually occasionally used in the Canary Islands). I'm so glad I did too. It was incredibly easy to make, literally just throwing a bunch of stuff in the slower cooker and letting it do its thing. The end result was *amazing* and worthy of its new name!

Note: This would be delicious over a bed of Miracle Cauli-Rice (p. 320).

1. Turn on your slow cooker and set it to low.

2. In a medium mixing bowl, combine the tomatoes, peppers, olives, onion, garlic, oregano, and bay leaves. Season with a bit of salt and pepper. Taste, adjust seasoning, and pour half the mixture in the bottom of your slow cooker. Set the rest aside.

3. Season the pork with the cumin, as well as salt and pepper. It's a large piece of meat, so there's no need to be bashful.

4. Place a large, ovenproof sauté pan (large enough to hold the roast, with room to spare) on the stove, over a medium-hot temperature, to begin preheating.

PER SERVING
CALORIES: 864.6
FAT: 65.46
PROTEIN: 59.19
CARBS: 4.93
FIBER: 1.33
SUGAR ALCOHOLS: 0
NET CARBS: 3.6

MORE FACTS: P. 519

5. When the pan is hot, add the fat to the pan and swirl it around to coat the pan. Immediately place the pork in the pan and sear. Sear all sides. When all sides are nicely golden and seared, place the pork in the slow cooker. Pour the remaining vegetable mixture over the top of the pork.

6. Place the lid on the cooker and cook for 8 hours. Once cooked, carefully remove the pork from the slow cooker and remove the shoulder blade. Strain off the liquid and set aside.

7. Pull the meat apart with two forks, or chop it with large knife. Drizzle some of the remaining juice and fat over the meat for extra moisture if needed. Serve!

BLACK PEPPER BEEF AND BROCCOLINI

SERVES: 4 · · · PREP: 5 MIN · · · COOK: 7 MIN · · · TOTAL: 12 MIN

1 1/2 lb. (681 g) **tender boneless beef** (such as rib eye or tenderloin), cut into bite-sized cubes

1 lb. (454 g) **broccolini**, cut into florets and pieces about 1 inch (2.5 cm) long

1 small (110 g) **red onion**, diced

4 **garlic cloves**, minced

1 Tbsp (15 mL) minced **fresh ginger**

1 Tbsp (15 mL) **freshly cracked black pepper**

1 tsp (5 mL) **sesame oil**

1/4 cup (60 mL) **soy sauce** (or coconut aminos)

1/4 cup (60 mL) **rice wine vinegar**

2 Tbsp (30 mL) **sugar replacement**

1/4 tsp (1 mL) **glucomannan powder**

1 Tbsp (15 mL) **coconut oil**

2 Tbsp (30 mL) black (or white) **sesame seeds**

salt to taste

PER SERVING
CALORIES: 546.23
FAT: 33.63
PROTEIN: 38.8325
CARBS: 23.375
FIBER: 4.835
SUGAR ALCOHOLS: 7.5
NET CARBS: 11.04

MORE FACTS: P. 522

I was once asked for PF Chang's clone recipes. I thought it was a cute idea, so I set out to create a batch of recipes based around those flavors and cooking techniques. Here I present a really nice Black Pepper Beef, a slightly sweet and spicy beef stir-fried with broccolini and finished with a glucomannan-thickened soy-based sauce (glucomannan is a naturally occurring fiber which comes from the konjac plant). The glucomannan is completely optional to the recipe, but that little tiny bit of fiber will thicken the sauce, allowing it cling to the beef and broccolini florets. It'll also resemble the PF Chang's tastes and textures... *just that much more.*

Beef Cut Note: I used a cubed rib eye steak in this recipe, but any tender cut will do quite nicely. Tenderloin, flat iron, New York, and flank would also be nice alternatives.

1. In a large-sized mixing bowl, combine beef, broccolini, diced onions, garlic, ginger, black pepper, and sesame oil. Add some salt to taste, and combine the mixture. Set aside.

2. In a small mixing bowl, combine soy sauce, rice wine vinegar, sweetener, and glucomannan powder. Whisk until the glucomannan and sweetener are dissolved. Set aside.

3. Heat a large wok over high heat. (If you do not have a wok, this can be done in two large sauté pans, placed over two hot burners.) This is intended to be done *very* fast, over very high heat. If the pan is not hot enough, or too many ingredients are added, then the pan cools down and the food steams, rather than sears. This is why two pans (with twice the surface area) can work in place of a large wok.

4. Once your wok, or two pans, is very hot, add coconut oil and quickly swirl to coat the bottom. Immediately add the beef mixture, evenly spreading the ingredients along the bottom of the wok, making a single layer. Allow the ingredients to sear for about 1 minute. Mix the ingredients and spread them back into a single layer. Repeat this process, evenly searing the mixture and then mixing again. The beef will overcook quickly, so this should only take about 3 minutes in order to maintain a nice medium rare.

5. Once everything has been quickly seared, pick up the soy mixture. Give it one last mix, to make sure any glucomannan or sweetener hasn't stuck to the bottom. Pour it evenly over the ingredients. It should immediately boil. Toss the ingredients to coat with the mixture. Allow the mixture to continue cooking for about 2 more minutes, mixing occasionally.

6. If the sauce isn't thick enough for your tastes, dissolve about 1/4 teaspoon (1 mL) of glucomannan powder in 1 tablespoon (15 mL) of soy sauce and add to the beef.

7. After no more than about 6 or 7 total minutes, the sauce should be nicely thickened and the beef should be about a medium rare. Garnish with sesame seeds and serve with Miracle Cauli-Rice (p. 320)!

ALMOND CASHEW CHICKEN

SERVES: 6 · · · PREP: 15 MIN · · · COOK: 7 MIN · · · TOTAL: 22 MIN

4 (681 g) **boneless chicken breasts** (skin optional), sliced into thin strips

16 (304 g) **shiitake mushrooms**, stemmed and quartered

1 small (110 g) **onion**, diced

2 (101 g) **celery ribs**, diced

1/2 cup (120 mL) **snow peas**, fibrous stem and string removed

4 **garlic cloves**, minced

1 Tbsp (15 mL) minced **fresh ginger**

1 tsp (5 mL) **crushed red chili flakes** (optional)

1/4 cup (60 mL) **soy sauce** (or coconut aminos)

1/4 cup (60 mL) **rice wine vinegar**

2 Tbsp (30 mL) **sugar replacement**

1/4 tsp (1 mL) **glucomannan powder**

1 Tbsp (15 mL) **coconut oil**

1/4 cup (60 mL) **slivered almonds**, toasted

1/4 cup (60 mL) **roasted cashew halves**

1/4 bunch (25 g) coarsely chopped **fresh cilantro**

salt and **pepper** to taste

1. In a large-sized mixing bowl, combine chicken, mushrooms, diced onions, celery, snow peas, garlic, ginger, chili flakes (optional), and some salt to taste. Combine the mixture. Set aside.

2. In a small mixing bowl, combine soy sauce, rice wine vinegar, sweetener, and glucomannan powder. Whisk until the glucomannan and sweetener are dissolved. Set aside.

3. Heat a large wok over high heat. If you do not have a wok, this can be done in two large sauté pans, placed over two hot burners. This is intended to be done *very* fast, over very high heat. If the pan is not hot enough, or too many ingredients are added, then the pan cools down and the food steams, rather than sears. This is why two pans (with twice the surface area) can work in place of a large wok.

4. Once your wok, or two pans, is very hot, add coconut oil and quickly swirl to coat the bottom. Immediately add the chicken mixture, evenly spreading the ingredients along the bottom of the wok, making a single layer. Allow the ingredients to sear for about 1 minute. Mix the ingredients and spread them back into a single layer. Repeat this process, evenly searing the mixture and then mixing again. The chicken will overcook quickly, so this should only take about 3 minutes.

5. Once everything has been quickly seared, pick up the soy mixture. Give it one last mix, to make sure any glucomannan or sweetener hasn't stuck to the bottom. Pour it evenly over the ingredients. It should immediately boil. Toss the ingredients to coat with the mixture. Allow the mixture to continue cooking for about 2 more minutes, mixing occasionally.

6. If the sauce isn't thick enough for your tastes, dissolve about 1/4 teaspoon (1 mL) of glucomannan powder in 1 tablespoon (15 mL) of soy sauce and add to the chicken.

PER SERVING
CALORIES: 279.89
FAT: 11.44
PROTEIN: 28.14
CARBS: 16.68
FIBER: 3.21
SUGAR ALCOHOLS: 5
NET CARBS: 8.47

MORE FACTS: P. 525

7. After no more than about 6 or 7 total minutes, the sauce should be nicely thickened and the chicken should be cooked through. At the last minute, toss in the almonds, cashews, and chopped cilantro. Mix in and serve with Miracle Cauli-Rice (p. 320)!

Chicken 'n' Dumplings

SERVES: 8 · · · PREP: 20 MIN · · · COOK: 1 HR · · · TOTAL: 1 HR 30 MIN

2 Tbsp (30 mL) **fat** (tallow, ghee, bacon fat, etc.)

1 small (110 g) **onion**, diced

1 (50 g) **celery rib**, cut into small cubes

1 small (27 g) **carrot**, peeled and cut into small cubes

4 **garlic cloves**, minced

1 tsp (5 mL) chopped **fresh thyme**

4 cups (960 mL) **chicken stock or broth**

1 Tbsp (15 mL) **glucomannan powder** (optional)

4 (681 g) **boneless chicken breasts** (skin optional)

1 **bay leaf**

1 1/4 cups (300 mL) **almond flour**

1/4 cup (60 mL) **coconut flour**

1/4 cup (60 mL) **tapioca flour**

1 Tbsp (15 mL) ground **white or black chia seeds**

1 Tbsp (15 mL) **baking powder**

1/2 tsp (2 mL) **salt**

1/2 cup (120 mL) chilled, **unsalted butter**, cut into cubes

1 large **egg**

1/2 cup (120 mL) **unsweetened almond milk**

salt and **pepper** to taste

PER SERVING
CALORIES: 529.53
FAT: 39.77
PROTEIN: 27.2
CARBS: 19.73
FIBER: 9.19
SUGAR ALCOHOLS: 0
NET CARBS: 10.55

MORE FACTS: P. 525

I'm a complete and total chicken and dumplings nut. I grew up on this stuff, with a family recipe handed down by my grandmother. Later in life, my mother discovered dumplings made from the famous mix in the yellow box, which my brother and I loved. My father stood firm on the old family recipe (with dumplings more like super-thick noodles). To this day, our family has an annual chicken and dumplings day in January, to get the family together, and like my childhood, the recipes alternate from year to year.

In trying to come up with a suitable replacement, I was never able to create a dumpling that didn't totally disintegrate in the liquid, but I recalled a type of dumpling that is baked, rather than simmered or steamed. Trying a tasty biscuit recipe that I'd developed, I cut little disks, covered a tray full of a thickened chicken soup base and baked it up. AMAZING! The flavors and textures were incredible! They weren't the soft, silky dumplings that the famous boxed blend creates or the fat, chewy noodles from my grandmother, but this cross between a dumpling and a potpie *truly* hits the spot and is the first time I feel I've found a suitable replacement. One of the few recipes that dips its toe over 10 net carbs, but... the outcome is worth the occasional splurge.

1. Heat a large soup pot over medium heat.

2. When warm, add the fat and swirl it around. Quickly add the onion, celery, carrot, garlic, and thyme with just a bit of salt and pepper. Cook until the onions are translucent (about 3 to 5 minutes).

3. While the vegetables sweat, whisk the optional glucomannan powder into the cold chicken stock until it dissolves.

4. Add the chicken stock, chicken, and bay leaf to the vegetables and bring up to a slow simmer. Turn the heat to low and allow to simmer for about 35 minutes.

5. While the chicken base simmers, preheat oven to 375°F (191°C).

6. In a medium-sized mixing bowl, combine the almond flour, coconut flour, tapioca flour, ground chia seeds, baking powder, and salt. Cut in the chilled butter cubes until the cubes are about the size of peas. Add the egg and stir in the almond milk until the dough pulls away from the side of the bowl. Dough should be somewhat wet but dry enough to form shapes.

7. Dust countertop or a piece of parchment paper with almond flour. Place the dough on the almond flour and roll into a log about 1 to 2 inches (3 to 4 cm) thick. Press the sides so that it's more a long square with flat top, bottom, and sides. Cut 16 square biscuits from the log by slicing every 3/4 of an inch (2 cm) or so.

8. Taste the chicken soup base and adjust seasoning. The chicken should be soft but not falling apart. Remove from the stove and pour into a deep 13" x 9" x 2" casserole pan (33 x 23 x 5 cm). Cover the chicken mixture by evenly distributing the 16 biscuits over the top of the hot liquid. Push them about halfway into the liquid.

9. Place the pan in the oven and bake for about 22 minutes or until the top is nice and golden. Remove from the oven and allow to rest for about 5 minutes. Serve!

Ginger Shrimp with Snap Peas, Peppers, and Bamboo Shoots

SERVES: 4 · · · PREP: 15 MIN · · · COOK: 7 MIN · · · TOTAL: 22 MIN

1 lb. (454 g) **shrimp (31/35)**, peeled and deveined

1 small (110 g) **onion**, diced

1 small (74 g) **red bell pepper**, stem removed, seeded and cut into bite sized squares

1/2 cup (120 mL) **bamboo shoots**

1/2 cup (120 mL) **snap peas**, fibrous stem and string removed

4 **garlic cloves**, minced

1 tsp (5 mL) **crushed red chili flakes** (optional)

1 Tbsp (15 mL) **fresh ginger**, minced

1/4 cup (60 mL) **soy sauce** (or coconut aminos)

1/4 cup (60 mL) **rice wine vinegar**

2 Tbsp (30 mL) **sugar replacement**

1/4 tsp (1 mL) **glucomannan powder**

1 Tbsp (15 mL) **coconut oil**

4 whole (60 g) **green onions** (scallions), sliced

salt and **pepper** to taste

PER SERVING
CALORIES: 216.95
FAT: 5.35
PROTEIN: 24.84
CARBS: 17.79
FIBER: 2.06
SUGAR ALCOHOLS: 7.5
NET CARBS: 8.23

MORE FACTS: P. 526

Like several of the other Asian-fusion super-fast stir-fries in this book, this is a new flavor profile and a different selection of lovely textures and colors. The base sauce is still the same, resulting in a delicious, thick, and slightly sweet soy sauce–based sauce.

1. In a large mixing bowl, combine shrimp, diced onions, peppers, bamboo shoots, snap peas, garlic, ginger, optional chili flakes, and some salt to taste. Combine the mixture. Set aside.

2. In a small mixing bowl, combine soy sauce, rice wine vinegar, sweetener, and glucomannan powder. Whisk until the glucomannan and sweetener are dissolved. Set aside.

3. Heat a large wok over high heat. If you do not have a wok, this can be done in two large sauté pans placed over two hot burners. This is intended to be done very fast, over very high heat. If the pan is not hot enough, or too many ingredients are added, then the pan cools down and the food steams, rather than sears. This is why two pans can work in place of a large wok.

4. Once your wok, or two pans, is very hot, add coconut oil and quickly swirl to coat the bottom. Immediately add the shrimp mixture, evenly spreading the ingredients along the bottom of the wok, making a single layer. Allow the ingredients to sear for about 1 minute. Mix the ingredients and spread them back into a single layer. Repeat this process, evenly searing the mixture and then mixing again. The shrimp will overcook quickly, so this should only take about 3 minutes.

5. Once everything has been quickly seared, pick up the soy mixture. Give it one last mix, to make sure any gluconmannan or sweetener hasn't stuck to the bottom. Pour it evenly over the ingredients. It should immediately boil. Toss the ingredients to coat with the mixture. Allow the mixture to continue cooking for about 2 more minutes, mixing occasionally.

6. If the sauce isn't thick enough for your taste, dissolve about 1/4 teaspoon (1 mL) of glucomannan powder in 1 tablespoon (15 mL) of soy sauce and add to the shrimp.

7. After no more than about 6 or 7 total minutes, the sauce should be nicely thickened and the shrimp should be cooked through. At the last minute, toss in the scallions. Mix in and serve with Miracle Cauli-Rice (p. 320)!

STUFFED DOUBLE-CUT PORK CHOPS

SERVES: 4 · · · PREP: 15 MIN · · · COOK: 25 MIN · · · TOTAL: 6 HR

1 1/2 cups (360 mL) **water**

1/4 cup (60 mL) **kosher salt** (or 2 Tbsp [30 mL] table salt)

4 **garlic cloves**, crushed

1/2 **small onion**, chopped

1 **bay leaf**

1 sprig **fresh thyme**

1/2 Tbsp (8 mL) **freshly cracked black pepper**

2 1/2 cups (600 mL) **ice water**

4 (1.8 kg [.45 kg each]) **double-cut pork chops**, frenched

1/2 lb. (227 g) **raw bulk Italian sausage** (sweet or spicy)

2 Tbsp (30 mL) **light oil** (coconut oil, olive, ghee, or bacon fat!)

salt and **freshly cracked pepper** to taste

PER SERVING
CALORIES: 821.52
FAT: 68.6
PROTEIN: 45.37
CARBS: 0.96
FIBER: 0.36
SUGAR ALCOHOLS: 0
NET CARBS: 0.6

MORE FACTS: P. 526

This is a serious pork chop! There's no fooling around with this one. I like to call it the "Over the Top Chop"! This double-cut pork chop has been brined and then stuffed with sausage. I do believe that this treatment renders about as moist and flavorful a pork chop as one could create. I really don't know that I know how to make a better chop!

Note: Most grocery stores do have butchers who will cut specific things for you if they have the product in the cooler. It may not hurt to call ahead, but my gut tells me that finding a full bone-in pork loin isn't that difficult. Then, explain that you want it cut "double-cut and frenched." This means that they will cut the chop every *two* ribs, rather than just one (like most pork chops). Frenched means that they clean the fat and sinew from around the bone, making an attractive appearance.

1. In a large pot (large enough for a gallon of liquid), bring your 1 1/2 cups (360 mL) of water to a boil. Add the salt and whisk the water until the salt dissolves. Remove the water from the heat and add the cloves, onion, bay leaf, thyme and cracked black pepper. Allow it to sit for about 15 minutes to cool. Add the ice water and stir. Make sure the brine is cold.

2. Add the pork to the brine. Make sure the pork is completely submerged. If it's not, you can weigh the pork down, or add a little more ice water. Brine the pork for between 2 and 10 hours. Any brining is good, even an hour. Longer is better, up to 12 hours. After 12 hours, the pork starts to deteriorate.

3. When the pork has been brined, remove it from the brine and wash thoroughly under cold water. Discard the brine. It cannot be reused.

4. Preheat your oven to 400°F (204°C).

5. With a sharp knife, make an incision between the bones, cutting deeply into the center of the pork chop but not cutting through the other side. You can use a small, sharp knife to cut in either direction, within the pork, to create a large slot or cavity within the pork chop. Just be careful not to break through any portion of the other side. You want a deep and wide pocket without holes. You can stick your finger in the incision and push around to tear a slightly larger pocket as well.

6. Divide your raw sausage into four even lumps. With your fingers, stuff the pork chops as full as you can. Really force it in there while being careful not to break or split the chops. The pork chop will begin to bulge a bit. That's ok. Force it in there.

7. At this point, it's best to let the pork sit at room temperature for about an hour or two prior to cooking. Allow this time if possible. Four hours is best. This will make the pork cook more evenly and hold more moisture.

8. Dry the pork well and then lightly season with a little salt and pepper.

9. Preheat a large skillet or ovenproof sauté pan over high heat. Add your oil to the pan and swirl it around to coat the pan. Quickly place your pork chops into the pan, making sure there is enough space between them. Lower your temperature to medium-high heat and allow the pork to sit on each side for about 1 to 2 minutes, creating a nice golden sear on the outside.

10. Once each side has been nicely colored, place the entire pan in the oven. Allow to roast in the oven for about 15 minutes but check it after 12.

11. Once the internal temperature of the pork reaches 160°F (71°C), remove from the oven. Poking it will result in a very firm pork chop. Cover the pork with foil and allow it to rest for 10 minutes before serving. Serve!

Over the Top Chop!

Sweet 'n' Spicy Chicken

SERVES: 4 · · · PREP: 5 MIN · · · COOK: 7 MIN · · · TOTAL: 12 MIN

4 (681 g) **boneless chicken breasts** (skin optional), sliced into thin strips

1 small (110 g) **onion**, diced

1 small (74 g) **red bell pepper**, stem removed, seeded, and cut into bite sized squares

4 **garlic cloves**, minced

1 Tbsp (15 mL) minced **fresh ginger**

1 Tbsp (15 mL) **crushed chilies** or **chili paste**

1 tsp (5 mL) **sesame oil**

1 tsp (5 mL) **crushed red chili flakes** (optional)

1/4 cup (60 mL) **soy sauce** (or coconut aminos)

1/4 cup (60 mL) **rice wine vinegar**

2 Tbsp (30 mL) **sugar replacement**

1/4 tsp (1 mL) **glucomannan powder**

1 Tbsp (15 mL) **coconut oil**

4 whole (60 g) **green onions** (scallions), sliced

2 Tbsp (30 mL) black (or white) **sesame seeds**

salt and **pepper** to taste

So many of the various quick stir-fries or dishes served in Asian restaurants are loaded with those pesky vegetables. While I love some good vegetables, oftentimes I just want the chicken and the sauce. Here's such a recipe! This has just enough veggies to give some color and taste, but not so much that it interferes with the tasty chicken and sauce. Perfect over a bed of Miracle Cauli-Rice (p. 320)!

1. In a large mixing bowl, combine chicken, diced onions, peppers, garlic, ginger, chilies, sesame oil, and some salt to taste. Combine the mixture. Set aside.

2. In a small mixing bowl, combine soy sauce, rice wine vinegar, sweetener, and glucomannan powder. Whisk until the glucomannan and sweetener are dissolved. Set aside.

3. Heat a large wok over high heat. If you do not have a wok, this can be done in two large sauté pans, placed over two hot burners. This is intended to be done very fast, over very high heat. If the pan is not hot enough, or too many ingredients are added, then the pan cools down and the food steams, rather than sears. This is why two pans can work in place of a large wok.

4. Once your wok, or two pans, is very hot, add coconut oil and quickly swirl to coat the bottom. Immediately add the chicken mixture, evenly spreading the ingredients along the bottom of the wok, making a single layer. Allow the ingredients to sear for about 1 minute. Mix the ingredients and spread them back into a single layer. Repeat this process, evenly searing the mixture and then mixing again. The chicken will overcook quickly, so this should only take about 3 minutes.

PER SERVING
CALORIES: 342.77
FAT: 12.4
PROTEIN: 39.06
CARBS: 18.2
FIBER: 2.86
SUGAR ALCOHOLS: 7.5
NET CARBS: 7.76

MORE FACTS: P. 527

5. Once everything has been quickly seared, pick up the soy mixture. Give it one last mix, to make sure any glucomannan or sweetener hasn't stuck to the bottom. Pour it evenly over the ingredients. It should immediately boil. Toss the ingredients to coat with the mixture. Allow the mixture to continue cooking for about 2 more minutes, mixing occasionally.

6. If the sauce isn't thick enough for your tastes, dissolve about 1/4 teaspoon (1 mL) of glucomannan powder in 1 tablespoon (15 mL) of soy sauce and add to the chicken.

7. After no more than about 6 or 7 total minutes, the sauce should be nicely thickened and the chicken should be cooked through. At the last minute, toss in the scallions. Mix in and serve with Miracle Cauli-Rice (p. 320). Garnish with sesame seeds!

Cheddar 'n' Onions Stuffed Bacon Wrapped Meatloaf

SERVES: 8 · · · PREP: 15 MIN · · · COOK: 45 MIN · · · TOTAL: 1 HR

1 lb. (454 g) **cheddar cheese**, cut into 1/2-inch rectangular sticks

2 Tbsp (30 mL) **cooking fat** (such as ghee, bacon fat, olive oil, coconut oil, etc.)

1 small (110 g) **red onion**, sliced

2 lbs. (908 g) **ground beef** (80 lean/20 fat)

2 large **whole eggs**, beaten

3 Tbsp (45 mL) **ground white chia seeds**

4 **garlic cloves**, minced

8 slices (200 g) **raw bacon**

salt and **pepper** to taste

PER SERVING
CALORIES: 786.27
FAT: 58.01
PROTEIN: 38.61
CARBS: 4.13
FIBER: 1.38
SUGAR ALCOHOLS: 0
NET CARBS: 2.75

MORE FACTS: P. 521

I have a recipe on my website called "Burger Balls," a cheddar-and-bacon-stuffed meatball intended for kids. It's a very popular recipe, as is meatloaf and pretty much anything wrapped in bacon. Never one to fear wrapping things in bacon, I thought this reimagined assortment of ingredients would be a fun addition for the whole family!

Note: Typically meatloaf recipes tend to have breadcrumbs in them, to help hold it together and also to absorb any fat or moisture that may leak out during the baking process. Historically, I've used crushed pork rinds to take their place, until I read about adding ground chia seeds to the base. I gave it a shot and will *never* look back. I used white chia seeds to mimic breadcrumbs, but any color will work. Chia seeds can hold upwards of ten times their own weight in moisture. Adding a little bit to a meatloaf recipe results in a meatloaf with an excellent texture and loads of moisture. While not required, it's *highly* encouraged.

1. Before you do anything, make sure your cheese is cut into half-inch sticks, roughly the size and shape of a finger. Place them in the freezer while you work on the rest of the ingredients. You aren't necessarily looking to *freeze* the cheese, so much as give it a nice chill.

2. Preheat oven to 450°F (232°C).

3. Place a sauté pan over medium heat on the stove. When it is warm, add cooking oil. When the oil begins to ripple in the pan, add onions. Season with a little salt and pepper. Cook for about 7 to 10 minutes or until soft and caramelized. Spread on a plate, in a thin layer, and place in the refrigerator to give a quick chill.

4. In a large mixing bowl, combine ground beef, eggs, ground chia, garlic, and a bit of salt and pepper. (Some

fresh herbs would be great at this point, but in keeping it basic to be family friendly, I've left them out; some fresh chopped thyme or rosemary would be delicious). Mix well.

5. On a piece of parchment paper or a baking tray, form a rectangle with the ground beef. It should be about 12" x 6" (30 x 15 cm).

6. Place the chilled cheese in the middle of the beef, in a straight line, and then top the cheese with the chilled onions.

7. Roll the beef around the cheese and onions, making sure that the filling is in the center of a rolled log and that the beef has formed a well-pressed and clean seal all the way around. Any melted cheese should not be allowed through an accidental opening as it cooks.

8. On a piece of parchment paper or a baking tray, lay a single slice of bacon. Then, parallel and slightly overlapping the first slice of bacon, lay a second slice of bacon. Continue this bacon "shingling" process, until you've used 8 slices of bacon. This process should result in a rectangular "sheet" of bacon.

9. Lay the ground beef log at the top of the sheet of bacon, making sure it's perpendicular to the strips of bacon. Tightly roll the log into the bacon sheet, making sure there is a clean seam at the bottom of the finished log.

10. Place the log on a parchment covered baking sheet, seam side down, and place in the oven. Bake for 10 minutes and then drop the temperature to 325°F (162°C) for about 35 more minutes or until the internal temperature is 155°F (68°C). Only poke with a thermometer, if you absolutely must. You will poke a hole and run the risk of a hot cheese geyser (not as fun as it sounds). Remove, cover with foil, and place in a warm area to rest for 10 to 15 minutes before slicing. Serve!

CHICKEN À LA MOMBIE

SERVES: 6 · · · PREP: 45 MIN · · · COOK: 15 MIN · · · TOTAL: 1 HR

6 (908 g) **boneless chicken breasts** (or equivalent thigh meat—skin optional)

2 Tbsp (30 mL) **cooking oil/fat** (ghee, olive oil, or even bacon fat!)

1 roughly 5-lb. (2.3 kg) **Spaghetti Squash**, pre-roasted and hot (p. 223)

1 recipe Thick, Goopy **Alfredo sauce** (about 2 cups [480 mL]) (p. 380)

18 leaves **fresh basil**, washed and hand torn

salt and **freshly cracked pepper** to taste

I have a follower on my Facebook page going by the alias of "Mombie Zoprano." I do not know her real name. It remains a mystery. I can only assume she's wanted in connection with all the missing gumball machines in the San Joaquin Valley. In any event, she popped onto my radar when I was added to the cookbook authoring team at Low Carbing Among Friends. She occasionally pops onto my Facebook page or sends me private messages announcing what she's just made herself that evening. She also shares a variety of recipes and things she's considering cooking. Her enthusiastic delivery can only be described as "sqwee-ing." Always a delight!

One of her ideas was for something along the lines of this here dish. Because the concept originated with a list stemming from Mombie, I've named it after her. Thanks for the inspiration, Mombie! I hope I've done your idea proud!

1. Butterfly the chicken breasts (or buy them that way). Lay a chicken breast on a flat cutting board. Place a knife parallel to the cutting board, about 1/2 inch (1 cm) above the surface. Slice into the breast, maintaining a slice that is parallel to the cutting board and essentially cuts the breast in half. Both top and bottom halves should be equal in thickness.

2. Once you've got thin sheets of chicken breast, place each piece between two sheets of plastic wrap and pound even thinner. You can use a mallet, rolling pin, or even the bottom of a saucepan. Just be careful to hit it flatly and evenly, or else you will make deep divots in the chicken. Ideally, the chicken will be a thin and even sheet of chicken breast when you are done.

3. Remove each slice from the plastic and *very* lightly season the chicken with salt and pepper. Set aside.

PER SERVING
CALORIES: 831.33
FAT: 64.02
PROTEIN: 47.14
CARBS: 14.78
FIBER: 2.4
SUGAR ALCOHOLS: 0
NET CARBS: 12.39

MORE FACTS: P. 523

4. **Note:** This recipe suggests that your sauce is already made and sitting warm on the stove, alongside your precooked spaghetti squash. Before cooking the chicken, be sure that the rest of the dish is ready, as the chicken cooks in minutes.

5. In a large, hot sauté pan, over medium-high heat, add your light oil.

6. When you see the oil begin to ripple, add your chicken. Depending on how the chicken was cut and pounded, you may be able to fit multiple pieces. However, you want a single layer of chicken with the entire side of each piece touching the bottom of the pan for a nice, hot searing effect.

7. After about 1 to 2 minutes of hot searing the chicken, flip and do the same thing on the other side. Once the chicken is nicely browned and cooked through, set it aside somewhere warm. Repeat this process with each piece of chicken until you have cooked it all.

8. Place a nice mound of spaghetti squash on six plates. Place a few basil leaves on the squash. Pile chicken on the top of the spaghetti squash and then finish with the Alfredo Sauce.

9. Serve!

ÜBER CRACK SLAW

SERVES: 4 · · · PREP: 20 MIN · · · COOK: 5 MIN · · · TOTAL: 25 MIN

1 1/2 lb. (681 g) **beef flank** (tenderloin, sirloin, or rib eye, etc., will work, as well)

1 Tbsp (15 mL) **minced fresh ginger**

4 **garlic cloves**, minced

2 Tbsp (30 mL) **sesame oil**

1 large (72 g) **carrot**, peeled

1 cup (240 mL) **snow peas**

1 small (304 g) head **Napa cabbage**

4 (60 g) **green onions** (scallions)

1/4 cup (60 mL) **soy sauce (or coconut aminos)**

2 Tbsp (30 mL) **spicy chili oil**

2 Tbsp (30 mL) **black sesame seeds** (or regular toasted sesame seeds)

salt and **pepper** to taste

Organization note: I *always* recommend reading the recipe first and then gathering the ingredients prior to cooking it. This recipe is no exception. The actual cooking time for this recipe is about 4 to 5 minutes, in a screaming hot pan. These ingredients are all cut very thin, with the idea being they will cook *really* quickly. If your ingredients aren't cut and ready to rock, you'll burn whatever is in the pan or just create a whole big scene... and who really wants that? Be prepared to wok it out!

PER SERVING
CALORIES: 636.15
FAT: 47.53
PROTEIN: 37.18
CARBS: 11.19
FIBER: 3.51
SUGAR ALCOHOLS: 0
NET CARBS: 7.69

MORE FACTS: P. 524

It's my understanding that the original "Crack Slaw" name comes from the addictive nature of this particular slaw. While I can't really do anything about the inception of the name, I have tried to give it a little boost. Just about every recipe I've seen for this amazing little dish is based on ground beef, cabbage, and variations of ginger, soy, and chilies. Yes, this is all tasty, quick, easy, and totally yum, but I see it as a bit of my job to take things and kind of twist them around and have a bit of fun with them.

I've chosen to take the same flavors and build something a little fresher and a little more vibrant. I've added a few more veggies and flavors, and combined them with a nice, very thinly cut flank steak. This is all finished with a spicy soy sauce, sesame oil, and black sesame seeds. It's these little tweaks which take it from Crack Slaw to ÜBER Crack Slaw.

1. Slice your flank steak into very thin strips against the grain. One trick is to have the thin flank steak in the freezer. Remove it and put it into the refrigerator about two hours prior to using. It will still be frozen but very easy to cut into thin strips with a knife. Slice and then add to a mixing bowl.

2. Add your garlic, ginger, and sesame oil to the mixing bowl with the beef. Mix well and set aside. By the time you get around to cooking it, it will be mostly defrosted.

3. Slice your carrots into very thin strips or "planks." Create a few small stacks of carrot strips and then cut them down into very thin sticks. To be all technical about it, you want carrot julienne. Set aside.

4. Peel the hard, fibrous string out of the snow peas and tear off the tops and bottom corners where the stem and weird little "feather" live. Create little stacks of 5 or so snow peas, then cut down into the stacks every 3 millimeters or so. You're also trying to make thin little snow pea sticks. Set these aside.

5. Cut your head of Napa cabbage into quarters, lengthwise, so that each quarter is still held together by the small stem at the base. Then, starting at the end opposite the stem, cut toward the stem every 2 or 3 millimeters, slicing each quarter into very thin strips. This will essentially shred the cabbage. Set aside.

6. Slice your green onions into thin little rings. Set aside.

7. Mix together your soy sauce with your hot chili oil. Many like to add a bit of sweet to this mixture. If you like a little sweet, feel free to whisk something sweet into this as well. Set aside.

8. Find your largest nonstick sauté pan or wok and get it screaming hot over high heat. Sprinkle your beef around the bottom of the pan, so that it's evenly spread, in a single layer. Do not touch the pan. Simply let it sear for about 1 minute. While it is searing, season the tops with a little bit of salt and pepper.

9. Evenly sprinkle your carrot sticks over the beef and toss the entire pan around, so the two ingredients are mixed. Let the pan sit for about 1 minute. Add a tiny bit of salt and pepper.

10. Evenly sprinkle your snow peas over the beef and carrots. Toss the pan around to mix. Let sit for 1 minute and add a tiny amount of salt and pepper.

11. Evenly sprinkle your cabbage and green onions over the ingredients in the pan. Toss everything together and let sit for about 30 seconds. Season with a little salt and pepper. Toss one more time and let sit for 30 seconds.

12. Add your soy mixture to the pan and toss everything until it's well coated and the cabbage has clearly begun to whither and wilt.

13. Divide your Über Crack Slaw between four plates or bowls. Garnish with the sesame seeds. Serve with more soy and chili oil for those that may need it. Enjoy!

Slow Cooker "Pot" Roast

SERVES: 6 · · · PREP: 20 MIN · · · COOK: 8 HR 20 MIN · · · TOTAL: 8 HR 40 MIN

4 lb. (1.8 kg) **beef chuck roast**

1 Tbsp (15 mL) **light oil** (such as coconut, olive, or ghee)

1 cup (240 mL) **red wine**, good quality

4 **garlic cloves**

10 sprigs **fresh thyme**

1 **bay leaf**

1 large (72 g) **carrot**, peeled and cut into chunks

2 ribs (101 g) **celery**, cut into chunks

1 small (110 g) **onion**, cut into chunks

1 small (420 g) **head cauliflower**, leaves removed and cut into florets

salt and **freshly cracked pepper** to taste

Most pot roasts I've had were large and soft pieces of meat, often in some kind of slightly thickened jus, and loaded with potatoes. This pot roast is similar, but with fauxtatoes (cute name for the cauliflower) instead! The method is essentially searing a piece of meat and throwing it into a slow cooker with some veggies, herbs, and red wine. Leave it alone for 8 hours. Return and add cauliflower, pushing it down into the jus. Let it sit for 20 more minutes. Serve!

1. Turn on your slow cooker, setting it to low.

2. Season your beef with a good layer of salt and pepper.

3. Heat a large sauté pan or skillet over medium-high heat. Add your oil to the pan and swirl it around. Quickly add your beef to the pan and sear it until a nice brown crust has formed. Flip it over and sear the other side. Continue flipping it until all sides have been properly seared. Add your beef to the slow cooker.

4. Pour your red wine into the still very hot pan with all the "stuff" stuck to the bottom. This should quickly boil, releasing some of those little flavor morsels into the hot wine. Swirl the pan around and use a wooden spoon to scrape anything else off the bottom of the pan into the wine. Pour the wine mixture over the top of the beef.

5. Add your garlic, thyme, and bay leaf to the slow cooker, making sure they are pushed into the liquid.

6. Add the rest of the vegetables except the cauliflower. Season with a bit of salt and pepper. Again, push these into the areas on the side of the roast as much as possible. You don't want much of it covering the roast. You want most of the veggies on the sides, surrounding the roast. As this all cooks, the meat and veggies will shrink, releasing their juices, creating an *amazing* flavor, as well as creating its own natural juices in which to cook! Getting everything as close to the bottom of the pot as is possible will help this process along.

PER SERVING
CALORIES: 835.03
FAT: 56.8
PROTEIN: 61.19
CARBS: 8.83
FIBER: 2.84
SUGAR ALCOHOLS: 0
NET CARBS: 5.99

MORE FACTS: P. 524

7. Add the lid and allow the ingredients to cook for 8 hours.

8. After 8 hours, add your cauliflower to the pot and push the florets under the surface of the liquid, as much as possible. Season with a bit of salt and pepper. Cover and allow to cook for 20 minutes. Serve!

Pan Roasted Beef Tenderloin Steak (a.k.a., How to Cook a Steak)

SERVES: 4 · · · PREP: 5 MIN · · · COOK: 15 MIN · · · TOTAL: 20 MIN

4 6- to 8-oz. (794 g) **thick-cut beef tenderloin steaks**, trimmed and brought up to room temperature

1 Tbsp (15 mL) lard or **olive oil**

1 Tbsp (15 mL) **butter**

salt and **pepper** to taste

One of the most common questions I've been asked, since the day I stepped into a professional kitchen is "How do I cook a steak?" Truth be told, there are a million ways, a variety of methods, a plethora of seasonings, many theories, etc. I'm going to suggest the following based on a beef tenderloin steak but suggest that the concepts can be applied to most cuts of a quickly cooked, grilled, sautéed, or roasted beef cut (nothing braised, smoked, or slow roasted, mind you; those are very different approaches). This recipe is a generalization but contains enough tips that they can be applied to several different cuts for a delicious, well-seasoned "beef-flavored" steak!

Beef purchasing thoughts: Beef is one of those things where you can spend *a lot* of money for aged Kobe beef; you can splurge for some organic, grass-fed beef (This is what I go for when I can find it. It's quite good for you, but is a touch more gamey and dry than you might be accustomed to.); or you can pick up whatever is on sale at the local store, etc. It depends on your price point as well as your dinner guests. Sometimes you want to impress; others… not so much. For me, personally, no matter what, I tend to buy a whole, large piece (tenderloin, prime rib, etc.) of meat, trim it, and break it into steaks myself. It's much cheaper this way. Then, I'm personally in the habit of vacuum packing and freezing my steaks for later use. Yes, this can diminish the quality of the meat, but not so much that it prevents me from doing it, to save some time and money down the road. I live in Mexico and tend to get my meat from Costco or a local restaurant distributor, but for those of you with access to great butchers or

PER SERVING
CALORIES: 544.85
FAT: 42
PROTEIN: 38.94
CARBS: 0
FIBER: 0
SUGAR ALCOHOLS: 0
NET CARBS: 0

MORE FACTS: P. 526

farmers, I suggest striking up conversations with them to see what's available. I've even heard of groups of neighbors getting together and buying whole or halves of cattle from local farmers and breaking them down themselves. This is a great way to get the best for less.

Beef seasoning thoughts: The whole of idea of crusts, marinades, rubs, spice blends, etc., tend to come from history, where refrigeration was scarce and a masking of the funky flavors of an old piece of meat needed done. Or the flavorings came from a method of preservation. Yes, these flavor blends *also* happen to taste really good, but if you've got access to a fresh cut of high-grade beef... you want to taste the beef! A properly cooked and juicy steak seasoned with nothing more than salt and pepper will always elicit the same response: "How did you cook this?! What did you season it with?!" When you say, "Salt and pepper," they won't believe you.

1. Beef tenderloin, and most cuts of meat for that matter, is a muscle. It likes to be relaxed when you cook it. It's more relaxed when it's warm than cold, straight from the refrigerator. It'll also cook more evenly if it's warm. Place your covered raw steaks on the countertop for about 30 minutes to an hour prior to cooking them. This isn't long enough for them to pick up any bacteria, so provided your kitchen is clean, no need to worry.

2. **Optional:** Some people tie a string around the steak at this point. They pull it nice and tight. They remove it when the steak is cooked and rested. This will create a more perfectly circular steak. I like my steak to be in the shape it came in, but if you want a round steak... go for it!

3. Preheat your oven to 450°F (232°C).

4. Preheat an ovenproof sauté pan over medium-high heat. Be sure to select a pan that is wide enough to allow for all four steaks with space between them. They should not touch one another in the pan. This will help with heat distribution.

5. Season your beef with salt and freshly cracked pepper. Your beef can likely handle more salt than you might think. Really coat your beef with a nice dusting of salt—don't go crazy, though... that's a nice piece of meat!

6. Look at your steaks and make a decision about which side of each steak is the most attractive. This will be the presentation side. Make a mental note.

7. Add your lard or olive oil (light olive oil or another flavorless, high smoke point oil is recommended) to the pan. Quickly swirl the oil around the pan. The oil should ripple but shouldn't burn or smoke.

8. Once you see nice rippling of the oil, add the butter to the pan. Give the pan a quick twirl, then place the attractive "presentation side" of the steaks face*down* in the sauté pan.

9. Allow the steaks to simply sit and sear in the pan for about 3 minutes. Try not to move them around, poke them, or swirl the pan around. I know it's tempting, but let the surface of the steak get nice and caramelized from the bottom of the pan. If there isn't a scorching or frying sound, then turn the heat up on the stove. If the pan isn't hot enough, the beef will steam rather than sear. This will create a gray lump of meat that won't retain as much of the juices. You must sear the presentation side of the beef to get a nice brown color.

10. Once the presentation side has a nice deep sear on it, flip each steak in the pan.

11. Let the steak sear for 1 minute.

12. Place the entire pan in the oven for about 5 minutes.

13. Poke the fleshy lump at the base of your palm, where it intersects with your thumb. Press this portion of your palm with your opposing index finger and make a mental note about the "spring" it gives back, when you poke it.

14. Open the oven and poke the smallest steak. It should spring or give back in a fashion very similar to the poking of your palm (poke the very center, or the hardest part of your palm, for a medium well). Alternately, use a meat thermometer in the thickest part of the steak (this makes a hole in the steak, allowing some juices to leak out, but… sometimes you gotta do what you gotta do). When the internal temperature of the smallest steak is 120°F (49°C) remove it from the oven. Normally, the steaks are all approximately the same size, so removing the entire pan is appropriate.

15. Remove the steaks from the pan and place to the side, in a warm location, on a plate. They will continue to carryover cook on their own. This should bring them up to a nice medium rare, while also allowing the muscle to relax again and the juices to settle within the meat. It's at this point I often hear, "But I want my steak to be HOT!" Yes, you can serve it fresh out of the oven, and it will be hotter on the surface, but it will also be cooler in the center and more juice will bleed out when cut. It's also true that more flavor exists when they are closer to human body temperature. Extreme heats and colds lose some of the flavor. A nice, warm, relaxed steak is the way to go.

16. **Final suggestion:** At this point, the pan has nice little bits of beefy goodness (known as *fond*) stuck to the bottom of the pan. Throw some mushrooms, capers, garlic, and black pepper in that pan. This will help pick up the fond. Then, hit the pan with a little red wine and some cream. If any juices have leaked out of the steaks, pour those juices into the pan. Cook for a moment, until the creamed mushrooms have thickened a bit. Place the mushrooms on a plate, and perhaps some grilled asparagus, and top it with a steak.

17. Enjoy!

Bacon-Wrapped Meat-Lovers'-Pizza-Stuffed Chicken Breast

SERVES: 2 · · · PREP: 20 MIN · · · COOK: 30 MIN · · · TOTAL: 50 MIN

1/4 cup (60 mL) **Marinara Sauce (p. 358)**

1 large (118 g) **chicken breast**, boneless and skinless

1 slice (28 g) **ham**

14 thin slices (28 g) **pepperoni**

2 oz. (56 g) **raw Italian sausage**

1/4 cup (60 mL) grated **Parmesan-Reggiano**

1/4 cup (60 mL) whole milk, low moisture **mozzarella**, grated

4 slices (100 g) **raw bacon**

salt and **pepper** to taste

This Bacon-Wrapped Meat-Lover's-Pizza-Stuffed Chicken Breast recipe is one of those borderline outlandish recipes that feels like junk food and tastes like weight gain, but... somehow it's not! This recipe is well within the boundaries of a low-primal way of eating. It's a bit difficult to make, due to the thin sheet of chicken breast that needs made, but once you've got the chicken, the rest is quite simple. Just add your ingredients, roll it, wrap it in bacon, add it to a hot pan, and bake! It is... *phenomenal*.

Note: Be careful with salt on this recipe. Most of the ingredients being used already have a good deal of salt added. You could probably get away with using zero salt, but a very light dusting of salt on the chicken might be appropriate.

1. Preheat oven to 425°F (218°C).

2. Standard tomato sauce, whether homemade or store bought, usually has a good deal of water added to it. First, start by placing the tomato sauce on the stove, in a small saucepot, over medium heat. Let it reduce by half while you assemble the rest of the ingredients. Once it's reduced to a thick paste, set it aside.

3. Butterfly the chicken breast (or buy it that way). Lay the chicken breast on a cutting board. Hold a knife parallel to the cutting board, about 1/2 inch (1 cm) above the surface. Slice into the breast, maintaining a slice that is parallel to the cutting board and essentially cuts the breast in half. *However*, do not cut through the entire breast. Also, be careful not to tear the meat or slice either side too thin.

PER SERVING
CALORIES: 566.06
FAT: 43.24
PROTEIN: 38.06
CARBS: 4.08
FIBER: 0.73
SUGAR ALCOHOLS: 0
NET CARBS: 3.35

MORE FACTS: P. 522

 MAIN DISHES

Both top and bottom halves should be equal in thickness. You want to stop slicing just prior to slicing through the opposing side of the breast. Once you've sliced almost through the breast, you can open it like a book. You essentially want to create a thin sheet of chicken.

4. Once you've got a thin sheet of chicken breast, place it between two sheets of plastic wrap and pound it even thinner. You can use a mallet, rolling pin, or even the bottom of a saucepan. Just be careful to hit it flatly and evenly, or else you will make deep divots in the chicken. Ideally, the chicken will be a thin and even sheet of chicken breast when you are done.

5. Very lightly season the chicken with salt and pepper. Place your slice of ham on the chicken. Spread your raw Italian chicken sausage evenly over the ham. Spread your tomato sauce evenly over the top of the sausage. Evenly distribute your pepperoni slices over the sauce. Mix your two cheeses. Then evenly spread over the sauce. Roll your chicken into a log. Try and roll it as tightly as possible. Set it aside.

6. Set your 4 bacon slices on a cutting board and cut them all in half. This will result in 8 short slices of bacon. Stretch them out a bit.

7. Lay one slice of bacon on the cutting board; then offset a second slice of bacon. Continue shingling the bacon, until you have a sheet of overlapping bacon slices.

8. Preheat a large ovenproof sauté pan over medium-high heat.

9. Lay the chicken log at the top of the sheet of bacon, making sure it's perpendicular to the strips of bacon. Tightly roll the log into the bacon sheet, making sure there is a clean seam at the bottom of the finished log.

10. Once the log is complete and the pan is hot, carefully place the seam side down in the sauté pan. Let it sear for about 30 seconds; then place the entire pan in the oven. Allow it to bake for roughly 20 to 30 minutes, depending on the size and thickness of the log.

11. Once the chicken has an internal temperature of 160°F (71°C), remove from the oven and allow to rest in the pan for 10 minutes before slicing.

12. Slice and serve! Delicious with more sauce, pasta, and a side of steamed broccoli!

Thai Green Chicken Curry

SERVES: 4 ··· PREP: 15 MIN ··· COOK: 15 MIN ··· TOTAL: 30 MIN

1 1/2 lb. (681 g) **boneless chicken**, cut into bite sized strips (breasts and/or thighs)

4 **garlic cloves**, minced

1 Tbsp (15 mL) minced **fresh galangal** (substitution: 1 Tbsp ginger)

1 Tbsp (15 mL) **sugar replacement**

1/4 cup (60 mL) **Green Curry Paste** (p. 482) (substitution: 2 Tbsp [30 mL] store bought)

2 Tbsp (30 mL) **coconut oil**

1 small (74 g) **green bell pepper**, seeded and diced

1 large (274 g) **Japanese eggplant**, cut into half moons

2 small (236 g) **green zucchini**, cut into half moons

1 1/2 cups (360 mL) **unsweetened coconut milk**

1/4 bunch (25 g) **cilantro**, washed and large stems removed

16 leaves **Thai basil**, hand torn (substitution: regular basil)

salt and **pepper** to taste

PER SERVING
CALORIES: 461.12
FAT: 28.16
PROTEIN: 39.92
CARBS: 14.23
FIBER: 3.81
SUGAR ALCOHOLS: 0.31
NET CARBS: 10.11

MORE FACTS: P. 527

This is my favorite Thai dish, hands down. I love it! It's action packed. It's fresh, brightly colored, filled with veggies, soft and scrumptious chicken, a little sweet, a good deal spicy, and outrageously aromatic. Making this at home, especially with a fresh and homemade curry paste, will cause your home to smell better than any home has ever smelled... *ever*. It's true!

1. In a large bowl, mix together your chicken, garlic, galangal, curry paste, sweetener, and a bit of salt and pepper. Set aside.

2. Heat your largest sauté pan (or wok if you have one) over high heat. When the pan is hot, add your coconut oil and swirl around to coat the pan. Immediately add your green peppers with a bit of salt and pepper. Sauté for about 1 minute.

3. Add your eggplant and zucchini to the pan and season with a bit of salt and pepper. Toss the three ingredients together; then let the mixture sit on high heat and sear for a minute or two. Flip it around and let sit for one more minute.

4. Sort of slide all the ingredients to one side of the pan, so about two-thirds of the pan is totally empty. Evenly sprinkle your chicken in this area and allow it to sear for about 1 minute. Toss the whole pan together and allow the ingredients to cook, sear, and pick up some color (caramelize or "turn brown") from the heat of the pan. This whole process is hot, fast, and smoky, while being fun and smelling *amazing*.

5. After about 2 minutes, add your coconut milk. The mixture *should* immediately boil rapidly. Turn the heat to medium-low and allow to simmer for about 4 to 8 minutes. The mixture should thicken, like a stew. Toss in the fresh cilantro and Thai basil at the last moment.

6. Taste and season with a bit of salt and pepper.

7. Serve!

JERK-INSPIRED PORK CHOP

SERVES: 4 · · · PREP: 10 MIN · · · COOK: 20 MIN · · · TOTAL: 30 MIN

1 **lime**

4 (880 g [220 g each]) **thick-cut pork chops**

1 tsp (5 mL) ground **allspice**

1 tsp (5 mL) ground **cayenne pepper**

1 tsp (5 mL) chopped **fresh thyme**

1 tsp (5 mL) **freshly cracked black pepper**

1/2 tsp (2 mL) ground **cinnamon**

1/4 tsp (1 mL) freshly ground **nutmeg**

4 **garlic cloves**, minced

2 Tbsp (30 mL) **coconut oil**

salt to taste

If you've never tried this before, try it. Right now. Seriously. Get into your car, go get the stuff, and start cooking. You'll be glad you did! Jerk seasoning is a mind-melting spice blend from Jamaica. Additionally, it's also a cooking method, but we're not going to cook over a barrel (you can if you want to, though). The foundation of a jerk seasoning blend is allspice and chilies (normally the scotch bonnet, which is amongst the hottest chili known to man—*OW!*). Beyond that, there are many other common spices. The end result is something packed with more aroma and flavor than my mind has ever been able to fully appreciate, much less process. It tries, gives up, and simply asks for more! This would also work for just about any pork chop, thick or thin. Chicken too!

Spice note: I've used cayenne in this recipe because it's readily available and probably already in your kitchen. However, if you can find a scotch bonnet (or two, if you dare!), remove the seeds, finely dice it, and add. Habaneros would also work. I *highly* recommend wearing rubber gloves, should you go down this road—you'll thank me later.

1. Preheat a grill.

2. Zest the lime with a zester or the fine side of a cheese grater. You can even use a vegetable peeler to remove the green outer layer of the lime. Do not use the white part though—it's called the pith and it's bitter—just get the green skin on the surface. If you use a peeler to make strips of zest, just make sure it's chopped fine. Add to a large bowl.

3. Juice the lime and add to the bowl.

PER SERVING
CALORIES: 696.63
FAT: 59
PROTEIN: 35.14
CARBS: 2.6
FIBER: 0.57
SUGAR ALCOHOLS: 0
NET CARBS: 2.03

MORE FACTS: P. 523

4. Add the remaining ingredients, including the pork and oil.

5. Season with salt to taste.

6. Grill until cooked through or a meat thermometer in the thickest part reads 140°F (60°C).

7. Cover the pork with foil and allow it to rest for 10 minutes before serving.

8. Serve!

TUNISIAN-SPICED RACK OF LAMB

SERVES: 4 · · · PREP: 10 MIN · · · COOK: 25 MIN · · · TOTAL: 2 HRS-ISH

1 **lemon**

1 tsp (5 mL) ground **coriander seed**

1 tsp (5 mL) ground **caraway seed**

1/2 tsp (2 mL) ground **cumin seed**

1/2 tsp (2 mL) ground **cayenne pepper**

4 **garlic cloves**, minced

2 Tbsp (30 mL) **light olive oil**

2 racks (1.6 kg) **lamb**, cleaned (frenched)

salt to taste

A friend of mine was the chef at a kosher Tunisian restaurant in Los Angeles. He was always talking about the food and influence from that region of the world. It's North Africa but with strong European ties, especially with the French. Sounds pretty interesting, right? The food is a kind of spicy Mediterranean. *Exoticy!*

What follows is a fairly simple but fantastically tender Tunisian-inspired oven-roasted rack of lamb. The photo contains the sauce known as Harissa (p. 370).

Note: Most lamb racks are purchased already cleaned (meaning the bones have the fat and sinew removed from between them), but if you get the full rack, ask your butcher to "french" it for you and watch as they clean it right up!

1. Zest the lemon with a zester or the fine side of a cheese grater. You can even use a vegetable peeler to remove the yellow outer layer of the lemon. Do not use the white part though; it's called the pith, and it's bitter. Just get the yellow skin on the surface. If you use a peeler to make strips of zest, just make sure it's chopped fine. It's a strong flavor, so only add about 1 teaspoon to a large mixing bowl.

2. Juice the lemon and add to the bowl, along with the remaining ingredients (except the lamb). Mix the spice blend together. Add the cleaned lamb racks to the bowl and thoroughly coat the racks with the spice blend.

3. Lamb racks are usually thinner on one side. In addition, it's generally good form to bring meats up to a warmer and more relaxed temperature. This will create a juicy and more evenly cooked piece of meat. At this point, leave the lamb in the bowl sitting on the countertop, to absorb flavors and warm up. Allow it to stay at room temperature for about 1 to 2 hours (no more than 4 though).

PER SERVING
CALORIES: 707.36
FAT: 38.71
PROTEIN: 80.04
CARBS: 2.42
FIBER: 0.5
SUGAR ALCOHOLS: 0
NET CARBS: 1.92

MORE FACTS: P. 524

4. Heat an oven to about 425°F (218°C).

5. Heat a very large ovenproof sauté pan.

6. Season the lamb racks with salt.

7. The top side of the rack has a fat cap. Place this side down in the pan. Sear it until you get a nice golden color.

8. When done searing the fat cap, stand the racks on their ends, so the bones intertwine like the fingers of two hands. Sear the top of the rounded portions of the two racks while they are balanced in this position.

9. Each rack has a thicker side. Now place the flat cut surface of the thicker side down in the pan until it's golden and seared.

10. Last, face the fat side of each rack up and place the entire pan directly into the oven.

11. Roast the racks for about 9 to 12 minutes (depending on size of racks and desired doneness). Check the internal temperature. I like mine on the rare side, so you can remove the racks at about 120°F (49°C) or 130°F (54°C) for a more medium to medium rare.

12. Remove the pan and cover with foil. Allow it to rest for 10 minutes before slicing and serving.

13. You can slice between each bone to carve little chops. If the bone gets in the way at the joints, just push hard through the bone. It'll go through. Enjoy!

Thai Red Curry Pork

SERVES: 4 · · · PREP: 15 MIN · · · COOK: 15 MIN · · · TOTAL: 30 MIN

1 approx. 1 1/4 lb. (568 g) **pork tenderloin roast**, cut into thin, bite-sized strips

4 **garlic cloves**, minced

1 Tbsp (15 mL) minced **fresh galangal** (substitution: 1 Tbsp ginger)

1 tsp (5 mL) ground **cinnamon**

1/4 tsp (1 mL) ground **cloves**

1/4 cup (60 mL) **Red Curry Paste** (p. 484) (substitution: 2 Tbsp [30 mL] store bought)

2 Tbsp (30 mL) **coconut oil**

1 small (74 g) **red bell pepper**, seeded and diced

1 large (274 g) **Japanese eggplant**, cut into cubes

1 1/2 cups (360 mL) **unsweetened coconut milk**

16 leaves **Thai basil**, hand torn (substitution: regular basil)

salt and **pepper** to taste

What follows is my interpretation of a pork curry recipe that I would get at a favorite Thai haunt just up the street from my battered old San Francisco apartment, in the Lower Haight district. It's thick and gloppy, while being rich with flavors, dense with coconut milk, spicy, and complicated. It's also little more than a quick stir-fry. If you have the stuff, the actual curry is mere minutes away. Go get the stuff!

Note: Photos taken with Miracle Cauli-Rice (p. 320) and was cooked with a Thai Red Curry Paste (p. 484).

1. In a large bowl, mix together your pork, garlic, galangal, cinnamon, cloves, curry paste, and a bit of salt and pepper. Set aside.

2. Heat your largest sauté pan (or wok if you have one) over high heat. When the pan is hot, add your coconut oil and swirl around to coat the pan. Immediately add your red bell peppers with a bit of salt and pepper. Sauté for about 1 minute.

3. Add your eggplant to the pan and season with a bit of salt and pepper. Toss the two ingredients together; then let the mixture sit on the high heat and sear for a minute or two. Flip it around and let sit for one more minute.

4. Sort of slide all the ingredients to one side of the pan, so about two-thirds of the pan is totally empty. Evenly sprinkle your pork in this area and allow it to sear for about 1 minute. Toss the whole pan together and allow the ingredients to cook, sear, and pick up some color (caramelize or "turn brown") from the heat of the pan. This whole process is hot, fast, and smoky, while being fun and smelling *amazing*.

PER SERVING
CALORIES: 400.74
FAT: 27.36
PROTEIN: 29.96
CARBS: 12.95
FIBER: 3.6
SUGAR ALCOHOLS: 0
NET CARBS: 9.35

MORE FACTS: P. 528

5. After about 2 minutes, add your coconut milk. The mixture *should* immediately boil rapidly. Turn the heat to medium low and allow to simmer for about 4 to 8 minutes. The mixture should thicken, like a stew. Toss in the fresh Thai basil at the last moment. Taste and season with a bit of salt and pepper.

6. Serve!

Fennel Horseradish Pork Spare Ribs

SERVES: 4 · · · PREP: 30 MIN · · · COOK: 5 HR · · · TOTAL: 24 HR

2 slabs (4.5 kg) **pork spare ribs** (about 5 lb. [2.3 kg] per slab)

1 **orange**

1/2 cup (120 mL) **prepared horseradish**

1 Tbsp (15 mL) whole **fennel seeds**

1 Tbsp (15 mL) **cayenne pepper**

4 **garlic cloves**, minced

1/4 cup (60 mL) **extra virgin olive oil**

salt and **freshly cracked pepper** to taste

This pork spare ribs recipe was *fantastic*! They were different than your standard dry-rubbed, smoked, and either sweet or vinegar-soaked ribs. These had more character to them, and the horseradish in the end just give it an earthy heat, pulling together the aroma from the orange and the sweet little pop from the fennel seeds. I was in Mexico when I cooked these, and Costco had a special on precut ribs. Each rib was individually cut, as opposed to a whole slab. I was annoyed, but they still turned out great. For the purposes of this recipe, I'm going to present it as if the rack had been whole (an intact slab of spare ribs will yield juicier results); my ribs were great but had too much barky, dry skin for each rib.

Note: Served with White BBQ Sauce (p. 364).

1. The day before the cook, you want to prepare and rub your ribs with a prepared paste. To begin, you'll want to peel the membrane off the inside (bony side) of the slab. This can be tricky to start, but once a corner has been loosened, the rest usually rips right off. The membrane is a slightly shiny, thick, paperlike layer covering the ribs. Slide a small knife into one corner of the ribs, just between the meat and membrane. I usually use a butter knife for this (a sharp knife may cut through the membrane, where I see this as more of a prying effect). Jiggle and push and shove the knife between the meat and membrane, sliding it from side to side until roughly 1 inch (2 1/2cm) of membrane has been loosened enough to hold on to. With a towel, grab the flap and, with consistent force, peel the membrane off the inside of the slab. It *should* come off in one nice tear. If it doesn't, continue the prying and pulling process until the entire membrane has been removed. Set it aside.

PER SERVING
CALORIES: 2,303.2
FAT: 150.48
PROTEIN: 216.44
CARBS: 9.36
FIBER: 2.5
SUGAR ALCOHOLS: 0
NET CARBS: 6.86

MORE FACTS: P. 519

2. With a sharp vegetable peeler, peel the outside of the orange. You want to remove *only* the orange outer layer, and none of the bitter white stuff (called *pith*). You want to remove about a third of the orange outer rind (called *zest*).

3. Cut the orange in half and juice it. Save the juice for the next day.

4. In a mixing bowl, mix together the horseradish, chopped orange zest, whole fennel seeds, cayenne, and freshly chopped garlic.

5. Rub the horseradish rub all over both sides of the slab. Wrap in plastic wrap and refrigerate overnight.

6. The next day, remove the ribs from the refrigerator and set them on the counter for about an hour before they go into the smoker.

7. Prepare your smoker. Preheat to between 215 and 235°F (102 to 113°C). This can be done in an oven without smoke and still tastes great, but it loses that smoky quality. Depending on your approach to the smoking process, you can also soak some hickory or other aromatic wood chips in some water at this point. Finally, put a drip pan filled with water on the rack beneath where the pork will go. Some of this water will evaporate, helping maintain moisture. It will also catch any fat, rather than causing flare-ups in the fire… or just making a big mess. Even if this is done on a pan in an oven, include a pan of water somewhere inside the oven.

8. Unwrap your ribs, season them with salt and pepper, and then place them in a safe spot, within the smoker, to begin the smoking process. Not too close to the heat! We want a low and slow cook. Find a spot which is not directly near the heat source.

9. Combine your fresh orange juice with an equal amount of extra virgin olive oil.

10. About once an hour, open the smoker and liberally brush your orange juice-olive oil mixture on both sides of the ribs.

11. The ribs should cook for about an hour per pound in the slab. When the ribs start to get dark from the sugar in the orange juice, wrap them in foil and place them back in the smoker until they are done. A five-pound rack will take approximately 5 hours. They will be done when the temperature of the ribs is between 175 and 185°F, on up as high as 200°F (80 to 85°C up to 93°C). The meat will have retracted by about a quarter to half an inch (1cm) and the meat will easily separate from the bones. Twist a rib to test!

12. Once the ribs are done, keep them in the foil and allow them to rest for about 20 minutes prior to slicing between each bone and serving. Serve!

Slow Cooker BBQ Beef Brisket

SERVES: 8 · · · PREP: 15 MIN · · · COOK: 8 HR · · · TOTAL: 8 HR 15 MIN

5 lb. (2.3 kg) **beef brisket**, trimmed

1 cup (240 mL) **Sweet 'n' Tangy BBQ Sauce** (p. 356)

2 Tbsp (30 mL) **cooking fat** (coconut, olive, or even bacon fat!)

salt and **pepper** to taste

I wanted to go with what I think slow cookers are used for: ease and simplicity. This recipe really has only two ingredients, takes only a few minutes to sear the meat, and... 8 hours later... you're done! Scrumtrulescent!

1. Trim any excess fat off your brisket (leave some fat). Cut into large pieces that will fit in your slow cooker. Season heavily with salt and pepper.

2. Add 1/2 of your BBQ sauce to the slow cooker and set it for a low cook.

3. Heat up a large sauté pan, over medium-high heat. Add a lightly flavored oil with a high smoke point. Coconut oil would work nicely. When the oil begins to ripple, add your pieces of meat (do not crowd the pan; you may need to do this in batches). The meat should sear nicely and develop some great flavors. Sear all sides of the meat. When the meat has been seared on all sides, place a piece in the slow cooker and drizzle a little of the remaining BBQ sauce on it. Then, place another piece, followed by more BBQ sauce. The idea is to get a little BBQ sauce between every piece of meat.

4. When all the brisket is within the slow cooker, add any remaining BBQ sauce.

5. Cover and allow to cook on low for 8 to 10 hours.

6. Slice and serve!

PER SERVING
CALORIES: 844.35
FAT: 66.76
PROTEIN: 51.67
CARBS: 5.93
FIBER: 1.33
SUGAR ALCOHOLS: 0
NET CARBS: 4.6

MORE FACTS: P. 527

Sides

o o o

I'm personally a bit strange about side dishes. Let's assume we have some lovely buttered broccoli as a side dish, and it's being served with a steak. To me, cooking a steak and cooking broccoli as two separate things is time consuming, and for the most part, when I'm just cooking dinner, I'm not out to impress anyone. So I cut my steak into cubes and sauté the cubes with broccoli and butter! The end result is a delicious, buttery steak and broccoli stir-fry! There's virtually no difference in taste or texture, but it's much quicker to throw together and uses less dishes. That said, the "side dish" is a big part of the dinner culture. Plus, not all sides work like this, and many of them are quite a bit of fun.

Let's go see what we've got on the side!

Simple Buttery Brussels Sprouts

SERVES: 8 · · · PREP: 10 MIN · · · COOK: 10 MIN · · · TOTAL: 20 MIN

2 lb. (908 g) **Brussels sprouts**

1/4 cup (60 mL) **fresh, whole butter**, cut into cubes, divided

salt and **pepper** to taste

This dish is about as basic and simple as can be but with an important restaurant twist. You'll get a sweet and properly cooked Brussels sprout, but it'll also be buttery and bright, vibrant green.

So often, roasted Brussels sprouts are these soft, brown, mushy balls of mini-cabbage. Instead, these are poached in salty boiling water, until *just* cooked (still slightly crunchy). This will season them all the way through. Then, they are plunged into ice water, where the cooking process is completely stopped, while the bright, vibrant color is preserved. Here, they are cut in half. It'll only take a few moments to cook them from here. With very little fuss, you can throw these in a sauté pan with some butter and toast 'em up! You'll get a hot, bright, sweet, and buttery Brussels sprout.

Just pure simple perfection.

1. Place a pot of salted water on the stove to boil. The water should be fairly salty.

2. Once the water boils, throw your Brussels sprouts into the water to boil. Let them boil for about 3 to 5 minutes. Remove the smaller ones first, and plunge them into a big bowl of ice water. Keep removing them from the water and adding to the ice water, from smallest to largest. They should be firm but cooked—*not* soft. You will continue cooking them later.

3. Once they are all in the ice water, let them stay in the ice water for about 10 minutes, until they are completely chilled all the way through. Remove them and drain them, so they are dry.

PER SERVING
CALORIES: 93.13
FAT: 5.5
PROTEIN: 3.41
CARBS: 9.08
FIBER: 3.41
SUGAR ALCOHOLS: 0
NET CARBS: 5.68

MORE FACTS: P. 531

4. Cut them in half, so that the stem stays intact on both halves. You can also trim any loose leaves and any brown or fibrous stem ends at this point. These can be tough.

5. Set aside to be cooked later or just cook them.

6. To cook, place a large nonstick sauté pan on the stove. Get it hot over medium-high heat. (**Note:** This could be done in two hot pans, or one very large hot pan. The idea is, if you add too many at once, the sprouts will cool the pan down too much and they will simmer, not *fry*.)

7. Add half of your butter to the pan and swirl it around, so the bottom is coated. It may start immediately browning. This is ok, but do not let it burn.

8. Even if the butter is not fully melted, add half of your dry Brussels sprout halves. Turn them all so they are all facing down in the pan and are only one layer deep. They should not be stacked, or else they will steam. They should be frying in the hot butter.

9. Let them fry for a few minutes, so the faces get nice and caramelized. Move them around the pan, so they cook evenly. Keep the pan hot.

10. Once they are cooked, season with a little salt and pepper. Toss and set aside.

11. Cook the other half of the Brussels sprouts in the remaining butter. Season and mix with the first batch and serve!

GREEN BEANS WITH TAPENADE

SERVES: 6 · · · PREP: 2 MIN · · · COOK: 5 MIN · · · TOTAL: 8 MIN

1 1/2 lb. (681 g) **green beans**, ends removed

1/2 cup (120 mL) **Black Olive Tapenade** (p. 352)

salt and **pepper** to taste

Here's a quick and easy side dish, but one filled with flavor and a touch of elegance. The concept is simple—green beans tossed with black olive tapenade!

1. In a medium-sized pot, boil about one gallon (3.8 L) of water, with about 2 to 3 tablespoons (30 to 45 mL) of salt.

2. Once the water is boiling, add the green beans to the water. Stir, then let boil for about 3 to 5 minutes (or until desired doneness—the crispier, the better!). While the beans boil, place a vegetable strainer in the sink. Also, place the tapenade into a medium-sized salad bowl and set aside.

3. When the beans are done, strain them through the strainer. Let them drip dry for about 1 minute. Once dry, toss them in the tapenade to evenly coat them. Season with salt and pepper to taste.

4. Serve!

PER SERVING
CALORIES: 85.61
FAT: 4.9
PROTEIN: 2.01
CARBS: 9.42
FIBER: 4.44
SUGAR ALCOHOLS: 0
NET CARBS: 4.97

MORE FACTS: P. 529

Garlicky BBQ Kale

SERVES: 8 · · · PREP: 5 MIN · · · COOK: 10 MIN · · · TOTAL: 15 MIN

Kale is one of those ingredients touted as a super-food. This purple and green leafy vegetable is related to broccoli, cauliflower, and Brussels sprouts. Kale has sprung onto the world health scene due to its enormous nutrient density. It's like… concentrated food! *So* much good stuff in those crisp, sweet leaves! It's also incredibly versatile, pretty, and pretty much grows everywhere. There's a strange aspect to kale though. It's sweet! It's actually got quite a high carb content to it. Just 4 ounces (100 g) of it has over 8 net carbs! To a follower of Paleo or primal trends, this is not an issue, but for those really counting every last little carb, 8 carbs for a decent-sized pile of greens is a hefty portion of the day's allotment.

In the end, I feel that the benefits of kale far outweigh the one minor drawback. I can't imagine someone experiencing any kind of negative response to kale. It's unfathomable to me to think that someone ate too much kale. After a good deal of thought and consideration, I decided to add a kale recipe and keep it simple.

1. Heat a large pot over medium heat.

2. Add bacon fat and turn the heat down to low. Add the garlic and stir until the garlic *just* begins to turn a very light brown. Immediately add the kale and BBQ sauce, with a little salt and pepper. Stir well, then place a lid on the top of the pot and allow the kale to slowly steam and braise in the liquid and kale juices that will develop. Let the kale "sweat" for about 5 to 10 minutes.

3. Taste, adjust seasoning, and serve!

2 Tbsp (30 mL) **fat** (like olive oil or bacon fat/lard)

12 **garlic cloves**, sliced into thin rings

1 1/2 lb. (681 g) **kale**, washed and very roughly chopped/sliced

1/4 cup (60 mL) **Sweet 'n' Tangy BBQ Sauce** (p. 356)

salt and **pepper** to taste

PER SERVING
CALORIES: 74.81
FAT: 3.6
PROTEIN: 2.55
CARBS: 10.26
FIBER: 1.7
SUGAR ALCOHOLS: 0
NET CARBS: 8.56

MORE FACTS: P. 528

Carrot-Squash Hash

SERVES: 8 · · · PREP: 10 MIN · · · COOK: 20 MIN · · · TOTAL: 30 MIN

1/4 cup (60 mL) **fresh whole butter**

1 lb. (454 g) **carrots**, peeled and diced

1 small (2 to 3 lb.) (1.1 kg) **kabocha squash**, peeled, seeded, and diced (substitution: acorn, buttercup, delicata, pumpkin)

1 medium (110 g) **onion**, diced

4 **garlic cloves**, minced

1 Tbsp (15 mL) chopped **fresh sage**

salt and **pepper** to taste

For the longest time, I was afraid of carrots. I'd read that, while fairly low in carbs, the carbs that *did* exist would blast my blood sugar at nearly the same rate as pure glucose! As a result, I (and *many* others) avoided carrots within a low-primal lifestyle.

Recently, I read an article discussing "The GI Carrot Myth," the general idea being that the original test resulting in cooked carrots having a glycemic index of 90+ was just wrong! Cooked carrots are actually closer to 30 or 40 (lower than a sweet potato). While this isn't new information, it's somehow less spectacular than saying that cooked carrots convert to sugar in the blood in a nanosecond. The myth has somehow persisted, even in my own mind, until recently.

Carrots are fine!

1. Preheat a large nonstick sauté pan. Add your butter and quickly swirl it around. A little light browning of the butter is ok. Don't burn it though. Before the butter is totally melted, add your cubed carrots and squash. Toss them in the butter to make sure the cubes are evenly coated. Then, spread them out along the bottom of the pan, so that there is as even a layer as possible. Season with salt and pepper.

2. Turn the heat down to medium low. About every 2 to 3 minutes, toss the veggies around, so a different group of mini-cubes will get exposure to the bottom of the pan. We're trying to brown up many of the cubes for color, texture, and flavor. Be careful not to burn them. They have a tendency to want to burn quickly. Watch it closely.

PER SERVING
CALORIES: 125.88
FAT: 5.52
PROTEIN: 1.08
CARBS: 10.26
FIBER: 2.56
SUGAR ALCOHOLS: 0
NET CARBS: 8.06

MORE FACTS: P. 529

3. Continue cooking until they are almost completely cooked through; this will take about 25–30 minutes with occasional tossing. Once they are nicely browned, add your onions and garlic with a bit more salt and pepper. Cook for a further 5 to 10 minutes, until the onions and garlic are cooked and translucent.

4. Taste some of the cubes and adjust the salt and pepper. This can handle a good amount of salt. When you're satisfied with the taste, toss some fresh herbs (sage is tasty!) into the mix and serve immediately.

Simple Southern-Style Braised Greens

SERVES: 8 · · · PREP: 20 MIN · · · COOK: 10 MIN · · · TOTAL: 30 MIN

8 slices (200 g) **raw bacon**, chopped (for bits)

1 1/2 lb. (681 g) **hearty, leafy bitter greens**, washed and cut into bite-sized ribbons

salt and **pepper** to taste

There are far more elaborate and time-consuming versions of this dish. You can add all sorts of other stuff, such as chilies, beer, molasses, ham hocks, vinegar, onions, apples, nuts, etc. While these things are all great (*really* great on occasion!), I'm going to go with a quick and dirty version, comprising of greens and... bacon! Nothing else!

Ultimately, what we have here is a bitter green. You can use any of the following for this recipe: kale, beet greens, chard, collards, mustard greens, or any other hearty green. With some kind of fat and the liquid that comes out of the greens themselves, the greens will wilt and mix with whatever you add to them. They lose a lot of their aggressive bitterness and become a very nice, soft, and *very* healthy dish. Serve as a side dish, as the base for a meat, as a snack, as a component for a future dip, etc.

A vegan variation might use something like olive oil, greens, garlic, apple cider vinegar, a cinnamon stick, toasted pecans, and apples.

PER SERVING
CALORIES: 157.06
FAT: 12.39
PROTEIN: 6.4
CARBS: 8.76
FIBER: 1.7
SUGAR ALCOHOLS: 0
NET CARBS: 7.06

MORE FACTS: P. 529

1. Cook the bacon in a fairly large-sized pot deep enough to cook all the greens at once (with a lid).

2. When crispy, strain the bacon bits and set aside. Save fat for another day. Do not clean the pot.

3. Add all the washed, cut, and dried greens to the pot and a thin layer of bacon fat.

4. Return the bacon bits to the pot.

5. Season with a small amount of salt and pepper and cover with a lid.

6. Let the greens steam themselves over a medium heat until they begin to wilt. This will take about 2 to 3 minutes. Stir the greens, to allow them to continue steaming evenly. Cover and let steam for a further 5 minutes.

7. Adjust the seasoning and serve!

CAULI-RICE

SERVES: 6 · · · PREP: 10 MIN · · · COOK: 5 MIN · · · TOTAL: 15 MIN

1 large head (840 g) **cauliflower**

salt and **pepper** to taste

When going to a low-primal way of eating, one of the very first things to go is rice. I love rice. It's delicious and comforting! Oh no! What now?!

Cauli-Rice is a rice substitute made out of cauliflower. When I first read about Cauli-Rice, I thought, *That's silly. It won't taste like rice!* I avoided it for the longest time simply because I didn't believe it could be a good substitute. Many months later, I had some leftover Indian curry. This seemed like a good opportunity to try it.

Surprisingly, it was great! It *completely* hit the spot. What I knew, but didn't realize, was that the rice is so much about the texture and to serve more as a vehicle for the stuff on top. Cauliflower is such a light taste, you can't really taste it. You just get that pleasing rice texture, some good nutrients, a little fiber, and... you get rice back!

It's so easy to make, and it's great with curries, in soups, as fried rice, with jambalaya, etc. Anywhere you'd use rice, you can use this!

(Ok, *not sushi*, but you get the point.)

1. Remove the leaves and core from the cauliflower.

2. With a cheese grater, grate the cauliflower over the largest grate section. An alternative is to put it into a food processor and pulse the cauliflower until it's small grains. You don't want to puree it, which is why I like the cheese grater method.

3. Place the grated cauliflower into microwaveable container, and season with salt and pepper.

PER SERVING
CALORIES: 35
FAT: 0.22
PROTEIN: 2.83
CARBS: 7.5
FIBER: 3.5
SUGAR ALCOHOLS: 0
NET CARBS: 4

MORE FACTS: P. 529

4. Cover with a lid or plastic wrap. If you use a lid, do not clamp it down. Simply place it on top, to allow some breathing. If plastic wrap is used, poke a few holes in the top. Steam needs to escape.

5. Microwave on high for 3 to 4 minutes. Remove and let sit for 1 more minute. (I don't have a microwave, so I usually use a Teflon pan, with a small amount of coconut oil in the pan. Over high heat, I sauté the Cauli-Rice for about 4 minutes, constantly tossing it around to cook it evenly. The end result is the same!)

6. Serve!

I Can't Believe That's Not Fried Rice

SERVES: 4 · · · PREP: 15 MIN · · · COOK: 15 MIN · · · TOTAL: 30 MIN

4 (60 g) **green onions** (scallions), cut into thin rings

2 Tbsp (30 mL) **toasted sesame oil**

1 Tbsp (15 mL) minced **fresh ginger**

2 **garlic cloves**, minced

1/2 lb. (227 g) **ham**, diced

1/2 cup (120 mL) **frozen peas and carrots**

4 large **whole eggs**, beaten

2 cups (480 mL) **Cauli-Rice** (p. 316)

1/4 cup (60 mL) **soy sauce** (or coconut aminos)

4 tsp (40 mL) **toasted sesame seeds**

salt and **pepper** to taste

When it's on the plate, in a bowl, or under a nice piece of chicken, it looks and tastes just like any other fried rice recipe. I've even made it for friends who were none the wiser. If you like fried rice and you look forward to it at your local Chinese or Japanese takeout joint, you will not be disappointed!

This is a fairly basic version, but it's common for me to add more stuff to it when I make it. Consider this recipe as a base. I'll often add zucchini, mushrooms, bean sprouts, green beans, onions, etc. You can also obviously add shrimp, Chinese BBQ pork, chicken, beef, duck, *Lap Cheong*... whatever!

Personal note: I have to confess that this is one of those that really gives me some portion-control issues. I think it's just the deep fondness I have for the real thing, but this is difficult to eat just a small amount of. I tend to want my bowl to be bottomless.

1. Preheat a wok or a large nonstick pan, over medium-high heat..

2. Set aside a small amount of the sliced green onions to be used as a garnish later.

3. Add sesame oil to the pan. Immediately add the ginger, garlic, and green onions. Stir quickly, making sure these ingredients do not burn. (It's a hot pan and these 3 ingredients are chopped very small. They will burn quickly.) Sauté for about 1 minute or until the garlic shows signs of turning brown (caramelizing). Add the ham, peas, and carrots. Sauté this mixture for a further 2 minutes. Pour the beaten eggs evenly around the pan. With a wooden spoon or a rubber spatula, cut and turn the eggs and veggies for about 1 minute. Eggs should be lightly cooked but not dry. Add the Cauli-Rice and soy sauce to the mixture. Continue cooking and stirring until mixed evenly and heated through. Season with salt and pepper.

4. Garnish with toasted sesame seeds and fresh, sliced green onions. Serve.

PER SERVING
CALORIES: 291.67
FAT: 18.59
PROTEIN: 21.92
CARBS: 11.49
FIBER: 3.42
SUGAR ALCOHOLS: 0
NET CARBS: 8.07

MORE FACTS: P. 532

It´s everything that you
want it to be!

Miracle Cauli-Rice

SERVES: 10 · · · PREP: 10 MIN · · · COOK: 10 MIN · · · TOTAL: 20 MIN

4 8-oz. packets (908 g) **Miracle Rice®**

1 large (840 g) **head cauliflower**

1 Tbsp (15 mL) **light flavored oil** (for sautéing, such as coconut, olive, or ghee)

salt and **pepper** to taste

Miracle Rice® or *shirataki* rice is a very low-carbohydrate Japanese rice substitute made from the devil's tongue yam (also known as the elephant yam or konjac yam). The end result is a product that is essentially net carb and calorie free. It's also gluten free, soy free, and sugar free. It's made primarily of fiber, which the body doesn't absorb. In the end, they are very small little "pearls," more along the lines of an Israeli couscous in terms of shape and texture than rice, but it definitely does a fine job of being "rice" too!

Probably my personal favorite way to make "rice" is to combine Cauli-Rice with Miracle Rice. In my mind, I get some of the nutrient benefits of the cauliflower. I also get the flavor (which I *do* like), in addition to some textural contrasts. The Miracle Rice stretches the carbs, allowing me to have a slightly larger portion with my fried rice, curry, jambalaya, what-have-you. It's more... *for less*!

Note: Miracle Rice® or *shirataki* rice can be found online fairly easily. You can also find it in many grocery stores, as well as Asian supermarkets.

1. Pour the contents of the rice bags into a strainer and get rid of the liquid. Once the rice is in a strainer, run it under cold water for a good minute or two. Wash that fishy odor off of it. Then, let it drip dry for a bit.

2. While the rice drip dries, remove the leaves and core from the cauliflower. With a cheese grater, grate the cauliflower over the largest grate section. An alternative is to put it into a food processor and pulse the cauliflower until it's small grains; you don't want to puree it, which is why I like the cheese grater method.

PER SERVING
CALORIES: 33
FAT: 1.33
PROTEIN: 1.7
CARBS: 4.5
FIBER: 2.1
SUGAR ALCOHOLS: 0
NET CARBS: 2.4

MORE FACTS: P. 530

3. Preheat a large nonstick pan. Add your rice to the pan and stir-fry to dry off the grains and tighten them up a bit. I've read that you do not need to oil these; there are no carbs to stick to the pan. However, I always add a little light olive, sesame or coconut oil, to them, just to be on the safe side. Cook them over very high heat for about 2 or 3 minutes, tossing them around until they're dry. Evidently, if you do not coat them with oil, when they are sufficiently dry, they will squeak, like a basketball player stopping abruptly.

4. When they appear dry, add your cauliflower to the pan and season with a little salt and pepper. (Alternately, you can place the cauliflower in a microwaveable container with a little salt and pepper. Cover with a lid or plastic wrap. If you use a lid, do not clamp it down. Simply place it on top, to allow some breathing. If plastic wrap is used, poke a few holes in the top. Steam needs to escape. Microwave on high for 3 to 4 minutes. Remove and let sit for 1 more minute. Fold into the dry Miracle Rice.)

5. If you're using the sauté pan, cook for about 3 to 4 more minutes or until the cauliflower is cooked through.

6. Serve!

COCONUT CAULI-RICE

SERVES: 12 · · · PREP: 10 MIN · · · COOK: 10 MIN · · · TOTAL: 20 MIN

1 1/2 cup (360 mL) **shredded unsweetened coconut**

4 8-oz. packets (908 g) **Miracle Rice®**

1 large (840 g) **head cauliflower**

4 **garlic cloves**, minced

1 Tbsp (15 mL) **coconut oil**

1/4 bunch (25 g) **cilantro**, washed and large stems removed, chopped

salt and **pepper** to taste

Here's another fun Cauli-Rice dish. This one is very at home in tropical dishes, where coconut would make a great base. Sure, this conjures images of the Caribbean, but this would make for a fantastic bed underneath a wide variety of curies and blends from Southeast Asia as well. A Jerk Pork Chop (p. 298), Ropa un Poco Vieja (p. 268), or some Green Thai Chicken Curry (p. 296). Each of these would be perfectly complemented by this fragrant side dish.

1. Preheat oven to 325°F (162°C).

2. Spread coconut on a baking sheet in a thin layer and bake in preheated oven. The flakes will toast very quickly and won't take more than 5–10 minutes. After a few minutes, stir the coconut to help ensure even color. Remove when toasted and set aside.

3. Pour the contents of the rice bags into a strainer and get rid of the liquid. Once the rice is in a strainer, run it under cold water for a good minute or two. Wash that fishy odor off of it. Then, let it drip dry for a bit.

4. While the rice drip dries, remove the leaves and core from the cauliflower. With a cheese grater, grate the cauliflower over the largest grate section. An alternative is to put it into a food processor and pulse the cauliflower until it's small grains; you don't want to puree it, which is why I like the cheese grater method.

PER SERVING
CALORIES: 89.31
FAT: 7.12
PROTEIN: 2.46
CARBS: 7.16
FIBER: 3.81
SUGAR ALCOHOLS: 0
NET CARBS: 3.35

MORE FACTS: P. 529

5. Preheat a large nonstick pan. Add your rice to the pan and stir-fry it, to dry and tighten the grains up a bit. I've read that you do not need to oil these; there are no carbs to stick to the pan. However, I always add a little light olive, sesame or coconut oil, to them, just to be on the safe side. Cook them over very high heat for about 2 or 3 minutes, tossing them around until they're dry. Evidently, if you do not coat them with oil, when they are sufficiently dry, they will squeak, like a basketball player stopping abruptly.

6. When they appear dry, add your garlic and cauliflower to the pan and season with a little salt and pepper. Cook for about 3 to 4 more minutes or until the cauliflower is cooked through.

7. At the last minute, add the toasted coconut and fresh cilantro. Toss together and serve!

Sweet Potato and Celeriac au Gratin

SERVES: 8 · · · PREP: 20 MIN · · · COOK: 1 HR · · · TOTAL: 1 HR 20 MIN

1 1/2 lb. (681 g) **sweet potatoes**

1 giant (681 g) **celery root**

1 Tbsp (15 mL) **butter**

1 1/4 cups (300 mL) **heavy whipping cream**

1 1/2 cups (360 mL) grated **Parmesan**

1/2 tsp (2 mL) **freshly ground nutmeg**

salt and **pepper** to taste

I love sweet potatoes. I think they're amazing in just about every way I've ever had them. In this case, I've paired them with celeriac. This is done for two reasons. 1. I like the color contrast of the two colors alternating in the slices. It's purdy! 2. Celeriac is lower in carbs than sweet potatoes but has a tendency to get a bit lost in the flavor. As a result, it lowers the carbs of the dish while carrying the flavors and textures of the sweet potatoes, as well as the luscious cream and cheese!

In terms of flat out flavor, this is 10 out of 10. I'm usually fairly critical of my recipes and do my best to portray them honestly and as I see them. This is probably in my top 10 of all recipes in this book. It's a treat to die for, but due to the higher than usual carb content, that's just it: it's a *treat*.

Note: I use a Japanese mandolin to cut the potatoes really thin. You could do this with a knife, but be careful and keep the slices as thin and consistent as possible.

1. Preheat oven to 350°F (177°C).

2. Peel and slice your celeriac and sweet potatoes with a mandolin. Make two separate piles. Then, separate each pile into four piles. You should now have eight piles, all about the same size.

3. Butter the inside of a baking pan (I used a 9" x 9" x 2" square [23 x 23 x 5 cm]).

PER SERVING
CALORIES: 331.14
FAT: 20.61
PROTEIN: 10.29
CARBS: 26.83
FIBER: 4.21
SUGAR ALCOHOLS: 0
NET CARBS: 22.61

MORE FACTS: P. 530

4. Start by placing a thin, consistent layer of celeriac slices. It should entirely cover the bottom of the pan. Sprinkle a small amount of salt on the layer. Next, add a thin, consistent layer of sweet potatoes. Make sure your layers are even and not thicker in the middle. Season with a little salt and pepper. Drizzle 1/4 cup (60 mL) of cream fairly evenly around the layer. Sprinkle 1/4 cup (60 mL) of grated Parmesan cheese over the sweet potatoes. Finally, give it a light dusting of nutmeg. Repeat these steps, alternating layers and seasoning each layer with a little salt, pepper, nutmeg, and a bit of cream and Parmesan. When done, top with the final 1/4 cup (60 mL) of cream and a 1/2 cup (120 mL) of Parmesan cheese.

5. Place your pan, uncovered, in the oven and allow to bake for about 45 minutes. When a knife easily enters the center of the dish, it is ready. If it gets prematurely dark, feel free to cover with a bit of aluminum foil, but be sure to poke some holes in it. It may take a bit more than an hour, depending on how thick you made it, but it will get there.

6. When done, remove it from the oven and allow it to sit for 15 minutes before slicing. This will allow it to firm up a bit.

Simple Buttery Broccoli

SERVES: 6 · · · PREP: 5 MIN · · · COOK: 5 MIN · · · TOTAL: 10 MIN

1 large (840 g) **bunch broccoli**, including stalks, cut into florets

1/4 cup (60 mL) **fresh whole butter** (half a stick), cut into small cubes

salt and **pepper** to taste

Food isn't complicated. People make it complicated.

Broccoli is delicious all on its own. It's a little sweet, with a great texture and a bright vibrant greenness that just screams "I'M A VEGETABLE!!!" There are so many recipes that are mixes and blends of a wide variety of vegetables, commonly known as *medleys*. Some have fruits and nuts mixed with heaps of spices and herbs.

Properly cooked broccoli, with a little salt and fresh butter, can be a *wonderful* side dish to just about any meal on its own! Yes, you can add a million things to this, but that kills the point. Yes, a little garlic and lemon zest would be delightful. Yes, some toasted pecans, orange zest, and a few chopped, dried cranberries might be interesting. Broccoli smothered in Goopy Alfredo sauce (p. 380) sounds inviting. Bacon, a whisper of mustard, a sprinkle of rosemary, and some roasted mushrooms also sound great, but...

...sometimes the broccoli wants to be the star. Let's give it a monologue to be proud of.

Note: I'm a big fan of broccoli stems. When you cut the florets off of the large broccoli trunk, you're left with something that looks like what the Jolly Green Giant might use for lumber... if he were a very, very small giant. Cut off the bigger branches, then with a vegetable peeler, peel the hard, fibrous skin on the outside. You'll eventually get a beautiful, bright, almost white-green core. This is the "broccoli heart" and it's delicious! Cut the center core into pieces about the same size as the florets and cook it right along with them. Enjoy!

PER SERVING
CALORIES: 114.33
FAT: 7.79
PROTEIN: 3.91
CARBS: 9.21
FIBER: 3.69
SUGAR ALCOHOLS: 0
NET CARBS: 5.53

MORE FACTS: P. 530

1. In a mixing bowl, place your cubed butter. Allow it to soften while you cook the broccoli.

2. Steam or cook the broccoli in salted boiling water. If you do steam it, dust it with a little salt prior to being added to the steamer. Cook until tender; then remove and strain out any excess liquid.

3. Add the hot broccoli to the fresh cubes of butter and toss the bowl around, coating the broccoli with freshly melted butter. Add a little salt and pepper to the broccoli as you move it around the bowl.

4. Serve!

Garlicky Baby Broccoli with Bacon

SERVES: 4 · · · PREP: 5 MIN · · · COOK: 35 MIN · · · TOTAL: 40 MIN

4 slices (100 g) **raw bacon,** chopped (for bits)

12 **garlic cloves,** sliced into 1/8-inch (1 mm) thick "chips"

1 lb. (454 g) **baby broccoli**

salt and **pepper** to taste

Broccolini, or "baby broccoli" as its sometimes called, is actually a cross between a Chinese vegetable called *gai-lan* and regular ol' broccoli. Its stalk is longer, totally edible, it has smaller florets, and the whole thing is just a bit sweeter. It looks like it's really becoming quite popular. Even the Jolly Green Giant is making a play!

This is a new ingredient for me, but I wanted to play with it and make something simple but tasty. That usually involves bacon. But I wanted to take it one step further: GARLIC! So, I made my little garlic chips, added some bacon, then sautéed the raw broccolini in the sweet and salty crunchy blend of ingredients, added a little salt and pepper, and... BEST BOWL OF BABY BROCCOLI EVER!

1. In a sauté pan, over medium heat, cook the bacon until crispy.

2. Remove the bacon from the bacon grease and set aside, while leaving the grease in the hot pan.

3. Over very low heat, in the pan with the bacon grease, add the garlic chips and slowly let them fry and turn a light golden brown—the slower, the better. This can take upwards of 30 minutes and require some careful attention (while you do other things). Do not let this burn or turn too dark. It becomes bitter *very* quickly.

4. Remove the garlic from the bacon fat and set aside on a paper towel to dry.

PER SERVING
CALORIES: 165.19
FAT: 11.25
PROTEIN: 6.1
CARBS: 10.73
FIBER: 2.84
SUGAR ALCOHOLS: 0
NET CARBS: 7.89

MORE FACTS: P. 530

5. Remove about half of the garlic-infused bacon fat and set aside (save and cook with it another day!).

6. Add your broccoli to the pan and season with a little salt and pepper. Sauté in the garlicky bacon fat for about 4 minutes or until tender. Add back your bacon bits and garlic chips. Sauté for 1 more minute, adjust seasoning, and serve!

MASHED CAULIFLOWER AND CELERY ROOT

SERVES: 8 · · · PREP: 5 MIN · · · COOK: 25 MIN · · · TOTAL: 30 MIN

1 large (840 g) **head cauliflower**, stem and leaves removed and cut into small florets

1 large (454 g) **celery root**, peeled and cut into chunks

4 **garlic cloves**

1 cup (240 mL) **heavy whipping cream**

1/2 cup (120 mL) **fresh whole butter** (one stick), cubed

salt and **pepper** to taste

All over the low-primal world you'll see mashed cauliflower as the primary replacement for mashed potatoes. That's fine... and good... and it totally works. Oftentimes, people will toss a potato into the mix to add a little potato-y texture. Again, this is fine, but it will definitely boost the carbs. I wanted to do something that would give it a little textural variety but without using potatoes. Instead, I used celery root, also known as celeriac. It's got a very neutral taste and a smooth consistency when pureed. It's got a slight celery taste, but is very low carb and is an excellent companion to the cauliflower. I *highly* recommend it! I've also added a bit of garlic, because... well... I just like garlic. This would be excellent with fresh herbs, cheeses, bacon, etc. Anything you'd toss into your mashed potatoes, you could toss into this and it would be wonderful. Sour cream, perhaps? Mascarpone? Delectable!

1. In a medium-sized pot with a lid, add your cauliflower florets, celery root, garlic, cream, and a little salt and pepper. Place a lid on the pot and place it over medium heat.

2. When the cream begins to simmer, turn the heat down very low and keep a very slow, steady simmer.

3. Let the veggies steam in the cream, under the lid, for about 20 minutes or until the celery root is soft and squishy.

PER SERVING
CALORIES: 254.89
FAT: 22.17
PROTEIN: 3.48
CARBS: 12.09
FIBER: 3.72
SUGAR ALCOHOLS: 0
NET CARBS: 8.38

MORE FACTS: P. 531

4. Mash the cauliflower in your favorite way. You can use a masher, a fork, a food processor, a hand mixer, etc. I used a ricer and pushed the contents through a medium-fine grain, which gives a mostly smooth texture, but with a slight graininess. While mashing/pureeing, add the fresh butter to the hot contents and also puree/mash with the butter. It will melt right in.

5. Adjust seasoning. Serve!

Pancetta-Wrapped Asparagus

SERVES: 4 · · · PREP: 10 MIN · · · COOK: 15 MIN · · · TOTAL: 25 MIN

1 bunch (227 g) **asparagus spears** (about 20 spears)

2 Tbsp (30 mL) **olive oil**

20 slices (250 g) **pancetta**, sliced into strips

salt and **pepper** to taste

This is a very simple but surprisingly elegant and extremely delicious little dish. Alone, it's wonderful, but you could also lean three of these onto a nice salad, with a goat cheese vinaigrette, a couple of toasted pine nuts, and a grilled half fig (just one!), and you'd have something impressive. It's quick and easy to prepare. The only things you need are asparagus, pancetta (Italian bacon!!), oil, salt, and pepper!

Note: I've left this simple, but there are many things you could do with this. A light squeeze of orange juice and a little orange zest tossed into the oil would be just delightful! As would some herbs. Rosemary, perhaps? A few chili flakes for a back-of-the-throat kicker if that's your thing. This is also just excellent if you grill it, but be careful; the pancetta wants to fall off. Be deliberate and clear in your movements and grill that stuff up! *Phenom-nom*!

1. Preheat your oven to 425°F (218°C). Place your baking tray in the oven to heat up.

2. Remove the fibrous and tough base of the asparagus spear. I usually just cut the base off the entire bundle, but many snap the spears in half, under the assumption that the asparagus knows where its own sweet spot lies; your call. Snap 'em or cut 'em. The base is tough but makes for a good soup!

3. Toss your asparagus in a little oil, salt, and pepper. Coat them well and evenly.

PER SERVING
CALORIES: 181.04
FAT: 18.61
PROTEIN: 8.47
CARBS: 2.32
FIBER: 1.72
SUGAR ALCOHOLS: 0
NET CARBS: 1.02

MORE FACTS: P. 531

4. Wrap each spear in pancetta. Set them on a plate with the seam side down.

5. Remove the hot baking tray from the oven and quickly place your asparagus spears on the tray, with the seam side down. Do it swiftly, before the tray cools off and the asparagus just steams. You want to hear that searing sound.

6. Place the tray in the oven. Bake for 8 to 14 minutes, depending on the thickness of the asparagus.

7. Remove from the oven and serve!

This is how italians wrap stuff in Bacon.

CREAMED SPINACH

SERVES: 6 · · · PREP: 15 MIN · · · COOK: 10 MIN · · · TOTAL: 25 MIN

2 lbs. (908 g) **fresh spinach leaves**, washed and stems removed

2 Tbsp (30 mL) **fat** (olive oil, butter, or even bacon fat)

1/2 small (35 g) **onion**, sliced

3 **garlic cloves**, minced

1 1/4 cups (300 mL) **heavy whipping cream**

1/4 tsp (1 mL) ground **nutmeg**

salt and **pepper** to taste

Creamed spinach, at its core, is little more than cream and spinach. A large bag of spinach is mostly air, followed by a lot of water, and then... the rest of it. Two full pounds of spinach will *look* like a lot, but when it's cooked and the air is removed and all the water evaporates, it shrivels into a small creamy mound of yum! One *could* just take a large pot full of cream, add the spinach with a bit of salt and pepper, then cook it until it's reduced, the cream thick and the entire concoction is coated with it. This is quick, easy, and delicious, while also being somewhat one-dimensional and a little lacking in vibrancy.

I'm going to suggest a few extra steps, but these will give us a slightly sweeter taste, with more developed flavors and a *much* brighter green color, creating a far more attractive side dish!

Random note: I *so* badly wanted to add bacon bits to this, but I decided to go minimalist. I also was feeling a bit bacon'ed out, if you can believe it! If you happen to trip while walking through the kitchen carrying bacon bits and a few are flung into the mix while it cooks, go ahead and leave them there. They'd be delicious!

1. Bring a medium-sized pot of water to a boil over high heat.

2. Gather a bowl with ice cubes and water, as well as a colander or straining device of some kind. Once the water boils, add a nice amount of salt. Place your spinach into the boiling water and allow it to swirl around for about 30 seconds. Remove the spinach with the strainer and immediately plunge it into the ice water. When it is thoroughly cooled, remove the spinach and squeeze it, by clinching it in your fists (or with a cloth), until all the water has been squeezed out. You should have a sizeable lump of bright green, cooked spinach. Coarsely chop the spinach and set aside.

PER SERVING
CALORIES: 250.18
FAT: 22.33
PROTEIN: 5.66
CARBS: 8.6
FIBER: 3.11
SUGAR ALCOHOLS: 0
NET CARBS: 5.49

MORE FACTS: P. 531

3. Place a large sauté pan over medium heat. Add oil, fat, or butter. When the oil ripples, add the garlic and onions with a little bit of salt and pepper. Cook until translucent, about 2 to 3 minutes. Add the spinach, cream, nutmeg, and a bit more salt and pepper. Turn the heat up to high; the liquid will evaporate more quickly. Cook, while stirring, until the cream thickens and clings to the spinach. About 4 to 5 minutes.

4. Taste, adjust seasoning, and serve!

5. **Optional:** Garnish with bacon bits.

Carrot and Parmesan Casserole

SERVES: 8 · · · PREP: 10 MIN · · · COOK: 35 MIN · · · TOTAL: 45 MIN

2 lb. (908 g) **carrots**, peeled and roll cut into large chunks

1/2 cup (120 mL) **heavy whipping cream**

1 medium (110 g) **onion**, diced

1 cup (240 mL) **grated Parmesan**, divided

4 **garlic cloves**, minced

1/4 tsp (1 mL) **ground nutmeg**

salt and **pepper** to taste

I wanted to see what would happen if I just took some well-cut carrots and threw them in the oven with some cream, cheese, and seasonings. I wanted something quick and simple, while also being super tasty. BOOM! I think we have a winner! Not the most attractive dish on the planet, but in terms of pure simplicity and flavor? Two thumbs up!

Note: This recipe uses a fun technique for cutting the carrots that is mostly irrelevant. It's called an *oblique* cut, or occasionally referred to as a roll cut or quarter cut. The cut works like this: Hold the knife at a 45-degree angle to the carrot and cut down. Roll the carrot a quarter of the way around and move it toward the knife one inch (2.5 cm) and cut. Again, roll the carrot 90 degrees and move another inch (2.5 cm) and cut, etc. Keep going, until you run out of carrot. It creates a quirky and interesting "rough chop" shape of carrot, which, for no clear cut (*tee-hee*) reason, I particularly enjoy doing!

1. Preheat oven to 350°F (177°C).

2. In a large mixing bowl, combine carrots, cream, onion, half of the Parmesan cheese, garlic, nutmeg, and some salt and pepper. Mix, so that the carrots are coated with the cream.

3. Pour the mixture into a greased 9" x 9" x 2" (23 x 23 x 5 cm) casserole pan and spread evenly. Top with the remaining Parmesan cheese.

PER SERVING
CALORIES: 158.8
FAT: 9.13
PROTEIN: 6.08
CARBS: 13.32
FIBER: 3.8
SUGAR ALCOHOLS: 0
NET CARBS: 9.53

MORE FACTS: P. 531

4. Bake for about 35 minutes or until the cheese is golden and the cream is thick and clings to the carrots. The carrots should be somewhat toothsome still. For those that love a good, soft carrot, you can optionally boil the carrots in salted water for about 7 to 10 minutes prior to baking, but I personally don't feel this step is necessary.

5. Scoop and serve!

HERBY ASPARAGUS AND MUSHROOMS

SERVES: 4 · · · PREP: 5 MIN · · · COOK: 10 MIN · · · TOTAL: 15 MIN

1/4 cup (60 mL) **fresh whole butter** (half a stick), cut into small cubes

1 lb. (454 g) **whole crimini** (or button) mushrooms, dirt removed with brush and stems removed

1 bunch (227 g) **asparagus spears**, tough stem ends removed

2 tsp (10 mL) **fresh oregano** (thyme, rosemary, sage, and/or marjoram), roughly chopped

salt and **pepper** to taste

A classic combination! These earthy flavors really complement one another and go extremely well with heartier cuts of meat like beef, lamb, and whole roasted chicken, turkey, etc. This particular side is nice because it's all done in one pan, fairly quickly. The trick is simply adding the ingredients to the pan in the right order and at the right times. This is finished with some fresh herbs and butter. Very rustic and simple, while also packing in a lot of flavor!

1. Heat a large sauté pan over medium-high heat.

2. Add 1 tablespoon (15 mL) of butter to the pan. Swirl the pan to coat the pan with butter. Quickly add the mushrooms. Season with a little salt and pepper. Sauté the mushrooms for about 5 minutes or until the mushrooms start to lose their water and shrivel a bit. Add your asparagus spears to the pan and sauté for a further 2 minutes. Lower the heat to a medium-low temperature.

3. At this point, make sure your stem ends are all facing up, like a series of very small mushroom bowls. Place a small amount of the herbs into each stem cavity, and then top the herbs with a small cube of fresh butter. Let the pan sit for 2 more minutes, as the butter melts the herbs into the mushrooms. Toss the ingredients in the pan.

4. Arrange the mushrooms and asparagus on four plates and serve!

PER SERVING
CALORIES: 142.59
FAT: 15.02
PROTEIN: 4.71
CARBS: 6.78
FIBER: 2.48
SUGAR ALCOHOLS: 0
NET CARBS: 4.3

MORE FACTS: P. 530

CARROT PUMPKIN MASH

SERVES: 8 · · · PREP: 15 MIN · · · COOK: 35 MIN · · · TOTAL: 50 MIN

Here's a really simple mashed pile of goodness which would be perfect under a nice piece of chicken or pork. Because it's such a simple base, a variety of different seasonings could be applied to help it match whatever else it may be served with. Add some maple flavoring, or a touch of orange juice and zest with a bit of cinnamon for some fun aroma. Go a different direction and add some cayenne pepper, fresh thyme, and smoky bacon bits for a nice spicy pork chop!

A lovely mash to serve as the basis for a dish is a wonderful, simple and comforting way to build a meal.

1/4 cup (60 mL) **fresh whole butter**

1 medium (110 g) **onion**, diced

4 **garlic cloves**, minced

1 small (2 to 3 lb.) (1.1 kg) **kabocha squash**, peeled, seeded, and cut into large pieces (substitution: acorn, buttercup, delicata, pumpkin)

1 lb. (454 g) **carrots**, peeled and cut into large pieces

1/2 cup (120 mL) **chicken stock** or **broth**

1 Tbsp (15 mL) thinly sliced **chives**

salt and **black pepper** to taste

1. In a medium-sized saucepan, melt the butter over medium heat. Add the onions and garlic with a bit of salt and pepper. Stir and cook until the onions are translucent, about 3 to 5 minutes.

2. Add the carrots and squash with a bit more salt and pepper. Stir to coat with the onion mixture.

3. Add the chicken stock and bring to a simmer. Reduce heat to low and add a lid. Allow to simmer for about 25 minutes or until vegetables are soft.

4. Pour off any extra liquid and set aside. Mash the vegetables using your favorite method, whether with a fork, masher, ricer, or food processor. Add back some of the liquid to adjust the consistency if it's too thick. Adjust seasoning with salt and pepper. Garnish with chives and serve!

PER SERVING
CALORIES: 126.66
FAT: 5.52
PROTEIN: 1.21
CARBS: 10.67
FIBER: 2.52
SUGAR ALCOHOLS: 0
NET CARBS: 8.14

MORE FACTS: P. 532

Southern Broccoli Pudding

SERVES: 10 · · · PREP: 20 MIN · · · COOK: 45 MIN · · · TOTAL: 1 HR 20 MIN

1 large (840 g) bunch **broccoli**, including stalks, cut into florets

3 Tbsp (45 mL) **butter**

1 medium (110 g) **onion**, diced

4 **garlic cloves**, minced

3 Tbsp (45 mL) **tapioca flour**

3/4 cup (180 mL) **heavy whipping cream**

1 cup (240 mL) **unsweetened almond milk**

1/2 lb. (227 g) **cheddar cheese**, grated

1 Tbsp (15 mL) **paprika**

2 tsp (10 mL) chopped **fresh thyme**

1 tsp (2g) **cayenne pepper**

4 large (200g) **whole eggs**

salt and **pepper** to taste

PER SERVING
CALORIES: 259.81
FAT: 20.09
PROTEIN: 11.37
CARBS: 10.72
FIBER: 2.83
SUGAR ALCOHOLS: 0
NET CARBS: 7.89

MORE FACTS: P. 529

This might be my personal favorite side dish in this book. The idea was originally part of a Thanksgiving post for my blog, which suggests this is a perfect dish for social gatherings. It's something like a cross between a pudding and a crustless quiche, but with the thickened cheese sauce as part of the whole shebang, it crosses into whole new realms of low-primal comfort food. The texture is simply sublime!

1. Preheat oven to 350°F (177°C). Grease a 2 1/2 quart (2.4 L) casserole dish and set aside.

2. Bring a large pot of water up to a boil, with about 8 to 12 cups (2 to 3 L) of salted boiling water. Have a large bowl filled with ice water sitting by its side.

3. Add your broccoli to the boiling water. Allow to boil for 1 minute. After 1 minute, remove the broccoli from the boiling water (using a colander or slotted spoon) and immediately place the veggies in the bowl of ice water. Make sure they are completely submerged. Stir them around, so they chill quickly. Leave the veggies in the ice water for about 5 minutes or until thoroughly chilled. If all the ice melts… add a little more! The veggies need to be completely and totally chilled. After the veggies have chilled, strain them through a colander and allow them to drip dry over a bowl or in the sink. You want to eliminate as much water as possible.

4. While the broccoli drip dries, place a medium-sized saucepan on the stove over medium heat. Melt the butter and add the onions and garlic with a bit of salt and pepper. Cook until the onions are translucent, about 3 to 5 minutes. Add the tapioca flour and stir in and cook for a further 3 to 5 minutes, stirring occasionally.

5. Quickly whisk in the cold cream and almond milk. Bring this mixture up to a slow simmer. Once it is simmering, whisk in the grated cheese, cayenne, paprika, and thyme. Taste the sauce and adjust with a bit of salt

and pepper.

6. In a medium mixing bowl, place your four eggs. Carefully and quickly whisk about 1/4 of the hot cheese sauce. Once this is whisked in, whisk in the remaining sauce.

7. Place your broccoli in the greased pan. Spread it into an even layer. Pour the hot cheese and egg sauce over the top of the broccoli. Bake for about 45 to 55 minutes or until golden, firm, and lightly puffed in the center. Remove and allow to rest for 15 minutes before serving.

8. Serve!

Parsnip-Almond Mash

SERVES: 6 · · · PREP: 5 MIN · · · COOK: 25 MIN · · · TOTAL: 30 MIN

1 lb. (454 g) **parsnips**, peeled and cut into chunks

1/2 cup (120 mL) **blanched almond flour**

1/4 cup (60 mL) unsweetened **almond milk**

1/4 cup (60 mL) **water**

1/4 cup (60 mL) **butter**

salt and **pepper** to taste

Almond meal absorbs warm water, much in the same way that polenta might. Therefore, it's kind of a fun ingredient to play with, but too much almond meal is akin to eating about a hundred nuts all at once. While those are delicious and tasty fats, it makes sense to add something to the almonds, to add body and some character. The parsnips really boost the carbs in this one, but for those a bit further up the carb ladder, I thought that parsnips made for a fun and aromatic addition.

1. In a small pot, over medium heat, add the parsnips, almond meal, milk, water, and a bit of salt and pepper. Stir, and place a lid on the pot. Allow it to simmer until the parsnips steam and soften.

2. Mash, puree, or rice the mixture with the fresh butter. This can be done with a fork, a mashing tool (for a rustic appearance), a food processor (for a smooth appearance), or a ricer (for a pleasant, consistent look and texture with a touch of graininess). There is no one "correct" method. Season with a bit of salt and pepper. Adjust consistency by adding a bit of warm almond milk to thin, should you choose to.

3. Serve!

PER SERVING
CALORIES: 178.77
FAT: 12.15
PROTEIN: 3.22
CARBS: 15.78
FIBER: 5.02
SUGAR ALCOHOLS: 0
NET CARBS: 10.76

MORE FACTS: P. 528

Green Beans, Almonds, and Peppers

SERVES: 4 · · · PREP: 15 MIN · · · COOK: 10 MIN · · · TOTAL: 25 MIN

This is a quick, bright, and tasty side dish. It seems to me that most people boil their vegetables, but this is completely unnecessary. The goal is simply to cook your veggies in a way that makes them healthy and delicious—sautéed in a little butter will do the trick. Especially if you use a nice, thin, fresh variety of green bean!

This simple side can go with just about anything. A spatchcocked chicken with a nice citrus compound butter would really do the trick!

The toasted almonds add nice texture and a little nutty variety! Couldn't we all use a little more nutty variety?

2 Tbsp (30 mL) **unsalted butter**

1 lb. (454 g) **green string beans**, ends and string removed

1 small (74 g) **red bell pepper**, thinly sliced

4 **garlic cloves**, minced

1/4 cup (60 mL) **sliced almonds**, toasted

salt and **pepper** to taste

1. Preheat a sauté pan over medium–high heat.

2. When the pan is hot, add the butter and green beans at the same time. Toss them in the pan to coat the green beans with butter. Season with salt and pepper.

3. Sauté the green beans for about 4 minutes.

4. Add the sliced red bell peppers and garlic. Season with a little more salt and pepper.

5. Sauté for another 4 minutes or until all the vegetables are cooked through. They should still be somewhat crisp and bright but cooked through.

6. At the last minute, add the toasted almonds to the pan. Mix them into the vegetables and then serve!

PER SERVING
CALORIES: 147.55
FAT: 10.2
PROTEIN: 3.55
CARBS: 12.02
FIBER: 5.17
SUGAR ALCOHOLS: 0
NET CARBS: 6.85

MORE FACTS: P. 530

Bacon-Sage Cauliflower "Au Gratin"

SERVES: 8 · · · PREP: 15 MIN · · · COOK: 30 MIN · · · TOTAL: 45 MIN

1 large (840 g) **head cauliflower**, stem and leaves removed and cut into small florets

1 recipe **Thick, Goopy Alfredo Sauce** (p. 380) (about 2 cups [480 mL])

1 Tbsp (15 mL) chopped **fresh sage**

1/4 cup (60 mL) real **bacon bits**

1/4 cup (60 mL) **almond flour**

1/4 cup (60 mL) grated **Parmesan cheese**

salt and **pepper**, to taste

PER SERVING
CALORIES: 389.24
FAT: 32.88
PROTEIN: 16.33
CARBS: 10.12
FIBER: 3.32
SUGAR ALCOHOLS: 0
NET CARBS: 6.8

MORE FACTS: P. 531

This is comfort food in the best possible way. I'm never fully sure what makes a particular dish "comfortable," but I feel confident in the stance that this particular dish exudes it. It's actually really quite simple. It's partially cooked cauliflower (boiled in salted water), then tossed with a cheese sauce, bacon, and fresh sage. It's then placed into a baking vessel, where it's topped with almond meal and more cheese. The end result is a soft, comforting mélange of cheesy, creamy, and bacon-y goodness. NOM[2]!!

Note: Because I operate a blog and have a sense of which are the most popular recipes, this is in the top five fairly easily.

1. Place a large pot full of water on the stove to boil.

2. Preheat your oven to 425°F (218°C).

3. If your Alfredo sauce is cold, warm it in a medium-sized saucepan.

4. Once your water is boiling, add a healthy amount of salt to the water. Add your cauliflower florets to the water and simmer for about 3 minutes. Strain the cauliflower, so that all the water is removed.

5. Stir the cauliflower into the Alfredo sauce. Add the sage and bacon bits as well. Once the cauliflower is evenly coated with the cheese sauce, pour it into a greased baking pan. I used a 9-inch round (24 x 4 cm) silicone baking pan, but a 9" x 13" (33 x 23 x 5 cm) casserole pan will work as well. All we're really doing is browning the top. It's all already mostly cooked at this point. Dust the top of the cauliflower with the almond meal and Parmesan cheese.

6. Bake in the oven for about 15 to 20 minutes or until the top is nice and toasty brown. Serve!

Sauces, Spreads, & Dippity Do's

○ ○ ○

This section alone could almost be its own miniature booklet. A simple chicken breast with poached broccoli is turned into a completely different meal when topped with an alfredo sauce—or perhaps a teriyaki sauce. Or a beurre blanc! A sauce can take a simple set of ingredients to a new culture or into a realm of complex flavors and textures. Dips and spreads are also ways to enhance crackers or veggie sticks, or take a basic sandwich and turn it into a panini! With the following thirty-five recipes, thousands of possible outcomes can occur, depending on what you choose to serve each of these with.

Blackberry Beurre Rouge

SERVES: 4 · · · PREP: 5 MIN · · · COOK: 25 MIN · · · TOTAL: 30 MIN

1 **shallot**, minced

1/2 cup (120 mL) good quality **red wine**

1/2 cup (120 mL) **fresh blackberries**, washed

1 Tbsp (15 mL) **homogenized heavy cream** (optional)

1/4 cup (60 mL) **chilled butter**, cut into about 12 small cubes

salt and **pepper** to taste

A beurre rouge (red butter) is a butter sauce made almost entirely from butter! Its origin is France and the method is essentially reducing red wine, to really concentrate the flavors. Once the wine is very dark burgundy, thick, and flavorful, cold butter is then whisked into the hot wine, carefully and methodically, so that the sauce emulsifies and thickens, rather than turning into a purple oil slick with some wine in it. I've left the sauce relatively pure, short of the addition of fresh blackberries to the reduction. This will add a bit more brilliance to the color, while also adding some sweet and a bit more character. Also, traditionally, there is no cream in the sauce. I've added it to this sauce because the homogenized cream helps the emulsion (something of "culinary training wheels"). Feel free to leave it out, but if you do, whisk quickly with firm determination and singularity of purpose!

1. In a small saucepan over medium heat, add shallots, wine, blackberries, and a bit of salt and pepper. Stir regularly while the liquid reduces to a fairly thick and lumpy syrup, roughly 1/4 cup (60 mL) in volume.

2. Over low heat, whisk in the 1 tablespoon (15 mL) of optional cream and then immediately add the first cube of butter, whisking it consistently through the warm syrup. You never want the butter to sit in one spot long enough for the fat to pool. You want it to continue moving and gliding through the sauce. Once the first cube of butter is almost completely melted, add the second cube of butter and continue whisking. Once the second cube of butter is almost melted, add the third cube. Continue in this manner until all the butter is used and you have a lovely, thick, and purple sauce. Taste it and adjust the seasoning with some salt and pepper.

3. Strain the blackberry seeds from the sauce and set in a warm place (a good one is to place it in a bowl with a warm wet towel beneath it). You want to keep the sauce warm, but if it's too hot, it will break. Think gentle and warm, like a baby's bottle.

PER SERVING
CALORIES: 148.74
FAT: 12.5
PROTEIN: 0.33
CARBS: 4.15
FIBER: 1
SUGAR ALCOHOLS: 0
NET CARBS: 3.15

MORE FACTS: P. 533

BEURRE BLANC

SERVES: 4 · · · PREP: 5 MIN · · · COOK: 25 MIN · · · TOTAL: 30 MIN

1 **shallot**, minced

3/4 cup (180 mL) good quality **white wine**

1 Tbsp (15 mL) **homogenized heavy cream** (optional)

1/4 cup (60 mL) **chilled butter**, cut into about 12 small cubes

salt and **pepper** to taste

A beurre blanc (white butter) is a butter sauce made almost entirely from butter! Its origin is France and the method is essentially reducing white wine, to really concentrate the flavors. Once the wine is reduced, tart, and concentrated, cold butter is then whisked into the hot wine, carefully and methodically, so that the sauce emulsifies and thickens, rather than turning into an oil slick with some wine in it. Traditionally, there is no cream in the sauce. I've added it to this sauce because the homogenized cream helps the emulsion (something of "culinary training wheels"). Feel free to leave it out, but if you do, whisk quickly and decidedly!

1. In a small saucepan over medium heat, add shallots, wine, and a bit of salt and pepper. Stir regularly while the liquid reduces to roughly 3 tablespoons (45 mL) in volume.

2. Over low heat, whisk in the 1 tablespoon (15 mL) of optional cream and then immediately add the first cube of butter, whisking it consistently through the warm syrup. You never want the butter to sit in one spot long enough for the fat to pool. You want it to continue moving and gliding through the sauce. Once the first cube of butter is almost completely melted, add the second cube of butter and continue whisking. Once the second cube of butter is almost melted, add the third cube. Continue in this manner until all the butter is used and you have a lovely, thick, and cream-colored sauce. Taste it and adjust the seasoning with some salt and pepper.

3. Set in a warm place (a good one is to place it in a bowl with a warm, wet towel beneath it). You want to keep the sauce warm, but if it's too hot, it will break. Think gentle and warm, like a baby's bottle.

PER SERVING
CALORIES: 152
FAT: 12.375
PROTEIN: 0.08
CARBS: 2.415
FIBER: 0
SUGAR ALCOHOLS: 0
NET CARBS: 2.42

MORE FACTS: P. 533

Sweet Thai Chili Sauce

SERVES: 4 · · · PREP: 3 MIN · · · COOK: 7 MIN · · · TOTAL: 10 MIN

A sweet Thai chili sauce is one of those perfect flavors where the sweet, salty, acid, and spice are all in perfect concert. I don't know how these flavors could be improved! This is *amazing* as a dip for... really anything! Brush it on some chicken before grilling. *Amazing*! In this book, it's used on chicken wings (p. 124) and fried shrimp (p. 136), but it's got loads of places it belongs. Make it. You won't be sorry!

1/2 cup (120 mL) **rice wine vinegar**

1/2 cup (120 mL) **sugar replacement**

1 Tbsp (15 mL) **crushed chilies** or **chili paste**

1 Tbsp (15 mL) **fresh minced ginger**

4 **garlic cloves**, minced

1 tsp (5 mL) **salt**

2 Tbsp (30 mL) **water**

1/2 tsp (2 mL) **glucomannan powder**

1. In a small saucepan, add the rice wine vinegar, sweetener, chilies, ginger, garlic, and salt. Bring the sauce up to a simmer over medium heat.

2. Once the sauce is up to a slow simmer, in a small mixing bowl, whisk together the water and glucomannan powder.

3. While whisking the hot sauce, pour the glucomannan mixture into the hot sauce. It should thicken within 2 to 3 minutes. This should give it a nice syrupy consistency.

4. Serve warm or chill it and refrigerate. It will thicken a bit more as it cools.

PER SERVING
CALORIES: 59.97
FAT: 0.26
PROTEIN: 0.21
CARBS: 33.75
FIBER: 0.69
SUGAR ALCOHOLS: 30
NET CARBS: 2.99

MORE FACTS: P. 532

Bacon, Cheddar, and Jalapeño Dip

SERVES: 6 · · · PREP: 15 MIN · · · COOK: 15 MIN · · · TOTAL: 35 MIN

2 Tbsp (30 mL) **fat** (olive oil, butter, or even bacon fat)

1 medium (110 g) **onion**, diced

2 **jalapeño peppers**, seeds and ribs removed, finely diced

4 **garlic cloves**, minced

1/2 lb. (227 g) **regular cream cheese** (not low fat)

1/2 lb. (227 g) **cheddar cheese**, grated and divided

1/2 cup (120 mL) **real bacon bits**

1/4 bunch (25 g) **cilantro**, washed, large stems removed and chopped

1/2 tsp (2 mL) ground **cumin seed**

1/2 tsp (2 mL) ground **coriander seed**

salt and **pepper** to taste

I love this dip. I LOOOoOOoOooOVE this dip! The day that I made this dip, I also whipped up a batch of Spicy Cumin-Cheddar Crackers (p. 468). On the days I do my cooking sessions, I cook between eight and fifteen recipes at the same time. In terms of determining which are my favorites, it largely comes down to which recipes were gone at the end of the day. This recipe, as well as the crackers, were totally gone. Vanished. Skeedoodled. Vamoosed. EATEN!

This recipe uses jalapeños, which aren't *that* spicy. I also suggest cutting out the ribs and seeds, which further eliminates the heat. In the end, this dip has a mild kick. Obviously, if you'd like to omit the heat, omit the peppers. However, on the flipside, if you want to *add* heat, you can double the peppers, or you can use different peppers, such as the fiery habanero! Finally, a little bit of your favorite hot pepper sauce in the cheese base won't hurt anything at all. As you're mixing the base, add a bit of your favorite chili sauce, taste it, and adjust seasoning before you top with cheese and bake!

1. Preheat oven to 400°F (204°C).

2. In a medium sauté pan, over medium heat, add your fat (bacon fat, butter, lard, or olive oil), onions, garlic, and diced jalapeños along with a little bit of salt and pepper. Sauté until the ingredients are soft and lightly colored (about 10 to 15 minutes). Remove and set aside.

PER SERVING
CALORIES: 366.65
FAT: 31.39
PROTEIN: 15.96
CARBS: 4.84
FIBER: 0.68
SUGAR ALCOHOLS: 0
NET CARBS: 4.18

MORE FACTS: P. 533

3. In a large mixing bowl, combine cream cheese, 1 1/2 cups (360 mL) of the cheddar cheese, bacon, cilantro, cumin, coriander, and a bit of salt and pepper. Add the veggies and mix the ingredients thoroughly.

4. Place the cream cheese mixture into an ovenproof casserole pan, or something roughly the size of a pie pan. Press the dip into the pan so it's got a flat top. Top the dip with the remaining cheddar cheese.

5. Bake the dip until the top is melted and lightly colored, about 15 minutes.

6. Serve hot!

BLACK OLIVE TAPENADE

SERVES: 12 · · · PREP: 5 MIN · · · COOK: 0 MIN · · · TOTAL: 5 MIN

1 cup (240 mL) **black olives** (like Kalamata), drained and pitted

1/4 cup (60 mL) **slivered almonds**, toasted

1/4 cup (60 mL) **extra virgin olive oil**

2 Tbsp (30 mL) coarsely chopped **capers**

2 **boneless anchovy filets**

1 Tbsp (15 mL) freshly squeezed **lemon juice**

1 tsp (5 mL) chopped **fresh rosemary**

1 tsp (5 mL) **fresh lemon zest** (peel)

2 **garlic cloves**, crushed

1/2 tsp (1 mL) **crushed red chili flakes**

salt and **pepper** to taste

Olive Tapenade (pronounced: toppin-odd) is little more than a coarsely pureed mixture of olives, capers, and other odds and ends. The fun and flavors really play into the "odds and ends" aspect of that particular mélange. This salty and lightly acidic concoction is usually used as a dip or spread, but is also great as a stuffing for a pork tenderloin or rubbed beneath the skin of a soon-to-be-roasted chicken. A very versatile recipe, this stuff is fantastic as is or as a part of a much bigger plan!

1. In a food processor, or with a mortar and pestle, process all the ingredients until the desired texture is achieved. I prefer mine to be a bit coarse, chunky, and rustic, but you can make this a fine puree should you seek such a thing.

2. Taste, and adjust seasoning with salt and pepper.

PER SERVING
CALORIES: 75.48
FAT: 7.14
PROTEIN: 0.96
CARBS: 1.95
FIBER: 0.86
SUGAR ALCOHOLS: 0
NET CARBS: 1.09

MORE FACTS: P. 534

ARTICHOKE PESTO DIP

SERVES: 8 · · · PREP: 5 MIN · · · COOK: 0 MIN · · · TOTAL: 5 MIN

This dip is so easy and so tasty and so absolutely yummy... it's so hard to believe that it's so acceptable for us to eat! Artichoke dips aren't uncommon, nor are artichoke dips with Parmesan and/or frozen spinach (all good combinations in their own right!). I just happened to have a bunch of basil lying around and a bunch of pesto in the freezer at the time. When I saw that, the whole thing just... clicked. I'm glad it did too! The end result is a thoroughly delicious and filling dip.

Enjoy it with Hazelnut-Parmesan Crackers (p. 466)!

1/2 cup (120 mL) **mayonnaise**

1/2 cup (120 mL) **sour cream**

1/2 cup (120 mL) **Pesto alla Genovese** (p.386)

8 whole (222 g) **artichoke hearts in oil**, cut into 8 wedges each

salt and **pepper** to taste

1. In a medium mixing bowl, mix the ingredients.

2. Season, taste, adjust seasoning, and serve!

PER SERVING
CALORIES: 261.21
FAT: 26.82
PROTEIN: 2.96
CARBS: 4.39
FIBER: 1.67
SUGAR ALCOHOLS: 0.03
NET CARBS: 2.69

MORE FACTS: P. 533

Orange Mojo

SERVES: 16 · · · PREP: 10 MIN · · · COOK: 0 MIN · · · TOTAL: 10 MIN

1 **orange**

3/4 cup (180 mL) **olive oil**

1 medium (110 g) **onion**, coarsely chopped

1/4 cup (60 mL) **freshly squeezed lime juice**

4 **garlic cloves**

1 tsp (5 mL) **salt**

1/2 tsp (1 mL) **crushed red chili flakes**

1/2 tsp (1 mL) ground **cumin seed**

1/2 tsp (1 mL) ground **coriander seed**

1/2 tsp (1 mL) **freshly cracked black pepper**

1/2 bunch (50 g) **fresh cilantro**, washed, stems removed, and chopped

PER SERVING
CALORIES: 100.05
FAT: 10.18
PROTEIN: 0.17
CARBS: 2.39
FIBER: 0.49
SUGAR ALCOHOLS: 0
NET CARBS: 2.09

MORE FACTS: P. 536

A *mojo* is a type of sauce originating in the Canary Islands, a Spanish archipelago just off the northwest coast of Africa. Some incredible flavors have been merged in this part of the world, combining local indigenous flora with a diverse set of cultures. A mojo is typically a bit spicy, with loads of olive oil and typically something on the sour side, be it vinegar or citrus juices. Garlic, onions, chilies, and herbs are often accomplices. In this particular case, we're going for a super tart drizzle of a sauce, perfect dribbled over a lonely chicken breast or used to spruce up and marinate a steak. These sauces are so vibrant and action packed, they can stand up to just about anything, while still bringing a touch of freshness even to a delicate fish. You know... just use a bit less! *wink*

Note: Makes about 2 cups, (480 mL) or sixteen 2-tablespoon (30 mL) servings.

1. With a zester, zest your orange. You can also use a vegetable peeler to peel the very outer orange layer of the orange (do not get the white pith; it's bitter). You want enough of the zest to create about 1 teaspoon (5 mL) of fresh zest. Juice the orange and place both the juice and the zest in a blender.

2. Add the olive oil, onion, lime juice, garlic, salt, chili flakes, cumin, coriander, and black pepper into the blender. Puree until fully liquefied.

3. Pour into a separate container and add the fresh cilantro. Stir it into the mojo.

PINEAPPLE SALSA

SERVES: 10 · · · PREP: 15 MIN · · · COOK: 0 MIN · · · TOTAL: 15 MIN

This is an absolutely terrific salsa. It's incredibly sweet and full of flavor—a perfect accompaniment to a simple pork chop or a nicely seared piece of fish. Because of its strong flavor, a little bit goes a long way! The nutrition is calculated at roughly 10 one-ounce (28 g) servings.

Note: A spectacular variation on this recipe can be made from grilling the ingredients prior to mixing them together. It loses some of the bright, vibrant tastes and colors, while picking up loads of character and depth.

1 cup (240 mL) **pineapple cubes** (fairly small dice)

2 small (148 g) **red bell peppers**, peeled and seeded

1 small (110 g) **red onion**, diced

4 **garlic cloves**, minced

1 Tbsp (15 mL) minced **fresh ginger**

2 **jalapeño peppers**, seeds and ribs removed, finely diced

1/4 bunch (25 g) **cilantro**, washed, large stems removed, and chopped

1/4 cup (60 mL) **lime juice**, freshly squeezed

salt to taste

1. In a medium-sized mixing bowl, combine the ingredients. This is best if left to sit for about one hour prior to eating, but it's ready immediately. Season to taste and serve!

PER SERVING
CALORIES: 22.17
FAT: 0.03
PROTEIN: 0.48
CARBS: 5.37
FIBER: 0.88
SUGAR ALCOHOLS: 0
NET CARBS: 4.49

MORE FACTS: P. 536

Sweet 'n' Tangy BBQ Sauce

SERVES: 16 · · · PREP: 5 MIN · · · COOK: 30 MIN · · · TOTAL: 35 MIN

1 cup (240 mL) **reduced sugar ketchup**

1 6-oz. can (168 g) **tomato paste**

1 cup (240 mL) **apple cider vinegar**

1/4 cup (60 mL) **liquid smoke**

2 Tbsp (30 mL) **sugar replacement**

2 Tbsp (30 mL) **unsweetened cocoa powder**

2 Tbsp (30 mL) **New Mexico chili powder**

2 Tbsp (30 mL) **smoked paprika**

1 tsp (5 mL) **yacon syrup**

salt and **pepper** to taste

A good BBQ sauce has some spice to it, a bit of smoki-ness, definitely some sweet, but above all, it should have tang! There should almost be pain coming from the inhalation of its vapor. I *love* a *very* strong and vin-egary BBQ sauce. The following recipe is somewhat toned down from what I would personally make (if you want to get closer to my personal preference, double the vinegar), but this recipe is by no means lacking in flavor. It's everything a good BBQ sauce should be, but without the unnecessary carbs.

All I can say is don't knock it till you've tried it!

Portion size: Makes about 2 cups, (480 mL) or sixteen 2-tablespoon (30 mL) servings.

1. Place all ingredients on the stove in a small saucepot, over medium-low heat.

2. Simmer for about 30 minutes (stirring occasionally) or until the sauce has thickened appropriately (keeping in mind it will thicken more when it cools). Season with salt and pepper.

3. Serve!

PER SERVING
CALORIES: 21.33
FAT: 0.49
PROTEIN: 0.82
CARBS: 6.54
FIBER: 1.33
SUGAR ALCOHOLS: 1.88
NET CARBS: 3.33

MORE FACTS: P. 534

Tomato and Roasted Pepper Cream

SERVES: 8 · · · PREP: 5 MIN · · · COOK: 5 MIN · · · TOTAL: 10 MIN

Oftentimes, you'll walk into an Italian restaurant and be offered a white sauce or a red sauce. You can order a pizza and have it red or white. Certainly red is the more common variety in these instances, but white is just as tasty! I'm here to tell you that the world isn't always so red and white. There are always going to be shades of pink. This is a *wonderful* accompaniment to zoodles, poured over a chicken breast, drizzled onto a bowl of buttered cauliflower, etc. It's got some pink from the tomatoes, as well as the slightly sweet roasted peppers. It's also got a little texture and smoky flavor coming from the bacon bits. Finally, there are the little speckles of fresh basil to tie the whole thing together. It's also *incredibly* fast to make—a perfect pairing with a plethora of meal ideas. Give it a shot!

1 Tbsp (15 mL) **butter**

4 **garlic cloves**, cut into thin rings

1/4 cup (60 mL) **real bacon bits**

2 medium (182 g) **tomatoes**, diced

2 small (148 g) **roasted bell peppers**, peeled, seeded, and diced

1 cup (240 mL) **heavy whipping cream**

16 leaves **fresh basil**, hand torn

salt and **pepper** to taste

1. In a sauté pan over medium heat, add your butter. Quickly add your chopped garlic and bacon bits to the pan. The very moment the garlic begins to turn brown, add your diced tomatoes and peppers to the pan, with some salt and pepper. Turn your heat up high and cook for about 2 minutes. Add your cream. Let the sauce reduce until it's the appropriate viscosity for a sauce (probably about 3 to 6 minutes, depending on how hot your pan is). Watch it, so it doesn't burn.

2. Once it's a nice thickness, taste it and adjust seasoning.

3. Finally, stir in your fresh basil leaves.

4. Serve!

PER SERVING
CALORIES: 139.54
FAT: 13.13
PROTEIN: 2.58
CARBS: 3.51
FIBER: 0.64
SUGAR ALCOHOLS: 0
NET CARBS: 2.87

MORE FACTS: P. 532

Marinara Sauce, A.K.A., Neapolitan Sauce, A.K.A., Napoli Sauce, A.K.A., La Salsa

SERVES: 8 · · · PREP: 5 MIN · · · COOK: 3 HRS · · · TOTAL: 3 HRS

1 Tbsp (15 mL) **extra virgin olive oil**

1 small (110 g) **onion**, diced

4 **garlic cloves**, cut into thin disks

1 28-oz. can (800 g) **San Marzano tomatoes**

16 leaves **fresh basil**, hand torn

salt and **pepper** to taste

The sauce that most Americans know as marinara is actually more in line with Neapolitan sauce, harking from Naples, Italy. Funnily enough, if you were an American in Naples and asked for "la salsa," you'd get marinara! It's sort of like how every other country calls soccer football, except the US, where we have an entirely different game we call football.

Napoli sauce is basically a tomato-based sauce, cooked with tomatoes and onions. That's about it!

This is also a chance to talk a little bit about canned San Marzano tomatoes. Legend has it that the first San Marzano tomato seeds were a gift from the King of Peru to the King of Naples sometime during the 1770s. These seeds were then planted near the city of San Marzano in the shadow of Mount Vesuvius. From these seeds, crossbreeding and careful selection led to the current-day San Marzano tomato.

Sometimes legends lie. The reality is far murkier, with the first actual printed mention of San Marzano tomatoes appearing in an American agricultural book put out by the USDA, which mentions them in cans in 1894. In 1902, some Italian documents mention that they are a cross between three other varieties: King Umberto, Fiaschella, and Fiascona.

PER SERVING
CALORIES: 41.43
FAT: 1.51
PROTEIN: 0.9
CARBS: 6.27
FIBER: 1.77
SUGAR ALCOHOLS: 0
NET CARBS: 4.51

MORE FACTS: P. 534

San Marzano tomatoes are grown in the volcanic soil of Mount Vesuvius near Naples, Italy. They are harvested when ripe, as the sun goes down. They are sweet, fleshy, high in pectin (which equates to thicker sauces), low in seeds, bright red, and easy to peel. Oh! And they look like an elongated Roma tomato.

The primary reason for San Marzano tomatoes being such a big deal is they are reliable and delicious. When it's not summertime and amazing local tomatoes are not available, these sweet tomatoes, canned at their absolute peak, are the way to go. Many chefs will do a little happy dance for the real thing. For *true* San Marzano tomatoes from Italy, look for the DOP seal, indicating "Designation of Origin." Seeds have traveled outside the region and are also canned, but they are not grown in the same soil or picked by the same standards. So, while many canned "San Marzano tomatoes" are actually spawned from the same seed, they are not the same thing. Buyer beware.

1. In a medium-sized saucepot, add your oil and place on the stove over medium-low heat. Watch the pot, so you don't burn the oil. Extra virgin oil burns really quickly and will make everything taste like burned oil.

2. THE MOMENT you see the surface of the oil ripple just a tiny bit, or become thinner, like water, as you roll it around the pan, add your garlic and onions, with a little salt and pepper. Stir until translucent and aromatic (about 5 minutes).

3. While the onions and garlic are sweating, open your can of San Marzanos and dump them into a large salad bowl. With both hands, grab each tomato and squeeze it. It will squish and become one with the puree. Do this to all the tomatoes, to create a thick and chunky tomato puddle.

4. Once the tomatoes are properly squooshed, pour them into the pot with the translucent garlic and onions.

5. Allow to simmer for upwards of three hours, over very low heat. Season with salt and pepper; tomatoes can take a lot of salt, so you can add *a little* more than may feel natural. Let the sauce simmer away until it is the appropriate consistency.

6. Finish by stirring in some fresh hand-torn basil at the last minute.

7. Serve!

Sweet 'n' Spicy Tomato Jam

SERVES: 12 · · · PREP: 15 MIN · · · COOK: 30 MIN · · · TOTAL: 45 MIN

1 Tbsp (15 mL) **coconut oil**

2 tsp (10 mL) ground **cumin seed**

1 tsp (5 mL) ground **coriander seed**

1 tsp (5 mL) ground **cinnamon**

1 tsp (5 mL) **chili flakes**

1 small (110 g) **onion**, diced

4 **garlic cloves**, cut into thin disks

2 tsp (10 mL) grated **fresh ginger**

1 lb. (454 g) **fresh tomatoes**, washed, dried and coarsely chopped

1/4 cup (60 mL) **sugar replacement**

2 tsp (10 mL) **yacon syrup**

1/2 bunch (50 g) **cilantro**, washed, large stems removed, and chopped

salt and **pepper** to taste

This tomato jam recipe comes from a restaurant that no longer exists. I am unsure who developed it, but it was on the menu when I worked there as a kid. I *loved* this stuff and made it regularly. I'm sure I used it wrong when I slathered it on my own meals, but I applied it, liberally, to almost everything. One of my favorites was to toss it with pasta and devour it when I got home—a strange combination, but one I ate often! The flavor combinations are also a bit strange. It's a difficult recipe to pinpoint in terms of ethnic origin. Is it Indian? Is it Moroccan? It initially feels like a sweet tomato jam from the southern United States, but then the spices and aromatics harking from other countries start teasing the olfactory nerves, resulting in a powerful mélange of exotic tastes and aromas. That's my way of saying... it's *tasty*!

Note: Makes about 1 1/2 cups (360 mL) of jam. The recipe is calculated for twelve 2-tablespoon (30 mL) portions.

1. Place a large sauté pan over medium heat on the stove. Add your oil.

2. Make sure you've got your onions, garlic, and ginger chopped and ready to toss into pan; watch for the oil to slightly ripple in the pan. When you see it ripple, add your dried spices (cumin, coriander, cinnamon, and chili flakes). Swirl them in the pan for no more than about 3 seconds or else they will burn. You want to toast them in the oil, not burn them. After 3 seconds quickly "save" the spices by throwing your onions, garlic, and ginger into the pan, and coat them with the hot, spiced oil.

PER SERVING
CALORIES: 26.93
FAT: 1.16
PROTEIN: 0.64
CARBS: 8.91
FIBER: 0.96
SUGAR ALCOHOLS: 5
NET CARBS: 2.95

MORE FACTS: P. 535

3. Add a little salt and pepper to the onion mixture. Sauté for about 2 minutes or until the onions become translucent.

4. Add your tomatoes, the sweetener and yacon syrup.

5. At this point, you want to cook the tomatoes until the whole thing reduces to the consistency of a jam-like spread. This can take anywhere between 15 and 45 minutes, depending on how quickly the tomatoes reduce. I suggest a fairly high heat and a wide sauté pan. This will evaporate the most water the fastest. Let it gurgle for a minute or two, then toss it around, and let it continue to gurgle. Just don't let the bottom burn. Alternately, you can put it on a very low heat (without a lid) and not need to watch it as closely. It'll take longer, but you'll have more freedom to do other things.

6. Once it's reduced, remove it from the stove and adjust the seasoning. Make sure it tastes good!

7. Spread it on a cookie tray and place it in the fridge to quickly cool it.

8. Once it's cool, sprinkle your chopped cilantro all over it, fold it in, and serve, save, or eat!

We be jammin'!

Dijon-Caper Cream Sauce

SERVES: 4 · · · PREP: 1 MIN · · · COOK: 5 MIN · · · TOTAL: 6 MIN

1/2 cup (120 mL) **heavy whipping cream**

2 Tbsp (30 mL) **Dijon mustard**, whole grain

2 tsp (10 mL) coarsely chopped **capers**

salt and **pepper** to taste

I eat a lot of mustard. In general, there are a lot of strong and spicy flavors that tend to go along with this way of eating. I suppose it's because strong, concentrated flavors like mustard have a big taste impact while having a very low impact on the blood sugar! As a result, I get a lot of herby and/or spicy dishes. Mustard seeds and capers are two ingredients that fall into this category quite well.

This is a very quick and simple sauce with virtually no carbs but a *ton* of flavor! This is great with all kinds of meat and fish, tossed with some cooked spaghetti squash, or as a dip for finger foods. Yum!

Cold note: These ingredients can be used in a variety of different ways, for different but similar taste sensations. For example, if you wanted a nice, light dip, you could whip the cream, like you would to make whipped cream. Rather than adding sugar, you can fold in the mustard, capers, salt, and pepper. This will give you a nice thick, chilled, light dip for veggies.

Hot note: What I *very* often do is sear a piece of fish or a steak. Or, even better, wrap it in bacon, then sear or roast it. When I'm done cooking the whatever it is, I'll remove it from the hot pan and set aside to rest. While it's resting and the hot pan still has little caramelized meat goodness (known in French kitchens as the *fond*) stuck to the bottom of the pan, some bacon fat, potentially little bits of spice in whatever the marinade may have been, etc., then, I'll add the cream, Dijon, capers, salt, and pepper to the hot pan. This will deglaze the pan and pick up all that extra flavor left over in the pan. This will add more richness and character to the sauce. Then, serve it with dinner!

PER SERVING
CALORIES: 109.12
FAT: 11.31
PROTEIN: 1.02
CARBS: 1.67
FIBER: 0.34
SUGAR ALCOHOLS: 0
NET CARBS: 1.33

MORE FACTS: P. 537

1. In a small sauce pan, over medium heat, add your ingredients.

2. Mix well and bring to a simmer.

3. Reduce the sauce for about 2 minutes or until thickened to the desired consistency.

4. Season and serve!

White BBQ Sauce

SERVES: 4 · · · PREP: 5 MIN · · · COOK: 0 MIN · · · TOTAL: 5 MIN

1/2 cup (120 mL) **mayonnaise**

1 Tbsp (15 mL) **lemon juice**, freshly squeezed

2 Tbsp (30 mL) **apple cider vinegar**

1 Tbsp (15 mL) **sugar replacement**

1 tsp (10 mL) **freshly cracked black pepper**

1 1/2 tsp (7 mL) **salt**

1/2 tsp (1 mL) **cayenne pepper**, ground

This is a great little sauce, especially for basting or brushing onto grilled meats (such as chicken, where most of it winds up!). It's an emulsified fat, which means it brushes on thick and lustrous but will quickly melt and meld the flavors in with the meats.

Note: It's good in combination with Horseradish-Fennel Spare Ribs (p. 304).

1. Mix it in a bowl.

2. Put it on stuff!

 Not to be confused with eggnog.

PER SERVING
CALORIES: 190.63
FAT: 20.91
PROTEIN: 0.74
CARBS: 4.87
FIBER: 0.24
SUGAR ALCOHOLS: 3.81
NET CARBS: 0.82

MORE FACTS: P. 535

Chunky Blue Cheese Dressing

SERVES: 12 · · · PREP: 5 MIN · · · COOK: 0 MIN · · · TOTAL: 5 MIN

Many store-bought salad dressings have added sugar in them (read labels!). The quality on the ingredients can also be questionable. Whenever I can, I like to make my own sauces and dressings. It doesn't take as long as you might think, and the flavors can just pop! Within this simple salad dressing, the large boulders of blue cheese have a tactile smoosh in a way that only a good, ripe, moldy cheese can. Its sticky, icky, blue-gray crumbles lumping up the pungent dressing makes for a perfect complement to a light salad... perhaps with a bit of fruit for a naughty splurge!

Try taking this dressing and tossing it with some baby romaine leaves, some walnuts, and a few cubes of apple or pear. Top it off with some more cheesy crumbles, and it's a sweet, funky paradise! Or just set a cup aside and dip your carrot sticks in it.

Note: This makes about twelve 2-tablespoon (30 mL) servings.

1/4 lb. (114 g) **quality Roquefort cheese,** crumbled and divided

1/4 cup (60 mL) **buttermilk**

1/4 cup (60 mL) **sour cream**

1/2 cup (120 mL) **mayonnaise**

1 Tbsp (15 mL) **apple cider vinegar**

salt and **freshly cracked pepper** to taste

1. In a bowl, squish together half of the cheese and the buttermilk with a fork, until it's a bit of a chunky paste.

2. Stir in the rest of the ingredients, including the remaining larger chunks of blue cheese.

3. Season with salt and pepper.

4. Serve or store!

PER SERVING
CALORIES: 108.28
FAT: 10.83
PROTEIN: 2.52
CARBS: 0.71
FIBER: 0.01
SUGAR ALCOHOLS: 0.02
NET CARBS: 0.69

MORE FACTS: P. 535

Balsamic Vinaigrette: More Than Just a Vinaigrette

SERVES: 4 · · · PREP: 1 MIN · · · COOK: 0 MIN · · · TOTAL: 1 MIN

6 Tbsp (90 mL) **extra virgin olive oil**

2 Tbsp (30 mL) **balsamic vinegar**

salt and **pepper** to taste

At its core, vinaigrette is an acidic liquid blended with fat. I believe it's supposed to additionally be emulsified, but I've worked in countless restaurants with nonemulsified vinaigrettes. (*Emulsified* means that the oil and fat were blended into a single slightly thicker, creamier liquid.) No one ever complained that their vinaigrette wasn't emulsified.

The standard ratio is three parts oil to one part vinegar. For a very standard red wine vinaigrette, for example, one would whisk together 1 tablespoon (15 mL) of red wine vinegar with 3 tablespoons (45 mL) of olive oil. Add a touch of salt and pepper. This would yield 1/4 cup (60 mL) of red wine vinaigrette.

There are umpteen bajillion different vinegars. Go to the grocery store and look at the vinegars and fats. You could purchase a strawberry-infused balsamic vinegar and whisk it into a walnut oil, for example. This would give a far more complex taste sensation, but we're still dealing with only a very basic ratio.

Are we cooking, yet?

We don't necessarily need to stop there! Lemon juice is also a very acidic liquid, much like vinegar. Oils aren't the only fats either. Whisking 1 tablespoon (15 mL) of fresh lemon juice into 3 tablespoons (45 mL) of warm goose/duck/chicken/bacon fat and tossing it on a spinach salad would be outstanding!

PER SERVING
CALORIES: 187
FAT: 18
PROTEIN: 0.03
CARBS: 1.35
FIBER: 0
SUGAR ALCOHOLS: 0
NET CARBS: 1.35

MORE FACTS: P. 535

Three parts fat to one part acidic liquid. (This is generally true, but I personally tend to do 2 to 1 for lemon juice and balsamic vinegar, which are less aggressive; this is a personal preference. I tend to like acidity.)

Armed with this very basic ratio, you can start really branching out and layering flavors. Imagine taking 1 tablespoon (15 mL) sherry vinegar and 2 tablespoons (30 mL) of olive oil, and whisking them together with another tablespoon of warm goose fat. Now, start whisking in some finely diced shallots, 1 tablespoon (15 mL) of whole grain mustard, 1 teaspoon (5 mL) of diced capers, and some fresh thyme. Try brushing this onto a bunch of vegetables before throwing them on the grill. YUMMO!

Now, we can try another direction. Let's take light champagne vinegar, add a little xylitol honey, some lightly flavored oil, a skosh of diced sweet onions, and sprinkle of fresh tarragon. Try that on a delicate salad with some grilled shrimp and a few toasted hazelnuts.

1. Whisk it!!

Not Pistou

SERVES: 12 · · · PREP: 10 MIN · · · COOK: 0 MIN · · · TOTAL: 10 MIN

2 lb. (908 g) **fresh assorted tomatoes**, diced

2 cups (480 mL) **fresh basil**, cut into chiffonade (about a large bunch's worth)

4 **garlic cloves**, minced

1 cup (240 mL) coarsely chopped **pine nuts**, toasted

2 cups (480 mL) grated **Parmesan cheese**

1/4 cup (60 mL) freshly squeezed **lemon juice**

1 cup (240 mL) good quality **extra virgin olive oil**

salt and **pepper** to taste

This is the best flavor combination on earth. Shockingly, it doesn't involve bacon or ketchup either! It's a wall of tomato and garlic flavor, punctuated with the nutty, salty cheese, the bright notes of the basil, and the texture of the toasted pine nuts. This is the stuff you'll find on the grilled bread at Italian restaurants. It's usually called bruschetta.

Now, let me say that I have zero recollection where I picked this up. It's just always been in my memory bank. Whoever taught it to me also said, "This is called *pistou*. It's like a French pesto." So I've echoed that same information to everyone I've made it for. Oh, how wrong I've been!

I just looked up the actual definition of *pistou* and... it's basically traditional Genovese pesto, but with the absence of pine nuts. *This* stuff... whatever you call it... has both pine nuts *and* a healthy dose of raw diced tomatoes!

This is great as a dip. It's also fantastic tossed with some zoodles (hot or sliced super thin and raw). Slather this stuff on a chicken breast, and you'll quickly understand its allure. Frankly... give me a spoon. I'll eat this stuff from a bowl! Whatever it is...

It's "Not Pistou."

PER SERVING
CALORIES: 325.78
FAT: 30.62
PROTEIN: 9.04
CARBS: 6.2
FIBER: 1.51
SUGAR ALCOHOLS: 0
NET CARBS: 4.7

MORE FACTS: P. 536

1. Blend the ingredients in a bowl. Season with salt and pepper; this recipe can handle a good amount of salt. Serve!

SPICY HOT COCKTAIL SAUCE

SERVES: 8 · · · PREP: 5 MIN · · · COOK: 0 MIN · · · TOTAL: 5 MIN

Cocktail sauce is most commonly a mixture of ketchup and horseradish. It's served with shrimp cocktail, obviously, but is also very common with oysters and other seafood. I like my cocktail sauce a bit on the hot and spicy side. So this recipe is presented how I, DJ Foodie, like my cocktail sauce. Feel free to tone it down or inject it with more fire! It should be obvious how to tweak this one.

Enjoy it! This particular cocktail sauce recipe takes but a minute to make, but... it's sooooo good!

Note: Makes about 1 cup (240 mL) of Cocktail Sauce.

2/3 cup (160 mL) **reduced sugar ketchup**

1/4 cup (60 mL) **prepared horseradish**

2 Tbsp (30 mL) freshly squeezed **lemon juice**

1 Tbsp (15 mL) **Tabasco sauce**

1 tsp (5 mL) **Worcestershire sauce**

4 **garlic cloves**, minced

salt and **pepper** to taste

1. Mix the ingredients in a bowl.

2. Serve!

PER SERVING
CALORIES: 11.2
FAT: .1
PROTEIN: .1
CARBS: 2
FIBER: .3
SUGAR ALCOHOLS: 0
NET CARBS: 1.7

MORE FACTS: P. 535

Harissa

SERVES: 8 · · · PREP: 5 MIN · · · COOK: 0 MIN · · · TOTAL: 5 MIN

2 Tbsp (30 mL) ground **cumin seed**

1 Tbsp (15 mL) **cayenne pepper**

1 Tbsp (15 mL) ground **coriander seed**

1 Tbsp (15 mL) ground **caraway seed**

1 Tbsp (15 mL) **salt**

1/4 cup (60 mL) chopped **fresh mint**

1/4 cup (60 mL) chopped **fresh cilantro**

2 Tbsp (30 mL) freshly squeezed **lemon juice**

1/2 cup (120 mL) good quality **olive oil**

4 **garlic cloves**, minced

PER SERVING
CALORIES: 136.66
FAT: 14.4
PROTEIN: 0.52
CARBS: 2.98
FIBER: 1.18
SUGAR ALCOHOLS: 0
NET CARBS: 1.8

MORE FACTS: P. 536

I don't remember where I was when I first tasted Harissa, I'm sad to say. Some part of me just feels like it's always been there when I've needed it. It's a spicy, exotic, complex blend of spices hailing from Tunisia (Northern Africa). Harissa is strongly chili based, using the piri piri chili. Mine still has a kick to it, but the spice has dropped back to basic cayenne, while the cumin has really been brought forward. Perhaps it's not a true Harissa, but I tend to prefer it balanced this way. It's still pretty fantastic, whatever you want to call it!

Normally, I'm a bit of a purist and prefer my meats and veggies to taste like their natural flavors. However, Harissa is so overwhelmingly delicious, that when I use it on something, it is what I want to taste! It's a sumptuous bounty of flavor! I really can't think of anything that couldn't benefit from a dab of Harissa. It's amazing as a marinade and a sauce. It's great on all meats and fishes. It's wonderful on veggies. I've even drizzled it all over pizza! Probably not great on ice cream, but that may be its only limitation. Try it. You'll be glad you did!

Note: Served with a Tunisian-Spice Rack of Lamb (p. 300) in the photo.

1. Put ingredients in a bowl; blend.

2. Serve with stuff! (Just make sure you stir it before you serve it. The goodies tend to settle at the bottom.)

A Lot Like Caesar Salad Dressing

SERVES: 6 · · · PREP: 10 MIN · · · COOK: 0 MIN · · · TOTAL: 10 MIN

Growing up, my family used to visit Mexico… a lot. In fact, I kind of live there and my parents have a house there. As early as I can remember, we would visit a restaurant in Puerto Vallarta at a hotel called Posada Rio Cuale. They had table-side service and did things like make big flaming table bombs (a crepe dish involving an orange, flaming waterfall of booze)… right there!

One of their famous table-side dishes was the famed Mexican Caesar Salad. I believe it is here that my mother realized one of the primary flavorings in a Caesar dressing was… ewwww… ANCHOVIES! (Truth be told, I like anchovies, but suspect bacon would be preferred by nine out of ten bacon enthusiasts.) As a result, we would visit the hotel and request our Caesar dressing be made with bacon, rather than anchovies. The rest was… more or less the same. Coddled eggs, mustard, bacon, lemon, Worcestershire, do a little dance, toss with croutons, lettuce, and… *voila*! Caesar salad!

Mine is actually even more basic than that. Its flavor is very similar to Caesar dressing but without the need to coddle your egg. In fact, it starts with mayonnaise ('cause… let's face it, you've likely got mayo on hand, but aren't sure where to find an egg that's been coddled). You can still do the little dance if you want to!

Note: Makes about six 2-tablespoon (30 mL) portions.

1. In a small mixing bowl, whisk together the ingredients.

2. Season to taste.

1/2 cup (120 mL) **mayonnaise**

2 **garlic cloves**, minced

2 Tbsp (30 mL) real **bacon bits**

1/4 cup (60 mL) grated **Parmesan cheese**

1 tsp (5 mL) **Worcestershire sauce**

salt and **pepper** to taste

PER SERVING
CALORIES: 153.45
FAT: 15.62
PROTEIN: 2.98
CARBS: 0.91
FIBER: 0.01
SUGAR ALCOHOLS: 0.04
NET CARBS: 0.85

MORE FACTS: P. 537

Orange-Rosemary Compound Butter

SERVES: 8 · · · PREP: 15 MIN · · · COOK: 0 MIN · · · TOTAL: 2 HR 15 MIN

1/2 cup (120 mL) **unsalted butter**

1 Tbsp (15 mL) chopped **fresh rosemary**

1 Tbsp (15 mL) **fresh orange zest** (peel)

salt and **pepper** to taste

Compound butters are flavored butters. They come in as many varieties as there are combinations of ingredients! I've been to fancy restaurants where the bread basket arrives, brimming with warm crackers, bread sticks, and mini loaves of whatever goodness may have danced through the baker's imagination the night before. It's not uncommon to see this cornucopia of carbs arrive with a variety of flavored butters—sometimes they are sweet, sometimes savory, sometimes they are spicy. Sometimes they are infused with cheeses and herbs. Other times they are very, very simple and really only used as a vehicle for some new ashy sea salt that's making the rounds.

One of my favorites comes from a restaurant in San Francisco. It's an homage to Winnie the Pooh. The breakfast dish is Sweet Corn Hushpuppies and Pooh Butter—whipped butter infused with honey... *get it?* I always thought it was cute.

This is a fairly simple and basic compound butter, more to serve as an introduction to compound butters. It's simply orange zest (the orange part of the skin, not the white part), rosemary—most any fresh herb would be great though—salt, pepper, and, of course, butter.

This is fantastic on fish, steak, pork, chicken, as a sandwich spread, tossed with fresh hot veggies, etc. There aren't many places where a little fat and a slight burst of fresh herby-citrus essence wouldn't be welcome. Make a log and bring it to your next neighborhood block party! (Just make sure you have a way to keep it cool; otherwise, it gets messy, quickly!)

Mix it, form it in plastic wrap, roll it, tighten it, chill it, slice it, and serve it!

PER SERVING
CALORIES: 204.55
FAT: 23.03
PROTEIN: 0.27
CARBS: 0.24
FIBER: 0.12
SUGAR ALCOHOLS: 0
NET CARBS: 0.12

MORE FACTS: P. 537

1. With an electric mixer, whip your softened butter. When it begins to lighten in color and increase in volume (because you're adding air to it), add the rest of your ingredients. Taste it and adjust the seasoning.

2. Take a sheet of plastic wrap, roughly 18" x 12" (45 x 30 cm), and lay it very flat on your countertop. Try and stretch out any folds or creases, so you have a very clean, flat sheet of plastic wrap. With a spoon or spatula, make a "log" of butter near one edge of the plastic wrap. You don't want to place it in the middle but about 1 inch (2.5 cm) inside the widest edge of the plastic wrap. The log should run parallel to this edge. The butter will be very soft at this point. Carefully cover the butter log with the 1-inch (2.5 cm) flap of plastic wrap. Continue carefully rolling the butter log, being sure not to apply any pressure to the center of the log. This may cause the butter to leak out the ends of the log.

3. Once your butter log has been formed, grab the two ends of the plastic wrap and pick up the log. While holding both sides of the log, swirl the butter log in front of you, like a jump rope. Do not let the ends of plastic twist within your fingers. The goal is to twist the butter log around and around, while tightening the ends of the plastic wrap. This will squeeze the butter into a firm, tight log. Take your two ends of the plastic wrap and fold them under the newly tightened log and place it in the refrigerator to cool.

4. In 2 to 3 hours, it should firm up into a solid log of compound butter. Slice little disks of butter, remove the plastic wrap from each flavorful medallion, and serve!

MAYONNAISE

SERVES: 32 · · · PREP: 10 MIN · · · COOK: 0 MIN · · · TOTAL: 10 MIN

1 large **whole egg**

1 large **egg yolk**

1 tsp (5 mL) **Dijon mustard**

2 Tbsp (30 mL) **lemon juice**, freshly squeezed

1 1/2 cup (360 mL) **olive oil**

1 Tbsp (15 mL) **sugar replacement**

water (to adjust consistency)

salt and **pepper** to taste

Mayonnaise is about as ubiquitous a sauce as there is. It's in almost all sandwiches and is used as the base for *many* salad dressings. It's what holds egg, chicken, and tuna salad together. In many ways, mayonnaise is what makes the world go round. Mayonnaise is an emulsion. An emulsion is a mixture of two different liquids, mixed together, that ordinarily shouldn't be mixed together. This is a fancy way of saying "oil and water blended together." Mayonnaise is awesome for a low-primal way of eating. It's got virtually no carbs and has a lot of good fats. I'm showing the recipe for how to make it because it's not that hard, it lasts a while in the fridge, and the store-bought mayonnaises often have a lot of sugar added. Finally, I just think it tastes better!

Note: This can be done in a bowl, with a whisk. The process is the same, but it just takes longer and makes your arms really *really* tired.

Makes about 32 one-tablespoon (15 mL) servings.

1. In a food processor or blender, add your eggs, Dijon, lemon juice, and a dash of salt. Turn it on the slowest setting.

2. *Slowly* (painstakingly slowly, to begin with—literally, one drop at a time), pour the olive oil in a slow, thin stream, into the food processor or blender. The first 1/4 cup (60 mL) of oil should literally be one drop at a time. Once that's incorporated and the emulsion has officially formed, you can pour in a somewhat faster, although still very thin stream of oil.

PER SERVING
CALORIES: 93.82
FAT: 10.43
PROTEIN: 0.3
CARBS: 0.6
FIBER: 0.01
SUGAR ALCOHOLS: 0.47
NET CARBS: 0.12

MORE FACTS: P. 537

3. Continue to drizzle the oil, until about 1/3 of it has been used. Open the processor and add your sugar equivalent if you want to make a slightly sweet mayonnaise (think Miracle Whip). Also check the consistency. If it's getting too thick, you can add 1/2 teaspoon (2 mL) of water.

4. Return the lid and continue to drizzle the oil into the mayonnaise. As you add the oil, the mayonnaise will thicken. If it gets too thick, stop the processor and add another 1/2 tsp (2 mL) of water. Repeat this process until all the oil has been added.

5. Adjust seasoning with salt and pepper.

6. Transfer into an airtight container. Homemade mayonnaise will last in the fridge for about two weeks.

ROUILLE
(FANCY SPICY FRENCH MAYO)

SERVES: 8 · · · PREP: 1 MIN · · · COOK: 1 MIN · · · TOTAL: 2 HR

1/2 tsp (2 mL) **saffron threads**

1 cup (240 mL) **mayonnaise**

2 **garlic cloves**, minced

1/2 tsp (2 mL) **cayenne pepper**, ground

salt and **pepper** to taste

There just isn't a whole lot to say about *rouille*. It's a fancy French mayonnaise. I suppose that somewhat undermines it. It's a fancy French *aioli*, which is a fancy French mayonnaise with garlic. The only difference, really, between aioli and mayonnaise is the addition of garlic, but... that little change suddenly transcends a basic mayonnaise, creating a smooth, creamy, and mildly hot French elixir. If you add saffron (the most expensive spice on earth!) and a little cayenne to aioli, you suddenly have *rouille*!

When I was about nineteen, I was lucky to be hired into a famous San Francisco restaurant frequented by the likes of Robin Williams, Danny Glover, Jodie Foster, bands like Phish, and even Bill Clinton. We had a fish special one night, and the fish was topped with *rouille*. The chefs would create the special dishes, and then bring us the ingredients, where they would show us how to assemble the dishes. At that point, I'd never heard of *rouille* before. I was impressed!

At the end of the night, I needed to wrap up what I had left, add a cover, label, and date it, but I didn't know how to spell it! This was the days before iPhones. I couldn't just whip out my phone and ask the universe. I had to sheepishly ask my chef, "How do you spell *rouille*?" She just looked at me like I'd asked her how to get to my own home, sighed dejectedly, turned, and walked away, leaving me to fend for myself. Being that I was in a hurry to get out into the world and be nineteen, I wrote, "Roooo-eeeeee" and then promptly ran out into the night.

In the middle of the night, while we were out being young line cooks, the bosses would comb through our refrigerated ingredients and throw out anything old,

PER SERVING
CALORIES: 95.17
FAT: 10.45
PROTEIN: 0.32
CARBS: 0.48
FIBER: 0.03
SUGAR ALCOHOLS: 0.03
NET CARBS: 0.42

MORE FACTS: P. 537

SAUCES, SPREADS, & DIPPIDY DO'S

out of place, or unlabeled. They were serious about their high-quality, fresh ingredients and strict labeling policies! The next day, I walked in and found my *roooo-eeeeee* had gone missing! I still didn't really know what it was and didn't know how to make it and needed more. I panicked. Had the chef really thrown it away? I wondered what I should do. I walked up to her and asked her if she'd seen my rouille. She looked at me, tilted her head back, and laughed the kind of laugh that can't be controlled. She put her hand on my shoulder and explained that she'd been having a particularly tough time of things, and when she was combing through my stuff, she saw my spelling and was beyond delighted. It apparently caught her at such a rotten time, that the sheer absurdity of it lifted her spirits and completely changed the tenor of her day. She'd spent the morning showing everyone my "hysterical" joke and had just forgotten to put it back.

In other news, *rouille* is usually served with fish, traditionally served with Bouillabaisse (p. 162), and is also yummy on sandwiches and wraps. This hard-to-spell sauce is delicious!"

1. Soak your saffron threads in about 1 tablespoon (15 mL) of warm water. Let it sit for about 2 hours.

2. Mix your saffron and soaking liquid with mayonnaise, garlic, and cayenne. Season to taste with salt and pepper.

3. Serve!

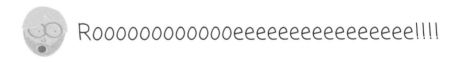 Rooooooooooooeeeeeeeeeeeeeeeeelllll

ROMESCO

SERVES: 8 · · · PREP: 10 MIN · · · COOK: 0 MIN · · · TOTAL: 10 MIN

2 small (148 g) **roasted red bell peppers**, peeled and seeded

2 Tbsp (30 mL) **tomato paste**

1 tsp (5 mL) **smoked paprika**

1 tsp (5 mL) **crushed red chili flakes**

4 **garlic cloves**, minced

2 Tbsp (30 mL) **extra virgin olive oil**

1/4 cup (60 mL) **blanched and slivered almonds**, toasted

2 Tbsp (30 mL) **red wine vinegar**

salt and **pepper** to taste

PER SERVING
CALORIES: 69.49
FAT: 5.74
PROTEIN: 1.51
CARBS: 3.59
FIBER: 1.26
SUGAR ALCOHOLS: 0
NET CARBS: 2.33

MORE FACTS: P. 538

Romesco is a thick nut and pepper sauce that comes from Northern Spain. In my mind, it belongs in the pesto family, but... it really doesn't. There's no cheese, it's not Italian, and... it's just not pesto. Those little factoids don't seem to stop me from holding it in my mind with Pesto (p. 386) and even the occasional Tapenade (p. 352)! Romesco is a really simple sauce to make, provided you've got the stuff lying around. I won't lie to you. It's *very* common for me to toast a bunch of slivered almonds and leave them in a jar. I go through them quickly, so they never really have time to go bad. I also tend to use roasted peppers from a jar that lives in my fridge. Yes, I bought them from a store. Don't tell anyone.

From there, it's really a matter of blending those two ingredients with a few other things. Then... ROMESCO!

This sauce is excellent with almost everything except dessert. It's stupendous with fish. This sauce is amazing with some simple grilled vegetables. It's perfectly matched with a meaty pork chop. Try a full dollop on a freshly grilled shrimp; then hold on to your chair. The list could go on!!

Makes about 8 two-tablespoon (30 mL) portions.

1. Dry the roasted peppers with a paper towel. Press out any extra moisture.

2. Add the ingredients to a food processor and puree until the desired consistency—some like smooth, while others like rustic. If it's too thick, thin with a touch more olive oil.

3. Season to taste. Serve!

THAI-STYLE PEANUT SAUCE

SERVES: 8 · · · PREP: 15 MIN · · · COOK: 15 MIN · · · TOTAL: 30 MIN

Peanut sauce is yum. Plain and simple. Its sweet, salty, fragrant, and thick gingery-ness always brings me comfort. It's yum. It's commonly served in Thai restaurants with grilled satays and a sweet cucumber salad. It's also quite tasty mixed with chilled noodles, for a peanut-y pasta salad! Slap some grilled shrimp on a pile of chilled peanut pasta salad, garnish with a few cilantro sprigs, and everyone in the neighborhood will come running! It can be used as the base for curries. It's great mixed with a little more lime juice and peanut oil, and used as a salad dressing! Serve it with grilled veggies or as the spread on a funky chicken sandwich!

1 Tbsp (15 mL) **coconut oil**

2 **garlic cloves**, minced

1 Tbsp (15 mL) minced **fresh ginger**

2 tsp (10 mL) **Red Curry Paste (p. 484)**

1/4 cup (60 mL) **natural peanut butter**

1/4 cup (60 mL) **unsweetened coconut milk**

1 Tbsp (15 mL) freshly squeezed **lime juice**

2 Tbsp (30 mL) **xylitol honey** (suggested, but optional)

salt and **chili flakes** to taste

1. Over medium-low heat, sauté the ginger, garlic, and curry paste in the oil until the garlic is translucent and the mixture is highly aromatic.

2. Add the remaining ingredients to the pan.

3. Simmer for 15 minutes.

4. If mixture is too thick (remember, it will thicken when it cools), thin the mixture with more coconut milk.

5. Taste and give final seasoning.

6. Remove and cool or serve warm!

PER SERVING
CALORIES: 84.58
FAT: 6.88
PROTEIN: 2.77
CARBS: 5.3
FIBER: 0.52
SUGAR ALCOHOLS: 2.25
NET CARBS: 2.53

MORE FACTS: P. 538

THICK, GOOPY ALFREDO SAUCE

SERVES: 6 · · · PREP: 15 MIN · · · COOK: 10 MIN · · · TOTAL: 25 MIN

2 cups (480 mL) **heavy whipping cream**

1/4 tsp (1 mL) freshly ground **nutmeg**

4 **garlic cloves**, minced

1/4 tsp (1 mL) **glucomannan powder** (optional)

2 cups (480 mL) grated **Parmesan**

salt and **pepper** to taste

Alfredo sauce is the famous sauce from fettuccini Alfredo that I'm sure we all know, love, and fantasize about from time to time (I know I do!). The original dish, popularized around one hundred years ago (1914), in Rome, Italy, was incredibly simple. It contained little more than fettuccini pasta, Parmesan cheese, and butter. Over the years, the dish and the sauce have become common items in restaurants and grocery stores around the world. It has also more commonly evolved to a creamy sauce, very often thickened with flour instead of cheese. In most of the restaurants I've worked in, this is how it was done. Start with hot cream, garlic, and nutmeg, then whisk in a roux (a cooked mixture of flour and butter). This thickens the cream. Then, I would add grated Parmesan cheese and whisk. This would simmer and gurgle away until it was the proper thickness. Then, it would get served!

The following recipe goes along the lines of the creamy-based sauce, but is thickened by reduction and cheese. While *far* from required, a bit of glucomannan powder can be added to thicken it.

Obviously, this is great with pasta, but it's also great on top of cooked vegetables. One of my personal favorites is a roasted chicken from the store. I'll dip the pieces of roasted chicken into the hot Alfredo sauce. I am mad, like a fox. Yum!

PER SERVING
CALORIES: 420.88
FAT: 39.06
PROTEIN: 14.34
CARBS: 4.5
FIBER: 0.12
SUGAR ALCOHOLS: 0
NET CARBS: 4.38

MORE FACTS: P. 537

1. Add the cream, nutmeg, and garlic to a small saucepan. Simmer the cream over low heat, until it begins to noticeably reduce in volume.

2. Glucomannan will help thicken the sauce. You won't need as much cheese or as much reduction of the sauce if you thicken it. If you choose to use it, whisk a tiny amount into some cold water and then whisk into the sauce while it simmers. It will thicken after about 2 to 3 minutes. Go light and add more, if you need it. Too much and it moved beyond "thick" and turns *slimy*.

3. Add the cheese to the cream mixture and whisk it in until it completely melts into a creamy sauce.

4. Continue to allow the sauce to simmer until it is the desired thickness.

5. Season with a small amount salt and pepper, and then serve!

BÉARNAISE SAUCE

SERVES: 8 · · · PREP: 5 MIN · · · COOK: 10 MIN · · · TOTAL: 15 MIN

1/4 cup (60 mL) **white wine vinegar**

1/4 cup (60 mL) good quality **white wine**

4 **shallots**, fine dice

4 large **egg yolks**

1 Tbsp (15 mL) **heavy whipping cream** (homogenized)

1 cup (240 mL) melted **fresh whole butter**

4 sprigs **fresh tarragon**, leaves only (chopped)

salt and **pepper** to taste

Béarnaise sauce is like a cooked mayonnaise with tarragon added to it. That's about as simple as I can put it. It *can* be a bit prickly to make, but it's got *enormous* flavor, is rich with healthy fats, and is extremely low-primal. It's also versatile. Put it on your eggs for breakfast or your steak at dinner!

In classical French cooking, there are five mother sauces. The five sauces are béchamel (thick, milky gravy), espagnole (thick, brown, and beefy gravy), velouté (thick chicken gravy), hollandaise (cooked, thick, eggy gravy) and tomate (thick tomato gravy). I feel like when I was in cooking school, I was taught that there were actually seven mother sauces, with the other two being mayonnaise (uncooked, thick, eggy gravy) and demi-glace (thick veal gravy made via reduction). The idea is, adding a few ingredients to each of these mother sauces will transform them into a totally new sauce. If you know how to make these seven sauces... you know how to make *thousands* of sauces!

Béarnaise sauce is a child of the mother sauce *hollandaise*. The method of preparation is essentially the same, with some minor variations (the biggest being the tarragon).

My béarnaise sauce recipe isn't a true béarnaise. It is, in fact, an abomination. Mine is thoughtfully constructed, tastes very similar, and just makes more sense to me as a fully realized sauce, even though most French chefs would like to speak French at me... *harshly*! The big changes are: I've omitted chervil, simply because it's such a challenge to find. If you do find it, add some. It's delightful! I'm also not using clarified butter. Instead, I'm using whole melted butter. Butter is roughly 80 percent butterfat, 19 percent water, and 1 percent "tasty butter bits" (milk solids). More often than not, water is needed to thin the sauce as it is built. Why not use the water in butter? The milk solids just add

PER SERVING
CALORIES: 247.96
FAT: 24.93
PROTEIN: 1.42
CARBS: 2.68
FIBER: 0.04
SUGAR ALCOHOLS: 0
NET CARBS: 2.65

MORE FACTS: P. 538

more flavor, so why remove them? Also, I know ghee is like the new butter, but... I suspect more people have old-school butter than ghee. It is also common to strain out the shallots. I never do this. I like them! Finally, I'm adding a smidgen of homogenized heavy cream. This is purely optional, but because a cooked egg–based emulsion can be such a fickle sauce, the store-bought homogenized cream helps the emulsion take place and hold.

Each of these variations take a step further away from a true béarnaise. Escoffier is probably turning in his grave, but he evolved food from his predecessors... I'm simply throwing in my spin!

1. Place a large pot of water on the stove to boil or the base of a double boiler.

2. In a separate nonreactive saucepot, place your vinegar, wine, and shallots. Bring to a simmer and reduce by just over half. Your shallots should be translucent, and you should have about 3 tablespoons (45 mL) of liquid.

3. Pour your wine mixture into a large nonreactive metal bowl or the top of a double boiler. Add your egg yolks and optional cream. Whisk this mixture together.

4. Place your egg mixture over the top of the water and whisk furiously while very slowly dripping in your melted butter. If the eggs start to cook or scramble too quickly, remove the sauce from above the boiling water while continuing to whisk and add more of the butter. Alternate putting the sauce above the water and removing it. You want to heat the eggs and cook the emulsion, but do it delicately, so as not to break the sauce or scramble the eggs.

5. Continue this process of slowly heating the bottom of the bowl or the top of the double boiler, while whisking the melted butter into it. The sauce should thicken and form something like a yellow mayonnaise. As you near the bottom of your butter, you will see some milky-looking water. Use this to thin the sauce to the desired consistency. You may not need it all.

6. Finally, add your chopped tarragon, salt, and pepper. Taste, adjust seasoning, and serve!

Contrary to popular opinion, this is not a mayonnaise made from bears.

Bacon Herb Cream Cheese Dip, a.k.a., Savory Fat Bomb

SERVES: 6 · · · PREP: 15 MIN · · · COOK: 0 MIN · · · TOTAL: 15 MIN

8 oz. (227 g) **regular cream cheese**, warmed and softened

2 **garlic cloves**, minced

1/2 cup (120 mL) **bacon fat**, room temperature (must be as cool as possible without solidifying)

1/2 cup (120 mL) grated **Parmesan chese**

1/4 cup (30 mL) **real bacon bits**

1 tsp (5 mL) chopped **fresh oregano**

salt and **pepper** to taste

This recipe actually began life as a "fat bomb," something you'll see more of in the sweeter section of this book. I was asked about my fat bomb recipes by another blogger, who asked if a savory fat bomb made sense. I thought about it and realized, "Sure! Why not?" So I set out to make this.

Many people following a low-primal philosophy tend to seek out higher fat recipes, or "boosts" to their daily fat numbers. Healthy fats provide quality energy. Fat is the densest form of energy, at 9 calories per gram (more than double carbohydrates or protein). Fat increases sense of satiety, especially within a diet comprised of few simple sugars. A small fat bomb can satisfy for several hours. Because of this satiety, overeating fat becomes uncomfortable and unlikely. There are many reasons for eating a fat bomb. Typically, a fat bomb is just eaten with a spoon, but this one doubles as an excellent dip.

1. Add the cream cheese to a food processor. Run the processor to loosen up the cream cheese. Add your garlic cloves as well as some salt and pepper (not too much salt, as the cheeses and bacon are already quite salty). Run the food processor.

2. *Very* slowly, pour a thin stream of liquid bacon fat through the hole in the top of the food processor until it is fully incorporated. A slow, thin stream is necessary, as it decreases the chance the emulsion will break. This process can be done with a whisk, but can be a lot of work.

3. Place the contents of the food processor into a bowl.

4. Add the remaining ingredients and fold into the mixture. Divide into six smaller portions and refrigerate. Much like peanut butter off a spoon, enjoy!

PER SERVING
CALORIES: 343.6
FAT: 34.33
PROTEIN: 7.49
CARBS: 2.35
FIBER: 0.14
SUGAR ALCOHOLS: 0
NET CARBS: 2.2

MORE FACTS: P. 538

PESTO ALLA GENOVESE

SERVES: 8 · · · PREP: 20 MIN · · · COOK: 0 MIN · · · TOTAL: 20 MIN

3 **garlic cloves**, diced

2/3 cup (160 mL) **extra virgin olive oil**

2 cups (480 mL) **fresh basil leaves** (about a large bunch's worth), packed, cleaned, and dried

2 tsp (10 mL) **lemon juice**

1/4 cup (60 mL) **pine nuts**, toasted

1/4 cup (60 mL) grated **Parmigiano Reggiano**

1/4 cup (60 mL) grated **Pecorino Romano**

salt and **pepper** to taste

Pesto (a word stemming from the Italian word for "pounded") is that bright green paste-like stuff that tastes great on pretty much everything. It's up there with bacon and ketchup, in terms of a perfect flavor. It's a very traditional sauce originating in Northern Italy. It's basically a mixture of basil, pine nuts, and cheese, but the combination is *oh* so much more than the sum of its parts!

Portion size: This particular recipe makes about a cup's (240 mL) worth of bright, vibrant, garlicky goodness. It's not uncommon for me to throw a few chili flakes in there... I like that little bit of zap! I'm counting each serving as 2 tablespoons (30 mL), for a total of 8 servings.

1. Add the garlic, salt, and half of the olive oil to a food processor with a sharp blade.

2. Pulse the processor and blend for 30 seconds.

3. Add the basil and lemon juice, then pulse for a further 30 seconds.

4. Add the pine nuts and cheeses, and then pulse to your desired consistency. If it's too thick, add more olive oil to adjust the consistency. I tend to like mine a bit on the pasty, rough side, but some like it smooth and saucy.

5. Use immediately or store covered with a thin layer of extra virgin olive oil. This will help prevent the pesto from turning brown and will allow it to last longer in the fridge.

PER SERVING
CALORIES: 213.29
FAT: 22.46
PROTEIN: 2.9
CARBS: 1.7
FIBER: 0.51
SUGAR ALCOHOLS: 0
NET CARBS: 1.19

MORE FACTS: P. 533

Pesto Cream Sauce

SERVES: 4 · · · PREP: 1 MIN · · · COOK: 19 MIN · · · TOTAL: 20 MIN

There are very few things I love more than pesto. Pesto can only really be heightened by the addition of cream. Ohhhh... *cream*. I often feel as if I could float through life on a green cloud of pesto cream. The bad news is, on occasion, I really try to! The good news is, pesto cream is really, really easy, and it's really that good. It's also like a rock-solid wall of calorie bomb. By and large, I don't count calories, but there are some foodstuffs that are so calorically dense, it becomes a bit irresponsible on my part not to point it out. This stuff is as good as it is genuinely fattening. Normally, I recommend fat and fat bombs, but within a heightened reason. The issue that I *personally* have with pesto cream is that I could drink it from a lavish goblet all day and never grow tired of it.

Portion control: Recipe makes about 1 cup (240 mL) of sauce, for about 1/4 cup (60 mL) per serving. Any less and it just feels like a *tease*.

2/3 cup (160 mL) **Pesto alla Genovese** (p. 386)

1 1/3 cup (320 mL) **heavy whipping cream**

salt and **pepper** to taste

1. Add the two ingredients to a pan and whisk over medium heat, until blended.

2. Once it simmers, turn to low heat and let it continue to simmer, reduce, and thicken. You can make it quicker by cooking over high heat, but you need to watch it and stir it.

3. When it's thick and gloopy, season to taste and then grab your lavish goblet and dance a little jig!

PER SERVING
CALORIES: 558.05
FAT: 59.29
PROTEIN: 5.29
CARBS: 4.6
FIBER: 0.68
SUGAR ALCOHOLS: 0
NET CARBS: 3.92

MORE FACTS: P. 534

Sun-Dried Tomato Pesto

SERVES: 8 · · · PREP: 10 MIN · · · COOK: 0 MIN · · · TOTAL: 10 MIN

1 cup (240 mL) **sun-dried tomatoes in oil**, oil drained off

4 **garlic cloves**, mince

2/3 cup (160 mL) **extra virgin olive oil**

2 tsp (10 mL) **lemon juice**

1/4 cup (60 mL) **pine nuts**, toasted

1/2 cup (120 mL) grated **Parmesan cheese**

salt and **pepper** to taste

The word *pesto* comes from the Genoese word *pestâ*, which means to pound or crush. Pesto is traditionally made with basil, pine nuts, garlic, olive oil, and Parmesan cheese. However, there are a million types and varieties of pesto. The root of the word is a verb and not a noun, so it's not really locked into any one ingredient. That said, most pesto I've seen tend to be some kind of ingredient blended with nuts, cheese, and oil.

Following that general pattern, you can take something like parsley and blend it with Asiago and walnuts. This gives you... parsley pesto! I've seen all kinds, from olive pesto to artichoke pesto, spicy arugula, chilies, etc. This one is for sun-dried tomatoes. It's phenomenally delicious and a little goes a long way.

1. Before adding your sun-dried tomatoes to your food processor, if they're not in oil or from a jar, make sure they are somewhat softened. Adding little rocks to your food processor might break it. If you've got nice, pliable, and soft tomatoes, great! If you've just dried them yourself, this is probably fine as well. Also, sun-dried tomatoes packed in oil will work quite nicely. However, if they've been sitting in your pantry or hanging out in a bulk bin, they might have become quite solid. If this is the case, put them in a bowl and pour a little hot water over them, then wrap the bowl in plastic wrap. This will slightly steam and soften them up a bit.

2. Let them sit for about 5 minutes and then pour off any excess water. We just need them soft enough not to spin around the machine but not rehydrated.

3. Add all ingredients in a food processor and pulse a few times. Continue pulsing until it's the consistency you like. You can make it a smooth paste or a rustic and chunky pesto; it's completely up to you.

4. Taste it, adjust seasoning, give it another pulse or two, then package or serve!

PER SERVING
CALORIES: 246.08
FAT: 24.56
PROTEIN: 3.69
CARBS: 4.67
FIBER: 0.91
SUGAR ALCOHOLS: 0
NET CARBS: 3.76

MORE FACTS: P. 534

Desserts

o o o

I've never had much of a sweet tooth, personally. However, I'd be lying if I said I didn't enjoy them. In fact, for years, it's been a habit to make ice cream, divide it into little containers, stash in the freezer, and eat one a night. In my very early days, fat bombs and chocolate bark were also enjoyed on a regular basis. Sweets and baked goods have a place within the low-primal landscape. While far from required, they're good to stave off a stressful moment, resolve a craving, or even just because it's a delicious end to a day! I've done my best to present a nice solid assortment of sweets, hopefully in a manner that will allow you to launch into your own sweet pursuits!

THAI PUMPKIN CUSTARD (SANKAYA)

SERVES: 8 · · · PREP: 10 MIN · · · COOK: 30 MIN · · · TOTAL: 40 MIN

1 small (2 to 3 lb.) (1.1 kg) **kabocha squash** (substitution: acorn, buttercup, delicata, pumpkin)

5 large **whole eggs**

3/4 cup (180 mL) **unsweetened coconut milk**

3/4 cup (180 mL) **sugar replacement**

1/2 tsp (2 mL) ground **cinnamon**

1/2 tsp (2 mL) **vanilla extract**

dash of **salt**

I'm a lover of pumpkins. Really all squash, to be honest: butternut, acorn, pumpkin, delicata, spaghetti, and... the kabocha! This Cambodian squash is much lower in carbs than most but appears to pack in just as much flavor as its cousins. With an edible rind and growing popularity, this squash is worth the hunt. I can find them year round at various Asian markets. They can also be found in the wintertime, at many farmers' markets. While somewhat obscure, they are *absolutely* worth tracking down!

Essentially, the top of the squash is popped, the seeds are scooped out, and then the cavity is filled with a sweetened coconut-egg mixture. Then, the whole thing is steamed in a steamer and split into wedges and served!

1. Add about 8 to 10 cups (about 2 L) of water to the base of a large steamer. Place this on the stove and bring to a boil.

2. Remove the top of the kabocha squash, like you would for a pumpkin at Halloween. Scrape the seeds off the bottom of the top, as well as scraping out the seeds from inside the squash. The inside should be nice and clean.

3. Whisk together the eggs, coconut milk, sweetener, cinnamon, vanilla, and salt. Whisk until the sweetener is fully dissolved. Pour the mixture into the cavity of the squash until it's full.

PER SERVING
CALORIES: 170.96
FAT: 9.67
PROTEIN: 6.59
CARBS: 36.26
FIBER: 0.76
SUGAR ALCOHOLS: 30
NET CARBS: 5.51

MORE FACTS: P. 539

4. Place the squash and lid into the steamer and cover. Turn the heat down to medium low and steam for about an hour. Do not open during this time, for fear the squash may crack.

5. After about an hour, the top of the custard should puff a bit. Pierce the custard with a wooden skewer, running it fairly deeply into the center. If it comes out clean, remove the squash and allow the custard to continue setting. Give it at least 45 minutes, and eat warm, if desired, but the best option is to chill the pumpkin in the refrigerator and then slice into wedges. Serve!

Chocolate OMM (One-Minute Muffin)

SERVES: 1 ··· PREP: 1 MIN ··· COOK: 1 MIN ··· TOTAL: 2 MIN

1 1/2 Tbsp (23 mL) **ground chia seed** (or 2 Tbsp [30 mL] flax meal)

2 Tbsp (30 mL) **almond flour**

1 Tbsp (15 mL) **sugar replacement**

1 Tbsp (15 mL) **unsweetened cocoa powder**

1/2 tsp (2 mL) **baking powder**

a dash of **salt**

1 large **egg**

1 Tbsp (15 mL) **melted butter**

PER SERVING
CALORIES: 275.08
FAT: 21.3
PROTEIN: 13.57
CARBS: 28.13
FIBER: 9.32
SUGAR ALCOHOLS: 15
NET CARBS: 3.81

MORE FACTS: P. 542

I left this as a simple chocolate OMM ratio because I wanted to point out a few directions that a raw batter like this could be taken. Try folding some raspberries and toasted almond slivers into it for a super-tasty treat! Try chopping up some erythritol sweetened chocolate bars and folding the chocolate chunks into the batter. This would become a truly hot, melty, gooey, double-chocolate delight... in 120 seconds! I know that some consider bananas to be the root of all evil, but with a small amount of freshly smooshed banana, maybe some natural banana flavoring, and a few toasted walnuts, a low-carb chocolate-banana treat is quickly within reach! Maybe throw some espresso grounds into the batter. Make a Morning Mocha Alert (MMA OMM)! Try putting a nice dollop of almond butter in the center before nuking it. Chocolate and almond butter! MMMMmmmm...

1. Combine your chia (or flax), almond flour, sweetener, cocoa powder, baking powder, and salt in a coffee mug or other microwaveable safe mold of some kind. I like to grease my mug first, but I don't think it's necessary.

2. Mix in your egg and melted butter.

3. Microwave on high for 60 seconds (90 seconds if using a weaker microwave or if you've added lots of other ingredients, like nuts, frozen berries, etc.).

4. Alternately, bake in a muffin tin at 350°F (177°C) for 13 to 15 minutes or until fully puffed in the center.

5. Eat and enjoy!

Plain ol' Vanilla OMM (One-Minute Muffin)

SERVES: 1 · · · PREP: 1 MIN · · · COOK: 1 MIN · · · TOTAL: 2 MIN

It seems that no matter what is presented, there's always someone that can't do this, can't do that, isn't able to absorb that, just wants it plain, etc. This is fine, common, and I love being able to present options and alternatives! One of the bigger issues related to many OMM varieties is the prevalence of flax, even as many others seek it out and love it! Flax does have a stronger flavor and is quite high in fiber. It tends to give a deeper "earthiness" to the muffins, a darker color, and hides more delicate flavors like vanilla.

So this recipe is on the lighter, more cakey side! It's using softer, finer ingredients with an overall more synergistic yum, resulting in a light and mellow OMM!

1 Tbsp (15 mL) **coconut flour**

1 Tbsp (15 mL) **almond flour**

1 Tbsp (15 mL) **vanilla whey protein** (sweetened with stevia)

1 Tbsp (15 mL) **sugar replacement**

1/2 tsp (15 mL) **baking powder**

a dash of **salt**

1 large **whole egg**

1 Tbsp (15 mL) **fresh whole butter**, melted

1/2 tsp (2g) **vanilla extract**

1. In a wide-mouthed coffee mug (or other microwave-safe mold of some kind), combine your coconut flour, almond flour, protein powder, sugar replacement, baking powder, and salt. I like to grease my mug first, but I don't think it's necessary.

2. Mix in your egg, melted butter, and vanilla.

3. Microwave on high for 60 seconds (90 seconds if using a weaker microwave, or if you've added lots of other ingredients, like nuts, frozen berries, etc.).

4. Alternately, bake in a muffin tin at 350°F (177°C) for 13 to 15 minutes or until golden.

5. Eat and enjoy!

PER SERVING
CALORIES: 209.1
FAT: 12.92
PROTEIN: 16.25
CARBS: 22.25
FIBER: 3.75
SUGAR ALCOHOLS: 15
NET CARBS: 3.5

MORE FACTS: P. 539

Pumpkin-Spice OMM with Maple Butter

SERVES: 1 · · · PREP: 5 MIN · · · COOK: 1 MIN · · · TOTAL: 6 MIN

Maple Butter:

1 Tbsp (15 mL) **butter**

1/2 tbsp (8 mL) **sugar-free maple syrup**

1 dash **salt**

Pumpkin OMM:

1 1/2 Tbsp (23 mL) **ground chia seed** (or 2 Tbsp [30 mL] flax meal)

2 Tbsp (30 mL) **hazelnut meal/flour** (substitute: almond flour)

2 Tbsp (30 mL) **sugar replacement**

1/2 tsp (2 mL) **baking powder**

1/2 tsp (2 mL) ground **cinnamon**

1/4 tsp (1 mL) freshly ground **nutmeg**

a dash ground **cloves**

a dash **powdered ginger**

a dash of **salt**

2 Tbsp (30 mL) **mashed pumpkin**

1 large **whole egg**

PER SERVING
CALORIES: 356.52
FAT: 29.19
PROTEIN: 11.82
CARBS: 43.04
FIBER: 9.13
SUGAR ALCOHOLS: 30
NET CARBS: 3.91

MORE FACTS: P. 540

Here we have a very simple pumpkin One-Minute Muffin. It's little more than a basic OMM recipe, but with the addition of some spices and a healthy spoonful of pumpkin puree. The end result is little more than a quick pumpkin yum, perfect for any time of the day!

The one thing that I personally feel makes this a bit on the special side is the partner in crime: maple butter! The reality is this is something I should have probably made its own recipe, rather than hiding it here, but... that's not the road I chose. Only you reading the Pumpkin OMM recipe will be privy to the maple butter, which is awesome slathered on a pork chop! It's *amazing* on a fresh, hot pumpkin OMM straight from the nuker. It's perfect melted on top of a thick stack of pancakes in the morning. Make a batch of this splendid butter and stash it in the freezer, in one big plastic-wrapped log. Just slice off a disk when you need some. You'll find it won't last long!

Maple Butter: The recipe for the maple butter is actually 1/2 cup (120 mL) butter (softened), a 1/4 cup (60 mL) sugar-free maple syrup, and a dash of salt. With a mixer, whip the butter until it's light in color and airy. Then, pour in the syrup, with a dash of salt, and whip until combined. Lay a sheet of plastic wrap on the counter, then spread your butter into a small log. Roll the log in the plastic wrap and refrigerate or freeze. This will make enough butter for about 6 to 8 OMMs. The amounts below are listed in this manner, so that I could keep the recipe as a single serving.

1. Read the notes about the Maple Butter, on the prceeding page. The best method for this is to make a large batch in advance and then use what you need for your OMM.

2. In a wide-mouthed coffee mug, combine your ground chia (or flax), hazelnut (or almond) flour, sugar replacement, baking powder, cinnamon, nutmeg, cloves, ginger, and salt. I like to grease my mug first, but I don't think it's necessary. Mix in your egg and pumpkin puree.

3. Microwave on high for 60 seconds (90 seconds if using a weaker microwave).

4. Alternately, bake in a muffin tin at 350°F (177°C) for 13 to 15 minutes or until golden.

5. Slather some maple butter on top. Eat and enjoy!

Frosted Carrot Cake OMM with Pecans

SERVES: 1 · · · PREP: 5 MIN · · · COOK: 1 MIN · · · TOTAL: 6 MIN

Carrot Cake OMM:

1 1/2 Tbsp (23 mL) **ground chia seed** (or 2 Tbsp [30 mL] flax meal)

2 Tbsp (30 mL) **almond flour**

2 Tbsp (30 mL) **sugar replacement**

1/2 tsp (2 mL) **baking powder**

1/2 tsp (2 mL) ground **cinnamon**

1/4 tsp (1 mL) ground **nutmeg**

a dash of **salt**

2 Tbsp (30 mL) grated **raw carrot**

1 Tbsp (15 mL) chopped **pecans**, toasted

1 large **whole egg**

1 Tbsp (15 mL) **melted butter**

1/2 tsp (2 mL) **vanilla extract**

Cream Cheese Frosting:

1 1/2 Tbsp (23 mL) **full-fat cream cheese**, warmed

1 Tbsp (15 mL) **fresh whole butter**, softened

3 Tbsp (45 mL) **powdered sugar replacement**

a dash **vanilla extract**

a dash **salt**

PER SERVING
CALORIES: 495.42
FAT: 43.05
PROTEIN: 14.54
CARBS: 81.9
FIBER: 9.15
SUGAR ALCOHOLS: 67.5
NET CARBS: 5.25

MORE FACTS: P. 540

Someone, somewhere, at some point in time, decided to do a poorly run test on cooked carrots, deeming them to be *incredibly* high glycemic, converting to glucose in the blood *much faster* than regular ol' table sugar! As a result, these fairly low-carb underground orange sticks have been passed over, time and time again, by people looking to maintain a stable level of blood sugar. I'm here to tell you… lies. ALL LIES!!

Carrots are fine. They are, in fact, good for you! Cooked, raw, peeled, or unpeeled, carrots are *not* going to hurt you. When I really stop and think about it, it's silly to think that someone, somewhere, at some point in time became obese by a carrot-heavy diet. I just really don't believe that to be true. They *may* have turned orange, though.

Carrots were once thought to have a GI of 90+ (pure glucose is 100, while table sugar is merely 65!). Current reports clock cooked carrots in at closer to 30 or 40, which is fairly low glycemic (lower than sweet potatoes).

These sweet carrot and pecan muffins attempt to capture the spirit of a fresh carrot cake smeared with a bit of cream cheese frosting! It's pretty amazing what can be done in sixty seconds!

Note: You can always powder sweetener in a coffee grinder.

1. In a wide-mouthed coffee mug, combine your chia (or flax), almond flour, sweetener, baking powder, cinnamon, nutmeg, and salt. I like to grease my mug first, but I don't think it's necessary.

2. Mix in your carrots, pecans, egg, butter, and vanilla.

3. Microwave on high for 60 seconds (90 seconds if using a weaker microwave).

4. Alternately, bake in a muffin tin at 350°F (177°C) for 13 to 15 minutes or until golden.

5. While the muffin is nuking, beat together your cream cheese, butter, powdered sugar replacement, vanilla, and salt. Make sure your cream cheese and butter are soft (leave out at room temperature for a while) before whipping, or else mixing will be difficult at best.

6. Slather some frosting on top. Eat and enjoy!

Now, with Pecans!

CHOCOLATE PUDDING PIE WITH MACADAMIA CRUST

SERVES: 8 · · · PREP: 20 MIN · · · COOK: 15 MIN · · · TOTAL: 6 HR 35 MIN

1 1/2 cups (360 mL) crushed, salted **macadamia nuts**

1 Tbsp (15 mL) **honey**

1/4 cup (60 mL) melted **fresh whole butter**

1 1/2 cups (360 mL) **heavy whipping cream**

2 1/2 cups (600 mL) unsweetened **almond milk**, divided

2 packets (about 4 1/2 to 5 tsp total) (14 g or 25 mL) **gelatin powder**

3/4 cup (180 mL) **unsweetened cocoa powder**

1 cup (240 mL) **sugar replacement**

1 Tbsp (15 mL) **vanilla extract**

a dash of **salt**

PER SERVING
CALORIES: 404.88
FAT: 40.72
PROTEIN: 6.38
CARBS: 37.22
FIBER: 4.91
SUGAR ALCOHOLS: 25
NET CARBS: 7.31

MORE FACTS: P. 539

Gelatin might be some of the weirdest stuff on earth, right up there with Aerogel and non-Newtonian fluids (i.e., cornstarch slurry). In simple terms, it's what gives Jell-O its shape and jiggle. It's usually bought in powdered form, but can also be bought in little sheets that feel like plastic. Dissolve these powders or sheets into a warm liquid and then let it chill. It will firm up the entirety of the liquid and become a jiggling gelatinous mass of bouncy wonkiness.

I first learned about using powdered gelatin back in culinary school, somewhere in the middle of the nineteenth century. I learned how to apply it to meats and fishes, an interesting branch of cookery known as *charcuterie*. Gelatin was used to firm things up, give shapes to meats and sauces that have no shape, suspending ingredients in "space," etc. Gelatin was fun but old school, and I never really used it in modern kitchens (of the early '90s), but I think it's seeing a bit of a revival.

This recipe is *very* simple to make and really doesn't use that many ingredients. The end result is deep and luxurious, without really breaking the carb bank. Oh... it's *tasty* too!

Nuts 'n' honey note: I use a little bit of honey in the crust. It's a tiny amount and really only serves to help the crust stay together. You could completely omit it and the recipe will still work, while also dropping each slice by about 2 net carbs. However, the crust will not stay as together and united. It will still work and be absolutely tasty, but it will be more crumbly. It's totally up to you!

1. Preheat oven to 325°F (163°C).

2. If your macadamia nuts are not crushed, place them in a large plastic bag with a resealable zipper. With a mallet or the edge of a pot or pan, whack at them until you have a squooshed bag of macadamia explosion. (I've tried this in a food processor, and for whatever reason, while you want a fine grain, the imperfect smashing method gives a better crust than macadamias pulverized in a food processor.)

3. Pour your crushed macadamias into a mixing bowl and add your honey (you can skip the honey, but it does help to hold the crust together) and melted butter. Mix the ingredients until the macadamias are well coated with the honey and butter.

4. Grease a 9-inch (23 x 4 cm) pie pan.

5. Press the nut mixture into the pie pan. Use the back of a spoon (or a tamper if you have one) to press the crusts firmly into the base and up the sides of the pan.

6. Bake the crusts for 12 minutes or until golden brown. Remove and allow to cool.

7. Combine cream and 2 cups (480 mL) of the almond milk in a medium saucepan over medium-low heat.

8. At the same time you add your milk to the stove, in a medium-sized mixing bowl, add your 1/2 cup (120 mL) remaining almond milk.

9. Sprinkle the gelatin powder evenly over the surface of the cold almond milk, in the mixing bowl. Allow it to bloom for about 5 minutes.

10. Into your hot milk mixture, whisk in your sugar equivalent, cocoa powder, vanilla, and a dash of salt. Whisk until the cocoa is ful-ly absorbed, lumps are gone, and the sugar equivalent has fully dissolved.

11. Once the mixture begins to simmer (but not boil), whisk the hot mixture into the blooming gelatin bowl. Whisk until the gelatin is completely dissolved.

12. Pour your warm mixture into the pie pan and place in the refrigerator to chill. Chilling takes between 4 to 6 hours.

13. Slice and serve with whipped cream!

THE FAMOUS MOCK DANISH

SERVES: 1 · · · PREP: 1 MIN · · · COOK: 2 MIN · · · TOTAL: 3 MIN

2 oz. (56 g) **regular cream cheese** (not low fat)

1 large **egg**

2 tsp (10 mL) **sugar replacement**

1/2 tsp (2 mL) **vanilla extract**

a dash **salt**

a dash **cinnamon** (optional)

There are some recipes that are here simply because this book would be incomplete without them. This is just such a recipe. I started my own personal journey into this way of eating several years ago. At the time, I didn't have a microwave. Actually, I was living in an apartment in Mexico and the apartment came with a *massive* microwave… that totally didn't work. It took up a huge amount of space and… near as I can tell, this was its only real accomplishment. As a result of starting down this road without a microwave, I had never tried classics like the One-Minute Muffin or… the Famous Mock Danish!

Both this and the One-Minute Muffin are recipes that exist and are handed down from one low-carber to the next… and onward and onward. Now, it's *my* turn to share these tasty treats!

1. In a small nonporous bowl, microwave the cream cheese for 15 seconds or less, just long enough to soften it. Make sure it's warm and *fully* softened, or else the eggs won't mix properly.

2. Add the egg and combine the two ingredients with a spatula until smooth.

3. Add the sweetener, vanilla, salt, and optional cinnamon. (I like it with cinnamon and a bit of nutmeg when plain but leave it out with eating it with fruit jelly.) Mix well.

4. Because I'm fussy, I transfer the ingredients into a 6-ounce ramekin (180 mL) to nuke, but you can continue to use the same bowl. Microwave for 90 seconds, rotating halfway through. It shouldn't be runny, but the center should still be a bit soft, for that *Danish* feeling. May need to nuke for a further 30 to 60 seconds.

PER SERVING
CALORIES: 272.02
FAT: 24.33
PROTEIN: 9.93
CARBS: 12.95
FIBER: 0
SUGAR ALCOHOLS: 10
NET CARBS: 2.95

MORE FACTS: P. 540

5. I use a spatula to pop mine out of the ramekin and placed it onto a plate, but, again, many just eat it right out of the bowl. Delicious hot or cold! Cover with jelly or sprinkle some more cinnamon and sweetener.

6. **Note:** I'm often asked how to do this without a microwave. Most people actually use it like a pancake batter, frying it in a little butter and then rolling some sugar-free jam into it and eating it like a sweetened taco.

STRAWBERRY-KIWI POPSICLES

SERVES: 6 · · · PREP: 10 MIN · · · COOK: 0 MIN · · · TOTAL: 4 HR

2 (152 g) **kiwis**, peeled and coarsely chopped

1 1/2 cup (360 mL) **water, divided**

2 tsp (5 mL) **vanilla extract, divided**

5 Tbsp (75 mL) **sugar replacement, divided**

1 cup (240 mL) sliced **strawberries**

a few dashes of **salt** (at different times)

Living in Mexico for as long as I have, I have run across a million varieties of something called *agua fresca* (fresh water). In essence, they are a fruit or a mixture of fruit, mashed, soaked, chopped, and/or pureed then mixed with *lots* of water and sugar. Some also use nuts, grains, and spices, but most are just a mixture of fruit, water, and sugar. For all intents and purposes, lemonade is an *agua fresca*!

See, sugar, much like salt, is a flavor enhancer. It tends to take the flavors and aromas from an ingredient and stretch it. This is how a watermelon, mixed with gallons of water and some sugar, can bring cool refreshment to a large body of people! It's inexpensive, fun, tasty, and brings a smile to many more faces than just the lone watermelon ever could!

The same exact idea and method applies here! By taking a fruit and mixing it with your favorite sweetener, then stretching with water, cream, or yogurt, and a bit of salt, you can freeze yummy little frozen snack-y sticks of goodness! The stretch-ability of the sweetener and salt has a fantastic little side effect for us low-primalists. It dilutes the carbs naturally found in the fruits, allowing us to eat full-flavored popsicles made from actual fruits! Through this method, you can eat a wider variety of fruits than you might ordinarily eat while staying low-primal. I can envision a mellow yellow pineapple pop. Can't you?!

In addition to being cool on a hot day, inexpensive fun for the whole family, a great way to tickle the taste buds with forbidden fruit, and being a fun way to play with foods, popsicles also have two other *fantastic* benefits. By nature, they are rooted in portion control. It's not like a bottomless barrel of ice cream. It's just a sin-

PER SERVING
CALORIES: 28.01
FAT: 0
PROTEIN: 0.5
CARBS: 18.5
FIBER: 1.17
SUGAR ALCOHOLS: 12.5
NET CARBS: 4.83

MORE FACTS: P. 541

gle *ice-olated* pop! Finally… popsicles last! You can make a big batch and stash them in the freezer, where they'll live for weeks and months! This means you can make a variety of flavors and save them up for a bright and sunny day!

1. In a blender, puree the kiwis with 3/4 cup (180 mL) water, 1 tsp (5 mL) vanilla, 3 Tbsp (45 mL) sweetener, and a bit of salt. You don't want to puree for too long, as the seeds will turn the whole mixture a dark, ugly color—just long enough to break them up. You can strain the seeds out if you like a more consistent, perfect green, but I opted to leave them in. It has a great *kiwi* appearance.

2. Evenly divide the mixture into the molds. The liquid should rise about halfway. Place in the freezer *without* their handles.

3. When the kiwi mixture has frozen, puree the strawberries with the remaining 3/4 cup (180 mL) water, 1 tsp (5 mL) vanilla, 2 Tbsp (30 mL) sweetener, and a bit of salt in a blender.

4. Pour the strawberry mixture into the molds. Fit your handles into the base of the molds and freeze until solid.

5. To remove from the molds, hold under hot tap water for about 15 seconds. The pops… pop right out!

Coco-Cocoa-Walnut Bark

SERVES: 2 ··· PREP: 1 MIN ··· COOK: 1 MIN ··· TOTAL: 30 MIN

2 Tbsp (30 mL) **coconut oil**, liquefied

1 Tbsp (15 mL) **unsweetened cocoa powder**

1 Tbsp (15 mL) **powdered sugar replacement**

1 Tbsp (15 mL) toasted, broken **walnut bits**

a dash **salt**

1 Tbsp (15g) **heavy whipping cream** (homogenized)

Within the world of low-primal eating, there are certain concepts that can't be ignored. There are certain recipes and types of foodstuffs that are seen again and again, over and over. One of them is the One-Minute Muffin (p. 393). Another is the Famous Mock Danish (p. 400). Another is *Bark*. No, not like the dog... *more like the tree*!

It's actually a bit of a wonder food. It's really no surprise that it's as popular as it is. It's got about four very clear characteristics that qualify it as a superfood, in my humble opinion. It's quick and easy to make. It quenches that sweet tooth, as well as the one seeking chocolate. It's made with good fats, which leave people feeling satisfied for hours. It's versatile. I've seen people toss all kinds of things into their barks. This creates an endless variety!

I've seen people infuse them with flavored oils and extracts. I've seen all varieties of nuts. I've seen all varieties of sweeteners. I've seen people throw dried fruits into it. I've seen people experiment with different colors, making white barks too. Such a simple thing, but it fills so many needs. Oh, did I mention? It's delicious!

1. Mix together the liquefied coconut oil with the cocoa powder, sugar equivalent, chopped walnuts, and a dash of salt.

2. Whip in the cream and stir until the whole thing is a nice thick, creamy, chocolaty-looking sauce.

3. Spread onto a sheet of wax paper, about 1/4 inch (8 mm) thick and refrigerate.

4. Once it cools, snap off pieces and enjoy as desired!

PER SERVING
CALORIES: 176.32
FAT: 17.77
PROTEIN: 1.26
CARBS: 2.79
FIBER: 1.16
SUGAR ALCOHOLS: 0.5
NET CARBS: 1.13

MORE FACTS: P. 541

Bark Bark!

LEMONGRASS-SCENTED COCONUT-LIME SORBET

SERVES: 6 · · · PREP: 15 MIN · · · COOK: 40 MIN · · · TOTAL: 55 MIN

1 cup (240 mL) **sugar replacement**

1/4 tsp (1 mL) **guar gum** (optional)

1/4 tsp (1 mL) **xanthan gum** (optional)

1/2 tsp (2 mL) **salt**

2 13.5-oz. cans (756 g) **coconut milk**

1 Tbsp (15 mL) minced **fresh galangal** (substitution: 1 Tbsp [15 mL] minced ginger)

1 Tbsp (15 mL) minced **lemongrass** (substitution: 1 tsp [5 mL] lemon zest)

4 **kaffir lime leaves,** cut into ribbons (substitution: 1 tsp [5 mL] lime zest)

2 tsp (10 mL) **fresh lime juice**

3 Tbsp (45 mL) **vegetable glycerine,** food grade (optional)

This is actually really quite easy to make. It just requires steeping the aromatics in the coconut milk with the sweetener. It's heated, then left to sit for about an hour. Finally, it's strained, cooled, and placed into an ice cream machine where it is churned into a frozen treat!

Texture note: The absence of real sugar slightly changes the texture of frozen desserts. The mouthfeel is just a little bit off (but *far* from unpleasant). You can approximate that sensation by adding vegetable glycerin and guar and/or xanthan gums. This will give you a texture and mouthfeel closer to the sorbets you're familiar with. If you leave them out, the end result will be very delicious, but will be harder to scoop, a little more crystallized, and the melting sensation in your mouth will result in a little less viscosity. I like to place them in the fridge for about an hour before I eat them. This softens them without melting them—*much* more pleasant!

Portion control: I'm a big fan of portioning, especially when it comes to this kind of sweet treat. I simply load them into little freezer-friendly dishes (mine are 6.5-oz cups [195 mL]), and put them into the freezer, like sweet little dessert cartridges. When I want one, I just grab one.

Note: This recipe is designed for a 2-quart (1.9 L) ice cream machine.

PER SERVING
CALORIES: 283.62
FAT: 26.77
PROTEIN: 2.85
CARBS: 37.59
FIBER: 0.39
SUGAR ALCOHOLS: 33.33
NET CARBS: 3.87

MORE FACTS: P. 539

1. In a dry bowl, blend together your powdered sugar equivalent, with the two gums and a dash of salt. (If using a liquid sweetener, skip this step. The idea is to more evenly distribute the gums into the powder, to prevent clumping.)

2. In a saucepot, over low heat, bring the coconut milk, galangal, lime leaves, and lemon grass up to a slow simmer.

3. Whisk your sugar equivalent, two gums, and dash of salt into the warm mixture. Turn off the heat and steep for 1 hour, stirring once or twice.

4. After an hour, strain your aromatics from the coconut milk through a sieve.

5. Chill the mixture.

6. When the mixture has been chilled, whisk in your fresh lime juice and vegetable glycerin.

7. Add mixture to your ice cream machine and follow instructions on the machine.

8. Serve fresh, or pack in the freezer for later!

Blackberry-Basil Sorbet

SERVES: 8 · · · PREP: 15 MIN · · · COOK: 30 MIN · · · TOTAL: 45 MIN

1 cup (240 mL) **water**

1 cup (240 mL) **sugar replacement**

1/4 tsp (1 mL) **guar gum** (optional)

1/4 tsp (1 mL) **xanthan gum** (optional)

1/2 tsp (2 mL) **salt**

3 cups (720 mL) **fresh blackberries**, washed

16 leaves **fresh basil**, cut into ribbons (chiffonade)

2 tsp (10 mL) fresh **lemon juice**

3 Tbsp (45 mL) **vegetable glycerine**, food grade (optional)

I make a lot of ice cream. I generally make it about twice a week and have covered hundreds of different flavors. However, it doesn't just stop with ice "cream," per se. There are other similar concoctions that are just as delicious. There are granitas, sorbets, sherbets, frozen custards, popsicles, frozen yogurts, etc. This one is a sorbet. It's also a little different than a standard strawberry sorbet too! Firstly, I use blackberries. It's also got a really surprisingly pleasant basil essence rippling through it. It seemed like a good idea, but… as it churned in my ice cream machine, my hopes fell and I started to doubt myself. Then, when I popped the lid and tasted it… it was *fantastic*! Perfectly balanced and delicious. The basil complemented the flavors more than I'd originally hoped, without ever being overwhelming—cool, fresh, light, and utterly fantastic.

Texture note: The absence of real sugar slightly changes the texture of frozen desserts. The mouthfeel is just a little bit off (but *far* from unpleasant). You can approximate that sensation by adding vegetable glycerin and guar and/or xanthan gums. This will give you a texture and mouthfeel closer to the sorbets you're familiar with. If you leave them out, the end result will be very delicious, but will be harder to scoop, a little more crystallized, and the melting sensation in your mouth will have a little less viscosity. Fun, right?!

Second note: I mention chiffonade of basil. It's basically basil that's been cut into strips. Stack basil leaves on top of one another, like a deck of cards. With a sharp knife, slice the stack every 1/8 of an inch (3mm) to produce basil chiffonade.

Third note: This recipe is designed for a 2-quart (1.9 L) ice cream machine.

PER SERVING
CALORIES: 48.68
FAT: 0.38
PROTEIN: 0.77
CARBS: 31.01
FIBER: 3.28
SUGAR ALCOHOLS: 25
NET CARBS: 2.74

MORE FACTS: P. 541

1. Place your water on the stove to boil in a small saucepan.

2. This one is a bit tough. I don't know what sweetener you're using, but ideally it's a powdered form of sweetener. Assuming this is the case, blend it with your salt. If you're using the guar and xanthan gums, also add them to the sugar equivalent and evenly mix it into the powder. This will help mix it into the liquid more evenly later.

3. Add your sugar equivalent mixture to the boiling water, to make sure it's been dissolved. Set aside to cool.

4. Puree your blackberries in a blender. Add a small amount of sweetened water, to help the blending process, should you need it.

5. I personally like to strain out the seeds and feel it gives the sorbet a more pleasant texture, but this is completely optional. Strain the blackberry puree through a fine mesh strainer if you like.

6. Whisk together your cooled, sweetened water, your berry puree, the lemon juice, basil, and vegetable glycerine.

7. Follow the instructions on your ice cream machine from this point forward.

8. Eat and enjoy!

ALMOND PANNA COTTA WITH STRAWBERRIES AND KIWI

SERVES: 6 · · · PREP: 10 MIN · · · COOK: 30 MIN · · · TOTAL: 4 HR

Almond Panna Cotta:

1 cup (240 mL) **heavy whipping cream**

1 cup (240 mL) unsweetened **almond milk,** divided

1 (12 g) **vanilla bean,** split lengthwise (or 2 tsp [10 mL] vanilla extract)

1/4 cup (60 mL) **sugar replacement**

a dash of **salt**

1 packet (about 2 1/4 to 2 1/2 tsp) (7 g or 13 mL) **gelatin powder**

Strawberry-Kiwi Salsa:

1 pint (480 mL) **strawberries,** washed and diced

2 each (182 g) **kiwi fruits,** peeled and diced

1/4 cup (60 mL) **slivered almonds,** toasted

2 tsp (10 mL) fresh **lemon juice**

a dash **salt**

This recipe actually caught me off guard. It was FAR greater than I remembered. I've had panna cotta many times in my life. I made it way back in cooking school, etc. I've always loved it but had completely forgotten about it. Such a pleasant reminder!

Gelatin, being a clear, flavorless, jiggly substance derived from the collagen of animals (probably best not to ask) is *more* than appropriate for a low-primal way of life.

This particular panna cotta recipe follows the basic ratios for panna cotta. The primary difference being it's sugar free and partially made with almond milk. This is both to reduce the carbs but also to supply a bridge between the strawberry, kiwi, and almond salsa. I had several people over when I made this, and it was quite popular to say the least!

1. Combine cream and 3/4 cup (180 mL) of the almond milk in a medium saucepan.

2. Split the vanilla bean in half. Scrape the seeds from the vanilla bean. Add the bean and seeds to the milk and cream.

3. Bring the milk to a very slow simmer. Remove the milk from the heat and whisk the sugar and salt into the milk. Make sure it dissolves. Keep warm but set aside.

4. In a medium-sized mixing bowl, add your 1/4 cup (60 mL) remaining almond milk.

5. Sprinkle the gelatin powder evenly over the surface of the almond milk. Allow it to bloom for about 5 minutes.

PER SERVING
CALORIES: 225.25
FAT: 18.46
PROTEIN: 4.17
CARBS: 20.36
FIBER: 2.97
SUGAR ALCOHOLS: 8.33
NET CARBS: 9.06

MORE FACTS: P. 541

6. While holding a strainer, strain your hot milk mixture into the gelatin mixture. This process will strain out the vanilla pods and any large fragments that may have broken off.

7. Whisk the warm milk mixture into the gelatin mixture. Make sure both the sugar equivalent and gelatin is completely dissolved.

8. Pour your warm mixture into six 6-ounce cups (180 mL) or ramekins.

9. Chill the panna cotta until firm (about 4 hours).

10. While the panna cotta firms up, you can make the salsa. To make the salsa, simply blend the ingredients together.

11. When the panna cotta is firm, serve in the same dish it was chilled in. Or you can unmold them by floating them in a bath of warm water for about 30 seconds. Then, flip them upside down to release them. Be careful when you do this; they're jiggly!

12. Serve with a nice spoonful or two of the salsa!

A strawberry-kiwi toupéel

TRIPLE CHOCOLATE EVERYTHING WADS

SERVES: 6 · · · PREP: 10 MIN · · · COOK: 0 MIN · · · TOTAL: 1 HR 10 MIN

1/2 cup (120 mL) melted fresh whole **butter**

1 tsp (5 mL) **vanilla extract**

1 cup (240 mL) **powdered sugar replacement**

1/2 cup (120 mL) **unsweetened cocoa powder**

1/4 cup (60 mL) **cacao nibs**

1/4 cup (60 mL) chopped **pecans**, toasted

1/4 cup (60 mL) **sugar-free chocolate chips** or chunks (I typically cut up a ChocoPerfection Bar)

1/4 cup (60 mL) unsweetened **shredded coconut**, toasted

a dash of **salt**

Here's a simple and delectable way to enjoy chocolate in a raw "no-bake cookie" form. If memory serves, the backbone for this recipe actually started as a haystack cookie recipe that I picked up from Laura Dolson, over at the excellent section on low-carb diets at About.com. I tweaked it to allow it to more match my own personal tastes; I upped the chocolate quotient and added some nuts. I went for an "everything wad," much in the same way some bagel shops have everything bagels.

The end result is calm and cool wads of crunchy goodness!

1. In a medium mixing bowl, combine the ingredients. Mix well.

2. Onto a large plate or baking tray, scoop the dough into 1-inch (2.5 cm) balls.

3. Chill. Eat when firm (about an hour).

PER SERVING
CALORIES: 269.67
FAT: 26.63
PROTEIN: 3.96
CARBS: 51.17
FIBER: 8.13
SUGAR ALCOHOLS: 40
NET CARBS: 3.04

MORE FACTS: P. 543

WHIPPED CREAM

SERVES: 8 · · · PREP: 5 MIN · · · COOK: 0 MIN · · · TOTAL: 5 MIN

Who doesn't love whipped cream?! I feel slightly silly including it in my list of recipes, but because it's so delicious and so acceptable within this way of eating, I started to feel slightly silly *not* including it. Whipped cream is soft, light, sweet, great on almost anything, and completely welcome to this way of eating, even at the induction level! Take a few fresh berries and dip them. Top a nice pudding with it. Use it with crepes. Use it within a trifle recipe. Eat it right off the whisk!

Tip: Cold cream, a chilled bowl, and a cold whisk will make a better whipped cream.

Tip two: Typically, cream about doubles in volume. So, for 1 cup (240 mL) of whipped cream, use 1/2 cup (120 mL) of cream. For 4 cups (960 mL) of whipped cream, start with 2 cups (480 mL) of cream.

1. Whisk the cream, sugar equivalent, and vanilla in a cold bowl with a cold whisk.

2. Whip until it begins to stiffen. When you remove the whisk and a firm peak holds in place, you are done. Do not over whip the cream. If you over mix you begin to make a sweetened butter, which gets a strange texture and isn't as lovely.

3. Serve!

1/2 cup (120 mL) **heavy whipping cream**

1 Tbsp (15 mL) **sugar replacement**

1/2 tsp (2 mL) **vanilla extract**

PER SERVING
CALORIES: 52.03
FAT: 5.5
PROTEIN: 0.31
CARBS: 2.34
FIBER: 0
SUGAR ALCOHOLS: 1.88
NET CARBS: 0.47

MORE FACTS: P. 545

Salted Brown Butter Fat Bomb

SERVES: 6 · · · PREP: 10 MIN · · · COOK: 1 HR · · · TOTAL: 1 HR 10 MIN

1 1/2 cup (360 mL) **heavy whipping cream**

8 oz. (227 g) **full-fat cream cheese**, preferably warmed

1/2 cup (120 mL) **powdered sugar replacement**

1 tsp (5 mL) **salt**

There's a concept in cookery for brown butter or even *blackened* butter. Butter has what's called "milk solids" in it (including lactose, a form of milk sugar). It's also got butterfat and water. When you cook butter, it will start to caramelize and eventually burn. As it caramelizes, the flavors deepen and become more complex and reminiscent of the caramel flavor that we all likely know and love!

Butter, in its store-bought form, is mostly all fat. I wanted more milk solids to caramelize. In order to create a whole, tasty dessert, whose flavor stems from a single ingredient, that ingredient needs to be pronounced. The only way I could conceive to get enough caramelized flavor was to either caramelize *a lot* of butter, then skim off most of the butterfat (ghee, essentially) or start with heavy cream! We all know that butter comes from cream. If I started with cream, I'd get a lot more milk solids, thus... more flavor! YAY!

This is where this recipe becomes a bit tricky and odd, but if the idea of a spoonful of *Salted Caramel Cheesecake* sounds appealing to you, and you're willing to work for it... you can have it! Those that have actually sought this out and made it have declared that the time and effort were worth it. The flavor is indeed quite special!

Note: Sorry for the lengthy explanation on the reduction and breaking of the cream. It needs to be done slowly... *oh* soo slowly... and carefully watched; otherwise, it burns or boils over. It's a bit tricky, but in my opinion *very* worth it.

PER SERVING
CALORIES: 334.75
FAT: 34.88
PROTEIN: 3.53
CARBS: 19.88
FIBER: 0
SUGAR ALCOHOLS: 16.67
NET CARBS: 3.22

MORE FACTS: P. 541

1. Place the heavy cream on the stove, over low heat, to start reducing. Do not try to go too fast or hurry the process, because the cream will boil up the sides of the pot and overflow and make a big mess of your kitchen. You need to go with a very low simmer and just let it gurgle away for a while. It can take a good hour or two, but, in my personal opinion, it's worth it! The end result of these steps really is something almost magical.

2. Reduce the cream until it breaks and starts to color. (*Breaking* means that it will stop looking like cream. It will separate into clear liquid fat with stuff floating in it; this is a good thing, in this case.) *Do not* burn it. There's a point at which it's too dark and becomes bitter. Look for something that resembles a nice "sand at the beach" (floating in yellow butter fat). Much darker than a nice sandy color and it gets bitter. Too light in color and the flavors are not developed as well as they could be. It's a very fine line! It should be light brown/tan.

3. Once it's like little pebbles and the color of sand at the beach, set it aside. Keep it warm but not hot.

4. Add all ingredients to a food processor, except the warm browned butter. You can do this with a bowl and a whisk, but it's touchy. The food processor is the way to go.

5. Turn on the food processor.

6. With the processor running, *slowly* pour the melted butter into the cream cheese. It should emulsify and make something that looks almost like tan-colored mayonnaise. Pour *very* slowly, in a thin stream, to start. After the first 1/4 cup (60 mL) has been added, you may pour a little more quickly (still slowly though).

7. Divide into six small cups with lids. Chill completely before adding the lids.

8. Store in the refrigerator.

Sweet 'n' Spicy Fat Bomb

SERVES: 6 · · · PREP: 10 MIN · · · COOK: 5 MIN · · · TOTAL: 15 MIN

8 oz. (227 g) **full-fat cream cheese**, preferably warmed

1/2 cup (120 mL) **powdered sugar replacement**

1 tsp (5 mL) grated **fresh ginger**

1 tsp (5 mL) ground **cinnamon**

1/2 tsp (2 mL) ground **cloves**

1/4 tsp (1 mL) freshly ground **nutmeg**

3/4 cup (180 mL) **coconut oil**

I don't know what you call these things. No Bake Cheesecake in a Cup? Refrigerator Candy? Fat Bombs? Clouds? I've seen them come in a variety of shapes, sizes, and names.

In the end, the concept is pretty simple. Take cream cheese and blend it with fat, flavor, and something sweet. Eat! I love them because they are tasty, quick, easy to make, easy to eat, and cure any sweet desires. I know many people eat them to boost their fat intake. I often use them as a vehicle for coconut oil, rather than a morning shot or an oil slick floating in my coffee. I make these in all sorts of flavors. This one is *really* tasty. It's like a spiced cheesecake!

1. Add all ingredients to a food processor, except the coconut oil.

2. Turn on the food processor.

3. With the processor running, slowly pour the coconut oil into the cream cheese. It should emulsify and make something that looks almost like mayonnaise. Pour *very* slowly, in a thin stream, to start. After the first 1/4 cup has been added, you may pour a little more quickly (still slowly though).

4. Divide into six small cups with lids.

5. Refrigerate.

6. Eat!

PER SERVING
CALORIES: 372
FAT: 36.98
PROTEIN: 2.32
CARBS: 18.65
FIBER: 0.28
SUGAR ALCOHOLS: 16.67
NET CARBS: 1.7

MORE FACTS: P. 545

Vanilla Fat Bomb

SERVES: 6 · · · PREP: 10 MIN · · · COOK: 0 MIN · · · TOTAL: 10 MIN

This was one of the first recipes on my website, but I never actually promoted it or shared it heavily on the blog, thinking it wasn't much of a recipe. It's really just a simple and silly concoction taking only a minute to make.

One day, on a lark, I shared it on my Facebook page. BOOM!

It was like a (fat) bomb went off. That thing spread far and wide, resulting in the most traffic my website has ever had (as of this printing, I still haven't topped it). This recipe makes something along the lines of a basic cheesecake-flavored mousse. It's soft, sweet, and tasty. It's also a great base for other flavors. People fold and add all sorts of things to this one. This recipe is great for the end of the day or a snack. It satisfies a sweet tooth and the fat helps to satiate for hours. In retrospect...

Yeah, OK. ...I get it.

1. Add the first four ingredients to a food processor. If you don't have one, you can do this with a whisk and a bowl.

2. Turn on the food processor.

3. With the processor running, add the cream in a medium-slow and deliberate steady stream. This will whip the cream with the cream cheese. This will add air and will result in something like a cheesecake mousse once it chills.

4. Portion into cups and chill.

8 oz. (227 g) **full-fat cream cheese**, preferably warmed

1/2 cup (120 mL) **powdered sugar replacement**

a dash of **salt**

1 tsp (5 mL) **vanilla extract**

1/2 cup (120 mL) **heavy whipping cream**

PER SERVING
CALORIES: 199.84
FAT: 20.22
PROTEIN: 2.7
CARBS: 18.8
FIBER: 0
SUGAR ALCOHOLS: 16.67
NET CARBS: 2.13

MORE FACTS: P. 540

Raspberry-Cream Cheese Swirl Frozen Custard

SERVES: 6 · · · PREP: 30 MIN · · · COOK: 0 MIN · · · TOTAL: 1 HR 30 MIN

1/2 cup (120 mL) **heavy whipping cream**

1/2 cup (120 mL) unsweetened **almond milk**

3/4 cup (180 mL) **powdered sugar replacement**

3/4 tsp (4 mL) **xanthan gum** (optional)

a dash of **salt**

6 large **egg yolks**

1 tsp (5 mL) **vanilla extract**

12 oz. (341 g) **full-fat cream cheese**, room temperature

2 Tbsp (30 mL) **vegetable glycerin** (optional)

1 pint (240 mL) **raspberries**, washed

1 tsp (5 mL) fresh **lemon juice**

Somewhere early on in my experience with low-glycemic foods, I discovered that ice cream was a perfect tool for my newfound way of life. It was fairly easy to make, it was incredibly easy to portion and store in the freezer, a near infinite variety of flavors could be made, it was almost always excellent, and it somehow seemed a fitting way to end each day! I've made hundreds of flavors, but this one is easily in my top ten. It takes a few extra steps, but the contrasting swirls really make it worth it!

Note: Sugar, aside from adding sweetness to ice cream, also has behavioral properties that make it ideal for the scoopable texture and mouthfeel of ice cream. Sugar-free ice creams tend to freeze *very* hard and lose a lot of the soft, creamy texture. As a result, I've learned that making frozen custards (with cooked egg yolks) helps the texture a lot. A little xanthan gum and vegetable glycerin both aid the texture as well. These second two aren't required and don't alter the flavor, but the little addition really helps to create the perfect scoop and mouthfeel that many seek in an ice cream experience.

1. Bring a wide-mouthed pot or a base for a double boiler full of water up to a boil.

2. Combine cream and almond milk in a medium saucepan. Bring up to a very light simmer.

3. Combine the sweetener, xanthan gum, and salt. Mix them, so the xanthan is evenly distributed within the powder. Set aside.

4. Place the egg yolks and vanilla into a nonreactive metal bowl with a diameter just a bit wider than the mouth of the pot of boiling water (or the top of the double boiler). Whisk until they have a lemony color.

PER SERVING
CALORIES: 371.9
FAT: 31.76
PROTEIN: 7.40
CARBS: 40.24
FIBER: 3.67
SUGAR ALCOHOLS: 30
NET CARBS: 6.57

MORE FACTS: P. 542

DESSERTS

5. Add a little bit of the hot liquid into the egg yolks, while whisking (about 1 ounce or 30 mL). This will temper the eggs. Keep whisking while adding more of the hot liquid, adding a little more and a little faster, each moment. You want to add and whisk to incorporate the hot liquid without creating scrambled eggs. Keep whisking while pouring, until all the liquid has been incorporated.

6. Add the sweetener-xanthan mix, and whisk it in.

7. Place bowl (or double boiler) over the mouth of the boiling water and continue to whisk. Whisk well, consistently and constantly, moving around the edges of the bowl, or else you'll develop cooked/scrambled egg bits around the edge. If the bowl gets too hot, remove it from the heat for a moment and keep whisking. Never let scrambled eggs form. Alternate the location of the bowl, moving from the cool countertop back to the hot steam, slowly raising the heat of the egg mixture to about 165°F (74°C).

8. Once the mixture reaches about 165°F (74°C), has no frothy bubbles, and is noticeably thick, remove it from the heat and whisk in the room-temperature cream cheese and vegetable glycerin. The mixture will be quite thick and smooth (and delicious!).

9. Chill the mixture overnight (or, if you're in a hurry, like I usually am, I pour it into my ice cream machine, while still warm, which wears on the machine).

10. Once chilled, pour the mixture into your ice cream machine, following the instructions for your specific machine.

11. While the machine churns and chills the frozen custard base, puree the raspberries and lemon juice in a blender or food processor. Through a fine sieve, strain the seeds from the raspberry puree. Chill while the custard continues to churn.

12. When the custard base is "soft-serve ready," remove two-thirds of it and place in the freezer. To the remaining third, add the raspberry puree and turn the ice cream machine back on. It should quickly (10 to 15 minutes, depending on machine) form a nice raspberry ice cream. Once the raspberry ice cream forms, remove the original custard from the freezer. Scoop the raspberry ice cream on top of it and spread it to cover the cream cheese ice cream. Now, with a plastic spatula, fold the two flavors together, until an obvious swirl has formed.

13. Freeze or scoop into individual containers with lids and freeze!

SPONGE CAKE

SERVES: 4 · · · PREP: 15 MIN · · · COOK: 20 MIN · · · TOTAL: 35 MIN

4 large **whole eggs**, room temperature

1/2 tsp (2 mL) fresh **lemon juice**

1 Tbsp (15 mL) **coconut flour**

2 Tbsp (30 mL) **sugar replacement**

1 tsp (5 mL) **vanilla extract**

1 dash (1g) **salt**

This recipe actually began life as a blunder. I was fairly new to baking with coconut flour, but was feeling as if I'd finally understood it. I set out to produce a light and fluffy Angel Food Cake. My thinking was, I could aerate the eggs and the whole thing would bake and be held in place with the wee bit of coconut flour. It baked and rose like the glorious fantasy I had in mind... and just as quickly it deflated and fell... taking my low-primal baking prowess right along with it. Rather than stomp around, I renamed it *Sponge Cake* and declared it a delicious victory!

Since then, I've used it in all many of different things, such as Trifles (p. 436), strawberry shortcake, and even a Jelly Roll coated Ice Cream Bombe (**Plug Alert:** You'll need to check out my website for that one!). This is a great and versatile little recipe!

1. Preheat oven to 350°F (177°C).

2. Grease a pan. I used a standard loaf pan, but might suggest this would work well in a cake pan, if you want a fairly thin, tasty, cakey disc of some sort.

3. Separate the eggs into 4 yolks and 4 whites.

4. Whip the egg whites with the lemon juice, until firm peaks can be formed. Set aside.

5. Whisk together the sweetener, coconut flour, salt, vanilla, and egg yolks. Once it's a nice consistent lemon color, gently fold in 1/4 of the egg white mixture. Once the first 1/4 has been folded in, fold in another 1/4 of the egg white mixture. Continue adding portions of the egg whites, while folding, until you have a large delicate cloud of light yellow eggs.

6. Pour your egg cloud into your prepared pan and bake for 20 minutes, or until golden brown.

7. Remove from the oven and allow to cool.

8. Top, cut, stack, etc. It's up to you!

PER SERVING
CALORIES: 82.3
FAT: 5.19
PROTEIN: 6.94
CARBS: 2.31
FIBER: .75
SUGAR ALCOHOLS: .5
NET CARBS: 1.05

MORE FACTS: P. 542

Cook, Learn, and Experiment

This book is a compilation between the most popular recipes on my website, as well as several new ones which only appear in this book. The following recipe, however, was actually posted on the Holistically Engineered (www.HolisticallyEngineered.com) website, run by super-talented fellow blogger *Karen Sorenson*.

At the time she asked me to do it, I had only been blogging for a few months. To be asked by such a big blogger to contribute to her site was huge, so I set out to really bring it.

Over a year later, I still love what I contributed to her site. Rather than edit it down, like so many of the other recipes, I'm leaving this one intact, because it really shines a light on a variety of techniques, but it *also* shows the enthusiasm and passion with which I pursue cooking. My hope is that not only will you read the following passage and pick up some tasty new tricks, but also pick up the bug I've been infected with, which is a true and deep desire to *cook, learn, and experiment*.

Great pies may result!

Salted Brown Butter Pecan Pie with Chocolate Ganache

SERVES: 8 · · · PREP: 20 MIN · · · COOK: 90 MIN · · · TOTAL: 8 HR

We're going to get down and dirty with a Salted Brown Butter Pecan Pie topped with Chocolate Ganache and Whipped Cream. Oh yeah!

I should say, however, that this is a *long* slice of pie! Don't let the length intimidate you. I could've easily written this as a short and sweet recipe but chose to make it educational. It's instructional, rather than simple-step oriented. Ultimately, the pie does take a lot of time and patience, but the actual steps involved aren't that time-consuming or dramatic. It's just a lot of hang time.

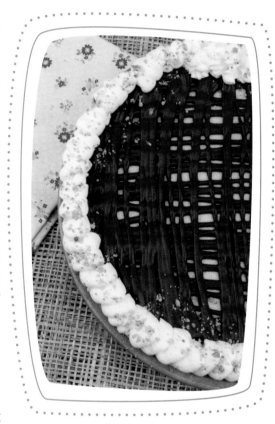

In any event, this recipe is quite a lot of fun! It utilizes some interesting techniques, which allow us to get a caramel flavor without any sugar! On top of being a sugar-free pie, it's also gluten free, grain free, and very low carb!

Some of the interesting topics we'll cover are:

- Nut crusts
- Caramel flavor without sugar (hint: it comes from cream)
- Emulsions
- Gelatin
- Chocolate
- Finally, the recipe itself!

Bored-to-tears note: For those that just want the goods, you can just skip all my rambling drivel and ballyhoo and skip to the recipe at the bottom of my gargantuan gastronomic treatise. However, for those wanting to take a deeper peek into a pie than you've ever done... read on!

Nut Crusts

First, we'll get into the nut crust. Nut crusts are an incredible way to go. Sure, I've had people complain and lament that they miss their tender, flakey crusts. I get it, but I also recognize that nut crusts are texturally interesting and delectable in their own right. They're also just about impossible to mess up!

If you take about 1 1/2 cup (360 mL) of just about any kind of nut and pulverize it, then mix it with 1/4 cup (60 mL) melted butter, you've got a solid crust. Simply push the "dough" into the base of a pie pan, prebake it, and fill it up. What results is a pie by every definition I know! Sure, it's a little on the crumbly side, but it's absolutely scrumptious, you can slice cleanly through it, it provides plenty of structure, it lends a pleasant texture, and it looks fantastic! I'll often add seasonings to it—perhaps a dash of salt, a dribble of vanilla, and even a tablespoon of honey to help bind it.

GASP! HONEY?!

Yep! One measly little tablespoon of honey spread across eight or so slices of pie doesn't add much in the way of flavor or carbs, but it *does* help to keep the crust in one piece. Have you ever touched honey? It's sticky! The sugar acts like a glue, binding it all together.

Nuts I've tried: pecans, walnuts, coconut, peanuts, macadamias, almonds, and hazelnuts. One of the strangest aspects of this is that smashing the nuts myself tends to yield the best crust! I really don't know why this is, but... it is.

I've tried pulverizing the nuts in a food processor. This works well and is quick! I've tried using pre-ground meals and flours. This is also quite easy to do, but is a little more costly. Each of these methods results in a nice and even crust, but it tends to be crumbly and doesn't hold together quite as well. For a crust that really seems to hold its own, oddly, the best method is to take whole nuts, chop them a bit, then place them in a large bag, and whack at them with a rolling pin, mallet, or the bottom of a pan. It's just as good for crust making as it is for releasing stress! Just whack the bag until the nuts are evenly pulverized but not nut butter-fied.

Coconut note: Coconuts don't really pulverize like other nuts. I've found this can work as a pure layer of compressed shredded coconut with a little honey, but it works best blended with another nut.

Caramel Flavor

There is a very distinct flavor that comes from the slow, methodical burning of sugars. A deep and complex essence rises from the otherwise clean, clear sweet of pure crystalline sucrose. How would one go about achieving a similar flavor without sugar? This question vexed me for a while, but then it hit me one day. BUTTER!

You can brown butter, which will give a similarly deep and rich flavor, but without all the carbs! The problem with butter, unfortunately, is that it's almost all butterfat! This isn't a problem from a macronutrient standpoint, but one concerned with the stuff within it! Butter is approximately 80 percent butterfat, 19 percent water, and only 1 percent stuff. The "stuff" (generally referred to as "milk solids" or "serum solids") is where the flavor lives! That mixture of tasty goodness is made of lactose (milk sugars), caseins, whey proteins, and minerals.

For the purposes of our pie, it's only the milk solids that we want to caramelize. With such a tiny overall percentage, it's going to take colossal amounts of butter to make our pie taste like anything but straight-up glorious butter!

One option would be to take a mountain of butter and cook it until the water completely evaporates. You can pour off the rest of the butterfat and use it for cooking. It is toasted clarified butter—ghee, to be more specific. What milk solids remain at the bottom of your pot can be further browned for yummy awesomeness. Unfortunately, this is a mammoth feat and totally unrealistic, unless you're a restaurant with a full staff and a major need for ghee.

Another, far more realistic approach would be to brown cream. Butter is made from cream after all, is it not? Just churn the stuff and you'll get butter! AHA!

If you take cream and place it on the stove over very low heat, the water will eventually evaporate. Again, we will be left with a mixture of butterfat and milk solids. However, *this* time, the ratio is stacked *much* more in our flavor. Cream has about 3 to 4 times the milk solids but near double the water. If you eliminate the water, your new ratio is about 7 to 8 times milk solids to butterfat. *Much* better! WOO-HOO!

Caramelizing these milk solids and then sweetening them will render a tasty caramel-flavored concoction!

Emulsions

Here we're going to get deeper into the scientific fun! Have you ever heard the phrase "cream rises to the top"? This is because cream is mostly fat, which has a lower density than water. This means it weighs less than water by volume. As a result, it floats to the top much in the same way oil floats above vinegar. It doesn't want to mix or stay put.

Most creams purchased in the store are homogenized. This means that the cream can no longer rise to the top! The homogenization process—a high-pressurized process pushing milk/cream through small, tapered tubes, shrinking the fat globules—creates a colloid emulsion. The end result? The tiny little globules of fat have been evenly dispersed and distributed within the "water," creating a smooth and consistent cream, which will never separate. Mayonnaise is another colloid emulsion; it occurs when fat is whipped with water and eggs.

Breaking an emulsion is the term cooks and foodies use for screwing up a mayonnaise, buerre blanc, or hollandaise sauce. It's usually followed by throwing a pan, stomping around, and swearing a lot. It's so easy to do! Most of the time, breaking an emulsion is a bad thing, because getting the emulsion to start can be such a pickle! Not this time. We *want* to break the cream!

At this point, you're probably asking yourself why I'm going through all of this. Two reasons:

1. It's hopefully interesting reading.
2. In order for us to make our brown butter pie with cream, we're going to need to break the cream's emulsion. We need to break it so that we can caramelize the milk solids. Then, we're going to re-emulsify it, with eggs and more homogenized cream.

There is a method to this madness!

Store-bought heavy cream is emulsified by engineered machines. It is designed not to separate, which makes this process a little strange. If you take a stick of butter and melt it, the emulsion breaks immediately. Breaking a store-bought cream requires time and patience.

The first step? Put cream on the stove!

Cream has a tendency to sit there, getting hotter and hotter, looking back at you with docile innocence… until you look away. When you least expect it, it will rage up into a bubbling frenzy of white foam, flowing over the edge of your pot, and making a big mess of your stove.

You know it's true. Pesky cream!

To stop this from happening, place a wooden spoon across the top of your pan. When the frenetic cream hits the spoon, it will immediately calm down and settle to the bottom of the pan. I also suggest bringing the cream up to a boil… *slowly*.

Once the cream is up and simmering, just let it gurgle away for a while. It can take a good hour or two, but, in my own personal opinion, it's worth it. The end result of these steps really is something almost magical. Reduce the cream (evaporate the water out of it) until it breaks and starts to color. DO NOT burn it. There's a point at which it's too dark and becomes bitter. Look for something that resembles a nice "sand at the beach" (floating in yellow butter fat). Much darker than a nice sandy color and it gets bitter. Too light in color and the flavors are not developed as well as they could be. It's a very fine line! It should be light brown/tan.

Once it's like little pebbles and the color of sand at the beach, set it aside. Keep it warm but not hot. We now have the basis for our caramel flavor, via a browned and broken cream emulsion. We're cooking now!

Gelatin

Gelatin might be some of the weirdest stuff on earth, right up there with aerogel and non-Newtonian fluids (i.e., cornstarch slurry). In simple terms, it's what gives Jell-O its shape and jiggle. It's usually bought in powdered form but can also be bought in little sheets that feel like plastic. Dissolve these powders or sheets into a warm liquid and then let it chill. It will firm up the entirety of the liquid and become a jiggling, gelatinous mass of bouncy wonkiness.

I first learned about using powdered gelatin back in culinary school, somewhere in the middle of the nineteenth century. I learned how to apply it to meats and fishes, an interesting branch of cookery known as *charcuterie*. Gelatin was used to firm things up, give shapes to meats and sauces that have no shape, suspend ingredients in "space," etc.

Gelatin was fun but old school, and I never really used it in modern kitchens (of the early '90s). I think it's seeing a bit of a revival (and rightly so... it's good for you!).

A little while back, I was trying to think of induction-friendly dessert recipes and thought panna cotta would do the trick. Panna cotta is little more than sweetened cream held into a molded shape with gelatin. That day, I made all sort of other desserts, but the Panna Cotta (p. 410) was the clear winner. This got me to thinking about gelatin and all its applications. It can really be applied to anything with water in it: sweet *or* savory. A little gives you a little structure and jiggle, and a lot will give you something firm and solid. It is odorless and tasteless. So it's little more than a gel, which would work in a glass of water, a bowl of ginger-infused chicken broth and freshly suspended cilantro leaves, as well as strawberry juice and cocoa powder mixed with cream and almond milk.

So, what is it? Where does it come from? You really probably don't want to know (short answer: animal skins, bones, and connective tissues... bleh).

We're going to use the gelatin to firm up a brown butter custard emulsion that we're about to make! This is done by "blooming" the gelatin in cold liquid while heating the rest. Blooming means we're going to sprinkle the unflavored gelatin powder evenly over the surface of (just about any) cold liquid. This allows the granules to plump in an even fashion, without clumping. It won't work properly if the liquid is warm.

In this case, we're going to make a custard base with egg yolks, almond milk, and cream. We're then going to briskly whisk the warm brown butter solution into the eggs, which will once again suspend the tiny fat globules within the water—an emulsion. We'll whisk this new brown butter custard into the blooming gelatin and pour the whole thing into our prebaked crust.

Time to chill out!

Chocolate

We're about to have some fun! We're going to make a sugar-free chocolate ganache. Ganache is a mixture of chocolate and cream, which is used as a glaze or a chocolate filling. A small amount of cream will yield something firm and perfect for a filling or layer between cakes. A larger amount of cream will yield something softer and more pliable. Even more and you have a decadent chocolate sauce—break out the strawberries!

Sugar-free chocolate can be a bit tough, unless using some of the more nefarious sugar alcohols, like sorbitol and mannitol, both of which are "technically" sugar free from a legal labeling standpoint, but they both have fairly significant impacts on blood sugar, as well as...

...too much of these sugar alcohols and you might offend your fellow guests with your periodic contributions to the room. (Many experience some gastrointestinal distress when they eat too many sugar alcohols.) This is why I often suggest an erythritol-based sweetener, which is all natural and has virtually no impact on blood sugar.

What I really like about this approach is it makes a delicious chocolate ganache, it's incredibly easy to make, and it's incredibly low-primal.

All we're going to do is heat up some cream, dissolve our sweetener into it, pour it over chopped up unsweetened chocolate, whisk it until melted, and... that's it! Hot ganache! The recipe I'm giving will firm up into a semisolid state—perfect for topping a pie.

When the ganache is warm, it will be pourable. It will thicken as it cools. Pour your warm ganache into a squirt bottle and quickly go back and forth over the top of the pie. This is how I convince people I know what I'm doing when the reality is it's just quick random squirting. Go up and down one way, then turn the pie 90 degrees and do it again—elegant lattice art!

This method tends to leave messy edges. This is where a little whipped cream comes in handy around the rim.

Maybe a few crumbled pecans to cover any blemishes and we have a massively delicious, super interesting, nearly impossible feat of pie!

1. First, start by putting a small pot on the stove. Measure out 2 cups (480 mL) of cream and place it on the stove to slowly reduce. Be careful not to let it boil over. The reduction process can take over an hour but can go faster if you're attentive, stir often, and watch it over a higher heat. I tend to go super slow and just go do other things around the house.

2. Reduce the cream until it breaks and starts to color. Look for something that resembles a nice "sand at the beach" (floating in yellow butter fat). Much darker than a nice sandy color and it gets bitter. Too light in color and the flavors are not developed as well as they could be. It's a very fine line! It should be light brown/tan.

3. Once it's like little pebbles and the color of sand at the beach, set it aside. Keep it warm but not hot.

4. Preheat oven to 325°F (163°C).

5. If your pecans are not crushed, place them in a large plastic (sandwich style) bag. With a mallet or the edge of a pot or pan, whack at them until you have a squooshed bag of pecan explosion. (I've tried this in a food processor, and for whatever reason, the imperfect smashing method gives a better crust than nuts cleanly pulverized in a food processor.)

6. Pour your crushed pecans into a mixing bowl, and add your honey (you can skip the honey, but it does help to hold the crust together) and melted butter. Mix the ingredients until the nuts are well coated with the honey and butter.

7. Grease a 9-inch (23 x 5 cm) pie pan.

8. Press the nut mixture into the pie pan. Use the back of a spoon (or a tamper if you have one) to press the crust firmly into the base and up the sides of the pan. Really get in there and press it firm.

9. Bake the crust for 12 minutes or until golden brown. Remove and allow the crust to cool.

10. In a large measuring cup, mix together 1 1/2 cup (360 mL) heavy cream (reserving one last 1/2 cup [120 mL] for the ganache) and the 1 1/2 cup (360 mL) unsweetened almond milk.

4 cups (960 mL) **heavy cream**, divided

1 1/2 cups (360 mL) **finely crushed pecans**

1/4 cup (60 mL) **melted butter**

1 Tbsp (15 mL) **honey** (optional)

1 1/2 cup (360 mL) **unsweetened almond milk**

2 packets (14g or 25 mL) of **gelatin** (about 4 1/2 to 5 tsp total)

1 1/4 cup (300 mL) **sugar replacement**, divided

1 tsp (5 mL) **vanilla extract**

1 tsp (5 mL) **salt**

6 large **egg yolks**

2 1/2 oz. (70 g) **unsweetened baking chocolate squares**, broken and chopped

1 Tbsp (15 mL) **butter**, cubed

PER SERVING
CALORIES: 659.39
FAT: 67.39
PROTEIN: 9.05
CARBS: 49.22
FIBER: 3.63
SUGAR ALCOHOLS: 37.5
NET CARBS: 8.1

MORE FACTS: P. 542

11. Pour 1/2 cup (120 mL) of your cream-almond milk blend into a large mixing bowl. Evenly sprinkle your gelatin over the entire surface area of the cream-almond mixture in the mixing bowl. Set the bowl aside, to allow the gelatin to bloom.

12. Place a large pot of water or the base of a double boiler on the stove to boil.

13. Pour the remaining cream-almond milk mixture into a saucepan and bring it up to a very low simmer. Once it simmers, whisk in your vanilla, 1 cup (240 mL) of the sugar replacement, and salt. Whisk until the sugar and salt have completely dissolved.

14. Put your egg yolks into the top of a double boiler, or in the base of a mixing bowl that is wider than the mouth of the pot of water on your stove. Whisk the eggs until they are broken and a little frothy. Pour a small amount of your hot sweetened cream-almond milk mixture into the egg yolks and briskly whisk. This act (called *tempering*) will prevent scrambled eggs. As you whisk, continue pouring the hot liquid into the yolks. Be sure you continue whisking as you do this, or else you'll end up with scrambled eggs (or very small egg particles).

15. When you are done whisking the cream-almond milk mixture into the eggs, *slowly* whisk in your broken browned-cream mixture. It's imperative that you do this carefully. Do not just dump it in there and whisk it, as it will stay broken. We need to re-emulsify this broken solution into the egg yolk mixture. Start by pouring a slow stream of the butterfat into the yolk mixture while whisking. Continue pouring and whisking until you get to the browned, grainy lumps at the bottom. Pour these in as well! When you are done, you should have a *delicious* light yellow mixture with little browned sandy flecks spread throughout.

16. Place this bowl over the top of your boiling water and continue whisking, so that it slowly heats up but without the edges of the bowl ever cooking the eggs. Keep it moving in the bowl. If the bowl gets too hot, remove it from the top of the water for a minute, while whisking, then place it back over the top of the water. The heat from the steam will "cook" the bottom of the bowl at approximately 212°F (100°C). When the mixture coats the back of a spoon and/or hits a temperature of about 165°F (74°C), you can remove it from the stove.

17. Pour your hot custard base over the top of your bloomed gelatin and whisk. Whisk until the gelatin is completely dissolved.

18. Pour your custard mixture into your prepared piecrust and place in the refrigerator to cool. Allow it to chill for about 6 hours (or overnight).

19. To make your ganache, heat up your remaining 1/2 cup (120 mL) cream on the stove. Once your cream is hot and is about to simmer, whisk in your 1/4 cup (60 mL) remaining sugar replacement until it has dissolved.

20. Place your chopped chocolate pieces and butter cubes into a small mixing bowl. Pour your hot cream mixture over the chocolate and whisk it in the bowl until the chocolate is fully melted and incorporated.

21. Pour your chocolate into a squirt bottle and squirt parallel lines of chocolate over the top of the pie, until half of the ganache is gone. Turn the pie about 90 degrees and spread the other half in a similar manner, but beware the inevitable spray that occurs near the end of the chocolate! (If you don't have a squirt bottle, you can just spread this in an even layer over the top of the pie with a spatula.)

22. Chill the pie for about 30 minutes, to allow the chocolate to firm up.

23. At this point, your pie is done! You can add some whipped cream around the rim, to hide the "seams," but this is totally optional.

24. Slice and eat! (**Tip:** If you heat a knife under hot tap water for 30 seconds, then wipe it dry and slice the pie, you'll get a cleaner slice. Heat and dry the blade between each slice for clean, perfect slices!)

25. Enjoy!

*Net carb count: 8.1 net carbs (per serving—yields 8 large servings). Omitting the optional honey drops the net carbs to 5.98 net carbs, per slice (1/8 of the pie).

Raspberry Mocha Sorbet

SERVES: 16 · · · PREP: 5 MIN · · · COOK: 2 MIN · · · TOTAL: 20 MIN

3/4 cup (180 mL) **powdered sugar replacement**

1/3 cup (80 mL) **unsweetened cocoa powder**

3/4 tsp (4 mL) **xanthan gum** (optional)

a dash of **salt**

2 cups (480 mL) **hot espresso** and/or **strong coffee**

1 pint (480 mL) **raspberries**, washed

2 Tbsp (30 mL) **vegetable glycerin** (optional)

I make a lot of ice cream. This particular batch was a Raspberry Mocha Sorbet... a bit of a departure from my normal fare. Normally, I go with frozen custards and then toss wacky stuff into it, like toasted pine nuts, rosemary, and orange zest, or a crazy salted brown butter. It's fairly unusual for me to make a granita, sorbet, or sherbet, but I am always playing with new ideas. I would best describe the taste as "like being kicked in the tongue by a chocolate Easter bunny." It's a *seriously* strong flavor, almost overwhelming to eat, but I confess to absolutely loving it!

It's three incredibly potent flavors, but the end result is a strong, sweet, perfumed, lightly bitter, and perferctly balanced member of the iced desserts family.

One of the key aspects to this particular flavor lies in its strength. After one small scoop, I'm done. It overwhelms the senses. Portion control... baked right in!

Two large scoops would be overkill.

Note: Sugar, aside from adding sweetness to ice creams, also has behavioral properties that make it ideal for the scoopable texture and mouthfeel of ice cream. Sugar-free ice creams tend to freeze *very* hard and lose a lot of the soft and smooth texture. As a result, I've learned that making frozen custards (with cooked egg yolks) helps the texture a lot, due to the lecithin within the yolks. A little xanthan gum and vegetable glycerin both aid the texture as well. While this recipe isn't a frozen custard, the xanthan and vegetable glycerin *can* both really help the texture. They aren't required and don't alter the flavor, but the little addition really helps to create the perfect scoop and mouthfeel that many seek in a sorbet experience.

PER SERVING
CALORIES: 23.24
FAT: 0.5
PROTEIN: 0.6
CARBS: 14.7
FIBER: 1.95
SUGAR ALCOHOLS: 11.25
NET CARBS: 1.5

MORE FACTS: P. 545

1. In a small mixing bowl, combine powdered sweetener, cocoa powder, xanthan gum, and salt. Mix, so that the xanthan is evenly distributed within the powder. This helps prevent clumping.

2. In a medium pot on the stove, bring the strong coffee to a low simmer.

3. Whisk the powder mixture into the coffee until dissolved and the liquid has somewhat thickened. Chill the liquid in the refrigerator.

4. While the liquid chills, puree the raspberries in a blender or food processor. Through a fine sieve, strain the seeds from the raspberry puree. Whisk the vegetable glycerin into the puree. Chill.

5. Once all liquids are chilled, pour them into an ice cream machine. Follow the instructions for your machine.

6. Some time later, once the proper texture has been achieved, remove from the machine and freeze in one large freezer-proof container, or several small ones.

7. Enjoy!

CRÈME PÂTISSIÈRE (PASTRY CREAM)

SERVES: 18 · · · PREP: 1 MIN · · · COOK: 15 MIN · · · TOTAL: 16 MIN

1 1/2 cups (360 mL) **heavy whipping cream**

1 1/2 cup (360 mL) unsweetened **almond milk**

1 (12 g) **vanilla bean**, split lengthwise (or 2 tsp [10 mL] vanilla extract)

3/4 cup (180 mL) **sugar replacement**

3 Tbsp (45 mL) **tapioca flour**

1 tsp (5 mL) **glucomannan powder**

a dash of **salt**

9 large **egg yolks**

I *love* pastry cream! This is the magical pudding-like custard you'll find inside a cream-filled doughnut, éclair, cream puff, pastry tart, cream horn, or a nice full Boston cream pie! One of my absolute favorite desserts is one called *mille-feuille* (pronounced something like "meel fwee," it means "thousand leaves"), which is alternating puff pastry and crème pâtissière, which is then frosted, usually with some kind of fun berry or chocolate design. I tried to make this for years, always running into issues of consistency. It would be too thin, or it would turn chunky, or it would simply be a custard. I had to reach outside of typical low-carb ingredients into something occasionally found in the Paleo landscape to achieve the desired consistency. The tapioca flour slightly boosts the carb counts, but... in return, I get pastry cream! Hello, true trifles!

Note: Makes roughly eighteen 1/4-cup (60 mL) servings.

Second note: Resulting in a total of about 4 1/2 cups (1 L), I readily admit that this recipe is quite large. The primary reason for its size is the small amount of glucomannan in relation to its strength. The glucomannan is a powerful thickener, but it takes on some bizarre qualities in too high a concentration. If I were to write this recipe as a much smaller recipe, then it would ask for 1/4 tsp (1 mL) of glucomannan, which really dramatically decreases the margin for error. My suggestion is to have a plan for lots of pastry cream for the first try. Be prepared to make a super huge trifle or two Boston cream pies, with hungry mouths nearby. Once you see how it works, then tweak the recipe the second time and cut it into thirds, resulting in only about 1 1/2 cups (360 mL), or about six 1/4-cup (60 mL) servings.

PER SERVING
CALORIES: 105.1
FAT: 9.86
PROTEIN: 1.95
CARBS: 12.51
FIBER: 0.31
SUGAR ALCOHOLS: 10
NET CARBS: 2.2

MORE FACTS: P. 544

Third note: The texture is thick, like a pudding, but it still somewhat pools. For a slightly thicker mixture that holds up as a filling in something like a cake, add 1 to 2 more tablespoons of tapioca flour.

Fourth note: Another trick to create a lighter, thicker cream that can also be piped is to fold in whipped cream. This will thicken and aerate the pastry cream.

Fifth note: Just sayin' hi!

1. Combine cream and almond milk in a medium saucepan. Split the vanilla beans lengthwise, and scrape the seeds from the vanilla bean. Add the pod and seeds to the milk and cream. Bring the milk to a slow simmer.

2. While the liquid heats, in a separate small mixing bowl, combine the sweetener, tapioca, glucomannan, and salt. Mix them together and set aside.

3. In a separate large mixing bowl, whisk the eggs well. Set aside.

4. Strain the hot liquid, to remove the vanilla pods.

5. Very, very slowly, whisk the hot milk mixture into the egg yolks. Whisk quickly, so as to incorporate the hot liquid evenly, without cooking or scrambling the eggs. This is called tempering the eggs. Once the liquid has been incorporated into the eggs, pour the milk-egg mixture back into the saucepan and return to a low heat.

6. Whisk the powder mixture into the hot liquid. Make sure it dissolves.

7. Stir consistently until the sauce thickens. The temperature should be at or just above 165°F (74°C). Whatever you do, do not boil this mixture. The cream will thicken a bit more as it chills.

8. Pour into a wide and shallow container, like a casserole pan. Place in the refrigerator to cool. It is ready when it is fully chilled, about 2 to 4 hours.

Strawberry and Whipped Sour Cream Trifle

SERVES: 4 · · · PREP: 10 MIN · · · COOK: 0 MIN · · · TOTAL: 10 MIN

1 1/2 cup (360 mL) **strawberries**, washed, stems removed, and diced

3 Tbsp (45 mL) **powdered sugar replacement**, divided

a dash of **salt**

1/2 cup (120 mL) **heavy whipping cream**

1/2 cup (120 mL) **sour cream**

1 tsp (5 mL) **vanilla extract**

1 recipe **Sponge Cake (p. 420)**

1 cup (240 mL) **Pastry Cream (p. 434)**

Note: This recipe is designed for little 1-cup (240 mL) portions. In the photos, I'd found some pretty cool little 8 oz. plastic cups, but obviously this recipe can be cut and scaled and divided into family sized or even larger sizes for things like potlucks. Just make more of the ingredients and layer it all into a nice big bowl and share with friends and family!

PER SERVING
CALORIES: 368.28
FAT: 31.62
PROTEIN: 9.89
CARBS: 32.94
FIBER: 2.18
SUGAR ALCOHOLS: 21.75
NET CARBS: 9.01

MORE FACTS: P. 543

This one comes from my memory as a kid. I started working in restaurants at about fourteen years old, but prior to that, I cooked at home quite often. I ran an underground candy-making business, focusing primarily on hard-candy suckers, but I'd also build houses and various shapes and molds with chocolates. I was known to whip up Chicken and Dumplings (p. 274) or Cioppino (p. 165) for the family. I also remember making trifles. Oh, how I *loved* trifles! As a kid, whipping up one of these brightly colored, layered desserts, in this large fancy glass bowl we had—to me, it was *fancy*. I'm not sure if I understood high-end foods at that age. I just knew that this was the best thing I knew how to make. If I was looking to impress someone with my twelve-year-old culinary prowess, I would whip up a trifle, making my own lady fingers, macerating my own berries, thickening my own pudding (from a box—you know... I was a kid!), etc. I'd carefully layer it all together and then strut, swagger, and gloat. Perfection!

1. In a small mixing bowl, combine the strawberries with 1 tablespoon (15 mL) of sweetener and salt. Mix together and set aside.

2. In a medium bowl, whip the cream, sour cream, vanilla, 2 Tbsp (30 mL) of the sweetener, and salt. Whip to stiff peaks and set aside.

3. Cut the sponge cake into 12 pieces (I cut circles, with a cookie cutter, to match the shape of my cups, but really any shape will do).

4. Place one piece of sponge cake in the bottom of a cup. Top it with a heaping tablespoon of pastry cream and whipped sour cream. Also add about 2 tablespoons (30 mL) of berries. Repeat this process two more times, topping with the remaining berries. Enjoy!

Almond Joy Thumbprint Cookies

SERVES: 8 · · · PREP: 25 MIN · · · COOK: 15 MIN · · · TOTAL: 1 HR

1/2 cup (120 mL) **unsalted butter**, room temperature and divided

1 cup (240 mL) **unsweetened almond butter**

3/4 cup (180 mL) **powdered sugar replacement**, divided

2 large **whole eggs**

1 tsp (5 mL) **vanilla extract**

1/4 cup (60 mL) **coconut flour**

a dash of **salt**

1/2 cup (120 mL) **heavy whipping cream**

2 1/2 oz. (70 g) **unsweetened baking chocolate squares**, broken and chopped

1/4 cup (60 mL) **unsweetened** shredded **coconut**

I've personally never had a huge sweet tooth, but when I did enjoy something sweet, sweetened coconut was often high on my list. Thankfully, coconut is not only delicious, but it's also good for us! I wanted to recreate the basic flavors in the Almond Joy candy bar, knowing that the combination works and also contains ingredients which tend to have low natural sugars and lots of good fats and flavors. Welcome to these tantalizing Almond Joy Thumbprints!

Serving size: The cookies can really be made any size. As printed, the intention is to make roughly 24 cookies, resulting in 3 cookies per serving.

1. Preheat oven to 350°F (177°C).

2. Line two baking sheets with parchment paper or silicone mats.

3. Cut a 1 tablespoon (15 mL) slice of butter and set it in the refrigerator to cool. Add the remaining butter, almond butter, and 1/2 cup (120 mL) of sweetener to a medium-sized mixing bowl. Preferably with an electric mixer, whip until the mixture is creamed or nicely aerated and the color has lightened.

4. Whip in the eggs and vanilla.

5. Add the coconut flour and salt to the mixing bowl, and combine until a nice dough has formed.

6. Scoop the dough into 1-inch (2.5 cm) balls with a cookie or ice cream scoop. Place about 2 inches (5 cm) apart on the prepared baking sheets. Press a thumbprint into the center of each ball, about 1/2 inch (1 cm) deep.

PER SERVING
CALORIES: 544.94
FAT: 52.31
PROTEIN: 11.56
CARBS: 34.94
FIBER: 7.56
SUGAR ALCOHOLS: 22.5
NET CARBS: 4.88

MORE FACTS: P. 543

7. Bake the cookies until the edges are golden, about 15 minutes. Remove and allow to cool.

8. While the cookies cool, make your chocolate ganache by heating up your cream on the stove. Once your cream is hot and is just about to simmer, whisk in your remaining 1/4 cup (60 mL) sweetener, until it has dissolved.

9. Take your chilled tablespoon of butter and cut it into 9 small cubes.

10. Place your chopped chocolate pieces and butter cubes into a small mixing bowl. Pour your hot cream mixture over the chocolate and whisk it in the bowl, until the chocolate is fully melted and incorporated.

11. Pour your warm chocolate into a pastry bag with a large tip. Pipe a nice even glob of chocolate into the indentation of each cooled cookie.

12. While the chocolate is still warm and soft, sprinkle the shredded coconut over the tops.

13. Allow the cookies to fully cool, so that the chocolate hardens to a fudge consistency. Enjoy!

SNICKERDOODLES

SERVES: 6 · · · PREP: 25 MIN · · · COOK: 15 MIN · · · TOTAL: 1 HR

1/2 cup (120 mL) **unsalted butter**, room temperature and divided

3/4 cup + 2 Tbsp (210 mL) **powdered sugar replacement**, divided

1 large **whole egg**

1 tsp (5 mL) **vanilla extract**

3/4 cup + 1 Tbsp (195 mL) **almond flour**

2 1/2 Tbsp (38 mL) **coconut flour**

2 1/2 Tbsp (38 mL) **tapioca flour**

2 1/2 Tbsp (38 mL) ground **white chia seeds**

1 1/2 tsp (8 mL) **baking powder**

a dash of **salt**

1 tsp (5 mL) **cinnamon**, ground

This one has kind of a funny backstory. Having just discovered how wonderful a little bit of tapioca flour is in baking, I decided I was the king of the universe. I threw a bunch of ingredients together (almond flour, coconut flour, tapioca flour, and some ground chia seeds) and dubbed it "DJ's Magic Mix." The plan was for it to be my personal baking blend that my recipes would revolve around. I set out, armed with my new magic mix, to bake a wide and far-reaching variety of cookies with it. I believe I tried about 14 different cookie recipes with my magic mix and... they were almost all dry, scratchy, and a bit on the inedible side... except for *this* tasty cookie right here! (Ok, and the Mexican Wedding Cookies [p. 442].) This is why the amounts are all a bit askew. The end results, however, were every bit as snickerdoodle as a snickerdoodle ever was!

Serving size: The cookies can really be made any size. As printed, the intention is to make roughly 18 cookies, resulting in 3 cookies per serving.

1. Preheat oven to 400°F (204°C).

2. To a medium-sized mixing bowl, add the butter and 3/4 cup (180 mL) of sweetener. Preferably with an electric mixer, whip until the mixture is creamed, or nicely aerated and the color has lightened.

3. Whip in the eggs and vanilla.

4. Add the almond, coconut, tapioca, and chia flours with the baking powder and salt to the mixing bowl. Combine until a nice dough has formed.

5. On a plate, or in a pie pan, combine the remaining 2 tablespoons (30 mL) of sweetener, with the cinnamon.

PER SERVING
CALORIES: 418.08
FAT: 40.65
PROTEIN: 6.24
CARBS: 45.19
FIBER: 4.72
SUGAR ALCOHOLS: 35
NET CARBS: 5.47

MORE FACTS: P. 543

6. Scoop the dough into 1-inch (2.5 cm) balls with a cookie or ice cream scoop. Drop each ball onto the plate with the sweetened cinnamon powder and then place about 2 inches (5 cm) apart on the prepared baking sheet. Repeat until each dough ball has been coated and arranged.

7. Bake the cookies until the edges are golden, about 10 minutes. Remove and allow to cool. Enjoy!

Mexican Wedding Cookies

SERVES: 6 · · · PREP: 5 MIN · · · COOK: 15 MIN · · · TOTAL: 45 MIN

1/2 cup (120 mL) **unsalted butter**, room temperature and divided

1/2 cup (120 mL) **powdered sugar replacement**, divided

1 cup + 2 Tbsp (270 mL) **almond flour**

2 Tbsp (30 mL) **coconut flour**

2 Tbsp (30 mL) **tapioca flour**

2 Tbsp (30 mL) ground **white chia seeds**

1 tsp (5 mL) **vanilla extract**

a dash of **salt**

These hard, white, little ball cookies are some of my favorites. They're almond flavored and coated with a soft, white powdered sweetener, traditionally sugar. While these are, indeed, eaten at Mexican weddings (known as *biscochitos*), they're also found quite often on the dinner buffet of many countries around the world on a variety of holidays. This type of cookie is also known as Russian tea cakes, Italian wedding cookies, butterballs, and even moldy mice. The origin is murky, but it's generally believed these were brought to Mexico by European nuns, back in the day.

Serving size: The cookies can really be made any size. As printed, the intention is to make roughly 18 cookies, resulting in 3 cookies per serving.

Cooling note: Because I tend to use a powdered erythritol blend, there is a very slight cooling sensation when these cookies are enjoyed. Interestingly, on this particular cookie, I find it to be a quite pleasant complement!

1. Preheat oven to 350°F (177°C).

2. Line a baking sheet with parchment paper or silicone mats.

3. To a medium-sized mixing bowl, add the butter and 1/4 cup (60 mL) of sweetener. Preferably with an electric mixer, whip until the mixture is creamed or nicely aerated and the color has lightened in color.

4. Mix in the almond, coconut, tapioca, chia flour and vanilla with a dash of salt to the mixing bowl and combine until a nice dough has formed. You may need to add a teaspoon or two (5 mL) of water to get it to form a dry, cohesive dough, as opposed to moist crumbles.

PER SERVING
CALORIES: 428.59
FAT: 42.42
PROTEIN: 6.08
CARBS: 29.58
FIBER: 4.58
SUGAR ALCOHOLS: 20
NET CARBS: 5

MORE FACTS: P. 544

 DESSERTS

5. Scoop the dough into 1-inch (2.5 cm) balls with a cookie or ice cream scoop. Place about 2 inches (5 cm) apart on prepared baking sheet.

6. Bake the cookies until golden, about 15 minutes. Remove and allow to cool.

7. Once the cookies are cool, toss them with the remaining powdered sweetener. (They are usually rolled in the sweetener on a plate, but I just put them all in a paper bag with the sweetener and lightly toss it all around.)

SPICED PUMPKIN PIE WITH GINGERBREAD CRUST

SERVES: 8 · · · PREP: 20 MIN · · · COOK: 1 HR 5 MIN · · · TOTAL: 1 HR 25 MIN

Crust:

3/4 cup + 3 Tbsp (225 mL) **almond flour**

3 Tbsp (45 mL) **coconut flour**

3 Tbsp (45 mL) **tapioca flour**

3 Tbsp (45 mL) ground **white chia seeds**

1/2 tsp (2 mL) **baking powder**

1/2 tsp (2 mL) ground **cinnamon**

1/4 tsp (1 mL) freshly ground **nutmeg**

1/4 tsp (1 mL) ground **cardamom**

a dash of ground **cloves**

a dash of **salt**

1/4 cup (60 mL) **sugar-free maple syrup** (xylitol based nutrition used)

1 Tbsp (15 mL) **yacon syrup** (substitute: blackstrap molasses)

2 tsp (10 mL) grated **fresh ginger**

1 tsp (5 mL) **vanilla extract**

Pumpkin Filling:

1 15-oz. can (420 g) **mashed pumpkin**

3/4 cup (180 mL) **sugar replacement**

3 large **whole eggs**

1/2 cup (120 mL) heavy whipping **cream**

1/2 cup (120 mL) unsweetened **almond milk**

1/2 cup (120 mL) **sugar-free maple syrup** (xylitol based nutrition used)

1 Tbsp (15 mL) **yacon syrup** (substitute: blackstrap molasses)

2 tsp (10 mL) grated **fresh ginger**

1/2 tsp (2 mL) ground **cinnamon**

1/4 tsp (1 mL) ground **allspice**

a dash of ground **cloves**

a dash of **salt**

Anyone that follows my blog knows that I'm a pumpkin lover. I'm not quite sure what it is, but really just about any of the winter squashes are fantastic, whether sweet or savory. This little pumpkin pie recipe falls dead center into the world of things I love. Not only does it have the soft and luxuriously comforting pumpkin filling, but it's also got a sweet and spicy gingerbread crust... just to take it to a whole new level!

Back in the day, I used to try and think of a catchphrase or some kind of quip that could encapsulate my style of cooking. One of my favorite lines has always been, "Not afraid to taste good!" That line applies in spades with this recipe. This is a pie that's not afraid to taste good!

PER SERVING
CALORIES: 244.98
FAT: 15.59
PROTEIN: 7.57
CARBS: 46.6
FIBER: 6.02
SUGAR ALCOHOLS: 28.88
NET CARBS: 11.17

MORE FACTS: P. 546

Crusty note: While the crust is excellent, I readily admit it's got some wonky ingredients in it. A quick alternative would be to take just about any nut—hazelnuts, pecans, almonds, etc.—and crush them. With 1 1/2 cups (360 mL) of crushed nuts mixed with 1/4 cup (60 mL) of melted butter and about 2 tsp (10 mL) of honey, mix it, press it into a pan, and par-bake for about 10 to 12 minutes at 350°F (177°C) for a less exotic but easier to attain little crust... and you'll still have something super tasty!

* Nutrition note: Technically, the yacon syrup is nonglycemic, meaning it has no impact on the blood. However, I was unable to find any nutrition labels that listed yacon with any fiber (it acts similar to fiber in the blood). It's my belief that the yacon is actually discounted in this recipe, rending each slice at 8.95 net carbs, but I can't readily prove it. In either case, this is calculated at 8 large slices. Have a smaller slice for a less carby impact!

1. Preheat oven to 325°F (163°C).

2. In a medium-sized mixing bowl, combine the almond, coconut, tapioca, and chia flours with the baking powder, cinnamon, nutmeg, cardamom, and a dash of salt.

3. Add the wet maple syrup, yacon, fresh ginger, and vanilla extract. Combine and form into a dough.

4. Grease a 9-inch (23 x 5 cm) pie pan and press the dough evenly into the pan, making sure there are no cracks or creases. Bake the crust for 5 minutes, just enough to set it. Remove and set aside to cool.

5. In a large mixing bowl, combine pumpkin, sweetener, eggs, cream, almond milk, maple and yacon syrups, ginger, cinnamon, allspice, cloves, and salt. Whisk until well combined.

6. Pour the pie filling into the pie and bake at 325°F (163°C) for 1 hour. Remove and allow to cool. Slice and serve!

MISSISSIPPI MUD PIE

SERVES: 12 · · · PREP: 30 MIN · · · COOK: 30 MIN · · · TOTAL: 8 HR

Chocolate Piecrust:

3 cups (720 mL) **almond flour**

1/2 cup (120 mL) **unsweetened cocoa powder**

1/4 cup (60 mL) **powdered sugar replacement**

1 Tbsp (15 mL) **tapioca flour**

1/2 tsp (2 mL) **salt**

1 large **egg**

3 Tbsp (15 mL) **melted butter**

Chocolate Ganache Layer:

1/2 cup (120 mL) **heavy whipping cream**

1/4 cup (60 mL) **sugar replacement**

2 1/2 oz. (70 g) **unsweetened baking chocolate squares,** broken and chopped

1 Tbsp (15 mL) **butter**

Chocolate Pudding Layer:

1 1/2 cups (360 mL) **heavy whipping cream**

2 1/2 cup (600 mL) unsweetened **almond milk** divided

2 packets (about 4 1/2 to 5 tsp, total) (14g or 25 mL) **gelatin powder**

3/4 cup (180 mL) **unsweetened cocoa powder**

1 cup (240 mL) **sugar replacement**

1 Tbsp (15 mL) **vanilla extract**

a dash of **salt**

Whipped Cream Topping:

1 cup (240 mL) **heavy whipping cream**

2 Tbsp (30 mL) **powdered sugar replacement**

1 tsp (5 mL) **vanilla extract**

If you like chocolate... like *a lot* of chocolate... A LOT, you'll *love* this pie—a chocolate crust with a deep dark chocolate ganache and chocolate pudding layers. The whipped cream on top is really only there to breathe a twinge of levity into the whole thing! This pie was so named because the thick and sludgy chocolate was reminiscent of the banks of the Mississippi River. This particular pie is actually an assemblage of other recipes in this book. Short of the crust, this pie is a layer of the chocolate ganache used in the Brown Butter Pie (p. 423) and Thumbprint Cookies (p. 438), plus the Chocolate Pudding from the Chocolate Pudding Pie (p. 398). The whipped cream is... well, it's Whipped Cream (p. 413). The fun in this pie is the layering and the bringing together of other concepts and ideas to form a whole new recipe. Fun, right?

Serving notes: Unlike the other pies, where I list 8 servings, this particular pie has 3 layers and is built tall, resulting in far more pie than with the other pies. Each of these 12 slices is quite ample.

PER SERVING
CALORIES: 474.42
FAT: 45.81
PROTEIN: 11.82
CARBS: 45.33
FIBER: 7.27
SUGAR ALCOHOLS: 29.17
NET CARBS: 8.9

MORE FACTS: P. 546

Chocolate Piecrust

1. Preheat oven to 300°F (149°C).

2. In a medium-sized mixing bowl, combine the almond flour, cocoa powder, sweetener, tapioca flour, and salt. Mix well and then add the egg and melted butter. Combine and mix until a nice ball forms. Roll the ball between two pieces of greased parchment or plastic wrap, until it's about an inch thick. Cover and refrigerate the dough for about 20 minutes.

3. Grease a 9" x 2" pie pan (23 x 5 cm).

4. Remove the dough from the refrigerator and, again, between two pieces of plastic wrap or greased parchment paper, roll the dough thinner, until it is wide enough to cover the pie pan, plus about 1 inch (2.5 cm) on all sides. Gently place the dough in the pie pan and push it into place, building up the rim and crimping the edges so that the piecrust stands about a full inch (2.5 cm) above the top of the pie pan. It will be taller than your standard pie. Be very careful to make sure there are no cracks and weaknesses in the crust.

5. Bake the crust for about 15 minutes or until firm and solid. Remove and cool.

Chocolate Ganache Layer

6. To make your ganache, heat up your cream on the stove. Once your cream is hot and is *just* about to simmer, whisk in your sugar replacement until it has dissolved.

7. Place your chopped chocolate pieces and butter cubes into a small mixing bowl. Pour your hot cream mixture over the chocolate, and whisk it in the bowl until the chocolate is fully melted and incorporated.

8. Evenly spread this chocolate mixture into the bottom of the chocolate piecrust. Place in the refrigerator to speed up the cooling process. Allow at least an hour before adding the warm pudding layer. The ganache must feel relatively solid.

Chocolate Pudding Layer

9. Combine cream and 2 cups (480 mL) of the almond milk in a medium saucepan over medium-low heat.

10. At the same time that you add your milk to the stove, in a medium-sized mixing bowl, add your 1/2 cup (120 mL) remaining almond milk.

11. Sprinkle the gelatin powder evenly over the surface of the cold almond milk, in the bowl. Allow it to bloom for about 5 minutes.

12. Into your hot milk mixture, whisk in your sugar replacement, cocoa powder, vanilla, and a dash of salt. Whisk until the cocoa is fully absorbed, lumps are gone, and the sugar equivalent has fully dissolved.

13. Once the mixture begins to simmer (but not boil), whisk the hot mixture into the blooming gelatin bowl. Whisk until the gelatin is completely dissolved.

14. Check to make sure your chocolate ganache layer has firmed up. Once it has, pour your warm mixture into the pie pan and place in the refrigerator to chill. Chilling takes between 4 to 6 hours.

Whipped Cream Layer

15. Whisk the cream, sweetener, and vanilla in a cold bowl with a cold whisk.

16. Whip until it begins to stiffen. When you remove the whisk and a firm peak holds in place, you are done. Do not over whip the cream.

17. Spread the whipped cream over the top of the chilled pie. Slice and serve!

Sparkling Gelled Layered Strawberries and Cream

SERVES: 14 · · · PREP: 30 MIN · · · COOK: 30 MIN · · · TOTAL: 12 HR

2 cups (480 mL) **sugar-free cream soda**

5 packets (about 11 2/3 tsp) (35g or 58 mL) **gelatin powder**, divided

1 pint (480 mL) **strawberries**, washed and leaves removed

1 cup (240 mL) **sugar replacement**, divided

3 cups (720 mL) **heavy whipping cream**

3 cups (720 mL) **unsweetened almond milk**

3 **vanilla beans**, 2 split lengthwise (or 2 Tbsp [30 mL] vanilla extract)

a dash of **salt**

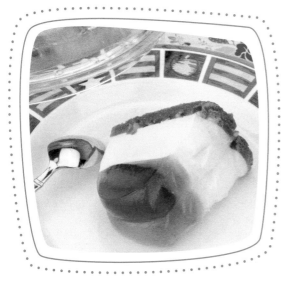

PER SERVING
CALORIES: 193.22
FAT: 18.367
PROTEIN: 3.61
CARBS: 20.4
FIBER: 0.67
SUGAR ALCOHOLS: 16.4
NET CARBS: 3.33

MORE FACTS: P. 544

This recipe is less a recipe and more a quick lesson in gelatin. Gelatin has a long history, with clear and detailed recipes for aspics appearing in literature over seven hundred years ago. Gelatin has made appearances on the tables of some of the history's most elite. At one time, gelatin-based dishes were regal and opulent and usually based around meats or fish. The process of refining the gelatin and extracting it from bones, skins, antlers, feet, and connective tissues of animals took time and tremendous effort. It was only served to the special few who could afford it. The use of gelatin was a sign that the host or hostess had the means to support a kitchen staff with the skill and time to create such a dish. This gave rise to beautiful and artistic gelatin recipes, formed in equally beautiful and expensive molds in the shapes of everything from fish to castles and fortresses complete with doors, windows, and crenellated turrets!

It wasn't until about a hundred years ago that flavored and powdered gelatins began appearing in typical households. A combination of flavored powdered gelatin, refrigeration, and an army of salesmen handing out free Jell-O recipes was the impetus for the spread.

Gelatin is extremely good for you. It's loaded with protein. It helps to improve digestion and can help with food allergies and various intolerances. It's excellent for bone and joint health. It's great for hair, nails, and teeth, while also improving the elasticity of skin. It's also great for weight loss. It's thought to increase the production of natural human growth hormones and boost metabolism. I don't want to bog this down in details, but suffice it to say gelatin is some good stuff. I suggest doing some reading up and finding some good quality gelatin.

One of the most common questions I'm asked in regards to gelatin is "Can I use the grass-fed stuff the same way as the regular gelatin in packets?" The answer is yes... probably.

There are *some* powdered gelatins, largely used as supplements, one of which is called "collagen hydrolysate." Collagen hydrolysate does not gel, but it does have fantastic health benefits and merits looking into. Most gelatins will gel. My overall point is that once you've got a refined, unflavored powdered gelatin, it will behave just like any other refined, unflavored powdered gelatin. Just make sure you're using the same amounts.

A standard packet of gelatin contains about 2 1/3 teaspoons (11.5 mL) of gelatin powder, weighing 7 grams. This is a bit less than a standard tablespoon (15 mL). For those who have managed to get their hands on sheets of gelatin, different sheets mean different things and have different blooms. It could be anywhere from 3 to 5 sheets per packet. Read the box or ask the source about gelling strength as it relates to a packet of gelatin.

A packet of gelatin will gel just about any liquid, including plain old-fashioned watery water.

- **1 cup of water** will gel quite firmly into a block.
- **2 cups of water** will gel into a firm shape, which can still be unmolded, but it's a far nicer and softer consistency than at 1 cup. This is the ratio we'll be focused on.
- **3 cups of water** will thicken and take on a strange viscosity. It won't hold its shape and can't be unmolded.

In order for gelatin to work, it must be first soaked in cold liquid to "bloom" for about 5 to 10 minutes. Hot liquids will not work, as the outside of the grain will swell, leaving the center without the ability to do so. Cold liquids allow for an even blooming. Once the gelatin has bloomed, it can then be added to hot liquids.

Again, just about any liquid can be used, from coffee, to alcohol, to fruit juices, creams, and water. There are, however, some tropical fruits which have an enzyme called "bromelin" that will prevent the gelatin from gelling, such as pineapple, kiwi, and even fresh ginger. Heating the juice(s) will destroy the enzyme, which will allow the gelatin to set.

I wanted to create an interesting and fun recipe that showcases several of the more interesting aspects of gelatin. In this case, I used three different primary liquids and layered them, including some fresh fruit in and amongst the layers.

The topmost layer was created with a stevia and erythritol sweetened cream soda, which had the gelatin added and was placed in a mold, where fresh strawberries were gently placed. This created the top-most "window" into the overall Strawberries and Cream layered gelatin dessert.

The second layer makes up the bulk of the dessert and is little more than a sweetened, vanilla-flavored panna cotta, or a vanilla-flavored gel of cream and almond milk.

The final layer is a blend of strawberry puree with some sweetener and a bit of water. For extra texture, I also added freshly diced strawberries.

This whole dessert took very little actual hands-on time to create, but there is a good 4 to 6 hours of hang time between each layer, while the layers chill and gel. If the previous layer hasn't fully gelled, then the new warm gelatin will simply mix in and ruin the effect.

Serving size: Makes about fourteen 6-ounce (180 mL) portions.

1. In a medium-sized mixing bowl, place 1/2 cup (60 mL) of chilled cream soda. Evenly spread 1 packet of gelatin over the full surface of the soda, making sure not to overlap much. There should be a clean, even layer of gelatin.

2. In a medium-sized sauce pan, on medium heat, bring the remaining 1 1/2 cups (180 mL) of soda up to just before it simmers. Keep it hot but don't let it boil.

3. Once the gelatin has bloomed (about 5 minutes), whisk the hot soda into the bowl with the gelatin, making sure that it's whisked well and that the gelatin has fully dissolved.

4. Pour the warm liquid into an 11-cup gelatin mold and place in the refrigerator to chill.

5. While the gelatin chills, take 7 or 8 of the strawberries and set them aside. Puree the remaining strawberries in a blender with 1/4 cup (60 mL) of sweetener and a dash of salt. Place this puree in a measuring cup in the refrigerator. Make sure you have 1 cup of puree.

6. With the remaining 7 or 8 strawberries, cut a 1/4-inch (.6 cm) section straight from the middle of each. These will look a bit like 7 or 8 red hearts. Dice the remaining strawberry sides and save.

7. After about 1 hour, check the soda to see if it has begun thickening. Once it begins to thicken, gently rest the 7 or 8 strawberry hearts on top of the thickening gel. If it's too thick, the strawberries won't submerge and if it's too thin, they'll sink and move around too much. Just watch for the right consistency and then layer them in a lovely little pattern. Place back in the refrigerator to chill completely through, about 2 to 3 hours.

8. Combine cream and 3/4 cup (180 mL) of the almond milk in a medium saucepan.

9. Split the vanilla bean in half. Scrape the seeds from the vanilla bean. Add the bean and seeds to the milk and cream.

10. Bring the milk to a very slow simmer. Remove the milk from the heat and whisk the sugar and salt into the milk. Make sure it dissolves. Keep warm, but set aside.

11. Once the soda is fully gelled, begin the vanilla cream layer.

12. In a large mixing bowl, place 1 1/2 cups (360 mL) of chilled, unsweetened almond milk. Evenly spread 3 packets of gelatin over the full surface of the almond milk, making sure not to overlap much. There should be a clean, even layer of gelatin.

13. In a large-sized saucepan, over medium heat, bring the cream, remaining 3/4 cup (180 mL) of sweetener, the remaining 1 1/2 cups (180 mL) of almond milk, split vanilla beans, and the dash of salt up to just before it simmers. Keep it hot but don't let it boil. Let it steep for 20 minutes, whisking it and making sure the sweetener has fully dissolved.

14. Strain the sweetened cream, to remove the large vanilla pods, and then whisk the hot, strained cream into the bowl with the gelatin, making sure that its whisked well and that the gelatin has fully dissolved.

15. At this point, allow the cream mixture cool to room temperature before adding to the previous layer. It prevents any melting, mixing, or blending of the two layers.

16. Gently pour the cool creamy liquid onto the top of the chilled soda and strawberries and place in the refrigerator to chill overnight. This is a lot of gelatin and will need a good 6 to 8 hours of chill time. Do not cover it.

17. The next day, add about 1/4 cup (60 mL) of strawberry puree and 1/4 cup (60 mL) water to a small mixing bowl. Evenly spread 1 packet of gelatin over the full surface of the strawberry water, making sure not to overlap much. There should be a clean, even layer of gelatin.

18. In a medium-sized saucepan, on medium heat, bring 3/4 cup (180 mL) of water up to a boil. Once it boils, quickly whisk it into the strawberry water with the gelatin, making sure the gelatin is fully dissolved. Once it's dissolved, add the remaining 3/4 cup (180 mL) of strawberry puree and the diced strawberries from the day before. Mix this together, so that the gelatin and strawberries are evenly distributed. Pour this evenly onto the top of the cream layer of the gelatin mold. Place in the refrigerator and allow it to chill completely through, about 3 more hours.

19. Once it is thoroughly chilled, submerge the bottom of the mold in a large bowl of hot water. Do not let any of the water touch the gelatin or seep over the edge. Place a platter over the top of the mold and carefully, and with clear determination, flip both the mold and platter, in unison, over, so that the mold is sitting upside down on the platter. Carefully remove the mold. Slice into it by warming a knife blade under hot tap water. Once the blade is hot, wipe off the water and make a slice! Repeat this process of warming and drying the blade, making slices in the dessert.

20. Serve!

BLUEBERRY-CREAM CHEESE EGGY McFOO

SERVES: 1 ··· PREP: 5 MIN ··· COOK: 25 MIN ··· TOTAL: 35 MIN

2 Tbsp (30 mL) **golden flaxseed meal** (or 1 1/2 Tbsp [23 mL] ground chia seed)

2 Tbsp (30 mL) **almond flour**

2 Tbsp (30 mL) **sugar replacement**, divided

1/2 tsp (2 mL) **baking powder**

2 large **eggs**

1 tsp (5 mL) melted **butter**

2 oz. (58 g) regular **cream cheese**, room temperature

2 Tbsp (30 mL) fresh or frozen **unsweetened blueberries**

1/2 tsp (2 mL) **vanilla extract**

2 dashes of **salt**

I'm really torn on this one. I can't decide if it's brilliant or a total misfire. It's a tiny bit of extra work, but it's also undeniably delicious! The end result is something like a cross between a mock Danish, an actual Danish, and a pot pie! It's potentially a misfire because, frankly, the batter can be a bit grumpy and a challenge to work with. Thankfully, it's going to taste fantastic no matter what you do, but it can vary pretty wildly in how it will look when it's done. At its heart, it's a berry and cream cheese–stuffed egg muffin, spawned by the concept of baking a breakfast sandwich as an all-inclusive pastry-like animal. Tinkering with different fillings, such as pumpkin, various berries, chocolate, apples, as well as savory options like ham and cheese, I believe the concept is definitely sound. Again, the batter can have its own agenda. The trick, really, is to let the fiber in the batter somewhat gel and thicken before adding the fillings and topping it off with more batter. Do this and you have an outstanding dessert, snack, or breakfast pastry with all the charm and grace of the real thing!

1. Preheat oven to 350°F (177°C).

2. In a small mixing bowl, combine flax or chia with the almond flour, 1 tablespoon (15 mL) of the sweetener, baking powder, and a dash of salt. Mix together. Add the eggs and melted butter and mix. Set aside. You want the batter to sit for about 4 minutes. It will slightly thicken.

3. While the batter thickens, grease a ramekin or other ovenproof small baking pan, such as a large muffin pan, pot-pie pan, etc.

PER SERVING
CALORIES: 529.71
FAT: 44.63
PROTEIN: 16.06
CARBS: 42.83
FIBER: 6
SUGAR ALCOHOLS: 30
NET CARBS: 6.83

MORE FACTS: P. 544

4. In a small mixing bowl, combine the cream cheese, blueberries, vanilla, a dash of salt, and the remaining 1 tablespoon (15 mL) of sweetener. Mix until just combined; there's no reason to go willy-nilly with it.

5. Pour half the thickened batter into the baking pan or ramekin. Carefully place your filling in the center of the batter, without any of it touching the rim, pushing it somewhat deeper into the center of the batter, letting the batter rise up a bit around it. The filling needs to be completely detached from the edge. Cover the filling with the remaining batter.

6. Bake for 22 to 27 minutes or until golden. Remove from the oven and allow to set for about 5 minutes before removing from the pan. Enjoy!

BLUEBERRY BREAD PUDDING

SERVES: 12 · · · PREP: 15 MIN · · · COOK: 1 HR · · · TOTAL: 2 HR

Bread Pudding:

1/2 cup (120 mL) **coconut flour**

1/2 cup (120 mL) **almond flour**

1/2 cup (120 mL) **vanilla whey protein powder** (sweetened with stevia)

1 1/4 cup (300 mL) **sugar replacement**, divided

4 tsp (40 mL) **baking powder**

1 **orange**

14 large eggs, divided

1/2 cup (120 mL) **melted butter**

1 1/2 cup (360 mL) **fresh or frozen blueberries**, unsweetened

1 1/2 cups (360 mL) **heavy whipping cream**

1 cup (240 mL) unsweetened **almond milk**

1 Tbsp (15 mL) **yacon syrup** (substitute: blackstrap molasses)

1 Tbsp (15 mL) **vanilla extract**

a dash of **salt**

Cream Cheese Frosting:

1/4 cup + 2 Tbsp (90 mL) **full-fat cream cheese**, warmed

1/4 cup (60 mL) **fresh whole butter**, softened

3/4 cup (180 mL) **powdered sugar replacement**

1/2 tsp (2 mL) **vanilla extract**

a dash of **salt**

PER SERVING
CALORIES: 401
FAT: 33.5
PROTEIN: 16
CARBS: 51.3
FIBER: 3.3
SUGAR ALCOHOLS: 40
NET CARBS: 7.9

MORE FACTS: P. 545

I love bread pudding. I can't state it any more clearly or accurately than that. It's such a wonderful and comforting way to either begin a day or end one. In a sense, it's a French toast casserole! This particular recipe uses my standard magic mega-batter to make a big loaf of bread. Then, it's cubed up and tossed with some blueberries, a bit of orange zest, and some sweet custard, where it's baked again. Absolutely delicious by itself, it's also fantastic with Crème Anglaise (p. 458), some sugar-free pancake syrup, or even some sweet no-sugar added jams or jellies (orange marmalade is a favorite of mine). In this particular case, I've opted to plunk a tasty ball of cream cheese frosting onto it. A bit sweet but so, *so* delicious!

1. Preheat oven to 350°F (177°C).

2. Grease a 13" x 9" (33 x 23 x 5 cm) casserole pan.

3. In a medium mixing bowl, sift together coconut flour, almond meal, protein powder, 1/2 cup (120 mL) sweetener (if powdered), baking powder, and salt.

4. With a zester, zest your orange. You can also use a vegetable peeler to peel the very outer orange layer of the orange (do not get the white pith; it's bitter). You want enough of the zest to create about 1 teaspoon (5 mL) of fresh zest. If using a vegetable peeler, chop the orange rind creating a finer zest and set aside. Juice the orange.

5. Add 8 of the eggs, the orange zest, the orange juice, and all of the melted butter. If using a liquid sweetener, add it now. Mix until combined. If the batter is still too thick, add up to 1/4 cup (60 mL) of water, cream, coconut milk, or almond milk to thin it out. It should look like thick pancake batter.

6. Pour the batter into the prepared pan and bake for 24 to 28 minutes or until golden. Remove from the oven and turn it off.

7. Once the bread has baked, remove it from the pan and let it cool. Wash the casserole pan, dry it, and grease it again.

8. Cut the bread into cubes the size of croutons. In a large bowl, combine the bread cubes and blueberries. Mix them and pour into the prepared casserole pan. Make sure they are distributed evenly through the bottom of the pan.

9. In a large bowl, combine the remaining 6 eggs, cream, almond milk, the remaining 3/4 cup (180 mL) sweetener, yacon syrup, vanilla, and a dash of salt. Whisk this mixture very well. Pour it evenly over the top of the bread cubes. Allow the cubes to soak up the custard base. At this point, it can take about an hour to let the cubes absorb the eggs. I typically place another casserole pan on top of the cubes, to submerge them in the custard, and place in the refrigerator for about an hour (or overnight). The cubes have a tendency to want to float on top, so it helps to have something to hold them down.

10. Once an hour has passed and the cubes have absorbed the custard base, again preheat oven to 350°F (177°C).

11. Bake for about 40 to 50 minutes or until it has set. It should start to color a nice brown on the top as well.

12. Remove from the oven and let rest for at least 15 minutes before slicing.

13. While the bread pudding is resting, in a medium mixing bowl, beat together your cream cheese, butter, powdered sweetener, vanilla, and salt. Make sure your cream cheese and butter are soft (leave out at room temperature for a while) before whipping or mixing will be difficult at best.

14. Slice your bread pudding, and plop some frosting on top. Eat and enjoy warm!

CRÈME ANGLAISE (VANILLA CUSTARD SAUCE)

SERVES: 12 · · · PREP: 1 MIN · · · COOK: 15 MIN · · · TOTAL: 16 MIN

1 cup (240 mL) **heavy whipping cream**

1 cup (240 mL) unsweetened **almond milk**

1 **vanilla bean**, split lengthwise (or 2 tsp [10 mL] vanilla extract)

1/2 cup (120 mL) **sugar replacement**

a dash **salt**

6 large **egg yolks**

PER SERVING
CALORIES: 101.02
FAT: 9.86
PROTEIN: 1.95
CARBS: 9.57
FIBER: 0.08
SUGAR ALCOHOLS: 8.33
NET CARBS: 1.15

MORE FACTS: P. 542

Crème anglaise is a smooth, sweet, and custardy vanilla sauce, probably coming from Ancient Rome, where eggs would be used as a thickener. Seen another way, this vanilla custard sauce could also be looked at as… melted vanilla ice cream! If you were to take this sauce and load it into an ice cream machine, you'd have something wonderful going on. It's a bit heavy and eggy as a vanilla ice cream, but that doesn't stop it from being delicious. I personally actually really like it this way. Frozen custards make a great sugar-free ice cream!

Normally, the eggs and sugar are beaten together, prior to adding the hot dairy. However, because of the fickle sugar replacements in a sugar-free world, I'm changing tradition in an attempt to ensure that the sugar equivalent is truly dissolved. Don't hate me in the morning!

Recipe makes roughly twelve 1/4-cup (60 mL) servings.

1. Combine cream and almond milk in a medium saucepan. Scrape the seeds from the vanilla bean. Add the bean and seeds to the milk and cream. Bring the milk to a slow simmer.

2. Remove the milk from the heat and whisk the sweetener and salt into the milk. Make sure it dissolves.

3. In a separate bowl, whisk the eggs well. Very, very slowly, whisk the hot milk mixture into the egg yolks. Whisk quickly, so as to incorporate the hot liquid evenly, without cooking or scrambling the eggs.

4. Once the liquid has been incorporated into the eggs, pour the milk–egg mixture back into the saucepan and return to low heat.

5. Stir consistently until the sauce thickens and coats the back of a spoon thickly. The temperature should be at above 165°F (74°C). Whatever you do, do not boil this mixture. Strain the sauce. Serve warm or chill!

Bakery

○ ○ ○

Baked goods are one of the greatest hits people feel when giving up grains. Time and time again, I see people stating how impossible it feels to give up bread. The loss of a sandwich is simply too much for some people to bear! While I realize I've got little baked odds and ends scattered throughout this book, these are the straight up savory breads that make for a lovely sandwich or panini. Some of these are incredible options for a bread basket over the holidays or as a base concept for a wider range of muffins and buns. Throw some tasty crackers into that bread basket, wouldja?!

With the baked items in this book, there's no need to give up that sandwich!

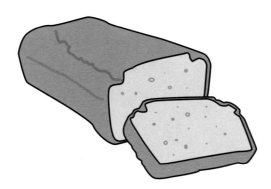

Savory Zucchini, Bacon, and Herb OMM

SERVES: 1 · · · PREP: 2 MIN · · · COOK: 1 MIN · · · TOTAL: 3 MIN

For years, I lived down in Mexico with a broken microwave. I'd read and read about the One-Minute Muffins in all the various low-carb forums but never had the opportunity to try one. I finally moved into an apartment with a working microwave and gave one a shot. Wow! What had I been missing?!

Since then, I've been making all sorts of flavors! I wanted to try something different though. No more sweet flavors, and no just plain breads either. I wanted something interesting and unique, the kind of thing you could serve in place of a bread basket during a nice meal and *no one* will question you about the lack of bread; they'll just gobble *these* tasty things down and beg for more!

2 Tbsp (30 mL) **flaxseed meal** (or 1 1/2 Tbsp [23 mL] ground chia seed)

2 Tbsp (30 mL) **almond flour**

2 Tbsp (30 mL) grated **Parmesan**

1/2 tsp (2 mL) **baking powder**

a dash of **salt**

2 Tbsp (30 mL) grated **zucchini**

1 Tbsp (15 mL) **chopped toasted pecans**

1 large **whole egg**

1 tsp (5 mL) melted **bacon fat**

1 Tbsp (15 mL) **real bacon bits**, divided

1/2 tsp (2 mL) chopped **fresh thyme**, divided

3 Tbsp (45 mL) **full-fat cream cheese**, warmed

1. In a wide-mouthed coffee mug, combine your flax (or chia), almond flour, Parmesan, baking powder, and salt. I like to grease my mug first, but I don't think it's necessary.

2. Squeeze the water out of your zucchini by squeezing it within your fist, over the sink. Un-clump the zucchini, so it is back in strand form. Mix in your zucchini, pecans, egg, bacon fat, half of the bacon bits, and half of the thyme.

3. Microwave on high for 60 seconds (90 seconds if using a weaker microwave).

4. Alternately, bake in a muffin tin at 350°F (177°C) for 13 to 15 minutes or until golden.

5. Garnish with a nice layer of cream cheese and then sprinkle the remaining bacon bits and thyme!

PER SERVING
CALORIES: 518.77
FAT: 44.32
PROTEIN: 23.68
CARBS: 11.93
FIBER: 6.48
SUGAR ALCOHOLS: 0
NET CARBS: 5.45

MORE FACTS: P. 547

Paleo Bread

SERVES: 8 · · · PREP: 10 MIN · · · COOK: 45 MIN · · · TOTAL: 1 HR 15 MIN

1 tsp (5 mL) **coconut oil**

4 large **eggs**, separated

2 1/2 tsp (12 mL) **apple cider vinegar**

1 cup (240 mL) smooth, unsweetened **almond butter**

1/4 cup (60 mL) unsweetened **almond milk**

1/4 cup (60 mL) **coconut flour**

1 tsp (5 mL) **baking soda**

1/2 tsp (2 mL) **salt**

Looking around the Internet, there are several variations of *Paleo bread*: a loaf of bread built primarily around nuts and aerated eggs, and leavened by a chemical reaction occurring between sodium bicarbonate (baking soda) and acid (apple cider vinegar). Because I always like to give credit if the inspiration comes from another source, in this case, I'll give credit to Danielle Walker of *Against All Grain* fame! Her specific recipe served as the basis for this one, even as this is a fairly common ratio for Paleo bread.

The following recipe has been altered from its original source to decrease the number of impact carbs while still staying within Paleo guidelines.

Note: This recipe works best when working with room-temperature eggs and almond butter. While being easier to work with, more air will also be trapped by the mixture during the beating and folding processes.

1. Preheat oven to 300°F (149°C).

2. Grease an 8 1/2" x 4 1/2" (21 x 11 cm) loaf pan with the coconut oil.

3. In an electric mixer, whip the egg whites with the vinegar. Whip until peaks form. Set aside.

4. In a separate bowl, beat the almond butter, egg yolks, and almond milk until lighter in color and nicely aerated. It will look like a beige pancake batter. (**Note:** Almond butters come in a wide variety of viscosities; if the batter is too firm, add a touch more almond milk.) Add coconut flour, baking soda, and salt. Mix until lumps are gone.

PER SERVING
CALORIES: 252.41
FAT: 19.11
PROTEIN: 10.94
CARBS: 8.55
FIBER: 5.53
SUGAR ALCOHOLS: 0
NET CARBS: 3.02

MORE FACTS: P. 547

5. With a large plastic spatula, remove approximately 1/4 of the egg white mixture and add to the almond mixture. Fold the mixture in until most of the lumps are gone. Be careful and thorough to scrape the bottoms and evenly fold the mixture. Take a second 1/4 of the egg white mixture and add to the almond mixture. Again, fold the mixture until the lumps are gone. Repeat this process two more times, until the egg white mixture has been evenly folded into the almond butter mixture.

6. Gently pour the batter into the loaf pan. Give the pan a small jiggle to smooth the top. Place the pan in the oven. Bake for 45 to 50 minutes. Like a soufflé, this is somewhat sensitive, so be careful not to bang around or open the oven door and create a big change in temperature within the oven. Do not open the door for at least the first 35 to 40 minutes. Once the top is nice and golden and a toothpick comes out clean, remove from the oven and place on a rack.

7. After about 20 minutes, turn the pan over and carefully remove the loaf from the pan.

8. Allow to cool fully before slicing.

9. Enjoy!

Patty's Pattypan Cupcakes

SERVES: 6 · · · PREP: 5 MIN · · · COOK: 15 MIN · · · TOTAL: 20 MIN

6 medium (180 g) **yellow pattypans**

1/4 cup +2 Tbsp (90 mL) ground **white chia seeds**

1/2 cup (90 mL) **almond flour**

2 tsp (10 mL) **baking powder**

a dash of **salt**

3/4 cup (180 mL) **goat cheese**, divided

4 large **whole eggs**

1/2 cup (120 mL) chopped **pecans**, toasted

1/4 cup (60 mL) grated **raw carrot**

2 Tbsp (30 mL) **melted butter, lard, or bacon fat**, divided

1 tsp (10 mL) chopped **fresh rosemary**

2 Tbsp (30 mL) **heavy whipping cream**

salt and **pepper**, to taste

PER SERVING
CALORIES: 402.79
FAT: 33.72
PROTEIN: 17.82
CARBS: 10.61
FIBER: 6.35
SUGAR ALCOHOLS: 0
NET CARBS: 4.26

MORE FACTS: P. 547

This recipe was developed and is here for a few reasons. Its origins started as I mulled over a way to develop a playful recipe, poking fun at Patty Strilaeff, one of the originators of StalkerVille.net, a recipe aggregation site devoted to real food with a heavy primal slant. I love their endless selection and have a good hundred of my own recipes bumping around her system. I've communicated with Patty several times and have always found her to be wonderfully pleasant, but a bit of a stickler for the rules. Two rules: No sugar alcohols... and no cupcakes! It was summertime and the summer pattypan squash were abundant, and I had a flash of a Pattypan Cupcake, without those infernal sugar alcohols (which Patty later accepted. YAY!). I love Patty and knew she'd understand the wink and nudge included along with this recipe. Beyond my loving nod to StalkerVille, this is also a straight-up delicious recipe and stunning to look at. It's also just a fun cupcake with a twist, in a day and age when cupcakes have almost become played out. Good times!

1. Preheat oven to 350°F (177°C).

2. Grease a standard 6-muffin muffin pan.

3. Wash the pattypans and cut a nice 1/4-inch (8 mm) sliver right from the middle of each. This will later serve as a garnish. Grate the rest of the pattypans with a cheese grater. Add a bit of salt to the grated squash and set aside.

4. In a medium-sized mixing bowl, combine ground chia, almond flour, baking powder, and salt.

5. Squeeze any extra water from the grated pattypans and discard the water. Add the patty pans to the mixing bowl. Crumble about 1/4 cup (60 mL) of the goat cheese into the mixing bowl, along with the eggs, pecans, grated carrots, 1 tablespoon (15 mL) of fat, and rosemary. Mix well.

6. Evenly divide the batter into the 6 prepared muffin cups and bake for 12 to 14 minutes or until golden.

7. While the cupcakes bake, preheat a medium-sized pan over medium-high heat. Season your 6 pattypan slivers with a bit of salt and pepper. Place your 1 remaining tablespoon (15 mL) of fat into the hot pan. Immediately add the slivers and sear each side of the pattypans, creating a nice golden sear on both sides. Remove and set aside.

8. In a small mixing bowl, combine the remaining goat cheese with the cream and a bit of salt and pepper. Mix until nice and smooth. The cupcakes can't be too hot when they're frosted, or it'll melt the frosting. When they're room temperature, frost the cupcakes. Garnish with any chopped nuts or herbs you have floating around.

9. Upload the recipe to StalkerVille and giggle!

CRISPITY HAZELNUT PARMESAN CRACKER

SERVES: 4 · · · PREP: 15 MIN · · · COOK: 45 MIN · · · TOTAL: 1 HR

1 cup (240 mL) **hazelnut flour** (or almond flour)

1/2 cup (120 mL) grated, densely packed **Parmesan cheese**

1 **egg white**

2 **garlic cloves**, minced

2 tsp (10 mL) chopped **fresh oregano** (thyme, rosemary, sage and/or marjoram)

salt, **pepper**, and **chili flakes** to taste

We have words like *crispy* to describe a certain texture. To really hone in on words for this specific texture, you can play with it and say something like "crispity crunch"! That denotes a slightly more positive textural experience. Unfortunately, I'm unaware of a word that describes the sheer delight I experienced when I bit down on my first hazelnut-Parmesan cracker. It was possibly the most pleasing toothy nibble that I'd experienced on a low-primal diet. If a word like *beautiful* could be used to describe a texture, I would describe these crackers as... beautiful.

Note: This recipe will make one batch for a single cookie tray, resulting in roughly 45 small (not tiny) crackers. Roughly... Wheat Thin–sized. For two trays... double the recipe!

1. Preheat oven to 275°F (135°C).

2. Combine ingredients in a bowl and mix until a ball of dough has formed.

3. Crumble the dough evenly around a greased sheet of parchment paper or foil. Place another sheet above it, and roll out the dough so that the crumbles form a single thin sheet. Remove the top sheet and play with the dough. It's pretty malleable, so if there are any cracks, you can just push the cracks together. I also pushed the edges in and together and broke off "dangleys" and pushed them into the main body of the dough. In the end, I had a nice rectangular sheet of dough.

PER SERVING
CALORIES: 240.38
FAT: 20.64
PROTEIN: 9.78
CARBS: 6.12
FIBER: 3.07
SUGAR ALCOHOLS: 0
NET CARBS: 3.05

MORE FACTS: P. 547

4. Using a cutting/dividing device (pizza cutter, bench scraper, butter knife, etc.) cut through the dough to form 48 little rectangles. This isn't an exact science, and you can adjust the shapes and sizes in any way you see fit. However, if you want precision, you can always measure the rectangle and do a little math. You can also use a ruler or some other straight guide, place it on the dough, and run your cutting device along the guide. With math and a good guide, you can create a perfect batch of squares. I'm more rustic myself and wing it.

5. Place the parchment or foil on a cookie/thin baking tray.

6. Bake for roughly 45 minutes, but start checking at 30 minutes. It will crisp on the edges first. You are essentially looking to melt the cheese within the cracker, then remove the moisture. The cracker will darken and firm up. When the sheet is the same even, slightly darker color across the enter sheet (the edges and the center are all the same color), remove the sheet from the oven.

7. Let the sheet cool; then pick up the crackers and snap where the perforations were cut.

8. Crackers!

Spicy Cumin Cheddar Crackers

SERVES: 4 · · · PREP: 15 MIN · · · COOK: 45 MIN · · · TOTAL: 1 HR

1 cup (240 mL) **almond flour**

1/2 cup (120 mL) grated **cheddar cheese**

1 **egg white**

2 **garlic cloves**, minced

1/2 tsp (2 mL) ground **cumin seed**

1/2 tsp (2 mL) ground **coriander seed**

1/2 tsp (2 mL) powdered **ancho pepper**

1/4 tsp (1 mL) powdered **cayenne pepper**

salt and **freshly cracked black pepper** to taste

This one came after a request from my own mother (she wanted something to dip into gua- camole). Using the Hazelnut-Parmesan Cracker (p. 466) as a platform, I used that same ap- proach, but with a different nut and seasoning blend. The end result? A more Latin-vibed crack- er. To verify, I made some salsa and tried it. DELICIOUS! I can only imagine this with some- thing like a hot, gooey Cheddar and Jalapeño Dip (p. 350)!

1. Preheat oven to 275°F (135°C).

2. Combine ingredients in a bowl, along with a bit of salt and pepper. Mix until a ball of dough has formed.

3. Crumble the dough evenly around a greased sheet of parchment paper or foil. Place another sheet above it, and roll out the dough so that the crumbles form a sin- gle thin sheet. Remove the top sheet and play with the dough. It's pretty malleable, so if there are any cracks, you can just push the cracks together. I also pushed the edges in and together and broke off "dangleys" and pushed them into the main body of the dough. In the end, I had a nice rectangular sheet of dough.

4. Using a cutting/dividing device (pizza cutter, bench scraper, butter knife, etc.) cut through the dough to form 24 little rectangles. Then, cut each rectangle into two triangles. This isn't an exact science, and you can adjust the shapes and sizes in any way you see fit. How- ever, if you want precision, you can always measure the rectangle and do a little math. You can also use a ruler or some other straight guide, place it on the dough, and run your cutting device along the guide. With math and a good guide, you can create a perfect batch of squares or triangles. I'm more rustic myself and wing it.

PER SERVING
CALORIES: 221.73
FAT: 18.31
PROTEIN: 10.21
CARBS: 7.19
FIBER: 3.24
SUGAR ALCOHOLS: 0
NET CARBS: 3.95

MORE FACTS: P. 548

5. Place the parchment or foil on a cookie/thin baking tray.

6. Bake for roughly 45 minutes, but start checking at 30 minutes. It will crisp on the edges first. You are essentially looking to melt the cheese within the cracker, then remove the moisture. The cracker will darken and firm up. When the sheet is the same even, slightly darker color across the enter sheet (the edges and the center are all the same color), remove the sheet from the oven. Too dark and it starts to get bitter.

7. Let the sheet cool; then pick up the crackers and snap where the perforations were cut.

8. Crackers!

Garlic-Herb Fauxcaccia

SERVES: 6 · · · PREP: 5 MIN · · · COOK: 25 MIN · · · TOTAL: 30 MIN

1 cup (240 mL) **flaxseed meal** (or 3/4 cup [180 mL] ground chia seed)

1 cup (240 mL) **almond flour**

1 1/2 Tbsp (23 mL) **baking powder**

1 Tbsp (15 mL) chopped **fresh rosemary**

1 tsp (5 mL) **crushed red chili flakes**

1 tsp (5 mL) **salt**, divided

8 large **whole eggs**, beaten

1/4 cup (60 mL) **extra virgin olive oil**

12 **garlic cloves**, minced

This is one of my most popular recipes. It started as a One-Minute Muffin and grew into this, as I experimented and tinkered. OMMs are little more than a quick-bread batter, microwaved in a cup. Within 60 seconds, a full muffin can be "baked," resulting in a warm, fresh muffin! However, if you take the same batter, place it into a ceramic cup, and bake it for 14 minutes... the same thing results! It just takes longer. There is *one* extra benefit, which is caramelization. Because the heat is external, the outside of the muffin browns, creating a more complex flavor. Other than that, same exact muffin!

I wanted to conduct a test by making a big batch of basic unsweetened OMM batter infused with a few herbs and loads of sweet garlic. I wanted something resembling a focaccia, but without yeast or wheat. I wanted it quick-bread style. Let's just say... it worked! IT WORKED WONDERS!! Delicious! Try some with dinner, or... slice it for *amazing* sandwiches!

1. Preheat oven to 350°F (177°C).

2. In a medium bowl, combine flax (or chia), almond flour, baking powder, rosemary, chili flakes, and half of the salt. Mix well.

3. Add the eggs, olive oil, and garlic to the mix. Mix well.

4. Grease a 9" x 9" (23 x 23 x 5 cm) square baking pan. Pour the batter into the pan. With a spatula, smooth it out so that it is evenly distributed throughout the pan. Sprinkle the remaining salt over the top of the batter.

5. Bake for about 20 to 25 minutes or until lightly golden brown and nicely puffed.

6. Place on a rack and cool for at least 10 minutes before slicing. Serve!

PER SERVING
CALORIES: 374.83
FAT: 31.08
PROTEIN: 16.72
CARBS: 13.01
FIBER: 7.47
SUGAR ALCOHOLS: 0
NET CARBS: 5.54

MORE FACTS: P. 548

ONE-MINUTE CHEDDAR BUNS

SERVES: 4 · · · PREP: 15 MIN · · · COOK: 40 MIN · · · TOTAL: 2 HR

1 cup (240 mL) **flaxseed meal** or 3/4 cup [180 mL] ground chia seeds

2 tsp (10 mL) **baking powder**

4 large **whole eggs**

1 Tbsp (15 mL) **olive oil**

1/2 cups (120 mL) shredded **cheddar/colby blend**

2 **garlic cloves**, minced

1/2 tsp (2 mL) chopped **fresh thyme**

salt, fresh cracked pepper, and **chili flakes,** to taste

This recipe is based off of the "One Minute Muffin." OMM's are everywhere that you see a low-carb recipe. They are called a "one-minute" muffin, because they are nuked for a minute, in a microwave. That's it! The method is really quite simple. Put your ingredients in a coffee mug, or any other nonporous and microwave safe container, swirl them around, place the cup in the microwave for one minute. Nuke it. Let it sit for another minute and then ... eat!

The core ratio can be adjusted in an infinite number of ways. You can add sweeteners to it, berries, nuts, spices, citrus rinds, chocolate chips, food colors, etc. You can also add cheese, herbs, garlic, chilies, etc. This "muffin" can be made sweet or savory.

It also takes the shape of anything you put it in. In the photos, you'll see that I have little round ones and bigger square ones. The smaller ones were nuked in little 6.5 oz glass cups that I stash homemade ice cream in. The bigger ones were nuked in microwaveable plastic tupperware-like containers. Once you make the batter, you can spray the container with some spray (or butter it up!), then pour the batter into it. You can expect it to rise about double or triple the height of the batter.

You can eat them hot and fresh or cool them down. You can also split them in half to use for sandwiches. I literally cannot believe I waited 3 years to give these a shot. Maybe microwaves aren't so bad, after all!

Note: This recipe makes 4 large "coffee cup" sized buns, 4 sandwich squares or about 6 small "buns".

PER SERVING
CALORIES: 276.51
FAT: 21.25
PROTEIN: 15.88
CARBS: 9.9
FIBER: 8.02
SUGAR ALCOHOLS: 0
NET CARBS: 1.88

MORE FACTS: P. 548

1. Grease your microwaveable containers.

2. In a medium sized mixing bowl, combine all ingredients.

3. Divide the batter evenly between your containers.

4. Microwave on high for 4 minutes (one minute, per serving).

5. Allow the containers sit in the microwave for 1 more minute.

6. Enjoy!

Orange and Sage Scented Bacon-Cranberry Muffins

SERVES: 6 · · · PREP: 5 MIN · · · COOK: 15 MIN · · · TOTAL: 20 MIN

1/4 cup (60 mL) **coconut flour**

1/4 cup (60 mL) **almond flour**

1/4 cup (60 mL) **vanilla whey protein powder** (sweetened with stevia)

1/4 cup (60 mL) **sugar replacement**

2 tsp (10 mL) **baking powder**

a dash of **salt**

1 **orange**

4 large **eggs**

1/4 cup (60 mL) **melted butter or bacon fat**

6 oz. (168 g) **fresh cranberries**

1/4 cup (60 mL) **real bacon bits**

1 tsp (5 mL) chopped **fresh sage**

PER SERVING
CALORIES: 220.96
FAT: 14.51
PROTEIN: 12.5
CARBS: 20.94
FIBER: 4.29
SUGAR ALCOHOLS: 10
NET CARBS: 6.65

MORE FACTS: P. 548

Here we have another entry with my favorite mega-batter! Again, the idea is to showcase how a single recipe or ratio of ingredients can be used in a wide variety of ways. This recipe was originally conceived as something befitting a holiday dinner spread, allowing friends and family, normies and low-primal enthusiasts alike, to break bread at the same time. The end result is something a little sweet, with fantastic flavor and a texture a bit like a buttery corn bread. It's yum!

1. Preheat oven to 350°F (177°C).

2. Grease a standard 6-muffin muffin pan.

3. In a medium mixing bowl, sift together coconut flour, almond meal, protein powder, sweetener (if powdered), baking powder, and salt.

4. With a zester, zest your orange. You can also use a vegetable peeler to peel the very outer orange layer of the orange (do not get the white pith; it's bitter). You want enough of the zest, to create about 1/2 tsp (2 mL) of fresh zest. If using a vegetable peeler, chop the orange rind, creating a finer zest, and set aside. Juice the orange.

5. Add the eggs, orange zest, orange juice, and melted butter. If using a liquid sweetener, add it now. Mix until combined. If the batter is still too thick, add up to 2 tablespoons (30 mL) of water, cream, coconut milk, or almond milk to thin it out. It should look like thick pancake batter. Fold in the cranberries, bacon bits, and sage.

6. Evenly divide the batter into the 6 prepared muffin cups and bake for 12 to 14 minutes or until golden.

7. Enjoy!

Everything Else

○ ○ ○

Here we have the misfits, the ragamuffins, and the uncategorizable. These are the recipes that aren't a baked good, sauce, dessert, or soup, but are still quite very important and deserve to be included. The crepes alone are almost worth the price of admission! Some of the other recipes in this book rely on the two curry pastes, and a nice leaf tucked into these cheesy taco shells makes for an amazing, crisp, and leak-free taco shell. Enjoy the odd ducks!

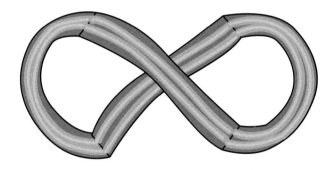

ALL-PURPOSE RICOTTA CREPES

SERVES: 7 · · · PREP: 5 MIN · · · COOK: 30 MIN · · · TOTAL: 35 MIN

1/2 cup (120 mL) whole milk **ricotta cheese**

4 large **eggs**, beaten

2 Tbsp (30 mL) **sugar replacement** (optional)

a dash of **salt**

2 Tbsp (30 mL) **unsalted butter**

These crepes are extremely versatile. They're tougher than your standard soft and svelte French crepe. They can handle a little more thrown at them. They're also very neutral, from a taste perspective. They're more a texutre or "purpose" than they are a "flavor." I use them for all kind of things—as a crepe, filled with sugar-free jams, shmears, and berries, but also as a wrap.

It's not at all uncommon for me to put a slice of turkey into one of these things, then cheese, a slice of tomato, some lettuce, and mustard. Roll it up. Deli wrap! I've used them in place of tortillas for enchiladas. You can roll them up really tightly and slice them into noodles too! Toss these with some zucchini strips, sauce, and cheese, and it's very pasta-like... low-primal style!

Makes roughly 6 to 8 crepes.

1. Add the ricotta, eggs, optional sweetener, and salt into a blender. Blend until combined and smooth. Set aside.

2. Heat a lightly buttered crepe or nonstick sauté pan over medium-low heat.

3. Depending on the size of the pan, add just short of 1/4 cup (60 mL) of batter to the pan and spread it evenly. If necessary, pick up the pan and deliberately tilt it in a variety of directions, directing the flow of the batter around the base of the pan until it completely covers the base of the pan, like a very thin pancake.

4. Once the edges start to brown and curl, loosen the crepe with a spatula and flip it to brown the other side. Repeat this process, placing each completed crepe on a paper towel.

5. Serve hot or layer between paper towels and refrigerate or freeze for later use.

PER SERVING
CALORIES: 100.29
FAT: 6
PROTEIN: 5.71
CARBS: 5.14
FIBER: 0
SUGAR ALCOHOLS: 4.29
NET CARBS: 0.86

MORE FACTS: P. 549

Oh Crêpe!

CHEDDAR TACO SHELLS

SERVES: 6 · · · PREP: 1 MIN · · · COOK: 20 MIN · · · TOTAL: 21 MIN

2 lbs. (908 g) **cheddar cheese**, grated

A really common question is, "What do I do in place of a tortilla?" One obvious answer is one of the many low-carb tortillas on the market. And while these are great, tasty, and obviously fit the bill, they also tend to be made of wheat products and qualify as a processed food. I've got a solid Cheddar Cracker (p. 468) that does a solid job of replacing the taste and texture of a wheat-based cracker but without grains! This tends to fill the void for some. For others, there's always the old, "Wrap it in a leaf!" Baby romaine leaves, leaves of Bibb lettuce, iceberg lettuce, and even cabbage all make for nice handy little holders for your taco fixin's. Again, this answer doesn't satisfy those that pine for the *crunch* of a crispity taco shell.

For you, I offer this cheddar-based taco shell!

These shells can be a bit fussy to make and hot oil tends to get everywhere, but they are also a lot of fun to make! They're delicious and quite toothsome to boot! The crunch isn't quite as quick to crisp as a baked or fried corn tortilla taco shell, but, come on... let's be realistic here. This is a taco shell made *entirely* out of fried cheese. Is this *really* that much of a sacrifice!?

Serving size note: 2 lbs. (908 g) of cheese should make about 12 shells, depending on thickness and size.

Nutrition disinformation: I don't really know how to calculate this. Easily half of the fat (and calories) are rendered from the cheese and poured off. These are nowhere near as calorically dense as the nutrition information will have you believe.

PER SERVING
CALORIES: 601.62
FAT: 49.57
PROTEIN: 37.33
CARBS: 1.83
FIBER: 0
SUGAR ALCOHOLS: 0
NET CARBS: 1.83

MORE FACTS: P. 549

1. Take a large pot and place it on the countertop with a thick wooden spoon forming a bridge through the center of the open space. You will eventually hang your melted cheese on this "spoon bridge." (I have a really thick-handled wooden spoon, which is also somewhat flat. This works perfect, in that it's about 3/4-inch (18 mm) wide and forms taco shells with flat bottoms. They stand up on their own!)

2. Heat a small- to medium-sized nonstick sauté pan over medium heat.

3. Evenly sprinkle your grated cheese around the base of the pan. Continue to cook over low-medium heat. The cheese will melt and melt together. It will eventually begin to fry and darken. Once the cheese has a firm, crispy look to it, but before it burns, pry it out with a heat-resistant plastic spatula and *immediately* drape it over your spoon and quickly adjust it so that equal portions of the cheese are hanging down both sides of the spoon. Be *very* careful as the pan also likely contains a lot of hot oil. Let this oil drip into the pot (and not on yourself).

4. Allow it to rest for a few minutes or until it's sufficiently chilled.

5. Repeat the process to make more taco shells.

6. Enjoy!

Loose 'n' Spicy Hot Chicken Italian Sausage

SERVES: 10 · · · PREP: 20 MIN · · · COOK: 0 MIN · · · TOTAL: 20 MIN

2 lbs. (908 g) **chicken meat**, skinless and boneless (assorted)

1 lb. (454 g) raw **bacon**

4 **garlic cloves**, minced

1 Tbsp (15 mL) whole **fennel seed**

1 Tbsp (15 mL) freshly cracked **black pepper**

1 Tbsp (15 mL) **crushed red chili flakes**

1 Tbsp (15 mL) **paprika**

2 tsp (10 mL) **salt**

Sausages are basically an emulsified blend of fat and meat stuffed into a natural casing (usually intestines) and then cooked.

Huh?

Sausages are meat that has been blended with fat, in a cold environment (so the fat doesn't melt). This is done in a way that combines the meat with the fat and keeps the meat moist when it cooks, rather than having the fat melt out and leak away, leaving behind a mealy mixture of cooked ground meat. A good sausage has chunks of visible meat and fat, but cooks up solid and moist!

This recipe is a loose sausage meat. I use it for all sorts of things, from "pasta" sauces to frittata fillings, as an ingredient in my Poorly Cooked Eggs (p. 116), as stuffing, for sandwich fillings, etc. The list goes on.

Again, sausage is meat and fat. You could go strictly chicken and use the chicken skin ground as the fat. This would work. I'm a big fan of bacon, so I tend to grind raw bacon in with my chicken meat. This is also how my recipe will be written. However, if you want to substitute the bacon for chicken skin, go for it! Just make sure the skin is fairly well cut up before you grind it.

Note: For all chicken, use 2 1/4 lb. (1 kg) chicken to 3/4 lb. (1/3 kg) chicken skin, rather than the ratio shown below. The rest of the recipe is the same!

PER SERVING
CALORIES: 325.04
FAT: 23.47
PROTEIN: 25.14
CARBS: 2.3
FIBER: 0.86
SUGAR ALCOHOLS: 0
NET CARBS: 1.44

MORE FACTS: P. 549

1. Chill bowl large enough for mixing 3 lb. (1.4 kg) of meat, as well as your meat grinder and any grinder attachments.

2. Cut the chicken and bacon into 1-inch (2.5 cm) chunks or lengths.

3. Mix in the chilled bowl with the remainder of the ingredients.

4. Grind the meat through a course grinder.

5. Grind it again! You want to grind it twice.

6. Pack in an airtight container and allow the flavors to marry overnight.

7. Wrap the meat and save for later, use in a recipe, freeze, or portion into ten patties and panfry them!

THAI GREEN CURRY PASTE

SERVES: 16 · · · PREP: 15 MIN · · · COOK: 0 MIN · · · TOTAL: 15 MIN

1 Tbsp (15 mL) **coriander seed**

1 tsp (10 mL) **white peppercorns**

1 **lime**

15 (101 g) **fresh green Thai chilies**, seeds removed (substitution: jalapeño or Serrano peppers)

1 1/2 Tbsp (23 mL) chopped **fresh galangal** (substitution: 1 Tbsp [15 ml] ginger)

4 **shallots**, chopped

1 Tbsp (15 mL) **shrimp paste** (substitution: 1 Tbsp [15 mL] fish sauce)

1 stalk (67 g) **lemongrass**, white part only, sliced thin

1/4 bunch (25 g) **cilantro**, washed (use cilantro stems too)

16 leaves **Thai basil** (substitution: regular basil)

8 **kaffir lime leaves**, chopped (substitution: 1 tsp [5 mL] lime zest)

1 Tbsp (15 mL) **sugar replacement**

1 tsp (4g) **salt**

PER SERVING
CALORIES: 12.8
FAT: 0.13
PROTEIN: 0.44
CARBS: 3.93
FIBER: 0.46
SUGAR ALCOHOLS: 0.94
NET CARBS: 2.53

MORE FACTS: P. 550

Among my favorite of all Thai flavors is that of a green curry. Frankly, there isn't a huge difference between a green and red curry paste. Most of the ingredients overlap, but there are some key differences:

- It's green, meaning it uses green chilies instead of red ones.
- It tends to be *much* fresher, with fresh chilies (rather than dried) and fresh herbs.
- It's got less of a shelf life; use it quickly!
- It also tends to be a little bit sweet.

If I were being truly honest with myself, I think I tend to lean toward green curries *because* they are a bit on the sweeter side. The tongue really only has five senses, and as various ones raise and become more pronounced, the overall sensation is enhanced. I could almost go so far as to say the flavor is better! I do believe all humans seek out sweeter things (not *just* humans, but us too). Adding a little sweet tends to enhance and improve flavors up to a point. There does come a point where sweet becomes sickening, or it becomes dessert. In the case of green curries, we're talking about something with a slightly sweet taste profile, with a very fresh flavor, wild aromas, and a good amount of heat.

Storage tip: This has a lot of fresh ingredients in it, so it's perishable. It's got some acid in it, which helps it last a little longer, but I wouldn't leave it in the fridge for more than a week. I have mine in series of tiny freezer-safe containers in the freezer. They hold up well in there.

Serving size: Recipe makes about 1 cup (240 mL) of paste. Serving size is roughly 1 tablespoon (15 mL).

1. Toast your coriander and white peppercorns. Place a sauté pan or skillet on the stove over medium heat. When the pan is hot, add your spices. Toast for about 2 minutes. The mixture should be quite aromatic, but do *not* let them burn. Remove them from the pan and allow to cool.

2. Once your spices are cool, grind them. This can be done in a mortar and pestle. I use an old beat-up coffee grinder. Alternately, you can also purchase pre-ground spices and toast them, but blend them together before toasting. Then, toast in a hot dry pan for maybe 30 seconds to a minute or until aromatic.

3. With a zester or a peeler, zest the very outer layer of the lime. Do *not* get any of the white part. You really only need about 6 good strips, for a total of about 1 teaspoon (5 mL) chopped. If a peeler was used, chop the zest and set aside. Juice the lime and set aside. Discard the rest of the lime.

4. In a food processor (or mortar and pestle for the real deal), combine all ingredients and process until the consistency of a paste.

THAI RED CURRY PASTE

SERVES: 16 · · · PREP: 15 MIN · · · COOK: 0 MIN · · · TOTAL: 15 MIN

10 whole **Thai dried chilies**

1 Tbsp (15 mL) **coriander seed**

2 tsp (10 mL) **cumin seed**

1 tsp (5 mL) **black peppercorns**

10 (67 g) **fresh red Thai chilies**, seeds removed
(substitution: Fresno or serrano peppers)

1 1/2 Tbsp (23 mL) **fresh galangal**, chopped
(substitution: 1 Tbsp [15 mL] ginger)

4 **shallots**, chopped

1 Tbsp (15 mL) **shrimp paste** (substitution: 1
Tbsp [15 mL] fish sauce)

8 **kaffir lime leaves**, chopped (substitution: 1
tsp [5 mL] lime zest)

1 stalk (67 g) **lemongrass**, white part only,
sliced thin

1/4 cup (60 mL) chopped **cilantro stems**

1 tsp (4g) **salt**

This recipe is a bit different than most in this book. There are no real tricks to it, and it's not directly low-carb in any specific way. However, like any good spice blend or potent ingredient, it packs a lot of punch for very little effect on blood sugar. A little goes a long way!

A curry paste is a fresh and vibrant blend of ingredients, most dominantly chilies, spices, and herbs. This can form the backbone or a backdrop (depending on the usage) for *many* different recipes. Plop a little into a peanut sauce to give it some more depth of character. Sauté some chicken and eggplant with it, just plain, and you've got a nice flavorful kick of flavors. Heat up some shrimp in some coconut milk with some lime juice, a little more fish sauce, some fresh cilantro, and a blend of tomatoes, peppers, squash, and mushrooms for an out-of-this-world shrimp and coconut soup!

Probably the most difficult part of this recipe is finding the ingredients. I'll list substitutions in the ingredient list where I can. Ultimately, the closer to the true ingredients you get, the more authentic your paste will be. Outside of ingredient procuring, the rest of the process is simply "throw it in a food processer and process!" That said, a mortar and pestle is the true and proper way to do this.

This particular blend is a scaled down and "basic" red paste. There are regional variations that can be explored. My thinking when developing this recipe was to keep it simple while still holding true to a red curry paste. This way, the peripheral ingredients could be added for specific and unique dishes. Some of the common additions to various red pastes are: white peppercorns, cinnamon, fish sauce, mace, nutmeg, and cloves. For an even more basic curry paste, you can eliminate the cilantro roots, coriander, cumin, and peppercorns.

PER SERVING
CALORIES: 18.2
FAT: 0.47
PROTEIN: 0.55
CARBS: 3.87
FIBER: 0.9
SUGAR ALCOHOLS: 0.94
NET CARBS: 2.96

MORE FACTS: P. 550

Storage tip: This has a lot of fresh ingredients in it, so it's perishable. It's got some acid in it, which helps it to last a little longer, but I wouldn't leave it in the fridge for more than a week. I have mine in series of tiny freezer safe containers in the freezer. They hold up well in there.

Serving size: Recipe makes about 1 cup (240 mL) of paste. Serving size is roughly 1 tablespoon (15 mL).

1. Split the dried chilies and remove the seeds. Soak the flesh in hot water for about 20 minutes.

2. While the chilies are soaking, toast your coriander, cumin, and peppercorns. Place a sauté pan or skillet on the stove over medium heat. When the pan is hot, add your black peppercorns. Toast for about 1 minute. Add your coriander seeds and toast for about 1 minute. Finally, add your cumin seeds and toast for about 1 minute. The mixture should be quite aromatic. Do *not* let them burn. Keep the pan moving, as they toast. Remove them from the pan and allow to cool.

3. Once your spices are cool, grind them. This can be done in a mortar and pestle. I use an old beat-up coffee grinder. Alternately, you can also purchase pre-ground spices and toast them, but blend them together before toasting. Then, toast in a hot dry pan for maybe 30 seconds to a minute or until aromatic.

4. In a food processor (or mortar and pestle for the real deal), combine all ingredients and process until the consistency of a paste.

Bacon Wrapped Bacon

SERVES: 8 · · · PREP: 15 MIN · · · COOK: 3 HR 30 MIN · · · TOTAL: A DAY OR TWO + 4 HR

1 slab lean **pork belly** (about 4 lbs) (1.8 kg)

1 cup (240 mL) **Sweet 'n' Tangy BBQ Sauce** (p. 356)

1 cup (240 mL) **chicken stock** or **broth**

16 slices (400 g) **raw bacon**

salt and **pepper** to taste

Note: A good portion of the fat in this recipe is removed before it is eaten, but I have no way to calculate the final macronutrient amount. Thankfully, most of us aren't afraid of fat, so it shouldn't be a problem. For those counting fat grams and/or calories, the fat and calories presented are likely double the real numbers.

Pork belly is a wonderful ingredient. It's what all American "streaky" bacon is made from. However, pork belly is absolutely delicious in its own right. It's very common in Asian preparations, where it is braised (cooked in liquid for several hours) and then cut into cubes and stir-fried into a wide variety of amazing dishes. The absolute best pork belly I've personally ever had was a sweet, Hoisin sauce–braised pork belly, served as a steak-sized portion. It was dripping with sweet sauce cascading down its sides into an equally delicious bed of braised yet crunchy Asian greens. Braising is a cooking method that slowly breaks down the muscle, resulting in a softened meat. The ribbons of pure, perfect fat lose their greasy qualities and take on an almost custard-like texture. Combined with the flavors infused through the marinating and braising, this becomes something both rustic and elegant, comforting but startling, bold but... Yeah, okay: *bold*. I've opted to take it into a smoky BBQ realm, braising it in chicken broth and BBQ sauce. The sweet flavors and the smoke match the added-later strips of actual bacon, as it is fried in its own fat and then roasted and served with a wonderful BBQ Pork Broth.

I would very likely serve this as an appetizer, probably with something like a small bed of Garlicky BBQ Kale (p. 311). I may even serve it as a dinner, with something like roasted carrots, garlic, and onions. However, because I couldn't decide, I've opted to place it with "Everything Else," back here at the end of the book—a perfect way to sign off; a smoky, fatty coda to a book otherwise known as *The Big Book of Bacon*.

1. Cut the pork belly into 8 perfect squares (or as close as you can get).

PER SERVING
CALORIES: 18.2
FAT: 0.47
PROTEIN: 0.55
CARBS: 3.87
FIBER: 0.9
SUGAR ALCOHOLS: 0.94
NET CARBS: 2.96

MORE FACTS: P. 549

2. Rub the pieces with the BBQ sauce and place in a covered bowl or tray and put in the refrigerator to marinate overnight (or roughly 12 hours).

3. After the pork has marinated, remove it from the refrigerator and place it into a large soup pot. Add the marinade and the chicken stock. Place the pot on the stove and bring to a very low simmer. Cover the pot and allow the contents to simmer for roughly 2 1/2 to 3 hours. Be sure to check the pork and turn the pieces over from time to time. Braise until the belly is very soft to the touch and the meat tears easily.

4. Once the meat is soft and cooked, remove it from the BBQ broth and place it onto a large baking tray, such as a cookie tray. Pour your BBQ broth into a bowl or container and place, uncovered, in the refrigerator.

5. If your belly had skin on it, peel it off at this point and discard. Evenly distribute the cooked belly pieces on the tray, with a space between each piece. Place another baking tray on top of the pork. Weigh down the top tray with bricks, stacks of plates, of whatever you may have that is heavy and can evenly distribute the weight on top of the pork belly. The goal is to evenly flatten the pieces of pork as they cool. This will make wrapping them and evenly cooking them easier when frying them up later. Remember, we want to flatten them but not squish them. Place the weighted trays of pork into the refrigerator to cool.

6. Once the pork is fully chilled, it is ready to be fried. I typically vacuum pack pieces of it at this point and freeze them for a rainy day. Basically, it's here in the process that they can be wrapped in plastic and saved for dinner or cooked.

7. If you're ready to cook, remove the sauce from the refrigerator. It will have formed a solid layer of fat on the top. With a spoon (or your fingers), remove this layer of fat and discard. Place the rest of the sauce in a saucepan and bring it up to a simmer on the stove. We want to reduce it by simmering it until some of the water evaporates, concentrating the flavors and thickening the sauce up. I think this is nice as a broth, so reduce it by about half.

8. While the sauce reduces, preheat the oven to 400°F (204°C).

9. Season each piece of pork belly with a bit of salt and pepper. Then, wrap each piece in two slices of bacon, making sure the seam for each piece is on the bottom.

10. Heat two large ovenproof sauté pans. Once the pans are hot, place four pieces of pork in each pan, making sure there is space between each piece and that the bacon seams are facedown. Turn the heat down to low or medium low and allow the pork to fry for about 6 minutes. It should have a nice color and begin crisping.

11. Place the two pans in the oven for about 8 more minutes. This will allow the pork to heat through. Once the 8 minutes are up, remove from the oven and flip the bellies, so that the top is now down in the pan. Place them on two burners over low to medium low for about 4 to 5 more minutes, to allow the top to crisp up.

12. Before serving, flip the pieces back over. Serve on a plate with your accoutrements of choice. Distribute the BBQ Pork Broth of the top of each plate and serve!

Random Story Time: I used to work with a Mexican dude named Saul. Saul didn't speak English very well, but… he was taking classes, tried really hard and was a wonderful guy! One day, I was trying to think of the Spanish word for "bacon." I had a big handful of raw bacon and held it up to Saul and said, "Hey, Saul … how do you say this?" and pointed at it. Saul stopped everything he was doing, as his face turned up into thoughtful kerfuzzle. He thought and thought. After about a minute, he started pacing around the kitchen. I'd never SEEN someone work so hard to think of a word. He kept saying, "I don't know! It's been a while. I'll think of it!"… then he'd stomp around, frustrated, dejected… and completely lost in thought. Finally, after what felt like a full 10 minutes of theatrics, the light bulb turned on, immediate and bright! His eyes opened wide and he looked at me, like he had the cure for cancer and said … "Bacon??!"

The whole kitchen just blew up in an uproar! Saul had thought I was quizzing him!

Saul, if you get this … the answer I was looking for was … "*Tocino*".

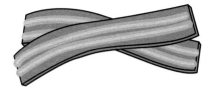

Back of the Book

...

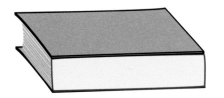

Shopping List

Meats

Most any and all muscle meats, in any amounts.

However, be aware that eggs, some organ meats (offal), and some seafood have small amounts of carbohydrates. You can still eat substantial portions of these ingredients, but you will need to count those carbs toward your daily limit.

Some examples:

Eggs = approximately half a carb each
Shrimp = about 4 carbs per pound (so about 1 carb per 4 large shrimp)
Oysters = about 2.5 carbs each
Beef Liver = about 1 carb per ounce (16 carbs per pound)
Also, some other meaty things to watch out for...

Bacon, ham, sausages, salami, deli meats, etc.—you'll need to read the packages for these products. Again, you may eat substantial portions of these items, but you'll need to shop around and find a product that suits your way of eating. This category of meat product often has sugar in their brines, marinades, and cures, as well as carb-y and wonky fillers and preservatives in some of the sausages and highly processed lunch meats. Talk to your butcher.

Fruits, Veggies and Legumes

Item	Carbs	Item	Carbs	Item	Carbs	Item	Carbs
Alfalfa sprouts	0	Avocado	2.17	Brussels sprouts	5	Honeydew melon	8.28
Broccoli rabe/rapini	0	Zucchini/Summer Squash	2.17	Raspberries	5.45	Peaches	9
Mushrooms	1	Eggplant	2.37	Strawberries	5.6	Peas	9
Asparagus	1.49	Tomatoes	2.74	Casaba melon	5.67	Oranges	10
Radish	1.72	Cauliflower	2.86	Rutabagas	5.7	Plums	10
Celery	1.82	Cucumber	2.99	Celeriac/Celery root	5.77	Apple	12
Greens/Lettuces		Peppers	3.05	Pumpkin	6.03	Blueberries	12
Endive	.19	Cabbage	3.29	Carrots	6.25	Leeks	12
Watercress	1	Green beans	3.64	Beets	6.62	Pears	12
Boston/Butter	1.23	Jicama	3.92	Spaghetti squash	6.93	Pineapple	12
Romaine	1.28	Broccoli	3.95	Watermelon	7.15	Parsnips	13
Mesclun/Mixed	1.29	Okra	4	Cranberries	7.27	Cherries	14
Spinach	1.47	Tomatillos	4	Onions	7.5	Beans, fava (cooked)	14
Iceberg	1.99	Fennel	4.27	Papaya	7.89	Potatoes, red	14
Arugula	2	Blackberries	4.86	Cantaloupe	7.99	Beans, kidney (cooked)	16
Chard	2	Artichokes	4.94	Kale	8	Beans, navy (cooked)	16
Collard	2	Turnips	4.92			Corn, sweet yellow	16
Mache	2					Grapes	16
Mustard	2					Potatoes, russet	17
						Sweet potatoes	17
						Beans, pinto (cooked)	18
						Bananas	20
						Beans, garbanzo (cooked)	20

Nuts and Seeds

Flax seeds	.44	Coconut, dried, unsweetened	2.24	Cashews	8.4
Pecans	1.12	Peanuts	2.24	Chestnuts	12.32
Brazil nuts	1.38	Pine nuts	2.24		
Macadamia nuts	1.4	Poppy seeds	2.24		
Chia seeds	1.68	Pumpkin seeds	2.52		
Coconut, raw meat	1.68	Almonds	2.8		
Hazelnuts	1.96	Sesame seeds	3.08		
Walnuts	1.96	Sunflower seeds	3.08		
		Pistachios	5.04		

Fats and Oils

Good Fats				Bad Fats
Flaxseed oil	225°F (107°C)	Cocoa butter	400°F (204°C)	Margarine
Butter, whole	250 to 300°F (121 to 149°C)	Almond oil	420°F (216°C)	Shortening
		Hazelnut oil	431°F (221°C)	Canola Oil
Sesame oil, unrefined	350°F (177°C)	Palm oil	455°F (235°C)	Corn oil
Coconut oil, unrefined	352°F (177°C)	Coconut oil, refined	450°F (232°C)	Soybean oil
Lard	370°F (188°C)	Sesame oil, semirefined	450°F (232°C)	Cottonseed oil
Olive oil, extra virgin	375°F (191°C)	Olive oil, extra light	468°F (242°C)	Vegetable oil
Olive oil, virgin	391°F (199°C)	Butter, clarified (ghee)	485°F (252°C)	

Dairy

Butter	0	Blue cheese	2.22	Cream cheese, full fat	3.88
Brie	.42	Provolone cheese	2.35	Feta cheese	4
Goat cheese	1	Ricotta cheese, full fat	2.84	Half and half	4.13
Cheddar cheese	1.23	Heavy cream	2.94	Plain yogurt, full fat	4.49
American cheese	2	Sour cream, full fat	3.48	Skim milk	4.87
Mozzarella cheese, whole milk, low moisture	2	Parmesan cheese	3.52	Milk	5.33
		Cottage cheese, full fat	3.56	Swiss cheese	5.33

Spices and Herbs

Basil, fresh, chopped	.01	Fennel seed	.24	Cumin seed	.66
Chives, fresh	.01	Coriander seed, ground	.26	Black pepper	.76
Cilantro, fresh, chopped	.01	Thyme, ground	.27	Cardamom, ground	.8
Oregano, fresh, chopped	.01	Basil, dried, ground	.28	Tarragon, ground	.86
Green Onions	.04	Ginger, fresh	.32	White pepper	.86
Parsley	.04	Paprika	.38	Garlic, fresh, chopped (about 1 carb per clove)	.93
Dill Weed, fresh	.05	Oregano, ground	.42	Allspice, ground	1
Rosemary, fresh	.05	Curry powder	.5	Pumpkin pie spice	1.08
Sage, fresh	.1	Vanilla extract	.5	Poultry seasoning	1.1
Tarragon, fresh	.1	Cloves, ground	.54	Ginger, ground	1.16
Thyme, fresh	.1	Cinnamon, ground	.56	Onion powder	1.5
Sage, ground	.14	Nutmeg, ground	.56	Garlic powder	1.89
Parsley, dried	.15	Cayenne pepper	.6		
Caraway seed	.24	Mace, ground	.6		

Low-Primal Powders

* Coconut Flour
* Almond Flour
* Hazelnut Meal/Flour
* Glucomannan Powder (a thickener)
* Arrowroot Starch/Flour (a thickener)
* Tapioca Flour (a thickener good for baking)
* Stevia-Sweetened or Unsweetened Whey Protein Powder (typically vanilla)
* Gelatin Powder (I prefer grass fed.)
* Cocoa Powder
* Ground Chia Seeds (I typically grind my own in a coffee grinder.)
* Ground Flaxseed Meal (I typically grind my own in a coffee grinder.)

Nonlow-Primal Powders

Soy Flour

Oat Fiber

Resistant Wheat Starch

Gluten Free Oat Flour

* Xanthan Gum

Guar Gum

Wheat Protein Isolate 5000

Wheat Protein Isolate 8000

Vital Wheat Gluten

Lupin Flour

Peanut Flour

Baking Mixes/Prepared Powders

Low-Carb Flours and Bake Mixes

Sugar-Free Gelatin Desserts

Sugar-Free Pudding Desserts

Nonlow-Primal Sweeteners

* Liquid Sucralose
* Sugar-Free Syrups (like you'd see at a coffee shop)

Polydextrose Fiber

Low-Primal Sweeteners

* Swerve Sweetener (a premade blend and my personal favorite: www.SwerveSweetener.com)
* Erythritol
* Inulin
* Tagatose
* Yacon Syrup (For making brown sugar)
* Xylitol Honey

Stevia Products

Fats/Oils

* Lard (I typically use bacon fat, though.)
* Olive Oil (look for the real deal; a lot of what is available isn't actually pure olive oil.)
* Coconut Oil
* Butter

Red Palm Oil

Ghee

Condiments

* Reduced Sugar Ketchup
* No-Sugar-Added Jams and Jellies
* Xylitol Pancake Syrup
* Maple Syrup
* Sugar-Free BBQ Sauce
* Tomato Sauce
* Salsa
* Almond Butter
* Peanut Butter
* Mustard

Hot Sauce

Coconut Aminos

Prepared Products

* Erythritol-Sweetened Chocolate Bars
* Erythritol-Sweetened Snack and Protein Bars
* Xylitol Breath Mints

Low-Carb Tortillas

Low-Carb Pita Breads

Canned Stuff

* Coconut Milk
* Pumpkin Puree
* Black Organic Soybeans
* Erythritol-Sweetened Soda

Other Stuff

* Almond Milk, unsweetened
* Cacao Nibs
* Shirataki Noodles and Rice
* Chia Seeds
* Apple Cider Vinegar
* Flavor Extracts and Oils

Cacao Butter

Erythritol-Sweetened Chocolate Chips

Kelp Noodles

NOTES

Beverages Nutrition Facts

Horchata · p.82

	CA	FAT	P	C	F	SA	NC
approximately 12 cups (2832g) water, divided	0	0	0	0	0	0	0
1 3/4 cups (254g) blanched almonds	1473	127	56	50.8	26.3	0	24.5
3/4 cup (109g) cashews	602	48	19.6	36	3.3	0	32.7
1/2 cup (72g) white sesame seeds	412	36	13	17	8.5	0	8.5
2 tsp (6g) fresh lime zest, finely chopped	3.8	0	.1	1.3	.1	0	1.3
2 sticks (16g) cinnamon	38	0	0	12	8	0	4
1 tsp (2g) freshly grated nutmeg	11	1	0	1	0	0	1
1 1/2 cups (360g) sugar equivalent (to taste)	0	0	0	360	0	360	0
1 Tbsp (13g) vanilla extract	37	0	0	2	0	0	2
1/2 tsp (2g) salt	0	0	0	0	0	0	0
Totals (of 12 servings):	2578	212.7	88.7	480	46.1	360	74
Per Serving:	214.9	17.7	7.4	40	3.8	30	(6.2)

Coconut, Orange, and Chia · p.86

	CA	FAT	P	C	F	SA	NC
1 1/3 cups (320g) almond milk, unsweetened	60	4.7	2.7	4	1.3	0	2.7
2/3 cup (151g) coconut milk, unsweetened	266	29.3	2.7	5.3	0	0	5.3
2 Tbsp (30g) sugar equivalent	0	0	0	30	0	30	0
1 Tbsp (12g) chia seeds	60	4	2	4	4	0	0
1 Tbsp (16g) fresh orange juice	7	0	0	1.5	0	0	1.5
2 tsp (13g) yacon syrup (or blackstrap molasses)	13.3	0	0	7.3	0	0	7.3
1/2 tsp (1.5g) fresh orange zest, finely chopped	1	0	0	.3	0	0	.3
a dash of salt	0	0	0	0	0	0	0
Totals (of 2 servings):	408	38	7.4	52.5	5.4	30	17.2
Per Serving:	204	19	3.7	26.3	2.7	15	(8.6)

Spiced Masala Chai Tea · p.87

	CA	FAT	P	C	F	SA	NC
2 cups (474g) water	0	0	0	0	0	0	0
1/4 cup (60g) sugar equivalent	0	0	0	60	0	60	0
1/2 tsp (2g) vanilla extract	0	0	0	0	0	0	0
1/2 tsp (1g) cinnamon, ground	0	0	0	0	0	0	0
1/4 tsp (.25g) cloves, ground	0	0	0	0	0	0	0
1/4 tsp (.25g) cardamom, ground	0	0	0	0	0	0	0
1/4 tsp (.25g) black pepper, ground	0	0	0	0	0	0	0
1/4 tsp (.25g) fennel seeds, ground	0	0	0	0	0	0	0
1/4 tsp (.25g) nutmeg, ground	0	0	0	0	0	0	0
1/4 tsp (.25g) salt	0	0	0	0	0	0	0
1/2 tsp (1g) fresh ginger, grated	0	0	0	0	0	0	0
2 cups (480g) almond milk, unsweetened	90	7	4	6	2	0	4
4 black tea bags	0	0	0	0	0	0	0
Totals (of 4 servings):	90	7	4	66	2	60	4
Per Serving:	22.5	1.8	1	16.5	.5	15	(1)

Sweet Lassi · p.94

	CA	FAT	P	C	F	SA	NC
1 cup (226g) plain Greek yogurt, unsweetened	260	22	8	10	0	0	10
1/2 cup (90g) ice cubes	0	0	0	0	0	0	0
2 Tbsp (30g) sugar equivalent	0	0	0	30	0	30	0
1/2 tsp (.5g) rose water	0	0	0	0	0	0	0
1/4 tsp (.25g) cardamom, ground	.8	0	0	.2	.1	0	.1
a dash of salt	0	0	0	0	0	0	0
Totals (of 1 servings):	260.8	22	8	40.2	.1	30	10.1
Per Serving:	260.8	22	8	40.2	.1	30	(10.1)

CA= Calories / **FAT**= Fat / **P**=Protein / **C**= Carbohydrates / **F**= Fiber / **SA**= Sugar Alcohols / **NC**= Net Carbs

Luxurious Eggnog — p.89

	CA	FAT	P	C	F	SA	NC
2 1/2 cups (595g) heavy whipping cream	2052	220	12.5	17.5	0	0	17.5
1 1/2 cup (360g) almond milk, unsweetened	67.5	5.3	3	4.5	1.5	0	3
1/3 cup (80g) sugar equivalent	0	0	0	80	0	80	0
1 (12g) vanilla bean, split lengthwise (or 2 tsp vanilla extract)	23	0	0	1	0	0	1
1/2 tsp (1g) cinnamon, ground	2.5	0	0	.8	.5	0	.3
1/4 tsp (.5g) nutmeg, freshly ground	2.6	.2	0	.3	.1	0	.1
a dash of salt	0	0	0	0	0	0	0
6 large (300g) whole eggs	429	30	13	3	0	0	3
Totals (of 8 servings):	2577	255.4	28.6	107.1	2.1	80	24.9
Per Serving:	322.1	31.9	3.6	13.4	.3	10	(3.1)

Chocolate Shake — p.92

	CA	FAT	P	C	F	SA	NC
4 cups (720g) ice cubes	0	0	0	0	0	0	0
3 cups (714g) heavy whipping cream	2463	264	15	21	0	0	21
1 recipe (145g) chocolate sauce (about 1/2 cup)	322.7	33.8	5.9	59.8	7.3	45	7.58
1/4 cup (60g) sugar equivalent	0	0	0	60	0	60	0
a dash of salt	0	0	0	0	0	0	0
Totals (of 4 servings):	2785	297.8	20.9	140.8	7.3	105	28.52
Per Serving:	696.4	74.5	5.2	35.2	1.8	26.25	(7.13)

Chocolate Sauce — p.92

	CA	FAT	P	C	F	SA	NC
1/4 cup (22g) unsweetened cocoa powder	49	4.5	4.3	12.5	7.3	0	5.3
1/3 cup (79g) heavy whipping cream, divided	273	29.3	1.7	2.3	0	0	2.3
3 Tbsp (45g) sugar equivalent	0	0	0	45	0	45	0
a dash of salt	0	0	0	0	0	0	0
Totals (of 4 servings):	322.7	33.8	5.9	59.8	7.3	45	7.6
Per Serving:	80.7	8.5	1.5	15	1.8	11.3	(1.9)

Spicy Hot Chocolate — p.88

	CA	FAT	P	C	F	SA	NC
1 cup (240g) unsweetened almond milk	45	3.5	2	3	1	0	2
3/4 cup (179g) heavy whipping cream	615	66	3.8	5.3	0	0	5.3
1 tsp (4g) vanilla extract	11.5	0	0	.5	0	0	.5
1/4 cup (60g) sugar equivalent	0	0	0	60	0	60	0
3 Tbsp (16g) unsweetened cocoa powder	36.8	3.4	23.2	9.4	5.5	0	3.9
1/2 tsp (1g) cinnamon, ground	2.5	0	0	.8	.5	0	.3
1/2 tsp (2g) ancho pepper, New Mexico chili, or cayenne, powdered	5.6	.2	.2	1	.4	0	.6
a dash of salt	0	0	0	0	0	0	0
1 shot (28g) espresso (optional)	5	0	0	0	0	0	0
Totals (of 2 servings):	722.1	73.1	29.2	70	7.4	60	12.5
Per Serving:	361.1	36.5	14.6	35	3.7	30	(6.3)

Cucumber-Ginger Water — p.90

	CA	FAT	P	C	F	SA	NC
1 one-inch piece (11g) fresh ginger	9	0	0	2	0	0	2
1 (301g) English cucumber	46.3	0	0	11.6	1.7	0	9.8
1 gallon (3776g) cold water	0	0	0	0	0	0	0
a dash of salt	0	0	0	0	0	0	0
Totals (of 16 servings):	55.3	0	0	13.6	1.7	0	11.8
Per Serving:	3.5	0	0	.9	.1	0	(.7)

Watermelon Agua Fresca — p.84

	CA	FAT	P	C	F	SA	NC
8 cups (1216g) seedless watermelon cubes or balls, divided	368	0	8	88	8	0	80
6 cups (1440g) water	0	0	0	0	0	0	0
1/2 cup (120g) sugar equivalent	0	0	0	120	0	120	0
1/4 cup (61g) lime juice, freshly squeezed	15.3	0	.3	5.3	.3	0	5
1/2 tsp (2g) salt	0	0	0	0	0	0	0
Totals (of 10 servings):	383.3	0	8.3	213.3	8.3	120	85
Per Serving:	38.3	0	.8	21.3	.8	12	(8.5)

CA= Calories / **FAT**= Fat / **P**=Protein / **C**= Carbohydrates / **F**= Fiber / **SA**= Sugar Alcohols / **NC**= Net Carbs

Breakfast Nutrition Facts

Baked Eggs with Spinach, Sun-Dried Tomatoes, and Goat Cheese — p.98

	CA	FAT	P	C	F	SA	NC
1/4 lb. (116g) spinach, washed and stems removed	26.6	.4	3.3	4.1	2.5	0	1.6
1 Tbsp (14g) butter	100	11	0	0	0	0	0
4 large (200g) eggs	284	20	24	1.7	0	0	1.7
1/4 cup (28g) sun-dried tomatoes in oil, oil drained off, sliced into strips	58.5	3.8	1.5	6.5	1.5	0	5
1/4 cup (112g) crumbled goat cheese	407	33.6	24.6	3.4	0	0	3.4
1/4 cup (60g) heavy whipping cream	205	22	1.3	1.8	0	0	1.8
2 sprigs (2g) fresh thyme, stems removed	2	0	.1	.5	.3	0	.2
salt and pepper	0	0	0	0	0	0	0
Totals (of 4 servings):	1084	90.8	54.8	17.8	4.2	0	13.6
Per Serving:	271	22.7	13.7	4.5	1.1	0	(3.4)

Rosemary, Ham, and Swiss Frittatas — p.102

	CA	FAT	P	C	F	SA	NC
1/2 cup (57g) bacon bits	200	12	24	0	0	0	0
1/2 lb. (227g) ham, cubed	356	16	46.7	4	0	0	4
1/2 lb. (227g) Swiss cheese, cubed	862	63.3	61.4	12.1	0	0	12.1
1 Tbsp (2g) fresh rosemary, chopped	2.6	.1	.1	.4	.3	0	.1
4 large (200g) eggs	286	20	26	2	0	0	2
1 1/4 cups (298g) heavy whipping cream	1026	110	6.3	8.8	0	0	8.8
2 Tbsp (30g) Dijon mustard, whole grain	24.7	1.2	1.5	2.9	1.2	0	1.7
salt and freshly cracked pepper to taste	0	0	0	0	0	0	0
Totals (of 4 servings):	2758.6	222.6	165.9	30.2	1.5	0	28.7
Per Serving:	689.6	55.7	41.5	7.6	.4	0	(7.2)

Grain-Free Pancakes — p.96

	CA	FAT	P	C	F	SA	NC
1/4 cup (28g) coconut flour	124	3	7	18	12	0	6
1/4 cup (28g) almond meal	160	14	6	6	3	0	3
1/4 cup (28g) vanilla whey protein powder (sweetened with stevia)	100	0	26	0	0	0	0
1/4 cup (60g) sugar equivalent	0	0	0	60	0	60	0
2 tsp (8g) baking powder	10	0	0	2	0	0	2
a dash of salt	0	0	0	0	0	0	0
4 large (200g) eggs	284	20	24	1.7	0	0	1.7
1/4 cup (56g) melted butter	400	44	0	0	0	0	0
2 Tbsp (28g) butter, ghee, or lard (for pan/griddle)	200	22	0	0	0	0	0
Totals (of 4 servings):	1278	103	63	87.65	15	60	12.7
Per Serving:	319.5	25.8	15.8	21.9	3.8	15	(3.2)

Nutty Chia Fauxtmeal — p.118

	CA	FAT	P	C	F	SA	NC
1/2 cup (120g) almond milk, unsweetened	22.5	1.8	1	1.5	.5	0	1
2 Tbsp (30g) heavy whipping cream	102	11	.6	.9	0	0	.9
2 Tbsp (30g) sugar-free pancake syrup	0	0	0	0	0	0	0
1/4 tsp (1g) vanilla extract	2.9	0	0	.1	0	0	.1
1/4 cup (28g) hazelnut flour (can substitute almond meal)	180	17	4	5	3	0	2
2 Tbsp (15g) chia seeds	70	4.5	3	7	6	0	1
1 Tbsp (10g) slivered almonds, toasted	52.6	4.6	2	1.8	.9	0	.9
1 Tbsp (6g) chopped pecans, toasted	42.8	4.4	.6	.9	.6	0	.3
1/4 tsp (.5g) cinnamon, ground	1.2	0	0	.4	.3	0	.1
a dash of nutmeg	0	0	0	0	0	0	0
a dash of salt	0	0	0	0	0	0	0
Totals (of 1 servings):	474.6	43.3	11.2	17.6	11.3	0	6.3
Per Serving:	474.6	43.3	11.2	17.6	11.3	0	(6.3)

CA= Calories / **FAT**= Fat / **P**=Protein / **C**= Carbohydrates / **F**= Fiber / **SA**= Sugar Alcohols / **NC**= Net Carbs

Bacon Pancake Wedgie — p.103

	CA	FAT	P	C	F	SA	NC
1/4 cup (28g) coconut flour	124	3	7	18	12	0	6
1/4 cup (28g) almond meal	160	14	6	6	3	0	3
1/4 cup (28g) vanilla whey protein powder (sweetened with stevia)	100	0	26	0	0	0	0
1/4 cup (60g) sugar equivalent	0	0	0	60	0	60	0
2 tsp (8g) baking powder	10	0	0	2	0	0	2
a dash of salt	0	0	0	0	0	0	0
4 large (200g) eggs	284	20	24	1.7	0	0	1.7
1/4 cup (56g) melted bacon fat, divided	400	44	0	0	0	0	0
1/2 cup (57g) real bacon bits	200	12	24	0	0	0	0
Totals (of 4 servings):	1278	93	87	87.7	15	60	12.7
Per Serving:	319.5	23.3	21.8	21.9	3.8	15	(3.2)

Coconut Flour OMM French Toast — p.108

	CA	FAT	P	C	F	SA	NC
1/4 cup (28g) coconut flour	124	3	7	18	12	0	6
1 Tbsp (15g) sugar equivalent	0	0	0	15	0	15	0
2 tsp (8g) baking powder	10	0	0	2	0	0	2
a dash of salt	0	0	0	0	0	0	0
8 large (400g) eggs, divided	572	40	52	4	0	0	4
3/4 cup (180g) unsweetened almond milk, divided	33.8	2.6	1.5	2.3	.8	0	1.5
1 tsp (4g) vanilla extract	11.5	0	0	.5	0	0	.5
1/4 cup (56g) butter, melted	400	44	0	0	0	0	0
1/2 cup (119g) heavy whipping cream	410	44	2.5	3.5	0	0	3.5
1/4 cup (56g) butter	400	44	0	0	0	0	0
Totals (of 4 servings):	1967.8	177.6	63	45.3	12.8	15	17.5
Per Serving:	490.5	44.4	15.8	11.3	3.2	7.8	(4.4)

Torta di Rotello — p.100

	CA	FAT	P	C	F	SA	NC
3 cups (336g) almond meal	1920	168	72	72	36	0	36
1 tsp (3g) arrowroot (optional)	9.5	0	0	2.4	.1	0	2.3
1/2 tsp (2g) salt	0	0	0	0	0	0	0
4 large (200g) eggs, divided	284	20	24	1.7	0	0	1.7
2 Tbsp (28g) butter	200	22	0	0	0	0	0
1 lb. (464g) spinach, washed and stems removed	106	1.6	13.1	16.3	9.8	0	6.5
1/2 lb. (232g) cream cheese	794	79	14	9	0	0	9
1/2 lb. (232g) whole milk, low-moisture mozzarella	737	58	51	4.6	0	0	4.6
1/4 lb. (116g) grated Parmesan cheese	500	33.6	44.1	4.64	0	0	4.6
3/4 lb. (348g) sliced Genoa salami	1350	114	73.1	3.5	0	0	3.5
4 (292g) roasted peppers, dried with paper towels	91.8	0	2.9	17.8	5.9	0	11.8
3/4 lb. (348g) sliced turkey breast	361	7	59.2	13.9	0	0	13.9
salt and pepper to taste	0	0	0	0	0	0	0
Totals (of 12 servings):	6355	504.1	353.4	145.8	51.8	0	94
Per Serving:	529.6	42	29.5	12.2	4.3	0	(7.8)

Orange-Walnut Strata — p.104

	CA	FAT	P	C	F	SA	NC
1/4 cup plus 2 Tbsp (42g) coconut flour	186	4.5	10.5	27	18	0	9
1/4 cup plus 2 Tbsp (42g) almond meal	240	21	9	9	4.5	0	4.5
1/4 cup plus 2 Tbsp (42g) vanilla whey protein powder (sweetened with stevia)	150	0	39	0	0	0	0
3/4 cup (180g) sugar equivalent, divided	0	0	0	180	0	180	0
1 Tbsp (12g) baking powder	15	0	0	3	0	0	3
a dash of salt	0	0	0	0	0	0	0
14 large (700g) eggs, divided	994	70	84	5.8	0	0	5.8
1/4 cup plus 2 Tbsp (84g) melted butter	600	66	0	0	0	0	0
1 (140g) orange	69	0	0	18	3	0	15
1 lb. (464g) cream cheese	1554	154	27.4	17.6	0	0	17.6
1 cup (100g) coarsely chopped walnut bits	654	65	15	14	7	0	7
1 tsp (4g) vanilla extract	11.5	0	0	.5	0	0	.5
1 1/2 cup (357g) heavy whipping cream	1231	132	8	10.5	0	0	10.5
Totals (of 10 servings):	5705	513.1	192.9	285.4	32.5	180	72.9
Per Serving:	475.4	42.8	16.1	23.8	2.7	15	(6.1)

CA= Calories / **FAT**= Fat / **P**=Protein / **C**= Carbohydrates / **F**= Fiber / **SA**= Sugar Alcohols / **NC**= Net Carbs

Caramelized-Apple Topped Grain-Free Pancakes p.112

	CA	FAT	P	C	F	SA	NC
1 medium (161g) apple	77	0	0	21	2	0	19
1/4 cup (54g) butter, ghee, or lard (for sautéing and pan/griddle), divided	400	44	0	0	0	0	0
a dash of cinnamon	0	0	0	0	0	0	0
a dash of nutmeg	0	0	0	0	0	0	0
a dash of salt	0	0	0	0	0	0	0
1/4 cup (28g) coconut flour	124	3	7	18	12	0	6
1/4 cup (28g) almond meal	160	14	6	6	3	0	3
1/4 cup (28g) vanilla whey protein powder (sweetened with stevia)	100	0	26	0	0	0	0
1/4 cup (60g) sugar equivalent	0	0	0	60	0	60	0
2 tsp (8g) baking powder	10	0	0	2	0	0	2
4 large (200g) eggs	284	20	24	1.7	0	0	1.7
1/4 cup (56g) melted butter	400	44	0	0	0	0	0
1/4 cup (25g) toasted walnuts, chopped	163	16.3	3.8	3.5	1.8	0	1.8
Totals (of 4 servings):	1718.5	141.3	66.8	112.2	18.8	60	33.4
Per Serving:	429.6	35.3	16.7	28	4.7	15	(8.4)

Spiced Nut-N-Honey Granola p.106

	CA	FAT	P	C	F	SA	NC
1 cup (99g) chopped pecans	684	71	9	14	10	0	4
1/2 cup (60g) chopped walnuts	392	39	9	8	4	0	4
1/2 cup (73g) slivered almonds	421	36.5	16	15.4	7.5	0	7.9
1/2 cup (36g) flaked coconut, unsweetened	200	20	4	8	8	0	0
1/2 cup (56g) almond meal	320	28	12	12	6	0	6
1/4 cup (26g) flax meal (or ground chia seed)	120	9	6	8	8	0	0
1/4 cup (57g) pepitas (pumpkin seeds)	296	24	18.8	7.5	2.3	0	5.3
1/4 cup (32g) sunflower seeds	186	16	6.3	7.8	3	0	4.8
1/4 cup (56g) melted butter	400	44	0	0	0	0	0
1/2 cup (120g) sugar equivalent	0	0	0	120	0	120	0
1 tsp (7g) honey	21.3	0	0	5.7	0	0	5.7
1 tsp (2g) cinnamon	4.9	0	.1	1.6	0	1.1	.6
1 tsp (4g) vanilla	11.5	0	0	.5	0	0	.5
1/2 tsp (1g) nutmeg	5.3	.4	.1	.5	.2	0	.3
1/2 tsp (2g) salt	0	0	0	0	0	0	0
1/4 cup (60g) water	0	0	0	0	0	0	0
Totals (of 4 servings):	3063.1	287.9	81.1	208.9	49	121.1	38.9
Per Serving:	765.8	72	20.3	52.2	12.2	30.3	(9.7)

Mini Crab, Asparagus, and Pepper Frittatas p.110

	CA	FAT	P	C	F	SA	NC
1 small (74g) red bell pepper	22.9	0	.7	4.4	1.5	0	3
1 bunch (227g) asparagus spears, tough stem ends removed	45.7	16	5.1	8.5	5.1	0	3.4
1 Tbsp (14g) butter	100	11	0	0	0	0	0
2 tsp (2g) fresh tarragon, roughly chopped	2	0	.1	.5	.3	0	.2
3 large (150g) eggs	214	15	19.5	1.5	0	0	1.5
1 cup (238g) heavy whipping cream	821	88	5	7	0	0	7
8 oz. (227g) lump crab meat, drained and shells removed	232	3.4	45.4	0	0	0	0
salt and freshly cracked pepper, to taste	0	0	0	0	0	0	0
Totals (of 8 servings):	1438.2	133.4	75.8	21.9	6.8	0	15.1
Per Serving:	179.8	16.7	9.5	2.7	.9	0	(1.9)

Eggy McFoo p.114

	CA	FAT	P	C	F	SA	NC
2 Tbsp (13g) golden flaxseed meal (or ground chia)	60	4.5	3	4	4	0	0
2 Tbsp (14g) almond meal	80	7	3	3	1.5	0	1.5
1/2 tsp (2g) baking powder	2.5	0	0	.5	0	0	.5
a dash of salt	0	0	0	0	0	0	0
2 large (100g) eggs	144	10	6.5	.5	0	0	.5
1 tsp (4g) melted butter, ghee, or lard	33.3	3.7	0	0	0	0	0
3 oz. (85g) ham	131	6	17.5	1.5	0	0	1.5
2 oz. (57g) cheddar cheese	225	18.6	14	.7	0	0	.7
Totals (of 1 servings):	676.9	49.8	44	10.2	5.5	0	4.7
Per Serving:	676.9	49.8	44	10.2	5.5	0	(4.7)

CA= Calories / **FAT**= Fat / **P**=Protein / **C**= Carbohydrates / **F**= Fiber / **SA**= Sugar Alcohols / **NC**= Net Carbs

Poorly Cooked Eggs — p.116

	CA	FAT	P	C	F	SA	NC
12 large (600g) eggs	858	60	26	6	0	0	6
3 cups (714g) heavy whipping cream	2463	264	16	21	0	0	21
1 Tbsp (14g) butter	100	11	0	0	0	0	0
1 bunch (227g) asparagus, tough stem ends removed then sliced into little 1/4-inch (1.2 cm) coins	45.7	16	5.1	8.5	5.1	0	3.4
1/2 lb. (227g) ham, cubed	356	16	46.7	4	0	0	4
1/2 lb. (227g) cheddar cheese, cubed	914	75.7	56.8	3.4	0	0	3.4
salt and pepper to taste	0	0	0	0	0	0	0
Totals (of 6 servings):	4738.2	442.7	150.6	42.9	5.1	0	37.8
Per Serving:	789.7	73.8	25.1	7.2	.9	0	(6.3)

Appetizers and Snacks Nutrition Facts

Grilled Chicken Satay — p.146

	CA	FAT	P	C	F	SA	NC
1 1/2 lb. (681g) boneless skinless chicken breasts, cut into strips	809	20.7	144	0	0	0	0
4 (12g) garlic cloves, minced	16	0	0	4	0	0	4
1 Tbsp (6g) fresh ginger, minced	4.8	0	.1	1.1	.1	0	1
2 tsp (10g) red curry paste	15	0	1	2	0	0	2
1/4 cup (57g) coconut milk, unsweetened	100	11	1	2	0	0	2
2 tsp (4g) turmeric, ground	14.2	0	.6	2.6	.8	0	1.8
1 Tbsp (15g) lime juice, freshly squeezed	3.8	0	.1	1.3	.1	0	1.3
18 bamboo skewers, soaked in water for 30 minutes	0	0	0	0	0	0	0
salt, pepper, and chili flakes to taste	0	0	0	0	0	0	0
2 Tbsp (28g) coconut oil, for grilling	240	24	0	0	0	0	0
Totals (of 6 servings):	1203.1	55.7	147.7	13	1	0	12
Per Serving:	200.5	9.3	24.6	2.2	.2	0	(2)

Stuffed Bacon-Wrapped Shrimp — p.130

	CA	FAT	P	C	F	SA	NC
1 lb. (454g) shrimp (16/20), peeled, with the tails left on, and deveined	481	9.1	90.8	4.5	.3	0	4.3
1 lb. (454g) raw Italian sausage (spicy or sweet)	908	64.1	74.8	10.7	0	0	10.7
8 slices (200g) bacon	916	90	24	2	0	0	2
salt and pepper to taste	0	0	0	0	0	0	0
Totals (of 4 servings):	2305.2	163.2	189.6	17.2	.3	0	16.9
Per Serving:	576.3	40.8	47.4	4.3	.1	0	(4.2)

Sweet Thai Chili Wings — p.124

	CA	FAT	P	C	F	SA	NC
2 lb. (908g) wings and drumettes	2015	145	163	0	0	0	0
1/4 (60g) cup sweet Thai chili sauce	119	.5	.4	67.5	1.4	60	6
salt and pepper to taste	0	0	0	0	0	0	0
Totals (of 4 servings):	968	51.3	105.6	30.3	10.8	0	19.5
Per Serving:	242	12.8	26.4	7.6	2.7	0	(4.9)

CA= Calories / **FAT**= Fat / **P**=Protein / **C**= Carbohydrates / **F**= Fiber / **SA**= Sugar Alcohols / **NC**= Net Carbs

Baked Coconut Shrimp — p.122

	CA	FAT	P	C	F	SA	NC
1/2 cup (44g) unsweetened coconut, shredded	240	24	4	12	8	0	4
3 Tbsp (21g) almond meal	120	10.5	4.5	4.5	2.3	0	2.3
1 Tbsp (8g) tapioca flour	25	0	0	6.5	0	0	6.5
1 large (50g) egg	71	5	6	.4	0	0	.4
1 Tbsp (14g) coconut milk	25	2.8	.3	.5	0	0	.5
1 Tbsp (15g) lime juice	3.8	0	.1	1.3	.1	0	1.3
1 tsp (2g) fresh lime zest, minced	1.9	0	0	.5	.2	0	.3
1 lb. (454g) shrimp (16/20), peeled, with the tails left on, and deveined	481	9.1	90.8	4.5	.3	0	4.3
salt and pepper to taste	0	0	0	0	0	0	0
Totals (of 4 servings):	968	51.3	105.6	30.3	10.8	0	19.5
Per Serving:	242	12.8	26.4	7.6	2.7	0	(4.9)

Thai Grilled Beef Skewers — p.128

	CA	FAT	P	C	F	SA	NC
1 1/2 lb. (681g) beef tenderloin, sirloin, or rib eye, cut into strips	1680	123	133	0	0	0	0
1/4 cup (72g) fish sauce	25.2	0	3.6	2.9	0	0	2.9
1 Tbsp (6g) fresh ginger, minced	4.8	0	.1	1.1	.1	0	1
4 (12g) garlic cloves, minced	16	0	0	4	0	0	4
1 Tbsp (5g) lemongrass, minced	5	0	.1	1.3	0	0	1.3
2 Tbsp (31g) lime juice, freshly squeezed	7.6	0	.1	2.6	.1	0	2.6
1 Tbsp (21g) yacon syrup (optional)	20	0	0	11	0	0	11
1 Tbsp (15g) sweetener	0	0	0	15	0	15	0
18 bamboo skewers, soaked in water for 30 minutes	0	0	0	0	0	0	0
salt, pepper, and chili flakes to taste	0	0	0	0	0	0	0
2 Tbsp (28g) coconut oil, for grilling	240	24	0	0	0	0	0
Totals (of 6 servings):	1998.6	147	137.5	37.9	.2	15	22.7
Per Serving:	333.1	24.5	22.9	6.3	0	2.5	(3.8)

Bacon-Cheddar BBQ Pork Sliders — p.126

	CA	FAT	P	C	F	SA	NC
1 1/2 lb. (681g) ground pork	1789	144	144	0	0	0	0
2 Tbsp (30g) Dijon mustard	24.8	1.2	1.5	2.9	1.2	0	1.7
3 (9g) garlic cloves, minced	13	0	1	3	0	0	3
1 Tbsp (7g) paprika (preferably smoked)	20.2	.9	1.1	3.9	2.6	0	1.3
1 tsp (2g) cayenne pepper, ground	5.7	.3	.3	1	.3	0	.7
1 tsp (1g) fresh thyme, chopped	1	0	.1	.2	.1	0	.1
12 slices (300g) raw bacon	1374	135	36	3	0	0	3
1 small (110g) onion, sliced into strips	44	0	1	10	2	0	8
12 (389g) mini one-minute cheddar buns	110	85	65.5	39.6	32.1	0	7.5
3/4 cup (114g) sugar-free BBQ sauce	170	5.9	4.9	35.6	8	0	27.6
1 cup (95g) prepared Sweet Sugar-Free Coleslaw	113	10.4	1.3	5.6	2.4	0	3.2
salt and pepper to taste	0	0	0	0	0	0	0
Totals (of 4 servings):	4662.1	383.5	257.2	104.9	48.7	0	56.2
Per Serving:	1165	95.9	64.3	26.2	12.2	0	(14)

Shrimp Scampi — p.141

	CA	FAT	P	C	F	SA	NC
1 lb. (454g) shrimp (16/20), peeled, with the tails left on, and deveined	481	9.1	90.8	4.54	.3	0	4.3
1/4 cup (56g) cold butter, divided	400	44	0	0	0	0	0
8 (24g) garlic cloves	32	0	0	8	0	0	8
2 Tbsp (28g) dry vermouth	45	0	0	3.5	0	0	3.5
1 Tbsp (15g) lemon juice	3.8	0	.1	1.3	.1	0	1.3
1 Tbsp (3g) chives	1	0	0	0	0	0	0
salt and pepper to taste	0	0	0	0	0	0	0
Totals (of 4 servings):	963.1	53.1	90.9	17.4	.3	0	17
Per Serving:	240.8	13.3	22.7	4.3	.1	0	(4.3)

CA= Calories / **FAT**= Fat / **P**=Protein / **C**= Carbohydrates / **F**= Fiber / **SA**= Sugar Alcohols / **NC**= Net Carbs

Sweet Thai Chili Shrimp   p.136

	CA	FAT	P	C	F	SA	NC
1/2 cup (56g) coconut flour	248	6	14	36	24	0	12
1 Tbsp (8g) tapioca flour	25	0	0	6.5	0	0	6.5
1 large (50g) egg	71	5	6	.4	0	0	.4
2 Tbsp (30g) club soda (or water)	0	0	0	0	0	0	0
1 lb. (454g) shrimp (31/35), peeled and deveined	481	9.1	90.8	4.5	.3	0	4.3
oil for frying (coconut or lard)	0	0	0	0	0	0	0
1/4 (60g) cup sweet Thai chili sauce	119	.5	.4	67.5	1.4	60	6
2 Tbsp (11g) fresh, chopped cilantro	2.5	.1	.2	.4	.3	0	.1
8 large (45g) lettuce leaves (butter, romaine, cabbage, ice burg, etc.)	8	.2	.6	1.6	1	0	.6
salt and pepper to taste	0	0	0	0	0	0	0
Totals (of 4 servings):	955.7	20.9	112	117	27	60	29.9
Per Serving:	238.9	5.2	28	29.2	6.7	15	(7.5)

Chinese Spare Ribs   p.134

	CA	FAT	P	C	F	SA	NC
2 slabs (4540g) pork spare ribs (about 5 lb. per slab)	8580	544	862	0	0	0	0
1/4 cup (58g) rice wine vinegar	100	0	0	2.8	0	0	2.8
1/4 cup (64g) soy sauce (or coconut aminos)	33.8	0	3.3	5.5	.5	0	5
1/4 cup (36g) loosely packed raisins	108	.3	1	28.8	1.3	0	27.5
2 Tbsp (24g) sesame seeds, divided	135	11.5	4.1	6.2	3.4	0	2.9
2 Tbsp (30g) sweetener	0	0	0	30	0	30	0
1 Tbsp (14g) sesame oil	130	14	0	0	0	0	0
1 Tbsp (6g) crushed chilies or chili paste	19.1	1	.7	3.4	1.6	0	1.5
1 Tbsp (6g) Chinese Five-spice	54	6	0	.2	0	0	.2
1 Tbsp (6g) ginger, chopped	4.8	0	.1	1.1	.1	0	1
4 (12g) garlic cloves	16	0	0	4	0	0	4
salt and pepper to taste	0	0	0	0	0	0	0
Totals (of 6 servings):	9182.3	577.6	871.8	82	6.9	30	44.8
Per Serving:	1530	96.3	145.3	13.7	1.1	5	(7.5)

Miniature Crab Cakes   p.132

	CA	FAT	P	C	F	SA	NC
8 oz. (227g) firm, fresh, raw white fish (cod, halibut, sole, shrimp, scallop, lobster, etc.)	232	3.4	45.4	0	0	0	0
1 large (50g) egg, chilled	71.5	5	6.5	.5	0	0	.5
1/2 cup (119g) heavy whipping cream	410	44	2.5	3.5	0	0	3.5
1 lb. (454g) lump crab meat, drained and shells removed	464	6.7	90.8	0	0	0	0
1 small (74g) red bell pepper, seeded and finely diced	22.9	0	.7	4.4	1.5	0	3
4 whole (60g) green onions (scallions), cut lengthwise into thin strips and divided	19.2	0	1.2	4.2	1.8	0	2.4
1 tsp (2g) smoked paprika	6.7	.3	.4	1.3	.9	0	.5
1/2 tsp (1g) cayenne pepper, ground	2.8	.2	.2	.5	.2	0	.3
1 cup (202.5g) pine nuts	1363	138	27	27	7.5	0	19.5
1/4 cup (56g) fresh whole butter, divided	400	44	0	0	0	0	0
salt and fresh-cracked pepper to taste	0	0	0	0	0	0	0
Totals (of 6 servings):	2993.3	241.6	174.7	41.5	11.8	0	29.6
Per Serving:	498.9	40.3	29.1	6.9	2	0	(4.9)

Whole Artichoke   p.120

	CA	FAT	P	C	F	SA	NC
12 cups (2880g) water	0	0	0	0	0	0	0
3 cups (706g) white wine	0	0	0	0	0	0	0
1 cup (240g) lemon Juice	0	0	0	0	0	0	0
1/4 cup (73g) salt	0	0	0	0	0	0	0
5 (15g) garlic cloves, sliced	0	0	0	0	0	0	0
5 to 10 (15g) thyme sprigs	0	0	0	0	0	0	0
1 bay leaf	0	0	0	0	0	0	0
1 Tbsp (6g) peppercorns	0	0	0	0	0	0	0
4 medium (512g) artichokes	240	0	16	52	28	0	24
Totals (of 4 servings):	240	0	16	52	28	0	24
Per Serving:	60	0	4	13	7	0	(6)

CA= Calories / **FAT**= Fat / **P**=Protein / **C**= Carbohydrates / **F**= Fiber / **SA**= Sugar Alcohols / **NC**= Net Carbs

Blackened Chicken Tenders p.142

	CA	FAT	P	C	F	SA	NC
2 Tbsp (14g) paprika	40.5	1.8	2.1	7.8	5.2	0	2.7
1 Tbsp (6g) freshly cracked black pepper	16	0	1	4	2	0	2
1 Tbsp (5g) cayenne pepper	17	1	1	3	1	0	2
4 (12g) garlic cloves, minced	16	0	0	4	0	0	4
2 tsp (2g) fresh thyme, chopped	2	0	.1	.5	.3	0	.2
1 tsp (1g) fresh oregano, chopped	1	0	.1	.2	.1	0	.1
1 Tbsp (18g) salt	0	0	0	0	0	0	0
2 tsp (10g) sugar equivalent	0	0	0	10	0	10	0
1 1/2 lb. (681g) boneless and skinless chicken breasts, cut into strips	809	20.7	144	0	0	0	0
1/2 cup (112g) fresh whole butter (one stick), melted	800	88	0	0	0	0	0
Totals (of 6 servings):	1701.8	111.6	149.2	27.6	8.6	8	11
Per Serving:	283.6	18.5	24.9	4.6	1.4	1.3	(1.8)

BBQ'd Bacon-Wrapped Basil Shrimp p.145

	CA	FAT	P	C	F	SA	NC
1 lb. (454g) shrimp (16/20), peeled and deveined	481	9.1	90.8	4.5	.3	0	4.3
1/4 cup (38g) Sugar-Free BBQ Sauce	56.8	2	1.6	11.9	2.7	0	9.2
6 slices (150g) raw bacon	687	67.5	18	1.5	0	0	1.5
18 leaves (7g) fresh basil	1.7	.1	.2	.2	.2	0	.1
18 bamboo skewers, soaked in water for 30 minutes	0	0	0	0	0	0	0
salt, pepper, and chili flakes to taste	0	0	0	0	0	0	0
2 Tbsp (28g) coconut oil for grilling	240	24	0	0	0	0	0
Totals (of 6 servings):	1466.7	102.6	110.7	18.1	3.1	0	15
Per Serving:	244.5	17.1	18.4	3	.5	0	(2.2)

Tod Man Pla (Thai Fish Cakes) p.138

	CA	FAT	P	C	F	SA	NC
1 1/2 lb. (681g) firm, fresh, raw white fish (cod, halibut, sole, shrimp, scallop, lobster, etc.)	696	10.1	136	0	0	0	0
3 (99g) egg whites	48	0	12	0	0	0	0
1 Tbsp (6g) fresh ginger, minced	4.8	0	.1	1.1	.1	0	1
4 (12g) garlic cloves, minced	0	0	0	0	0	0	0
1 Tbsp (15g) red curry paste	22.5	0	1.5	3	0	0	3
1/4 cup (72g) fish sauce	25.2	0	3.6	2.9	0	0	2.9
10 (10g) fresh kaffir lime leaves, cut into very thin strips (lime zest is an acceptable substitute)	8	0	0	1	0	0	1
1/2 lb. (227g) green string beans, ends and string removed, cut into thin little disks	70.4	.3	2.7	16.2	7.7	0	8.5
1 small (74g) red bell pepper, seeded and cut into small dice	22.9	0	.7	4.4	1.5	0	3
2 Tbsp (28g) light oil (for sautéing, such as coconut, olive, or ghee)	240	24	0	0	0	0	0
salt and freshly cracked pepper to taste	0		0	0	0	0	0
Totals (of 6 servings):	1137.9	34.4	156.9	28.6	9.3	0	19.3
Per Serving:	189.7	5.7	26.2	4.8	1.6	0	(3.2)

Bacon-Wrapped Rosemary-Skewered Scallops p.140

	CA	FAT	P	C	F	SA	NC
18 sprigs (72g) fresh rosemary	0	0	0	0	0	0	0
9 slices (225g) raw bacon	1030	101	27	2.3	0	0	2.3
18 jumbo (504g) sea scallops	443	5	85.7	10.1	0	0	10.1
salt and pepper to taste	0	0	0	0	0	0	0
Totals (of 6 servings):	1474	106.3	112.7	12.3	0	0	12.3
Per Serving:	245.7	17.7	18.8	2.1	0	0	(2.1)

CA= Calories / **FAT**= Fat / **P**=Protein / **C**= Carbohydrates / **F**= Fiber / **SA**= Sugar Alcohols / **NC**= Net Carbs

Soups & Stews Nutrition Facts

Jambalaya — p.172

Ingredient	CA	FAT	P	C	F	SA	NC
2 Tbsp (28g) unsalted butter	200	22	0	0	0	0	0
1 medium (110g) onion, diced	44	0	1	10	2	0	8
4 (12g) garlic cloves, peeled	16	0	0	4	0	0	4
1 (51g) celery rib, diced	0	0	0	0	0	0	0
1 small (74g) green bell pepper, diced	22.9	0	.7	4.4	1.5	0	3
1/2 tsp (1g) guar gum (optional)	3.3	0	0	.9	.9	0	0
1/2 tsp (1g) xanthan gum (optional)	5	0	0	1.2	1.2	0	0
2 cups (448g) chicken stock or broth	31.4	.6	4.5	3	0	0	3
2 (364g) large ripe tomatoes, coarsely chopped	66	0	4	14	4	0	10
1 lb. (454g) ham, diced	713	32.1	93.5	8	0	0	8
3 bay leaves	0	0	0	0	0	0	0
4 (340g) Andouille links (or other Creole/Cajun smoked sausage; I often use Spanish chorizo), sliced into thick rings	560	24	52	12	4	0	8
1 1/2 lb. (680g) whole boneless chicken breasts (or equivalent thigh meat, skin optional)	1169	61.2	142	0	0	0	0
1 Tbsp (8g) chili powder	25.1	1.4	1	4.4	2.7	0	1.7
2 tsp (2g) fresh thyme, chopped	2	0	.1	.5	.3	0	.2
16 (454g – 1lb.) large shrimp, peeled and deveined	481	9.1	90.8	4.5	.3	0	4.3
salt and pepper to taste	0	0	0	0	0	0	0
Totals (of 8 servings):	3339.7	150.3	390.4	66.9	16.8	0	50.1
Per Serving:	417.5	18.8	48.8	8.4	2.1	0	(6.3)

Thai Hot and Sour Shrimp — p.150

Ingredient	CA	FAT	P	C	F	SA	NC
1 lb. (454g) shrimp (16/20), peeled, with the tails left on, and deveined	481	9.1	90.8	4.5	.3	0	4.3
2 Tbsp (28g) coconut oil, divided	240	24	0	0	0	0	0
1 medium (110g) onion, diced	0	0	0	0	0	0	0
4 (12g) garlic cloves	0	0	0	0	0	0	0
1 one-inch (22g) piece of galangal (Thai ginger—ginger is an acceptable substitute), peeled and sliced into 8 chunks	0	0	0	0	0	0	0
1 (22g) lemongrass stalk, 1/2-inch rough chop from the white portion	0	0	0	0	0	0	0
3 (3g) fresh kaffir lime leaves, roughly chopped (or 1/2 tsp fresh lime zest)	0	0	0	0	0	0	0
1 (188g) red Thai chili, roughly chopped	0	0	0	0	0	0	0
5 cups (896g) chicken broth	62.7	1.2	9	6	0	0	6
1/2 lb. (227g) crimini, shiitake, oyster, or button mushrooms, washed and sliced into wedges	61.6	0	6.8	9.8	2.3	0	6.8
1 small (118g) green zucchini	19	.4	1.5	4	1.5	0	2.6
2 Tbsp (31g) fresh lime juice	7.6	0	.1	2.6	.1	0	2.5
2 Tbsp (36g) fish sauce	12.6	0	1.8	1.4	0	0	1.4
1/4 bunch (25g) fresh cilantro, very coarsely chopped	5.8	.1	.6	.9	.7	0	.7
1/4 bunch (25g) fresh basil, very coarsely chopped	5.8	.1	.6	.9	.7	0	.7
salt and pepper to taste	0	0	0	0	0	0	0
Totals (of 6 servings):	2050.1	152.4	115.5	48.6	11.3	0	37.8
Per Serving:	341.7	25.4	19.3	8.1	1.9	0	(6.3)

CA= Calories / **FAT**= Fat / **P**=Protein / **C**= Carbohydrates / **F**= Fiber / **SA**= Sugar Alcohols / **NC**= Net Carbs

Curried Chicken and Apple "Mulligatawny" p.152

	CA	FAT	P	C	F	SA	NC
2 Tbsp (28g) ghee or coconut oil	240	24	0	0	0	0	0
1 lb. (454g) boneless chicken, light or dark meat, cubed	539	13.8	96.6	0	0	0	0
1 small (110g) onion, diced	44	0	1	10	2	0	8
2 ribs (101g) celery, diced	16	0	1	3	2	0	1
1 small (72g) carrot, diced	29.3	0	.6	6.8	2.3	0	4.5
4 (12g) garlic cloves, minced	16	0	0	4	0	0	4
2 tsp (4g) grated fresh ginger	3.2	0	.1	.7	.1	0	.6
1 Tbsp (6g) yellow curry powder	40	2	2	8	4	0	4
6 cups (1120g) chicken broth	78.4	1.5	11.2	7.6	0	0	7.6
2 medium (322g) apples (such as golden delicious)	154	0	0	42	4	0	38
1 Tbsp (15g) fresh lemon juice	3.8	0	.1	1.3	.1	0	1.3
1 tsp (2g) minced fresh lemon zest	1.9	0	0	.5	.2	0	.3
1/4 bunch (25g) fresh cilantro, very coarsely chopped	5.8	.1	.6	1	.7	0	.7
salt and pepper to taste	0	0	0	0	0	0	0
Totals (of 8 servings):	1171.9	41.4	113.1	84.8	15.3	0	70
Per Serving:	195.3	6.9	18.8	14.1	2.6	0	(11.7)

Cream of Roasted Garlic, Cauliflower, and Bacon p.160

	CA	FAT	P	C	F	SA	NC
4 slices (100g) raw bacon, chopped	458	45	12	1	0	0	1
12 (36g) garlic cloves, sliced into 1/8-inch thick "chips"	48	0	0	12	0	0	12
1 head (840g) large cauliflower, stem and leaves removed, and cut into small florets	210	1.3	17	45	21	0	24
2 cups (448g) chicken stock or broth	31.4	.6	4.5	3	0	0	3
1 1/2 cups (357g) heavy whipping cream	1231	132	7.5	10.5	0	0	10.5
salt and pepper to taste	0	0	0	0	0	0	0
Totals (of 6 servings):	1978.9	178.9	41	71.5	21	0	50.5
Per Serving:	329.8	29.8	6.8	11.9	3.5	0	(8.4)

Smoked Salmon Chowder p.154

	CA	FAT	P	C	F	SA	NC
2 cups (448g) chicken stock or broth	31.4	.6	4.5	3	0	0	3
1 small (110g) onion, diced	44	0	1	10	2	0	8
2 (101g) celery ribs, diced	16	0	1	3	2	0	1
4 (12g) garlic cloves, minced	16	0	0	4	0	0	4
1 bay leaf	0	0	0	0	0	0	0
4 slices (100g) raw bacon, chopped	458	45	12	1	0	0	1
1 cup (116g) Hubbard squash, cut into 1/4- to 1/2-inch cubes	46	1	2	10	3	0	7
1 small (74g) red bell pepper, seeded and diced	22.9	0	.7	4.4	1.5	0	3
1 tsp (2g) smoked paprika (non-smoked is fine)	6.7	.3	.4	1.3	.9	0	.5
2 1/2 cups (595g) heavy whipping cream	2052	220	12.5	17.5	0	0	17.5
8 oz. (227g) smoked salmon, cut into cubes	976	68.1	90.8	0	0	0	0
salt and pepper to taste	0	0	0	0	0	0	0
Totals (of 6 servings):	3669.6	335	124.9	54.3	9.3	0	44.9
Per Serving:	611.6	55.8	20.8	9.1	1.6	0	(7.5)

Turkey Meatball Soup with Kale and Roasted Peppers p.178

	CA	FAT	P	C	F	SA	NC
2 Tbsp (25g) butter, divided	200	22	0	0	0	0	0
1 small (110g) onion, diced and divided	44	0	1	10	2	0	8
4 (12g) garlic cloves, minced and divided	16	0	0	4	0	0	4
1 lb. (454g) ground turkey	676	37	79	0	0	0	0
1 large (50g) egg	71	5	6	.4	0	0	.4
1 Tbsp (4g) ground chia seed (optional)	17.5	1.3	.8	1.8	1.5	0	.3
1 Tbsp (2g) fresh chopped sage	2.62	.1	.1	.4	.3	0	.1
1/2 lb. (227g) kale, washed and very roughly chopped	113	2.3	6.8	22.7	4.5	0	18.2
2 small (148g) roasted bell peppers, peeled, seeded, and sliced	45.9	0	1.5	8.9	3	0	5.9
6 cups (1120g) chicken broth	78.4	1.5	11.2	7.6	0	0	7.6
salt and pepper to taste	0	0	0	0	0	0	0
Totals (of 6 servings):	1264.9	69.1	106.3	55.7	6.7	0	44.4
Per Serving:	210.8	11.5	17.7	9.3	1.1	0	(7.4)

CA= Calories / **FAT**= Fat / **P**=Protein / **C**= Carbohydrates / **F**= Fiber / **SA**= Sugar Alcohols / **NC**= Net Carbs

Taco Soup
p.157

	CA	FAT	P	C	F	SA	NC
1 lb. (454g) ground beef (80 lean/20 fat)	1153	90.8	77.2	0	0	0	0
2 (364g) large ripe tomatoes, diced	66	0	4	14	4	0	10
1 14-oz. can (216g) baby corn, drained and cut into 1/2-inch portions	62.5	0	5	10	5	0	5
1 small (110g) onion, diced	44	0	1	10	2	0	8
4 (12g) garlic cloves, minced	16	0	0	4	0	0	4
1 (6.67g) jalapeño pepper, diced and seeds removed	2	0	.1	.4	.2	0	.2
2 Tbsp (30.5g) freshly squeezed lime juice	7.6	0	.1	2.6	.1	0	2.6
1/2 bunch (50g) cilantro, washed, large stems removed, and chopped	11.5	.3	1.1	1.9	1.5	0	.4
6 cups (1120g) chicken broth	78.4	1.5	11.2	7.6	0	0	7.6
1 cup (230g) sour cream	444	45	5	8	0	0	8
2 whole (272g) avocado, peeled and sliced	554	42	6	24	18	0	6
1 cup (113g) shredded cheddar/Colby cheese blend	443	36	27	3	0	0	3
salt and pepper to taste	0	0	0	0	0	0	0
Totals (of 8 servings):	2882.2	215.6	137.7	85.5	30.7	0	54.8
Per Serving:	360.3	27	17.2	10.7	3.8	0	(6.8)

Manhattan Chowder
p.158

	CA	FAT	P	C	F	SA	NC
4 lb. (1816g) small to medium clams (Quahog, littleneck, or cherrystone)	1343	18.2	236	54.5	0	0	54.5
4 slices (100g) raw bacon, chopped	458	45	12	1	0	0	1
4 (12g) garlic cloves, minced	16	0	0	4	0	0	4
1 tsp (2g) chili flakes	6.3	.3	.2	1.1	.7	0	.4
1 cup (232g) good quality white wine	190	0	0	7	0	0	7
1 small (110g) onion, diced	44	0	1	10	2	0	8
1 small (74g) red bell pepper, diced	22.9	0	.7	4.4	1.5	0	3
2 (101g) celery ribs, diced	16	0	1	3	2	0	1
1 small (72g) carrot, peeled and diced	29.3	0	.6	6.8	2.3	0	4.5
2 (364g) large ripe tomatoes, diced	66	0	4	14	4	0	10
2 cups (448g) chicken stock or broth (maybe a bit more)	31.4	.6	4.5	3	0	0	3
1 bay leaf	0	0	0	0	0	0	0
10 springs (10g) fresh thyme	2.6	.1	.1	.4	.3	0	.1
salt and pepper to taste	0	0	0	0	0	0	0
Totals (of 6 servings):	2226.5	64.2	260.2	109.2	12.7	0	93.5
Per Serving:	371.1	10.7	43.4	18.2	2.1	0	(15.6)

CA= Calories / **FAT**= Fat / **P**=Protein / **C**= Carbohydrates / **F**= Fiber / **SA**= Sugar Alcohols / **NC**= Net Carbs

Sopa Sin Tortilla
p.168

	CA	FAT	P	C	F	SA	NC
8 cups (1792g) chicken stock or broth	125	2.3	17.9	12.1	0	0	12.1
2 (1135g) pork tenderloins, cut into halves and cleaned (or 2 1/2 lbs. equivalent pork shoulder, cut into 4 large chunks)	1237	22.7	238	0	0	0	0
1 Tbsp (14g) lard or favorite cooking oil	119	13.5	0	0	0	0	0
1 Tbsp (6g) cumin, ground	22.5	1.3	0	2.6	.7	0	2
1 Tbsp (6g) coriander, ground	17.9	1.1	.7	3.3	2.5	0	.8
2 large (364g) ripe tomatoes, coarsely chopped	66	0	4	14	4	0	10
1/2 (105g) 7-oz. can chipotle peppers in adobo sauce	60	1.5	3	12	9	0	3
1 medium (110g) onion, diced	44	0	1	10	2	0	8
4 (12g) garlic cloves, peeled	16	0	0	4	0	0	4
1/4 cup (61g) freshly squeezed lime juice	15.3	0	.3	5.3	.3	0	5
1 bunch (100g) cilantro, washed and chopped	23	.5	2.2	3.7	2.9	0	.8
2 whole (272g) avocado, peeled and sliced	554	42	6	24	18	0	6
1 1/2 cup (35g) pork rind pieces	200	11.3	20	0	0	0	0
1 cup (230g) sour cream	444	45	5	8	0	0	8
1 cup (132g) Monterey jack cheese, cubed	492	40	32.3	.9	0	0	.9
salt and pepper to taste	0	0	0	0	0	0	0
Totals (of 8 servings):	3436.6	181.2	330.7	100	39.3	0	60.6
Per Serving:	429.6	22.7	41.3	12.5	4.9	0	(7.6)

Bouillabaisse
p.162

	CA	FAT	P	C	F	SA	NC
1/2 cup (108g) extra virgin olive oil, divided	955	108	0	0	0	0	0
1 cup (232g) white wine, good quality	190	0	0	7	0	0	7
1 small (110g) onion, peeled and diced	44	0	1	10	2	0	8
4 each (12g) garlic cloves, minced	16	0	0	4	0	0	4
2 medium (182g) tomatoes, diced	32	0	2	8	2	0	6
1 bulb (234g) fennel, diced	73	0	3	17	7	0	10
1 bay leaf	0	0	0	0	0	0	0
1/2 tsp (0g) saffron threads	0	0	0	0	0	0	0
1 tsp (1g) fresh thyme, chopped	1	0	.1	.2	.1	0	.1
1/2 tsp (1g) fresh orange zest (peel)	1	0	0	.2	.1	0	.1
1/2 tsp (1g) cayenne pepper, ground	2.8	.2	.2	.5	.2	0	.3
1 1/2 lb (681g) halibut fillets	696	10.1	136	0	0	0	0
32 medium-sized (448g) clams, fresh and alive	331	4.5	58.2	13.4	0	0	13.4
32 medium-sized (512g) mussels, fresh and alive	385	9	53.7	17.9	0	0	17.9
4 fillets (681g) dover sole	618	8.4	129	2	0	0	2
1 lb (454g) shrimp	481	9.1	90.8	4.5	.3	0	4.3
1 cup (211g) Rouille	761	83.6	2.6	3.8	.3	.25	3.3
salt and fresh cracked pepper, to taste	0	0	0	0	0	0	0
Totals (of 8 servings):	4588.8	232.9	477.3	88.5	12	.25	76.4
Per Serving:	573.6	29.1	59.7	11.1	1.5	0	(9.6)

CA= Calories / **FAT**= Fat / **P**=Protein / **C**= Carbohydrates / **F**= Fiber / **SA**= Sugar Alcohols / **NC**= Net Carbs

Curried Cauliflower · p.170

	CA	FAT	P	C	F	SA	NC
2 Tbsp (28g) ghee or coconut oil, divided	200	22	0	0	0	0	0
1 one-inch (22g) piece of ginger, divided	17.6	0	.4	4	.4	0	3.5
3 (9g) garlic cloves, diced	13	0	1	3	0	0	3
1 tsp (2g) garam masala	7	0	0	1	1	0	0
2 tsp (4g) ground turmeric	14.2	.4	.3	2.6	.8	0	1.8
1 tsp (2g) ground cumin seed	7.5	.4	0	.9	.2	0	.7
1 tsp (2g) ground coriander seed	6	.4	.2	1.1	.8	0	.3
1 tsp (2g) chili flakes	6.3	.3	.2	1.1	.7	0	.4
1 head (840g) large cauliflower, chopped and divided	210	1.3	17	45	21	0	24
2 cups (470g) vegetable stock	24	0	0	6	0	0	6
1 13.5-ounce (381g) can coconut milk	750	81	8.4	10.1	0	0	10.1
1 tsp (5g) lemon juice	1.3	0	0	.4	0	0	.4
6 sprigs (15g) cilantro leaves, fresh whole	3.5	0	0	.8	.5	0	.3
salt and pepper to taste	0	0	0	0	0	0	0
Totals (of 6 servings):	1261.2	105.9	27.7	76	25.54	0	50.4
Per Serving:	210.2	17.7	4.6	12.7	4.3	0	(8.4)

Lazy Cioppino · p.165

	CA	FAT	P	C	F	SA	NC
1/2 cup (108g) extra virgin olive oil, divided	955	108	0	0	0	0	0
1 cup (232g) white wine, good quality	190	0	0	7	0	0	7
1 small (110g) onion, peeled and diced	44	0	1	10	2	0	8
4 each (12g) garlic cloves, minced	16	0	0	4	0	0	4
2 medium (182g) tomatoes, diced	32	0	2	8	2	0	6
1 bulb (234g) fennel, diced	73	0	3	17	7	0	10
2 ribs celery, diced	16	0	1	3	2	0	1
1/2 tsp (1g) chili flakes	3.1	.2	.1	.6	.3	0	.2
1 each (0g) bay leaves	0	0	0	0	0	0	0
32 medium-sized (448g) clams, fresh and alive	331	4.5	58.2	13.4	0	0	13.4
32 medium-sized (512g) mussels, fresh and alive	385	9	53.8	17.9	0	0	17.9
1 lb (454g) shrimp	481	9.1	90.8	4.5	.3	0	4.3
1 1/2 lb (681g) halibut fillets	696	10.1	136	0	0	0	0
Juice of one lemon (46g)	11.5	0	.2	4	.2	0	3.8
1 tsp (1g) fresh thyme, chopped	1	0	.1	.2	.1	0	.1
1/2 tsp (1g) fresh lemon zest (peel)	1	0	0	.3	.1	0	.1
salt and fresh cracked pepper, to taste	0	0	0	0	0	0	0
Totals (of 8 servings):	3236.9	140.9	346.4	89.9	14	0	75.8
Per Serving:	404.6	17.6	43.3	11.2	1.8	0	(9.5)

CA= Calories / **FAT**= Fat / **P**=Protein / **C**= Carbohydrates / **F**= Fiber / **SA**= Sugar Alcohols / **NC**= Net Carbs

NUTRITION FACTS

Albondigas p.148

	CA	FAT	P	C	F	SA	NC
1/2 lb. (227g) ground beef, pork, or turkey	576	45.4	38.9	0	0	0	0
1/2 lb. (227g) raw Mexican chorizo	1028	85.9	54.3	4.5	0	0	4.5
1 large (50g) egg	71	5	6	.4	0	0	.4
1 Tbsp (4g) ground chia seed (optional)	17.5	1.3	.8	1.8	1.5	0	.3
6 (18g) garlic cloves, chopped and divided	24	0	0	6	0	0	6
2 tsp (4g) cumin, ground	15	.9	0	1.8	.4	0	1.3
1 tsp (2g) coriander seed, ground	6	.4	.2	1.1	.8	0	.3
1/2 tsp (1g) cinnamon, ground	2.5	0	04	.8	.5	0	.3
6 cups (1120g) chicken broth	78.4	1.5	11.2	7.6	0	0	7.6
1 medium (110g) onion, diced	44	0	1	10	2	0	8
1 medium (91g) tomato, diced	16	0	1	4	1	0	3
2 ribs (101g) celery, diced	16	0	1	3	2	0	1
1 small (72g) carrot, peeled and diced	29.3	0	.6	6.8	2.3	0	4.5
1 Tbsp (14g) lard or other cooking oil	120	12	0	0	0	0	0
1/4 bunch (25g) fresh cilantro, very coarsely chopped	5.8	.1	.6	.9	.7	0	.7
salt and pepper to taste	0	0	0	0	0	0	0
Totals (of 6 servings):	2050.1	152.4	115.5	48.6	11.3	0	37.8
Per Serving:	341.7	25.4	19.3	8.1	1.9	0	(6.3)

Mexican Gazpacho p.176

	CA	FAT	P	C	F	SA	NC
2 lb. (908g) fresh assorted tomatoes, cut into chunks	164	0	10	34.9	10	0	24.9
1 (301g) English cucumber, peeled, seeded, and cut into chunks	122	0	13.6	18.2	4.5	0	13.6
1 (70g) sweet red onion, cut into chunks	28	0	1	7	1	0	6
1 small (74g) red bell pepper, seeded and cut into chunks	22.9	0	.7	4.4	1.5	0	3
4 (12g) garlic cloves	16	0	0	4	0	0	4
2 Tbsp (31g) lemon juice, freshly squeezed	7.6	0	.1	2.6	.1	0	2.5
2 Tbsp (30g) red wine vinegar	5.7	0	0	.1	0	0	.1
1/4 cup (54g) extra virgin olive oil, good quality	477	54	0	0	0	0	0
1/4 lb. (114g) cherry tomatoes, washed, dried, and halved or quartered	20.6	0	1.3	4.4	1.3	0	3.1
8 sprigs (20g) cilantro leaves, fresh whole, stems removed	4.7	0	0	1	.7	0	.3
1/4 cup (58g) sour cream	111	11.3	1.3	2	0	0	2
1/2 tsp (1g) cumin, ground	3.8	.2	0	.4	.1	0	.3
1 whole (136g) avocado, peeled and sliced	227	21	3	12	9	0	3
salt and pepper to taste	0	0	0	0	0	0	0
Totals (of 8 servings):	1211.9	86.5	31	91.1	28.2	0	62.9
Per Serving:	151.5	10.8	3.9	11.4	3.2	0	(7.9)

CA= Calories / **FAT**= Fat / **P**=Protein / **C**= Carbohydrates / **F**= Fiber / **SA**= Sugar Alcohols / **NC**= Net Carbs

Sinful Crimini of Mushroom Soup							p.174
	CA	FAT	P	C	F	SA	NC
8 slices (200g) raw bacon, chopped	916	90	24	2	0	0	2
1 medium (110g) onion, diced	44	0	1	10	2	0	8
2 (6g) garlic cloves, minced	8	0	0	2	0	0	2
1 lb. (454g) crimini (portobello with the gills removed or button) mushrooms, washed and sliced into little wedges	122	0	13.6	18.2	4.5	0	13.6
1 tsp (1g) fresh rosemary, chopped	.9	0	0	.1	.1	0	.1
1 1/2 cups (336g) chicken stock or broth	23.5	.4	3.4	2.3	0	0	2.3
2 Tbsp (34g) Worcestershire sauce	26.5	0	0	6.7	0	0	6.7
3/4 cup (179g) heavy whipping cream	615	66	3.8	5.3	0	0	5.3
1/4 cup (16g) parsley leaves, washed	2.9	0	.3	.5	.3	0	.3
3 Tbsp (41g) extra virgin olive oil	358	40.5	0	0	0	0	0
salt and pepper to taste	0	0	0	0	0	0	0
Totals (of 6 servings):	2118.3	197	46	47	6.9	0	40.1
Per Serving:	353	32.8	7.7	7.8	1.2	0	(6.7)

Salads Nutrition Facts

Cucumber Mint Salad							p.182
	CA	FAT	P	C	F	SA	NC
2 (602g) English cucumbers, sliced into very thin rings	92.6	0	0	23.2	0	0	23.2
1 small (110g) red onion, very thinly sliced	44	0	1	10	2	0	8
1/4 cup (56.5g) Greek yogurt, plain and full fat	65	5.5	2	2.5	0	0	2.5
2 Tbsp (30.5g) freshly squeezed lime juice	7.6	0	.1	2.6	.1	0	2.6
1/4 cup (22g) fresh mint, leaves sliced thin	9.7	.2	.7	1.8	1.5	0	.2
salt and pepper to taste	0	0	0	0	0	0	0
Totals (of 8 servings):	218.9	5.7	3.8	40.1	3.6	0	36.5
Per Serving:	27.4	.7	.5	5	.5	0	(4.6)

Sweet 'n' Creamy Coleslaw							p.200
	CA	FAT	P	C	F	SA	NC
8 cups (560g) cabbage, shredded (about 1/2 head)	136	0	8	36	18	0	18
1/4 cup (28g) carrot, peeled and grated	11.2	0	.2	2.6	.9	0	1.7
1/2 cup (110g) mayonnaise	750	83.5	2.4	4.8	.1	3.8	1
2 Tbsp (31g) fresh lemon juice	7.6	0	.1	2.6	.1	0	2.5
2 Tbsp (30g) sweetener	0	0	0	30	0	30	0
salt and pepper to taste	0	0	0	0	0	0	0
Totals (of 8 servings):	905.3	83.5	10.7	76	19.1	33.8	23.2
Per Serving:	113.2	10.4	1.3	9.5	2.4	4.2	(2.9)

CA= Calories / **FAT**= Fat / **P**=Protein / **C**= Carbohydrates / **F**= Fiber / **SA**= Sugar Alcohols / **NC**= Net Carbs

Chilled Soy-Lime Flank Steak Salad — p.198

	CA	FAT	P	C	F	SA	NC
1 1/2 lb. (681g) beef flank, tenderloin, sirloin, or rib eye, cut into 4 portions	1680	123	133	0	0	0	0
2 Tbsp (28g) coconut oil or ghee	240	24	0	0	0	0	0
4 cups (188g) shredded romaine lettuce	31.8	.6	15.7	6.3	3.9	0	2.4
1 small (74g) red bell pepper, seeded and cut into thin slices	22.9	0	.7	4.4	1.5	0	3
1 small (70g) sweet red onion, cut into thin slices	28	0	1	7	1	0	6
1/4 bunch (25g) cilantro, washed and large stems removed	5.8	.1	.6	.9	.7	0	.2
1 Tbsp (14g) toasted sesame oil	130	14	0	0	0	0	0
1 Tbsp (14g) hot chili oil	130	14	0	0	0	0	0
3 Tbsp (41g) avocado, macadamia, or a light olive oil	358	40.5	0	0	0	0	0
1 Tbsp (15g) sweetener	0	0	0	15	0	15	0
2 Tbsp (30.5g) fresh lime juice	7.6	0	.1	2.6	.1	0	2.5
3 Tbsp (48g) Japanese soy sauce (shoyu) or coconut aminos	25.3	0	2.5	4.1	.4	0	3.8
2 tsp (4g) fresh ginger, grated	3.2	0	.1	.7	.1	0	.6
2 Tbsp (24g) sesame seeds, toasted	135	11.5	4.1	6.2	3.4	0	2.8
salt and pepper to taste	0	0	0	0	0	0	0
Totals (of 4 servings):	2798.4	227.8	158.3	47.4	11.1	15	21.4
Per Serving:	699.6	56.9	39.6	11.9	2.7	3.8	(5.3)

Colorful Asian Slaw — p.183

	CA	FAT	P	C	F	SA	NC
1 small head (304g) Napa cabbage, shredded	80	0	4	12	4	0	8
2 small (148g) red bell peppers, seeded and sliced thin	45.9	0	1.5	8.9	3	0	5.9
1 small (72g) carrot, peeled and sliced into very thin strips	29.3	0	.6	6.8	2.3	0	4.5
1 cup (63g) snow peas, sliced into very thin strips	26	0	2	5	2	0	3
1 small (110g) red onion, sliced thin	44	0	1	10	2	0	8
4 whole (60g) green onions (scallions)	19.2	0	1.2	4.2	1.8	0	2.4
1/4 cup (64g) soy sauce	33.8	0	3.3	5.5	.5	0	5
1/4 cup (58g) rice wine vinegar	100	0	0	2.8	0	0	2.8
1 Tbsp (6g) chopped fresh ginger	4.8	0	.1	1.1	.1	0	1
4 (12g) garlic cloves, minced	16	0	0	4	0	0	4
2 Tbsp (28g) sesame oil	260	28	0	0	0	0	0
2 Tbsp (30g) sweetener	0	0	0	30	0	30	0
2 Tbsp (24g) black sesame seeds (or regular toasted sesame seeds)	135	11.5	4.1	6.2	3.4	0	2.9
salt and pepper to taste	0	0	0	0	0	0	0
Totals (of 6 servings):	794.5	39.5	17.7	96.4	19	30	47.4
Per Serving:	132.4	6.6	3	16.1	3.2	5	(7.9)

Thai Cucumber Salad — p.187

	CA	FAT	P	C	F	SA	NC
2 (602g) English cucumber, sliced into very thin rings	92.6	0	0	23.2	3.5	0	19.7
1 small (110g) red onion, very thinly sliced	44	0	1	10	2	0	8
2 (13g) jalapeño peppers, seeds removed and thinly sliced	4	.1	.2	.8	.4	0	.4
1/4 cup (60g) rice wine vinegar	19.8	0	0	4.2	0	0	4.2
1/4 cup (60g) sweetener	0	0	0	60	0	60	0
2 Tbsp (36g) fish sauce	12.6	0	1.8	1.4	0	0	1.4
1 tsp (4g) salt	0	0	0	0	0	0	0
Totals (of 8 servings):	173	.1	3	99.6	5.8	60	33.8
Per Serving:	21.6	0	.4	12.5	.7	7.5	(4.2)

CA= Calories / **FAT**= Fat / **P**=Protein / **C**= Carbohydrates / **F**= Fiber / **SA**= Sugar Alcohols / **NC**= Net Carbs

Shrimp and Mango Stuffed Tomato — p.190

	CA	FAT	P	C	F	SA	NC
2 lb. (908g) shrimp (31/35), peeled and deveined	962	18.2	181	9.1	.6	0	8.5
2 Tbsp (28g) coconut oil	240	24	0	0	0	0	0
4 small (454g) tomatoes (about 1/4 lb. each)	82.3	0	5	17.5	5	0	12.5
1 (70g) sweet red onion, very thinly sliced	28	0	1	7	1	0	6
1 small (74g) roasted red bell pepper, seeded and very thinly sliced	22.9	0	.7	4.4	1.5	0	3
1 small (392g) mango, peeled, cored, and sliced thin	135	1	1	35	4	0	34
2 Tbsp (31g) fresh lime juice	7.6	0	.1	2.6	.1	0	2.5
1/2 bunch (50g) cilantro, washed, large stems removed, and chopped	11.5	.3	1.1	1.9	1.5	0	.4
salt and pepper to taste	0	0	0	0	0	0	0
Totals (of 8 servings):	1489.9	43.4	190.6	77.5	13.6	0	66.9
Per Serving:	186.2	5.4	23.8	9.7	1.7	0	(8.4)

Sausage, Tomato, and Fresh Mozzarella Tower — p.188

	CA	FAT	P	C	F	SA	NC
1 lb. (454g) raw Italian Chicken Sausage	1083	78.2	83.8	7.7	2.9	0	4.8
1 lb. (454g) assorted fresh tomatoes	82.3	0	5	17.5	5	0	12.5
1 lb. (454g) fresh mozzarella cheese	1120	80	80	0	0	0	0
2 Tbsp (16g) chopped capers	3.7	.2	.3	.8	.5	0	.3
2 Tbsp (30g) fresh lemon juice	7.6	0	.1	2.6	.1	0	2.5
1 tsp (2g) minced fresh lemon zest	1.9	0	0	.5	.2	0	.3
2 tsp (2g) chopped fresh oregano	2	0	.1	.5	.3	0	.2
2 (6g) garlic cloves, minced	8	0	0	2	0	0	2
1/4 cup (54g) extra virgin olive oil	477	54	0	0	0	0	0
salt and pepper to taste	0	0	0	0	0	0	0
Totals (of 4 servings):	2786.6	212.4	169.4	31.6	9	0	22.6
Per Serving:	696.7	53.1	42.4	7.9	2.2	0	(5.7)

The Great Wedge — p.193

	CA	FAT	P	C	F	SA	NC
1 small head (324g) iceberg lettuce, washed	45	0	3	10	4	0	6
2 oz. (56g) quality Roquefort cheese, crumbled	206	17.4	12.3	1.1	0	0	1.1
1/2 lb. (227g) cherry tomatoes, washed, dried, and halved or quartered	41.2	0	2.5	8.7	2.5	0	6.2
1/4 cup (28g) bacon bits	100	6	12	0	0	0	0
1/4 cup (16g) parsley leaves, washed	2.9	0	.3	.5	.3	0	.3
1 Tbsp (14g) extra virgin olive oil	119	13.5	0	0	0	0	0
1/2 cup (118g) blue cheese dressing	433	43.3	10	2.9	0	.1	2.8
salt and pepper to taste	0	0	0	0	0	0	0
Totals (of 6 servings):	948.2	80.2	40.1	23.2	6.8	.1	16.4
Per Serving:	237.1	20	10	5.8	1.7	0	(4.1)

Greatest Salad Ever! — p.180

	CA	FAT	P	C	F	SA	NC
4 cups (188g) mixed baby greens, washed	31.8	.6	2.4	6.3	3.9	0	2.4
1 lb. (454g) fresh mozzarella, cubed	1120	80	80	0	0	0	0
1 lb. (454g) fresh tomatoes, cubed	82.3	0	5	17.5	5	0	12.5
16 leaves (6g) fresh basil, hand torn	1.5	.1	.2	.2	.1	0	.1
1/4 cup (64g) balsamic vinegar	56	0	.3	10.8	0	0	10.8
1/4 cup (54g) extra virgin olive oil	477	54	0	0	0	0	0
4 (605g) 5 to 6 oz. boneless chicken breasts, cubed (or equivalent thigh meat, skin optional)	1040	54.5	127	0	0	0	0
2 (6g) garlic cloves, minced	8	0	0	2	0	0	2
8 slices (200g) raw bacon, chopped	916	90	24	2	0	0	2
salt and pepper to taste	0	0	0	0	0	0	0
Totals (of 4 servings):	3733.7	279.1	238.9	38.7	9	0	29.7
Per Serving:	933.4	69.8	59.7	9.7	2.3	0	(7.4)

CA= Calories / **FAT**= Fat / **P**=Protein / **C**= Carbohydrates / **F**= Fiber / **SA**= Sugar Alcohols / **NC**= Net Carbs

Mixed Greens with Blackberries, Bacon, and Goat Cheese — p.191

	CA	FAT	P	C	F	SA	NC
1 cup (144g) fresh blackberries, washed	62	1	2	18	8	0	10
4 cups (284g) mixed greens, washed and dried	30	0	2	6	2	0	4
1/4 cup (22g) fresh mint leaves, washed and dried	9.7	.2	.7	1.8	1.5	0	.2
1/4 cup (28g) bacon bits	100	6	12	0	0	0	0
1/4 cup (30g) broken walnut halves	196	19.6	4.5	4	2	0	2
2 Tbsp (32g) balsamic vinegar	28	0	.1	5.4	0	0	5.4
1/4 cup (54g) extra virgin olive oil	477	54	0	0	0	0	0
1/4 cup (112g) goat cheese	407	33.6	24.6	3.4	0	0	3.4
salt and pepper to taste	0	0	0	0	0	0	0
Totals (of 4 servings):	1311.1	114.5	45.9	38.5	13.5	0	25
Per Serving:	327.8	28.6	11.5	9.6	3.4	0	(6.2)

Green Beans, Asparagus, and Heartichoke Salad — p.184

	CA	FAT	P	C	F	SA	NC
1 bunch (227g) asparagus, fibrous ends removed	45.7	16	5.1	8.5	5.1	0	3.4
1/2 lb. (227g) green beans, ends removed	70.4	.3	2.7	16.2	7.7	0	8.5
8 whole (221.84g) artichoke hearts in oil, drained and cut into 8 wedges, each	264	18.8	7.1	23	11.2	0	11.8
1/4 cup (34g) toasted pine nuts	227	23	4.5	4.5	1.3	0	3.3
1 Tbsp (8g) drained and coarsely chopped capers	1.9	.1	.2	.4	.2	0	.2
2 (6g) garlic cloves, crushed	8	0	0	2	0	0	2
2 tsp (2g) fresh oregano, chopped (thyme, rosemary, sage, and/or marjoram)	2	0	.1	.5	.3	0	.2
1/4 cup (54g) good quality extra virgin olive oil, divided	477	54	0	0	0	0	0
2 Tbsp (31g) freshly squeezed lemon juice	7.6	0	.1	2.6	.1	0	2.5
salt and pepper to taste	0	0	0	0	0	0	0
Totals (of 6 servings):	794.5	39.5	17.7	96.4	19	30	47.4
Per Serving:	132.4	6.6	3	16.1	3.2	5	(7.9)

Greek Salad — p.192

	CA	FAT	P	C	F	SA	NC
1 lb. (454g) fresh assorted tomatoes, cut into thin slices or wedges	82.3	0	4.5	17.5	4.5	0	13
1 (301g) English cucumber, seeded and cut into small cubes	122	0	13.6	18.2	4.5	0	13.6
1 small (70g) sweet red onion, very thinly sliced	28	0	1	7	1	0	6
1 small (74g) red bell pepper, seeded and cut into small cubes	22.9	0	.7	4.4	1.5	0	3
1/4 cup (60g) chopped Kalamata olives	27.5	.4	3.5	4.2	2.5	0	1.8
2 tsp (2g) chopped fresh oregano	2	0	.1	.5	.3	0	.2
2 (6g) garlic cloves, minced	8	0	0	2	0	0	2
2 Tbsp (31g) fresh lemon juice	7.6	0	.1	2.6	.1	0	2.5
2 Tbsp (30g) red wine vinegar	5.7	0	0	.1	0	0	.1
1/2 cup (108g) extra virgin olive oil	955	108	0	0	0	0	0
1 lb. (454g) feta cheese, cut into cubes	1198	96.9	63.6	18.2	0	0	18.2
salt and pepper to taste	0	0	0	0	0	0	0
Totals (of 8 servings):	2460.2	205.2	87.2	74.7	14.4	0	60.3
Per Serving:	307.5	25.7	10.9	9.3	1.8	0	(7.5)

Curried Chicken Salad — p.186

	CA	FAT	P	C	F	SA	NC
1 1/2 lb. (681g) cooked chicken meat, diced	1628	93.4	186	0	0	0	0
1/2 small (35g) red onion, diced	14	0	.5	3.5	.5	0	3
1/2 cup (51g) diced celery	0	0	0	0	0	0	0
1/4 cup (36g) chopped raisins	123	.3	1.3	32.8	1.5	0	31
2 tsp (4g) curry powder	.8	0	0	.2	.1	0	.1
1 cup (109g) mayonnaise	750	83.5	2.4	1.3	.1	.3	1
1/4 cup (36g) toasted slivered almonds	210	18.3	8	7.3	3.8	0	3.5
2 tsp (10g) fresh lemon juice	2.5	0	0	.9	0	0	.1
1/2 bunch (50g) cilantro, washed, large stems removed, and chopped	11.5	.3	1.1	1.9	1.5	0	.4
salt and pepper to taste	0	0	0	0	0	0	0
Totals (of 4 servings):	2741.6	195.6	200	47.7	7.4	.3	40.1
Per Serving:	685.4	48.9	50	11.9	1.9	.1	(10)

CA= Calories / **FAT**= Fat / **P**=Protein / **C**= Carbohydrates / **F**= Fiber / **SA**= Sugar Alcohols / **NC**= Net Carbs

TAKING OUT THE CARBAGE

The Famous Cobb Salad — p.194

	CA	FAT	P	C	F	SA	NC
1 cup (50g) chopped Belgian endive	8	0	0	2	2	0	0
1 cup (34g) coarsely chopped watercress	4	0	1	0	0	0	0
1 cup (72g) shredded iceberg lettuce	10	0	1	2	1	0	1
1 cup (47g) shredded romaine lettuce	8	.2	4	1.6	1	0	.6
4 (344g) cooked and chilled chicken breast halves (skin on if possible)	568	12	108	0	0	0	0
12 slices (336g) bacon, precooked and crispy	84	36	12	0	0	0	0
2 (100g) hard-boiled eggs, peeled and chopped or cut in half	155	11	12	1	0	0	1
4 oz. (112g) quality Roquefort cheese, crumbled	413	34.7	24.6	2.2	0	0	2.2
1/2 lb. (227g) cherry tomatoes, washed, dried, and halved or quartered	41.2	0	2.5	8.7	2.5	0	6.2
2 whole (272g) avocados, peeled and sliced or diced	554	42	6	24	18	0	6
4 whole (60g) green onions (scallions), sliced	19.2	0	1.2	4.2	1.8	0	2.4
2 (6g) garlic cloves, minced	8	0	0	2	0	0	2
1 Tbsp (15g) Dijon mustard	12.4	.6	.7	1.5	.6	0	.9
1 Tbsp (15.25g) freshly squeezed lemon juice	3.8	0	.1	1.3	.1	0	1.3
2 Tbsp (30g) red wine vinegar	5.7	0	0	.1	0	0	.1
1/4 cup (54g) good quality extra virgin olive oil	477	54	0	0	0	0	0
salt and pepper to taste	0	0	0	0	0	0	0
Totals (of 6 servings):	2372	190.5	173.1	50.7	27	0	23.7
Per Serving:	395.3	31.7	28.9	8.5	4.5	0	(4)

The Famous Salad Niçoise — p.196

	CA	FAT	P	C	F	SA	NC
2 Tbsp (30g) Dijon mustard	24.8	1.2	1.5	2.9	1.2	0	1.7
2 Tbsp (31g) freshly squeezed lemon juice	7.6	0	.1	2.6	.1	0	2.5
4 sprigs (2g) chopped, fresh tarragon leaves	2	0	.1	.5	.3	0	.2
1 (3g) garlic clove, minced	4	0	0	1	0	0	1
2 Tbsp (20g) finely diced shallots	14	0	0	4	0	0	4
2 tsp (5g) chopped capers	1.2	.1	.1	.3	.2	0	.1
1/2 cup (108g) extra virgin olive oil	0	0	0	0	0	0	0
1/2 lb. (227g) green beans, ends removed	70.4	.3	2.7	16.2	7.7	0	8.5
4 cups (220g) butter-head (a.k.a., Boston or Bibb) lettuce	28.3	0	2.7	5.4	2.7	0	2.7
1/4 cup (45g) coarsely chopped assorted French olives	47	3.2	.5	2.7	1.4	0	1.4
1/2 lb. (227g) cherry tomatoes, halved or quartered	41.2	0	2.5	8.7	2.5	0	6.2
16 (32g) boneless anchovy filets	67.2	3.2	9.3	0	0	0	0
4 (672g) super fresh tuna steaks (yellowfin [ahi] or albacore)	725	6.7	154	0	0	0	0
1 Tbsp (14g) lard, olive oil, or ghee	120	12	0	0	0	0	0
4 (200g) hard-boiled eggs, peeled and chopped or cut in half	310	22	24	2	0	0	2
salt and pepper to taste	0	0	0	0	0	0	0
Totals (of 4 servings):	1463.4	48.6	198.1	46.3	16	0	30.3
Per Serving:	365.9	12.2	49.5	11.6	4	0	(7.6)

CA= Calories / **FAT**= Fat / **P**=Protein / **C**= Carbohydrates / **F**= Fiber / **SA**= Sugar Alcohols / **NC**= Net Carbs

Lunch Nutrition Facts

ChupaChorueso: Cheese-Stuffed Cheese with Mexican Sausage
p.208

	CA	FAT	P	C	F	SA	NC
4 oz. (113g) cheddar cheese, grated	451	37.2	28	1.4	0	0	1.4
2 oz. (56g) hot pepper Monterey jack cheese, grated	220	18	12	2	0	0	2
2 oz. (56g) queso fresco, crumbled	199	15.7	12.7	1.7	0	0	1.7
4 oz. (113g) raw Mexican chorizo, crumbled and cooked	514	42.9	27.1	2.3	0	0	2.3
Totals (of 1 servings):	1384	113.8	79.9	7.3	0	0	7.3
Per Serving:	1384	113.8	79.9	7.3	0	0	(7.3)

Spicy Cheese-Stuffed Burger
p.204

	CA	FAT	P	C	F	SA	NC
1/4 cup (54g) ghee, bacon fat, or lard, divided	477	54	0	0	0	0	0
1 (65g) Poblano pepper, seeds removed and diced	13	.1	.6	3	1.1	0	1.9
1 (7g) jalapeño pepper, seeds removed and diced	2	0	.1	.4	.2	0	.2
3 (9g) garlic cloves, diced	13	0	1	3	0	0	3
1 small (110g) onion, diced	44	0	1	10	2	0	8
1 1/2 lb. (681g) ground beef	768	60.5	51.5	0	0	0	0
1 large (50g) egg	72	5	6.5	.5	0	0	.5
2 tsp (4g) cumin, ground	15	.9	0	1.8	.4	0	1.3
1 tsp (2g) coriander seed, ground	6	.4	.2	1.1	.8	0	.3
8 oz. (227g) Oaxaca cheese, grated	808	63.6	52.2	6.6	0	0	6.6
2 medium (182g) tomato, sliced	32	0	2	8	2	0	6
1 whole (136g) avocado, peeled and sliced	277	21	3	12	9	0	3
1 cup (230g) sour cream	444	45	5	8	0	0	8
1/4 bunch (25g) fresh cilantro, large stems removed, divided	5.8	.1	.6	.9	.7	0	.7
salt and pepper to taste	0	0	0	0	0	0	0
Totals (of 6 servings):	2978	250.6	123.6	55.3	16.3	0	39.5
Per Serving:	496.3	41.8	20.6	9.2	2.7	0	(6.6)

Sandwich Wraps
p.216

	CA	FAT	P	C	F	SA	NC
8 (47g) All-Purpose Crepes	87.8	5.3	5	1	0	0	1
2 Tbsp (30g) Dijon mustard	24.8	1.2	1.5	2.9	1.2	0	1.7
6 (31.33g) lettuce leaves, washed and dried	5.3	.1	.4	1.1	.7	0	.4
4 slices (112g) ham	182	10.1	19	4.5	1.1	0	3.4
4 slices (112g) cheddar cheese	462	36.2	33.6	.7	0	0	.7
4 slices (32g) cooked bacon	175	13.8	11.5	.3	0	0	.3
1 small (91g) tomato, cut into 10 wedges	16	0	1	4	1	0	3
salt and pepper to taste	0	0	0	0	0	0	0
Totals (of 2 servings):	954.2	66.6	72	14.4	4	0	10.5
Per Serving:	477.1	33.3	36	7.2	2	0	(5.2)

Pizza Pucks
p.212

	CA	FAT	P	C	F	SA	NC
4 oz. (114g) regular cream cheese (not low-fat), softened	388	38.7	6.9	4.4	0	0	4.4
2 large (100g) whole eggs	143	10	13	1	0	0	1
1/2 cup (50g) Parmesan cheese, grated and divided	215	14.5	19	2	0	0	2
3/4 lb. (341g) mozzarella (whole milk, low moisture), grated and divided	1082	85.1	74.9	6.8	0	0	6.8
1 tsp (1g) fresh oregano, chopped	1	0	.1	.2	.1	0	.1
4 (12g) garlic cloves, minced	16	0	0	4	0	0	4
4 oz. (112g) raw Italian sausage	259	18.7	20.1	1.8	.7	0	1.2
1 cup (230g) marinara sauce	110	4	2.4	16.7	4.7	0	12
1/4 cup (28g) real bacon bits	100	6	12	0	0	0	0
24 thin slices (48g) pepperoni	236	20.6	10.3	0	0	0	0
salt, pepper, and chili flakes to taste	0	0	0	0	0	0	0
Totals (of 4 servings):	2553.3	197.6	158.6	37	5.5	0	31.5
Per Serving:	638.3	49.4	39.6	9.3	1.4	0	(7.9)

CA= Calories / **FAT**= Fat / **P**=Protein / **C**= Carbohydrates / **F**= Fiber / **SA**= Sugar Alcohols / **NC**= Net Carbs

Italian Turkey Club — p.202

	CA	FAT	P	C	F	SA	NC
1 sheet (624g) grain-free focaccia	1689	140	76.3	50.1	22.8	0	27.2
1/2 cup (193g) Pesto alla Genovese (homemade or store-bought pesto)	853	89.8	11.6	6.8	.3	0	6.6
1 1/2 lb. (681g) sliced turkey	681	13.6	122	13.6	0	0	13.6
12 slices (96g) cooked bacon	526	41.3	34.6	1	0	0	1
1 medium (91g) tomato, sliced thin	16	0	1	4	1	0	3
salt and pepper to taste	0	0	0	0	0	0	0
Totals (of 6 servings):	3765.2	285.2	246.1	75.5	24.1	0	51.4
Per Serving:	627.5	47.5	41	12.6	4	0	(8.6)

Pulled Pork — p.206

	CA	FAT	P	C	F	SA	NC
1/4 cup (60g) yellow mustard	49.5	2.3	3	5.8	2.4	0	3.4
2 Tbsp (30g) yacon syrup	40	0	0	22	0	0	22
1 small (110g) onion, cut into chunks	44	0	1	10	2	0	8
12 (36g) garlic cloves, tips removed	48	0	0	12	0	0	12
1 pork butt, bone in (also known as shoulder or Boston butt) (about 5 to 6 lb.) (2724g)	6420	492	468	0	0	0	0
2 Tbsp (14g) paprika	40.5	1.8	2.1	7.8	5.2	0	2.7
1 Tbsp (5g) cayenne pepper	17	1	1	3	1	0	2
1 Tbsp (2g) fresh thyme, chopped	2.6	.1	.1	.4	.3	0	.1
1 Tbsp (6g) fresh cracked black pepper	16	0	1	4	2	0	2
2 Tbsp (36g) salt	0	0	0	0	0	0	0
Totals (of 8 servings):	6677.6	497.3	476.1	65.1	12.9	0	52.2
Per Serving:	834.7	62.2	59.5	8.1	1.6	0	(6.5)

Greasy Pork Sandwich — p.210

	CA	FAT	P	C	F	SA	NC
2 Tbsp (13g) golden flaxseed meal (or 1 1/2 Tbsp (10g) ground chia seed)	60	4.5	3	4	4	0	0
2 Tbsp (14g) almond meal	80	7	3	3	1.5	0	1.5
1 large (50g) egg	72	5	6.5	.5	0	0	.5
1 tsp (4.67g) melted butter	33.3	3.7	0	0	0	0	0
1/2 tsp (2g) baking powder	2.5	0	0	.5	0	0	.5
3 slices (84g) deli ham	136	7.6	14.3	3.4	.8	0	2.5
3 slices (84g) bacon, precooked and crispy	28	9	3	0	0	0	0
1 large (50g) egg	72	5	6.5	.5	0	0	.5
2 Tbsp (30g) heavy whipping cream	102	11	.6	.9	0	0	.9
1 Tbsp (14g) bacon fat or butter	100	11	0	0	0	0	0
salt and pepper to taste	0	0	0	0	0	0	0
Totals (of 1 servings):	474.6	43.3	11.2	17.6	11.3	0	6.3
Per Serving:	474.6	43.3	11.2	17.6	11.3	0	(6.3)

Chicken Nuggets — p.214

	CA	FAT	P	C	F	SA	NC
1 cup (216g) high smoke point oil (see recipe notes)	1910	216	0	0	0	0	0
1 1/2 cup (168g) almond flour	960	84	36	36	18	0	18
1 cup (100g) finely grated Parmesan cheese	431	29	38	4	0	0	4
2 tsp (2g) chopped fresh oregano (thyme, rosemary, sage and/or marjoram)	2	0	.1	.5	.3	0	.2
4 (12g) garlic cloves, minced	16	0	0	4	0	0	4
1 large (50g) egg	72	5	6.5	.5	0	0	.5
1 1/2 lb. (681g) boneless chicken (I used breast, but thigh will work, as well; skin is optional), cut into cubes	1171	61.3	143	0	0	0	0
salt, pepper, and chili flakes to taste	0	0	0	0	0	0	0
Totals (of 8 servings):	4562.3	395.3	223.6	45	18.3	0	26.7
Per Serving:	570.3	49.4	28	5.6	2.3	0	(3.3)

CA= Calories / **FAT**= Fat / **P**=Protein / **C**= Carbohydrates / **F**= Fiber / **SA**= Sugar Alcohols / **NC**= Net Carbs

Pasta Nutrition Facts

Chicken Noodles with Asparagus, Artichokes, and Pine Nuts p.218

	CA	FAT	P	C	F	SA	NC
3/4 cup (156g) ice cubes	0	0	0	0	0	0	0
3 Tbsp (18g) egg white powder	45	0	13.5	0	0	0	0
6 oz. (168g) skinless chicken breast, chilled and cubed	185	1.4	38.4	0	0	0	0
2 cups (448g) chicken stock or broth	31.4	.6	4.5	3	0	0	3
1/2 cup (112g) fresh whole butter, cut into about 12 cubes and divided	800	88	0	0	0	0	0
4 (12g) garlic cloves, crushed	16	0	0	4	0	0	4
1 bunch (227g) asparagus, cut into thin slices	45.7	16	5.1	8.5	5.1	0	3.4
3 whole (83g) artichoke hearts in oil, drained and cut into 8 wedges each	99	7.1	2.7	8.6	4.2	0	4.4
1/4 cup (34g) pine nuts, toasted	227	23	4.5	4.5	1.3	0	3.3
1 Tbsp (8g) capers, drained and coarsely chopped	1.9	.1	.2	.4	.2	0	.2
1/4 tsp (.5g) crushed red chili flakes	1.6	.1	.1	.3	.1	0	.2
1/4 cup (25g) Parmesan-Reggiano cheese, grated	107	7.3	9.5	1	0	0	1
16 leaves (6g) fresh basil, hand torn	1.5	.1	.2	.2	.1	0	.1
salt and pepper to taste	0	0	0	0	0	0	0
Totals (of 4 servings):	1562.1	143.6	78.6	30.5	11	0	19.5
Per Serving:	390.5	35.9	19.7	7.6	2.8	0	(4.9)

Stir-Fried Peanut Chicken with Kelp Noodles p.220

	CA	FAT	P	C	F	SA	NC
24 oz. (680g) kelp noodles	36	0	0	6	6	0	0
1 Tbsp (15g) lime juice, freshly squeezed	3.8	0	.07	1.3	.1	0	1.3
1 1/2 lb. (681g) boneless chicken, cut into strips	809	20.7	144.	0	0	0	0
4 (12g) garlic cloves, minced	16	0	0	4	0	0	4
1 Tbsp (6g) fresh ginger, minced	4.8	0	.1	1.1	.1	0	1
2 Tbsp (28g) coconut oil	240	24	0	0	0	0	0
1/4 large (210g) bunch broccoli, including stalks, cut into florets	71.5	.7	5.9	13.8	5.5	0	8.3
1 small (74g) red bell pepper, seeded and sliced very thin	22.9	0	.7	4.4	1.5	0	3
1 large (72g) carrot, peeled and cut into thin strips (or grated with grater)	29.3	0	.6	6.8	2.3	0	4.5
1/2 medium (55g) red onion, very thinly sliced	22	0	.5	5	1	0	4
1/2 cup (120g) peanut sauce	338	27.5	11.1	21.2	2.1	9	10.1
1/4 bunch (25g) cilantro, washed and large stems removed	5.8	.1	.6	.9	.7	0	.2
2 whole (30g) green onions (scallions), cut lengthwise into thin strips	9.6	0	.6	2.1	.9	0	1.2
1/4 cup (37g) peanuts, toasted and chopped	207	18	9.5	6	3	0	3
salt and pepper to taste	0	0	0	0	0	0	0
Totals (of 4 servings):	1816.3	91	174.5	72.7	23.2	9	40.5
Per Serving:	454.1	22.8	43.6	18.2	5.8	2.3	(10.1)

Zucchini Fettuccini, a.k.a. ZOODLES!!! p.226

	CA	FAT	P	C	F	SA	NC
4 small (472g) green zucchini and/or summer squash, cut into zoodles	76	1.5	5.8	16.1	5.8	0	10.2
1/4 cup (28g) real bacon bits	100	6	12	0	0	0	0
1 Tbsp (14g) lightly flavored oil (like olive oil, ghee, or bacon fat)	100	11	0	0	0	0	0
salt and pepper to taste	0	0	0	0	0	0	0
Totals (of 4 servings):	276	18.5	17.8	16.1	5.8	0	10.2
Per Serving:	69	4.6	4.5	4	1.5	0	(2.6)

Roasted Spaghetti Squash p.223

	CA	FAT	P	C	F	SA	NC
1 roughly 5-lb. (930g) spaghetti squash	252	0	6	60	12	0	48
1/4 cup (56g) fresh whole butter, softened	400	44	0	0	0	0	0
salt and black pepper to taste	0	0	0	0	0	0	0
Totals (of 6 servings):	652	44	6	60	12	0	48
Per Serving:	108.7	7.3	1	10	2	0	(8)

CA= Calories / **FAT**= Fat / **P**=Protein / **C**= Carbohydrates / **F**= Fiber / **SA**= Sugar Alcohols / **NC**= Net Carbs

Singapore-Style Noodles p.230

	CA	FAT	P	C	F	SA	NC
16 oz. (454g) tofu shirataki noodles, angel hair (non-tofu is fine too!)	80	2	4	12	8	0	4
1 lb. (454g) boneless chicken, cut into strips	539	13.8	96.6	0	0	0	0
16 large (454g) shrimp, peeled and deveined	481	9.1	90.8	4.5	.3	0	4.3
2 Tbsp (12g) yellow curry powder, divided	40	2	2	8	4	0	4
4 (12g) garlic cloves, minced	16	0	0	4	0	0	4
1 Tbsp (6g) fresh ginger, minced	4.8	0	.1	1.1	.1	0	1
4 large (200g) whole eggs	286	20	26	2	0	0	2
2 Tbsp (28g) coconut oil	240	24	0	0	0	0	0
1/4 large (210g) bunch broccoli, including stalks, cut into florets	71.5	.7	5.9	13.8	5.5	0	8.3
1 small (74g) red bell pepper, seeded and sliced very thin	22.9	0	.7	4.4	1.5	0	3
1 cup (104g) mung bean sprouts	31	0	3	6	2	0	4
1/2 medium (55g) onion, very thinly sliced	22	0	.5	5	1	0	4
1/4 bunch (25g) cilantro, washed and large stems removed	5.8	.1	.6	.9	.7	0	.2
2 whole (30g) green onions (scallions), cut lengthwise into thin strips	9.6	0	.6	2.1	.9	0	1.2
salt and pepper to taste	0	0	0	0	0	0	0
Totals (of 4 servings):	1850.4	71.7	230.8	63.9	24	0	39.9
Per Serving:	462.6	17.9	57.7	16	6	0	(10)

Crepe Fettuccine with Tomatoes, Fresh Mozzarella, and Pesto p.224

	CA	FAT	P	C	F	SA	NC
15 (752g) all-purpose ricotta crepes	1404	84	80	12	0	0	12
2 Tbsp (28g) olive oil	240	24	0	0	0	0	0
1 lb. (454g) assorted fresh cherry tomatoes, cut into halves and quarters	82.3	0	5	17.5	5	0	12.5
1/2 tsp (1g) crushed red chili flakes	3.2	.2	.1	.6	.3	0	.3
1/4 cup (97g) Pesto alla Genovese (homemade or store-bought pesto)	426	44.9	11.6	6.8	.3	0	6.6
1 lb. (454g) fresh mozzarella, removed from water and cubed (or use bocconcini)	1120	80	80	0	0	0	0
1/4 cup (25g) Parmesan-Reggiano cheese, grated	107	7.3	9.5	1	0	0	1
16 leaves (6g) fresh basil	1.5	.1	.2	.2	.1	0	.1
salt and fresh cracked pepper to taste	0	0	0	0	0	0	0
Totals (of 4 servings):	3385.3	240.4	186.4	38	5.7	0	32.4
Per Serving:	846.3	60.1	46.6	9.5	1.4	0	(8.1)

Meat Lover's Lasagna p.228

	CA	FAT	P	C	F	SA	NC
1 1/2 lb. (681g) chicken breasts, scaloppini style	809	20.7	144	0	0	0	0
1 Tbsp (14g) olive oil	119	13.5	0	0	0	0	0
1 lb. (454g) ground beef	1153	90.8	77.2	0	0	0	0
1 lb. (454g) raw Italian sausage	1564	140	64	4	0	0	4
1 26-oz. jar (737g) no-sugar-added pasta sauce	420	30	12	36	12	0	24
3 cups (300g) Parmesan cheese, grated and divided into two parts	1293	87	114	12	0	0	12
1 cup (248g) whole-milk ricotta cheese	432	0	28	8	0	0	8
2 large (100g) whole eggs	143	10	13	1	0	0	1
2 lb. (908g) whole milk low-moisture mozzarella, grated	2240	160	160	0	0	0	0
15 (752g) all-purpose ricotta crepes	1404	84	80	12	0	0	12
salt and pepper to taste	0	0	0	0	0	0	0
Totals (of 12 servings):	9577.7	636	693.1	73	12	0	61
Per Serving:	798.1	53	57.8	6.1	1	0	(5.1)

CA= Calories / **FAT**= Fat / **P**=Protein / **C**= Carbohydrates / **F**= Fiber / **SA**= Sugar Alcohols / **NC**= Net Carbs

Main Dishes Nutrition Facts

Ropa un Poco Vieja — p.268

	CA	FAT	P	C	F	SA	NC
2 medium (182g) tomatoes, diced	32	0	2	8	2	0	6
2 small (148g) red bell peppers, peeled, seeded, and sliced into strips	45.9	0	1.5	8.9	3	0	5.9
1 small (110g) onion, sliced	44	0	1	10	2	0	8
1/2 cup (90g) assorted olives with pimento, coarsely chopped	93.9	6.3	.9	5.4	2.7	0	2.7
4 (12g) garlic cloves, minced	16	0	0	4	0	0	4
2 tsp (2g) fresh oregano, coarsely chopped	2	0	.1	.5	.3	0	.2
2 bay leaves	0	0	0	0	0	0	0
1 5- to 6-lb. (2724g) pork butt, bone in (also known as shoulder or Boston butt)	6420	492	468	0	0	0	0
1 Tbsp (6g) cumin seed, ground	23	1.3	0	2.6	.7	0	2
2 Tbsp (28g) fat (tallow, ghee, bacon fat, etc.)	240	24	0	0	0	0	0
salt and pepper to taste	0	0	0	0	0	0	0
Totals (of 8 servings):	6916.8	523.7	473.5	39.4	10.6	0	28.8
Per Serving:	864.6	65.5	59.2	4.9	1.3	0	3.6

Fennel Horseradish Pork Spare Ribs — p.304

	CA	FAT	P	C	F	SA	NC
2 slabs (4540g) pork spare ribs (about 5 lb. per slab)	8580	544	862	0	0	0	0
1 (140g) orange	69	0	0	18	3	0	15
1/2 cup (120g) prepared horseradish	48	1.2	1.2	13.3	3.6	0	9.7
1 Tbsp (6g) fennel seeds, whole	20.7	.9	1	3.1	2.4	0	.7
1 Tbsp (5g) cayenne pepper	17	1	1	3	1	0	2
4 (12g) garlic cloves, minced	0	0	0	0	0	0	0
1/4 cup (54g) extra virgin olive oil	477	54	0	0	0	0	0
salt and freshly cracked pepper to taste	0	0	0	0	0	0	0
Totals (of 4 servings):	9212.8	601.9	865.8	37.4	10	0	27.4
Per Serving:	2303	150.5	216.4	9.4	2.5	0	6.9

Chicken Puttanesca — p.246

	CA	FAT	P	C	F	SA	NC
1/4 cup (54g) extra virgin olive oil, divided	477	54	0	0	0	0	0
4 (681g) boneless chicken breasts (skin optional)	809	20.7	144	0	0	0	0
4 (12g) garlic cloves, minced	16	0	0	4	0	0	4
1 small (110g) red onion, diced	44	0	1	10	2	0	8
1/2 cup (90g) assorted Italian olives, pitted and very coarsely chopped	93.9	6.3	.9	5.4	2.7	0	2.7
1 Tbsp (8g) capers, drained and coarsely chopped	1.9	.1	.2	.4	.2	0	.2
4 (8g) boneless anchovy filets, coarsely chopped	16.8	.8	2.3	0	0	0	0
1/2 tsp (1g) crushed red chili flakes	3.2	.2	.1	.6	.3	0	.3
1 lb. (454g) assorted fresh tomatoes, diced	82.3	0	5	17.5	5	0	12.5
salt and pepper to taste	0	0	0	0	0	0	0
Totals (of 4 servings):	1544.9	82.1	154.4	37.8	10.2	0	27.6
Per Serving:	386.2	20.5	38.6	9.5	2.6	0	6.9

Seared Scallops with Almond-Parsnip Mash & Blackberry Beurre Rouge — p.248

	CA	FAT	P	C	F	SA	NC
20 jumbo (560g) sea scallops	492	5.6	95.2	11.2	0	0	11.2
1 Tbsp cooking fat (such as ghee, olive oil, bacon fat, lard, etc.)	100	11	0	0	0	0	0
20 fresh (36g) blackberries, washed	15.5	.3	.5	4.5	2	0	2.5
2 fresh sage leaves, very thinly sliced and divided	1.3	.1	0	.3	.1	0	.1
1/4 cup toasted slivered almonds	210	18.3	8	7.3	3.8	0	3.5
2 Tbsp (28g) butter	200	22	0	0	0	0	0
1/2 full recipe Almond-Parsnip Mash	536	36.4	9.7	47.3	15.1	0	32.3
1 full recipe Beurre Rouge	595	50	1.3	16.6	4	0	12.6
salt and pepper to taste	0	0	0	0	0	0	0
Totals (of 4 servings):	2151.4	143.6	114.7	87.1	25	0	62.2
Per Serving:	537.8	35.9	28.7	21.8	6.2	0	15.5

CA= Calories / **FAT**= Fat / **P**=Protein / **C**= Carbohydrates / **F**= Fiber / **SA**= Sugar Alcohols / **NC**= Net Carbs

Spicy Burger Casserole — p.240

	CA	FAT	P	C	F	SA	NC
2 small (148g) red bell peppers, stems removed and seeded	45.9	0	1.5	8.9	3	0	5.9
2 (130g) Poblano peppers, stems removed and seeded	26	.2	1.1	6	2.2	0	3.8
1 cup (240g) water	0	0	0	0	0	0	0
1/2 cup (120g) almond milk, unsweetened	22.5	1.8	1	1.5	.5	0	1
1/4 cup (56g) fresh whole butter	400	44	0	0	0	0	0
2 Tbsp (28g) fat (olive oil, butter, or even bacon fat!)	240	24	0	0	0	0	0
1 medium (110g) onion, diced	44	0	1	10	2	0	8
2 (27g) jalapeño peppers, seeds and ribs removed, finely diced	8	.2	.4	1.6	.7	0	.8
4 (12g) garlic cloves, minced	16	0	0	4	0	0	4
2 lb. (908g) ground beef (80 lean/20 fat)	2306	181	154	0	0	0	0
1 tsp (2g) cumin seed, ground	7.5	.4	0	.9	.2	0	.7
1 tsp (2g) coriander seed, ground	6	.4	.2	1.1	.8	0	.3
1 1/2 cups (168g) almond flour	960	84	36	36	18	0	18
1 lb. (454g) mild cheddar cheese, grated and divided	1804	148	112	5.5	0	0	5.5
salt and pepper to taste	0	0	0	0	0	0	0
Totals (of 8 servings):	5887	485.3	307.6	75.4	27.5	0	48
Per Serving:	735.9	60.7	38.4	9.4	3.4	0	(6)

Pork Carnitas — p.238

	CA	FAT	P	C	F	SA	NC
1 approximately 5 to 6 lb. (2724g) pork butt, bone-in (also known as shoulder or Boston butt)	6420	492	468	0	0	0	0
12 (36g) garlic cloves, sliced into thin slivers	48	0	0	12	0	0	12
1/2 cup (122g) fresh lime juice	30.5	0	.5	10.5	.5	0	10
salt and pepper to taste	0	0	0	0	0	0	0
Totals (of 8 servings):	6498.5	492	468.5	22.5	.5	0	22
Per Serving:	812.3	61.5	58.6	2.8	.1	0	(2.8)

Brisket with Shrooms and Fennel — p.244

	CA	FAT	P	C	F	SA	NC
5 lb. (2270g) beef brisket, fat trimmed off	6287	502	406	0	0	0	0
16 sprigs (64g) fresh rosemary	0	0	0	0	0	0	0
12 (36g) garlic cloves	48	0	0	12	0	0	12
1/2 cup (116g) red wine, good quality	98.6	0	0	3.2	0	0	3.2
1/4 cup (64g) balsamic vinegar	56	0	.3	10.8	0	0	10.8
2 lb. (908g) (about 24 large) whole crimini (or button) mushrooms, dirt removed with brush	245	0	27.2	36.3	9.1	0	27.2
2 bulbs (468g) fennel, cut into 8 wedges each	146	0	6	34	14	0	20
2 Tbsp (27g) olive oil	238	27	0	0	0	0	0
salt and pepper to taste	0	0	0	0	0	0	0
Totals (of 8 servings)	7120.3	529.2	440.3	96.2	23.1	0	73.2
Per Serving:	890	66.2	55	12	2.9	0	(9.1)

Chicken with Pancetta and Mushrooms — p.258

	CA	FAT	P	C	F	SA	NC
1 cup (224g) chicken stock or broth	15.7	.3	2.2	1.5	0	0	1.5
8 leaves (2g) fresh sage, divided	2.6	.1	.1	.4	.3	0	.1
1 lb. (454g) crimini or button mushrooms, halved or quartered	122	0	6.8	9.1	2.3	0	6.8
2 cups (164g) cubed eggplant	40	0	2	10	6	0	4
1/4 cup (54g) olive oil, divided	477	54	0	0	0	0	0
4 (12g) garlic cloves, minced	16	0	0	4	0	0	4
1 Tbsp (8g) capers, drained and coarsely chopped	1.9	.1	.2	.4	.2	0	.2
4 (681g) boneless chicken breasts (skin optional)	809	20.7	144	0	0	0	0
8 slices (100g) pancetta, sliced into strips	175	13.8	11.5	.3	0	0	.3
1/2 cup (112g) chilled whole butter (one stick), cut into about 12 cubes	800	88	0	0	0	0	0
salt and pepper to taste	0	0	0	0	0	0	0
Totals (of 4 servings)	2460.9	177	167.7	25.8	8.8	0	17
Per Serving:	615.2	44.2	41.9	6.4	2.2	0	(4.2)

CA= Calories / **FAT**= Fat / **P**=Protein / **C**= Carbohydrates / **F**= Fiber / **SA**= Sugar Alcohols / **NC**= Net Carbs

Coq au Vin — p.250

	CA	FAT	P	C	F	SA	NC
1 large (about 6 lb.) (2724g) chicken, cut into 8 pieces	3042	204	288	0	0	0	0
4 oz. (100g) salt pork (or bacon), cut into cubes	513	50.4	13.4	1.1	0	0	1.1
1 lb. (454g) mushrooms, dirt removed with brush	122	0	13.6	18.2	4.5	0	13.6
16 (128g) pearl onions, peeled	60	2	2	8	1	0	7
2 large (144g) carrots, peeled and cut into chunks	58.5	0	1.1	13.5	4.5	0	9
2 cups (464g) burgundy wine	394	0	0	12.6	0	0	12.6
4 (12g) garlic cloves, crushed	16	0	0	4	0	0	4
1 (50.5g) celery rib, cut into chunks	8	0	.5	1.5	1	0	.5
10 sprigs (10g) fresh thyme	2.6	.1	.1	.4	.3	0	.1
1 bay leaf	0	0	0	0	0	0	0
1/4 cup (56g) whole butter, cut into about 12 cubes	400	44	0	0	0	0	0
salt and freshly cracked black pepper to taste	0	0	0	0	0	0	0
Totals (of 4 servings):	4617.2	300.5	318.7	59.3	11.3	0	48
Per Serving:	1154	75.1	79.7	14.8	2.8	0	(12)

Smoked Paprika Chicken — p.252

	CA	FAT	P	C	F	SA	NC
1 lb. (454g) assorted fresh tomatoes, cut into rustic chunks	82.3	0	5	17.5	5	0	12.5
2 small (148g) roasted red peppers, peeled, seeded, and cut into rustic chunks	45.9	0	1.5	8.9	3	0	5.9
1 medium (110g) onion, cut into rustic chunks	44	0	1	10	2	0	8
2 Tbsp (30g) red wine vinegar	5.7	0	0	.1	0	0	.1
1 Tbsp (7g) smoked paprika (regular is fine)	20.2	.9	1.1	3.9	2.6	0	1.3
1 Tbsp (2g) fresh thyme, chopped	2.6	.1	.1	.4	.3	0	.1
4 (12g) garlic cloves, minced	16	0	0	4	0	0	4
1 approximately 3 lb. (1336g) whole chicken	2886	212	228	0	0	0	0
1/4 cup (36g) blanched and slivered almonds, toasted	210	18.3	8	7.3	3.8	0	3.5
salt and pepper to taste	0	0	0	0	0	0	0
Totals (of 4 servings):	3313.2	231.3	244.6	52.1	16.6	0	35.5
Per Serving:	828.3	57.8	61.2	13	4.1	0	(8.9)

Oven-Roasted Spatchcock Chicken — p.264

	CA	FAT	P	C	F	SA	NC
2 tsp (2g) fresh thyme, chopped	2	0	.1	.5	.3	0	.2
2 tsp (1g) fresh rosemary, chopped	1.8	.1	0	.3	.2	0	.1
2 tsp (2g) fresh oregano, chopped	2	0	.1	.5	.3	0	.2
1/2 tsp (1g) crushed red chili flakes	3.2	.2	.1	.6	.3	0	.3
4 (12g) garlic cloves, minced	16	0	0	4	0	0	4
1/4 cup (56g) light oil (such as coconut, olive, or ghee)	480	48	0	0	0	0	0
1 (1336g) whole chicken	2886	212	228	0	0	0	0
salt and pepper to taste	0	0	0	0	0	0	0
Totals (of 2 servings):	3391	260.3	228.4	5.8	1	0	4.8
Per Serving:	1695	130.2	114.2	2.9	.5	0	(2.4)

Cheddar 'n' Onions Stuffed Bacon Wrapped Meatloaf — p.282

	CA	FAT	P	C	F	SA	NC
1 lb. (454g) cheddar cheese, cut into 1/2-inch rectangular sticks	1804	148	112	5.5	0	0	5.5
2 Tbsp (27g) cooking fat (such as ghee, bacon fat, olive oil, coconut oil, etc.)	955	27	0	0	0	0	0
1 small (110g) red onion, sliced	44	0	1	10	2	0	8
2 lb. (908g) ground beef (80 lean/20 fat)	2306	181	154	0	0	0	0
2 large (100g) whole eggs, beaten	143	10	13	1	0	0	1
3 Tbsp (22.5g) ground chia seeds	105	6.8	4.5	10.5	9	0	1.5
4 (12g) garlic cloves, minced	16	0	0	4	0	0	4
8 slices (200g) raw bacon	916	90	24	2	0	0	2
salt and pepper to taste	0	0	0	0	0	0	0
Totals (of 8 servings):	6290.2	464.1	308.9	33	11	0	22
Per Serving:	786.3	58	38.6	4.1	1.4	0	(2.8)

CA= Calories / **FAT**= Fat / **P**=Protein / **C**= Carbohydrates / **F**= Fiber / **SA**= Sugar Alcohols / **NC**= Net Carbs

Black Pepper Beef and Broccolini — p.270

	CA	FAT	P	C	F	SA	NC
1 1/2 lb. (681g) tender boneless beef (such as rib eye or tenderloin), cut into bite-sized cubes	1680	123	133	0	0	0	0
1 lb. (454g) broccolini, cut into florets and pieces about 1 inch (2.5cm) long	154	0	12.4	29.9	11.4	0	18.6
1 small (110g) red onion, diced	44	0	1	10	2	0	8
4 (12g) garlic cloves, minced	16	0	0	4	0	0	4
1 Tbsp (6g) fresh ginger, minced	4.8	0	.1	1.1	.1	0	1
1 Tbsp (6g) freshly cracked black pepper	16	0	1	4	2	0	2
1 tsp (5g) sesame oil	40	4	0	0	0	0	0
1/4 cup (64g) soy sauce (or coconut aminos)	33.8	0	3.3	5.5	.5	0	5
1/4 cup (58g) rice wine vinegar	100	0	0	2.8	0	0	2.8
2 Tbsp (30g) sweetener	0	0	0	30	0	30	0
1/4 tsp (1g) glucomannan powder	0	0	0	0	0	0	0
1 Tbsp (14g) coconut oil	120	12	0	0	0	0	0
2 Tbsp (24g) black (or white) sesame seeds	135	11.5	4.1	6.2	3.4	0	2.9
salt to taste	0	0	0	0	0	0	0
Totals (of 4 servings):	2184.9	134.5	155.3	93.5	19.3	30	44.2
Per Serving:	546.2	33.6	38.8	23.4	4.8	7.5	(11)

Baked Salmon with Fennel, Leeks, and Cauliflower — p.242

	CA	FAT	P	C	F	SA	NC
1 (108g) lemon	7.6	0	.1	2.6	.1	0	2.5
1/4 cup (54g) extra virgin olive oil, good quality	477	54	0	0	0	0	0
1 large head (840g) cauliflower, cut into large florets	210	1.3	17	45	21	0	24
1 bulb (234g) fennel, cut into 6 wedges	73	0	3	17	7	0	10
1 (89g) white part of leek, cut into 6 disks	54	0	1	13	2	0	11
1 3-lb. (1362g) side of salmon (or two smaller ones)	2546	163	272	0	0	0	0
1/4 cup (60g) Dijon mustard, whole grain	49.5	2.3	3	5.8	2.4	0	3.4
salt and pepper to taste	0	0	0	0	0	0	0
Totals (of 6 servings):	3418.6	221.1	296.5	83.5	32.5	0	50.9
Per Serving:	569.8	36.9	49.4	13.9	5.4	0	(8.5)

Slow Cooker Brisket 'n' Cabbage — p.256

	CA	FAT	P	C	F	SA	NC
1/4 cup (62g) coarse kosher or sea salt	0	0	0	0	0	0	0
1 Tbsp (6g) black peppercorns	16	0	1	4	2	0	2
1/4 (2g) cinnamon stick	4.9	0	.1	1.6	1.1	0	.6
2 bay leaves	6.3	.2	.2	1.5	.5	0	1
2 whole (1g) cloves	3.2	.2	.1	.6	.3	0	.3
2 whole (1g) allspice berries	2.6	.1	.1	.7	.2	0	.5
2 whole (1g) juniper berries	2.6	.1	.1	.7	.2	0	.5
1 small (110g) white onion, diced	44	0	1	10	2	0	8
2 ribs (101g) celery, diced	16	0	1	3	2	0	1
1 small (72g) carrot, peeled and diced	29.3	0	.6	6.8	2.3	0	4.5
2 Tbsp (30g) Dijon mustard, whole grain	24.8	1.2	1.5	2.9	1.2	0	1.7
5 lb. (2270g) beef brisket	6287	502	406	0	0	0	0
1 large head (908g) green cabbage	218	2	11	49	21	0	28
salt to taste	0	0	0	0	0	0	0
Totals (of 8 servings):	6655.4	505.9	423.3	80.8	32.8	0	48
Per Serving:	831.9	63.2	52.9	10.1	4.1	0	(6)

Bacon-Wrapped Meat-Lovers'-Pizza-Stuffed Chicken Breast — p.294

	CA	FAT	P	C	F	SA	NC
1/4 cup (61.25g) tomato sauce	34	2.3	.8	3.1	.8	0	2.3
1 large (118g) chicken breast, boneless and skinless	130	1	27	0	0	0	0
1 slice (28g) ham	45.6	2.5	4.8	1.1	.3	0	.8
14 thin slices (28g) pepperoni	138	12	6	0	0	0	0
2 ounces (56g) raw Italian sausage	129	9.4	10	.9	.3	0	.6
1/4 cup (25g) Parmesan-Reggiano cheese, grated	107	7.3	9.5	1	0	0	1
1/4 cup (28g) whole milk, low moisture mozzarella, grated	89	7	6	1	0	0	1
4 slices (100g) raw bacon	458	45	12	1	0	0	1
salt and pepper to taste	0	0	0	0	0	0	0
Totals (of 2 servings):	1132.1	86.5	76.1	8.2	1.5	0	6.7
Per Serving:	566.1	43.2	38.1	4.1	.7	0	(3.4)

CA= Calories / **FAT**= Fat / **P**=Protein / **C**= Carbohydrates / **F**= Fiber / **SA**= Sugar Alcohols / **NC**= Net Carbs

Paella Mixta — p.262

	CA	FAT	P	C	F	SA	NC
16 medium-sized (224g) clams, fresh and alive	165	2.2	29.1	6.7	0	0	6.7
1 head (840g) large cauliflower	210	1.3	17	45	21	0	24
4 (202g) celery ribs, cut into large dice	32	0	1	6	4	0	2
2 small (148g) red bell peppers, seeded and cut into large dice	45.9	0	1.5	8.9	3	0	5.9
1 small (110g) onion, cut into large dice	44	0	1	10	2	0	8
1/2 cup (80g) frozen peas and carrots	38	0	2	8	2	0	6
4 (12g) garlic cloves, minced	16	0	0	4	0	0	4
1/2 tsp (1g) crushed red chili flakes	3.2	.2	.1	.6	.3	0	.3
1/2 tsp (0g) saffron threads	0	0	0	0	0	0	0
4 (340g) Spanish chorizo links (or a hot Italian sausage)	560	24	57	12	4	0	8
1 (1336g) whole chicken, cut into 8 pieces	2886	212	228	0	0	0	0
2 cups (448g) hot chicken stock or broth	31.4	.6	4.5	3	0	0	3
16 (454g) large shrimp	481	9.1	90.8	4.5	.3	0	4.3
salt and pepper to taste	0	0	0	0	0	0	0
Totals (of 8 servings):	4513.4	249.4	432	108.7	36.5	0	72.2
Per Serving:	564.2	31.2	54	13.6	4.6	0	(9)

Cuban Stuffed Pork Loin — p.266

	CA	FAT	P	C	F	SA	NC
1 (140g) fresh orange, washed	5.8	0	.1	1.5	.7	0	.8
1 (67g) fresh lime, washed	1.5	.1	.2	.2	.1	0	.1
1/2 cup (90g) kosher salt (or 5 Tbsp standard table salt)	0	0	0	0	0	0	0
3 lb. (1362g) pork loin, boneless and center cut	2532	150	276	0	0	0	0
1/2 cup (90g) assorted olives with pimento, coarsely chopped	93.9	6.3	.9	5.4	2.7	0	2.7
1/4 cup (36.25g) raisins, chopped	123	.3	1.3	32.8	1.5	0	31.3
1 Tbsp (8g) capers, drained and coarsely chopped	1.9	.1	.2	.4	.2	0	.2
4 (12g) garlic cloves, minced	16	0	0	4	0	0	4
2 tsp (2g) fresh oregano, coarsely chopped	2	0	.1	.5	.3	0	.2
1 Tbsp (6g) cumin seed, ground	23	1.3	0	2.6	.7	0	2
2 Tbsp (28g) fat (tallow, ghee, bacon fat, etc.)	240	24	0	0	0	0	0
salt and pepper to taste	0	0	0	0	0	0	0
Totals (of 6 servings):	3039.3	182.1	278.7	47.4	6.2	0	41.2
Per Serving:	506.6	30.3	46.5	7.9	1	0	(6.9)

Chicken à la Mombie — p.284

	CA	FAT	P	C	F	SA	NC
6 (907.5g) boneless chicken breasts (or equivalent thigh meat—skin optional)	1560	81.7	190	0	0	0	0
2 Tbsp (28g) light oil (coconut, olive, or even bacon fat!)	240	24	0	0	0	0	0
1 roughly 5-lb. (930g) spaghetti squash, pre-roasted and hot	652	44	6	60	12	0	48
1 recipe (448g) low-carb Alfredo sauce (about 2 cups)	2533	234	86.1	28.5	2.2	0	26.3
18 leaves (6.4g) fresh basil, washed and hand torn or sliced	1.5	.1	.2	.2	.1	0	.1
salt and freshly cracked pepper to taste	0	0	0	0	0	0	0
Totals (of 6 servings):	4988	384.1	282.8	88.7	14.4	0	74.3
Per Serving:	831.3	64	47.1	14.8	2.4	0	(12.4)

Jerk-Inspired Pork Chop — p.298

	CA	FAT	P	C	F	SA	NC
1 (67g) lime	3.82	0	.1	1.3	.1	0	1.3
4 (880g) thick-cut pork chops (double cut with bone-in, preferably)	2504	211	139	0	0	0	0
1 tsp (2g) allspice, ground	5.3	.2	.1	1.4	.4	0	1
1 tsp (2g) cayenne pepper, ground	5.7	.3	.3	1	.3	0	.7
1 tsp (1g) fresh thyme, chopped	1	0	.1	.2	.1	0	.1
1 tsp (2g) freshly cracked black pepper	5.3	0	.3	1.3	.7	0	.7
1/2 tsp (1g) cinnamon, ground	2.5	0	0	.8	.5	0	.3
1/4 tsp (.5g) nutmeg, freshly ground	2.6	.2	0	.3	.1	0	.1
4 (12g) garlic cloves, minced	16	0	0	4	0	0	4
2 Tbsp (28g) coconut oil	240	24	0	0	0	0	0
salt to taste	0	0	0	0	0	0	0
Totals (of 4 servings):	2786.5	236	140.5	10.4	2.3	0	8.1
Per Serving:	696.6	59	35.1	2.6	.6	0	(2)

CA= Calories / **FAT**= Fat / **P**=Protein / **C**= Carbohydrates / **F**= Fiber / **SA**= Sugar Alcohols / **NC**= Net Carbs

Slow Cooker Cochinita Pibil — p.254

	CA	FAT	P	C	F	SA	NC
1 (140g) orange	69	0	0	18	3	0	15
1 3 1/2 oz. box (about 1/3 cup) (100g) achiote paste	185	2.5	5	35	13.1	0	21.9
2 (27g) jalapeno peppers, seeds removed	8	.2	.4	1.6	.7	0	.8
2 tsp (4g) cumin seed, ground	15	.9	0	1.8	.4	0	1.3
1 tsp (2g) coriander seed, ground	6	.4	.3	1.1	.8	0	.3
1 tsp (2g) cinnamon, ground	4.9	0	.1	1.6	1.1	0	.6
1/2 tsp (1g) cloves, ground	3.2	.2	.1	.6	.3	0	.3
1/2 bunch (50g) cilantro, washed and stems removed	11.5	.3	1.1	1.9	1.5	0	.4
12 (36g) garlic cloves, sliced into 1/8th inch thick "chips"	48	0	0	12	0	0	12
1/2 cup (122g) lime juice, freshly squeezed	30.5	0	.5	10.5	.5	0	10
1 (2724g) pork butt, bone-in (also known as shoulder or Boston butt, about 5 to 6 lb.)	6420	492	468	0	0	0	0
3 (112g) banana leaves (optional but recommended)	0	0	0	0	0	0	0
salt and pepper to taste	0	0	0	0	0	0	0
Totals (of 8 servings):	6801.2	496.4	475.4	84.1	21.5	0	62.5
Per Serving:	850.1	62.1	59.4	10.5	2.7	0	(7.8)

Tunisian-Spiced Rack of Lamb — p.300

	CA	FAT	P	C	F	SA	NC
1 (108g) lemon	7.6	0	.1	2.6	.1	0	2.5
1 tsp (2g) coriander seed, ground	6	.4	.2	1.1	.8	0	.3
1 tsp (2g) caraway seed, ground	6.7	.3	.4	1	.8	0	.2
1/2 tsp (1g) cumin seed, ground	3.8	.2	0	.4	.1	0	.3
1/2 tsp (1g) cayenne pepper, ground	2.8	.2	.2	.5	.2	0	.3
4 (12g) garlic cloves, minced	16	0	0	4	0	0	4
2 Tbsp (28g) light olive oil	240	24	0	0	0	0	0
2 racks (1589g) lamb, cleaned (frenched)	2546	129	319	0	0	0	0
salt to taste	0	0	0	0	0	0	0
Totals (of 4 servings):	2829.5	154.8	320.1	9.7	2	0	7.7
Per Serving:	707.4	38.7	80	2.4	.5	0	(1.9)

Über Crack Slaw — p.286

	CA	FAT	P	C	F	SA	NC
1 1/2 lb. (681g) beef flank (tenderloin, sirloin, or rib eye, etc., will work, as well)	1680	123	133	0	0	0	0
1 Tbsp (6g) fresh ginger, chopped	4.8	0	.1	1.1	.1	0	1
4 (12g) garlic cloves, minced	16	0	0	4	0	0	4
2 Tbsp (28g) sesame oil	260	28	0	0	0	0	0
1 large (72g) carrot, peeled	29.3	0	.6	6.8	2.3	0	4.5
1 cup (63g) snow peas	26	0	2	5	2	0	3
1 small (304g) head Napa cabbage	80	0	4	12	4	0	8
4 (60g) green onions (scallions)	19.2	0	1.2	4.2	1.8	0	2.4
1/4 cup (64g) soy sauce	33.8	0	3.3	5.5	.5	0	5
2 Tbsp (28g) hot chili oil	260	28	0	0	0	0	0
2 Tbsp (24g) black sesame seeds (or regular toasted sesame seeds)	135	11.5	4.1	6.2	3.4	0	2.9
salt and pepper to taste	0	0	0	0	0	0	0
Totals (of 4 servings):	2544.6	190.5	148.7	44.8	14	0	30.7
Per Serving:	636.2	47.6	37.2	11.2	3.5	0	(7.7)

Slow Cooker "Pot" Roast — p.288

	CA	FAT	P	C	F	SA	NC
4 lb. (1816g) beef chuck roast	4480	328	356	0	0	0	0
1 Tbsp (14g) light oil (such as coconut, olive, or ghee)	120	12	0	0	0	0	0
1 cup (232g) red wine, good quality	197	0	0	6.3	0	0	6.3
4 (12g) garlic cloves	16	0	0	4	0	0	4
10 sprigs (10g) fresh thyme	2.6	.1	.1	.4	.3	0	.1
1 bay leaf	0	0	0	0	0	0	0
1 large (72g) carrot, peeled and cut into chunks	29.3	0	.6	6.8	2.3	0	4.5
2 ribs (101g) celery, cut into chunks	16	0	1	3	2	0	1
1 small (110g) onion, cut into chunks	44	0	1	10	2	0	8
1 small (420g) head cauliflower, leaves removed and cut into florets	105	.7	8.5	22.5	10.5	0	12
salt and freshly cracked pepper to taste	0	0	0	0	0	0	0
Totals (of 6 servings):	5010.2	340.8	367.1	53	17	0	36
Per Serving:	835	56.8	61.2	8.8	2.8	0	(6)

CA= Calories / **FAT**= Fat / **P**=Protein / **C**= Carbohydrates / **F**= Fiber / **SA**= Sugar Alcohols / **NC**= Net Carbs

Almond Cashew Chicken — p.272

Ingredient	CA	FAT	P	C	F	SA	NC
4 (681g) boneless chicken breasts (skin optional), sliced into thin strips	809	20.7	144	0	0	0	0
16 (304g) shiitake mushrooms, stemmed and quartered	103	1.5	6.8	20.6	7.6	0	13
1 small (110g) onion, diced	44	0	1	10	2	0	8
2 (101g) celery ribs, diced	16	0	1	3	2	0	1
1/2 cup (32g) snow peas, fibrous stem and string removed	13	0	1	2.5	1	0	1.5
4 (12g) garlic cloves, minced	16	0	0	4	0	0	4
1 Tbsp (6g) fresh ginger, minced	4.8	0	.1	1.1	.1	0	1
1 tsp (2g) crushed red chili flakes (optional)	6.4	.3	.2	1.1	.5	0	.6
1/4 cup (63.75g) soy sauce (or coconut aminos)	33.8	0	3.3	5.5	.5	0	5
1/4 cup (58g) rice wine vinegar	100	0	0	2.8	0	0	2.8
2 Tbsp (30g) sweetener	0	0	0	30	0	30	0
1/4 tsp (1g) glucomannan powder	0	0	0	0	0	0	0
1 Tbsp (14g) coconut oil	120	12	0	0	0	0	0
1/4 cup (36g) slivered almonds, toasted	210	18.3	8	7.3	3.8	0	3.5
1/4 cup (34g) roasted cashew halves	196	15.8	2	11.3	1	0	10.3
1/4 bunch (25g) coarsely chopped fresh cilantro	5.8	.1	.6	.9	.7	0	.2
salt and pepper to taste	0	0	0	0	0	0	0
Totals (of 6 servings):	1679.4	68.7	168.9	100.1	19.3	30	50.8
Per Serving:	279.9	11.4	28.1	16.7	3.2	5	(8.5)

Ham 'n' Cheddar Chicken — p.260

Ingredient	CA	FAT	P	C	F	SA	NC
1 large (118g) chicken breast, boneless and skinless	130	1	27	0	0	0	0
2 slices (56g) ham	91.3	5	9.5	2.2	.6	0	1.7
1/2 cup (50g) cheddar cheese, grated	210	16.7	12.5	.8	0	0	.8
4 slices (100g) raw bacon	458	45	12	1	0	0	1
salt and pepper to taste	0	0	0	0	0	0	0
Totals (of 2 servings):	889.8	67.7	61.02	4	.6	0	3.4
Per Serving:	444.9	33.9	30.51	2	.3	0	(1.7)

Chicken 'n' Dumplings — p.274

Ingredient	CA	FAT	P	C	F	SA	NC
2 Tbsp (28g) fat (tallow, ghee, bacon fat, etc.)	240	24	0	0	0	0	0
1 small (110g) onion, diced	44	0	1	10	2	0	8
1 (50.5g) celery rib, cut into small cubes	8	0	.5	1.5	1	0	.5
1 small (28g) carrot, peeled and cut into small cubes	11.2	0	.2	2.6	.9	0	1.7
4 (12g) garlic cloves, minced	16	0	0	4	0	0	4
1 tsp (1g) fresh thyme, chopped	1	0	.1	.2	.1	0	.1
4 cups (896g) chicken stock or broth	62.7	1.2	9	6	0	0	6
1 Tbsp (15g) glucomannan powder (optional)	0	0	0	15	15	0	0
4 (681g) boneless chicken breasts (skin optional)	809	20.7	144	0	0	0	0
1 bay leaf	0	0	0	0	0	0	0
1 1/4 cups (140g) almond flour	800	70	30	30	15	0	15
1/4 cup (84g) coconut flour	372	9	21	54	36	0	18
1/4 cup (30g) tapioca flour	100	0	0	26	0	0	26
1 Tbsp (7g) ground white or black chia seeds	35	2.5	1.5	3.5	3	0	.5
1 Tbsp (12g) baking powder	15	0	0	3	0	0	3
1/2 tsp (2g) salt	0	0	0	0	0	0	0
1/2 cup (227g) chilled, unsalted butter, cut into cubes	1628	184	2	0	0	0	0
1 large (50g) egg	71.5	5	6.5	.5	0	0	.5
1/2 cup (120g) unsweetened almond milk	22.5	1.8	1	1.5	.5	0	1
salt and pepper to taste	0	0	0	0	0	0	0
Totals (of 8 servings):	4236.2	318.1	217.6	157.9	73.5	0	84.4
Per Serving:	529.5	39.8	27.2	19.7	9.2	0	(10.6)

Prime Rib — p.236

Ingredient	CA	FAT	P	C	F	SA	NC
1 10-lb. (4540g) prime rib, bone in (about 4 ribs)	8832	736	512	0	0	0	0
1/4 cup (56g) fat (tallow, ghee, bacon fat, etc.)	480	48	0	0	0	0	0
salt and pepper to taste	0	0	0	0	0	0	0
Totals (of 8 servings):	9312	784	512	0	0	0	0
Per Serving:	1164	98	64	0	0	0	(0)

CA= Calories / **FAT**= Fat / **P**=Protein / **C**= Carbohydrates / **F**= Fiber / **SA**= Sugar Alcohols / **NC**= Net Carbs

TAKING OUT THE CARBAGE

Ginger Shrimp with Snap Peas, Peppers, and Bamboo Shoots — p.276

	CA	FAT	P	C	F	SA	NC
1 lb. (454g) shrimp (31–35), peeled and deveined	481	9.1	90.8	4.5	.3	0	4.3
1 small (110g) onion, diced	44	0	1	10	2	0	8
1 small (74g) red bell pepper, stem removed, seeded and cut into bite sized squares	22.9	0	.7	4.4	1.5	0	3
1/2 cup (60g) bamboo shoots	6.5	0	1	1	.5	0	.5
1/2 cup (32g) snap peas, fibrous stem and string removed	13	0	1	2.5	1	0	1.5
4 (12g) garlic cloves, minced	16	0	0	4	0	0	4
1 tsp (2g) crushed red chili flakes (optional)	6.4	.3	.2	1.1	.5	0	.6
1 Tbsp (6g) fresh ginger, minced	4.8	0	.1	1.1	.1	0	1
1/4 cup (63.75g) soy sauce (or coconut aminos)	33.8	0	3.3	5.5	.5	0	5
1/4 cup (58g) rice wine vinegar	100	0	0	2.8	0	0	2.8
2 Tbsp (30g) sweetener	0	0	0	30	0	30	0
1/4 tsp (1g) glucomannan powder	0	0	0	0	0	0	0
1 Tbsp (14g) coconut oil	120	12	0	0	0	0	0
4 whole (60g) green onions (scallions), sliced	19.2	0	1.2	4.2	1.8	0	2.4
salt and pepper to taste	0	0	0	0	0	0	0
Totals (of 4 servings):	867.8	21.4	99.4	71.2	8.2	30	32.9
Per Serving:	217	5.4	24.8	17.8	2.1	7.5	(8.2)

Pan Roasted Beef Tenderloin Steak — p.290

	CA	FAT	P	C	F	SA	NC
4 6- to 8-oz. (795g) thick-cut beef tenderloin steaks, trimmed and brought up to room temperature	1960	143	155	0	0	0	0
1 Tbsp (14g) olive oil	119	13.5	0	0	0	0	0
1 Tbsp (14g) butter	100	11	0	0	0	0	0
salt and pepper to taste	0	0	0	0	0	0	0
Totals (of 4 servings):	2179.4	168	155.8	0	0	0	0
Per Serving:	544.9	42	38.9	0	0	0	(0)

Stuffed Double-Cut Pork Chops — p.278

	CA	FAT	P	C	F	SA	NC
1 1/2 cups (0g) water	0	0	0	0	0	0	0
1/4 cup (0g) kosher salt (or 2 Tbsp table salt)	0	0	0	0	0	0	0
4 (0g) garlic cloves, crushed	0	0	0	0	0	0	0
1/2 (0g) small onion, chopped	0	0	0	0	0	0	0
1 bay leaf	0	0	0	0	0	0	0
1 sprig (0g) fresh thyme	0	0	0	0	0	0	0
1/2 Tbsp (0g) freshly cracked black pepper	0	0	0	0	0	0	0
2 1/2 cups (0g) ice water	0	0	0	0	0	0	0
4 (1816g) double-cut pork chops, frenched)	2504	211	139	0	0	0	0
1/2 lb. (227g) raw bulk Italian sausage (sweet or spicy)	541	39.1	41.9	3.8	1.4	0	2.4
2 Tbsp (28g) light oil (coconut oil, olive, ghee, or bacon fat!)	240	24	0	0	0	0	0
salt and freshly cracked pepper to taste	0	0	0	0	0	0	0
1 Tbsp (14g) coconut oil	120	12	0	0	0	0	0
4 whole (60g) green onions (scallions), sliced	19.2	0	1.2	4.2	1.8	0	2.4
salt and pepper to taste	0	0	0	0	0	0	0
Totals (of 4 servings):	3286.1	274.4	181.5	3.8	1.4	0	2.4
Per Serving:	821.5	68.6	45.4	1	.4	0	(.6)

Herb Pork Tenderloin Roast — p.234

	CA	FAT	P	C	F	SA	NC
2 Tbsp (26g) olive oil	239	26	0	0	0	0	0
1/2 Tbsp (1g) fresh rosemary	1.3	.1	0	.2	.1	0	.1
1 tsp (1g) fresh thyme	0	0	.1	.5	.3	0	.2
1 tsp (1g) fresh oregano	0	0	.1	.5	.3	0	.2
1 tsp (2g) fresh lemon zest	1.9	0	0	.5	.2	0	.3
1 Tbsp (15g) lemon juice, freshly squeezed	3.8	0	.1	1.3	.1	0	1.3
4 (12g) garlic cloves, minced	16	0	0	4	0	0	4
2 1 1/4 lb. (1135g) pork tenderloins, cleaned of sinew and extra fat	1237	22.7	238	0	0	0	0
salt and pepper to taste	0	0	0	0	0	0	0
Totals (of 6 servings):	1499.3	48.8	238.7	7	1	0	6.1
Per Serving:	249.9	8.1	39.8	1.2	.2	0	(1)

CA= Calories / **FAT**= Fat / **P**=Protein / **C**= Carbohydrates / **F**= Fiber / **SA**= Sugar Alcohols / **NC**= Net Carbs

Sweet 'n' Spicy Chicken — p.280

	CA	FAT	P	C	F	SA	NC
4 (681g) boneless chicken breasts (skin optional), sliced into thin strips	809	20.7	144	0	0	0	0
1 small (110g) onion, diced	44	0	1	10	2	0	8
1 small (74g) red bell pepper, stem removed, seeded, and cut into bite sized squares	22.9	0	.7	4.4	1.5	0	3
4 (12g) garlic cloves, minced	16	0	0	4	0	0	4
1 Tbsp (6g) fresh ginger, minced	4.8	0	.1	1.1	.1	0	1
1 Tbsp (6g) crushed chilies or chili paste	19.1	1	.7	3.4	1.6	0	1.5
1 tsp (5g) sesame oil	40	4	0	0	0	0	0
1 tsp (2g) crushed red chili flakes (optional)	6.4	.3	.2	1.1	.5	0	.6
1/4 cup (64g) soy sauce (or coconut aminos)	33.8	0	3.3	5.5	.5	0	5
1/4 cup (58g) rice wine vinegar	100	0	0	2.8	0	0	2.8
2 Tbsp (30g) sweetener	0	0	0	30	0	30	0
1/4 tsp (1g) glucomannan powder	0	0	0	0	0	0	0
1 Tbsp (14g) coconut oil	120	12	0	0	0	0	0
4 whole (60g) green onions (scallions), sliced	19.2	0	1.2	4.2	1.8	0	2.4
2 Tbsp (24g) black (or white) sesame seeds	135	11.5	4.1	6.2	3.4	0	2.9
salt and pepper to taste	0	0	0	0	0	0	0
Totals (of 4 servings):	1371.1	49.6	156.2	72.8	11.4	30	31.1
Per Serving:	342.8	12.4	39.1	18.2	2.9	7.5	(7.8)

Thai Green Chicken Curry — p.296

	CA	FAT	P	C	F	SA	NC
1 1/2 lb. (681g) boneless chicken, cut into bite sized strips (breasts and/or thighs)	809	20.7	144	0	0	0	0
4 (12g) garlic cloves, minced	16	0	0	4	0	0	4
1 Tbsp (6g) fresh galangal, minced (substitution: 1 Tbsp ginger)	4.8	0	.1	1.1	.1	0	1
1 Tbsp (12g) sweetener	0	0	0	1	0	1	0
1/4 cup (60g) fresh green curry paste (substitution: 2 Tbsp store bought)	51.2	.5	1.8	12.2	1.9	.3	10.1
2 Tbsp (28g) coconut oil	240	24	0	0	0	0	0
1 small (74g) green bell pepper, seeded and diced	22.9	0	.7	4.4	1.5	0	3
1 large (274g) Japanese eggplant, cut into half moons	55	.5	2.5	13	8	0	5
2 small (236g) green zucchini, cut into half moons	38	.7	2.9	8	2.9	0	5.1
1 1/2 cups (339g) unsweetened coconut milk	600	66	6	12	0	0	12
1/4 bunch (25g) cilantro, washed and large stems removed	5.8	.1	.6	.9	.7	0	.2
16 leaves (6.4g) Thai basil, hand torn (substitution: regular basil)	1.5	.1	.2	.2	.1	0	.1
salt and pepper to taste	0	0	0	0	0	0	0
Totals (of 4 servings):	1371.1	49.6	156.2	72.8	11.4	30	31.1
Per Serving:	342.8	12.4	39.1	18.2	2.9	7.5	(7.8)

Slow Cooker BBQ Beef Brisket — p.306

	CA	FAT	P	C	F	SA	NC
5 lb. (2270g) beef brisket, trimmed	6287	502	406	0	0	0	0
2 Tbsp (28g) cooking fat (coconut, olive, or even bacon fat!)	240	24	0	0	0	0	0
1 cup (238g) homemade BBQ sauce	227	7.9	6.6	47.5	10.6	0	36.8
salt and pepper to taste	0	0	0	0	0	0	0
Totals (of 8 servings):	6754	534.1	413.4	47.5	10.6	0	36.8
Per Serving:	844.4	66.8	51.7	5.9	1.3	0	(4.6)

CA= Calories / **FAT**= Fat / **P**=Protein / **C**= Carbohydrates / **F**= Fiber / **SA**= Sugar Alcohols / **NC**= Net Carbs

Thai Red Curry Pork — p.302

	CA	FAT	P	C	F	SA	NC
1 approx. 1 1/4 lb. (537g) pork tenderloin roast, cut into thin, bite-sized strips	585	17	108	0	0	0	0
4 (12g) garlic cloves, minced	16	0	0	4	0	0	4
1 Tbsp (6g) fresh galangal, minced (substitution: 1 Tbsp ginger)	4.8	0	.1	1.1	.1	0	1
1 tsp (2g) cinnamon, ground	4.9	0	.1	1.6	1.1	0	.6
1/4 tsp (.25g) cloves, ground	0	0	0	0	0	0	0
1/4 cup (60g) fresh red curry paste (substitution: 2 Tbsp store bought)	72.8	1.9	2.2	15.5	3.6	0	11.9
2 Tbsp (28g) coconut oil	240	24	0	0	0	0	0
1 large (274g) Japanese eggplant, cut into cubes	55	.5	2.5	13	8	0	5
1 small (74g) red bell pepper, seeded and diced	22.9	0	.7	4.4	1.5	0	3
1 1/2 cups (339g) unsweetened coconut milk	600	66	6	12	0	0	12
16 leaves (6g) Thai basil, hand torn (substitution: regular basil)	1.5	.1	.2	.2	.1	0	.1
salt and pepper to taste	0	0	0	0	0	0	0
Totals (of 4 servings):	1602.9	109.5	119.8	51.8	14.4	0	37.4
Per Serving:	400.7	27.4	30	13	3.6	0	(9.4)

Sides Nutrition Facts

Garlicky BBQ Kale — p.311

	CA	FAT	P	C	F	SA	NC
2 Tbsp (28g) fat (like olive oil or bacon fat/lard)	200	22	0	0	0	0	0
1 1/2 lb. (681g) kale, washed and very roughly chopped/sliced	340	6.8	20.4	68.1	13.6	0	54.5
12 (36g) garlic cloves, sliced into thin rings	48	0	0	12	0	0	12
1/4 cup (38g) sugar-free BBQ sauce	10	0	0	2	0	0	2
salt and pepper to taste	0	0	0	0	0	0	0
Totals (of 8 servings):	598.5	28.8	20.4	82.1	13.6	0	68.5
Per Serving:	74.8	3.6	2.6	10.3	1.7	0	(8.6)

Parsnip-Almond Mash — p.342

	CA	FAT	P	C	F	SA	NC
1 lb. (454g) parsnips, peeled and cut into chunks	341	0	6.8	81.9	23.9	0	58
1/2 (56g) cup blanched almond meal	320	28	12	12	6	0	6
1/4 cup (60g) almond milk	11.3	.9	.5	.8	.3	0	.5
1/4 cup (60g) water	0	0	0	0	0	0	0
1/4 cup (54g) butter	400	44	0	0	0	0	0
salt and pepper to taste	0	0	0	0	0	0	0
Totals (of 6 servings):	1072.6	72.9	19.3	94.7	30.1	0	64.5
Per Serving:	178.8	12.2	3.2	15.8	5	0	(10.8)

CA= Calories / **FAT**= Fat / **P**=Protein / **C**= Carbohydrates / **F**= Fiber / **SA**= Sugar Alcohols / **NC**= Net Carbs

Green Beans with Tapenade — p.310

	CA	FAT	P	C	F	SA	NC
1 1/2 lb. (681g) green beans, ends removed	211	.8	8.2	48.6	23.2	0	25.4
1/2 cup (119g) black olive tapenade	302	28.6	3.9	7.9	3.5	0	4.4
salt and pepper to taste	0	0	0	0	0	0	0
Totals (of 6 servings):	513.7	29.4	12.1	56.5	26.7	0	29.9
Per Serving:	85.6	4.9	2	9.4	4.4	0	(5)

Simple Southern-Style Braised Greens — p.314

	CA	FAT	P	C	F	SA	NC
8 slices (200g) raw bacon, chopped (for bits)	916	90	24	2	0	0	2
1 1/2 lb. (681g) hearty, leafy bitter greens, washed and cut into bite-sized ribbons	340	9.1	27.2	68.1	13.6	0	54.5
salt and pepper to taste	0	0	0	0	0	0	0
Totals (of 8 servings):	1256.5	99.1	51.2	70.1	13.6	0	56.5
Per Serving:	157.1	12.4	6.4	8.8	1.7	0	(7.1)

Southern Broccoli Pudding — p.340

	CA	FAT	P	C	F	SA	NC
1 large (840g) bunch broccoli, including stalks, cut into florets	286	2.8	23.5	55.3	22.1	0	33.2
3 Tbsp (54g) butter	300	33	0	0	0	0	0
1 medium (110g) onion, diced	44	0	1	10	2	0	8
4 (12g) garlic cloves, minced	16	0	0	4	0	0	4
3 Tbsp tapioca flour	75	0	0	19.5	0	0	19.5
3/4 cup (179g) heavy whipping cream	615	66	3.8	5.3	0	0	5.3
1 cup (240g) unsweetened almond milk	45	3.5	2	3	1	0	2
1/2 lb. (227g) cheddar cheese, grated	902	74.4	56	2.8	0	0	2.8
1 Tbsp (7g) paprika	20.2	.9	1.1	3.9	2.6	0	1.3
2 tsp (2g) chopped fresh thyme	2	0	.1	.5	.3	0	.2
1 tsp (2g) cayenne pepper	5.7	.3	.3	1	.3	0	.7
4 large (200g) whole eggs	286	20	26	2	0	0	2
salt and pepper to taste	0	0	0	0	0	0	0
Totals (of 10 servings):	2598.1	200.9	113.7	107.2	28.3	0	78.9
Per Serving:	259.8	20.1	11.4	10.7	2.8	0	(7.9)

Carrot-Squash Hash — p.312

	CA	FAT	P	C	F	SA	NC
1/4 cup (56g) fresh whole butter	400	44	0	0	0	0	0
1 lb. (454g) carrots, peeled and diced	184	0	3.6	42.6	14.2	0	28.4
1 small (2 to 3 lb.) (1135g) kabocha squash, peeled, seeded, and diced (substitution: acorn, buttercup, delicata, pumpkin)	360	0	4	28	4	0	24
1 medium (110g) onion, diced	44	0	1	10	2	0	8
4 (12g) garlic cloves, minced	16	0	0	4	0	0	4
1 Tbsp (2g) chopped fresh sage	2.6	.1	.1	.4	.3	0	.1
salt and pepper to taste	0	0	0	0	0	0	0
Totals (of 8 servings):	1007.1	44.1	8.6	85	20.5	0	64.5
Per Serving:	125.9	5.5	1.1	10.6	2.6	0	(8.1)

Cauli-Rice — p.316

	CA	FAT	P	C	F	SA	NC
1 large head (840g) cauliflower	210	1.3	17	45	21	0	24
salt and pepper to taste	0	0	0	0	0	0	0
Totals (of 6 servings):	210	1.3	17	45	21	0	24
Per Serving:	35	.2	2.8	7.5	3.5	0	(4)

Coconut Cauli-Rice — p.322

	CA	FAT	P	C	F	SA	NC
1 1/2 cup (132g) shredded unsweetened coconut	720	72	12	36	24	0	12
1 Tbsp (14g) light oil (for sautéing, such as coconut, olive, or ghee)	120	12	0	0	0	0	0
4 8-oz. packets (908g) Miracle Rice	0	0	0	0	0	0	0
4 (12g) garlic cloves, minced	16	0	0	4	0	0	4
1 large (840g) head cauliflower	210	1.3	17	45	21	0	24
1/4 bunch (25g) cilantro, washed and large stems removed, chopped	5.8	.1	.6	.9	.7	0	.2
salt and pepper to taste	0	0	0	0	0	0	0
Totals (of 12 servings):	1071.8	85.5	29.6	85.9	45.7	0	40.2
Per Serving:	89.3	7.1	2.5	7.2	3.8	0	(3.4)

CA= Calories / **FAT**= Fat / **P**=Protein / **C**= Carbohydrates / **F**= Fiber / **SA**= Sugar Alcohols / **NC**= Net Carbs

Green Beans, Almonds, and Peppers p.343

	CA	FAT	P	C	F	SA	NC
2 Tbsp (28g) unsalted butter	200	22	0	0	0	0	0
1 lb. (454g) green string beans, ends and string removed	140	.5	5.4	32.4	15.4	0	16.9
1 small (74g) red bell pepper, thinly sliced	22.9	0	.7	4.4	1.5	0	3
4 (12g) garlic cloves, minced	16	0	0	4	0	0	4
1/4 cup (36g) sliced almonds, toasted	210	18.3	8	7.3	3.8	0	3.5
salt and pepper to taste	0	0	0	0	0	0	0
Totals (of 4 servings):	590.2	40.8	14.2	48.1	20.7	0	27.4
Per Serving:	147.6	10.2	3.6	12	5.2	0	(6.8)

Garlicky Baby Broccoli with Bacon p.328

	CA	FAT	P	C	F	SA	NC
4 slices (100g) raw bacon, chopped (for bits)	458	45	12	1	0	0	1
12 (36g) garlic cloves, sliced into 1/8-inch thick "chips"	48	0	0	12	0	0	12
1 lb. (454g) baby broccoli	154	0	12.4	29.9	11.4	0	18.6
salt and pepper to taste	0	0	0	0	0	0	0
Totals (of 4 servings):	660.8	45	24.4	42.9	11.4	0	31.6
Per Serving:	165.2	11.3	6.1	10.7	2.8	0	(7.9)

Sweet Potato and Celeriac au Gratin p.324

	CA	FAT	P	C	F	SA	NC
1 1/2 lb. (681g) sweet potatoes	583	0	10.2	138	20.5	0	117
1 giant (681g) celery root	288	0	8.7	61.1	13	0	48.1
1 Tbsp (14g) butter	100	11	0	0	0	0	0
1 1/4 cups (298g) heavy whipping cream	1026	110	6.3	8.8	0	0	8.8
1 1/2 cups (150g) Parmesan cheese, grated	646	43.5	57	6	0	0	6
1/2 tsp (1g) freshly ground nutmeg	5.3	.4	.1	.5	.2	0	.3
salt and pepper to taste	0	0	0	0	0	0	0
Totals (of 8 servings):	2649.1	164.9	82.3	214.6	33.7	0	180.9
Per Serving:	331.1	20.6	10.3	26.8	4.2	0	(22.6)

Simple Buttery Broccoli p.326

	CA	FAT	P	C	F	SA	NC
1 large (840g) bunch broccoli, including stalks, cut into florets	286	2.8	23.5	55.3	22.1	0	33.2
1/4 cup (56g) fresh whole butter (half a stick), cut into small cubes	400	44	0	0	0	0	0
salt and pepper to taste	0	0	0	0	0	0	0
Totals (of 6 servings):	686	46.8	23.5	55.3	22.1	0	33.2
Per Serving:	114.3	7.8	3.9	9.2	3.7	0	(5.5)

Miracle Cauli-Rice p.320

	CA	FAT	P	C	F	SA	NC
4 8-oz. packets (908g) Miracle Rice®	0	0	0	0	0	0	0
1 large (840g) head cauliflower	210	1.3	17	45	21	0	24
1 Tbsp (14g) light oil (for sautéing, such as coconut, olive, or ghee)	120	12	0	0	0	0	0
salt and pepper to taste	0	0	0	0	0	0	0
Totals (of 10 servings):	330	13.3	17	45	21	0	24
Per Serving:	33	1.3	1.7	4.5	2.1	0	(2.4)

Herby Asparagus and Mushrooms p.338

	CA	FAT	P	C	F	SA	NC
1/4 cup (56g) fresh whole butter (half a stick), cut into small cubes	400	44	0	0	0	0	0
1 lb. (454g) whole crimini (or button) mushrooms, dirt removed with brush and stems removed	122	0	13.6	18.2	4.5	0	13.6
1 bunch (227g) asparagus spears, tough stem ends removed	45.7	16	5.1	8.5	5.1	0	3.4
2 tsp (2g) fresh oregano (thyme, rosemary, sage, and/or marjoram), roughly chopped	2	0	.1	.5	.3	0	.2
salt and pepper to taste	0	0	0	0	0	0	0
Totals (of 4 servings):	570.3	60.1	18.8	27.1	9.9	0	17.2
Per Serving:	142.6	15	4.7	6.8	2.5	0	(4.3)

CA= Calories / **FAT**= Fat / **P**=Protein / **C**= Carbohydrates / **F**= Fiber / **SA**= Sugar Alcohols / **NC**= Net Carbs

Bacon-Sage Cauliflower "Au Gratin" — p.344

	CA	FAT	P	C	F	SA	NC
1 large (840g) head cauliflower, stem and leaves removed and cut into small florets	210	1.3	17	45	21	0	24
1 recipe (448g) low-carb Alfredo sauce (about 2 cups)	2533	234	86.1	28.5	2.2	0	26.3
1 Tbsp (2g) fresh sage, chopped	2.6	.1	.1	.4	.3	0	.1
1/4 cup (28.4g) bacon bits	100	6	12	0	0	0	0
1/4 cup (28g) almond meal	160	14	6	6	3	0	3
1/4 cup (25g) Parmesan-Reggiano cheese, grated	107	7.3	9.5	1	0	0	1
Totals (of 8 servings):	3114	263.1	130.6	80.9	26.5	0	54.4
Per Serving:	389.2	32.9	16.3	10.1	3.3	0	(6.8)

Carrot and Parmesan Casserole — p.336

	CA	FAT	P	C	F	SA	NC
2 lb. (908g) carrots, peeled and roll cut into large chunks	368	0	7.1	85.1	28.4	0	56.7
1/2 cup (119g) heavy whipping cream	410	44	2.5	3.5	0	0	3.5
1 medium (110g) onion, diced	44	0	1	10	2	0	8
1 cup (100g) grated Parmesan cheese, divided	431	29	38	4	0	0	4
4 (12g) garlic cloves, minced	16	0	0	4	0	0	4
1/4 tsp (.25g) ground nutmeg	0	0	0	0	0	0	0
salt and pepper to taste	0	0	0	0	0	0	0
Totals (of 8 servings):	1270.4	73	48.6	106.6	30.4	0	76.2
Per Serving:	158.8	9.1	6.1	13.3	3.8	0	(9.5)

Simple Buttery Brussels Sprouts — p.308

	CA	FAT	P	C	F	SA	NC
2 lb. (908g) Brussels sprouts	345	0	27.2	72.6	27.2	0	45.4
1/4 cup (56g) fresh, whole butter, cut into cubes, divided	400	44	0	0	0	0	0
salt and pepper to taste	0	0	0	0	0	0	0
Totals (of 8 servings):	745	44	27.2	72.6	27.2	0	45.4
Per Serving:	93.1	5.5	3.4	9.1	3.4	0	(5.7)

Pancetta-Wrapped Asparagus — p.332

	CA	FAT	P	C	F	SA	NC
1 bunch (227g) asparagus spears (about 20 spears)	45.7	16	5.1	8.5	5.1	0	3.4
2 Tbsp (28g) olive oil	240	24	0	0	0	0	0
20 slices (250g) pancetta, sliced into strips	438	34.4	28.8	.8	0	0	.8
salt and pepper to taste	0	0	0	0	0	0	0
Totals (of 4 servings):	724.1	74.4	33.9	9.3	5.1	0	4.2
Per Serving:	181	18.6	8.5	2.3	1.3	0	(1.1)

Creamed Spinach — p.334

	CA	FAT	P	C	F	SA	NC
2 lb. (908g) fresh spinach leaves, washed and stems removed	208	0	27.2	36.3	18.2	0	18.2
2 Tbsp (28g) fat (olive oil, butter, or even bacon fat)	240	24	0	0	0	0	0
1/2 small (35g) onion, sliced	14	0	.5	3.5	.5	0	3
3 (9g) garlic cloves, minced	12	0	0	3	0	0	3
1 1/4 cups (298g) heavy whipping cream	1026	110	6.3	8.8	0	0	8.8
1/4 tsp (.25g) nutmeg, ground	0	0	0	0	0	0	0
salt and pepper to taste	0	0	0	0	0	0	0
Totals (of 6 servings):	1501.1	134	34	51.6	18.7	0	32.9
Per Serving:	250.2	22.3	5.7	8.6	3.1	0	(5.5)

Mashed Cauliflower and Celery Root — p.330

	CA	FAT	P	C	F	SA	NC
1 large (840g) head cauliflower, stem and leaves removed and cut into small florets	210	1.3	17	45	21	0	24
1 large (454g) celery root, peeled and cut into chunks	192	0	5.8	40.7	8.7	0	32
4 (12g) garlic cloves	16	0	0	4	0	0	4
1 cup (238g) heavy whipping cream	821	88	5	7	0	0	7
1/2 cup (112g) fresh whole butter (one stick), cubed	800	88	0	0	0	0	0
salt and pepper to taste	0	0	0	0	0	0	0
Totals (of 8 servings):	2039.1	177.3	27.8	96.7	29.7	0	67
Per Serving:	254.9	22.2	3.5	12.1	3.7	0	(8.4)

CA= Calories / **FAT**= Fat / **P**=Protein / **C**= Carbohydrates / **F**= Fiber / **SA**= Sugar Alcohols / **NC**= Net Carbs

Carrot Pumpkin Mash — p.339

	CA	FAT	P	C	F	SA	NC
1/4 cup (56g) fresh whole butter	400	44	0	0	0	0	0
1 medium (110g) onion, diced	44	0	1	10	2	0	8
4 (12g) garlic cloves, minced	16	0	0	4	0	0	4
1 small (2 to 3 lb.) (1135g) kabocha squash, peeled, seeded, and cut into large pieces (substitution: acorn, buttercup, delicata, pumpkin)	360	0	4	28	4	0	24
1 lb. (454g) carrots, peeled and cut into large pieces	184	0	3.6	42.6	14.2	0	28.4
1/2 cup (112g) chicken stock or broth	7.8	.2	1.1	.8	0	0	.8
1 Tbsp (3g) thinly sliced chives	1	0	0	0	0	0	0
salt and black pepper to taste	0	0	0	0	0	0	0
Totals (of 8 servings):	1013.3	44.2	9.7	85.3	20.2	0	65.1
Per Serving:	126.7	5.5	1.2	10.7	2.5	0	(8.1)

I Can't Believe That's Not Fried Rice — p.318

	CA	FAT	P	C	F	SA	NC
2 Tbsp (28.01g) toasted sesame oil	260	28	0	0	0	0	0
4 (60g) green onions (scallions), cut into thin rings	19.2	0	1.2	4.2	1.8	0	2.4
1 Tbsp (6g) minced fresh ginger	4.8	0	.1	1.1	.1	0	1
2 (6g) garlic cloves, minced	8	0	0	2	0	0	2
1/2 lb. (227g) ham, diced	356	16	46.7	4	0	0	4
1/2 cup (80g) frozen peas and carrots	38	0	2	8	2	0	6
4 large (200g) whole eggs, beaten	286	20	26	2	0	0	2
2 cups (200g) Cauli-Rice	70	2.7	5.7	15	7	0	8
1/4 cup (64g) soy sauce	33.8	0	3.3	5.5	.5	0	5
4 tsp (16g) toasted sesame seeds	90.4	7.7	2.7	4.2	2.2	0	1.9
salt and pepper to taste	0	0	0	0	0	0	0
Totals (of 4 servings):	1166.7	74.4	87.7	46	13.7	0	32.3
Per Serving:	291.7	18.6	21.9	11.5	3.4	0	(8.1)

Sauces, Spreads, and Dippity Do's Nutrition Facts

Sweet Thai Chili Sauce — p.349

	CA	FAT	P	C	F	SA	NC
1/2 cup (116g) rice wine vinegar	200	0	0	5.5	0	0	5.5
1/2 cup (120g) sugar replacement	0	0	0	120	0	120	0
1 Tbsp (6g) crushed chilies or chili paste	19.1	1	.7	3.4	1.6	0	1.5
4 (12g) garlic cloves, minced	16	0	0	4	0	0	4
1 Tbsp (6g) fresh minced ginger	4.8	0	.1	1.1	.1	0	1
1 tsp (4g) salt	0	0	0	0	0	0	0
2 Tbsp (30g) water	0	0	0	0	0	0	0
1/2 tsp (1 g) glucomannan powder	0	0	0	1	1	0	0
Totals (of 4 servings):	239.9	1	.8	135	2.7	120	12
Per Serving:	60	.3	.2	33.8	.7	30	(3)

Tomato and Roasted Pepper Cream — p.357

	CA	FAT	P	C	F	SA	NC
1 Tbsp (14g) butter	100	11	0	0	0	0	0
4 (12g) garlic cloves, cut into thin rings	16	0	0	4	0	0	4
1/4 cup (28g) real bacon bits	100	6	12	0	0	0	0
2 medium (182g) tomatoes, diced	32	0	2	8	2	0	6
2 small (148g) roasted bell peppers, peeled, seeded, and diced	45.9	0	1.5	8.9	3	0	5.9
1 cup (238g) heavy whipping cream	821	88	5	7	0	0	7
16 leaves (6g) fresh basil, hand torn	1.5	.1	.2	.2	.1	0	.1
salt and pepper to taste	0	0	0	0	0	0	0
Totals (of 8 servings):	1116.4	105.1	20.7	28.1	5.1	0	23
Per Serving:	139.5	13.1	2.6	3.5	.6	0	(2.9)

CA= Calories / **FAT**= Fat / **P**=Protein / **C**= Carbohydrates / **F**= Fiber / **SA**= Sugar Alcohols / **NC**= Net Carbs

Beurre Blanc p.348

	CA	FAT	P	C	F	SA	NC
1 (20g) shallot, minced	14	0	0	4	0	0	4
3/4 cup (174g) white wine, good quality	142	0	0	5.2	0	0	5.2
1 Tbsp (15g) homog- enized heavy cream (optional)	51.3	5.5	.3	.4	0	0	.4
1/4 cup (54g) chilled butter, cut into about 12 small cubes	400	44	0	0	0	0	0
salt and pepper to taste	0	0	0	0	0	0	0
Totals (of 4 servings):	608	49.5	.3	9.7	0	0	9.7
Per Serving:	152	12.4	.1	2.4	0	0	(2.4)

Artichoke Pesto Dip p.353

	CA	FAT	P	C	F	SA	NC
1/2 cup (110g) mayon- naise	750	83.5	2.4	1.3	.1	.3	1
1/2 cup (115g) sour cream	222	22.5	2.5	4	0	0	4
1/2 cup (194g) basil pesto	853	89.8	11.6	6.8	2.1	0	4.8
8 whole (222g) artichoke hearts in oil, cut into 8 wedges each	264	18.8	7.1	23	11.2	0	11.8
salt and pepper to taste	0	0	0	0	0	0	0
Totals (of 6 servings):	2199.9	188.4	95.7	29.1	4	0	25.1
Per Serving:	261.2	26.8	3	4.4	1.7	0	(2.7)

Blackberry Beurre Rouge p.346

	CA	FAT	P	C	F	SA	NC
1 (20g) shallot, minced	14	0	0	4	0	0	4
1/2 cup (58g) red wine, good quality	98.6	0	0	3.2	0	0	3.2
1/2 cup (72g) fresh blackberries, washed	31	.5	1	9	4	0	5
1 Tbsp (15g) homog- enized heavy cream (optional)	51.3	5.5	.3	.4	0	0	.4
1/4 cup (54g) chilled butter, cut into about 12 small cubes	400	44	0	0	0	0	0
salt and pepper to taste	0	0	0	0	0	0	0
Totals (of 4 servings):	595	50	1.3	16.6	4	0	12.6
Per Serving:	148.7	12.5	.3	4.2	1	0	(3.2)

Bacon, Cheddar, and Jalapeño Dip p.350

	CA	FAT	P	C	F	SA	NC
2 Tbsp (28g) fat (olive oil, butter, or even bacon fat)	240	24	0	0	0	0	0
1 medium (110g) onion, diced	44	0	1	10	2	0	8
2 (27g) jalapeño pep- pers, seeds and ribs removed, finely diced	8	.2	.4	1.6	.7	0	.8
4 (12g) garlic cloves, minced	16	0	0	4	0	0	4
8 oz. (227g) regular cream cheese (not low fat)	777	77.3	13.7	8.8	0	0	8.8
1/2 lb. (227g) cheddar cheese, grated and divided	902	74.4	56	2.8	0	0	2.8
1/2 cup (57g) real bacon bits	200	12	24	0	0	0	0
1/4 bunch (25g) cilantro, washed, large stems removed and chopped	5.8	.1	.6	.9	.7	0	.2
1/2 tsp (1g) cumin seed, ground	3.8	.2	0	.4	.1	0	.3
1/2 tsp (1g) coriander seed, ground	3	.2	.1	.6	.4	0	.1
salt and pepper to taste	0	0	0	0	0	0	0
Totals (of 6 servings):	2199.9	188.4	95.7	29.1	4	0	25.1
Per Serving:	366.7	31.4	16	4.8	.7	0	(4.2)

Pesto alla Genovese p.386

	CA	FAT	P	C	F	SA	NC
3 (9g) garlic cloves, diced	13	0	1	3	0	0	3
2/3 cup (144g) extra virgin olive oil	1273	144	0	0	0	0	0
2 cups (141g) fresh basil leaves (about a large bunch's worth), packed, cleaned, and dried	32.4	1.4	4.2	4.2	2.8	0	1.4
2 tsp (10g) lemon juice	2.5	0	0	.9	0	0	.8
1/4 cup (34g) pine nuts, toasted	227	23	4.5	4.5	1.3	0	3.3
1/4 cup (25g) Parme- san-Reggiano cheese, grated	107	7.3	9.5	1	0	0	1
1/4 cup (25g) Pecorino Romano cheese, grated	50	4	4	0	0	0	0
salt and pepper to taste	0	0	0	0	0	0	0
Totals (of 8 servings):	1706.3	179.7	23.2	13.6	4.1	0	9.5
Per Serving:	213.3	22.5	2.9	1.7	.5	0	(1.2)

CA= Calories / **FAT**= Fat / **P**=Protein / **C**= Carbohydrates / **F**= Fiber / **SA**= Sugar Alcohols / **NC**= Net Carbs

Black Olive Tapenade · p.352

	CA	FAT	P	C	F	SA	NC
1 cup (180g) black olives (like Kalamata), drained and pitted	187	12.6	1.8	10.8	5.4	0	5.4
1/4 cup (36g) slivered almonds, toasted	210	18.3	8	7.3	3.8	0	3.5
1/4 cup (54g) extra virgin olive oil	477	54	0	0	0	0	0
2 Tbsp (16g) capers, drained and coarsely chopped	3.7	.2	.3	.8	.5	0	.3
2 (4g) boneless anchovy filets	8.4	.4	1.2	0	0	0	0
1 Tbsp (15g) lemon juice, freshly squeezed	3.8	0	.1	1.3	.1	0	1.3
1 tsp (.67g) fresh rosemary, chopped	.9	0	0	.1	.1	0	.1
1 tsp (2g) fresh lemon zest (peel)	1.9	0	0	.5	.2	0	.3
2 (6g) garlic cloves, crushed	8	0	0	2	0	0	2
1/2 tsp (1g) crushed red chili flakes	3.2	.2	.1	.6	.3	0	.3
salt and pepper to taste	0	0	0	0	0	0	0
Totals (of 12 servings):	905.8	85.6	11.5	23.4	10.3	0	13.1
Per Serving:	75.5	7.1	1	2	.9	0	(1.1)

Sweet and Tangy BBQ Sauce · p.356

	CA	FAT	P	C	F	SA	NC
1 cup (256g) reduced sugar ketchup	80	0	0	16	0	0	16
1 6-oz. can (170g) tomato paste	139	1	7	32	7	0	25
1 cup (239g) apple cider vinegar	0	0	0	0	0	0	0
1/4 cup (60g) liquid smoke	0	0	0	0	0	0	0
2 Tbsp (30g) sugar replacement	0	0	0	30	0	30	0
2 Tbsp (11g) unsweetened cocoa powder	24.5	2.3	2.1	6.3	3.6	0	2.6
2 Tbsp (16g) New Mexico chili powdered	50.2	2.7	1.9	8.8	5.4	0	3.4
2 Tbsp (14g) smoked paprika	40.5	1.8	2.1	7.8	5.2	0	2.7
1 tsp (7g) yacon syrup	7	0	0	3.7	0	0	3.7
salt and pepper to taste	0	0	0	0	0	0	0
Totals (of 16 servings):	341.2	7.8	13.2	104.6	21.3	30	53.3
Per Serving:	21.3	.5	.8	6.5	1.3	1.9	(3.3)

Sun-Dried Tomato Pesto · p.388

	CA	FAT	P	C	F	SA	NC
1 cup (110g) sun-dried tomatoes in oil, oil drained off	234	15	6	26	6	0	20
4 (12g) garlic cloves, mince	16	0	0	4	0	0	4
2/3 cup (144g) extra virgin olive oil	1273	144	0	0	0	0	0
2 tsp (10g) lemon juice	2.54	0	0	.9	0	0	.8
1/4 cup (34g) pine nuts, toasted	227	23	4.5	4.5	1.3	0	3.3
1/2 cup (50g) Parmesan-Reggiano cheese, grated	215	14.5	19	2	0	0	2
salt and pepper to taste	0	0	0	0	0	0	0
Totals (of 8 servings):	1968.6	196.5	29.5	37.4	7.3	0	30.1
Per Serving:	246.1	24.6	3.7	4.7	.9	0	(3.8)

Pesto Cream Sauce · p.387

	CA	FAT	P	C	F	SA	NC
2/3 cup (159g) basil pesto	1137	119	14.5	9.1	2.7	0	6.4
1 1/3 cup (317g) heavy whipping cream	1094	117	6.7	9.3	0	0	9.3
salt and pepper to taste	0	0	0	0	0	0	0
Totals (of 4 servings):	2232.2	237.1	21.2	18.4	2.7	0	15.7
Per Serving:	558.1	59.3	5.3	4.6	.7	0	(3.9)

Marinara Sauce · p.358

	CA	FAT	P	C	F	SA	NC
1 Tbsp (14g) extra virgin olive oil	120	12	0	0	0	0	0
1 small (110g) onion, diced	44	0	1	10	2	0	8
4 (12g) garlic cloves, cut into thin disks	16	0	0	4	0	0	4
1 28-oz. can (800g) San Marzano tomatoes	150	0	6	36	12	0	24
16 leaves (6g) fresh basil, hand torn	1.5	.1	.2	.2	.1	0	.1
salt and pepper to taste	0	0	0	0	0	0	0
Totals (of 8 servings):	331.5	12.1	7.2	50.2	14.1	0	36.1
Per Serving:	41.4	1.5	.9	6.3	1.8	0	(4.5)

CA= Calories / **FAT**= Fat / **P**=Protein / **C**= Carbohydrates / **F**= Fiber / **SA**= Sugar Alcohols / **NC**= Net Carbs

White BBQ Sauce   p.364

	CA	FAT	P	C	F	SA	NC
1/2 cup (110g) mayonnaise	750	83.5	2.4	1.3	.1	.3	1
1 Tbsp (155g) lemon juice, freshly squeezed	3.8	0	.1	1.3	.1	0	1.3
2 Tbsp (30g) apple cider vinegar	0	0	0	0	0	0	0
1 Tbsp (15g) sugar replacement	0	0	0	15	0	15	0
1 tsp (2g) freshly cracked black pepper	5.3	0	.3	1.3	.7	0	.7
1 1/2 tsp (4g) salt	0	0	0	0	0	0	0
1/2 tsp (1g) cayenne pepper, ground	2.8	.2	.2	.5	.2	0	.3
Totals (of 4 servings):	762.5	83.6	3	19.5	1	15.3	3.3
Per Serving:	190.6	20.9	.7	4.9	.2	3.8	(.8)

Chunky Blue Cheese Dressing   p.365

	CA	FAT	P	C	F	SA	NC
4 oz. (112g) quality Roquefort cheese, crumbled and divided	413	34.7	24.6	2.2	0	0	2.2
1/4 cup (61g) buttermilk	24.5	.5	2	3	0	0	3
1/4 cup (58g) sour cream	111	11.3	1.3	2	0	0	2
1/2 cup (110g) mayonnaise	750	83.5	2.4	1.3	.1	.3	1
1 Tbsp (15g) apple cider vinegar	0	0	0	0	0	0	0
salt and freshly cracked pepper to taste	0	0	0	0	0	0	0
Totals (of 12 servings):	1299.3	129.9	30.3	8.6	.1	.3	8.2
Per Serving:	108.3	10.8	2.5	.7	0	0	(.7)

Balsamic Vinaigrette   p.366

	CA	FAT	P	C	F	SA	NC
6 Tbsp (84g) extra virgin olive oil	720	72	0	0	0	0	0
2 Tbsp (32g) balsamic vinegar	28	0	.1	5.4	0	0	5.4
salt and pepper to taste	0	0	0	0	0	0	0
Totals (of 4 servings):	748	72	.1	5.4	0	0	5.4
Per Serving:	187	18	0	1.4	0	0	(1.4)

Sweet and Spicy Tomato Jam   p.360

	CA	FAT	P	C	F	SA	NC
1 Tbsp (14g) light oil (for sautéing, such as coconut, olive, or ghee)	120	12	0	0	0	0	0
2 tsp (4g) cumin seed, ground	15	.9	0	1.8	.4	0	1.3
1 tsp (2g) coriander seed, ground	6	.4	.2	1.1	.8	0	.3
1 tsp (2g) cinnamon, ground	4.9	0	.1	1.6	1.1	0	.6
1 tsp (2g) chili flakes	6.3	.3	.2	1.1	.7	0	.4
1 small (110g) onion, diced	44	0	1	10	2	0	8
4 (12g) garlic cloves, cut into thin disks	16	0	0	4	0	0	4
2 tsp (4g) fresh ginger, grated	3.2	0	.1	.7	.1	0	.6
1 lb. (454g) fresh tomatoes, washed, dried and coarsely chopped	82.3	0	5	17.5	5	0	12.5
1/4 cup (60g) sugar replacement	0	0	0	60	0	60	0
2 tsp (14g) yacon syrup	14	0	0	7.3	0	0	7.3
1/2 bunch (50g) cilantro, washed, large stems removed, and chopped	11.5	.3	1.1	1.9	1.5	0	.4
salt and pepper to taste	0	0	0	0	0	0	0
Totals (of 12 servings):	323.2	13.9	7.7	107	11.5	60	35.4
Per Serving:	26.9	1.2	.6	8.9	1	5	(3)

Spicy Hot Cocktail Sauce   p.369

	CA	FAT	P	C	F	SA	NC
2/3 cup (171g) reduced sugar ketchup	53.3	0	0	5.3	0	0	5.3
1/4 cup (60g) prepared horseradish	24	.6	.6	6.7	1.8	0	4.9
2 Tbsp (31g) lemon juice, freshly squeezed	7.6	0	.1	2.6	.1	0	2.5
1 Tbsp (12g) Tabasco sauce	.5	0	0	0	0	0	0
1 tsp (6g) Worcestershire sauce	4.4	0	0	1.1	0	0	1.1
4 (12g) garlic cloves, minced	0	0	0	0	0	0	0
salt and pepper to taste	0	0	0	0	0	0	0
Totals (of 8 servings):	89.9	.6	.8	15.8	2	0	13.8
Per Serving:	11.2	.1	.1	2	.3	0	(1.7)

CA= Calories / **FAT**= Fat / **P**=Protein / **C**= Carbohydrates / **F**= Fiber / **SA**= Sugar Alcohols / **NC**= Net Carbs

Harissa — p.370

	CA	FAT	P	C	F	SA	NC
2 Tbsp (12g) cumin seed, ground	45	2.6	0	5.3	1.3	0	4
1 Tbsp (5g) cayenne pepper	17	1	1	3	1	0	2
1 Tbsp (6g) coriander seed, ground	17.9	1.1	.7	3.3	2.5	0	.8
1 Tbsp (6g) caraway seed, ground	20	2	1.2	3	2.3	0	.7
1 Tbsp (18g) salt	0	0	0	0	0	0	0
1/4 cup (22g) fresh mint, chopped	9.7	.2	.7	1.8	1.5	0	.2
1/4 cup (22g) fresh cilantro, chopped	5.1	.2	.4	.9	.7	0	.2
2 Tbsp (31g) lemon juice, freshly squeezed	7.6	0	.1	2.6	.1	0	2.5
1/2 cup (108g) olive oil, good quality	955	108	0	0	0	0	0
4 (12g) garlic cloves, minced	16	0	0	4	0	0	4
Totals (of 8 servings):	1093.3	115.2	4.2	23.9	9.5	0	14.4
Per Serving:	136.7	14.4	.5	3	1.2	0	(1.8)

Not Pistou — p.368

	CA	FAT	P	C	F	SA	NC
2 lb. (908g) fresh assorted tomatoes, diced	164	0	10	34.9	10	0	24.9
2 cups (141g) fresh basil, cut into chiffonade (about a large bunch's worth)	32.4	1.4	4.2	4.2	2.8	0	1.4
4 (12g) garlic cloves, minced	16	0	0	4	0	0	4
1 cup (135g) pine nuts, toasted and coarsely chopped	909	92	18	18	5	0	13
2 cups (200g) Parmesan cheese, grated	862	58	76	8	0	0	8
1/4 cup (61g) lemon juice, freshly squeezed	15.3	0	.3	5.3	.3	0	5
1 cup (216g) extra virgin olive oil, good quality	1910	216	0	0	0	0	0
salt and pepper to taste	0	0	0	0	0	0	0
Totals (of 12 servings):	3909.3	367.4	108.5	74.4	18.1	0	56.4
Per Serving:	325.8	30.6	9	6.2	1.5	0	(4.7)

Pineapple Salsa — p.355

	CA	FAT	P	C	F	SA	NC
1 cup (165g) pineapple cubes (fairly small dice)	82	0	1	22	2	0	20
2 small (148g) red bell peppers, peeled and seeded	45.9	0	1.5	8.9	3	0	5.9
1 small (110g) red onion, diced	44	0	1	10	2	0	8
4 (12g) garlic cloves, minced	16	0	0	4	0	0	4
1 Tbsp (6g) fresh ginger, minced	4.8	0	.1	1.1	.1	0	1
2 (27g) jalapeño peppers, seeds and ribs removed, finely diced	8	.2	.4	1.6	.7	0	.8
1/4 bunch (25g) cilantro, washed, large stems removed, and chopped	5.8	.1	.6	.9	.7	0	.2
1/4 cup (61g) lime juice, freshly squeezed	15.3	0	.3	5.3	.3	0	5
salt to taste	0	0	0	0	0	0	0
Totals (of 10 servings):	221.7	.3	4.8	53.7	8.8	0	44.9
Per Serving:	22.2	0	.5	5.4	.9	0	(4.5)

Orange Mojo — p.354

	CA	FAT	P	C	F	SA	NC
1 (140g) orange	69	0	0	18	3	0	15
3/4 cup (162g) olive oil	1432	162	0	0	0	0	0
1 medium (110g) onion, coarsely chopped	44	0	1	10	2	0	8
1/4 cup (61g) freshly squeezed lime juice	15.3	0	.3	5.3	.3	0	5
4 (12g) garlic cloves	16	0	0	4	0	0	4
1 tsp (4g) salt	0	0	0	0	0	0	0
1/2 tsp (1g) crushed red chili flakes	3.2	.2	.1	.6	.3	0	.3
1/2 tsp (1g) cumin seed, ground	3.8	.2	0	.4	.1	0	.3
1/2 tsp (1g) coriander seed, ground	9	.2	.1	.6	.4	0	.1
1/2 tsp (1g) freshly cracked black pepper	2.7	0	.2	.7	.3	0	.3
1/2 bunch (50g) fresh cilantro, washed, stems removed, and chopped	11.5	.3	1.1	1.9	1.5	0	.4
1/2 bunch (50g) cilantro, washed, large stems removed, and chopped	11.5	.3	1.1	1.9	1.5	0	.4
Totals (of 16 servings):	1600.8	162.8	2.8	41.4	7.8	0	33.5
Per Serving:	200.1	20.4	.4	5.2	1	0	(4.2)

CA= Calories / **FAT**= Fat / **P**=Protein / **C**= Carbohydrates / **F**= Fiber / **SA**= Sugar Alcohols / **NC**= Net Carbs

Thick, Goopy Alfredo Sauce   p.380

	CA	FAT	P	C	F	SA	NC
2 cups (476g) heavy whipping cream	1642	176	10	14	0	0	14
1/2 tsp (1g) nutmeg, freshly ground	5.3	.4	.1	.5	.2	0	.3
4 (12g) garlic cloves, minced	16	0	0	4	0	0	4
1/4 tsp (.5g) glucomannan powder (optional)	0	0	0	.5	.5	0	0
2 cups (200g) Parmesan cheese, grated	862	58	76	8	0	0	8
salt and pepper to taste	0	0	0	0	0	0	0
Totals (of 6 servings):	2525.3	234.4	86.1	27	.7	0	26.3
Per Serving:	420.9	39.1	14.3	4.5	.1	0	(4.4)

A Lot Like Caesar Salad Dressing   p.371

	CA	FAT	P	C	F	SA	NC
1/2 cup (110g) mayonnaise	750	83.5	2.4	1.3	.1	.3	1
2 (6g) garlic cloves, minced	8	0	0	2	0	0	2
2 Tbsp (14g) bacon bits	50	3	6	0	0	0	0
1/4 cup (25g) Parmesan-Reggiano cheese, grated	107	7.3	9.5	1	0	0	1
1 tsp (6g) Worcestershire sauce	4.4	0	0	1.1	0	0	1.1
salt and pepper to taste	0	0	0	0	0	0	0
Totals (of 6 servings):	920.7	93.7	17.9	5.4	.1	.3	5.1
Per Serving:	153.5	15.6	3	.9	0	0	(.9)

Rouille (Fancy Spicy French Mayo)   p.376

	CA	FAT	P	C	F	SA	NC
1/2 tsp (0g) saffron threads	0	0	0	0	0	0	0
1 cup (110g) mayonnaise	750	83.5	2.4	1.3	.1	.3	1
2 (6g) garlic cloves, minced	8	0	0	2	0	0	2
1/2 tsp (1g) cayenne pepper, ground	2.8	.2	.2	.5	.2	0	.3
salt and pepper to taste	0	0	0	0	0	0	0
Totals (of 8 servings):	761.4	83.6	2.6	3.8	.3	.3	3.3
Per Serving:	95.2	10.5	.3	.5	0	0	(.4)

Mayonnaise   p.374

	CA	FAT	P	C	F	SA	NC
1 large (50g) whole egg	71.5	5	6.5	.5	0	0	.5
1 large (17g) egg yolk	53.9	4.6	2.7	.7	0	0	.7
1 tsp (5g) Dijon mustard	4.1	.2	.3	.5	.2	0	.3
2 Tbsp (31g) lemon juice, freshly squeezed	7.6	0	.1	2.6	.1	0	2.5
1 1/2 cup (324g) olive oil	286	324	0	0	0	0	0
1 Tbsp (15g) sugar replacement	0	0	0	15	0	15	0
water (to adjust consistency)	0	0	0	0	0	0	0
salt and pepper to taste	0	0	0	0	0	0	0
Totals (of 32 servings):	3002.2	333.8	9.6	19.3	.3	15	4
Per Serving:	93.8	10.4	.3	.6	0	.5	(.1)

Orange-Rosemary Compound Butter   p.372

	CA	FAT	P	C	F	SA	NC
1/2 cup (227g) unsalted butter	1628	184	2	0	0	0	0
1 Tbsp (2g) fresh rosemary, chopped	2.6	.1	.1	.4	.3	0	.1
1 Tbsp (6g) fresh orange zest (peel)	5.8	0	.1	1.5	.7	0	.8
salt and pepper to taste	0	0	0	0	0	0	0
Totals (of 8 servings):	1636.4	184.1	2.1	1.9	.9	0	1
Per Serving:	204.6	23	.3	.2	.1	0	(.1)

Dijon-Caper Cream Sauce   p.362

	CA	FAT	P	C	F	SA	NC
1/2 cup (119g) heavy whipping cream	410	44	2.5	3.5	0	0	3.5
2 Tbsp (30g) Dijon mustard, whole grain	24.8	1.2	1.5	2.9	1.2	0	1.7
2 tsp (5g) capers, drained and coarsely chopped	1.2	.1	.1	.3	.2	0	.1
salt and pepper to taste	0	0	0	0	0	0	0
Totals (of 4 servings):	436.5	45.2	4.1	6.7	1.4	0	5.3
Per Serving:	109.1	11.3	1	1.7	.3	0	(1.3)

CA= Calories / **FAT**= Fat / **P**=Protein / **C**= Carbohydrates / **F**= Fiber / **SA**= Sugar Alcohols / **NC**= Net Carbs

Béarnaise Sauce — p.382

	CA	FAT	P	C	F	SA	NC
1/4 cup (60g) white wine vinegar	11.3	0	0	.3	0	0	.3
1/4 cup (58g) white wine, good quality	47.6	0	0	1.7	0	0	1.7
4 (80g) shallots, fine dice	56	0	0	16	0	0	16
4 large (68g) egg yolks	215	17.9	10.9	2.5	0	0	2.5
1 Tbsp (15g) heavy whipping cream (homogenized)	51.3	5.5	.3	.4	0	0	.4
1 cup (224g) fresh whole butter, melted	1600	176	0	0	0	0	0
4 sprigs (2g) fresh tarragon, leaves only (chopped)	2	0	.1	.5	.3	0	.2
salt and pepper to taste	0	0	0	0	0	0	0
Totals (of 8 servings):	1983.7	199.5	11.4	21.4	.3	0	21.2
Per Serving:	248	24.9	1.4	2.7	0	0	(2.7)

Thai-Style Peanut Sauce — p.379

	CA	FAT	P	C	F	SA	NC
1 Tbsp (14g) coconut oil	120	12	0	0	0	0	0
2 (6g) garlic cloves, minced	8	0	0	2	0	0	2
1 Tbsp (6g) fresh ginger, minced	4.8	0	.1	1.1	.1	0	1
2 tsp (10g) red curry paste	15	0	1	2	0	0	2
1/4 cup (64g) natural peanut butter	400	32	20	12	4	0	8
1/4 cup (57g) unsweetened coconut milk	100	11	1	2	0	0	2
1 Tbsp (15g) lime juice, freshly squeezed	3.8	0	.1	1.3	.1	0	1.3
2 Tbsp (40g) xylitol honey (suggested, but optional)	25	0	0	22	0	18	4
salt and chili flakes to taste	0	0	0	0	0	0	0
Totals (of 8 servings):	676.6	55	22.2	42.4	4.2	18	20.2
Per Serving:	84.6	6.9	2.8	5.3	.5	2.3	(2.5)

Romesco — p.378

	CA	FAT	P	C	F	SA	NC
2 small (148g) roasted red bell peppers, peeled and seeded	45.9	0	1.5	8.9	3	0	5.9
2 Tbsp (32g) tomato paste	26	0	2	6	2	0	4
1 tsp (2g) smoked paprika	6.7	.3	.4	1.3	.9	0	.5
1 tsp (2g) crushed red chili flakes	6.4	.3	.2	1.1	.5	0	.6
4 (12g) garlic cloves, minced	16	0	0	4	0	0	4
2 Tbsp (27g) extra virgin olive oil	238	27	0	0	0	0	0
1/4 cup (36g) blanched and slivered almonds, toasted	210	18.3	8	7.3	3.8	0	3.5
2 Tbsp (30g) red wine vinegar	5.7	0	0	.1	0	0	.1
salt and pepper to taste	0	0	0	0	0	0	0
Totals (of 8 servings):	555.9	45.9	12.1	28.7	10.1	0	18.6
Per Serving:	69.5	5.7	1.5	3.6	1.3	0	(2.3)

Bacon Herb Cream Cheese Dip — p.384

	CA	FAT	P	C	F	SA	NC
8 oz. (227g) regular cream cheese, warmed and softened	777	77.3	13.7	8.8	0	0	8.8
2 (6g) garlic cloves, minced	8	0	0	2	0	0	2
1/2 cup (108g) bacon fat, room temperature (must be as cool as possible without solidifying)	955	108	0	0	0	0	0
1/2 cup (50g) Parmesan-Reggiano cheese, grated, densely packed	215	14.5	19	2	0	0	2
1/4 cup (28g) real bacon bits	100	6	12	0	0	0	0
1 tsp (2g) fresh oregano, stems removed and chopped	6.1	.2	.2	1.3	.9	0	.4
salt and pepper to taste	0	0	0	0	0	0	0
Totals (of 6 servings):	2061.6	206	44.9	14.1	.9	0	13.2
Per Serving:	343.6	34.3	7.5	2.4	.1	0	(2.2)

CA= Calories / **FAT**= Fat / **P**=Protein / **C**= Carbohydrates / **F**= Fiber / **SA**= Sugar Alcohols / **NC**= Net Carbs

Desserts Nutrition Facts

Thai Pumpkin Custard (Sankaya)
p.390

Ingredient	CA	FAT	P	C	F	SA	NC
1 small (2 to 3 lb.) (1135g) kabocha squash (substitution: acorn, buttercup, delicata, pumpkin)	360	0	4	28	4	0	24
5 large (250g) whole eggs	357	25	32.5	2.5	0	0	2.5
3/4 cup (170g) unsweetened coconut milk	300	33	3	6	0	0	6
3/4 cup (180g) sugar replacement	0	0	0	180	0	180	0
1/2 tsp (1g) cinnamon, ground	2.5	0	0	.8	.5	0	.3
1/2 tsp (2g) vanilla extract	5.8	0	0	.3	0	0	.3
dash of salt	0	0	0	0	0	0	0
Totals (of 8 servings):	1025.7	58	39.5	217.6	4.5	180	33
Per Serving:	171	9.7	6.6	36.3	.8	30	(5.5)

Plain ol' Vanilla OMM (One-Minute Muffin)
p.393

Ingredient	CA	FAT	P	C	F	SA	NC
1 Tbsp (7g) coconut flour	31	.8	1.8	4.5	3	0	1.5
1 Tbsp (7g) almond meal	40	3.5	1.5	1.5	.8	0	.8
1 Tbsp (7g) vanilla zero-carb whey protein	25	0	6.5	0	0	0	0
1 Tbsp (15g) sugar replacement	0	0	0	15	0	15	0
1/2 tsp (2g) baking powder	2.5	0	0	.5	0	0	.5
a dash of salt	0	0	0	0	0	0	0
1 large (50g) whole egg	71.5	5	6.5	.5	0	0	.5
1 tsp (5g) fresh whole butter, melted	33.3	3.7	0	0	0	0	0
1/2 tsp (2g) vanilla extract	5.8	.0	0	.3	0	0	.3
Totals (of 1 servings):	209.1	12.9	16.3	22.3	3.8	15	3.5
Per Serving:	209.1	12.9	16.3	22.3	3.8	15	(3.5)

Lemongrass-Scented Coconut-Lime Sorbet
p.406

Ingredient	CA	FAT	P	C	F	SA	NC
1 cup (200g) sugar replacement	0	0	0	200	0	200	0
1/4 tsp (.5g) guar gum (optional)	3.3	0	0	.9	.9	0	0
1/4 tsp (.5g) xanthan gum (optional)	5	0	0	1.2	1.2	0	0
1/2 tsp (1g) salt	0	0	0	0	0	0	0
2 13.5-oz. cans (756g) coconut milk	1488	160	16.7	20.1	0	0	20.1
1 Tbsp (6g) fresh galangal, minced (substitution: 1 Tbsp ginger)	4.8	0	.1	1.1	.1	0	1
1 Tbsp (5g) lemongrass, minced (substitution: 1 tsp lemon zest)	5	0	.1	1.3	0	0	1.3
4 (6g) kaffir lime leaves, cut into ribbons (substitution: 1 tsp lime zest)	1.5	.1	.2	.2	.1	0	.1
2 tsp (10g) fresh lime juice	2.5	0	0	.9	0	0	.8
3 Tbsp (44g) vegetable glycerine, food grade (optional)	191	0	0	0	0	0	0
Totals (of 6 servings):	1701.8	160.6	17.1	225.5	2.3	200	23.2
Per Serving:	283.6	26.8	2.9	37.6	.4	33.3	(3.9)

Chocolate Pudding Pie with Macadamia Crust
p.398

Ingredient	CA	FAT	P	C	F	SA	NC
1 1/2 cups (167.5g) macadamia nuts, crushed and salted	1202	127	13.8	23.8	15	0	8.8
1 Tbsp (21g) honey	64	0	0	17	0	0	17
1/4 cup (56g) melted fresh whole butter	400	44	0	0	0	0	0
1 1/2 cups (357g) heavy whipping cream	1231	132	7.5	10.5	0	0	10.5
2 1/2 cups (600g) almond milk, unsweetened and divided	112	8.8	5	7.5	2.5	0	5
2 packets (about 4 1/2 to 5 tsp total) (14g) gelatin powder	46.9	0	12	0	0	0	0
3/4 cup (65g) unsweetened cocoa powder	147	13.5	12.8	37.5	21.8	0	15.8
1 cup (200g) sugar replacement	0	0	0	200	0	200	0
1 Tbsp (12g) vanilla extract	34.6	0	0	1.5	0	0	1.5
a dash of salt	0	0	0	0	0	0	0
Totals (of 8 servings):	3239	325.8	51	297.8	39.3	200	58.5
Per Serving:	404.9	40.7	6.4	37.2	4.9	25	(7.3)

CA= Calories / **FAT**= Fat / **P**=Protein / **C**= Carbohydrates / **F**= Fiber / **SA**= Sugar Alcohols / **NC**= Net Carbs

Pumpkin-Spice OMM with Maple Butter — p.394

	CA	FAT	P	C	F	SA	NC
Maple Butter							
1 Tbsp (14g) butter	100	11	0	0	0	0	0
1/2 tbsp (8g) sugar-free maple syrup	0	0	0	0	0	0	0
1 dash salt	0	0	0	0	0	0	0
Pumpkin OMM							
1 Tbsp (14g) butter	100	11	0	0	0	0	0
1/2 Tbsp (8g) sugar-free maple syrup	0	0	0	0	0	0	0
1 1/2 (14g) Tbsp ground chia seed (or 2 Tbsp flax meal)	75	4.5	3	6	6	0	0
2 Tbsp (14g) hazelnut flour (substitute: almond meal)	90	8.5	2	2.5	1.5	0	1
2 Tbsp (30g) sugar replacement	0	0	0	30	0	30	0
1/2 tsp (2g) baking powder	2.5	0	0	.5	0	0	.5
1/2 tsp (1g) cinnamon, ground	2.5	0	0	.8	.5	0	.3
1/4 tsp (.5g) nutmeg, freshly ground	2.6	.2	0	.3	.1	0	.1
a dash cloves, freshly ground	0	0	0	0	0	0	0
a dash dried powdered ginger	0	0	0	0	0	0	0
a dash of salt	0	0	0	0	0	0	0
2 Tbsp (31g) mashed pumpkin	12.4	0	.3	2.5	1	0	1.5
1 large (50g) whole egg	71.5	5	6.5	.5	0	0	.5
Totals (of 1 servings):	356.5	29.2	11.8	43	9.1	30	3.9
Per Serving:	356.5	29.2	11.8	43	9.1	30	(3.9)

Frosted Carrot Cake OMM with Pecans — p.396

	CA	FAT	P	C	F	SA	NC
Carrot Cake OMM							
1 1/2 (14g) Tbsp ground chia seed (or 2 Tbsp flax meal)	75	4.5	3	6	6	0	0
2 Tbsp (14g) almond meal	80	7	3	3	1.5	0	1.5
2 Tbsp (30g) sugar replacement	0	0	0	30	0	30	0
1/2 tsp (2g) baking powder	2.5	0	0	.5	0	0	.5
1/2 tsp (1g) cinnamon, ground	2.5	0	0	.8	.5	0	.3
1/4 tsp (.5g) nutmeg, freshly ground	2.6	2	0	.3	.1	0	.1
a dash of salt	0	0	0	0	0	0	0
2 Tbsp (14g) raw carrot, grated	5.6	0	.1	1.4	.4	0	1
1 Tbsp (6g) pecans, chopped and toasted	42.8	4.4	.6	.9	.6	0	.3
1 large (50g) whole egg	71.5	5	6.5	.5	0	0	.5
1 tsp (4.67g) melted butter	33.3	3.7	0	0	0	0	0
1/2 tsp (2g) vanilla extract	5.8	0	0	.3	0	0	.3
Cream Cheese Frosting							
1 1/2 Tbsp (21g) full-fat cream cheese, warmed	72.8	7.3	1.3	.8	0	0	.8
1 Tbsp (14g) fresh whole butter, softened	100	11	0	0	0	0	0
3 Tbsp (38g) powdered sugar replacement	0	0	0	37.5	0	37.5	0
a dash vanilla extract	1	0	0	0	0	0	0
a dash salt	0	0	0	0	0	0	0
Totals (of 1 servings):	495.4	43.1	14.5	81.9	9.2	67.5	5.3
Per Serving:	495.4	43.1	14.5	81.9	9.2	67.5	(5.3)

The Famous Mock Danish — p.400

	CA	FAT	P	C	F	SA	NC
2 oz. (57g) regular cream cheese (not low fat)	194	19.3	3.4	2.2	0	0	2.2
1 large (50g) egg	72	5	6.5	.5	0	0	.5
2 tsp (10g) sugar replacement	0	0	0	10	0	10	0
1/2 tsp (2g) vanilla extract	5.8	0	0	.3	0	0	.3
a dash salt	0	0	0	0	0	0	0
a dash cinnamon (optional)	0	0	0	0	0	0	0
Totals (of 1 servings):	272	24.3	9.9	13	0	10	3
Per Serving:	272	24.3	9.9	13	0	10	(3)

Vanilla Fat Bomb — p.417

	CA	FAT	P	C	F	SA	NC
8 oz. (227g) full-fat cream cheese, preferably warmed	777	77.3	13.7	8.8	0	0	8.8
1/2 cup (100g) powdered sugar replacement	0	0	0	100	0	100	0
a dash of salt	0	0	0	0	0	0	0
1 tsp (4g) vanilla extract	11.5	0	0	.5	0	0	.5
1/2 cup (119g) heavy whipping cream	410v	44	2.5	3.5	0	0	3.5
Totals (of 6 servings):	1199	121.3	16.2	112.8	0	100	12.8
Per Serving:	199.8	20.2	2.7	18.8	0	16.7	(2.1)

CA= Calories / **FAT**= Fat / **P**=Protein / **C**= Carbohydrates / **F**= Fiber / **SA**= Sugar Alcohols / **NC**= Net Carbs

Strawberry-Kiwi Popsicles   p.402

	CA	FAT	P	C	F	SA	NC
2 (152g) kiwis, peeled and coarsely chopped	92	0	2	22	4	0	18
3/4 cup (180g) water	0	0	0	0	0	0	0
1 tsp (4g) vanilla extract	11.5	0	0	.5	0	0	.5
3 Tbsp (45g) sugar replacement	0	0	0	45	0	45	0
1 cup (166g) strawberries, sliced and cleaned	53	0	1	13	3	0	10
3/4 cup (180g) water	0	0	0	0	0	0	0
1 tsp (4g) vanilla extract	11.5	0	0	.5	0	0	.5
2 Tbsp (30g) sugar replacement	0	0	0	30	0	30	0
a few dashes of salt (at different times)	0	0	0	0	0	0	0
Totals (of 6 servings):	168.1	0	3	111	7	75	29
Per Serving:	28	0	.5	18.5	1.2	12.5	(4.8)

Coco-Cocoa-Walnut Bark   p.404

	CA	FAT	P	C	F	SA	NC
2 Tbsp (28g) coconut oil, liquefied	240	24	0	0	0	0	0
1 Tbsp (5g) unsweetened cocoa powder	12.3	1.1	1.1	3.1	1.8	0	1.3
1 Tbsp (15g) powdered sugar replacement	0	0	0	15	0	15	0
1 Tbsp (8g) broken and toasted walnut halves	49.1	4.9	1.1	1	.5	0	.5
a dash salt	0	0	0	0	0	0	0
1 Tbsp (15g) heavy whipping cream (homogenized)	51.3	5.5	.3	.4	0	0	.4
Totals (of 2 servings):	352.6	35.5	2.5	19.6	2.3	15	2.3
Per Serving:	176.3	17.8	1.3	9.8	1.2	7.5	(1.1)

Salted Brown Butter Fat Bomb   p.414

	CA	FAT	P	C	F	SA	NC
1 1/2 cup (357g) heavy whipping cream	1231	132	7.5	10.5	0	0	10.5
8 oz. (227g) full-fat cream cheese, preferably warmed	777	77.3	13.7	8.8	0	0	8.8
1/2 cup (100g) powdered sugar replacement	0	0	0	100	0	100	0
1 tsp (4g) salt	0	0	0	0	0	0	0
Totals (of 6 servings):	2008.5	209.3	21.2	119.3	0	100	19.3
Per Serving:	334.8	34.9	3.5	19.9	0	16.7	(3.2)

Almond Panna Cotta with Strawberries and Kiwi   p.410

	CA	FAT	P	C	F	SA	NC
Almond Panna Cotta							
1 cup (238g) heavy whipping cream	821	88	5	7	0	0	7
1 cup (240g) almond milk, unsweetened and divided	45	3.5	2	3	1	0	2
1 (12g) vanilla bean, split lengthwise (or 2 tsp vanilla extract)	23	0	0	1	0	0	1
1/4 cup (50g) sugar replacement	0	0	0	50	0	50	0
a dash of salt	0	0	0	0	0	0	0
1 packet (about 2 1/4 to 2 1/2 tsp) (7g) gelatin powder	23.5	0	6	0	0	0	0
Strawberry-Kiwi Salsa							
1 pint (357g) strawberries, washed and diced	114	1	2	27	7	0	20
2 each (182g) kiwi fruits, peeled and diced	112	0	2	26	6	0	20
1/4 cup (36g) blanched and slivered almonds, toasted	210	18.3	8	7.3	3.8	0	3.5
2 tsp (10g) lemon juice	2.5	0	0	.9	0	0	.8
a dash salt	0	0	0	0	0	0	0
Totals (of 6 servings):	1351.5	110.8	25	122.1	17.8	50	54.3
Per Serving:	225.3	18.5	4.2	20.4	3	8.3	(9.1)

Blackberry-Basil Sorbet   p.408

	CA	FAT	P	C	F	SA	NC
1 cup (237g) water	0	0	0	0	0	0	0
1 cup (200g) sugar replacement	0	0	0	200	0	200	0
1/4 tsp (.5g) guar gum (optional)	3.3	0	0	.9	.9	0	0
1/4 tsp (.5g) xanthan gum (optional)	5	0	0	1.2	1.2	0	0
1/2 tsp (1g) salt	0	0	0	0	0	0	0
3 cups (432g) fresh blackberries, washed	186	3	6	45	24	0	21
16 leaves (6g) fresh basil, cut into ribbons (chiffonade)	1.5	.1	.2	.2	.1	0	.1
2 tsp (10g) lemon juice	2.5	0	0	.9	0	0	.8
3 Tbsp (44g) vegetable glycerine, food grade (optional)	191	0	0	0	0	0	0
Totals (of 8 servings):	389.4	3.1	6.2	248.1	26.2	200	21.9
Per Serving:	48.7	.4	.8	31	3.3	25	(2.7)

CA= Calories / **FAT**= Fat / **P**=Protein / **C**= Carbohydrates / **F**= Fiber / **SA**= Sugar Alcohols / **NC**= Net Carbs

Chocolate OMM (One-Minute Muffin) p.392

	CA	FAT	P	C	F	SA	NC
1 1/2 (14g) Tbsp ground chia seed (or 2 Tbsp flax meal)	75	4.5	3	6	6	0	0
2 Tbsp (14g) almond meal	80	7	3	3	1.5	0	1.5
1 Tbsp (12g) sugar replacement	0	0	0	15	0	15	0
1 Tbsp (5g) unsweetened cocoa powder	12.3	1.1	1.1	3.1	1.8	0	1.3
1/2 tsp (2g) baking powder	2.5	0	0	.5	0	0	.5
a dash of salt	0	0	0	0	0	0	0
1 large (50g) egg	72	5	6.5	.5	0	0	.5
1 tsp (5g) melted butter	33.3	3.7	0	0	0	0	0
Totals (of 1 servings):	275.1	21.3	13.6	28.1	9.3	15	3.8
Per Serving:	275.1	21.3	13.6	28.1	9.3	15	(3.8)

Sponge Cake p.420

	CA	FAT	P	C	F	SA	NC
4 large (200g) whole eggs, room temperature	286	20	26	2	0	0	2
1/2 tsp (2g) lemon juice	.6	0	0	.2	0	0	.2
1 tbsp (7g) coconut flour	31	.8	1.8	4.5	3	0	1.5
2 tbsp (24g) sugar replacement	0	0	0	2	0	2	0
1 tsp (4g) vanilla extract	11.5	0	0	.5	0	0	.5
1 dash (1g) salt	0	0	0	0	0	0	0
Totals (of 4 servings):	329.2	20.8	27.8	9.2	3	2	4.2
Per Serving:	82.3	5.2	6.9	2.3	.8	.5	(1.1)

Crème Anglaise (Vanilla Custard Sauce) p.458

	CA	FAT	P	C	F	SA	NC
1 cup (238g) heavy whipping cream	821	88	5	7	0	0	7
1 cup (240g) almond milk, unsweetened	45	3.5	2	3	1	0	2
1/2 cup (100g) sugar replacement	0	0	0	100	0	100	0
1 (12g) vanilla bean, split lengthwise (or 2 tsp vanilla extract)	23	0	0	1	0	0	1
a dash salt	0	0	0	0	0	0	0
6 large (102g) egg yolks	323	26.9	16.4	3.8	0	0	3.8
Totals (of 12 servings):	1212.2	118.4	23.4	114.8	1	100	13.8
Per Serving:	101	9.9	2	9.6	.1	8.3	(1.2)

Salted Brown Butter Pecan Pie with Chocolate Ganache p.423

	CA	FAT	P	C	F	SA	NC
1 1/2 cups (149g) finely crushed pecans	1026	106	13.5	21	15	0	6
1/4 cup (54g) melted butter	400	44	0	0	0	0	0
1 Tbsp (21g) honey (optional)	64	0	0	17	0	0	17
3 1/2 cups (833g) heavy cream, divided	2873	308	17.5	24.5	0	0	24.5
1 1/2 cup (360g) unsweetened almond milk	67.5	5.3	3	4.5	1.5	0	3
2 packets (14g) of gelatin (about 4 1/2 to 5 tsp total)	46.9	0	12	0	0	0	0
6 large (102g) egg yolks	323	26.9	16.4	3.8	0	0	3.8
1 tsp (4g) vanilla extract	11.5	0	0	.5	0	0	.5
1 1/4 cup (300g) sugar replacement, divided	0	0	0	300	0	300	0
1 tsp (4g) salt	0	0	0	0	0	0	0
2 1/2 oz. (70g) unsweetened baking chocolate squares, broken and chopped	362	37.5	10	22.5	12.5	0	10
1 Tbsp (14g) butter, cubed	100	11	0	0	0	0	0
Totals (of 8 servings):	5275.2	539.1	72.4	393.8	29	300	64.8
Per Serving:	659.4	67.4	9.1	49.2	3.6	37.5	(8.1)

Raspberry-Cream Cheese Swirl Frozen Custard p.418

	CA	FAT	P	C	F	SA	NC
Raspberry–Cream Cheese Swirl Frozen Custard	0	0	0	200	0	200	0
1/4 tsp (.5g) guar gum (optional)	3.3	0	0	.9	.9	0	0
1/4 tsp (.5g) xanthan gum (optional)	5	0	0	1.2	1.2	0	0
1/2 tsp (1g) salt	0	0	0	0	0	0	0
2 13.5-oz. cans (756g) coconut milk	1488	160	16.7	20.1	0	0	20.1
1 Tbsp (6g) fresh galangal, minced (substitution: 1 Tbsp ginger)	4.8	0	.1	1.1	.1	0	1
1 Tbsp (5g) lemongrass, minced (substitution: 1 tsp lemon zest)	5	0	.1	1.3	0	0	1.3
4 (6g) kaffir lime leaves, cut into ribbons (substitution: 1 tsp lime zest)	1.5	.1	.2	.2	.1	0	.1
2 tsp (10g) fresh lime juice	2.5	0	0	.9	0	0	.8
Totals (of 6 servings):	2231.4	190.6	44.4	241.4	22	180	39.4
Per Serving:	371.9	31.8	7.4	40.2	3.7	30	(6.6)

CA= Calories / **FAT**= Fat / **P**=Protein / **C**= Carbohydrates / **F**= Fiber / **SA**= Sugar Alcohols / **NC**= Net Carbs

Triple Chocolate Everything Wads — p.412

	CA	FAT	P	C	F	SA	NC
1/2 cup (112g) fresh whole butter melted	800	88	0	0	0	0	0
1 tsp (4g) vanilla extract	11.5	0	0	.5	0	0	.5
1 cup (240g) powdered sugar replacement	0	0	0	240	0	240	0
1/2 cup (43g) unsweetened cocoa powder	98	9	8.5	25	14.5	0	10.5
1/4 cup (56g) cacao nibs	260	24	8	20	18	0	2
1/4 cup (25g) pecans, toasted and chopped	171	17.8	2.3	3.5	2.5	0	1
1/4 cup (38g) sugar-free chocolate chips or chunks	157	9	3	12	9.8	0	2.3
1/4 cup (22g) toasted shredded coconut, unsweetened	120	12	2	6	4	0	2
a dash of salt	0	0	0	0	0	0	0
Totals (of 6 servings):	1618	159.8	23.8	307	48.8	240	18.3
Per Serving:	269.7	26.6	4	51.2	8.1	40	(3)

Snickerdoodles — p.440

	CA	FAT	P	C	F	SA	NC
1/2 cup (227g) unsalted butter, room temperature and divided	1628	184	2	0	0	0	0
3/4 cup + 2 Tbsp (210g) powdered sugar replacement, divided	0	0	0	210	0	210	0
1 large (50g) whole egg	71.5	5	6.5	.5	0	0	.5
1 tsp (4g) vanilla extract	11.5	0	0	.5	0	0	.5
3/4 cup + 1 Tbsp (91g) almond flour	520	45.5	19.5	19.5	9.8	0	9.8
2 1/2 Tbsp (17.5g) coconut flour	77.5	1.9	4.4	11.3	7.5	0	3.8
2 1/2 Tbsp (19g) tapioca flour	62.5	0	0	16.3	0	0	16.3
2 1/2 Tbsp (23g) white chia seeds, ground	125	7.5	5	10	10	0	0
1 1/2 tsp (6g) baking powder	7.5	0	0	1.5	0	0	1.5
a dash of salt	0	0	0	0	0	0	0
1 tsp (2g) cinnamon, ground	4.9	0	.1	1.6	1.1	0	.6
Totals (of 6 servings):	2508.5	243.9	37.5	271.1	28.3	210	32.8
Per Serving:	418.1	40.7	6.2	45.2	4.7	35	(5.5)

Almond Joy Thumbprint Cookies — p.438

	CA	FAT	P	C	F	SA	NC
1/2 cup (227g) unsalted butter, room temperature and divided	1628	184	2	0	0	0	0
1 cup (256g) unsweetened almond butter	1560	128	56	48	32	0	16
3/4 cup (180g) powdered sugar replacement, divided	0	0	0	180	0	180	0
2 large (100g) whole eggs	143	10	13	1	0	0	1
1 tsp (4g) vanilla extract	11.5	0	0	.5	0	0	.5
1/4 cup (28g) coconut flour	124	3	7	18	12	0	6
a dash of salt	0	0	0	0	0	0	0
2 1/2 oz. (70g) unsweetened baking chocolate squares, broken and chopped	362	37.5	10	22.5	12.5	0	10
1/2 cup (119g) heavy whipping cream	410	44	2.5	3.5	0	0	3.5
1/4 cup (22g) unsweetened coconut, shredded	120	12	2	6	4	0	2
Totals (of 8 servings):	4359.5	418.5	92.5	279.5	60.5	180	39
Per Serving:	544.9	52.3	11.6	34.9	7.6	22.5	(4.9)

Strawberry and Whipped Sour Cream Trifle — p.436

	CA	FAT	P	C	F	SA	NC
1 1/2 cup (249g) strawberries, washed, stems removed, and diced	79.5	0	1.5	19.5	4.5	0	15
3 Tbsp (45g) powdered sugar replacement, divided	0	0	0	45	0	45	0
a dash of salt	0	0	0	0	0	0	0
1/2 cup (119g) heavy whipping cream	410	44	2.5	3.5	0	0	3.5
1/2 cup (116g) sour cream	222	22.3	2.5	4	0	0	4
1 tsp (4g) vanilla extract	11.5	0	0	.5	0	0	.5
1 recipe (245g) Sponge Cake	329	20.8	27.8	9.2	3	2	4.2
1 cup (240g) pastry cream	420	39.5	7.8	50	1.2	40	8.8
Totals (of 4 servings):	1473.1	126.5	39.5	131.8	8.7	87	36
Per Serving:	368.3	31.6	9.9	32.9	2.2	21.8	(9)

CA= Calories / **FAT**= Fat / **P**=Protein / **C**= Carbohydrates / **F**= Fiber / **SA**= Sugar Alcohols / **NC**= Net Carbs

Mexican Wedding Cookies — p.442

	CA	FAT	P	C	F	SA	NC
1/2 cup (227g) unsalted butter, room temperature and divided	1628	184	2	0	0	0	0
1/2 cup (120g) powdered sugar replacement, divided	0	0	0	120	0	120	0
1 cup + 2 Tbsp (126g) almond flour	720	63	27	27	13.5	0	13.5
2 Tbsp (14g) coconut flour	62	1.5	3.5	9	6	0	3
2 Tbsp (15g) tapioca flour	50	0	0	13	0	0	13
2 Tbsp (18g) white chia seeds, ground	100	6	4	8	8	0	0
a dash of salt	0	0	0	0	0	0	0
1 tsp (4g) vanilla extract	11.5	0	0	.5	0	0	.5
Totals (of 6 servings):	2571.5	254.5	36.5	177.5	27.5	120	30
Per Serving:	428.6	42.42	6.1	29.6	4.6	20	(5)

Crème Pâtissière (Pastry Cream) — p.434

	CA	FAT	P	C	F	SA	NC
1 1/2 cups (357g) heavy whipping cream	1231	132	7.5	10.5	0	0	10.5
1 1/2 cup (360g) almond milk, unsweetened	67.5	5.3	3	4.5	1.5	0	3
1 (12g) vanilla bean, split lengthwise (or 2 tsp vanilla extract)	23	0	0	1	0	0	1
3/4 cup (180g) sugar replacement	0	0	0	180	0	180	0
3 Tbsp (23g) tapioca flour	75	0	0	19.5	0	0	19.5
1 tsp (4g) glucomannan powder	10	0	0	4	4	0	0
a dash of salt	0	0	0	0	0	0	0
9 large (153g) egg yolks	484	40.3	24.6	5.7	0	0	5.7
Totals (of 18 servings):	1891.8	177.5	35.1	225.2	5.5	180	39.7
Per Serving:	105.1	9.9	2	12.5	.3	10	(2.2)

Sparkling Gelled Layered Strawberries and Cream — p.450

	CA	FAT	P	C	F	SA	NC
2 cups (480g) sugar-free cream soda	0	0	0	6	0	6	0
1 pint (357g) strawberries, washed and leaves removed	114	1	2	27	7	0	20
1 cup (240g) sugar replacement, divided	0	0	0	240	0	240	0
3 cups (714g) heavy whipping cream	2463	264	16	21	0	0	21
3 cups (720g) unsweetened almond milk	135	10.5	6	9	3	0	6
5 packets (about 11 2/3 tsp) (35g) gelatin powder, divided	117	0	30.1	0	0	0	0
a dash of salt	0	0	0	0	0	0	0
3 (36g) vanilla beans, 2 split lengthwise (or 2 Tbsp [30 mL] vanilla extract)	69	0	0	3	0	0	3
Totals (of 14 servings):	2898.3	275.5	54.1	306	10	246	50
Per Serving:	193.2	18.4	3.6	20.4	.7	16.4	(3.3)

Blueberry-Cream Cheese Eggy McFoo — p.454

	CA	FAT	P	C	F	SA	NC
2 Tbsp (13g) golden flaxseed meal (or ground chia)	60	4.5	3	4	4	0	0
2 Tbsp (14g) almond meal	80	7	3	3	1.5	0	1.5
2 Tbsp (30g) sugar replacement, divided	0	0	0	30	0	30	0
1/2 tsp (2g) baking powder	2.5	0	0	.5	0	0	.5
2 large (100g) eggs	144	10	6.5	.5	0	0	.5
1 tsp (4g) melted butter	33.3	3.7	0	0	0	0	0
2 oz. (57g) regular cream cheese, room temperature	194	19.3	3.4	2.2	0	0	2.2
2 Tbsp (19g) fresh or frozen unsweetened blueberries	9.9	.1	.1	2.4	.5	0	1.9
1/2 tsp (2g) vanilla extract	5.8	0	0	.3	0	0	.3
a dash of salt	0	0	0	0	0	0	0
Totals (of 1 servings):	529.7	44.6	16.1	42.8	6	30	6.8
Per Serving:	529.7	44.6	16.1	42.8	6	30	(6.8)

CA= Calories / **FAT**= Fat / **P**=Protein / **C**= Carbohydrates / **F**= Fiber / **SA**= Sugar Alcohols / **NC**= Net Carbs

Blueberry Bread Pudding — p.456

	CA	FAT	P	C	F	SA	NC
Bread Pudding							
1/2 cup (56g) coconut flour	248	6	14	36	24	0	12
1/2 cup (56g) almond meal	320	28	12	12	6	0	6
1/2 cup (56g) vanilla whey protein powder (sweetened with stevia)	200	0	52	0	0	0	0
1 1/4 cup (300g) sugar replacement, divided	0	0	0	300	0	300	0
4 tsp (16g) baking powder	20	0	0	4	0	0	4
1 (140g) orange	69	0	0	18	3	0	15
1/2 cup (112g) melted butter	800	88	0	0	0	0	0
1 1/2 cup (233g) fresh or frozen blueberries, unsweetened	118	1.5	1.5	28.5	6	0	22.5
1 1/2 cups (357g) heavy whipping cream	1231	132	8	10.5	0	0	10.5
1 cup (240g) almond milk, unsweetened	45	3.5	2	3	1	0	2
1 Tbsp (15g) yacon syrup (substitute: black-strap molasses)	20	0	0	11	0	0	11
1 Tbsp (12g) vanilla extract	34.6	0	0	1.5	0	0	1.5
a dash of salt	0	0	0	0	0	0	0
Cream Cheese Frosting							
1/4 cup + 2 Tbsp (85g) full-fat cream cheese, warmed	291	29	5.1	3.3	0	0	3.3
1/4 cup (56g) fresh whole butter, softened	400	44	0	0	0	0	0
3/4 cup (180g) powdered sugar replacement	0	0	0	180	0	180	0
1/2 tsp (2g) vanilla extract	5.8	0	0	.3	0	0	.3
a dash of salt	0	0	0	0	0	0	0
Totals (of 12 servings):	4811.8	402	192.8	615.1	40	480	95.1
Per Serving:	401	33.5	16	51.3	3.3	40	(7.9)

Sweet 'n' Spicy Fat Bomb — p.416

	CA	FAT	P	C	F	SA	NC
8 oz. (227g) full-fat cream cheese, preferably warmed	777	77.3	13.7	8.8	0	0	8.8
1/2 cup (100g) powdered sugar replacement	0	0	0	100	0	100	0
1 tsp (2g) fresh ginger, grated	1.6	0	0	.4	0	0	.3
1 tsp (2g) cinnamon, ground	4.9	0	.1	1.6	1.1	0	.6
1/2 tsp (1g) cloves, ground	3.2	.2	.1	.6	.3	0	.3
1/2 tsp (1g) nutmeg, freshly ground	5.3	.4	.1	.5	.2	0	.3
3/4 cup (168g) coconut oil	1440	144	0	0	0	0	0
Totals (of 6 servings):	2232	221.9	13.9	111.9	1.7	100	10.2
Per Serving:	372	37	2.3	18.7	.3	16.7	(1.7)

Raspberry Mocha Sorbet — p.432

	CA	FAT	P	C	F	SA	NC
3/4 cup (180g) powdered or granular sugar replacement	0	0	0	180	0	180	0
1/3 cup (29g) unsweetened cocoa powder	65.3	6	5.7	16.7	9.7	0	7
3/4 tsp (1.5g) xanthan gum (optional)	7.5	0	0	1.5	1.5	0	0
a dash of salt	0	0	0	0	0	0	0
2 cups (480g) hot espresso and/or strong coffee	9.6	0	0	0	0	0	0
1 pint (312g) raspberries, washed	162	2	4	37	20	0	17
2 Tbsp (29g) vegetable glycerin (optional)	127	0	0	0	0	0	0
Totals (of 16 servings):	371.8	8	9.7	235.2	31.2	180	24
Per Serving:	23.2	.5	.6	14.7	2	11.3	(1.5)

Whipped Cream — p.413

	CA	FAT	P	C	F	SA	NC
1/2 cup (119g) heavy whipping cream	410	44	2.5	3.5	0	0	3.5
1 Tbsp (15g) sugar replacement	0	0	0	15	0	15	0
1/2 tsp (2g) vanilla extract	5.8	0	0	.3	0	0	.3
Totals (of 8 servings):	416.3	44	2.5	18.8	0	15	3.8
Per Serving:	52	5.5	.3	2.3	0	1.9	(.5)

CA= Calories / **FAT**= Fat / **P**=Protein / **C**= Carbohydrates / **F**= Fiber / **SA**= Sugar Alcohols / **NC**= Net Carbs

Mississippi Mud Pie p.446

	CA	FAT	P	C	F	SA	NC
Chocolate Piecrust							
3 cups (336g) almond flour	1920	168	72	72	36	0	36
1/2 cup (43g) unsweetened cocoa powder	98	9	8.5	25	14.5	0	10.5
1/4 cup (60g) powdered sugar replacement	0	0	0	60	0	60	0
1 Tbsp (8g) tapioca flour	25	0	0	6.5	0	0	6.5
1/2 tsp (2g) salt	0	0	0	0	0	0	0
1 large (50g) egg	72	5	6.5	.5	0	0	.5
3 Tbsp (42g) melted butter	300	33	0	0	0	0	0
Chocolate Ganache Layer							
2 1/2 oz. (70g) unsweetened baking chocolate squares, broken and chopped	362	37.5	10	22.5	12.5	0	10
1/2 cup (119g) heavy whipping cream	410	44	2.5	3.5	0	0	3.5
1/4 cup (60g) sugar replacement	0	0	0	60	0	60	0
1 Tbsp (14g) butter	100	11	0	0	0	0	0
Chocolate Pudding Layer							
1 1/2 cups (357g) heavy whipping cream	1231	132	7.5	10.5	0	0	10.5
2 1/2 cup (600g) almond milk, unsweetened and divided	112	8.8	5	7.5	2.5	0	5
2 packets (about 4 1/2 to 5 tsp, total) (14g) gelatin powder	46.9	0	12	0	0	0	0
3/4 cup (65g) unsweetened cocoa powder	147	13.5	12.8	37.5	21.8	0	15.8
1 cup (200g) sugar replacement	0	0	0	200	0	200	0
1 Tbsp (12g) vanilla extract	34.6	0	0	1.5	0	0	1.5
a dash of salt	0	0	0	0	0	0	0
Whipped Cream Topping							
1 cup (238g) heavy whipping cream	821	88	5	7	0	0	7
2 Tbsp (30g) powdered sugar replacement	0	0	0	30	0	30	0
1 tsp (1g) vanilla extract	11.5	0	0	.5	0	0	.5
Totals (of 12 servings):	5693.1	549.8	141.8	544	87.3	350	106.8
Per Serving:	474.4	45.8	11.8	45.3	7.3	29.2	(8.9)

Spiced Pumpkin Pie with Gingerbread Crust p.444

	CA	FAT	P	C	F	SA	NC
3/4 cup + 3 Tbsp (105g) almond flour	600	52.5	22.5	22.5	11.3	0	11.3
3 Tbsp (21g) coconut flour	93	2.3	5.3	13.5	9	0	4.5
3 Tbsp (23g) tapioca flour	75	0	0	19.5	0	0	19.5
3 Tbsp (27g) white chia seeds, ground	150	9	6	12	12	0	0
1/2 tsp (2g) baking powder	2.5	0	0	.5	0	0	.5
1/2 tsp (1g) cinnamon, ground	2.5	0	0	.8	.5	0	.3
1/4 tsp (.5g) nutmeg, freshly ground	2.6	.2	0	.3	.1	0	.1
1/4 tsp (.25g) cardamom, ground	0	0	0	0	0	0	0
a dash cloves, freshly ground	0	0	0	0	0	0	0
a dash of salt	0	0	0	0	0	0	0
1/4 cup (60g) sugar-free maple syrup (xylitol based nutrition used)	50	0	0	19	0	17	2
1 Tbsp (15g) yacon syrup (substitute blackstrap molasses)	20	0	0	11	0	0	11
2 tsp (4g) fresh ginger, grated	3.2	0	.1	.7	.1	0	.6
1 tsp (4g) vanilla extract	11.5	0	0	.5	0	0	.5
1 15-oz. can (420g) mashed pumpkin	175	0	3.5	35	14	0	21
3/4 cup (180g) sugar replacement	0	0	0	180	0	180	0
3 large (150g) whole eggs	214.	15	19.5	1.5	0	0	1.5
1/2 cup (119g) cream, heavy whipping	410	44	2.5	3.5	0	0	3.5
1/2 cup (120g) almond milk, unsweetened	22.5	1.8	1	1.5	.5	0	1
1/2 cup (120g) sugar-free maple syrup (xylitol based nutrition used)	100	0	0	38	0	34	4
1 Tbsp (15g) yacon syrup (substitute: blackstrap molasses)	20	0	0	11	0	0	11
2 tsp (4g) fresh ginger, grated	3.2	0	.1	.72	.1	0	.6
1/2 tsp (1g) cinnamon, ground	2.5	0	0	.81	.5	0	.3
1/4 tsp (.5g) allspice, ground	1.3	.1	0	.48	.1	0	.4
a dash cloves, freshly ground	0	0	0	0	0	0	0
a dash of salt	0	0	0	0	0	0	0
Totals (of 8 servings):	1959.8	124.8	60.6	372.8	48.2	231	93.6
Per Serving:	245	15.6	7.6	46.6	6	28.9	(11.7)

CA= Calories / **FAT**= Fat / **P**=Protein / **C**= Carbohydrates / **F**= Fiber / **SA**= Sugar Alcohols / **NC**= Net Carbs

Bakery Nutrition Facts

Savory Zucchini, Bacon, and Herb OMM

p.461

	CA	FAT	P	C	F	SA	NC
2 Tbsp (13g) flaxseed meal (or 1/2 Tbsp ground chia seed)	60	4.5	3	4	4	0	0
2 Tbsp (14g) almond meal	80	7	3	3	1.5	0	1.5
2 Tbsp (13g) Parmesan cheese, grated	53.9	3.6	4.8	.5	0	0	.5
1/2 tsp (2g) baking powder	2.5	0	0	.5	0	0	.5
a dash of salt	0	0	0	0	0	0	0
2 Tbsp (23g) zucchini, grated	3.6	.1	.3	.8	.3	0	.5
1 Tbsp (6g) chopped toasted pecans	42.8	4.4	.6	.9	.6	0	.3
1 large (50g) whole egg	71.5	5	6.5	.5	0	0	.5
1 tsp (5g) bacon fat, melted	33.3	3.7	0	0	0	0	0
1 Tbsp (7g) real bacon bits, divided	25	1.5	3	0	0	0	0
1/2 tsp (.5g) fresh thyme, chopped and divided	.5	0	0	.1	.1	0	.1
3 Tbsp (43g) full-fat cream cheese, warmed	145	14.5	2.6	1.7	0	0	1.7
Totals (of 1 servings):	518.8	44.3	23.7	11.9	6.5	0	5.5
Per Serving:	518.8	44.3	23.7	11.9	6.5	0	(5.5)

Crispity Hazelnut Parmesan Cracker

p.466

	CA	FAT	P	C	F	SA	NC
1 cup (112g) hazelnut flour (or almond flour)	720	68	16	20	12	0	8
1/2 cup (50g) Parmesan-Reggiano cheese, grated, densely packed	215	14.5	19	2	0	0	2
1 (33g) egg white	16	0	4	0	0	0	0
2 (6g) garlic cloves, minced	8	0	0	2	0	0	2
2 tsp (2g) fresh oregano (thyme, rosemary, sage and/or marjoram), rough chop	2	0	.1	.5	.3	0	.2
salt, pepper, and chili flakes to taste	0	0	0	0	0	0	0
Totals (of 4 servings):	961.5	82.5	39.1	24.5	12.3	0	12.2
Per Serving:	240.4	20.6	9.8	6.1	3.1	0	(3.1)

Paleo Bread

p.462

	CA	FAT	P	C	F	SA	NC
1 tsp (5g) coconut oil	40	4	0	0	0	0	0
1 cup (256g) smooth almond butter	1560	125	56	48	32	0	16
4 large (200g) eggs, separated	284	20	24	1.7	0	0	1.7
2. 1/2 tsp (12g) apple cider vinegar	0	0	0	0	0	0	0
1/4 cup (60g) almond milk, unsweetened	11.3	.9	.5	.8	.3	0	.5
1/4 cup (28g) coconut flour	124	3	7	18	12	0	6
1 tsp (4g) baking soda	0	0	0	0	0	0	0
1/2 tsp (2g) salt	0	0	0	0	0	0	0
Totals (of 8 servings):	2019.3	152.9	87.5	68.4	44.3	0	24.2
Per Serving:	252.4	19.1	10.9	8.6	5.5	0	(3)

Patty's Pattypan Cupcakes

p.464

	CA	FAT	P	C	F	SA	NC
6 medium (180g) yellow pattypans	29	.6	2.2	6.2	2.3	0	3.9
1/4 cup +2 Tbsp (54g) white chia seeds, ground	300	18	12	24	24	0	0
1/2 cup (56g) almond meal	320	28	12	12	6	0	6
2 tsp (8g) baking powder	10	0	0	2	0	0	2
a dash of salt	0	0	0	0	0	0	0
3/4 cup (180g) goat cheese, divided	815	67.2	49.3	6.7	0	0	6.7
4 large (200g) whole eggs	286	20	26	2	0	0	2
1/2 cup (50g) pecan halves, toasted and chopped	342	35.5	4.5	7	5	0	2
1/4 cup (28g) raw carrot, grated	11.3	0	.3	2.8	.8	0	2
2 Tbsp (28g) melted butter, lard, or bacon fat, divided	200	22	0	0	0	0	0
1 tsp (1g) fresh rosemary, chopped	.9	0	0	.1	.1	0	.1
2 Tbsp (30g) heavy whipping cream	102	11	.6	.9	0	0	.9
Totals (of 6 servings):	2416.7	202.3	106.9	63.7	38.1	0	25.6
Per Serving:	402.8	33.7	17.8	10.6	6.4	0	(4.3)

CA= Calories / **FAT**= Fat / **P**=Protein / **C**= Carbohydrates / **F**= Fiber / **SA**= Sugar Alcohols / **NC**= Net Carbs

Spicy Cumin-Cheddar Crackers — p.468

	CA	FAT	P	C	F	SA	NC
1 cup (112g) almond flour	640	56	24	24	12	0	12
1/2 cup (50g) cheddar cheese, grated	210	16.7	12.5	.8	0	0	.8
1 (33g) egg white	16	0	4	0	0	0	0
2 (6g) garlic cloves, minced	8	0	0	2	0	0	2
1/2 tsp (1g) cumin seed, ground	3.8	.2	0	.4	.1	0	.3
1/2 tsp (1g) coriander seed, ground	3	.2	.1	.6	.4	0	.1
1/2 tsp (1g) ancho pepper, powdered	2.8	.1	.1	.5	.2	0	.3
1/4 tsp (.5g) cayenne pepper, powdered	2.8	.1	.1	.5	.2	0	.3
salt and freshly cracked black pepper to taste	0	0	0	0	0	0	0
Totals (of 4 servings):	886.9	73.2	40.9	28.8	13	0	15.8
Per Serving:	221.7	18.3	10.2	7.2	3.24	0	(4)

Garlic-Herb Fauxcaccia — p.470

	CA	FAT	P	C	F	SA	NC
1 cup (104g) flaxseed meal (or 3/4 cup ground chia seed)	480	36	24	32	32	0	0
1 cup (112g) almond flour	640	56	24	24	12	0	12
1 1/2 Tbsp (18g) baking powder	22.5	0	0	4.5	0	0	4.5
1 Tbsp (2g) fresh rosemary, chopped	2.6	.1	.1	.4	.3	0	.1
1 tsp (2g) crushed red chili flakes	6.4	.3	.2	1.1	.5	0	.6
1 tsp (4g) salt, divided	0	0	0	0	0	0	0
8 large (400g) whole eggs, beaten	572	40	52	4	0	0	4
1/4 cup (54g) extra virgin olive oil	477	54	0	0	0	0	0
12 (36g) garlic cloves, minced	48	0	0	12	0	0	12
Totals (of 6 servings):	2249	186.5	100.3	78.1	44.8	0	33.2
Per Serving:	374.8	31.1	16.7	13	7.5	0	(5.5)

Orange and Sage Scented Bacon-Cranberry Muffins — p.474

	CA	FAT	P	C	F	SA	NC
1/4 cup (28g) coconut flour	124	3	7	18	12	0	6
1/4 cup (28g) almond meal	160	14	6	6	3	0	3
1/4 cup (28g) vanilla whey protein powder (sweetened with stevia)	100	0	26	0	0	0	0
1/4 cup (60g) sugar replacement	0	0	0	60	0	60	0
2 tsp (8g) baking powder	10	0	0	2	0	0	2
a dash of salt	0	0	0	0	0	0	0
1 (140g) orange	69	0	0	18	3	0	15
4 large (200g) eggs	284	20	24	1.7	0	0	1.7
1/4 cup (56g) melted butter or bacon fat	400	44	0	0	0	0	0
6 oz. (168g) fresh cranberries	77.9	0	0	19.9	7.6	0	12.2
1/4 cup (28g) real bacon bits	100	6	12	0	0	0	0
1 tsp (1g) chopped fresh sage	.9	0	0	.1	.1	0	.1
Totals (of 6 servings):	1325.8	87	75	125.7	25.7	60	39.9
Per Serving:	221	14.5	12.5	20.9	4.3	10	(6.7)

One-Minute Cheddar Buns — p.472

	CA	FAT	P	C	F	SA	NC
1 cup (104g) flaxseed meal or 3/4 cup ground chia seeds	480	36	24	32	32	0	0
2 tsp (8g) baking powder	10	0	0	2	0	0	2
4 large (200g) whole eggs	286	20	26	2	0	0	2
1 tbsp (14g) olive oil	100	11	0	0	0	0	0
1/2 cups (57g) cheddar/colby cheese blend, shredded	221	18	13.5	1.5	0	0	1.5
2 each (6g) garlic cloves, minced	8	0	0	2	0	0	2
1/2 tsp (.5g) fresh thyme, chopped	.5	0	0	.1	.1	0	0
salt, fresh cracked pepper and chili flakes, to taste	0	0	0	0	0	0	0
Totals (of 4 servings):	1106	85	63.5	39.6	32.1	0	7.5
Per Serving:	276.5	21.3	15.9	9.9	8	0	(1.9)

CA= Calories / **FAT**= Fat / **P**=Protein / **C**= Carbohydrates / **F**= Fiber / **SA**= Sugar Alcohols / **NC**= Net Carbs

Everything Else Nutrition Facts

Basic All-Purpose Ricotta Crepes
p.476

	CA	FAT	P	C	F	SA	NC
1/2 cup (124g) ricotta cheese, whole milk	216	0	14	4	0	0	4
4 large (200g) eggs, beaten	286	20	26	2	0	0	2
2 Tbsp (30g) sugar replacement (optional)	0	0	0	30	0	30	0
a dash of salt	0	0	0	0	0	0	0
2 Tbsp (28g) unsalted butter	200	22	0	0	0	0	0
Totals (of 7 servings):	702	42	40	36	0	30	6
Per Serving:	100	6	5.7	5.1	0	4.3	.9

Bacon-Wrapped Bacon
p.486

	CA	FAT	P	C	F	SA	NC
1 slab lean pork belly (about 4 lb.) (1816g)	9406	962	163	0	0	0	0
1 cup (152g) Homemade BBQ Sauce	170	3.9	6.6	52.3	10.6	15	26.7
1 cup (224g) chicken stock or broth	15.7	.3	2.2	1.5	0	0	1.5
16 slices (400g) raw bacon	1832	180	48	4	0	0	4
salt and pepper to taste	0	0	0	0	0	0	0
Totals:	11425	1146	220.3	57.8	10.6	15	32.2
Per Serving:	1428	143.3	27.5	7.2	1.3	1.9	4

Loose and Spicy Hot Chicken Italian Sausage
p.480

	CA	FAT	P	C	F	SA	NC
2 lb. (908g) chicken meat, skinless and boneless (assorted)	1079	27.6	193	0	0	0	0
1 lb. (454g) bacon	2079	204	54.5	4.5	0	0	4.5
4 (12g) garlic cloves, minced	16	0	0	4	0	0	4
1 Tbsp (6g) fennel seed, whole	20.7	.9	1	3.1	2.4	0	.7
1 Tbsp (6g) freshly cracked black pepper	16	0	1	4	2	0	2
1 Tbsp (6g) crushed red chili flakes	19.1	1	.7	3.4	1.6	0	1.8
1 Tbsp (7g) paprika	20.2	.9	1.1	3.9	2.6	0	1.3
2 tsp (4g) salt	0	0	0	0	0	0	0
Totals (of 10 servings):	3250.	234.7	251.4	23	8.6	0	14.4
Per Serving:	325	23.5	25.1	2.3	.9	0	1.4

Cheddar Taco Shells
p.478

	CA	FAT	P	C	F	SA	NC
2 lb. (908g) cheddar cheese, grated	3609	297	224	11	0	0	11
Totals (of 6 servings):	3609.7	297.4	224	11	0	0	11
Per Serving:	601.6	49.6	37.3	1.8	0	0	1.8

CA= Calories / **FAT**= Fat / **P**=Protein / **C**= Carbohydrates / **F**= Fiber / **SA**= Sugar Alcohols / **NC**= Net Carbs

Thai Red Curry Paste p.484

	CA	FAT	P	C	F	SA	NC
10 (28g) Thai dried chilies, whole	89	5	3	16	8	0	8
1 Tbsp (6g) coriander seed, ground	17.9	1.1	.7	3.3	2.5	0	.8
2 tsp (4g) cumin seed, ground	15	.9	0	1.8	.4	0	1.3
1 tsp (2g) black peppercorns	5.3	0	.3	1.3	.7	0	.7
10 (66.7g) fresh red Thai chilies, seeds removed (substitution: Fresno or serrano peppers)	20	.4	.9	4	1.9	0	2.1
1 1/2 Tbsp (9g) fresh galangal, chopped (substitution: 1 Tbsp ginger)	7.2	0	.2	1.6	.2	0	1.4
4 (80g) shallots, chopped	56	0	0	16	0	0	16
1 Tbsp (17g) shrimp paste (substitution: 1 Tbsp fish sauce)	8	0	2	0	0	0	0
8 (12.8g) kaffir lime leaves, chopped (substitution: 1 tsp. lime zest)	2.9	.1	.4	.4	.3	0	.1
1 stalk (67g) lemongrass, white part only, sliced thin	66.3	0	1.3	16.8	0	0	16.8
1/4 cup (15g) cilantro stems, chopped	3.5	0	0	.8	.5	0	.3
1 tsp (4g) salt	0	0	0	0	0	0	0
Totals (of 16 servings):	291.2	7.5	8.9	61.9	14.5	0	47.4
Per Serving:	18.2	.5	.6	3.9	.9	0	(3)

Thai Green Curry Paste p.482

	CA	FAT	P	C	F	SA	NC
1 Tbsp (6g) coriander seed, ground	17.9	1.1	.7	3.3	2.5	0	.8
1 tsp (2g) white peppercorns	5.3	0	.3	1.3	.7	0	.7
1 (67g) lime	3.8	0	.1	1.3	.1	0	1.3
15 (101g) fresh green Thai chilies, seeds removed (substitution: jalapeño or Serrano peppers)	30	.6	1.4	6	2.9	0	3.2
1 1/2 Tbsp (9g) fresh galangal, chopped (substitution: 1 Tbsp ginger)	7.2	0	.2	1.6	.2	0	1.4
4 (80g) shallots, chopped	56	0	0	16	0	0	16
1 Tbsp (17g) shrimp paste (substitution: 1 Tbsp fish sauce)	8	0	2	0	0	0	0
8 (12.8g) kaffir lime leaves, chopped (substitution: 1 tsp lime zest)	2.9	.1	.4	.4	.3	0	.1
1 stalk (67g) lemongrass, white part only, sliced thin	66.3	0	1.3	16.8	0	0	16.8
1/4 bunch (25g) cilantro, washed (use cilantro stems too)	5.8	.1	.6	.9	.7	0	.2
16 leaves (6g) Thai basil (substitution: regular basil)	1.5	.1	.2	.2	.1	0	.1
1 Tbsp (15g) sugar replacement	0	0	0	15	0	15	0
1 tsp (4g) salt	0	0	0	0	0	0	0
Totals (of 16 servings):	204.7	2	7.1	62.8	7.4	15	40.4
Per Serving:	12.8	.1	.4	3.9	.5	.9	(2.5)

CA= Calories / **FAT**= Fat / **P**=Protein / **C**= Carbohydrates / **F**= Fiber / **SA**= Sugar Alcohols / **NC**= Net Carbs

INDEX

B